MW00359111

# Research Methods in Human Ecology/ Home Economics

# Research Methods in Human Ecology/ Home Economics

BY JOHN TOULIATOS and NORMA H. COMPTON

IOWA STATE UNIVERSITY PRESS / AMES

**To PAULA and KARA and to BILL and ANNE**

---

**JOHN TOULIATOS** is professor of family studies and home economics at Texas Christian University. Previously he was on the faculty and served as head of the Department of Family and Child Development and director of the Child Study Center at Auburn University. In addition to publishing numerous research articles in child development, family relations, psychology, social work, and education, he is senior author of *Approaches to Child Study* and *Handbook of Family Measurement Techniques.*

**NORMA H. COMPTON** is professor of family studies at Purdue University. She has served as dean of the School of Consumer and Family Sciences at Purdue University, dean of the School of Home Economics at Auburn University, and as director of the Institute for Research on Man and His Personal Environment and head of the Clothing and Textiles Department at Utah State University. She is author of numerous research publications and senior author of *Foundations of Home Economics Research: A Human Ecology Approach.*



Composed by Iowa State University Press
Printed in the United States of America



First edition, 1988

---

**Library of Congress Cataloging-in-Publication Data**

Touliatos, John.
Research methods in human ecology/home economics.

Bibliography: p.
Includes index.
1. Home economics—Research. 2. Human ecology—Research. I. Compton, Norma H. II. Title.
TX165.T67 1988 640'.72 87-29895
**ISBN 0-8138-0719-0**

# Contents

# Preface

This book is intended to serve as a basic text for students in their first research methods course in human ecology/home economics. That course may be offered at the junior or senior level or during the first year of graduate work. As an introductory text, it presupposes little or no knowledge of statistics or tests and measurements.

Leaders in the field have challenged the profession to give higher priority to research activity and the training of scholars, emphasizing that research is the foundation of any profession. We wrote *Research Methods in Human Ecology/Home Economics* in response to this challenge. More specifically, our objectives in preparing the book were to help students become more intelligent consumers of the research literature and to familiarize them with procedures for planning and conducting their own studies. With human ecology as a unifying theoretical framework and the inclusion of a wide range of methodologies, the book will enable students specializing in different areas within human ecology/home economics units to translate into action some of the profession's research goals and guidelines discussed in the second chapter.

Structurally, this book is organized into six parts: research foundations, data collection methods, research strategies, data preparation and analysis, research communication, and ethical and professional responsibilities. Part 1 (Chaps. 1–5) focuses on the meaning of science and research; a human ecology perspective to home economics; and basic considerations in planning research, including detailed treatments of selecting and formulating a research problem and reviewing the literature.

Part 2 (Chaps. 6–7) addresses the selection and construction of measuring instruments and discusses various data collection techniques for research, such as observation, questionnaires, and interviews.

Part 3 (Chaps. 8–12) covers different strategies employed in research, including experiments, field studies, surveys, using existing data, and evaluation studies. Although Part 2 and Part 3 overlap somewhat, we have separated chapters dealing primarily with data collection techniques from those on research strategies to show that no single method of gathering data is necessarily identified with a particular type of research (e.g., observation can be used in experiments or nonexperimental field studies). Our classification of research strategies into two broad categories, experimental and nonexperimental, is no more or less satisfactory than those proposed by others. All such classification systems are artificial and never completely adequate, but some type of categorization is needed for an introductory text. With this two-way classification system, there are inevitably more subtypes (and chapters) under the nonexperimental rubric (e.g., field studies, surveys, historical research). We placed the chapter on evaluation studies last in the sequence because some of these investigations may involve either experimental or nonexperimental approaches.

Part 4 (Chaps. 13–14) covers preparation of data and data analysis.

Part 5 (Chaps. 15–16) discusses research proposals and reports. Chapter 15 includes examples of a dissertation proposal and a proposal for extramural funding.

Part 6 (Chaps. 17–18) deals with ethical and professional responsibilities of researchers in human ecology. Placement of this material at the back of the book does not imply that these issues are any less important than others discussed in the text.

To elaborate on certain points we have made and to give suggestions for further reading, we have provided notes at the end of each chapter. Synopses of research reports that illustrate various research methods covered in the book are also presented at the ends of the chapters in Part 3. These sample reports were chosen from the different specializations within human ecology. As such, they are multidisciplinary in nature in terms of the researchers, journals, and monographs represented. Other articles may be added by faculty and students.

Touliatos has assumed responsibility for writing Chapters 1 and 3–16. Compton has written Chapters 2, 17, and 18 and has selected and prepared synopses of the 20 research reports.

We are indebted to many people for their encouragement, support, and assistance during the preparation of this book. Thanks are extended to Barry Perlmutter for his comments and criticisms during the latter stages of the project. The helpful suggestions of Arnold Barkman, Bob Demaree, Art Bedeian, and Byron Lindholm are also gratefully acknowledged.

We deeply appreciate the capable assistance of Carol Kramer (secretary, Department of Family Studies and Home Economics, Texas Christian University) and Dianne Cherry (administrative assistant-to-the-dean, School of Consumer and Family Sciences, Purdue University). We likewise acknowledge the splendid cooperation of the Mary Couts Burnett Library at Texas Christian University, particularly Acquisitions, Interlibrary Loan, Automated Information Retrieval Services, and the Funding Information Center. For their conscientious work and editorial guidance, we express our appreciation to Bill Silag, managing editor, and Carla Tollefson, manuscript editor, at Iowa State University Press. We thank Peggy Sturgill, who typed the manuscript. Finally, we are grateful to the authors and publishers who granted us permission to reprint their material. We are especially indebted to Harv Joanning, associate professor of human development and family studies, Texas Tech University, and to Libby Blume, assistant professor and discipline coordinator of child development, Mercy College of Detroit, for allowing us to include their proposals in Chapter 15.

PART 1

# Research Foundations

CHAPTER 1

# Science and Research Defined

Since science provides the most dependable means of understanding the interaction of people with their environment and of generating new knowledge about human-environment relations,[1] it is appropriate to consider the characteristics of science, to investigate research as an aspect of science, and to explore the relationship of theory to research.

## CHARACTERISTICS OF SCIENCE

### Definition of Science

When asked the question, What is science? students commonly conjure up thoughts of laboratories, test tubes, caged animals, computers, and people in white coats. They might mention familiar scientific laws or specific content in a science course they have taken. It is not surprising that students fail to agree on a definition or description of science. Although *science* is a familiar term, it is employed in many contexts and it is not clearly understood by all. Indeed, philosophers specializing in the philosophy of science and scientists themselves hold differing views of science.

Conant (1951, 25), former president of Harvard University, has defined science as "an interconnected series of concepts and conceptual schemes that have developed as a result of experimentation and observation and are fruitful of further experimentation and observations." Sax (1968, 7) has viewed science both as a method and an attitude. As a method:

> Empirical sciences consist of controlled observations. . . . Observations are controlled by eliminating or reducing the effects of irrelevant or extraneous variables by means of apparatus, tests, examinations,

> instruments, or specialized techniques. These observations are combined to form *theoretical systems* that are useful in explaining and predicting the relationships between the observations.

As an attitude:

> Science consists of a willingness to examine and, if need be, to modify or repudiate one's own beliefs, ideas, or methods as new or more reliable evidence is obtained. The attitude is one that encourages the scientist to control and reduce biases, to be as precise as possible, to verify or disprove his beliefs empirically, and to organize empirically obtained data into a meaningful body of theoretical knowledge.

Although there is no universal definition of science, it is necessary for us to reach a common understanding of the concept. In this book, science will refer to an attitude and a method. Science is a way of thinking, a way of looking at nature that involves certain principles and guidelines. Science is an objective, accurate, and systematic method of human inquiry with the aim of obtaining the most reliable data possible and organizing it into a meaningful body of theoretical knowledge.

## Assumptions of Science

Some assumptions are fundamental to scientific endeavors. Usually left unstated and taken for granted by scientists, these premises are very important. Sjoberg and Nett (1968, 23–28) described a minimum set of assumptions that underlie scientific investigation. These assumptions have been summarized here.

1. *There is order in the natural world.* Phenomena in the physical and social world are not random or capricious; the universe is lawful and predictable. As such, there is no need for dependence on supernatural forces to explain conditions. We are capable of understanding nature and ourselves.

2. *Knowledge is superior to ignorance.* Knowledge is preferable even when the consequences of new data threaten the status quo and are emotional and possibly traumatic. Conversely, ignorance is undesirable and detrimental to our well-being.

3. *There is a communication tie between the scientist and external reality,* and this human-environment link is maintained through sense impressions. Science is based on empiricism, or evidence that is the product of our experiences with the physical, biological, and social world as perceived through the sense organs (i.e., empirical assumption).

4. *There are cause-and-effect relationships within the physical and the social orders.* This notion assumes that the occurrence of some events is preceded or accompanied by the occurrence of other events. Although all

scientists do not agree on a rigidly interpreted determinism based upon absolute certainty, they are guided by the concept of levels of probability.

5. *The scientist is motivated to acquire scientific knowledge by a desire to improve society.* Science is not a dehumanizing activity, but rather it may help humans realize their potential and improve their condition. (Although improved quality of life is often a by-product of science, some scientists who feel that science should be neutral and concentrate only on the understanding of physical and human phenomena might take issue with this assumption.)

6. *The scientist, as an observer, is a reliable "instrument" for scientific activities.* While science does not offer complete immunity against errors that nonscientists make in day-to-day inquiry, scientists can obtain reliable information and/or develop systematic methods to help them perceive, remember, compare, compute, differentiate, and integrate. This may require the development of sophisticated instrumentation to extend the capabilities of scientists and reduce their errors.

7. *The social conditions necessary for scientific activity can be sustained.* Scientific freedom and the tolerance of free inquiry, as well as direct support for science by society, are essential for the pursuit of knowledge. The underwriting of scientific activity is expected by scientists.

## Aims of Science

There are four major aims of science: description, explanation, prediction, and progress. The initial step in any scientific undertaking is *description* of phenomena in answer to the question, What? In other words, scientists must first know what is out there: what the essential characteristics of the phenomena are and the extent to which they exist.

Description may be molecular (micro) or molar (macro), depending on the thing or event being studied. For example, physicists, who are interested in atomic and subatomic particles, deal primarily with detailed, molecular explanations. The same can be said for chemists. Conversely, sociologists, who study group behaviors, are concerned more with larger units of behavior or molar descriptions. Ethnologists, who investigate cultures, deal with even larger units of descriptions on the molecular-molar dimension. At times, however, within a given discipline there are different levels of description. In psychology, a physiological psychologist operates at a more molecular level than a child psychologist, although the latter might engage in molecular descriptions in an attempt to adequately describe diminutive aspects of behavior before pursuing molar descriptions of a child's behavior.

The two levels of description can be complementary and are dictated by the needs of the discipline and the types of questions under investigation. By being overly molecular in their descriptions, scientists may run the risk of providing too much information, including irrelevant details, thereby wasting valuable time. If their descriptions are excessively molar, scientists may fail to observe relevant data and provide a picture that is too vague and therefore meaningless.

The second aim of science is *explanation.* After obtaining an accurate description, scientists need to answer the question, Why? For instance, if the data show that there are lower achievement levels among children from single-parent as opposed to intact homes, scientists want to know why this is so. An explanation gives significance and meaning to the description by telling the conditions under which things and events come about, what causes them, and the previously verified principles or laws that determine their occurrence.

The third aim of science is *prediction.* Scientists are not content to describe and explain phenomena; they want to take what they know and predict future events under certain conditions. Typically, they speak in terms of probabilities rather than absolute predictions.

The fourth aim of science is *progress.* Scientific work is often undertaken to influence the future in some positive way. Its objective is change—remedial or developmental action that will improve the quality of life.

## The Scientific Method

Of the different ways of generating and testing the truth of statements about events in the world, the scientific mode is superior primarily because of the foundation upon which it is based. That foundation is the *scientific method*—a set of procedures or steps used to approach and solve problems.[2] The actual number of steps and terms that describe them vary somewhat from one author to the next. However, the general pattern is as follows:

1. Casually observing phenomena
2. Clarifying a problem
3. Formulating hypotheses
4. Developing and applying a design or methodology to test the hypotheses
5. Testing of hypotheses
6. Further testing and refining of results
7. Explaining results and drawing conclusions

The process begins with casual observation of a phenomenon or event and the feeling that there is a need to resolve a problem or answer a question. Next, a more precise identification and definition of the problem are made, and hypotheses (conjectural statements) are formulated based upon the preliminary observations. A design is then developed to test the hypotheses, the hypotheses are verified or refuted, and the results are subjected to further tests and refinements. Ultimately, the results are explained and integrated with previously established concepts and theories of science.

Although the steps are listed in order and are normally pursued in that sequence, the scientist may or may not follow this chronology. The scientist may choose to pursue the steps out of order, to go back and forth between steps, or to work on two or more steps at one time. The stages are not discrete; the completion of one step is not required before the next is begun. In addition, the scientific method is cyclical. It may be necessary to discard or modify hypotheses, which will require additional data collection, testing, and so forth.

## RESEARCH AS AN ASPECT OF SCIENCE

Research is undertaken to explore new areas, describe situations and events, and explain phenomena. Sound research is essential to the development and refinement of science.

*Research* has been defined simply as "a systematic way of asking questions" (Drew and Hardman 1985, 3) and more elaborately as "a careful inquiry or examination to discover new information or relationships and to expand and to verify existing knowledge" (Rummel 1964, 2).[3] Since definitions of this kind are somewhat abstract, Best (1981, 18–20)* has summarized some of the most important characteristics of research to clarify its methodology.

- Research is directed toward the solution of a problem. The ultimate goal is to discover cause-and-effect relationships between variables, though [for lack of enough evidence to establish one of cause-and-effect] researchers often have to settle for the useful discovery of a systematic relationship.

- Research emphasizes the development of generalizations, principles, or theories that will be helpful in predicting future occurrences. Research usually goes beyond the specific objects, groups, or situations investigated and infers characteristics of a target population from the sample observed. Research is more than information retrieval, the simple gathering of information. Although many school research departments gather and tabulate statistical information that may be useful in decision making, these activities are not properly termed research.

*John W. Best, RESEARCH IN EDUCATION, © 1981, pp. 18–20. Adapted by permission of Prentice-Hall, Englewood Cliffs, New Jersey.

- Research is based upon observable experience or empirical evidence. . . . Research rejects revelation and dogma as methods of establishing knowledge and accepts only what can be verified by [or deduced from] observation.

- Research demands accurate observation and description. Researchers use quantitative, numerical measuring devices, the most precise form of description. When this is not possible or appropriate, they use qualitative, or nonquantitative, descriptions of their observations. They select or devise valid data-gathering procedures and, when feasible, employ appropriate mechanical, electronic, or psychometric devices to refine observation, description, and analysis of data.

- Research involves gathering new data from primary or first-hand sources or using existing data for a new purpose. Teachers frequently assign a so-called research project that involves writing a paper dealing with the life of a prominent person. The students are expected to read a number of encyclopedias, books, or periodical references, and synthesize the information in a written report. This is not research, for the data are not new. Merely reorganizing or restating what is already known and has already been written, valuable as it may be as a learning experience, is not research. It adds nothing to what is known.

- Although research activity may at times be somewhat random and unsystematic, it is more often characterized by carefully designed procedures, always applying vigorous analysis. Although trial and error are often involved, research is rarely blind, shotgun investigation—trying something to see what happens.

- [An effective] researcher knows what is already known about the problem and how others have investigated it. He or she has searched the related literature carefully, and is also thoroughly grounded in the terminology, the concepts, and the technical skill necessary to understand and analyze the data gathered.

- Research strives to be objective and logical, applying every possible test to validate the procedures employed, the data collected, and the conclusions reached. The researcher attempts to eliminate personal bias [in conducting the study]. There is no attempt [in the design of the study] to persuade or to prove an emotionally held conviction. The emphasis is on testing rather than on proving the hypothesis. Although absolute objectivity is as elusive as pure righteousness, the researcher tries to suppress bias and emotion in his or her analysis.

- Research involves the quest for answers to unsolved problems. Pushing back the frontiers of ignorance is its goal.

- [While originality is a quality of good research, it is also worthwhile to deliberately repeat previous important studies], using identical or similar procedures, with different subjects, different settings, and at a different time. This process is *replication,* a fusion of the words *repetition* and *duplication.* Replication is always desirable to confirm or to raise questions about the conclusions of a previous study. . . .

- Research is characterized by patient and unhurried activity. It is rarely spectacular and researchers must expect disappointment and discouragement as they pursue the answers to difficult questions.

- Research is carefully recorded and reported. Each important term is defined, limiting factors are recognized, procedures are described in detail, references are carefully documented, results are subjectively recorded, and conclusions are presented with scholarly caution and restraint. The written report and accompanying data are made available to the scrutiny of associates or other scholars. Any competent scholar will have the information necessary to analyze, evaluate, and even replicate the study.

- Research sometimes requires courage. The history of science reveals that many important discoveries were made in spite of the opposition of political and religious authorities. The Polish scientist Copernicus (1473–1543) was condemned by church authorities when he announced his conclusion concerning the nature of the solar system. His theory that the sun, not the earth, was the center of the solar system, in direct conflict with the older Ptolemaic theory, angered supporters of prevailing religious dogma, who viewed his theory as a denial of the story of creation as described in the book of Genesis. Modern researchers in such fields as genetics, sexual behavior, and even business practices have also aroused violent criticism from those whose personal convictions, experiences, or observations were in conflict with some of the research conclusions.

## Classification of Research

There is no single, consistent way to classify research. It can be classified according to purpose (e.g., exploratory, descriptive, casual), application (basic, applied), strategy (historical, survey), degree of experimental control (experimental, nonexperimental), time dimension (cross-sectional, longitudinal), setting (laboratory, field), data collection procedure (interview, observation), character of data collected (quantitative, qualitative), and data analysis technique (correlational, factor analytic). Usually, there is overlap among these categories. For example, an investigation may have an applied goal, involve participants of different ages, use paper-and-pencil questionnaires to examine the subjects cross-sectionally, and require correlational analyses of the data.

No single system of classification can be acceptable in all situations. However, the two types of research presented here, classified primarily by application, will provide a framework for later discussion and illustration of the various data collection techniques and research strategies that can be used in conducting such studies.

### Basic Research

*Basic research,* sometimes called pure or fundamental research, is conducted for the sake of science. Normally carried on in structured laboratory settings, it is "done to test theory, to study relations among phenomena to understand the phenomena, with little or no thought of application of the results of research to practical problems" (Kerlinger 1979, 283). The emphasis is on problems as abstractions, not as utilitarian matters. Fundamental research seeks only to discover basic truths or principles. Although basic research usually yields findings that eventually can be applied to practical problems outside the domain of science, this type of research is not expected to produce results that have immediate application.

Interestingly, one empirical study in medicine has examined the relative effects of basic and applied research on practice. Comroe and Dripps (1976) asked physicians to select research articles that contained significant bodies of knowledge that had to be developed before 10 major clinical advances could be made in the last 30 years. They found that physicians identified significantly more reports of basic than nonbasic research as having a greater impact on medical practice.

### Applied Research

Applied research includes most of the features of basic research but differs in terms of its goals. *Applied research* is directed toward the practical application of scientific knowledge and toward the solution of specific problems. Its justification is in the immediate value of results.

Kerlinger (1979, 287–88) has commented on the significance of applied research:

> Applied research is indispensable and often highly significant in two or three ways. First, it can, as intended, provide information that will help lead to problem solution. Second, it can sometimes suggest new or different lines of basic research. For instance, an unexpected relation between two variables may be discovered in a survey of opinions. This relation may suggest the alteration of a theory being tested in basic research. The needs of applied research can also stimulate basic methodological research. The need for more appropriate forms of analysis

in studying such phenomena as school achievement, occupational status, later-life success, and similar variables apparently helped to reinforce the development of multivariate analysis, especially multiple regression analysis and path analysis. Third, and perhaps even more important, applied research sometimes has a heuristic quality. It can lead to theory development and basic research. It is often rich in potential hypotheses that cry out for testing and theoretical underpinning.

Action Research. One form of applied research that is especially relevant to human ecology is called *action research.* Its primary objectives are social action and the improvement of practice. Its major focus is on local applicability. Rapoport (1985, 280) points out that, under the best circumstances, action research can yield *both* improved practice and increased knowledge. He views modern action research as consisting of a "family of approaches having at its core the joining together within a project or program two agenda: to advance an action program through the use of scientific knowledge, and to advance knowledge through studying the workings of the action program."

Action research projects arise from different conditions (Rapoport 1985, 281–82): agency thrust, researcher thrust, and external pressure. An agency (e.g., social service agency, school) that has developed a program may feel that research input would be beneficial. Or a researcher who has a theory may wish to develop his or her ideas through collaboration with an action agency. Certain external pressures, such as social ferment or mandated program evaluation, may also serve as stimuli for these investigations.

Action research requires a close working relationship between the researcher and the action agent. The researcher and the practitioners in the setting (as well as clients, in some cases) participate in the definition of problems, establishment of research goals, selection or development of measuring instruments, collection of data, and interpretation of findings.

Although methodological difficulties may result from the researcher's loss of autonomy in these collaborative projects, benefits may accrue from action studies. The problems investigated are likely to be significant; the practitioners, who have been involved in each phase of the research process, view the data as "theirs" and are more likely to accept them as relevant and translate them into action; and the training received in carrying out the study gives the practitioners a greater understanding and appreciation of research and increases their organization's internal capability for conducting future investigations.[4]

Both basic and applied research are important to science and should be viewed as representing a continuum rather than a dichotomy. They overlap considerably in that the two approaches seek the discovery of scientific truth and lead to the solution of human problems, in spite of the disinterest of basic research in stated, short-term, utilitarian goals.

## RELATION OF THEORY TO RESEARCH

### Nature and Functions of Theory

The maturity of an academic discipline is generally gauged by the extent to which it has developed a solid foundation for the construction of theories. Although *theory* means slightly different things to different people,[5] the definition of theory presented here is adequate for our needs, acknowledging that it is but one of several that might be proposed. Selltiz, Wrightsman, and Cook (1976, 581) define theory as "a statement of the relationships that exist among concepts." (See Chap. 2 for a more comprehensive definition.)

Theory has three basic functions. First, it organizes and synthesizes existing facts and information. In this descriptive capacity, theory arranges everything that is known about a phenomenon and places it in a logical and understandable framework. Second, it enables the researcher to see certain relationships that are not apparent from examination of any datum taken alone, and it mediates application of knowledge to new situations. Third, theory serves as a guide for the discovery of new facts by pinpointing questions to be answered and by specifying the kinds of data that should be collected. It provides a basis for predicting what will happen when certain events occur.

#### Example: Theory of Achievement Motivation

McClelland et al. (1953) advanced a theory on the nature of origins of achievement motivation, or *n* Achievement, which continues to attract the attention of researchers. Essentially, McClelland et al. (1953, 275) argued that human motives, such as achievement motivation, are learned:

> They develop out of repeated affective experiences connected with certain types of situations and types of behavior. In the case of achievement motivation, the situations should involve "standards of excellence," presumably imposed on the child by the culture, or more particularly by the parents as representatives of the culture, and the behavior should involve either "competition" with those standards of excellence or attempts to meet them which, if successful, produce positive affect, or if unsuccessful, negative affect. It follows that those cultures of families which stress "competition with standards of excellence" or which insist *that the child be able to perform certain tasks*

*well by himself*—such cultures or families should produce children with high achievement motivation.

The theory implied that socialization practices that stress competition in situations involving standards of excellence (achievement training) and put the child on his or her own (independence training) influence the development of achievement motivation. This line of thinking suggested the direction that their research should take. As McClelland et al. (1953, 276) stated: "The research problem then boils down to an attempt to discover whether individuals with high or low *n* Achievement scores have in fact been treated differently by their families as they were growing up. Our hypothesis is that individuals with high achievement motivation will have been forced to master problems on their own more often and earlier than individuals with low achievement motion."

Theory and research are inextricably linked (Fig. 1.1). On the one hand, theory guides research. In the McClelland et al. example, theory provided a blueprint for action. With very few exceptions, research includes some type or level of theory, whether explicit or implicit.[6] The theory may be well defined in the literature or exist as a vague hunch or informed guess in the researcher's mind. On the other hand, research tests and stimulates theory, contributes to the refinement of methods and procedures, and leads to the development of more adequate theory.

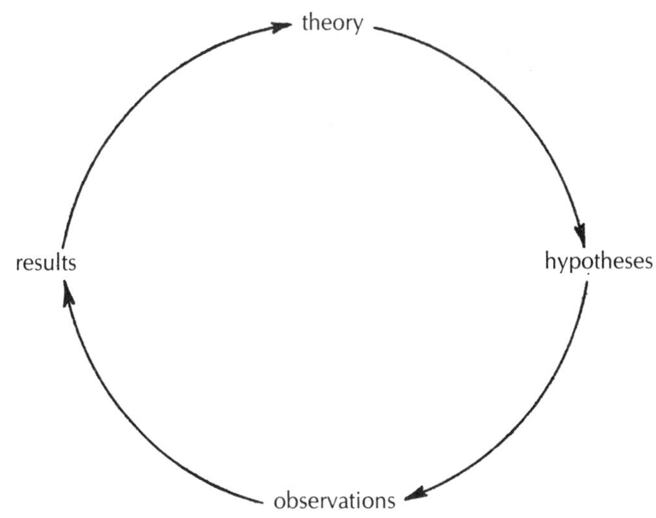


**Figure 1.1.** The relationship of theory to research.

In the case of achievement motivation, numerous researchers have examined the origins of this human need by using McClelland's original framework. Over the years, the findings of these studies have led to the development of new techniques for the measurement of achievement motivation and to the derivation of related but more comprehensive theories (e.g., including identification of different types of achievement motivation, accounting for sex differences) as well as to voluminous research testing the newer ideas. Theory is not static; it is continuously evaluated and changed.

### Characteristics of Useful Theories

Useful theories are typically compatible with existing knowledge, including previously validated theories, and with empirical observations made relative to them. They have heuristic value measured by the degree to which they stimulate research.

A useful theory is explicit, with all concepts clearly defined and related to each other in a logical manner. It is parsimonious, or stated in the simplest terms possible, with verifiable generalizations. Hypotheses generated are generally empirically testable by independent investigators. However, a theory is not tested directly; the hypotheses within the theory are tested. If the hypotheses comprising a theory are supported, confidence is gained in the validity of the overall theory, but the theory is never fully proven. Data that are in agreement with it only support, not prove, the theory. The next empirical test could disprove it! Actually, a theory that cannot be proven wrong is not very useful because it has the potential for becoming self-sustaining dogma. Turner (1986) reminds us that when a theory is rejected, science has advanced because theories that survive refutation offer, *for the time being,* the most accurate picture of the world.

## The Place of Theory in Research

There are differences of opinion regarding the relative importance of theory and observation (or data) in research. Some scholars believe that it is necessary to theorize first and only then engage in empirical checks to test the theory. Others are more oriented toward discovery or after-the-fact explanation. In their way of thinking, theory evolves after careful consideration of all facts and reflects only a summary of concrete observations.

These two points of view are referred to as the *hypothetico-deductive* and the *inductive* approaches, respectively. Generally, deduction or deductive reasoning begins with broad statements from which specific statements are derived, following the pattern: If this is so, and that is so, then this must also be so. Induction or inductive reasoning moves from particular instances to more general rules.

## Theory-then-Research

The difference between the hypothetico-deductive and the inductive orientations is reflected in two major strategies: theory-then-research and research-then-theory. The theory-then-research strategy, exemplifed by Popper (1963), is outlined by Reynolds (1971, 144):

1. Develop an explicit theory in either axiomatic or process description form.
2. Select a statement generated by the theory for comparison with the results of empirical research.
3. Design a research project to "test" the chosen statement's correspondence with empirical research.
4. If the statement derived from the theory does not correspond with the research results, make appropriate changes in the theory or the research design and continue with the research (return to step 2).
5. If the statement from the theory corresponds with the results of the research, select further statements for testing or attempt to determine the limitations of the theory (the situations where the theory does not apply).

## Research-then-Theory

In contrast, Merton (1957,103) contends that the preferred approach to developing a scientific body of knowledge is research-then-theory. He argues: "It is my central thesis that empirical research goes far beyond the passive role of verifying and testing theory; it does more than confirm or refute hypotheses. Research plays an active role: it performs at least four major functions which help shape the development of theory. It initiates, it reformulates, it deflects, and it clarifies theory."

Merton gives examples of the four impacts of research on theory development. In the course of testing a hypothesis, the investigator may notice an unanticipated or anomalous pattern that provokes curiosity, calls for initiation of another direction of inquiry, and culminates in a new or extended theory. This process has been labeled *serendipity* by Merton. Another possibility is that new data generated by research may press for elaboration of a conceptual scheme and lead to recasting of theory. New methods of research also may help refocus theoretic interest on the growing points of research, possibly where there is an abundance of statistical data. Or the requirements of research for clarification of concepts and quantification sometimes help raise conceptual issues that may go undetected or be delayed in theoretical inquiry.

According to Reynolds (1971, 140), the research-then-theory strategy follows this sequence:

1. Select a phenomenon and list all the characteristics of the phenomenon.

2. Measure all the characteristics of the phenomenon in a variety of situations (as many as possible).
3. Analyze the resulting data carefully to determine if there are any systematic patterns among the data "worthy" of further attention.
4. Once significant patterns have been found in the data, formalization of these patterns as theoretical statements constitutes the laws of nature (axioms, in Bacon's terminology).

The controversy over the place of theory in the research process has not retarded scientific progress. Research has and will continue to flourish under both strategies because the difference exists more in belief than in actuality (Nagel 1961).

## NOTES

1. See Wallace (1971, 11–16) for a brief description of three additional modes of generating and testing knowledge (authoritarian, mystical, and logico-rational).

2. The scientific method is not completely without controversy (Kaplan 1964). Some scholars argue that there is not one rigid set of logical rules that all scientists (e.g., physical scientists, psychologists, mathematicians) can follow to make their undertakings truly scientific. As Conant (1951, 45) has written, "There is no such thing as *the* scientific method." Undoubtedly, the wide disparity among the sciences calls for different methods. On the other hand, an equally convincing case can be made that there are sufficient common features in scientific inquires conducted in different fields (Goldstein and Goldstein 1984; Van Dalen 1979).

3. Technical research terms are introduced through the book. Due to space limitations, a glossary has not been included in the book, but the reader is referred to Miller and Wilson's (1983) little paperback, *A Dictionary of Social Science Methods,* which defines over 1000 research-related terms. It is an excellent companion volume for any beginning research text. Another useful sourcebook for definitions of research terms is the *Handbook of Research and Quantitative Methods in Psychology* by Yaremko et al. (1986).

4. Action research is discussed in more detail by Argyris, Putnam, and Smith (1985), Chein, Cook, and Harding (1948), Ketterer, Price, and Politser (1980), Lewin (1946), Peters and Robinson (1984), Rapoport (1985), and Sanford (1970).

5. The term *theory* has sometimes been used interchangeably with *model.* In this book, however, a distinction is made between the two. A model is "an abstraction from reality that serves to order and simplify our view of the reality while still representing its essential characteristics" (Nachmias and Nachmias 1987, 519). Both theories and models are ways of conceptualizing the world around us, but there are some differences between them, as Van Dalen (1979, 56) explains:

> Models are analogies (this thing is like that thing) and therefore can tolerate some facts that are not in accord with the real phenomena. A theory, on the other hand, is supposed to describe the facts and relationships that exist, and any facts that are not compatible with the theory invalidate the theory. In summary, some scholars argue that models are judged by

their usefulness and theories by their truthfulness; models are not theories but tools that are used as a basis for formal and rigorous theory construction.

A common example of a model is the use of the globe as a model of the earth. A miniature and simplified reproduction of the real thing, the globe represents important features in a way that is readily understood (e.g., oceans, continents, mountain ranges). In addition to this type of physical replica, models can be graphic representations (e.g., interior designer's renderings), mathematical equations, and other symbols that order, simplify, and represent reality. More recently, the computer has been used as a model of human behavior.

Another term, *paradigm,* has been used in connection with theory and model. According to Smith (1975, 240), a paradigm "stands for the entire constellation of beliefs, values, techniques, and so on shared by members of a given community. . . . Paradigms are the assumptions or conceptualizations—either explicit or implicit—underlying any data, theory, or method. Paradigms act, therefore, as 'world views' suggestive of research questions or problems." In a sense, a paradigm is like a "super theory." Some examples are S-R learning theory, exchange theory, and utility theory. See Kuhn (1970) and Reynolds (1971) for further information.

6. For a brief discussion of levels of theory, see Nachmias and Nachmias (1987, 40–46). Their classification, from lowest to highest level, includes ad hoc classificatory systems, taxonomies, conceptual frameworks, and theoretical systems.

Greenwald et al. (1986) examine the conditions under which theory can obstruct research progress. Although these authors believe theory is essential to research, they point out that when theory testing is a goal, there is always danger that the theory may blind the investigator to potentially meaningful observations.

CHAPTER 2

# A Human Ecology Perspective for Home Economics

## UNIFYING MODELS

Schools or departments of home economics/human ecology/human resources/human development/consumer and family sciences or those with other related titles are people-oriented components of their universities. The question is often raised whether programs in these units represent one academic discipline or a series of separate disciplines and professions. This question is related to the generalist-specialist issue. Actually, programs and degrees are usually offered in seemingly diverse specializations such as child development; family relations; dietetics; nutrition; food science; restaurant, hotel and institutional management; home management; family or consumer economics; consumer affairs; retailing or fashion merchandising; clothing and textiles; housing and equipment; and interior design. Home economics education programs feature a more generalist orientation. However, a unifying framework exists for the specializations within all of these programs. They are in the business of serving families and consumers, primarily in relation to their food, clothing, and shelter and their interaction among themselves and their families and with their physical environment.

### A Model for Human Ecology Professions

A visual representation of a unifying framework for the specializations offered within human ecology and related departments or schools is suggested in Figure 2.1, which symbolizes dynamic plant-like relationships with interrelated parts that function as a whole.

The theoretical frameworks for the applied programs in human ecol-

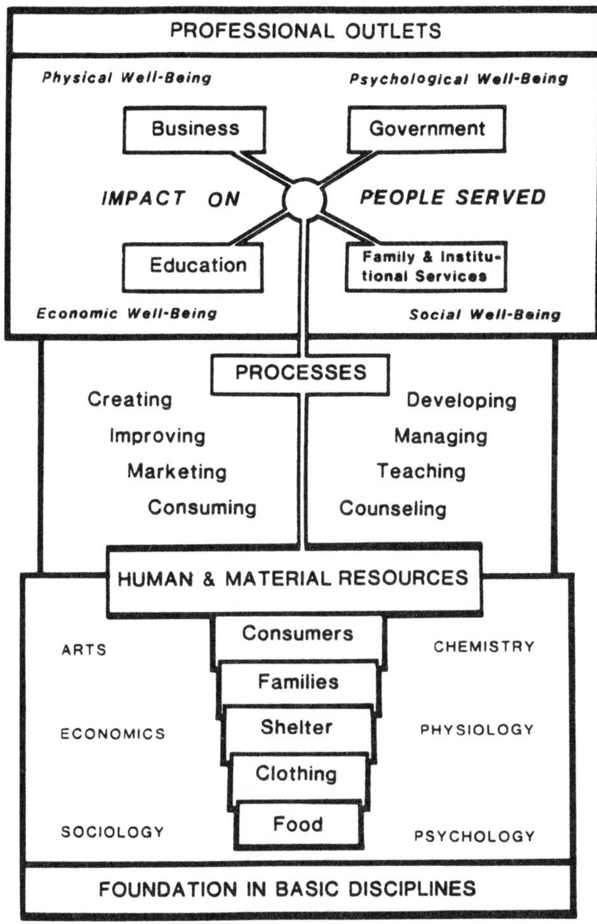


**Figure 2.1.** A model for human ecology professions.

ogy and related departments have their foundations in the *basic disciplines.* The primary disciplines represented in Figure 2.1 (art, economics, sociology, etc.) are also reflected in the academic backgrounds of many of the faculty of these departments. Teaching, research, and extension faculty coordinate and apply knowledge from these and other foundation disciplines as they deal with the *processes* of creating, improving, marketing, and consuming food, clothing, and shelter products. Faculty in these departments also focus on the personal development of family members and prepare teachers and counselors to help families manage their *human and material resources.* Graduates of applied programs in human ecology and related departments engage in the same processes when they move into *professional careers* in business, government, education, or family and institutional services. The end result, the final mission, is the *impact* that these professionals make on the quality of life in terms of improved physical, economic, psychological, and social well-being of the families and consumers they serve.

### An Integrative Model for Human Ecology Research

Another way of unifying the specializations within these units is to regard the food, clothing, and shelter products, as well as families and consumers, as components of the near environment that interact with one another. This *human ecology* perspective is the focus of this book, with human ecology defined as the study of human beings in interaction with their near environment, including their home (its design, furnishings, and equipment), wearing apparel, food, family, and community (including institutions such as hotels, restaurants, and nursing homes).

To carry its objective of improving the well-being of families through education, research, and community service, human ecology applies and synthesizes theories from the physical and behavioral sciences, humanities, and/or the arts. Its researchers may work as part of a team with members of their own or other disciplines on complex social problems requiring multidisciplinary approaches toward improving the quality of living in an increasingly polluted environment. Of course, an individual researcher may decide to concentrate on research within any single field of study without regard for its relationship to the others. However, the overall focus in human ecology research should be on the whole if it is to be a dynamic research enterprise in tune with today's demands.

## DEVELOPMENT OF HUMAN ECOLOGY

### Biology

*Ecology* is the "study of interrelations between organisms and their environment" (Hawley 1950). Biologists first analyzed environment-behavior relations, focusing on the interdependence of plant and animal groups occupying the same habitat. Many of the key concepts and methods of modern bioecology can be traced to Charles Darwin's work, *The Origin of the Species,* first published in 1859.

### Sociology

Sociologists later applied the contributions made in bioecology to the study of human communities (McKenzie 1925; Park and Burgess 1921,

1925). The focus of their studies was on the human ecosystem comprised of the city and its surrounding agricultural areas. They viewed the spatial and economic organization of the city as the primary index of human adaptation to the environment.

## Psychology

Roger Barker is credited with the first major attempt to apply an ecological perspective to the discipline of psychology, extending ecology from the macro to the micro level (Barker 1960, 1968). He replaced demographic methods of analysis with finer observations of interpersonal behavior and individualized subject-report data. Barker developed an environment-behavior unit, the *behavior setting,* in which cyclical patterns of activity occurring within specific time intervals and spatial boundaries are described. Examples of such behavioral settings are dormitory lounges, restaurants, and baseball games.

During the 1970s, the shrinkage of natural resources and deterioration of environmental quality prompted widespread concern about the environment. Psychologists rediscovered the large-scale physical environment and collaborated with architects and planners in studying its impact on behavior.

Two areas of psychology have emerged that are directly concerned with the relationship between human behavior and elements of the architectural and natural environment. *Ecological psychology* emphasizes the collective processes by which groups adapt to physical and social resources available in the environment. *Environmental psychology* focuses more on intrapersonal processes, such as perception, cognition, and learning, that mediate the impact of the environment on the individual (Stokols 1977, 6).

## Environmental Design and Planning

According to Craik (1968), the initiative in the development of research in environmental psychology has come primarily from the areas of environmental design and planning. Since World War II, however, the discipline of psychology has contributed by moving from the seclusion of the laboratory and seeking problems in the real world to examine and to expand the usefulness of its concepts and methods.

## Home Economics

The field of home economics also has historical roots in ecology. Pioneers in home economics considered the name human ecology for their field but abandoned it at the beginning of this century. Ellen H. Richards defined home economics as "the study of the laws, conditions, principles and ideals which are concerned on the one hand with man's physical environment and on the other hand with his nature as a social being, and a study specially of the relation between these two factors" (Lake Placid Conference on Home Economics 1902, 70–71). In recent years, numerous college units of home economics have focused on this human-environment relationship. In 1971 *The Annual Guides to Graduate Study* added a section of "institutions offering graduate work in human development and home economics, including child development, clothing and textiles, and household economics and management." That publication states: "These sciences have in part grown out of or replaced some formerly isolated academic areas and now constitute a single study of human ecology and are therefore presented here as a new discipline for the first time."

**AAHE Goals and Guidelines**

In 1970 the Association of Administrators of Home Economics (AAHE) sponsored a major nationwide endeavor to examine the current status of research in its fields and to project directions for future research emphases. Using an ecological model as a base, three task forces worked on broad-scope objectives within different areas of emphasis:

*Task Force I:* Physical/biological aspects of man and his environment
*Task Force II:* Sociopsychological needs and development of human beings
*Task Force III:* Relation between man and the technological setting in which he develops and lives

Five major research goals were presented to a group of active researchers and administrators as the framework for a research workshop in March 1970. Broad research problem areas and specific research questions were developed for each goal (Schlater 1970, 15). The five goals and suggested research problem areas are as applicable today as they were when they were formulated, but the word *people's* should be substituted for the word *man's*. The goals are:

*Goal I:* Improve the conditions contributing to man's psychological and social development
*Goal II:* Improve the conditions contributing to man's physiological health and development
*Goal III:* Improve the physical components of man's near environment
*Goal IV:* Improve consumer competence and family resource use
*Goal V:* Improve the quality and availability of community services which enrich family life

## New Initiatives

In 1981 the United States Department of Agriculture's Science and Education Administration established a national steering committee, with representatives from land-grant colleges and universities and other organizations, to identify high-priority initiatives for research, extension, and higher education programs in home economics (United States Department of Agriculture 1981). Four major thrusts that are similar to the 1970 research goals were determined: (1) family economic stability and security, (2) energy and environment, (3) food, nutrition, and health, (4) family strengths and social environment. The original document should be consulted for listing of new initiatives for each thrust that suggest specific areas for research.

## NCA-5

In 1983, based upon the research priorities framework of the 1981 National Plan for New Initiatives in Home Economics and the Researchable Topics Survey of the National Association of Extension Home Economics, NCA-5 (Committee of Agriculture Experiment Station Home Economics Administrators in the North Central Region) outlined and reaffirmed five research thrusts as priority areas for Home Economics Agriculture Experiment Station–supported research regionally and nationally. These thrusts, revised in 1985 and approved by NCA-5 in January 1986, are as follows:

*Family Economic Stability and Financial Security.* Families are faced with increasingly complex decisions involving demands on their resources during times of economic stress and change. Specific programs of research are needed to develop and extend information about:

- the impact of economic change (i.e., unemployment, limits on credit availability, high interest rates) on the family unit.
- optimizing the family's real income through household production, home-based and other self-employment and paid employment.
- the effects of current family resource decisions on the family's future.

*Family Food, Consumption, Nutrition and Health.* Ensuring quality food products and adequate nutrient intakes are critical for optimal health and development. Specific programs of research are needed to develop and extend information about:

- the nutrient bioavailability, nutrient interrelationships, and nutrient requirements for optimal health.
- the function, nutrient composition, quality, and stability of available and developing food products.

- the effects of nutrient imbalances on the nutritional status and the behavior of particular high risk groups, such as infants, children, pregnant or lactating women, and the elderly.

*Family Energy and Environmental Resource Utilization.* Continuing increases in energy costs and limited energy availability are burdening families' budgets and creating special hardships for limited income families. The effective and efficient use of environmental resources in everyday living is a primary task of families. Specific programs of research are needed to:

- develop methods of direct assessment of home energy consumption.
- determine and document the cost-effective benefits of home energy conserving devices and approaches.
- design and evaluate passive solar energy support in moderate and low income housing.
- assess the effects of pollutants of food, clothing and air on high risk family members (e.g., pregnant women, fetuses, young children and aged adults).

*Family Strengths and the Social Environment.* Family life-styles and stages in the family life cycle significantly influence family function and optimal development. Specifically, research is needed that extends information about how families cope with stress. Topics would include the following:

- how families can identify and manage the stress of a radically changing social and economic environment.
- parenting skills that promote the optimal development of children.
- the transition to initial parenting and non-traditional parenting situations.
- the impact of an aging population on the family.
- the use of support systems (e.g., day care, nursing homes, family and community support) in reducing family stress.

*Family and High Technology.* Rapid societal shifts toward the increased use of high technology and the concomitant reduction in the cost of microcomputers and other high technology devices for the home are increasingly affecting families. Specific programs of research are needed to rapidly extend and develop information about:

- the utilization of microcomputers and other high technology equipment in the home for managerial, environmental control, educational and family support purposes.
- the use of computers and special control devices in the home in the

production of goods and services for families.

- the impact of high technology on family function, stress and well-being, including social interaction, and individual development of patterns. This would also include the potential role of high technology (both in terms of devices and information processing and communication and control techniques) in optimizing the family's interaction with larger societal units, e.g., school, community, and governmental agencies.

## MULTIDISCIPLINARY NATURE OF HUMAN ECOLOGY

It should be evident from the brief summaries of the contributions of biology, sociology, psychology, environmental design and planning, and home economics to human ecology that the field is multidisciplinary in nature. However, more than any other discipline, home economics appears to have incorporated human ecology as a unifying framework for its numerous specializations. The continuing reorganizing and renaming of home economics units as departments, schools, or colleges of human ecology attest to this trend. These units are also becoming more multidisciplinary in terms of recruiting faculty with doctoral degrees in the more basic disciplines of physiology, chemistry, sociology, psychology, architecture and design, and economics, for example, who bring with them different theories and methodologies for applicatoin to the study of environment-behavior relationships. These faculty complement the backgrounds of the more traditional home economics/human ecology faculty with degrees in applied fields focusing on the physical (product) aspects of the home environment, such as clothing, textiles, housing and interior design, equipment, and foods.

Proshansky, Ittelson, and Rivlin (1970, 51) have outlined four identifying and defining features of environmental science: (a) it deals with the human-ordered and defined environment; (b) it grows out of pressing social problems; (c) it is multidisciplinary in nature; and (d) it includes study of human beings as an integral part of every problem.

Bronfrenbrenner (1979, 16) believes that there has been relatively less attention given by psychologists to the environmental aspects of the human environment equation: "To assert that human development is a product of interaction between the growing human organism and its environment is to state what is almost a commonplace in behavioral science. . . . What we find in practice . . . is a marked asymmetry, a hypertrophy of theory and research focusing on the properties of the person and only the most rudimentary conception and characterization of the environment in which the person is found."

## CONCEPTUAL AND THEORETICAL FRAMEWORKS

In Chapter 1 it was emphasized that theory and research are intertwined—that all research includes some type or level of theory, whether explicit or implicit. This linkage merits repeating here. Science was defined in the first chapter as "an interconnected series of concepts and conceptual schemes" (Conant 1951, 25). Theories are built from such a body of relationships among variables. Kerlinger (1986,9) describes theory as a "set of interrelated constructs (concepts), definitions, and propositions that present a systematic view of phenomena by specifying relations among variables, with the purpose of explaining and predicting the phenomena."

Theory and practice are not antagonistic in science. A good theory is very practical. As Leonardo de Vinci said, "Those who are enamoured of practice without science are like a pilot who goes into a ship without rudder or compass and never has any certainty where he is going."

Because of the multidisciplinary nature of human ecology, examples of concepts and theories from numerous disciplines are presented in this text.[1] In referring to environmental psychology, Proshansky, Ittelson, and Rivlin (1970) point out that interdisciplinary theory, in either a single research problem area or an entire field of study, is fraught with many difficulties. Problems are analyzed in accordance with the theorist's definition of a problem, and researchers vary in their fundamental training in and orientation to human-environment phenomena.

The following examples of conceptual or theoretical frameworks are not intended to be all-inclusive but to serve as an indication of some of the recent thinking in human ecology and to illustrate the forms that such frameworks can take. It is hoped that students will develop their own framework after a thorough study of the concepts basic to their major field of interest, thereby contributing to further theory development through research.

### Ecosystems

A. G. Tansley (1935, 284) originated the term *ecosystem* when he wrote: "The more fundamental conception is . . . the whole system. . . . Not only the organism-complex, but also the whole complex of physical factors forming what we call the environment . . . are the basic units of nature on the face of the earth. . . ." He emphasized that these ecosystems may be of different kinds and sizes.

### Processes for Human Transactions with the Environment

The areas of research in environmental psychology have been classified into three basic kinds of human transactions with the environment (Stokols

1977). The basic concepts discussed by numerous other theorists in the broad areas of human-environment interaction can be grouped within these three classifications of processes: orientation, operation, and evaluation. Ecosystem concepts summarized in the remainder of this chapter follow these classifications. The concepts and related theories are being applied and tested through research in human ecology/home economics and its numerous specializations, as well as in other disciplines, as the research examples accompanying this text illustrate.

### Orientation Processes

*Orientation processes* are those by which people perceive where they are, predict what will happen there, and decide what to do.

Environmental Perception. *Environmental perception* is the process of apprehending, through our senses, the physical environment that is immediately present. It is one of the most essential psychological processes by which we adapt to the environment. It forms the foundation for all of our knowledge about the world around us. It focuses upon settings and places and upon the factors influencing the impressions that observers form of their environment. Environmental perception is of particular relevance to the fields of architecture, environmental design, and interior design. It also parallels and draws upon concepts and methods used in the more highly developed research on person perception, which analyzes one's perceptions and evaluations of other people. Researchers in human ecology/human economics have studied the effects of clothing on person perception.

Environmental Cognition. *Environmental cognition* consists of the storage, organization, and recall of features of the environment that are not immediately present. Pioneering work in this area was undertaken by Lynch (1960), a professor of urban planning. In *The Image of the City,* he details his investigations of residents' images of three American cities (Boston, Jersey City, and Los Angeles), based upon asking them for directions and requesting them to sketch maps of their cities. Since Lynch's studies, geographers and psychologists have sought to learn more about the nature of the processes involved in the formation of mental maps. The products of these processes have been called mental maps, environmental images, schemata, and most frequently, cognitive maps. Downs and Stea (1973) define *cognitive mapping* as a process that enables us to collect, organize, store, recall, and decode information about the relative location and attributes of features of the geographic environment. The cognitive map portrays a particular person's representation of the environment.

Personality and the Environment. The trait model of personality has guided most of the previous research on personality and the environment, with lack of consideration of the situational influences on person-environment relationships (Windley 1975). In recent years, however, Craik (1973) referred to two major thrusts of personality-environment research: (a) personal styles of relating to the everyday physical environment (*environmental dispositions*) and (b) the use of established personality inventories to predict people's use and modification of the physical environment, including its reciprocal impact. Environmental dispositions studied have included pastoralism and urbanism, privacy preference, thing-person orientation, arousal seeking, and internal versus external locus of control.

### Operation Processes

*Operation processes* refer to the processes by which people act upon (modify or respond to) their surroundings, including their responses to environmental stressors such as noise and crowding. In this respect, there has been a relative lack of product-oriented studies (Cone and Hayes 1976). Some theorists would label these behavioral phenomena as functional adaptations and coping mechanisms.

Proxemics: Human Spatial Behavior. The study of human spatial behavior was launched by E. T. Hall (1966). This behavior has been examined in relation to privacy, personal space, territoriality, and crowding, with emphasis on the conceptual linkages among them. Sommer (1969) has demonstrated the relationships between types of activity being performed and the formality or informality of the setting. Generally, research on spatial behavior emphasizes the ways people utilize the environment to fulfill needs and achieve goals.

Environmental Stressors. Conditions in the environment result in stress to the extent that they tax or exceed the individual's adaptive resources. In the literature, two kinds of stress have been differentiated: systemic stress and psychological stress.

*Systemic stress* evolved in medically oriented research and emphasized the physiological aspects of stress. Pioneering work in the area is credited to Hans Selye (1956, 1976), who defined systemic stress as the nonspecific response of the body to any environmental demands made on it. Selye called the body's systemic response to stressful conditions the *general adaptation syndrome* (GAS). The GAS is the body's effort to function in a steady state while under stress. *Homeostasis,* the term used for the body's ability to maintain steady functioning despite changing external conditions, has been expanded by researchers to include psychological functioning.

*Psychological stress* has been the focus of more recent research studies (Lazarus 1966; Lazarus and Cohen 1977). In psychological stress, the individual appraises the personal meaning and significance of the stressor. Lazarus and his colleagues (Folkman and Lazarus 1980) have identified two major types of coping strategies for dealing with stressful situations. Problem-faced coping takes place when people either alter the stressful condition in the environment and/or change their behavior in dealing with the stress. Emotion-focused coping occurs when people reduce or better tolerate their emotional reactions to the stressful situation.

Environmental stressors being studied include noise, temperature, air pollution, and crowding. It should be emphasized that systemic and psychological stress are not mutually exclusive concepts; psychological stress may include aspects of systemic stress. They may be considered as emphasizing different aspects of a single stress reaction.[2]

Information Overload and Environmental Stress. Our electronic age has created a totally new environment, one that requires a wide range of awareness and of participation and involvement with things and people on a global scale. This age of constant communication is continually and subtly altering our perceptual senses as all aspects of our experience interact. Toffler (1970) referred to these rapid changes as future shock. Cohen (1978) advanced a model of environmental stress in terms of *information overload.* According to this model, when unpredictable and uncontrollable environmental stressors increase the demands placed on an individual's attention capacity for a prolonged period, the attention capacity will decrease, showing cognitive fatigue. This theory has been applied in studies of environmental stress, including the psychological effects of crowding.

Learned Helplessness and Environmental Stress. The theory of learned helplessness was originally developed in experimental psychology and has been applied by some environmental psychologists to determine why people who are unable to control stressful conditions tend to show low levels of persistence and tolerance for frustration when the stressful conditions no longer exist. The learned helplessness paradigm has been applied to assess the consequences of long-term exposure to aircraft noise on children's cognitive functioning, and to examine the experiences of the elderly in their housing environments.

**Evaluation Processes**

*Evaluation processes* include the ways in which people judge the quality of their environment. People's needs and goals provide the basis for judging the adequacy of various aspects of the environment.

Environmental Attitudes. *Environmental attitudes* include people's feelings of satisfaction or dissatisfaction with their environment. An important function of these attitudes is in the selection of residential environments in which to live. Considerable attention has been devoted recently to developing measuring techniques for environmental attitudes. The major techniques have been labeled *perceived environmental quality indices* (PEQI), which provide a quantitative measure of the quality of a particular physical setting, such as a housing development, a shopping center, or a hotel. Obviously, environmental attitudes play an important role in environmental design and planning.

Environmental Assessment. *Environmental assessment* is broader than environmental attitude. Research on environmental assessment is concerned with people's preferences regarding the future environment in addition to their attitudes toward their present surroundings. Numerous methodological devices have been developed for presenting environmental displays (simulations) and measuring people's responses to them. However, less attention has been paid to the development of theory (Stokols 1978). Exceptions include Wohlwill's (1976) extension of Berlyne's (1971) theory of aesthetics to environmental assessment and Kaplan's (1976) landscape preference prediction model. These theories suggest that concepts including complexity, coherence, and familiarity are determinants of environmental preferences.

Environmental assessment also includes *social impact assessment,* or the evaluation of proposed environmental changes on the physical and social well-being of user groups, where demographic and psychological criteria are used for forecasting the social and health consequences of environmental changes. (See Chap. 12 and **Research Synopsis 12.1**.)

## Human-Environmental Optimization

Through orientation, operation, and evaluation processes, individuals and groups guide their transactions with the environment in accordance with specified goals and plans toward human-environmental optimization. They try to achieve optimal environments to meet their needs and accomplish their goals. Thus, human-environmental optimization becomes an integrating theme for the study of human-environment interactions. It extends earlier concepts of behavior-environment fit and behavior-environment congruence.

## Information Rate

Environmental psychologists often describe and compare environments in terms of the concept of *information rate,* the amount of information contained or perceived in the environment per unit of time (Mehrabian 1976). The more information in the form of stimuli that must be processed by the observer, the higher the information rate. This information rate is also referred to as the *load* of an environment. A high-load environment has a high information rate, while a low-load environment has a low rate.

Environments are rated for load with numerous descriptive adjective pairs (e.g., large-scale–small-scale, complex–simple, novel–familiar, contrasting–similar, surprising–usual, heterogeneous–homogeneous, crowded–uncrowded, asymmetrical–symmetrical, random–patterned, dense–sparse). An environment described in terms of many of the left-hand terms would have a high load in contrast to one described with low-load right-hand terms. Information overload can lead to environmental stress; on the other hand, a low load can lead to boredom, and very low-load environments (e.g., solitary confinement) can result in serious impairment.

## HUMAN ECOLOGY/HOME ECONOMICS SPECIALIZATIONS AS ENVIRONMENTAL COMPONENTS

This chapter presents a *unifying* ecological framework for the specializations dealing with food, clothing, and shelter products as well as with families and consumers, who interact with each other and with these products of the environment. A few illustrations follow of the functioning of the specialized areas in human ecology/home economics as components of the environment. (See Chaps. 8–12 for synopses of actual research.)

### Food and Nutrition: Our Internal Environment

Food and nutrition (the process by which an individual takes in and utilizes food as energy) enable the individual to survive and adapt to the environment.

#### Energy

*Energy* can be regarded as a broad, unifying concept in studying people's relationships to their environment. Every event that takes place in the universe, whether physical, biological, or cultural, is an expression of energy.

According to the Second Law of Thermodynamics, *entropy* (an inactive or static condition in which energy may become useless) tends to increase as the universe becomes older. As entropy increases, the universe and all closed systems tend naturally to deteriorate—to move from a state of organization and differentiation to a state of chaos and sameness. But human beings are not isolated, closed systems. They take in food, which generates energy from outside themselves, and are, as a result, parts of that larger world that contains the sources of vitality or energy. They also take in information through their sense organs and act on the information received (Wiener 1954). This is in accord with the Second Law, which holds that living organisms can oppose the drift and move in a direction opposite to that specified for the cosmos as a whole, developing more complex structures and greater concentrations of energy.

## Homeostasis

The human organism combats entropy or resists the general stream of decay through the process of homeostasis. "It is the pattern maintained by this homeostasis which is the touchstone of our personal identity" (Wiener 1954, 96). Originally, this concept was applied to strictly physiological processes. It has since been applied to psychological and social areas. In the physiological sense, homeostasis consists of dynamic automatic forces operating within the organism to maintain a fairly rigid constancy or stability within its internal environment. These forces are under the control of the autonomic nervous system and therefore operate quite automatically. However, we can consciously assist the natural forces in some cases by altering our external or internal environment (i.e., through surgery, clothing and shelter provisions, etc.).

The nature of these forces that keep homeostasis operating can best be explained by the biochemist. The key word probably is *enzyme*. A prominent chemist once defined life as a system of cooperating enzyme reactions. As Cannon (1932, 289) indicated in his classic book, *The Wisdom of the Body:* "The blood proteins (on which the very existence of the normal blood volume depends), the blood calcium (of primary importance for the proper functioning of the neuromuscular system), and the red corpuscles of the blood (essential for the oxygen supply to the tissues) are examples of factors in the fluid matrix, all of which exhibit homeostasis to a surprising degree. Marked change in their concentrations brings about alarming disturbance in the organism."

## Food and Energy

The human being is an open energy system, taking energy from the environment and in turn utilizing that energy to interact with that environment by responding through his or her nervous system to environmental stimuli. The only form in which energy can be taken from the environment in significant amounts by higher animals, including man, is the chemical energy of food. This chemical energy is transformed into other forms of energy (mechanical, electrical, heat).

Few resources are tied as directly to survival as food. The principle of population is a principle of survival resting on the relation of numbers of people to food. Each human is designed to capture and transform the energy stored in foods into the complex processes of living, growing, and behaving.

### Nutrition and Communication

Humans, as open systems, combat entropy by taking in food to generate energy and by communicating with their environment, taking in information through their sense organs and acting on it. This communication and action is controlled by the nervous system.

The primary function of the nervous system is to adjust the organism to its environment. Such adjustment is achieved through (1) the coordination of sustaining systems, (2) learning or habit formation, and (3) reflective thought and planned adaptation. The autonomic nervous system functions to regulate visceral activities (hunger, sex, elimination) and to maintain their balanced coordination and stability (homeostasis). Emotions are also expressed through the autonomic nervous system.

The central nervous system, comprised of the brain and spinal cord, functions to maintain the adjustment and coordination of afferent and efferent nerve impulses. Afferent nerve fibers receive stimuli from the environment, in the form of visual, auditory, affectory, gustatory, and tactile sensations, and carry these sensory impulses to the central nervous system. Efferent nerve fibers convey outgoing or motor impulses from the central nervous system to organs of response, such as the muscles of limbs and the speech organs.

Normally the process of communication with one's environment proceeds as follows. Nerve cells have long thin threads leading from the spinal cord to the various muscles in the body. Messages (from sensory stimuli) are sent along this network, ordering muscles to perform their function (response). There is a gap between the end of the nerve fiber and the muscle. A chemical, acetylcholine, is released to send messages across this gap (or synapse). Once the message is delivered to the muscle cells, an enzyme in the blood fragments acetylcholine, and the stage is open for new communication.

Nutrition is important for central nervous system functioning as well as for maintaining homeostasis within the body by the autonomic nervous system. Learning may be a matter of protein synthesis within the neurons. The protein-producing system is poorly developed in mentally disordered persons. Mental disturbances invariably accompany the physical symptoms of pellagra, a disease associated with the absense of nicotinic acid, or niacin, in the diet. Similar disturbances may occur in beriberi, which is caused by a lack of vitamin $B_1$. There is a correlation between these B-complex vitamins and the functioning of the brain. The source of energy for the brain is the metabolism of sugar. These vitamins are coenzymes in the various steps of that metabolism. Whether the stresses on a brain are emotional or chemical (resulting from absence of dietary essentials), the consequential symptoms are apparently very similar.

## Clothing: The Second Skin and Portable Environment

### Perception

The human body and its extension through clothing has been referred to as both the subject and the object of perception (as both a stimulus and a response). As such, it is an intimate part of our near environment. McLuhan (1964) described fashion as an attempt to adjust the sensory life to a changing technological environment. Hence, the experiencing of not only a wide range of colors but also of many textures and sculptural shapes in dress relates to our desire to experience the environment in its entirety with all our senses.

Clothing has also been studied in relation to *person perception,* which analyzes one's perception of other people (Douty 1963). In discussing the psychological functions of clothing, Flugel (1950, 20) wrote: "The essential purpose of decoration is to beautify the bodily appearance so as to attract the admiring glances of others and to fortify one's self esteem."

### Proxemics: Human Spatial Behavior

The first and most basic form of human spatial behavior is the development of body boundaries (Melson, 1980, 75). Clothing becomes important in establishing self-awareness very early in life. Such awareness is at first related to kinesthetic sensations and awareness of the physical body. Clothes become closely identified with the body and affect sensations. Through the *differentiation process,* people learn to separate their bodies from their environment, and the clearness of this demarcation may have important behavioral implications throughout their lives, helping to maintain homeostasis. Clothing plays an important part in this demarcation. Clothing that extends the physical dimensions of one's body tends to be felt as part of the body. The stiffness, thickness, and strength of clothing fabrics are also imparted through body sensations.

Techniques have been developed for measuring the definiteness of a person's *body-image boundary* (limit or boundary that separates the body from the outside world). Compton (1964) demonstrated how clothing may compensate for weak body-image boundaries in some women.

### Environmental Adaptation

Clothing also serves as a means of adapting to outside environmental stressors and modifying energy consumption. An apparel textile may be viewed as an extension of a person's bodily heat-control mechanism because it helps the individual attain some degree of equilibrium (homeostasis) in a changing environment. Such thermal equilibrium relates to comfort. Thermal comfort is influenced by environmental factors of temperature, humidity, rate of air movement, and radiation intensity. An apparel textile serves as a barrier to heat transfer. It reduces the amount of heat lost from the body to the atmosphere and decreases the amount of heat absorbed by the body from the atmosphere. Textile fibers and air trapped within them are excellent insulators and poor conductors of heat.

Since clothing provides shelter and protection for the human body, it has become an important product for surviving in today's world. The space suit is an item of clothing, although those who have depended on it as a life-supporting, miniature spacecraft might think of it as an "engineered product" or a "moving house." Watkin's (1984) work emphasizes that the lines between clothing, products, and housing often cannot be clearly drawn.

## Housing: The Spatial Environment

Winston Churchill once said, "We shape our buildings and afterwards our buildings shape us." To McLuhan (1964), housing is an extension of a person's bodily heat-control mechanism, and techniques of heating and lighting give new flexibility and scope to this mechanism by enabling people to attain some degree of thermal and physiological equilibrium in a changing environment.

For thousands of years people had the open spaces in their natural environment for individual privacy and solitude. Today their homes are the last refuge they have from the hazards of street traffic and from the noise, stress, and dust of the outside world. Research to provide an understanding of how people use and respond to space is essential for designing and arranging physical home environments that promote the healthy psychological and social development and adjustment of people.

### Territoriality

Although studies on the relationships between humans and physical space have been conducted in many fields of social science, more is understood about animal spatial behavior. One of the most important concepts emerging from animal studies, territoriality, is also applicable to human societies. Territoriality is a basic characteristic of living organisms.

*Territory* is the space or area to which an animal or human lays claim and defends against others of the same species (Plihal and Brown 1969). An individual's or family's territory (usually consisting of the home and its grounds) may be protected by laws preventing its search or seizure, by installing fences or planting hedges, by constructing walls, and so forth. The psychologist Jung (1965, 2) believed that territory for humans is an expression of our basic need for roots: "The need for roots is the need for a sense of safety, identity, and belonging, a feeling of wanted security and steadiness. If a person has a physical area or territory which is his [or her] own, the familiarity of it, the feeling of being 'at home' or belonging there meets the need for roots. People may satisfy the need in other ways but territory is one way."

### Crowding

The degree of crowding in the rooms of a home is regarded as an important index of housing conditions. "Crowding or congestion is pollution of living space and we must look at human beings as potential environmental insults" (Linton 1968, 92). The same space may feel more or less crowded depending on how many people occupy it, how furniture and equipment are arranged in it, how its occupants organize themselves, and what types of activities or social interaction take place within it.

The concept of crowding may be as much an attitude on the part of people as it is physical in nature. Some recent studies suggest that individuals who commit violent crimes may have a low tolerance for crowding. Rates for violent crimes have been positively correlated with actual population densities in American cities (Ehrlich and Ehrlich 1970).

### Social Interaction

In addition to the importance of providing space for privacy, the organization of space is important for social interaction. In Merton's (1951, 181) opinion: "The dwelling unit is the locus of the initial socialization of the child; it is there that his character-structure is largely shaped. Not only are patterns of socialization typically enacted *within* the home; they appear in part to be oriented *toward* the house and its contents." Physical distance carries social interactional meaning, with people tending to arrange themselves at distances from one another on the basis of the social action in which they are engaged.

## Management and the Human Environment

Human-environmental optimization is an integrating theme for the study of human-environment interactions. Resources in the environment should be managed by individuals and groups to achieve this optimization.

Resource management is viewed as the extraction and transformation of environmental energy through the active processes of perceiving, spacing, valuing, and deciding. These processes, taken together, may be viewed as the means by which individuals, families, and other groups seek to maintain an adaptation level for environmental stimulation in order to achieve their goals (Melson 1980, 170).

Basic environmental resources of nutrients from food and fossil fuels are utilized to form the foundation upon which other energy transformations are built. Hannon (1975) estimated that the household sector of the economy consumes two-thirds of all U.S. energy consumed. It is important to consider the family's process of decision making with regard to energy resources. A major interdisciplinary study of energy use by families concluded that energy consumption is largely determined by the nondecisions of families—that the amount of energy needed for their activities is a *consequence* of the family's life-style (Morrison and Gladhart 1976).

All management problems involve the use of resources as inputs to produce some kinds of outputs. These resources usually have alternative uses, and a cost is sustained in using the resources. The output, or benefit, from using the resources also has value. Therefore, management seeks to minimize the costs and maximize the benefits associated with a given use of resources. This economic concept of utility has been adopted by many decision theorists. Utility is used as a measurement of the degree to which satisfaction (or attainment of objectives or goals) is obtained. Alternative choices or modes of action are compared to determine which choice yields the greatest amount of utility. Some decision problems are more easily quantified than others. For example, if an objective can be expressed in dollars, such as gross profit received, the degree of satisfaction of the objective is easily measured.

Consumption is a key concept within the economic framework. Output (or benefit) is viewed in terms of the consumption of goods and services that leads to family welfare. The household or consumer unit is used as a unit of reference in many economic surveys. Such surveys of consumption patterns over long periods of time are important in analyzing the family cycle fully. Economic concepts such as those involving control of expenditures and division of labor within the household affect power structure and roles within the family.

Management, however, consists of more than the economic management of resources to produce a high standard of living through consumption. Management should have as its end goal the encouragement of self-actualization of individuals and families. Beyond *having,* the focus should be on *being,* on providing an environment that will help each individual reach his or her full potential.

## The Family as an Ecosystem

The family is an example of an ecosystem—a group of organisms interacting with each other and their environment. Families, like organisms, do not exist in isolation; they occupy an environmental niche or microenvironment. Just as an ecosystem tends toward self-regulation, a family can learn to maintain itself somewhat like a balanced aquarium. Basic resources provide energy input that can be absorbed, stored, gradually consumed, and dissipated as heat. Associated with the flow of energy is a cycling of nutrients enabling the ecosystem to be balanced and self-contained. As a life-support system, the family receives physical sustenance from the natural environment and is dependent upon the social environment for its affectional and socialization needs.

An ecosystem is affected by an environmental catastrophe and by the invasion of a new species. The birth of each child, the addition of an in-law or stepparent, or the hospitalization or death of an individual family member affect some of the members more than others. Some individuals respond to opportunities afforded them, and others suffer restraints to their further development.

The better-adapted species in an ecosystem tend to survive and increase, while the less well-adapted ones are unable to survive the competition for space, nutrients, or other needs. The stability of an ecosystem, or its ability to adapt to invasion or catastrophe without a period of instability or major change, is related to its diversity. In the same manner, a family with little diversity among its members and its investment of resources is vulnerable to changing social and economic conditions.

Nature obtains stability by allowing energy to flow smoothly through the ecosystem, by retaining and recycling nutrients, and by encouraging diversity of species. Both the species and the environment have a remarkable ability to change. Since the family is not a closed system, it must be resilient and adaptable to change while maintaining its family organization as an ecosystem. The continued well-being of an ecosystem depends upon keeping the natural recycling mechanisms intact. The family needs to recognize that its resources are finite and must be conserved. The maintenance of environmental quality and the development of attitudes and values necessary to solve problems within the microenvironment can be a trust for one's children.

The family is also an important link in the global ecosystem. The relationship between persons and environment is a reciprocal one. Not only does the environment affect people's behavior but people, in turn, affect and reconstruct the environment. An interactional model is reflected in Kurt Lewin's (1936) classic dictum, B = f (P, E)—that behavior is a function of both the person and the environment.

## Consumer Service Environments

America has become a service economy, dominated by industries that perform rather than produce. It is predicted that there will be continued fast growth in service industries and service jobs, with data processing and hospitality leading the way (Albrecht and Zemke 1985).[3] Manufacturing goods will continue to be produced and consumed but fewer people will be required to produce them. In this new era, service itself becomes a product. Referring to definitions from the Census Bureau and the Department of Commerce, Albrecht and Zemke (1985, 3) apply the following four broad segments of the economy to the *service sector,* which consists of "industries whose output is intangible":

- Transportation, communication, and utilities.
- Wholesale and retail trade.
- Finance, insurance and real estate.
- Services—the fastest growing part of the "service sector," which includes business services such as housekeeping, barbering, and recreational services; and most of the non-profit areas of the economy.

**The Retailing Industry**

Blackwell and Talarzyk (1983) stress the importance of an understanding of life-style retailing to the achievement of high yields, and possibly even the survival of retail organizations, throughout the remainder of the decade. A life-style retail organization is one that bases its strategy and operations on the unique living patterns of its target customers rather than on demographics or merchandise strength. These authors cite restaurants as one of the best examples of life-style retailing. Other examples are provided from the fashion apparel field.

Store environments are among the environmental settings that have been studied by Mehrabian (1976). He concludes that "environmental conditions that make for maximum buying, namely, conditions that provide heightened arousal, heightened pleasure, and mild feelings of dominance, are the same as those which make a place fun for shoppers" (Mehrabian 1976, 287). Bargain stores and shopping centers are the most loaded environments. A good illustration is an atmosphere where shoppers experience themselves as part of a large bazaar-like atmosphere, as in large open-air markets and department store warehouse clearance sales. Filene's basement in Boston is cited as the classic example of a highly loaded and invariably crowded department store. This store buys merchandise from stores going out of business and sells it in its basement with a schedule of price markdowns. Dubbed the Smoke Pit, the basement is often a mob scene with customers undressing in the aisles and fighting with each other. The experience of "gambling for an exceptional buy" brings crowds day after day.

While some people like a highly loaded, arousing shopping environment, others prefer more moderate- or low-arousal settings that also promote high levels of pleasant and dominance feelings. Exclusive, high-status stores feature visually pleasant merchandise artfully displayed in uncrowded and well-organized (low-load) settings. The store personnel are also important in setting a pleasant atmosphere conducive to needs of clientele. Some large department stores feature uniform low-load displays that bore shoppers.

Mehrabian and Williams (1969), in studying persuasion, found that people are most susceptible to influence when they are highly aroused and feeling pleasant. "Stores can be readily designed to elicit this combination of feelings from their customers, thereby increasing customer suggestibility and purchasing" (Mehrabian 1976, 294).

### Hospitality and Tourism

Restaurants (an important part of tourism) provide one of the best examples of life-style retailing (Tigert, Lathrope, and Bleeg 1971). Mill and Morrison (1985) emphasize that from a marketing viewpoint, the segmentation of a target market by life-style provides a good picture of the characteristic likes and dislikes of the potential tourist.

An ideal restaurant should have characteristics similar to those of other retail establishments. All of these establishments must cause people to approach (enter), stay, and enjoy themselves. They should also consist of environments that range from highly loaded and extremely arousing to slightly loaded and relaxing. People may require recreational environments that compensate for the varying loads of their work settings (Mehrabian 1976).

Mehrabian (1976) describes bars and restaurants with varying environments: (1) Gourmet dining—"an intensely refined sensual and aesthetic experience" (p. 263). (2) Pseudo gourmet dining—food is not the central element but is secondary to high-status decor, service, and inflated prices characteristic of most gourmet restaurants. (3) Restaurant dining—the food served is but one aspect of an exciting evening that may include entertainment during the meal. (4) Functional dining—the main purpose is to ingest food with minimum delay, expense, and hassle.

## Notes

1. Suggested references for readers who desire more information on environmental theories and concepts are Canter (1977), Csikszentmihalyi and Rochberg-Halton (1981), Gibson (1979), Levy-Leboyer (1982), Rapoport (1982), Russell and Mehrabian (1976), Sims, Paolucci, and Morris (1972), Stokols (1982), and Wapner (1981).

2. For a more detailed discussion of environmental stress, see Holahan (1982).

3. The hospitality industry is a conglomerate of institutions that includes restaurants, hotels, resorts, and school food services. It encompasses food, lodging, and travel away from home.

CHAPTER 3

# Some Basic Considerations in Planning Research

## OVERVIEW OF THE RESEARCH PROCESS

Scientific research is research that more or less conforms to the scientific method discussed in Chapter 1. Most scientific research is characterized by an underlying sequence of activities. While certain aspects of the process may be less appropriate for some types of research than others, the sequence can be used as a general format from which an adequate proposal and study may be generated. As Harburg's map (Fig. 3.1) illustrates, the path of inquiry is frequently difficult and seldom as neat and orderly as a sequence might suggest.

Significant overlap in activities of the research process result in a blurring of boundaries between those activities (see Fig. 3.2). Seemingly discrete stages that define the process must be viewed within parameters dictated by the requirements of the overall product. An illustration of the appropriateness of returning to supposedly earlier stages during which the foundation was laid for the investigation is provided by examining overlap between the literature review and other components of the research process. Even during more advanced stages, such as following formulation of the hypothesis, generation of the research design, or interpretation of the findings, gaps in areas initially examined may become apparent. It is at junctures such as these that a return to the available literature may prove most valuable. It is often through this type of reexamination that the researcher finally develops a complete understanding of the issues being evaluated.

Research is cyclic and self-correcting. It begins with a problem, stimulated by theory and past research, and ends with tentative generalizations derived from results of the study. The generalizations ending one cycle are the beginning of the next cycle (i.e., a new problem). In other words, the

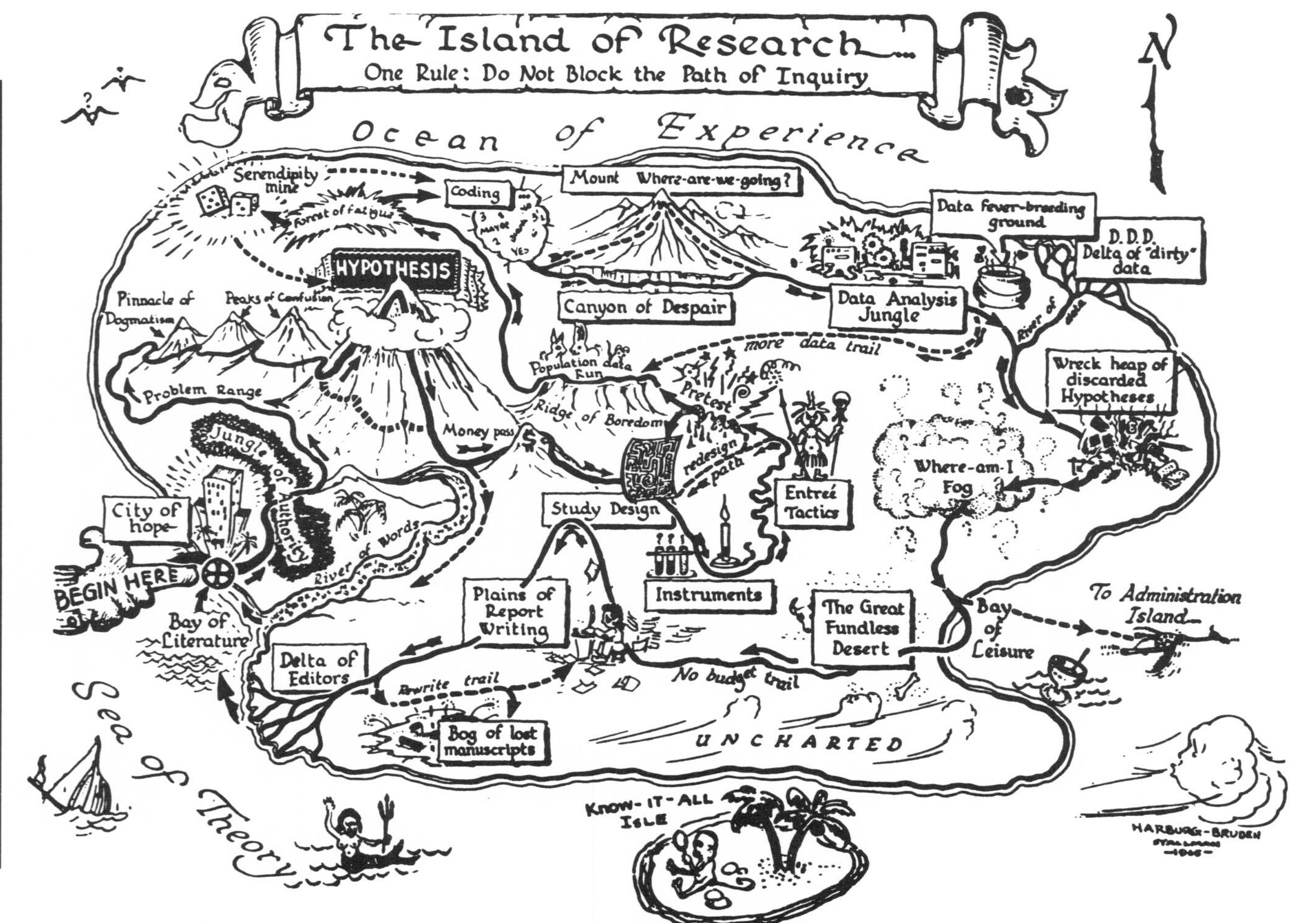


**Figure 3.1.** The Island of Research. (Reprinted by permission of *American Scientist,* journal of Sigma Xi, by Ernest Harburg, vol. 54, no. 4 [1966].)

succeeding study tests the generalizations of the previous research. If the generalizations are rejected, new ones are formulated and subjected to investigation. Before reformulation, however, the methods and procedures on which the generalizations are based are scrutinized carefully for possible deficiencies, and necessary changes in research design, measurement, and data analysis are incorporated. The cyclic and self-correcting nature of research explains why so many seemingly similar studies are reported in the literature. Research is never-ending; the process is constantly repeated with refinements.

## Major Components of the Research Process

There are several interrelated aspects of the research process that are deserving of individual examination. Each of these is considered in detail elsewhere in the text, but a listing and brief discussion of these processes are provided here as an overview.

### Selection of a Research Problem Area and Preliminary Literature Review

The initial step in research is to decide on a general area in which to work. Chapter 2 listed several broad research areas in human ecology associated with academic areas of study, but other sources of ideas also can be translated into legitimate research problems.

A preliminary literature review helps familiarize the researcher with what has already been published in the general problem area. At this stage of the literature search, the investigator draws primarily on sources that effectively summarize relevant theory and past research.

### Detailed Review of Literature

The purpose of the detailed literature review is to help the investigator arrive at a specific research problem and learn as much about that problem as possible. Narrowing down a broad area to a precise research problem can be a difficult task, especially for the beginning researcher. When defining the scope of a study, you must ask: Specifically, what do I plan to investigate? What is the exact question I wish to answer? The problem should be stated in specific terms and be capable of resolution, but it should not be so specific that it is trivial.

Once the problem has been identified, the investigator continues the literature review begun earlier but the search now focuses on theory and research *directly* related to the defined problem. The review takes on greater organization and detail in an attempt to identify all pertinent literature. Actual reports of research are consulted. During the literature review, the researcher also gleans methodological ideas for the study being planned.

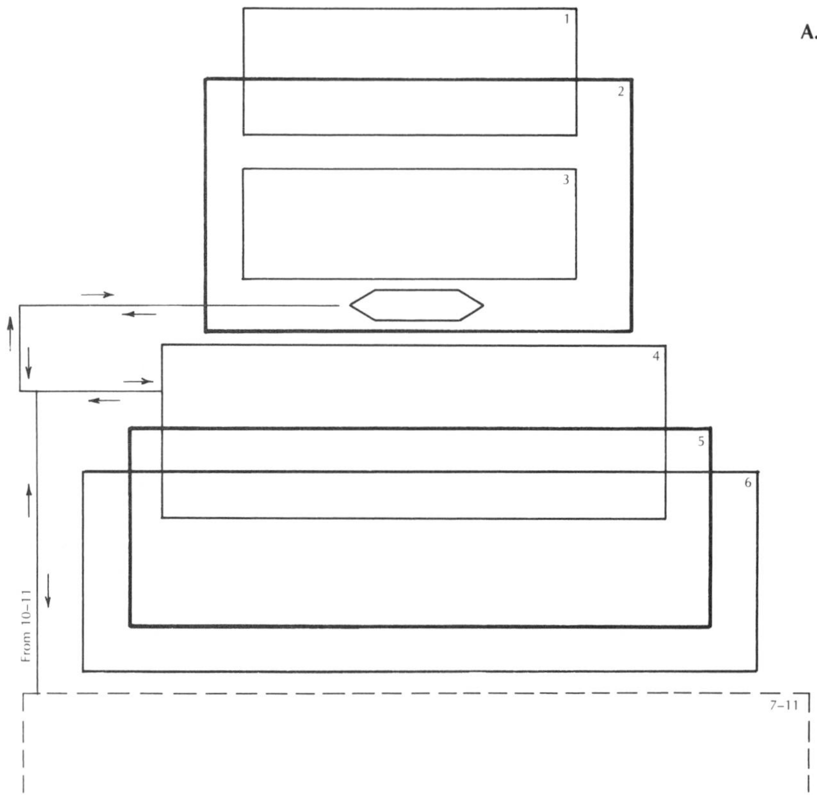


**Figure 3.2.** **A** and **B.** Overlapping components of the research process. **A.** In the general preparation for conducting the study (1–6), activities are limited to integrating available information into a cohesive structure: 1 = selection of a research problem area and preliminary review of the literature, 2 = detailed review of the literature, 3 = formulation of hypotheses or research questions, 4 = preparation of a research plan/proposal, 5 = development of a research design, 6 = procedures and instrumentation. Arrows connecting areas 2 and 4 indicate the need for continued review of the literature. **B.** From the implementation of the proposal through completion of the final report (7–11), activities are directed toward conducting the study and drawing conclusions: 7 = selection of sample, 8 = collection and preparation of data, 9 = analysis of data, 10 = interpretation of findings, 11 = completion of final research report. Arrows indicate exploratory post-hoc analyses and extended literature review during the final stages of the project. (Figure by Barry F. Perlmutter and John Touliatos)

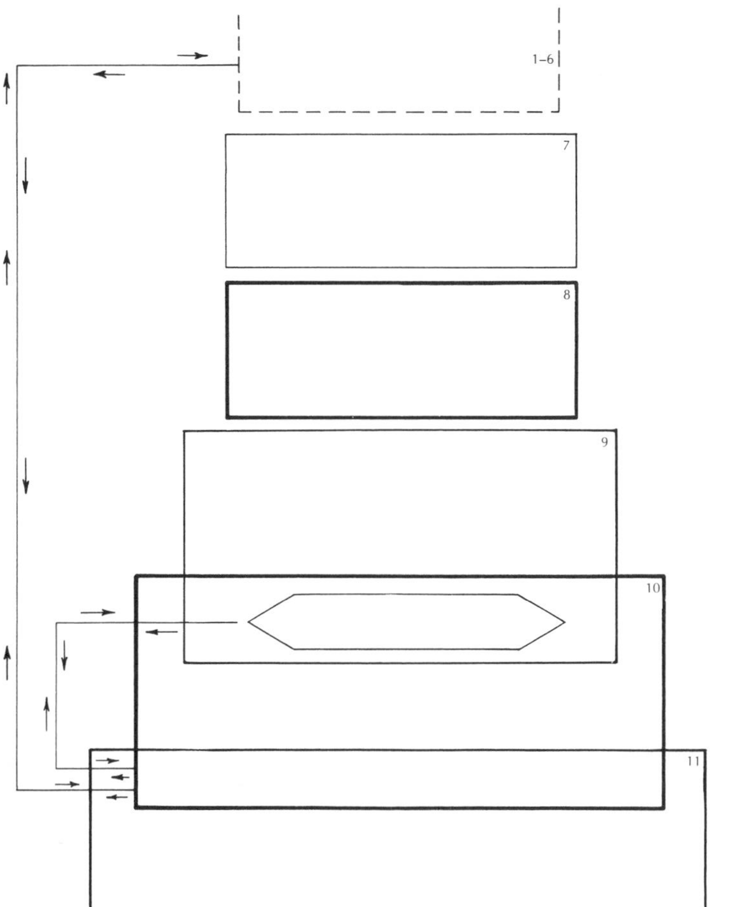


## Formulation of Hypotheses or Research Questions

Following immersion in the literature, the researcher is prepared to formulate hypotheses or research questions based upon existing theory and past studies.

## Preparation of a Research Plan/Proposal

A research plan of some kind should be developed after examining the literature and formulating hypotheses or research questions. When at least tentative hypotheses or questions have been posed, the investigator can identify variables and begin thinking in terms of sampling, instrumentation, and other design issues. The plan may take the form of a simple outline, a formal thesis or dissertation proposal, or a request for funding from a foundation or government agency.

If humans or animals are to be used in the research, it is necessary to consider ethical guidelines established for the protection of live subjects.[1] Review of proposed research projects by committees established by academic departments, universities, and research organizations ensures that procedures are ethically acceptable.

Putting the plan in writing forces the researcher to think through technical and ethical aspects of the investigation as well as more practical matters, such as timetables, costs, and potential obstacles, that may be encountered. It also facilitates evaluation of the intended study and serves as a "road map" for carrying out the project. A research proposal may be viewed as a working document that evolves into a research report as the study proceeds.

### Development of a Research Design

After a problem has been identified and hypotheses or research questions have been stated, the investigator is in a position to develop an overall context within which these hypotheses and questions may be addressed. The design indicates the specific situations and conditions to be examined, specifies data collection procedures expected to facilitate solution of the problem, and designates who the subjects will be and how they will be selected. Finally, it indicates the unit of analysis (e.g., individuals, groups, organizations) and type of statistical analyses possible.

### Procedures and Instrumentation

It is necessary to determine if there are available instruments such as questionnaires, interview schedules, and observational systems to adequately measure the variables under investigation. Adoption of an existing instrument that is technically sound and appropriate for the sample and study purposes not only saves time and effort but also facilitates interpretation of results in relation to findings of others who have previously used the same measuring device. If a suitable instrument cannot be identified, the investigator adapts an available measure or constructs a new one.

Even though an instrument may be chosen for which there are normative data and other technical information, it is a good idea to try it out on subjects similar to ones who will be included in the final sample. Pretesting helps the researcher evaluate study procedures and personnel as well as measuring instruments.

### Selection of Sample

The sample should be representative of the population to which the researcher wishes to generalize the findings. If an experimental treatment is to be applied, subjects are assigned to conditions at this point.

### Collection and Preparation of Data

Collecting data involves largely routine problems of public relations, administration, scheduling, and meticulous and efficient record keeping. The researcher exercises care to ensure that data are collected in an objective and uniform manner consistent with the study design and that they are recorded accurately in a suitable format. The primary investigator often delegates some or all of the responsibilities for data collection so that he or she can devote more time to other aspects of the project. If this is the case, the researcher carefully trains the observers, interviewers, or test monitors and supervises their performances throughout the study.

Following collection, raw data must be coded, scored, and put into a format appropriate for analysis.

### Analysis of Data

Statistical procedures are normally used to analyze data. (Results of the analyses are included in the Results section of the research report.)

### Interpretation of Findings

Following analyses, the researcher interprets the findings within the framework of existing theory and past research. (Interpretations are included in the Discussion section of the report.)

### Completion of Final Research Report

Although new information was added as the project proceeded, if a proposal was previously developed, a great deal of the work on the research report has already been done (e.g., introduction, literature review, method).

At this final stage, the research report is completed. The Results and Discussion sections are finalized. The Discussion section includes not only interpretation of the findings but also conclusions and possible recommendations. Also, last minute references are added, changes in other sections of the report are made, the abstract is written, and the title of the report (study) may be slightly revised so as to better represent the final product.

## CONCEPTS, VARIABLES, AND THEIR MEASUREMENT

Concepts (sometimes called constructs or hypothetical constructs) are necessary tools in theory building and research. A *concept* is a mental abstraction, a verbal device, or a label invented by the researcher to signify an object or process. Researchers use concepts as basic descriptive categories to interpret, structure, and explore the world around them. Social class, intelligence, achievement, and happiness are examples of concepts. Concepts are not observed directly; instead, they are judged or inferred from observations and measurements. Thus, it may be said that concepts are abstractions of the real world. Both concepts and the observations or measurements on which they are based are referred to as *variables,* which means they can have different values, such as differences in quantity, frequency, or size.

## Types of Variables

### Independent and Dependent Variables

The most important way to classify variables is as independent and dependent. In an experimental study, the *independent variable* is the factor that the researcher purposively manipulates in an attempt to determine its relationship to an observed outcome. It is often called the experimental or treatment variable. Since it is the variable from which a prediction is being based, it may also be referred to as the predictor variable. Knowledge of the values of the independent variable helps predict values of the dependent variable.

The *dependent variable* is the factor that is measured to ascertain the effect of the independent variable. It is frequently termed the criterion variable. If a researcher is examining the effects of an innovative teaching method on children's achievement, the independent variable is the new teaching methodology and the dependent variable is the measured change in students' achievement test scores attributable to the teaching. The independent variable is the presumed cause of changes in the dependent variable.

In nonexperimental studies, the terms independent and dependent variables are usually used even though they have less distinct meanings. The researcher does not manipulate anything as in an experiment; the manipulation or treatment has presumably already taken place. Differences between groups also may have already been created by biological and social influences, with the researcher merely seeking to discover a relationship among the variables. In these studies, the independent variable is the presumed causal, antecedent, or preexisting condition that can be related to consequent factors, or dependent variables. Categorization of independent and dependent variables is made on logical grounds and/or by the interests of the researcher. For example, in a study of family social climate and psychological adjustment of adolescents, the prevailing view might dictate that family social climate be designated the independent variable and adjustment the dependent variable.

### Organismic Variables

*Organismic variables* are characteristics that individuals have when they come to the research situation. Examples of preexisting attributes of research subjects are sex, intelligence, social class, and personality traits. In many, and perhaps most, studies, it is important that such variables as these be taken into account.

### Intervening Variables

*Intervening variables* are factors that underlie or mediate the relationship between the independent and dependent variables. Generally, the intervening variable is a hypothetical conception and cannot be seen, measured, or manipulated. The existence of these unobservable psychological processes (e.g., feelings, motivation, perception), assumed to intervene between cause-and-effect or stimulus-and-response variables, is inferred from observable behavior.

### Moderator Variables

A *moderator* is a variable that affects the relationship between the independent and dependent variables but does not have a direct role in a cause-and-effect sense. Prompted by theory or past studies suggesting that a moderator variable might alter the relationship between the dominant variables, the researcher singles out and measures or manipulates the moderator variable to determine if it in fact modifies or helps explain more about the relationship of the independent to the dependent variable. Sex of the subject, social class, IQ, and personality traits are examples of possible moderator variables. As an illustration, there is a possiblity that a relationship between two variables will be different for males and females or for individuals from different social classes.

### Control Variables

*Control variables* are variables whose effects are held constant, or removed either statistically or by other means, because they could intrude upon or confuse the relationship between the independent and dependent variables. Sex, age, intelligence, and social class are some of the variables that the researcher may choose to control for. For example, in an investigation of the effects of a certain type of instruction on learning, the researcher would probably want to control for intelligence.

### Continuous and Discrete Variables

A *continuous variable* is one that represents a continuum with graduated values, both whole and fractional units, from low to high. There are an indefinite number of possible values between any two adjacent points on the scale. If the variable is body weight, 175 and 176 pounds are adjacent values on the scale, but there still can be a number of intermediate values, such as 175.5 pounds or 175.51 pounds. Chronological time is another continuous variable that may take on an unlimited number of intermediate values. Since continuous variables are often expressed as whole numbers, they may appear to be discontinuous, but they are not. Measures of affiliation motivation, intelligence, parental attitudes toward child rearing, and height are other examples of continuous variables.

In contrast, a *discrete variable* has a finite number of potential values between any two points on the scale. Measurement is possible only in whole units and not fractional amounts. A family can have 1, 2, 3, 4, or more children but not 2.5 children. In other words, between the values of 2 and 4, there is only one other possible value, 3. Group size, number of family moves, and number of divorces in a county represent values that proceed by whole numbers and are therefore discrete variables.

Some discrete variables belonging to the nominal level of measurement (see next section) are two-category (dichotomous) or multiple-category (polytomous). They are also referred to as categorical variables (Kerlinger 1986) because the values represent categories, each of which is based upon having or not having one or more defining characteristics. It is an all-or-nothing consideration. Examples of dichotomous variables are sex of subject, white–nonwhite, legally married–unmarried, gainfully employed–unemployed, and alive–deceased. Thus, all subjects who are married are considered the same, put in the "married" subset, and assigned the same numeral, 1, in that category. Polytomous variables, having more than two subsets, include religious affiliation (e.g., Protestant, Catholic, Jewish) and country of birth (United States, Canada, Mexico, other). They are likewise handled by assigning 1s and 0s to individuals.

While it is impossible to change a discrete variable to a continuous variable (one cannot be 40% married or 26% female), a continuous variable can be converted to a discrete variable. Although there is a loss of information, age can be expressed as minor or adult, IQ as low or high, and weight as light, average, or heavy.

For the sake of simplicity, most of the examples of research given here have only a single independent and a single dependent variable or just one moderator variable. Although mathematics and statistics in years past imposed certain limitations and encouraged examination of only *the* independent variable and *the* dependent variable, recent developments in statistical theory, increased capacities of computers, and improvements in data processing technology have made the simultaneous study of many variables possible. This is especially important in human ecology, where research problems seldom lend themselves to explanation in terms of a single variable. The questions researchers ask are complex and require the investigation of several independent variables and one or more dependent variables or call for the inclusion of many control and moderator variables. One independent variable may explain only a small amount of variation in the dependent variable, whereas the introduction of additional independent variables may help account for more variation. Furthermore, certain events emerge only in interaction with others. Examining combinations of variables helps avoid the problem of partial answers and adds clarity to findings. Appropriate statistical techniques, referred to collectively as *multivariate analysis* (e.g., multiple regression, multiple analysis of variance, multiple factor analysis, path analysis), allow analysis of multiple causation and concomitance and should be considered when designing a study.

It is necessary to remember that *the researcher* classifies and designates variables as independent, dependent, and so on. The literature and the intent of a particular study help the researcher classify the variables. An independent variable in one investigation may be a dependent or moderator variable in another investigation, or what is a control variable in one may be a moderating variable in another. Classification of variables are not mutually exclusive. Sex, an organismic variable, could also be a control variable if its effects are controlled or a moderator variable if it helps explain the relationship between an independent and dependent variable. It can even be an independent variable. The same holds true for factors like age, social class, and educational level.

## Measurement of Variables

There is another basis for the classification of variables that has implications for the type of research questions that can be answered, the statistical procedures that can be used, and the interpretations that can be derived from the results of a study. Variables may be categorized according to the manner in which values are assigned to them, or put another way, by the numerical properties of the scales by which the variables are measured. Technically, we measure the indicators of variables. Measurement is the process of assigning numbers or other symbols to variables according to some set of rules. Empirical indicators are derived from operational definitions of a term (see Chap. 4). Four basic levels of measurement, forming a hierarchy of increasing complexity (Stevens 1951), are used in human ecology to convert concepts into variables: nominal, ordinal, interval, and ratio scales (Table 3.1).

### Nominal Scales

At the *nominal* (or classificatory) level, objects or individuals are classified into distinguishable, named categories with no implication of "more" or "less." Although numbers are usually assigned for labeling and classification purposes, any collection of meaningful symbols could be selected to denote the classes (e.g., A, B, C, D or 1, 2, 3, 4). If numbers are used, they are strictly qualitative and represent nothing more than simple designations

**Table 3.1. Characteristics of the Four Levels of Measurement**

| Level of Measurement | Characteristics: Classification | Order | Equal intervals | True zero point | Examples |
|---|---|---|---|---|---|
| Nominal | Yes | No | No | No | Sex of individual, "number" on football jersey |
| Ordinal | Yes | Yes | No | No | Rank in graduating class, academic degrees |
| Interval | Yes | Yes | Yes | No | Fahrenheit temperature, calendar dates |
| Ratio | Yes | Yes | Yes | Yes | Weight, length |

of type. Therefore, if we assign a 1 to a female and 2 to a male, a 1 is neither less nor more than a 2. Examples of such scales are the classification of people by marital status, religion, nationality, occupation, disease, hair color, or any other classification by which groups may be distinguished from one another by name. Objects can be classified nominally also (e.g., make of car, type of architecture, acid or alkaline solution, synthetic or natural fibers). Obviously, some classification systems involve two categories, and others involve more than two.

The only requirements for nominal scaling are that the categories be homogeneous and mutually exclusive. All of the members of any one classification must possess the property or characteristic being scaled, and they must differ from members of another classification. Since there is no indication that they represent more or less of the characteristic involved, the members within a category are regarded as equivalent with respect to the variable under study. (At this primitive level of measurement, statistical operations are limited to the counting of numbers or cases in the categories, calculation of mode, chi square, percentages, and certain coefficients of correlations.)

### Ordinal Scales

*Ordinal* (or ranking) *scales* give us more information than nominal scales. Not only do they imply class membership, but ordinal variables also reflect order of relation or position in an ordered series. Ordinal variables allow us to say that there is more or less of something, even though the exact distance between values is unknown and is not necessarily equal. There is no absolute zero point. The difference of more or less between categories permits the researcher to make judgments about one thing compared to another and to place variables in some order, such as most to least, highest to lowest, and best to worst, although it does not permit accurate absolute judgments.

Illustrations of ordinal scales include rank in graduation class, military ranks, academic degrees, ratings in a beauty contest, street numbers on houses, social class, and league standings of football teams. A classic example of an ordinal scale in human ecology research is the attitude or opinion questionnaire that asks for the subject's degree of agreement with statements: *strongly agree, agree, disagree,* or *strongly disagree.* If one subject circles *agree* for an item and a second subject circles *disagree,* we can say that the two respondents have different attitudes and that the first subject is in greater agreement with the statement. However, we cannot assume anything about the magnitude of difference in attitude between the research subjects. If a third subject circles *strongly agree,* we are able to say that the first one is in greater agreement with the statement than the second and that the third subject is in greater agreement than the first. There is no way to determine if the difference between the attitudes of the first and third subject is of the same magnitude as the difference between the first and second subject. We know only the ordered relationship: that the third research subject expressed the strongest agreement, the first subject ranked second, and the second subject ranked last in terms of agreement. Since the interval is unknown, addition, subtraction, multiplication, and division are not possible. (Appropriate statistics include the use of the median, percentile, rank-order coefficient of correlation, Kendall's $\tau$, and rank-order analysis of variance.)

## Interval Scales

In addition to possessing the properties of the nominal and ordinal scales, an *interval scale* has the characteristic of equal distances between any two numbers on the scale. Thus, we can make statements of sameness or differences, greater than or less than, *and* equal intervals between measurement points. Although a zero point may be arbitrarily defined for convenience, an interval variable does not have a true zero point. A classic example of interval measurement is Fahrenheit temperature. If the temperature for the past three days has been 10°, 20°, and 30°, respectively, it is appropriate to say that the differnce between the first and second is the same as the difference between the second and third days. The difference between the first and third days is twice the difference between the temperature of the first and second or second and third days. But we cannot say that it was twice as hot on the second day as the first day or that it was three times as hot on the third compared to the first day. Finally, zero degrees does not indicate a total lack of heat. (Interval measurement is amenable to a number of statistical operations not permitted with nominal and ordinal measures, including calculation of the mean of a distribution of scores.)

Most measuring instruments used in human ecology research (e.g., personality, intelligence, aptitude, achievement) yield scores that approximate interval quality reasonably well and are treated as such. Strictly speaking, they are usually only ordinal level. However, Kerlinger (1986,

403) has indicated that the assumption of equal intervals does not lead to a major problem in the interpretation of findings as long as researchers are alert to cases where there is gross inequality of intervals.

## Ratio Scales

A *ratio scale* combines all of the characteristics of nominal, ordinal, and interval scales—and in addition, it has a true zero point as its origin. It is the highest level of measurement. The inclusion of a fixed zero point offers a consistent starting point for measurement, allows us to indicate the actual quantity of the thing being measured, and permits ratio judgments. Physical properties such as weight, mass, volume, and length are of the ratio type. Ratio behavioral measurements include the number of trials required to learn a task and the reaction time or length of time to respond to a stimulus. We can say that a subject who took 2 seconds to respond to a stimulus reacted twice as fast as an individual who took 4 seconds. On no other measurement scale can such ratio statements be made. (All statistical procedures can be applied at this level.)

Variables that can be measured at a higher level can also be measured at a lower level, but the reverse is generally not true. Weight (ratio), for example, may be converted to ranks (ordinal) or collapsed into broad classes (nominal), such as heavy, medium, and light, and analyzed with statistical methods appropriate to the respective lower levels of measurement. Conversely, religious affiliation (nominal) cannot be transformed to the ordinal or interval level. Usually, the highest possible level of measurement is used to avoid the risk of supplying incomplete and potentially misleading information.

How does a researcher decide which scale is appropriate for a particular project? Manheim (1977) believes that it is necessary to balance the ideal with the feasible. He says that first, the kinds of statements required to answer a research question will indicate whether an ordinal or an interval scale is needed. The researcher must select or construct instruments that will provide appropriate measures of the variables. Second, the available measuring devices and the research data themselves may very well determine the scale that is appropriate or possible. Third, the degree of precision and accuracy desired may dictate the measurement scale that is to be used. Manheim explains that if (weaker) statistical tests appropriate for ordinal data are adequate for a study, it may be uneconomical to strive for interval data.

In the discussion of interval scales, it was indicated that most research instruments are really ordinal level but that they are treated as if they were interval level. Traditionally many authors have insisted that only certain statistical methods are appropriate to certain types of scales. (Some of these restrictions were mentioned at the end of the discussion of each measurement level.) In recent years, however, a growing number of scholars in the fields of measurement and statistics have assumed a more liberal position and have argued that researchers are safe in calculating any statistic on any data that have the properties of *at least* an ordinal level. (In actual practice, statistics like *r, t,* and *F,* appropriate for interval and ratio variables, are used by most investigators with ordinal-level data in order to gain the advantages of these statistical methods.)[2]

## Sampling

*Sampling* is a procedure in which the researcher uses a part of a population to draw conclusions about a whole population. Since sampling employs a number of technical terms, it is necessary to define a few of them before proceeding with the discussion.

### Related Terminology

*Population* (often called the universe) refers to a specified group of events, objects, or persons that meet a set of specifications or have a common measurable characteristic. All red oak trees, all automobiles on the road, all records in a file, all farms, all cats, all unwed mothers, and all American citizens over 65 years old are populations. For research purposes, a population should be carefully defined (e.g., all unwed mothers in Texas under 30 years of age as of 1 September 1986).

*Elements* are single units in any given population (e.g., individuals, households, societies, corporations). The entire full-time undergraduate student body at Texas Christian University is considered a population, and the elements of the population are the individual full-time undergraduates enrolled at that institution at the time the sample is drawn.

When all elements are selected from a population for study, it is a *census.* When only a subset or portion of a population is chosen for investigation, it is called a *sample.* A good sample is considered representative of the population.

Characteristics of a population are referred to as *parameters,* while corresponding characteristics of the sample are termed *statistics.* Sampling procedures permit the researcher to estimate the value of a parameter that is unknown from a sample statistic that he or she can measure. The researcher can also test hypotheses concerning the parameter. Estimates generated from such tests are referred to as *statistical inferences.*

### Advantages of Sampling

There are several advantages to sampling. First, it helps the researcher keep down costs. If fewer data are collected and processed, fewer personnel, less office space, and so forth are needed. The money that is saved with a smaller, manageable project can be spent more effectively in hiring better-qualified workers, providing more training and supervision of research personnel, and pursuing a more in-depth examination (e.g., longer interviews) and analysis of the variables under investigation. Second, when sampling is used, the time required for data collection is reduced, possibly avoiding some potential validity problems associated with the undesirable effects of changes over time that may be encountered with certain measures. Third, data can be analyzed more quickly and results disseminated sooner because fewer subjects are used than in a study of an entire population. Nevertheless, the investigator must keep in mind that the precision with which estimates of a parameter can be made depends upon sample size.

Lazerwitz (1968, 278–79) describes the desired characteristics of a sample:

> First of all, a proper sample must give a precise picture of the population from which it is drawn. Second, the sample must be obtained by a probability process. This permits the use of statistical procedures to describe and analyze the data of the sample and relate it to the population from which it came. Finally, the sample should be as small as precision considerations permit, as economical as possible, and gathered as swiftly as its various measurement techniques permit. . . . The sampling process not only should yield estimations of population means, percentages, and totals, but must also obtain measurements on subclasses of a population.

## General Considerations in Sample Design

*Sample design* is that part of the research design that is concerned with determining which elements of the population to study and how to select them. Several questions, including those listed here, must be answered prior to selecting a sample.

1. *What is the purpose of the study?* Sampling is no problem if the purpose of the investigation is limited to a particular class in Trinity Valley School or to a group of residents in the Candleridge housing tract. On the other hand, if the purpose is to generalize the findings beyond the particular class and to determine a procedure suitable for use with a larger group, sampling is important. In this regard, when testing for the statistical significance of results, most statistical techniques assume a random sample was used.

2. *What is the population to be studied?* A researcher may define the population as a fairly small group that can be studied in its entirety. Or the investigator may wish to sample a population, such as the customers of a given store, to determine their attitudes toward shopping in that store. On a

still larger basis, he or she may be interested in the nationwide acceptability of a particular food product.

3. *What is the sampling unit?* Is the unit to be studied individuals, families, schools, city blocks?

4. *Is a complete list of the individual elements of the population* (called a frame) *available?* Will permission be granted to use the list? If an accurate and up-to-date listing is not available, it may be necessary for the researcher to prepare one for the research project.

5. *What sample size is necessary?* There is a relationship between sample size and the desired level of precision of statistical analyses. *Precision* refers to the similarity of a sample value to a "true" population value. Other factors also have a bearing on the desired sample size.

6. *What type of sampling will be most appropriate?* Various types of probability and nonprobability sampling techniques are possible, and each has its advantages and disadvantages.

7. *Is the plan economically feasible?* Sample design requires a blending of sampling theory with the resources available. What is the timetable for the study? How widely scattered is the population? How will the data be collected? Will highly trained individuals be gathering the data? Do the administrators of cooperating agencies and programs understand research methodology?

In the planning of a particular study, many sampling considerations of a specific nature beyond those indicated above are bound to arise. As an example, in a household survey of Fort Worth, Texas, many rules have to be adopted for replacing or otherwise dealing with units that are temporarily vacant, refusals to participate, and so forth. Other issues may arise when inquiries that deal with sensitive matters (e.g., illegal activities, abortion, child abuse and neglect) are planned. When developing sampling procedures, it is often helpful for an investigator to search the literature for other studies that have dealt with similar issues.

## Types of Sampling

There are two basic types of sampling: probability and nonprobability. In *probability sampling,* each individual or element is chosen by chance methods and has an equal opportunity of being included in the sample. The probability is known (and is not zero). If, for example, 50 workers are drawn at random from a factory whose population is 400, the possibility of any worker being selected is 1 in 8 (50/400). Probability sampling provides the greatest assurance that a sample is representative of the population from which it is taken—i.e., that the sample values do not differ more than a certain amount from the true population values. If probability sampling is used, the researcher can minimize selection bias as well as estimate the margins of chance error and govern the size and design of the sample for the desired level of accuracy (Riley 1963).

In *nonprobability sampling,* units are not selected by chance procedures, and there is no way of knowing the probability of inclusion in the sample. Yet, nonprobability samples have a place in research, as the literature will attest.[3] There are some studies whose objectives do not call for a probability sample, such as when the investigation is designed strictly for analytical purposes and the data are not to be used for the purpose of generalizing to the population, when the study is purely exploratory, or when a sample is desired that is small enough for intensive analysis. Frequently, the risks involved in not employing a probability sample are outweighed by the advantages. The researcher may be able to use a more desirable method of data collection or gain access to a larger sample if a nonprobability design is chosen. On a more practical note, nonprobability sampling is almost without exception more convenient and economical. Although nonprobability sampling can give useful results, probability sampling procedures should be used whenever possible.

## Probability Sampling

Some of the major forms of probability sampling are simple random, systematic, stratified, and cluster sampling. Forms of nonprobability sampling are convenience, quota, purposive, and snowball sampling.

### Simple Random Sampling.

The basic probability sampling design is *simple random sampling;* all other methods of scientific sampling are variations of it. With this technique, each element or item in the total population (whether the population consists of consumers, bread, children, or houses) has an equal probability or chance of being included in the sample of that population. The lottery method is one way to approach simple random sampling. Each member of the population is assigned a unique number, the number is written on a slip of paper (all the same size, shape, color), the slips of paper are placed in a large bowl and mixed thoroughly, and a blindfolded person selects a slip of paper from the bowl. Since each slip represents a member of the population, the probability of picking each one is the same.

A far more efficient and preferable procedure is to use random numbers for sample selection. Tables of random numbers, available in most statistics books, are listed in columns of two, three, four, or more digits on consecutive pages (Ex. 3.1).

If a random sample of 50 is to be taken from a population of 300 people, the individuals in that population are first numbered from 1 to 300. Since the largest number assigned is three digits in this case, the researcher

| | | |
|---|---|---|
| 10097 | 98520 | 91499 |
| 37542 | 11805 | 80336 |
| 08422 | 83452 | 44104 |
| 99019 | 88685 | 12550 |
| 12807 | 99594 | 63606 |
| 66065 | 65481 | 61196 |
| 31060 | 80124 | 15474 |
| 85269 | 74350 | 94557 |
| 63573 | 69916 | 42481 |
| 73796 | 09893 | 23523 |

**Example 3.1.** A portion of a set of five-digit random numbers. (Reprinted from The Rand Corporation, *A Million Random Digits with 100,000 Normal Deviates,* Glencoe, Ill.: Free Press, 1955, p. 1. Used by permission.)

must use a table of random numbers containing at least three-digit numbers. If the random number has more than three digits, the last three digits can be used.

To determine the starting point on a random numbers table, the investigator closes his or her eyes, stabs the page with a pencil, and uses the number on which the pencil lands. If the pencil happens to land on or is closest to 10097 in Example 3.1, for example, that is the starting point. Beginning with 10097, then, each number (composed of the last three digits) that is less than 301 is noted. Since the first possible three-digit number is 10097, subject number 97 is selected for the sample. The next two numbers down the column, 542 and 422, do not correspond to any serial number in the population (1 to 300), so they are ignored. (It is permissible to go across, diagonally, or down columns as long as the decision is made in advance and the plan is used consistently.) The fourth, sixth, and seventh numbers in the left-hand column are less than 301, and subjects with these numbers are chosen. If the same number comes up again, it is not used. The researcher continues the procedure until all 50 subjects for the sample are selected. Persons with assigned numbers 97, 19, 65, 60, 124, 104, and 196 are chosen from our partial table of random digits and an additional 43 individuals are selected from the full table.

When properly carried out, a sufficiently large random sample is likely to be representative of the population. Systematic differences between the sample and population, such as those of social class, intelligence, and so on, tend to cancel each other out. Statistical procedures have been designed for estimating the required sample size and for judging the reliability of data based upon sample estimates. It is relatively easy to obtain a random sample, since it is not necessary to have knowledge of the characteristics of the population that might be important to a particular study. Many of the statistics that are widely used in research, such as the mean, standard deviation, and analysis of variance, assume that a random sample was used.

There are some difficulties that the researcher may encounter in selecting a random sample. A complete listing of the universe may not be available. There may be duplications on the list of the population that need to be eliminated (e.g., adults in a continuing education program may be enrolled in more than one course). Selecting a large random sample can be a laborious task. Another problem is that the sample may be widely scattered geographically, increasing the cost of the study if an interview method is used. Finally, a random sample may not provide sufficient cases for analyzing data from special subgroups.

Systematic Sampling. When a complete list of the elements of a population is available, it may be easier to select a random sample directly from that list rather than to go through the process of numbering each item and drawing random numbers. This variation of simple random sampling is advantageous when the population is extremely large or a large sample is to be drawn. *Systematic* (or serial) *sampling* can provide an equal opportunity for all units to be drawn if the first item is selected at random. This can be done by deciding what size sample is wanted, dividing the total number in the population by the desired sample size, and using this number as the basis for systematic selection. For example, if there are 400 schools from which to draw a systematic sample of 50 schools, 8 would be the size of the selection or sampling interval to be used. We would start by drawing at random (from a table of random digits) a number between 1 and 8; this number would be the first unit of the sample. We would continue by taking every eighth one on the list of schools—a random list is necessary—until the sample of 50 is completed. If the first selection is the seventh school, the sample would consist of schools numbered 7, 15, 23, 31, 39, 47, and so on.

How effective this sampling plan is depends on the type of list used. An alphabetical list probably is not random, since members of the same family and of certain ethnic groups may be clustered. If families are listed by income and ranked in descending order, the first 100 families would have higher incomes than other families farther down the list. Procedures are available to help avoid problems caused by systematic patterns in populations.[4]

Stratified Random Sampling. Often, the population to be sampled is heterogeneous; it is made up of a number of subpopulations or strata. Strata may be based on characteristics such as sex, age, ethnicity, socioeconomic status, occupation, and urban/rural residence. A good example of stratification is a city whose population includes three distinct ethnic groups. A random sample of persons from that population probably would not produce a proportionate number of representatives from each of the three strata. If a truly representative sample of the city's population is desired or if there is a special interest in comparing the three subgroups, stratified random sampling is beneficial.

In *stratified random sampling,* the population is first broken down into strata, and a random sample is selected from each stratum. Using our example of the city, let us say that there are 6000 whites, 3000 blacks, and 1000 Hispanics in the total population. If we decide on a proportional sample of 1/100 from each stratum, we will choose 60 whites, 30 blacks, and 10 Hispanics (6000/100, 3000/100, and 1000/100, respectively). Selection of subjects from each subgroup then follows simple random sampling procedures.

In contrast to *proportionate* stratified sampling described above, where each stratum is proportional to the population size of the stratum, *disproportionate* stratification produces an equal number of cases from each stratum regardless of the proportions in the population. Disproportionate sampling is warranted when precise comparisons among strata, and not the population as a whole, are the primary interest or when detailed analysis of one stratum is the researcher's objective. Returning to the example of the city with a tri-ethnic composition, we might decide to sample in different proportions and randomly select 30 whites, 30 blacks, and 30 Hispanics to optimize comparisons. Although it requires the weighting of results stratum by stratum, disproportionate stratified random sampling is an economical approach when one of the strata is substantially larger than the others because it helps avoid the collection and processing of unnecessarily large amounts of data from the more prominent group(s) in the population.

Stratified sampling ensures the inclusion of each essential group in the sample. Another advantage is that greater precision may be achieved with fewer cases than would be possible with a random sample. A further advantage is that the statistics applicable to random samples can be applied when the individual cases selected for each strata have been chosen at random.

Choosing the strata significant to the study might be difficult. It is important to know which factors to select as well as their relative frequency in the population. The factors must be potentially relevant to the research problem. If a sample is to be stratified on several factors, it may be difficult to find enough cases to meet the specifications.

Cluster Sampling. Samples are not always selected in units of one. Sometimes the sample unit consists of groups of elements, or clusters. These clusters may be geographic areas, buildings, farms, schools, classrooms, army platoons, industrial work groups, or families. *Cluster sampling* lends itself to situations where the population is naturally assembled into larger groupings (like these) and when it is difficult or impractical to prepare an accurate list of the elements that make up a target population.

Suppose that the research objective is to examine school readiness of 6-year-olds enrolled in public kindergarten programs throughout a state. Because of the logistics involved in selecting a random sample and administering a readiness test to kindergartners all over the state, cluster sampling, using a (kindergarten) class as the sampling unit, may be a more feasible alternative. After preparing a list of school districts in the state, the researcher selects a simple or stratified random sample of school districts. Next, the investigator lists the schools for each of the districts and takes a simple or stratified random sample of them. The researcher then takes a sample of the kindergarten classes in each of the schools and collects data from all of the youngsters in these classes (or in some cases from a sample of the children). The procedure moves through a series of stages, from sample to sample, until the researcher finally arrives at the unit of inquiry.

When cluster sampling is used to select individuals who reside in a specific geographic area, the method is referred to as *area sampling*. To survey a group of urban households, for example, the researcher moves from more inclusive to less inclusive sampling units, first sampling cities, then districts within cities, and finally households within districts. These methods are employed in most national surveys.

Cluster sampling allows the efficient accumulation of large samples because the clusters are grouped close together, thereby reducing travel and other research-related expenses as well as time needed to execute a study. Furthermore, this sampling technique is economical in that it requires the listing of clusters rather than individuals. In drawing a random sample of public school kindergarten children spread over the entire state, it is necessary to list every kindergartner (not an easy task), whereas in cluster sampling the researcher only lists the schools (or classes). Moreover, it is easier to obtain permission to impose on a few classes for research purposes than to disrupt the routines of 75 or 100 classrooms in many different school districts by randomly selecting a few students from each class.

Another advantage is that in certain studies, such as those designed to observe changes in population over time, the cluster sample may be used over and over again. Also, the method of cluster sampling is independent of other sampling classifications. Thus, after the clusters have been formed, the sample that is drawn from among the groupings may be a simple random sample, a systematic sample, a stratified random sample, or another cluster sample.

On the negative side, nonrepresentativeness of the sample may occur in cluster sampling at any of its stages. Additionally, calculated on a per case basis, it gives less precise estimates than simple random samples of the same size because of group tendencies toward homogeneity (e.g., people who live and work together tend to share many characteristics, including race, background, education, and income). There is no real advantage to the cluster sampling design unless the research subjects are geographically dispersed, so that there are consequent major cost and time gains.

### Nonprobability Sampling

Convenience Sampling. *Convenience sampling* (also called accidental sampling) consists of simply taking the cases that are available and continuing the process until a designated sample size is reached. The first 50 customers entering a store on a given day could be studied this way, or a college professor could study the students in class. The researcher who wishes to generalize to the larger population must assume (with considerable risk) that these customers are representative of all customers in the population being considered or that the professor's students represent college students in general. Otherwise, the conclusions would be limited to the 50 customers in the given store or to the students in those specific classes. Actually, there is no way of knowing how representative an accidental sample is of a larger population.

Why, then, are these convenience samples used? One reason is that, relative to random sampling, they are quick and inexpensive. This enables the investigator to draw very large samples that may help compensate for risk of bias. Another reason is that some researchers claim to be more concerned about the relationship between independent and dependent variables within the group studied than with the representativeness of results. They suggest, however, that if the findings of such investigations are repeated with new groups of subjects, confidence is gained in the generalization of the results. Also, although it cannot be supported by statistical sampling theory, some of these researchers argue that there is no good reason for assuming that college students included in accidental samples are different from the general population of college students or that nonhuman subjects in a laboratory study are different from all animals of a given species and strain.

Since it is not possible to specify the population to which findings can be generalized, the researcher using convenience samples must be cautious and extremely conservative (e.g., include qualifications) in drawing conclusions (Badia and Runyon 1982).

Quota Sampling. *Quota sampling* is the method employed in many marketing surveys and political polls involving sizeable populations over a large geographic area. With this type of sampling, the researcher begins by describing the population in terms of the dimensions assumed to be pertinent to the research problem. The characteristics typically taken into account are age, sex, marital status, ethnicity, occupation, socioeconomic level, and religion, although there are others. The researcher then determines the proportion of the population falling into each of the relevant classes, usually using data taken from a recent census. This specifies the quota for the sample so that the percentage of subjects in each class of the total sample will contain the same percentage of individuals making up the corresponding subset of the population. If it is known that 20% of the population is black, 20% of the sample would be black. If 50% of the population is male and 50% female, the sample drawn for investigation would be half male and half female. In reality, the quotas usually involve combinations of the various characteristics (e.g., males or females who are in different age categories, educational levels, ethnic groups).

Quota sampling resembles stratified random sampling except for one very important feature: randomization. When a quota sampling procedure is used in an interview study, the interviewer is instructed to locate a fixed number of individuals in each of the designated categories until his or her quota requirements are fulfilled. Choices within strata are not at random but rather by the judgment of the interviewer. Herein lies a fundamental problem. Since the interviewer has the freedom to select the research subjects, there may be a tendency (possibly unconscious) to sample those that are easily accessible, are friendly and cooperative, or are well dressed, leading to overrepresentation of some groups and underrepresentation of others. Persons who are at home during the day or who live on corner lots may be quite different from those who are not home until evening or those whose houses are located in the middle of a block.

There are other weaknesses in the quota method in addition to the bias introduced by the interviewer into the classification procedure. It is not easy for the interviewer to procure appropriate cases as the number of dimensions on which the quota is based increases. Smith (1975, 117) explains why it is extremely difficult to sample on more than three characteristics:

> This is because the number of variables (categories) to be filled is a multiplicative function of the number of values in each variable. For instance, if we wished to sample proportionate numbers of persons by sex, social class, and age where there are two sexes, three social classes, and two age divisions, we would have $2 \times 3 \times 2 = 12$ categories of respondents to select. But if we added the levels of religion, we double that number, and so on.

Another shortcoming of the method is that statistical theory of sampling error and confidence limits are not applicable because quota sampling does not employ random sampling at any stage. It is basically a convenience sampling approach. In spite of these drawbacks, quota sampling is more economical than random sampling in surveys of large populations and may be acceptable if the objective is to obtain typical opinions rather than precise statistics. The quality of a quota sample depends enormously on the training and skill of the person collecting the data, so it is essential that he or she have clear, simple, and complete instructions as to how to fill the quotas.

Purposive Sampling. *Purposive sampling* involves handpicking the cases to be included so that they appear to be representative of the population in which the researcher is interested. These subjective selections based upon assumed typicality (e.g., "average" individual, "representative" city) are made by an investigator who has considerable knowledge of the population and makes choices consistent with research objectives. Although the selections may result in some errors of judgment, it is assumed that these errors in selection will counterbalance each other.

An argument can be made that if the researcher can avoid bias in making the selections, his or her own judgment (by avoiding chance error) may yield a more accurate sample than a probability sample (Riley 1963). Unfortunately, there is no way to assess the accuracy of a purposive sample. Purposive sampling procedures are more appropriate for small than for large samples and should be considerd only if probability sampling is impractical. The primary weakness of this approach is that even experts differ on the best way to choose representative samples.

Snowball Sampling. In another type of nonprobability sampling, *snowball sampling,* the researcher starts with a few known cases and then selects additional subjects by asking sample participants to identify others with the characteristics in question. Each of the later subjects is requested to name others, and the process is repeated until a satisfactory sample size is achieved. This process is similar to a "chain letter." Researchers may resort to snowball sampling when a list of all persons in a population is unavailable and a systematic sampling frame cannot be applied. This is especially true with relatively rare populations, such as informal community leaders (who operate behind the scenes), the parents of stillborn babies, victims of domestic violence, drug users, runaway children, or defectors from religious cults. These people are often known to each other but not to researchers.

Sudman (1976) describes the use of snowball sampling as a means of obtaining a comparison (control) group of nonparticipants to investigate the effectiveness of social intervention programs. He gives the Job Corps and Manpower Training Programs as examples of social programs where the participants are self-selected and where good comparison groups of nonparticipants are usually unavailable. Requesting each group participant to identify a person like himself or herself who was not in the program may produce a comparison group that is similar in most respects except for exposure to the program. The same principle can be used in studies of juvenile delinquents where, for comparative purposes, a youngster can be asked to name a friend who is like him or her (age, race, sex) but who has never been in trouble with authorities.

## Animal Samples

Although the treatment of sampling so far has emphasized the use of human subjects in research, animals are often used instead of people in research, particularly in nutrition and behavioral studies. Although investigators who are interested in examining human development and behavior should use human subjects whenever possible for obvious purposes of generalization, animal studies do provide valuable clues about humans and lead to the discovery of principles that can be applied to people. Research with nonhuman species can be justified for several reasons: the greater control of heredity and environment, faster reproduction and development, and greater dependability of animals; and certain ethical limitations with human subjects (Matheson, Bruce, and Beauchamp 1974).

There are, however, some sampling-related problems associated with the use of nonhuman species. When ordering from commercial suppliers (small, freelance suppliers; pet stores; and pounds should be avoided), the researcher can designate the strain, sex, and age of the animals necessary for the research. But this is about as far as the investigator can go in specifying his or her needs. Using the albino variant of the brown rat (a common laboratory animal) as an example, Sidowski and Lockard (1966, 8–9) enumerate the problems a researcher may encounter when ordering animals for research:

> Freshly received animals are not uniform products from an automatic production line, nor are they a random sample from the world's population of rats. Animals suppliers differ greatly in such environmental practices as the ambient temperature, light-dark cycle, type of food, cage size and animal density, and the physical arrangement of food and water devices. . . . Since different animal suppliers employ different combinations of conditions, the same designated strain purchased from different suppliers is not a homogeneous population because of the different effects of two environments.

Furthermore, two shipments from the same company may not be strictly equivalent because they may use tiers of cages, with animals in the higher cages being exposed to more light, heat, and so on.

Although all of these factors cannot be controlled, Ellingstad and

Heimstra (1974) have suggested some ways to help combat potential problems. All animals should be obtained from the same supplier, since a shipment of rats, for instance, probably will come from the same large cage or from the same tier of cages. Preferably, the researcher should purchase all of the animals needed for a study in one shipment. If this is impossible, the investigator should be sure to use the same strain of animal and order them from the same supplier. The rules pertaining to the random assignment of humans to experimental groups (see Chap. 8) apply equally to the assignment of nonhuman animal subjects to different groups for study and should be closely followed. (See Chap. 17 for guidelines for the ethical use of animals in research.)

Some investigators order a few young animals and raise them in their own laboratories, thereby partially solving the difficulties created by the unknown effects of previous treatment. Though an expensive procedure, primarily because of space requirements, breeding and maintaining one's own laboratory animals permits the investigator to describe the conditions unique to the sample before the experiment and allows the replication of earlier studies.[5]

## Errors in Sampling

### Random Error

Random error arises from minor influences of an unknown nature. Such errors, sometimes referred to as "white noise," are also called chance errors. It is important to note that random error is merely assumed to exist. What is known is that different samples drawn from the same population rarely provide identical estimates of the population characteristic under investigation. Since sample results are based on only a part of the population and not on the whole population, they will, by chance, yield slightly different estimates.[6]

Random error is reduced by increasing sample size. The smaller the random error, the more confidence there is that the sample is indeed representative of the population and that generalizing from the sample to the population is warranted. This is especially important in survey research, although random error must also be considered in experimental studies.

Random error does not operate consistently in any particular direction, and it tends to cancel itself out over the sample (i.e., averages to zero). In a study to estimate the average income of a population, for example, some interviewees in the sample may overstate their income, some may understate it, and others may not know it or refuse to tell. The interviewer may even record the income incorrectly. Still, the net difference should be close to zero.

### Systematic Error

Systematic error is more serious than random error and results from imperfections in the research design or mistakes in the execution of a study. These procedural problems bias the sample in a direction away from the true population value. Failure of a sample of respondents to represent the target population can occur for different reasons, such as the use of a faulty sample design, the failure to carry out correctly a sound sampling plan, or the utilization of an inadequate sampling frame. An earlier example of systematic error was that some interviewers, when given the freedom to select subjects on their own, may avoid certain people and oversample some other types of people. Systematic error is especially troublesome because it is very difficult to detect and impossible to estimate.

## Population Estimates and Confidence Intervals

Because of the existence of sampling error, sample results can never be considered absolutely true for the population, but rather they are probably true within certain specifiable limits—that is, within certain *confidence intervals* and at a certain *confidence level.* A confidence interval represents the limits within which the researcher can make a statement as to where a population characteristic lies and has a given probability of being correct. It reflects the limits of error associated with studying the sample instead of the whole population under the same conditions and is expressed as so many points above and below the sample results. A confidence level refers to the likelihood, usually 95% or 99%, that the population score actually falls within that particular range. Thus, it is possible to say that you are 95% confident (or you give 19-to-1 odds) that the true population mean score is between 100 and 110.

## Sample Size

Other things being equal, large samples are generally more accurate than small samples. Therefore, it is advisable to use as large a sample *as is practical,* but a sample representative of its population is more important than the size of the sample. Ideally, a sample is a replica of the population. In actuality, each sample drawn differs from other possible samples and from the population. Imagine drawing sample after sample. Providing that the sample values give unbiased estimates (i.e., they are "on target"), as the number of samples increases, the mean of this distribution of sampling estimates should be very close to the actual mean of the whole population.

How does the researcher determine how large a sample should be? Sudman (1976) indicates that there are different ways of approaching this problem. First, to get a general idea, an inexperienced researcher can examine the literature to see what sample sizes have been used in the past by others studying similar research problems. Modal sample sizes will reflect current practices in the field and can aid in initial planning by checking one's judgment about suitable sample sizes against those of other more experienced investigators. The second strategy is more formal and is based upon the width of the confidence interval and the level of probability. It requires the researcher to balance the value of additional information with the costs of collecting that information.[7]

One consideration in sample size determination is the homogeneity, or similarity, of the population on the variable in question. The more homogeneous the group is, the smaller the sample can be. Although there is usually heterogeneity (variation) in populations studied in human ecology, if all of the members of a population are the same on the characteristic being investigated, there is no need for careful sampling. In this unlikely case, selecting any one person would be sufficient to study the population.

The number of categories by which the researcher wishes to analyze the data is also a factor that affects sample size. If multiple variables are being examined in a study and if subgroup breakdowns are used (e.g., sex, age), quite large samples are needed. Type of measurement used is another consideration, with continuous measures requiring larger samples than discrete measures because there are more points on a continous scale and fewer subjects per point. The type of sampling procedure chosen also affects sample size. For the same level of precision, simple random sampling, for instance, demands a much larger sample than does stratified sampling.

At some point, the statistical advantages of a larger sample must be weighed against the additional costs of gathering more data. A larger sample is dictated when the population is to be divided into subgroups for a comparison of various characteristics. Also, a larger sample helps to ensure that uncontrolled variables will be operating randomly. Conversely, a comprehensive study of a small sample might make a greater contribution than a more superficial study of a larger group. When time-consuming techniques (such as in-depth interviews and projective measures) are employed, a small sample is probably more feasible.

There are numerous formulas and tables available to assist researchers in determining the sample size necessary for different degrees of precision and for the confidence level desired, but a detailed discussion of these and other sampling issues is beyond the scope of this book.[8]

## RELIABILITY AND VALIDITY OF RESEARCH FINDINGS

A final consideration of researchers (and the bottom line in all investigations) is the reliability and validity of the results produced by a study.

## Reliability

The *reliability* of research findings refers to the consistency or repeatability of results. When another investigator, following the same procedures, using the same type of subjects, and employing identical methods of data analysis arrives at comparable results, we can say that the findings are reliable. The best way to assess reliability of results is by repeating, or replicating, a study.

## Validity

The *validity* of research findings indicates the trustworthiness of results or the soundness of the answers yielded by a study. The two primary forms of validity associated with scientific research are internal validity and external validity.[9] *Internal validity* refers to the internal procedures of an investigation. If the differences in scores are in fact attributable to differences in the characteristics you are measuring, you can rule out other probable sources of differences (i.e., spuriously produced differences). In true experiments, internal validity involves the question of whether the independent variable (the factor that has been manipulated) has really produced a change in the dependent variable (the behavior of the research subjects). If an experimental study has internal validity, we can say that the experimental manipulation, or treatment, made a difference and can eliminate other plausible, rival interpretations that might account for the results. Unfortunately, numerous extraneous variables, many of which cannot be completely eliminated, may influence the results by producing effects that are confounded with effects of the independent variable. *Confounding,* the most serious threat to internal validity, occurs when the effects of two or more variables are so intermixed that the researcher is unable to determine the effect due to each.

*External validity* refers to the representativeness and generalizability of research findings. In considering the external validity of a study, we are concerned about the relevance the results have beyond the confines of the investigation—that is, to the real world. To what extent can the researcher generalize his or her findings to other populations, settings, and variables? Can the results of a study of first graders be generalized to all first grade students? To all first graders in this school district? To first grade students in this elementary school? Or are the results limited only to the youngsters who participated in the study?

Setting and variable representativeness are other related concerns in external validity. In terms of setting (ecological) representativeness, will the relationship between variables hold for first graders in schools located in other neighborhoods, cities, or geographic regions? For example, if we are examining social development in the United States, Mexico, and Sweden, can we be sure that this variable means the same thing in Mexico and in Sweden as it does in the United States?

Rigorously controlled research, like laboratory experiments, has high internal validity and produces relatively conclusive results. However, these lab studies represent artificial, contrived, and frequently unrealistic situations that may have weaknesses related to external validity. Inevitably, as controls are tightened for the sake of internal validity, the maintenance of external validity becomes more problematic. Assuming issues related to internal validity can be controlled, research done in field settings would be expected to have greater external validity than studies conducted under laboratory conditions. When designing studies, researchers must attempt to reach a middle ground between the two validity demands in order to ensure a methodologically sound study whose findings can be generalized.

The reliability and validity of the measuring instruments used in research, as well as the reliability and validity of whole investigations, are important. The quality of the assessment tools used affects the reliability and validity of research findings.

## NOTES

1. In research, the people being investigated are called research subjects, or simply *subjects,* and are often referred to collectively as the *sample*. In survey research involving interviews or questionnaires, research participants are occassionally called respondents because they are responding to oral or written questions. Another term used synonymously with subjects in studies employing interviews is interviewees. In ethnographic investigations, people in the research setting may be referred to as informants, actors, or participants, depending on their roles. Subject will be used in most discussions throughout the book, but all of these terms will be employed interchangeably. For detailed presentations on the human subject in research, see Adair (1973), Rosenthal and Rosnow (1969, 1975), and Silverman (1977).

2. Borgatta and Bohrnstedt (1980), Gaito (1980), Gardner (1975), and Mitchell (1986) provide a full discussion of the controversy over Steven's (1951) levels of measurement/types of scales and their implications for statistics. Maxwell and Delaney (1985, 85) reflect the thinking of many researchers today when they write, "The dominant view seems to be that level of measurement, particularly the distinction between ordinal and interval, is irrelevant for statistics."

3. Different applications of nonprobability sampling are discussed by Chein (1981).

4. When a list is not random and has a systematic pattern, this is referred to as a problem of *periodicity*. See Cochran (1977) for more information.

5. Another benefit of breeding and raising one's own laboratory animals is the possibility of employing the *split-litter techique*. Consult Ellingstad and Heimstra (1974, 58) for an explanation of this procedure, which assures groups of comparable genetic constitution.

6. Samples are normally distributed within the population, with some samples better approximating properties of the population than others. Thus, depending on the particular elements that comprise the sample, the sample may accurately or inaccurately estimate the corresponding characteristics of the population.

The difference between a population estimate from repreated samples and the actual population value is called *sampling error* and is usually expressed as the *standard error.* The standard error indicates the extent to which and with what probability a sample estimate departs from a population value that would have been obtained if a complete census had been taken.

7. Refer to Cochran (1977, 78–88) for a good discussion of the steps in sample size determination using this second approach.

8. Among the many references on sampling, the following may be noted: Ackoff (1953); Biernacki and Waldorf (1981); Cochran (1977); Cohen (1977); Hansen, Hurwitz, and Madow (1953); Jaeger (1984); Kalton (1983b); Kish (1965); Lazerwitz (1968); Parten (1950); Raj (1972); Slonim (1960); Sudman (1976, 1986); and Yates (1981).

9. Described originally by Campbell and Stanley (1963), these two types of validity have been further subdivided. Refer to Cook and Campbell (1979) for details regarding the subtypes—*statistical conclusion validity* (whether the relationship found for the sample also holds for the population) as a special case of internal validity and *construct validity* (whether the measured variable reflects only the intended construct) as a special case of external validity. Another validity consideration in research is *ecological validity* (whether the study is carried out in a "real" social environment under natural conditions). This type of validity, which is related to external validity, has been discussed at length by Bronfenbrenner (1977).

CHAPTER 4

# Selecting and Formulating a Research Problem

Selecting a research problem does not usually present difficulties for seasoned researchers because studies they have already completed raise new questions and generate additional problems for investigation. Indeed, most established researchers complain that there is not enough time to pursue their many areas of interest. An entirely different situation often exists with beginning researchers. Although there is no shortage of research problems in human ecology, finding or recognizing these problems and formulating a specific one to investigate can pose obstacles for novice investigators.

## THE RESEARCH PROBLEM

There are numerous sources of research ideas that we hear about every day, including environmental concerns; consumer affairs; educational problems; and family, health, and social welfare issues. One's personal interests can also inspire researchable problems. But perhaps the single best way to identify fruitful problems for study is to specialize in a field of interest and learn as much about that area as possible. Extensive reading of the theoretical and research literature; lectures, seminars, and class discussions; and out-of-class exchanges of ideas with colleagues, instructors, and faculty advisers help identify unanswered questions for study. Several broad research problems for human ecology research mentioned in Chapter 2 should be beneficial to problem seekers. In the next chapter, a number of journals, bibliographies, indexes, abstracts, and handbooks are listed in the discussion of reviewing literature. These, too, are excellent sources of problems that merit investigation. To promote problem awareness, there is no substitute for familiarity with the accumulated knowledge in a field.

## Evaluating the Research Problem

After becoming acquainted with the field and crystallizing tentative ideas for research problems, the researcher must decide which problem should be pursued. A number of considerations are useful in evaluating the suitability of a research problem.

### Is the Problem of Interest to the Researcher?

Though not a sufficient reason to select a problem, a high degree of interest is helpful. The more personal appeal a problem has to the researcher, the greater the likelihood that the study will be well designed and carefully executed to completion. Such interest, however, should never bias the analyses, results, or conclusions of a study. For the novice researcher, the advantages of developing an interest in an ongoing research program in an academic department or institution and joining a team of faculty and students studying a particular area should not be ruled out. Their interest and enthusiasm in the cooperative project may be contagious and their guidance invaluable, particularly if this is the investigator's first attempt at research.

### Is the Problem Researchable?

Not all problems are amenable to research. For example, certain philosophical issues or questions involving value judgments cannot be empirically investigated. All research problems must be empirically grounded in order to generate evidence concerning the validity of the theory. It must be possible to collect relevant data for the conclusive resolution of a problem.

### Is the Problem Important?

Will solution of the problem contribute to the current fund of knowledge? Is it timely and does it fill a research gap? Will it help clear up contradictory findings in the literature? Will it validate a theoretical position? Will it help solve a practical problem?

Although uniqueness of a problem may be another consideration, by no means should a problem be discarded if it has been investigated in the past. Uniqueness or originality refer to both purpose *and* method. Complete originality in research is actually very rare. Repetition of some previous study is of value because it serves to verify research results and increases the generality of findings. It is especially important in most areas of human ecology, where experimental controls that characterize the physical sciences are often lacking. Repeating a project or extending it with improvements in measurement and statistical methodology may lead to different findings and greater contributions to theory. Studies carried out with refined instruments and/or to correct inadequate research design and inappropriate use of statistics are very worthwhile undertakings.

Data stored in data banks often have not been completely exploited by the original research effort; they may contain many unanswered questions that represent important research problems. Also, the development of new measuring instruments should not be overlooked as a legitimate research problem.

Although determining the significance of a research problem in advance may not be completely possible, the investigator should feel confident that the problem has some scientific value and is worthy of his or her expenditure of time, energy, and some resources.

### Is Research on the Problem Feasible?

Does the investigator have the necessary expertise to conduct the study? Is there sufficient time available to develop the requisite abilities if the investigator is lacking certain skills? If not, the researcher may choose to abandon the problem and select another or ask someone who has the competencies to collaborate in the project as a co-investigator or adviser. It is imperative that a researcher recognize his or her limitations before pursuing a problem.

The feasibility of a problem extends to other considerations. Is the size and scope of the project manageable? Are the required data accessible? Will permission be given to use a particular sample? If the problem is controversial, will there be opposition from individuals or groups? Are the necessary research procedures consistent with ethical guidelines? Are sound measuring instruments available or must they be constructed? Are resources such as funds, facilities (office and laboratory space, library, etc.), computer time, and clerical support available? Is the timetable for execution of the study compatible with the investigator's own schedule?

## Stating the Problem

The selection of a particular problem for study from a broad problem area is only the beginning of the research process. Before it can serve as a guide for designing and conducting an investigation, the problem must be stated clearly to indicate specifically what is being studied. Initially, some problems are too general or vague and require refinement before they are articulated satisfactorily for research purposes. Many beginning researchers have a tendency to state problems in overly broad terms. To provide a focus for research activity, the problem statement should be definitive and precise.

Here are several problems that have been restated from general to more manageable and researchable forms.

*Original:* The consumer decision process.

*Restatement:* (a) The purpose of this study is to examine the relationship of personality needs to the consumer decision process, or (b) Is there a relationship between personality needs and the consumer decision process?

*Original:* Soil release finishes on fabrics.

*Restatement:* (a) The objective of this investigation is to determine the effects of soil release finishes on the removal of soil from different fabrics, or (b) What are the effects of soil release finishes on the removal of soil from different fabrics?

*Original:* The self-concept of children.

*Restatement:* (a) This study is designed to investigate the relationship between a preschool child's self-concept and his or her social adjustment, or (b) What is the relationship between a preschool child's self-concept and his or her social adjustment?

*Original: Nutrition education in the public schools.*

*Restatement:* (a) The purpose of the study is to determine the effects of nutrition education on nutrition knowledge and dietary quality of high school students, or (b) What are the effects of nutrition education on nutrition knowledge and dietary quality of high school students?

A good problem statement is written unambiguously, usually but not always in the form of a question. Some authors prefer that the statement be put in interrogative form because the answer is what is being sought in the study, and it is important never to lose sight of this objective. Moreover, a problem presented as a question seems to facilitate the development of subproblems from the larger research problem. (Most studies include subproblems). Sometimes the problem is stated in the research report in both declarative and interrogative forms. For instance, The purpose of this study is to . . . Specifically, what are the effects of . . . ?

A good problem statement also asks about the relationship or difference between variables. The relationship can be explicitly expressed, as in, What is the relationship between _____ and _____? or the relationship can be implied, as in, What are the effects of _____ on _____? Referring to our consumer decision process example (as restated), a relationship between two variables, personality needs and consumer decision process, was explicitly expressed.

Finally, a problem statement should be researchable. That is, data necessary to answer the question must be available.

## HYPOTHESES AND RESEARCH QUESTIONS

Following statement of the problem (and subproblems) and at least a brief literature review, the next step is to construct a hypothesis (or hypotheses) or to formulate a research question (or questions). Research either attempts to test hypotheses or to answer research questions. Because they are used more frequently, hypotheses are discussed in relatively greater detail.

### Hypotheses

Derived from the problem statement(s), hypotheses are conjectures or educated guesses about the relationship between two or more variables. Hypotheses may stem from theory, findings of other studies, observations, or intuition or from a combination of these. Stated in advance of data collection, hypotheses point to the kinds of data to be collected and the methods by which they should be analyzed in addition to providing a framework for interpretation and discussion of findings.

A hypothesis typically contains the following characteristics:

1. It describes a relationship or difference between two or more variables.
2. It is stated simply and concisely in declarative form; clear, simple, operational terms that eliminate ambiguity are used.
3. It is specific and reflects the variables of interest.
4. It is value-free; judgmental words like *should, ought, bad,* and *better than* (as well as the researcher's own subjective preferences and biases) are excluded.
5. It is testable with available methods and can be found to be probably true or probably false.

#### Forms of the Hypothesis

There are two basic types of hypotheses: research and null. The *research hypothesis* (also called the alternate or working hypothesis) states that a difference or relationship *does* exist between the groups or measures being investigated. The *null hypothesis* (also called the statistical hypothesis) states that a difference or relationship *does not* exist. Both types are important in research.

The research hypothesis indicates what the investigator expects to support with the data collected. It is derived from theory or other evidence. For example, a research hypothesis might be that students taking Latin score higher on English achievement tests than students who do not take Latin. Since the research hypothesis cannot be tested directly with statistical procedures, it is translated into the null form, and the investigator attempts to disconfirm its negation. In terms of statistical logic, the way to obtain support for a proposition is to reject (or fail to find support for) the negative form of the proposition. If the opposite of the research hypothesis is rejected, the original research hypothesis, while not proven to be true, is indirectly supported.

Kidder and Judd (1986, 364) explain that in hypothesis testing the researcher assumes a role similar to that of a prosecutor in a criminal trial:

> A jury must make a decision whether or not a defendant is guilty of the crime of which he or she is accused. Before the trial begins and any arguments or evidence is heard, the defendant is entitled in the U.S. legal system to a "presumption of innocence," that the defendant did not commit the crime. The prosecutor would like the hypothesis of "guilty" confirmed by the jury, but the prosecutor must provide enough evidence to overrule this presumption of innocence beyond a reasonable doubt. Our legal system recognizes that it is not possible to prove the lack of innocence (i.e., the guilt) of a defendant conclusively, without any doubts whatsoever. So the requirement is that the prosecution must prove guilt beyond a reasonable doubt.
>
> Social scientists are engaged in a task quite analogous to that of the prosecutor. When they collect data from a sample, they wish to conclude that the hypothesis that motivated the research is correct (i.e., that two variables are related). So they start out with the presumption that their hypothesis is not true (the null hypothesis). They must then demonstrate, based on their sample of data, that this presumption is unlikely to be true in the population. Only then can they have reasonable confidence that their research hypothesis is in fact true in the population. Just as in the courtroom analogy, there will always remain the possibility that they have reached the wrong conclusion.

As a contradiction of the research hypothesis, the null hypothesis posits no difference, no effect, or no relationship between variables; indicates that any dfference found is attributable to chance; and subjects this supposition to a probability test. In effect, the null hypothesis can be considered the hypothesis the researcher would like to nullify through testing.

The statement of the null hypothesis determines the manner in which data are ultimately analyzed. The null hypothesis can be stated: X is less than Y, X is greater than Y, or X is not equal to Y. In the first and second examples the researcher evaluates the result of the statistical analysis by using what is referred to as a *one-tailed test*. In the third example a *two-tailed test* would be used.

To illustrate, suppose we are interested in the relationship of shoe size to intelligence. A one-tailed test would be generated by the hypothesis: People of higher intelligence tend to have larger feet. This hypothesis, evaluated at the $p < .05$ level, would be significantly supported only if our results indicated with a 95% certainty that it was true.

But suppose we were really interested in whether or not average shoe sizes differed between populations with high and low intelligence, regardless of which group had larger or smaller feet. In this instance a one-tailed test might not answer our research question. If our findings indicated that low intelligence persons had larger feet and we had used the one-tailed test stated above, our results would not have been significant, forcing us to reject our hypothesis and not allowing us to confirm the opposite position. A two-tailed test designed to evaluate results in either direction, on the other hand, would have allowed us to draw a more reasonable conclusion.

If you are really only interested in results from one direction or the other, however, a one-tailed test will result in significant findings more often. Using our example of shoe size and intelligence where we found that the low intelligence sample had larger feet, a two-tailed test evaluated at $p < .05$ would yield significant results only if the odds of finding a greater difference between the two variables was less than 2.5%. This is because we would also have accepted results where high intelligence persons had larger feet. Thus, we were evaluating whether the results were signficant at $p < .025$ on either end $(.025 + .025 = .05)$, with either high or low intelligence persons having the larger feet.

Examples of research hypotheses and their corresponding null hypotheses follow:

*Research:* There is a significant difference in the fabric preferences of men and women.

*Null:* There is no significant difference in the fabric preferences of men and women.

*Research:* There is a relationship between job satisfaction and marital adjustment.

*Null:* There is no relationship between job satisfaction and marital adjustment.

*Research:* There will be a difference in school readiness between children attending kindergarten and those not attending kindergarten.

*Null:* There will be no difference in school readiness between children attending kindergarten and those not attending kindergarten.

If the null hypothesis is rejected after testing, then, assuming both reliability and validity of the results, it is likely that some true difference or relationship exists. The statistically significant findings are presumed to be due to experimental factors, possibly the independent variables stated in the research hypothesis, and not to mere chance. Such results increase the confidence we have in the tenability of the research hypothesis. With rejection of the null hypothesis, the corresponding research hypothesis has survived a test of disconfirmation and is indirectly supported. As the research hypothesis survives more tests of disconfirmation in subsequent studies, the evidence for its support is strengthened.

If the null hypothesis is accepted, this (failure to reject it) means that the corresponding research hypothesis is not supported as stated. (The null and research hypotheses can never both be true or false.) The investigator must conclude that the results are not statistically significant and are probably explainable by chance.

But hypotheses are never completely proved or disproved. Different types of error may lead to rejection of hypotheses that are true and failure to reject hypotheses that are false (See Chap. 14). A null hypothesis is only rejected as implausible or accepted as plausible within certain arbitrary statistical limits.

## Research Questions

There are instances when researchers eschew formal hypotheses and choose to use only a problem statement phrased as a question. Research questions are frequently employed in descriptive studies. Some investigations are designed to discover relevant facts, describe conditions or practices, or examine relationships without regard for theoretical assumptions. In other studies, research questions, rather than hypotheses, are used when there is little background information in an area or no underlying theory, or when the investigator is faced with highly complex relationships among variables. A carefully worded problem statement in the form of a research question will suffice as long as it indicates clearly what variables are being examined and what information or answer is being sought. Even these investigations could benefit in many cases, however, from the use of formally stated hypotheses.

Some authors believe that, while specific hypotheses offer needed focus, such hypotheses narrow attention to the point of disregarding relevant information and oversimplify a problem by restricting its answer to either true or false through significance testing. Others think that unless a formal hypothesis is tested, the study does not represent legitimate research. In their estimation, research questions are not acceptable substitutes for hypotheses because they do not allow for the deduction of consequences. Proponents of formal hypotheses view research questions as an easy way out for the investigator who has not thoroughly reviewed the literature and is presumably unable to predict relationships between variables. (Of course, this is perhaps sometimes true, but by no means always so.)

There are valid arguments for and against the use of research questions instead of hypotheses. However, the most important issue is whether or not the problem is clear and precise, regardless of its form—research question, research hypothesis, or null hypothesis. A considerable amount of direction can be provided by explicitly stated research questions, and their use should not be discouraged in cases where they are deemed appropriate.[1]

## DEFINITION OF TERMS

In order to organize data to examine relationships among them, a researcher must make use of concepts. *Concepts* embody the important ideas of a field of study. Some concepts are quite close to the objects or facts they represent and need little definition. One's mental image of food may be easily illustrated by pointing to specific foods. Concepts such as intelligence, creativity, management, and attitude cannot be so easily related to the phenomena they represent. These higher-level abstractions are sometimes referred to as *constructs,* which are derived from concepts at a lower level of abstraction. When there is a wide distance between concepts or constructs and the empirical facts to which they refer, special care must be given to defining them, both in terms of the general meaning they are intended to convey and of the operations by which they will be represented in a study.

Although there are numerous ways to define terms,[2] two that are especially important in human ecology research are conceptual and operational definitions.

### Conceptual Definitions

A *conceptual definition* describes something in conceptual or hypothetical terms. It identifies a concept employing other concepts or conceptual expressions (not observable criteria), somewhat like a dictionary uses words to define other words. We can define "intelligence" as ability to think abstractly, "anxiety" as subjective fear, "effective marriage counseling" as counseling that promotes marital adjustment, and so on. How a concept (construct, variable) is defined within the context of a particular research problem is the researcher's prerogative. However, we must know what the definer means. Needless to say, it is helpful if the definition does not contradict common usage. An appraisal can be made regarding the intelligibility of a conceptual definition, but it cannot be judged true or false by someone else. Conceptual definitions help the researcher understand theory, develop research problems, and formulate hypotheses.

Nachmias and Nachmias (1987, 33) have listed the essential attributes of a good conceptual definition:

- A definition must delineate the unique attributes or qualities of that which is defined. It must be inclusive of all cases covered by it. At the same time, it should be exclusive of all cases *not* being denoted by it.
- A definition should not be circular; that is, it must not contain any part of the thing being defined. Defining "female" as a person having feminine qualities or "power" as a quality shared by powerful people does not enhance communication.
- A definition should be stated positively whenever possible. Defining "intelligence" as a property that lacks color, weight, and character obviously does not enhance communication because there are many other things that lack color, weight, and character.
- A definition should use clear terms. A term such as "conservative" means different things to different people, and unless there is an agreement on its meaning, it should not be used in a definition.

## Operational Definitions

In the research process, it is necessary to link concepts or constructs to the real world—to bridge the gap between the hypothetical and empirical reality. The translation of constructs into empirical terms is accomplished by the *operational definition.* Operational definitions enable the researcher to point to the things in the observable world that are being studied. They specify the activities or operations involved in measuring or manipulating variables.

An operational definition denotes how a variable is to be measured in a particular project. For instance, a researcher who is interested in conducting a study of children's aggression will find the conceptual definition of "aggression" of limited value when it is time to actually investigate the construct. The conceptual definition (which precedes the operational definition in a research report) helps describe the general nature of the phenomenon that is to be examined. It helps set the stage for what is to come, but it does not tell the investigator what data to collect. Subsequently, it is necessary to translate the construct into operational terms. The researcher must develop a second definition, one based on the *observable* characteristics of aggression. The investigator might stipulate hitting, kicking, biting, and cursing as indicators (indicants) of attributes contained within the concept of aggression and then locate or construct an observation schedule to record (measure) the occurrence of the behavior as operationally defined.

Using another example, if the variable is "academic achievement," it can be defined operationally as letter grades assigned by teachers for a reporting period, numerical scores on teacher-made exams, or scores on standardized achievement tests given annually. Technically, it is the demonstration of representative knowledge, skills, and behaviors by the students, as reflected in the grades or scores, that is the operational definition of academic achievement. However, since many operational definitions of the characteristics or qualities of people and things either lead to the development of assessment procedures or are measured by existing instruments that embody the operational definition, for ease of exposition we usually refer to the scores on these measures as the operational definition of the phenomenon. We simply say that X is the characteristic measured by the instrument, or the definition of X is given by the measuring device.

Suppose a researcher operationally defines academic achievement as student performance in three academic areas: language, mathematics, and reading. This stipulates what is to be measured. The investigator looks for a well-established instrument that assesses language, math, and reading achievement and decides on the *California Achievement Tests.* (There is no need to construct a new instrument if a suitable one is already available that assesses achievement as defined.) The specific operations involved in measuring academic achievement in this case are to administer the test to a group of subjects under standardized conditions, to score the subjects' responses to items according to directions in the manual (or have it machine scored), and to record the scores for each subject. The operational definition of academic achievement as the characteristic measured by the test, or as scores on this test, spells out exactly what the researcher must do to quantify the phenomenon.

An operational definition does not indicate how well the operations assess a given construct. We must assume that the investigator determined the adequacy of the operations (e.g., a measuring instrument) before it was adopted. It is important to note that *any* operational definition of a concept is not adequate just because the concept has been operationalized.

Some operational definitions are more satisfactory than others. There should be congruence between the conceptual and operational definition of a term. The definition should possess observability, and it should have theoretical import; that is, an operational definition should relate to a recognized theory or have the potential for incorporation in a theory.

No single operational definition can tap all of the diverse meanings of a construct. Still, the researcher must make an effort to determine the best combination of indicators to represent a construct. The indicators that are ultimately observed in a study will only be an approximation of the "true" measure of that construct (Van Dalen 1978). If for some reason, we do not subscribe to an investigator's conceptualization and operationalization, we should nevertheless have a clear idea of how to interpret the results because we will understand what the terms mean.

A construct may be measured in more than one way; that is, it may have more than one operational definition. All of its operational definitions define it, but in different ways, because of the theoretical notions that underlie each one. The researcher who was considering adequate measures of achievement could have selected the *Metropolitan Achievement Tests, Stanford Achievement Test,* or *Iowa Tests of Basic Skills,* to name a few, but chose to define academic achievement as scores on the *California Achievement Tests,* presumably because they seemed to be a valid measure relative to the purpose of the study. Using operational definitions employed in previous investigations enhances communication within the scientific community and facilitates the replication of studies and comparison of research findings. Practically everyone in education, psychology, and human development knows what the *California Achievement Tests* are and has access to technical information on the instrument and research using the instrument. They understand the operational definition of academic achievement selected by the investigator.

Other examples of constructs and some possible operational definitions of each follow:

**Intelligence:** scores on the *Wechsler Adult Intelligence Scale,* scores on the *Stanford-Binet Intelligence Scale,* scores on the *Kuhlman-Anderson Test*

**Anxiety:** readings of a galvanometer, scores on the *Manifest Anxiety Scale,* scores on the *Children's Manifest Anxiety Scale*

**Dietary quality:** interview responses to a 24-hour recall of food intake, written self-reports using a 7-day food diary, responses to a food frequency questionnaire, results of biochemical analyses

**Nutritional status:** loss of body weight (in an obese sample); reduction of serum lipid parameters, i.e., cholesterol, lipid protein profile (in a sample at risk for cardiovascular disease); combination of results of anthropometric measures (skinfold, percent body fat, height, weight), dietary quality measures, and biochemical analyses

**Child-rearing practices:** responses to the *Block Child-Rearing Practices Report;* answers to questions on the *Sears, Maccoby, and Levin Interview Schedule;* records of in-home observations from the *Fels Behavior Rating Scales*

**Clothing conformity:** scores on *Selker's Individual Clothing Conformity Inventory,* scores on *Russell's Clothing Atittudes Questionnaire,* scores on *Morrow's Clothing Preference Inventory*

**Social class:** ratings of subjects on *Hollingshead's Four Factor Index of Social Status,* ratings on *Duncan's Socioeconomic Index,* ratings on the *Siegel Prestige Scale*

**Self-concept:** scores on the *Sears Self-concept Scale,* scores on the

*Tennessee Self-concept Scale,* researcher's interpretation of subject's drawing of human figures

**Product appeal:** observation recordings of the ratio of purchasers to nonpurchasers of a product during an 8-hour period at a particular department store, responses to a telephone marketing survey concerning a new product

Operationalization (or operationism) extends to a variety of other procedures in research. It may refer to the details of an investigator's manipulation of variables, or *experimental operational definition.* In some studies, the researcher causes the phenomenon being defined to occur. If "frustration" is viewed as prevention from reaching a goal, the investigator might place an attractive food such as candy where it is visible but inaccessible to young children. The operational definition of frustration then would be placement of children in a room with five pieces of candy that are clearly visible but out of their reach.

In an animal study, "drive" might be operationally defined as hours of food deprivation or possibly the animal's blood sugar level. In an investigation of interpersonal relations between young adults, "conflict" can be defined as the state produced by placing two dormitory roommates in a situation where a positive alternative for one is a negative alternative for the other, and vice versa. These operational definitions tell the researcher how to induce a particular state. The details should be adequate enough for replication.

Other terms used in a study also require explicit definition. We need to know specifically who the study participants were. References to college students, retail managers, single-parent families, working mothers, nursery school children, school administrators, and upper middle class convey limited meaning. Detailed sample descriptions with clear definitions of terms like these are essential to our understanding of research. The importance of defining *all* terms in a study cannot be overemphasized.

### Operationism and Hypotheses/Research Questions

The discussion of hypotheses and research questions earlier in this chapter included examples that involved statements couched in conceptual (literary) terms. Now that operationism has been introduced, we can deal with operational hypotheses and research questions. Operational hypotheses and research questions are those in which indicators have been substituted for concepts so that the statements can be interpreted empirically. The researcher defines specifically the indicators for the variables, and it is clear what procedures, or operations, will be involved in testing the hypothesis or in answering the question. Taking one of our earlier examples, here are four ways that the same hypothesis can be posed:

*Research conceptual:* There is a relationship between job satisfaction and marital adjustment.

*Research operational:* There is a relationship between scores by female accountants on the *Minnesota Satisfaction Questionnaire* and the *Short Marital Adjustment Test.*

*Null conceptual:* There is no relationship between job satisfaction and marital adjustment.

*Null operational:* There is no relationship between scores by female accountants on the *Minnesota Satisfaction Questionnaire* and the *Short Marital Adjustment Test.*

Here are two ways that a related research question can be stated:

*Question conceptual:* Is there a relationship between job satisfaction and marital adjustment?

*Question operational:* Is there a relationship between scores by female accountants on the *Minnesota Satisfaction Questionnaire* and the *Short Marital Adjustment Test?*

There is a wide variation in the acceptable ways to make these statements. If mentioning the names of research instruments makes the formulation too cumbersome, reference to the measuring devices can be omitted, since the specific tools used will be noted elsewhere in the research report. For example, the research operational definition could be: There is a relationship between scores on self-report measures of job satisfaction and marital adjustment in female accountants. However communicated, it is important for the statement to indicate all of the variables being studied without going into too much detail. Good examples can be found in reputable research journals.

## NOTES

1. In many studies using research questions, the null hypothesis is implied; it is actually tested when the data are subjected to statistical analysis.

2. There are several good references on defining concepts, including Bierstedt (1959), Boring (1945), Ennis (1964), Hempel (1952), Kaplan (1964), Kendler (1981), Mandler and Kessen (1959), Margenau (1950), and Underwood (1957). Bridgman (1927), a physicist, is credited with originally proposing the idea of operational definitions.

CHAPTER 5

# Reviewing the Literature

Reviews of literature are becoming increasingly important in science because of the information explosion, the growing specialization, and the expansion of the number of outlets for the dissemination of research findings. Since past research helps shape the next generation of studies, the literature review is a fundamental activity in the research process. The cumulative nature of science requires accurate accounts of previous research for orderly knowledge building (Cooper 1984).

The literature review is a continuous process. After deciding on a general problem area or tentatively identifying a research problem, the investigator conducts a preliminary survey of the literature to become acquainted with relevant theory and past research. This facilitates the formulation of a more precise problem. The researcher then continues the review. At the more advanced stage of the literature survey, after the problem has been limited in size and scope, the investigator searches only for material that has a direct bearing on the project. This search continues until the study is completed and the research report is finalized.

## PURPOSE OF THE LITERATURE REVIEW

A survey of related literature is beneficial for several reasons. It helps delimit the research problem and state it more precisely. In addition, the review is a valuable source of information regarding the definition and operationalization of variables, the relationships among variables, and the ways in which the variables can be incorporated in hypotheses or research questions. A good review of research uncovers what has already been done in the area and identifies what remains to be done. Most research articles conclude with helpful suggestions for future research.

Only by making an intensive search can one determine whether or not a problem has been solved satisfactorily. The fact that a problem has been studied does not preclude another investigation, however. Valuable research may result from deliberate replication of a study. The conditions may be kept identical in order to verify the results, or they may be changed to provide for a comparison of two or more procedures. Repetition of studies at regular time intervals also allows the observation of trends and developments.

A survey of pertinent studies enables the researcher to know what others have tried and how successful their efforts have been. It gives the researcher insights into effective and ineffective methods and procedures (e.g., measurement, sampling) and provides ideas regarding possible modifications that will ensure a better designed project. A combination of creative and informed thinking can lead to new approaches in problem solving. The literature review alerts the investigator to possibilities that might have been overlooked in earlier studies, minimizes unanticipated difficulties, and saves time and effort in planning and executing the project.

Finally, the review aids in the interpretation of results. If the researcher's findings are in agreement with the results of other studies, he or she may have greater confidence in the conclusions. When results differ from the comparative data, the investigator will be stimulated to find out in what respects they differ and to explain possible reasons for the discrepancies.

## STEPS IN THE LITERATURE REVIEW

Although the literature search should be viewed as a continuous process, there are at least eight identifiable steps which most researchers follow:

1. Identifying general terms related to the topic
2. Consulting major textbooks, handbooks, encyclopedias, and other general sources for basic information and important references
3. Identifying more specific key terms or descriptors associated with the research problem
4. Locating indexes, abstracts, and retrieval systems that will help uncover related articles, books, and so forth
5. Identifying titles of relevant articles, reports, and monographs
6. Obtaining reference materials from libraries
7. Summarizing reports containing important information on the problem
8. Writing the review and preparing a list of references

The initial step in the review involves identification of some general terms that have been employed before to describe research on the topic. The potential variables in the study are the primary bases for the key terms. Professors and colleagues can usually help with suggestions of general terms.

Using these broad key words, the researcher consults secondary sources, such as major textbooks, handbooks, encyclopedias, and annual review series as well as journals specializing in literature reviews, for a coherent overview of the topic. (Materials in which the author is reporting or reviewing the work of others are called *secondary* sources; materials reporting findings directly from the person who carried out the study are referred to as *primary* sources.) *Meta-analyses* of topics, or the quantitative integration of empirical research literature, are especially valuable and should be sought (see Meta-analysis section at the end of this chapter). The summaries provided by all of these sources not only give a broad perspective of an area but also define significant technical terms and give important references for follow-up. This leads to the formulation of a problem statement and the development of a tentative outline or framework that will structure the search and assist the researcher in classifying and filing information that is accumulated.

Before the investigator can proceed further, it is necessary to compile a list of more specific key words, phrases, or descriptors related to the research problem. Good sources of common descriptors may be found in the *Library of Congress Subject Headings, Thesaurus of ERIC Descriptors,* and *Thesaurus of Psychological Index Terms.* Often the researcher will need to modify the original list of key words to make them compatible with the terms used by the particular index, abstract, or computer-retrieval system selected. The identification of key terms is requisite to a thorough search of the literature.

The next step is the identification of indexes, abstracts, and computer-search systems to help the researcher uncover important primary sources. Most indexes, abstracts, and computerized databases are organized according to descriptors or subject headings. Changes in technical terminology in a field can cause an inconvenience and present a special challenge for the reviewer. From time to time, new indexing terms are introduced, requiring the researcher to check less specific subject-search headings for earlier, related citations.

Once the titles of relevant sources have been found in the indexes and abstracts or have been generated by the computer, the researcher looks for the materials in the library and checks them out if they are available.[1] It is a good idea to begin with the most recent books or articles and work backward because the more contemporary materials have incorporated the most current thinking and research results and they include references of earlier, relevant sources.

The card catalog, which indexes a library's book holdings, is used to locate books. It is arranged alphabetically on 3″ × 5″ cards in rows of cabinet drawers. Each volume has an author, title, and subject card that includes standard information: the author's name; title of the book; publisher, date of publication, and edition; number of pages, inclusion of preface, bibliography, tables, illustrations; subject classifications; Library of Congress (LC) call number; and library call number. Most book collections are classified according to the Library of Congress or Dewey Decimal systems, both of which assign a code for each field and its subclassifications. Card catalogs are arranged in different ways, depending on the library. The author, title, and subject cards may be placed in one alphabet; the author and title cards may be put under one alphabet and the subject cards under another; or the three cards may be filed under three separate alphabets. Periodicals, government documents, microforms, and other special collections are usually cataloged separately.

Since no library, however large, can include all of the sources needed by the researcher, it may be necessary to borrow materials from another library. A good interlibrary loan service is essential to literature reviewing. Although numerous union lists are available that record book, journal, and microform holdings of libraries in the United States and Canada, over 3000 libraries use the Online Computer Library Center (OCLC) Interlibrary Loan Subsystem to identify area, state, regional, and national libraries that have certain books, journals, government documents, dissertations, theses, and microforms (Kilgour et al. 1972; La Grange 1981). This service, which catalogs millions of entries, facilitates ordering materials for the literature reviewer that are not held locally. Other libraries use comparable computer-based cataloging systems to handle interlibrary loans. Although most books can be borrowed for a limited time period, periodicals are usually not circulated, and a photocopy of the requested article is made for a small fee.

After the researcher has access to the materials, he or she should skim each source to determine if it is pertinent to the study. If so, careful notes should be taken to summarize material. Photocopies should be made of the most important references.

## The Literature Search as a Continuous Process

Throughout the study and until the final report is written, the researcher is on the lookout for the latest materials available on his or her topic. This requires checking the latest issues of relevant indexes and abstracts that serve as guides to published articles. Unfortunately, there is a time lag of anywhere from 2 to 18 months between the appearance of a paper in a professional journal and the publication of an index or abstract covering it.

One way to deal with this problem is to go to the shelves of unbound periodicals in the library and browse through the latest issues of journals that have already been found useful in the review. However, since researchers do not always have the luxury of time and their local libraries do not subscribe to all of the important journals, an even better solution to the problem of rapid access to the latest articles published is to read *Current Contents,* a weekly publication of the Institute for Scientific Information. *Current Contents* includes photoreproductions of the tables of contents of the latest issues of over 1000 journals. It is available in six different series, with some overlap among them: Social and Behavioral Sciences; Life Sciences; Clinical Practice; Physical and Chemical Sciences; Engineering, Technology, and Applied Sciences; and Agriculture, Biology, and Applied Sciences. Normally, the materials are no more than 6 to 10 weeks old when they appear in this publication. *Current Contents* includes an author index and addresses of authors to contact for reprints. (An online version of *Current Contents* is also available.)

The person conducting a review of literature should monitor studies in progress in areas related to the research problem. Through interaction with active researchers, one can learn about projects in various stages of completion at other institutions long before preliminary and formal reports are available. A letter or long distance telephone call to a recognized authority in an area can pay handsome dividends. Papers "in press" are another valuable source of information on current research that should be considered. Many journals list forthcoming articles in a section devoted to manuscripts accepted for publication. The researcher can contact the authors of these forthcoming papers and request preprints before they appear in the journal.

Papers presented at professional meetings are important reference sources that should not be overlooked. Researchers commonly present the findings of a study at an annual meeting before submitting the paper for publication. (Some papers are never submitted for publication and the report as a "paper presented" will be the *only* bibliographic record available.) The *Index to Social Sciences and Humanities Proceedings* (quarterly) and *Index to Scientific and Technical Proceedings* (monthly), both published by the Institute for Scientific Information, give the literature reviewer access to tables of contents of published conference proceedings, authors' names, and their organizational affiliations. *Conference Papers Index,* available on a monthly basis, is a similar publication whose information is derived from the printed programs of meetings rather than the published proceedings. Of course, the literature reviewers can borrow copies of program brochures brought back by professors and colleagues who have attended conferences dealing with various subject matter areas and themes, and examine the printed programs firsthand for titles of presentations and authors of materials that are of interest.

Staying informed of the latest books and monographs can be accomplished by examining publishers' catalogs and flyers, by looking at advertisements in professional journals that announce new publications or books in press, and by consulting *Forthcoming Books, Subject Guide to Forthcoming Books,* and *Publishers' Weekly.* The OCLC online system also records information on books about to be published. Once again, the search for relevant materials goes on until the research report is written.

It should be emphasized that information about a given study may be available in a number of slightly varied forms that correspond to stages of the publication cycle (Fig. 5.1). With some effort, the literature reviewer can gain access to information about a particular investigation at any of several different points in the publishing sequence.

## REFERENCE SOURCES

There are a variety of reference sources appropriate for literature searches in human ecology: books and monographs, periodicals and other serials, subject bibliographies, and dissertations and theses. Indexes and abstracts provide convenient guides to these reference materials and facilitate searching. A special category of documents called government publications is another important source of information when surveying the literature. More and more government documents as well as other nongovernment sources are being made available through micropublication. Another trend is the increased use of computer-based information retrieval. Computer searching is gradually replacing manual searching in most large or multidimensional literature reviews. Of course, the reference librarian is an excellent resource person for anyone undertaking a literature review.

### Books and Monographs

Books and monographs are cataloged in a library's card catalog system. The researcher who is interested in having access to book titles, including those not in the local library, can consult the *Cumulative Book Index, Library of Congress Catalog,* or *National Union Catalog.* To find out if a book is still in print, the researcher can check *Books in Print.*

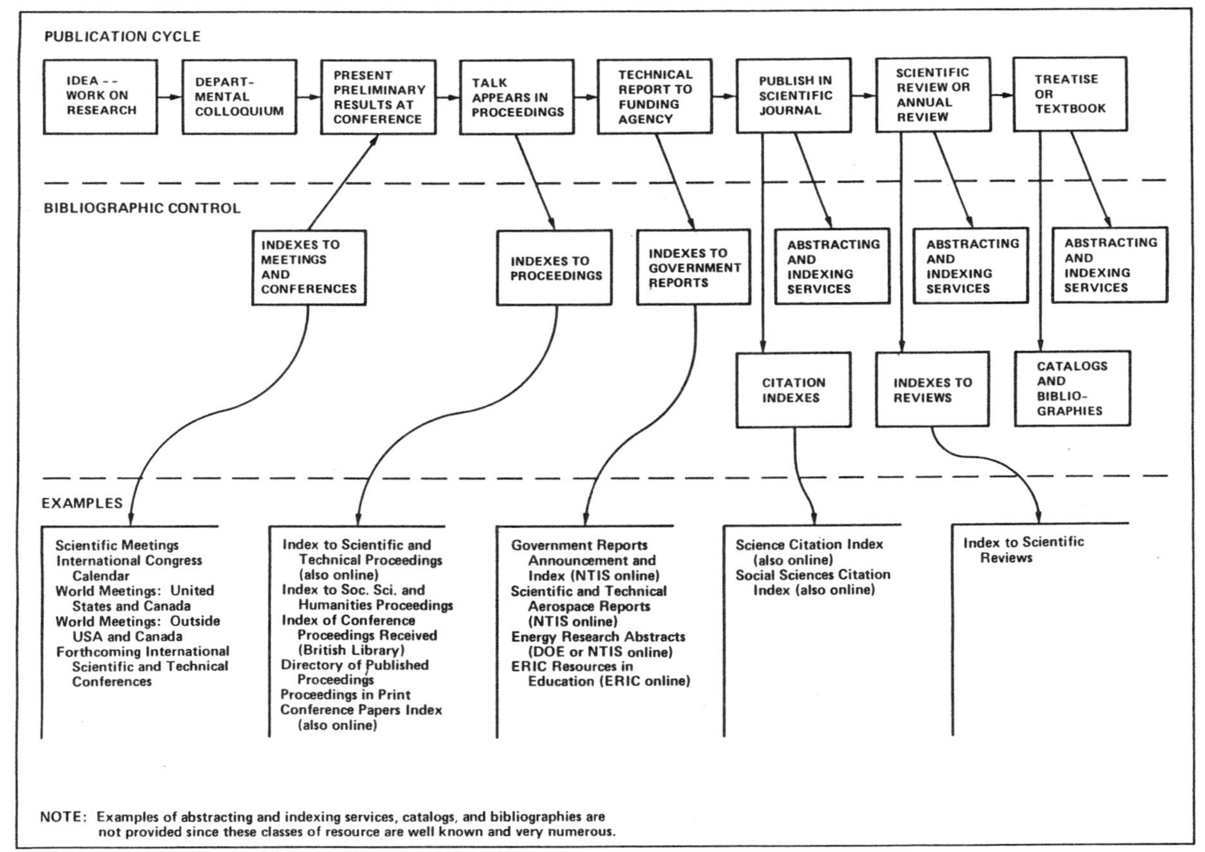


**Figure 5.1.** The scientific publication cycle. (From M. J. Bates, "Locating Elusive Science Information." Reprinted from *Special Libraries,* v. 75. no. 2 [April 1984], p. 116. © by Special Libraries Association. Used by permission.)

## Periodicals and Other Serials

*Periodicals* are journals and magazines that are published on a regular basis. *The Journal of Home Economics* and *Home Economics Research Journal* are examples of professional journals that are issued quarterly. Although periodicals are normally included in the card catalog, the library usually maintains a separate up-to-date listing of current journal holdings in the reference and/or serials section. Periodicals report new ideas and recent research results long before that information is available in books. They are primary sources of information on past studies.

The overwhelming task of browsing through dozens or even hundreds of individual journals searching for appropriate articles to include in a literature review is handled through the use of indexes, abstracts, and computer searching. Complete listings of available periodicals are found in *Ulrich's International Periodical Directory* and its companion volume, *Irregular Serials and Annuals: An International Directory,* as well as in *The Standard Periodicals Directory* and *The Serials Directory.*

Serials other than professional journals include annual review series or other reviews that are published on an irregular continuing basis. They discuss recent developments and the latest research findings within a subject matter area and contain extensive bibliographies. Contributors to these volumes are usually the leading authorities in the field. Evaluative overviews of different topics are presented every year or whenever a new volume is produced. Some reviews are *Annual Review of Nutrition, Annual Review of Psychology, Annual Review of Sociology, Annual Review of Public Health, Review of Child Development Research, Review of Research in Education, Annals of Child Development,* and *Advances in Nutritional Research.*

## Subject Encyclopedias

The search for reference material may also entail the use of *subject encyclopedias,* works which provide general but authoritative summaries on a topic. These brief summarizing discussions are helpful only in the initial phase of a literature review. Examples of subject encyclopedias are *International Encyclopedia of the Social Sciences; Encyclopedia of Aging; Encyclopedia of Educational Research; Encyclopedia of Environmental Science; McGraw-Hill Encyclopedia of Science and Technology; Encyclopedia of Textiles; Encyclopedia of Psychology; Concise Encyclopedia of Psychology; Encyclopedia of World Art; International Encyclopedia of Psychiatry, Psychology, Psychoanalysis, and Neurology;* and *Encyclopedia of Social Work.* Numerous volumes that are called encyclopedias lack sufficient treatment of topics to qualify technically as encyclopedias and are little more than dictionaries with expanded discussion.

## Subject Dictionaries

*Subject dictionaries* define the terminology in specialized fields. Some dictionaries that might be useful to researchers in human ecology are *Dictionary of Social Science Methods, Dictionary of Statistical Terms, Dictionary of Education, Comprehensive Dictionary of Psychological and Psychoanalytical Terms, Dictionary of Key Words in Psychology, Dictionary of the Biological Sciences, Fairchild's Dictionary of Textiles, Fashion Production Terms, Textile Glossary, Compilation of ASTM Standard Definitions, Fairchild's Dictionary of Fashions, The Dictionary of Retailing, Dictionary of Interior Design, Dictionary of Behavioral Science, Dictionary of the Social Sciences, Taber's Cyclopedic Medical Dictionary, International Dictionary of Medicine and Biology,* and *Dictionary of Nutrition and Food Technology.*

## Handbooks

*Handbooks* are heavily documented reference sources in a subject matter area. Usually these compendia synthesize and evaluate the literature with scholarly chapters on particular topics written by well-known authors. They include *Handbook of Social Psychology, Handbook of Aging and the Social Sciences, Handbook of Marriage and the Family, Handbook of Research on Teaching, Handbook of Research in Early Childhood Education, Handbook of Environmental Psychology,* and *Handbook of Child Psychology.*

## Subject Bibliographies

*Subject bibliographies* are a useful source of information during the early stages of the literature search. They provide the name of the author, the title, the publisher, the place of publication, the date of publication, and usually the number of pages in a work. Some also include annotations. If a bibliography is current, it can save the researcher a great deal of time in the library. Although available on almost any topic, bibliographies vary considerably in terms of their style, quality, and comprehensiveness. Because of their highly specialized nature and large number, no examples of subject bibliographies are provided here.

The *Bibliographic Index* is the primary guide to bibliographies in all areas. It gives citations for articles devoted entirely or in part to bibliography; books, parts of books, and pamphlets that provide bibliographies; and appended reference lists in articles and books. Besterman's *A World Bibliography of Bibliographies and of Bibliographical Catalogues, Calendars, Abstracts, Digests and the Like* is another good reference on bibliographies, although it does not include those that appear as parts of books and articles. The literature searcher also can gain access to bibliographies by checking the bibliography subdivision under the appropriate subject heading in the library's card catalog; by consulting periodical indexes and abstracts that cite bibliographic articles; by looking through the subject index of *Books in Print,* which includes a bibliography subheading for many different subjects; and by examining Sheehy's (1976) *Guide to Reference Books.* Every researcher should become acquainted with Sheehy's *Guide* and its *Supplements,* which list available bibliographies, encyclopedias, dictionaries, handbooks, and other reference sources within such subjects as children and youth, costume, consumerism, home economics, housing, interior design, marriage and the family, nutrition, and textiles.

## Dissertations and Theses

Doctoral dissertations and master's theses represent a source of studies that should not be overlooked when reviewing the literature. Occasionally an author will publish the findings of graduate research in a professional journal, but the majority of these investigations do not find their way into the periodicals. Dissertations are fairly easy to locate through *Dissertation Abstracts International,* the *Comprehensive Dissertation Index, American Doctoral Dissertations,* and the Dissertation Abstracts Online computerized database.[2] Master's theses, however, are relatively more difficult to identify. Some standard guides to available theses are *Master's Abstracts, Master's Theses in Education, Master's Theses in the Pure and Applied Sciences,* and *Guide to Lists of Master's Theses.* Master's theses written since 1980 can also be located through the Dissertation Abstracts Online service. Researchers who wish to examine dissertations and theses can purchase photocopies or microfilms from University Microfilms, Inc. In addition to the results reported by graduate students, both dissertations and theses contain comprehensive reviews of the literature that can provide good references on a particular topic.

## Indexes

*Indexes* are references that list materials in alphabetical order by subject heading or key word. These comprehensive guides to the literature allow the researcher to search through thousands of journals, whether or not they are in the library where the researcher normally works. They direct the literature reviewer to periodicals and other specific sources relevant to the research problem in much the same way that an index at the back of a book specifies where to find information on a topic in the volume or that the card catalog indicates where to look for a particular book in the library.

An index lists all of the periodicals searched, along with their dates, and gives a key to abbreviations used. Indexes do not present annotations of the contents of the documents, although in a few cases a reference source with "Index" in its title also provides abstracts (e.g., *Current Index to Journals in Education*). Some indexes that may be of interest to persons doing research in human ecology follow.

*Applied Science and Technology Index* deals with periodicals on construction engineering, trade, business, and related subjects. Among its subject headings are architecture, food and food industry, textile industry and fabrics, engineering, chemistry, and energy resources.

*Art Index* is a guide to art periodicals and museum bulletins. Its subject areas include archaeology, architecture, art history, arts and crafts, city planning, fine arts, graphic arts, industrial design, interior design, landscape design, photographs, and films.

*Arts and Humanities Citation Index* is a multidisciplinary index to the core literature of the arts and humanities. Like other citation indexes published by the Institute for Scientific Information (ISI), it is a system of four basic indexes that can be used interactively. References may be generated through knowledge of authors in the area of interest (*Citation Index*) or through a combination of key terms (*Permuterm Subject Index*). Complete bibliographical information for each article, including a listing of the references cited in the article, is available *(Source Index)*. It is also possible to locate publishing authors and their works by corporate or academic affiliation (*Corporate Index*).

*Bibliographic Index* is a bibliography of current subject bibliographies that have 50 or more citations.

*Bibliography of Hotel and Restaurant Administration* is an index of periodicals and books covering topics in the hospitality industries through 1985.

*Biological and Agricultural Index* covers agriculture, biological sciences, economics, ecology, food technology, and nutrition.

*Business Periodicals Index* lists journals in advertising, marketing, finance, investments, taxation, and insurance and in other specific businesses, industries, and trades. Some subject headings in this index that are closely related to human ecology include clothing and dress, consumer protection, family, fashion, merchandising, food service, houses, nutrition, and women.

*Clothing Index* covers periodical articles in areas such as social psychological aspects of clothing, costume and textile history, textile aesthetics and design, clothing construction, fashion merchandising and marketing, and textile science.

*Comprehensive Dissertation Index* is a compilation of dissertations accepted for doctoral degrees by U.S. institutions and some foreign universities, retrospective to 1861. The index is divided into disciplines, with complete citations provided under both author and subject entries. Unlike *Dissertation Abstracts International,* no abstracts are given.

*Cumulative Index to Nursing and Applied Health Literature* covers topics in nursing and other health-related areas.

*Education Index,* a cumulative index to educational journals in the English language, is devoted primarily to periodicals but also includes some monographs and yearbooks. It provides access to materials in administration and supervision, special education and rehabilitation, psychology and mental health, counseling, teaching methods, vocational education, tests and measurements, and educational research. Home economics education, nutrition education, and family life education are only a few subject headings that are of particular interest to researchers in human ecology.

*Humanities Index* is a comprehensive guide to periodical articles in archaeology and classical studies, history, language and literature, religion, theology, philosophy, literary and political criticism, and related subjects.

*Index Medicus* focuses on the literature in biomedicine, including periodical articles, letters, and editorials that have substantive contents. This work covers aging, mental health, personality development, nutrition, and other subjects in medicine that may be of interest to researchers in human ecology.

*Index to Social Sciences and Humanities Proceedings* offers complete bibliographic details of hundreds of proceedings each year in the social sciences and humanities.

*Inventory of Marriage and Family Literature* provides the most complete listing available of the periodical literature published in English on marriage and families. Over 100 subject categories are included, such as family policy, day care, economics and the family, divorce and separation, birth control, family life education, marriage counseling and therapy, and family financial counseling.

*Lodging and Restaurant Index* is a quarterly index of major periodicals in the hospitality, lodging, and restaurant industry published since 1985.

*Public Affairs Information Service Bulletin* includes a selective list of the latest books, journal articles, government publications, pamphlets, and reports of public and private agencies relating to social and economic conditions, public administration, and international relations. Among the subject headings are consumer protection, education, environment, family, housing, and food consumption.

*Readers' Guide to Periodical Literature* covers periodicals of general interest published in the United States.

*Science Citation Index* is an index to science, medicine, agriculture, technology, and the behavioral sciences. (See *Arts and Humanities Citation*

*Index* description for more information on ISI citation indexes.)

*Social Sciences Index* lists articles published by periodicals in anthropology, economics, environmental science, law and criminology, medical science, psychology, sociology, and related subjects.

*Social Sciences Citation Index* covers books, articles, conference reports, and book reviews from anthropology, business, communications, psychology, sociology, statistics, and urban studies. (See *Arts and Humanities Citation Index* description for more information on ISI citation indexes.)

*Statistical Reference Index* is a guide to American statistical publications from sources other than the federal government. It surveys and reviews current statistical publications issued by major associations, institutes, commercial publishers, and independent research centers in this country, as well as reports published by state government agencies and universities.

## Abstracts

A second type of systematized reference guide is the abstract. Like indexes, *abstracts* list references by topical areas, but they also provide brief, nonevaluative summaries of the sources. These annotations supply the literature reviewer with information so that he or she can decide whether or not to read the original source. The content summaries are quite helpful when the title does not clearly describe the materials covered in an article.

*Abstracts in Anthropology* is divided into four sections: ethnology, linguistics, archaeology, and physical anthropology. Its topics include acculturation, adaptation, authority and power, cultural change and stability, culture of poverty, ecology, ritual, and ceremony.

*Biological Abstracts* includes subjects ranging over all fields of the biological sciences, such as biochemistry, ecology, nutrition, food technology, gerontology, pediatrics, psychiatry, and public health. This work indexes journal articles, symposia, and proceedings.

*Chemical Abstracts* includes such topics as dyes and textile chemistry, foods, glass, clay products, enameled metals, building materials, fuels, waxes, and detergents.

*Child Development Abstracts and Bibliography* covers the areas of biology, health, and medicine; cognition learning and perception; social psychological, cultural, and personality studies; educational processes; psychiatry and clinical psychology; and history, theory, and methodology. Some specific topics included are day care, parent-child relations, sex differences, and nutrition.

*Current Index to Journals in Education* indexes the current periodical literature in education and provides brief abstracts of their contents. Compatible with the ERIC information-retrieval system, it covers hundreds of major education and education-related journals. The *Thesaurus of ERIC Descriptors* provides indexing terms appropriate for a search using this index.

*Dissertation Abstracts International* (formerly *Dissertation Abstracts*) includes abstracts of dissertations accepted by all universities in the United States, Canada, and some other countries. This reference is indexed by author and key word.

*Environmental Abstracts,* a collection of abstracts of literature dealing with the environment and human behavior, has 21 different categories, including air and noise pollution, chemical and biological contamination, food and drugs, environmental design and urban ecology, and environmental education.

*Food Technology Abstracts* contains information on foods, standards, laws, and regulations in the food industry.

*Gerontological Abstracts* covers research on aging and the literature dealing with the delivery of services to the elderly.

*Historical Abstracts* has sections on methodology and research methods, philosophy and interpretation of history, social and cultural history, economic history, sciences and technology, and geographical areas or countries.

*Home Economics Research Abstracts* is a series that compiles abstracts of dissertations and master's theses completed at colleges and universities offering graduate programs in home economics. Abstracts are organized into five areas: (a) art, housing, furnishings, and equipment; family economics; and home management; (b) textiles and clothing; (c) home economics education; (d) family relations and child development; and (e) foods and nutrition; institutional administration. Although this publication was discontinued at the end of 1981, it is a good source of materials for the years 1964–1978.

*Human Resources Abstracts* is a collection of abstracts of journal articles, books, and pamphlets dealing with research and action programs, legislative and community developments, and policy trends in the social services area. Some specific topical areas covered are minority group problems, employment, retirement, poverty, housing, and compensatory education.

*Journal of Human Services Abstracts* includes material dealing with the planning, management, and delivery of human services. Subject headings include adoption, foster care, food and nutrition service, housing, and vocational education.

*Master's Abstracts* provides a catalog of selected master's theses that are available on microfilm.

*Nutrition Abstracts and Reviews* includes materials dealing with the chemical composition of foodstuffs, vitamins, physiology of nutrition, human diet in relation to health and disease, and other topics related to nutrition.

*Psychological Abstracts* covers the literature in the major areas of psychology and related fields such as biology, business, education, medicine, psychiatry, social work, and sociology. Areas of psychology cited are general psychology, developmental psychology, social and experimental psychology, psychometrics, physical and psychological disorders, and educational and applied psychology. Most of the sources included are journal articles, although before 1980 this work included psychological dissertations, books, and book chapters. (These entries are still available through computer search of the *Psychological Abstracts* database). In addition to material listed under a variety of subjects related to human development, family relations, and marriage and family counseling, other literature of interest to human ecology researchers also is found under specific topical headings such as clothing fashions, consumer research, environment, housing, interior design, and nutrition. The most recent indexing terminology used is available in the *Thesaurus of Psychological Index Terms.*

*Rehabilitation Literature* contains abstracts of materials focusing on persons with disabilities, as well as full-length articles on rehabiliation-related topics.

*Resources in Education* (RIE) indexes and abstracts books, dissertations, speeches and conference proceedings, project and technical reports, and descriptions of ongoing programs in education and related areas. The source of key descriptions relevant to the search is the *Thesaurus of ERIC Descriptors.* RIE is a valuable reference because it includes materials that are not reported in professional journals and permits the early identification and acquisition of reports of interest. Most of the documents listed are available from the ERIC Document Reproduction Service in microfiche or paper copy.

*Sage Family Studies Abstracts* includes books, journal articles, pamphlets, government publications, and legislative research reports pertaining to the family.

*Sage Urban Studies Abstracts* covers the literature in the area of urban studies.

*Social Work Research and Abstracts* includes both original research papers and abstracts of articles previously published in social work and related fields. Material is organized according to fields of service (e.g., aging and the aged, family and child welfare, housing and urban development), social policy and action, service methods, the profession, history, and related fields of knowledge.

*Sociological Abstracts* covers the literature in sociology and related disciplines under major headings such as methodology, social psychology, group interactions, complex organization, social differentiation, urban structures and ecology, and sociology of education. Some specific subject areas that are of special interest to human ecology are demography, consumer behavior, family and socialization, and feminist studies.

*Women Studies Abstracts* contains abstracts of materials dealing wth women and women's issues, including family, sexuality, mental and physical health, employment, interpersonal relations, sex roles, and sex differences and similarities.

*World Textile Abstracts* covers areas such as fibers, yarns, fabrics, chemical and finishing processes, clothing and made-up goods, mill engineering, management, analysis, testing, quality control, and polymer science.

## Government Publications

Government publications are presented here as a separate group of reference sources because most government documents are not included in the abstracts and indexes already mentioned. Furthermore, many libraries separate the government holdings from other collections and also catalog them separately. Here are a variety of useful government documents, including indexes, abstracts, and sourcebooks for persons conducting research in human ecology.

*American Statistics Index* provides a comprehensive guide to the statistical publications of the U.S. government. It indexes and abstracts materials containing statistical data that may be significant to researchers.

*CIS Index,* published by the Congressional Information Service, indexes and abstracts working papers, reports of hearings, and publications of the U.S. Congress (excluding the *Congressonal Record).*

*Government Reports Announcements and Index,* a publication of the National Technical Information Service, abstracts and indexes research, development, and technical reports prepared under grants and contracts with federal, state, and local agencies.

*Historical Statistics of the United States: Colonial Times to 1970* contains annual data on the social, economic, and political life of this nation since colonial times. Since definitions of variables are consistent throughout the work, the examination of historical trends is possible.

*Index to U.S. Government Periodicals* covers publications by agencies of the federal government, some of which are not listed in materials described in earlier sections nor indexed in *Monthly Catalog* mentioned below. Some government periodicals indexed that are relevant to human ecology are *Aging, American Education,* and *Children Today.*

*Monthly Catalog of United States Publications* is the primary bibliography for U.S. documents. Published by the U.S. Superintendent of Documents, it lists new materials processed during the monthly period, without annotations.

*Statistical Abstract of the United States* summarizes important statistics on social, political, economic, and industrial organizations of this country. Prepared on an annual basis by the U.S. Bureau of the Census, it includes topics such as population, immigration, education, science, education, law enforcement, communications, and vital statistics. Statistical tables are prefaced by introductory narratives and are followed by references to the source of data and related publications.

*Statistical Reference Index* is a guide to American statistical publications from private organizations and institutes, independent research centers, and state government agencies and universities. This work includes both indexes and abstracts.

Two sources of international statistics that may be of value to persons doing research are the *Statistical Yearbook* and the *Demographic Yearbook*.

## Microforms

Increasingly more reference material for literature reviews is being made available to researchers through the means of microform. *Microforms* are photographed reductions of printed materials such as books, research reports, newspapers, theses, and dissertations. There are four different microformats: microfilm, microfiche, microcard, and microprint. Dissertations and other documents have been available on microfilm for many years. Microfiche is a transparent plastic film, usually 4″ × 6″, which holds 60 pages or more. The Educational Resources Information Center (ERIC), for example, has used microfiche successfully to fill orders for copies of research documents. Because of their reasonable cost, the U.S. government is issuing more and more of its documents in microfiche. Microcard is a 4″ × 6″ opaque card capable of holding 50 pages. Microprint is a 6″ × 9″ microcard that can include approximately 100 pages of printed material. More recently, super- and ultra-microfiche have been developed that contain up to 1000 pages of printed matter on one transparent card. Mechanical readers are necessary to illuminate and magnify the microforms. Reader printers are available that enable the researcher to make hard copy printouts of selected pages.

Some of the guides that list materials available as microforms include *Guide to Microforms in Print* and its companion, *Subject Guide to Microforms in Print; Serials in Microform; Master's Abstracts; Dissertation Abstracts International;* and *Microfilm Abstracts.* Microforms are durable and compact as well as economical.

## COMPUTER-BASED DATA RETRIEVAL

The information available in many of the indexes and abstracts already discussed may also be accessed through computerized retrieval. A literature review that is large and complex warrants searching for references via the computer. Other factors to be considered when deciding whether or not to run a computer search include the speed with which the material is needed, the coverage that is required for the particular literature survey, the accessibility of the desired information by other means, and the availability of automated information-retrieval services (Borchardt and Francis 1984).

After deciding that a computer search is justified and identifying certain key words that are related to the research problem, the researcher consults the person (usually a librarian) in charge of the library's computer-retrieval services. That person is called a *search-analyst.* The researcher explains the general nature of the study, suggests descriptors for the search, indicates the types of documents that will hopefully be retrieved, and gives the names of a few periodicals that are likely to include relevant articles. This information is then used to determine which databases should be tapped for the search. Since an abstracting service will require a special vocabulary, the search-analyst and researcher may examine appropriate thesauruses to identify other key terms that should be included.

Key terms must be selected carefully because a search that is too general will result in volumes of irrelevant references, and a search that is too narrow will miss some important ones. Borchardt and Francis (1984, 55) have emphasized that "no search will improve upon the key words used to designate the search." It is a good idea for the researcher to be familiar with a few pertinent articles that should be retrieved by the computer search. If these are not included among the references produced, the researcher is alerted to the possibility that something is wrong (e.g., different descriptors are needed) and that the search should be modified and rerun. In most cases, the information vendor delivers a printed bibliography to the researcher within 7 to 10 days. (A vendor is a company that makes databases within its data bank available to researchers and sells computer time for searching.)

### Computerized Databases for Human Ecology

There are several computer-assisted retrieval systems available to persons conducting research in human ecology. The researcher should consult the search-analyst, who will have catalogs describing all of the available computerized databases. A number of databases are general in nature and cut across different subject matter areas. Included in this category of multidisciplinary databases are COMPREHENSIVE DISSERTATION AB-

STRACTS, CRIS/USDA, ERIC, GPO MONTHLY CATALOG, MAGAZINE INDEX, PAIS INTERNATIONAL, SCISEARCH, and SOCIAL SCISEARCH. Since some computerized databases are more closely related to specific fields, a selective listing of databases for most areas within human ecology is provided in Table 5.1. (For an evaluation of many of these databases, see Brooks and Touliatos [in press]; Pfaffenberger, Franklin, and Echt 1983.)[3] Multiple database searching is usually a necessity in human ecology research.

## Advantages and Limitations of Computer Searches

As Brooks and Touliatos (in press) and Pfaffenberger, Franklin, and Echt (1983) point out, there are several advantages of using computer-based retrieval systems, including the following:

1. Computerized databases are usually more up-to-date than printed indexes and abstracts. In many cases, abstracting and indexing is done directly onto computer tape, which then produces the printed materials.
2. Computer searching eliminates the cumbersome task of looking through indexes and abstracts and copying citations. If the computer service prints brief summaries of the contents of the documents retrieved, the researcher can save additional time by locating for further study only those materials that seem to be directly related to the project.
3. Computer-based retrieval generates, with incredible speed, a comprehensive list of sources included in a particular index, thereby allowing the researcher to undertake a much broader search than would be possible if the work was done manually.
4. With the help of the computer, several different concepts can be searched simultaneously with relative ease. Many research problems in human ecology involve two, three, four or more concepts, which complicates a manual search.
5. The material included in a computer database may not be available elsewhere. It is not unusual for a computer database to include more material than its corresponding printed publications.
6. The search strategy can be immediately restructured as needed to generate the specific information desired.
7. The researcher does not need to know how to operate a computer to take full advantage of automated information-retrieval systems.

In spite of its numerous virtues, computer-based literature searching has some shortcomings (Brooks and Touliatos [in press]; Pfaffenberger, Franklin, and Echt 1983), including the following:

**Table 5.1. Selective Listing of Databases for Human Ecology**

| Family resource management/consumer studies | Fashion (design merchandising), clothing and textiles | Foods, nutrition, and dietetics | Restaurant and hotel management/hospitality services[a] | Housing and interior design[b] | Human development and family relations | Vocational home economics education |
|---|---|---|---|---|---|---|
| ABI/INFORM | ABI/INFORM | AGRIBUSINESS USA | ABI/INFORM | APPLIED SCIENCE AND TECHNOLOGY INDEX | AGELINE | ERIC |
| FAMILY RESOURCES DATABASE | CA SEARCH | AGRICOLA | MAGAZINE INDEX | ARTBIBLIOGRAPHIES MODERN | CATALYST RESOURCE ON THE WORK FORCE & WOMEN DATABASE | RIVE |
| F & S | F & S INDEX | AGRIS INTERNATIONAL | MANAGEMENT CONTENTS | COMPENDEX | ERIC | VECM |
| MAGAZINE INDEX | MAGAZINE INDEX | BIOSIS | PROMT | MAGAZINE INDEX | EXCEPTIONAL CHILD EDUCATION RESOURCES | |
| MARS | MANAGEMENT CONTENTS | CAB | TRADE AND INDUSTRY INDEX | MEDLINE | FAMILY RESOURCES DATABASE | |
| PROMT | MARS | CA SEARCH | | PSYCINFO | MEDLINE | |
| PSYCINFO | PROMT | ERIC | | | MENTAL HEALTH ABSTRACTS | |
| RBN | RBN | EXCERPTA MEDICA | | | PSYCINFO | |
| | TEXTILE TECHNOLOGY DIGEST | FOODS ADLIBRA | | | SOC ABSTRACTS | |
| | TRADE AND INDUSTRY INDEX | FSTA | | | SOCIAL SCISEARCH | |
| | | MAGAZINE INDEX | | | SOCIAL WORK ABSTRACTS | |
| | | MEDLINE | | | | |

[a]Databases dealing with food service are listed under Foods, nutrition, and dietetics.
[b]MEDLINE and PSYCINFO include sources examining the relationship between the built environment and human behavior.

1. Although an extensive bibliography may result from computer searching, the researcher must still locate and obtain the periodical articles and books before they can be used in the survey of literature.

2. Most computerized databases are fairly new and do not go back more than 10 years or so, although two widely used services, *Psychological Abstracts* and the ERIC database, are computerized back to 1967 and 1966, respectively. In addition, computerized databases may not include sources published in the last few weeks or so. Consequently, some degree of manual searching is always necessary.

3. Certain areas of research are not covered as well by one computer database as by others.

4. When more than one database is searched, there are often duplicate citations.

5. Reliance on the computer alone precludes browsing, serendipitous discoveries, and broad exposure to the literature that is possible with manual searching.

6. A highly trained intermediary, the search-analyst, is necessary to interface between the researcher and the computer (unless researchers can do the search with their own microcomputers by employing systems offered by certain vendors).

7. Although use of printed indexes and abstracts is free to faculty and students, there is usually a charge for computer searches. Fees may range from less than $10 to $50 or more.

## NOTE TAKING IN THE LITERATURE REVIEW

If the content of the material is considered relevant, the researcher should record the information in a systematic manner. Although it is impossible to photocopy everything, it is advisable to mechanically reproduce good reference lists, statistical tables, and major articles. Use of the copier not only saves time but also ensures accuracy and may be well worth the expense.

Even if the photocopier is used extensively, considerable note taking will be involved in a survey of literature. No single acceptable method exists for extracting and summarizing essential material from articles, chapters, books, and reports, but certain guidelines may help make the literature review go more smoothly:

1. Use 5″ × 8″ index cards. They are large enough to hold a great deal of information. If more than the front and back of a single card is needed, a second card can be stapled to the first one. Cards can be filed in a file box with alphabetical dividers or in an accordian file folder.

2. In the upper right-hand corner of the card, note an appropriate subject heading and underline it in red to allow convenient filing. If the source is a book, include the call number opposite the subject heading. This will help locate the material if it must be reread later.

3. Standardize the organization of the cards. A complete *bibliographic citation,* as it will ultimately appear in the reference list, serves as the "title" of the card. If the material is incorporated in the review, the bibliographic information can be typed directly from the card to the list of references when the survey is completed.

The summary itself is organized as an abstract under traditional headings, such as problem, subjects, method, and results and conclusions, but it also includes another heading: personal comments. The *problem* describes the purpose of the study and includes the hypotheses or research questions. The *subjects* section identifies the sample. Under *method* are included such items as measuring instruments used, procedures for manipulating variables, and statistical analyses performed. The *results and conclusions* section highlights the most important findings and the author's conclusions. A final section, *personal comments,* is reserved for the reviewer's evaluative notes regarding the study's procedures, technical questions, and so on. This is also an appropriate place for comments such as "best source on . . . ," "excellent reference list included," "good ideas for introductory section," "note sampling procedure used," or "see page 105 for summary of validity studies on . . ." The literature reviewer should always record his or her thoughts and never rely on memory.

The task of summarizing information from research articles is facilitated because most reports include a 100–150 word abstract. However, these prepared summaries must be expanded by the reviewer to include more detail if they are to be of maximum use in the survey of literature. Although including unnecessary information is a waste of time and effort, it is far better to have too much rather than too little information available when formal writing begins.

## WRITING THE LITERATURE REVIEW

Considerable advance planning is necessary before any writing is done. It is advisable to note all variables and combinations of variables or relationships under investigation in the current study and to list under these headings the specific sources examined that refer to each. "Classic" studies should be identified in the listing in some way (e.g., asterisked). Since "literature" includes both research and nonresearch sources, it is a good idea to have separate headings for research and conceptual/theoretical materials. Nonresearch articles and books are an important part of the survey of literature. Inevitably, some sources will be subsumed under multiple headings and will therefore be referred to in more than one place in the review.

Identifying the key variables contained in the research problem and listing the sources under these headings beforehand help ensure that the researcher will introduce a particular source at the appropiate point(s) in the review. Moreover, it makes it easier to group comparable studies that should be combined in some manner and discussed together. Different studies may have examined similar aspects of the current problem in much the same way. The overall objective of the literature review is to synthesize related materials, consolidating their presentation whenever possible rather than presenting the previous studies and papers author by author as uncoordinated summaries in chronological order.

At the beginning of the written review, it is beneficial to future readers if the researcher indicates the manner in which the review is organized. It is also good practice to point out how the literature was systematically investigated, including the abstracts, indexes, and computer databases used and the years covered as well as key words or descriptors employed in the search. If both manual and computerized searches were used, this should be indicated.

In lengthy reviews, the variable headings mentioned for initial grouping of sources may serve as the basis for subheadings in the literature write-up. Even if formal subheadings are not used, the review should be carefully structured. The researcher needs to summarize trends gleaned from the studies cited in one part or section of the review before proceeding to the next. Carefully constructed transition sentences provide continuity between sections. A summary section or a summarizing statement at the end of the whole review is necessary.

The length and detail of the written review is determined by the type of report being prepared. Literature reviews in theses and dissertations have traditionally been voluminous (typically handled as a separate chapter), whereas those intended for manuscripts reporting research for submission to professional journals are much shorter because of space limitations. In the latter, only the most relevant sources are cited to provide a context for the study.

Ordinarily, relevant theories are presented first in a literature review, followed by classic studies on the topic. As the sources cited relate closer and closer to the current investigation, they are described in relatively greater detail, giving not only the findings but possibly also information regarding sampling, measurement, and analyses. The pattern followed by the literature reviewer is from the general to the specific. It is imperative that the researcher strive to be selective and include only those sources that bear directly on the specific research problem. It is, after all, a review of *related* literature and not a report of every source consulted during the search. A literature survey should be restricted to essential sources that provide a foundaton for the study and logically lead to the statement of specific hypotheses or research questions.

There are many acceptable styles for preparing the literature review, each with its set of guidelines for organizing the material, citing references, and developing the reference list (see Chap. 16). Universities have their own preferred style for theses and dissertations, and professional journals likewise provide specifications for manuscript preparation.

Regardless of the style adopted, there are some steps that can be taken to increase the quality and usefulness of the review. First, outline the review of related literature before writing anything. This helps ensure that there is a coherent framework for presentation that is directly related to the problem. Second, be sure that the literature is up-to-date. There is no excuse for dependence on outdated references and omission of very recent ones simply because they were not yet included in the print abstracts or computer databases or were difficult to obtain through interlibrary loan. Third, all citations must be accurate. Bibliographic entries (and other information) on note cards completed during the literature search should be correct. If ever in doubt, double check the reference. There is nothing more annoying to a reader than trying to follow up an incorrect reference! Fourth, minimize direct quotations. Learn to paraphrase, using long quotes only when absolutely necessary. Fifth, plan on doing some rewriting. After a first draft of the literature review is prepared, set it aside for at least a few days and then reread it carefully, make editorial changes, and include any new material uncovered during the interim. The researcher should expect to be adding references up to the time that the total report is typed.

## THE LITERATURE REVIEW AS AN INDEPENDENT SCHOLARLY ACTIVITY

The discussion has proceeded as if the survey of related literature is a prelude to primary research, with the investigator beginning the next steps in the research process after the review is relatively complete. Although this is usually the case, research reviewing itself is a legitimate scholarly activity (Garfield 1987a, 1987b). Many reputable journals are devoted exclusively to the publication of literature reviews (e.g., *Marriage and Family Review, Review of Educational Research, Sociological Review, Psychological Bulletin),* evidence that carefully done reviews, like sound primary research, represent a contribution to a field. Additionally, journals that publish primary research are giving more space to articles reviewing the literature and, in some cases, are devoting entire issues to "state-of-the-art" literature reviews or decade reviews (e.g., *Home Economics Research Journal, Journal of Marriage and the Family*).

Independent scholarly reviews may take different forms. One form is the systematic, narrative survey of literature like the one described in this chapter. In summarizing and synthesizing past research and writing, its sole objective is the presentation of the current state of knowledge in an area and identification of questions that remain unanswered. No presentation of new primary research data follows. Another type of independent review surveys theories. It is designed to compare existing theories by examining their various features, and it often leads to the integration of ideas from different theories and to the reformulation of theory. Still another approach is the methodological review. It is aimed primarily at investigating and critiquing operational definitions, measurement techniques, and other aspects of research methodology that have been used in a problem area.

Ideally, a literature review that precedes a report of primary research combines elements of these three kinds of independent reviews. That is, it includes a consideration of related theories and at least some methodological evaluation of past studies in addition to surveying previous research from which generalizations will be inferred and hypotheses derived.

Two alternatives to the traditional narrative review are meta-analysis and the integrative research review.

## Meta-analysis

In recent years, an increasing number of literature reviewers have employed statistical methods like those used in individual studies to integrate findings across investigations. Glass calls this collection of techniques for quantitative literature reviewing *meta-analysis.* In Glass's (1977, 352) words, "The accumulated findings of dozens or even hundreds of studies should be regarded as complex data points, no more comprehensible without the full use of statistical analysis than hundreds of data points in a single study could be so casually understood." His meta-analytic procedure involves transforming the findings of each study included in the review to a common metric, coding characteristics of the individual studies, and then using statistical methods to examine overall and subsample effects, relationships among characteristics of the studies, and relationships among their results. Summary data from each study, not original data, are used in the analyses. Although most reviews of the literature continue to be done in the traditional literary fashion, meta-analytical reviews are being carried out with greater frequency because of their methodological rigor, replicability, and amenability to numerous statistical procedures, including multivariate analyses. (**Research Synopsis 12.4** illustrates the use of meta-analysis.)

Various procedures for combining and analyzing the results of a set of studies have been described elsewhere.[4]

## The Integrative Research Review

Jackson (1980) and Cooper (1984) propose a model for literature surveys that is especially well suited for reviews that do not introduce new data.[5] It includes most of the features of a good traditional narrative review, with strict adherence to scientific criteria, and also applies statistics to the research integration. Therefore, it combines the best of both the narrative and quantitative approaches. Called the *integrative research review,* this procedure views the literature survey as a research process that parallels the same rigorous methodology and concern with validity threats found in primary research.

According to Cooper (1984), there are five stages in the integrative review. The first stage, *problem formulation,* involves the development of conceptual and operational definitions. In a literature review, there are usually several operations defining a particular concept. In the second stage, *data collection,* the literature reviewer attempts to retrieve as much of an entire "population" of studies as possible using different methods of information retrieval (e.g., indexes, abstracts). Judgments are made regarding the quality of the studies retrieved in the third stage, *data evaluation.* This process is analogous to data editing and the identification of unreliable and invalid data in primary research. The fourth stage, *analysis and interpretation,* involves the application of quantitative inference procedures, such as meta-analysis, and the interpretation of results. In the fifth stage, *presentation of results,* the literature reviewer employs essentially the same structure for reporting integrative reviews as the researcher in primary research reports (introduction, method, results, and discussion). Cooper (1984, 7) believes that this objective, systematic approach results in "a replicable review that can create consensus among scholars and focus debate in a constructive fashion."

## NOTES

1. An excellent manual for utilization of library resources is Reed and Baxter's (1983) *Library Use.* Other helpful references include Bates (1984), Borchardt and Francis (1984), Frick (1980), Kennedy (1979), Kirk (1978), McMillan (1981), and Mann (1987).

2. Titles of dissertations in human ecology/home economics are also listed annually in an issue of the *Home Economics Research Journal* published by the American Home Economics Association. Previously, AHEA published *Titles of Dissertations and Theses Completed in Home Economics,* but this publication ceased in 1981.

3. Guidelines for effective computer searching in home economics are presented in Brooks and Touliatos (in press). Some other helpful sources on computer searching include Atherton and Christian (1977), Borg (1987, 41–62), Chen and Schweizer (1981), Kent (1977), Mann (1987, 80–102), and Perry and Dana (1985). The latest developments in online computer search systems are reported primarily in two professional journals, *Database* and *Online.*

There are several database directories. The major directories are *Data Base Directory* published by Knowledge Industries in cooperation with the American Society for Information Science, *Directory of Online Databases* published by Cuadra/Elsevier, and Williams's (1985) *Computer-readable Databases* distributed by the American Library Association. The latter is available in two volumes (vol. 1: *Science, Technology, and Medicine* and vol. 2: *Business, Law, Humanities, and Social Sciences*)). For an evaluation of these three directories, see Janke (1985).

4. It is impossible to do justice to a topic like meta-analysis in an introductory research text. For more information, see Bangert-Drowns (1986), Bullock and Svyantek (1985), Glass (1977), Glass, McGaw, and Smith (1981), Green and Hall (1984), Hunter, Schmidt, and Jackson (1982), Nurius and Yeaton (1987), Oliver and Spokane (1983), Rosenthal (1984), Strube and Hartmann (1983), and Wolf (1986). For a discussion of meta-ethnography, a method for synthesizing from qualitative studies, see Noblit and Hare (1988).

5. However, like meta-analysis, it can, but seldom does, serve as a prelude to reports of primary research.

PART 2

# Data Collection Methods

CHAPTER 6

# Selecting/Constructing Data Collection Instruments

This chapter examines some technical and practical considerations in selecting or constructing research instruments. As used here, *instrument* refers to any measuring device adopted for the purpose of data collection—observational system, questionnaire, interview schedule, and so on. The two major technical considerations in determining the adequacy of a research instrument are related to reliability and validity. More practical considerations also must be addressed by researchers. These are discussed under the heading of usability. The same considerations apply when the researcher is selecting an instrument that is already available, modifying an existing instrument, or constructing a new one for use in a study.

## RELIABILITY AND VALIDITY

The reliability and validity of research results were discussed in Chapter 3. This chapter focuses on the reliability and validity of assessment tools, the two most important factors in evaluating a particular instrument for data collection. There is a direct relationship between the quality of measuring instruments chosen for a study and the reliability and validity of that study's findings and the interpretations made from its findings. If an investigator has used instruments that provide accurate and consistent results and that serve the purposes for which they are intended, we are more likely to have confidence in the investigator's conclusions.

### Reliability

*Reliability* refers to the consistency with which an instrument measures something. A reliable instrument produces precise and stable scores, observations, and so on. If we measure the length and width of a desk top with a plastic ruler, we should obtain about the same dimensions today as we did yesterday. Our measuring instrument, the plastic ruler, is said to be reliable because it gives the same results when we compare (correlate) the dimensions yielded on two different occasions.

The relationship between the two results may be calculated by means of correlational analyses, typically using the Pearson product-moment correlation (see Chap. 14). This statistical procedure yields a numerical index, called a *correlation coefficient,* of the relationship between two sets of data. It is also commonly referred to as a *reliability coefficient.* Correlations of 1.00 signify a 1-to-1 relationship, or perfect reliability; correlations of zero indicate no reliability; and those between zero and 1.00 denote intermediate levels of reliability. While theoretically possible, a perfect correlation between two sets of scores is seldom attained when there are a large number of scores because of chance influences that are always present to some degree. But it is possible to achieve a reliability coefficient in the high .90s if the instrument is well constructed and administered under optimum conditions. Usually, most reliabilities are in the intermediate range, such as .65, .80, or .92. A strong association between the two measurements is an indication of high reliability and suggests that the instrument is providing information that is stable or relatively free from chance aspects of the trait or ability being measured.

Returning to the case of the plastic ruler, if we decided to use a measuring tape made of fabric to measure the desk top instead of the ruler, we might encounter some problems. The measuring tape may not be as reliable for assessing the dimensions of the top because we might stretch the tape too taut one time and not taut enough the next time. The measurements provided by the tape would not be as consistent as those by the plastic ruler. Using another example, this time involving an intelligence test, a person who receives an IQ score of 125 should obtain approximately the same score a week or two from now on an equivalent form of that instrument. If the person obtains an IQ score of 105 on the second administration, we would have to question the reliability of the test as well as the validity of the findings of any research using that measure.

Measures of physical characteristics tend to have higher degrees of reliability than measures of mental, psychological, and behavioral traits. Since human ecology research frequently employs psychological instruments, including measures of attitudes, interests, and opinions, researchers are justifiably concerned about the reliability of their assessment tools. (Reliability is very important because it is a basic characteristic that every instrument must possess if good research is to be achieved.) Of the nonphysical measuring devices, intelligence and achievement tests usually have higher reliabilities than personality inventories, behavior rating scales, and interviews because the latter instruments assess attributes that are generally less stable.

There are also numerous factors that affect reliability which are not directly related to the properties being measured. Among the extraneous factors that introduce at least some error of measurement into all assessment procedures and that could affect the stability of responses are the fluctuations in attention, memory, and effort of the subject and the influence of practice and of other outside experiences related to the traits being investigated. In addition to these chance factors, conditions such as the environmental setting of the testing or research room (e.g., lighting, ventilation, distractions) and the manner in which instructions are given to subjects before testing and data collection may affect reliability and influence research results. If a measuring device is overly sensitive to these potential sources of error, it is not a reliable instrument.

If it were possible to obtain a score uninfluenced by these chance events or conditions that intrude on the measurement process, we could know a person's "true" score. Unfortunately, the best estimate of this theoretical value is someone's obtained score—which can be higher or lower than the corresponding true score. The difference between an obtained score and the hypothetical true score is called the *error of measurement.* As the chance factors that contribute to unreliability (error of measurement) decrease, reliability increases.

When it is desirable to know how close an individual's obtained score is to his or her true score (i.e., the precision of an assigned value), the *standard error of measurement,* based on an instrument's reliability and its standard deviation, can be calculated. The standard error of measurement provides confidence intervals around a person's true score and allows a range of interpretation. Thus, if the reliability of an intelligence test is .91 and its standard deviation is 15, we can be confident that on the average an obtained score will be within ±4.5 points of the true score (107.5 to 116.5) 68% of the time and within ±9.0 points (103 to 121) 95% of the time.[1] If the standard error of measurement is zero, reliability is perfect.

## Estimating Reliability

There are four methods of estimating instrument reliability: test-retest, equivalent forms, internal consistency, and interrater techniques. Each procedure represents a different approach to reliability and gives different information about a measuring device. The use to which we put a particular instrument will dictate the type of reliability that is most essential. For example, if we are interested in determining the stability of performance over time, test-retest reliability would be appropriate. If equivalency of two present measurements is of interest, equivalent forms should be examined.

Test-retest Reliability. The test-retest method of estimating reliability involves administering the same instrument on more than one occasion to the same people under identical conditions and then comparing each individual's performance on the two administrations. This strategy provides a measure of stability across time. A high correlation coefficient indicates that the instrument assessed the same characteristic on both occasions and suggests that the measuring device is reliable. One advantage of the test-retest method is that only one form of the instrument is necessary. Some possible drawbacks are the influence of practice and memory from the initial assessment, variations in the subjects or in the physical conditions of the two test situations, and the maturation and experiences of subjects between sessions. The effects of memory are especially critical and may lead to spuriously high reliability coefficients. A common practice is to compromise between waiting long enough to offset the effects of the initial testing but not long enough for a significant amount of real change to take place in the subjects.

Equivalent Forms Reliability. Another means of assessing reliability is with the equivalent forms procedure. Sometimes referred to as alternate, or parallel, forms reliability, this technique necessitates two different but equal versions of an instrument. The parallel forms must use different items but measure the identical attributes in the same way. The alternate forms must be similar in content, number of items, level of difficulty, and other technical properties.

One form of the instrument is given to the subjects, followed closely by a second administration of an equivalent form. (Administration of the parallel form may be done at the same sitting.) A Pearson product-moment correlation is computed between the two sets of scores to determine the degree of relationship between them. The resulting reliability coefficient is often called a *coefficient of equivalence.*

Although the equivalent forms reliability estimate helps overcome the recall effects that frequently plague the test-retest method, achieving equivalency of forms is usually very difficult. Evidence of alternate forms reliability is necessary if one form is to be used as a pretest and the other as a posttest in a study (see Chap. 8).

Internal Consistency Reliability. The reliability of a test also can be determined from a single administration of an instrument. The *split-half* reliability estimate subdivides the measure into two halves so that all odd-numbered items are scored as a test and all even-numbered items are scored as a test. The Pearson product-moment correlation is then employed to correlate the scores made by each subject on one half of the items with those made by each subject on the other half. The Spearman-Brown prophecy formula subsequently must be applied to estimate the reliability for the whole test from the obtained correlation between the two halves of the measure. Since the length of an instrument is generally related to its reliability, with longer tests being more reliable, the correlation between the two halves will be an underestimate requiring correction by this formula. The split-half method denotes the equivalence of the two parts, or the degree to which two subsamples of the test domain seem to be homogeneous (i.e., measure the same property).

There are other internal consistency procedures that examine the relationship of responses on each item to responses on every other item and to the test as a whole. One method that determines item response patterns is the *Kuder-Richardson formula* (Kuder and Richardson 1937), which yields an average reliability based upon all possible split-half coefficients, without splitting the measure in half. This reliability estimate is appropriate only for instruments whose items have just two response categories (e.g., *yes–no, true–false*) or can be scored as right or wrong. If the response format is not dichotomous but is arranged as a multipoint continuum (e.g., *strongly agree, agree, disagree, strongly disagree*), Cronbach's (1951) *coefficient alpha* is used. The results of the Cronbach test of interitem consistency are interpreted like those derived from the Kuder-Richardson formulas.

Interrater Reliability. The degree of similarity between the scores, ratings, or observations by two or more independent judges is also a measure of reliability. Considerable agreement between the judgments denotes high interrater reliability. Conversely, inconsistency in the judgments indicates low interrater reliability. In a study using a rating scale, two people rate the same subject with the instrument, and the ratings of one judge are compared with those of the other; a correlation coefficient is calculated to reflect the congruence between the two independent ratings. A similar procedure is used to determine interscorer reliability when projective personality measures or unstructured interviews are used in data collection. Interrater reliability depends on the similarity of the scores given by two or more judges to the projective stories or to interpretations of subject responses in an interview situation.

The concept of interrater reliability is analogous to interobserver reliability in observational studies, where observers code defined behaviors or events using an observational system, rating scale, or checklist. Interobserver reliability also can be calculated in nonbehavioral studies, such as when anthropometric data like skinfold measurements of young children are made by two people. Interobserver reliability is usually established by having two persons independently record their impressions of identical stimuli and then comparing the results of the observations to determine agreement.

Although there are several ways to estimate reliability in observational research, one common practice is simply to calculate an interobserver agreement percentage by using the formula[2]

$$\frac{\text{number of agreements}}{\text{number of agreements} + \text{disagreements}} \times 100$$

A more detailed explanation of the theory of reliability, as well as a comprehensive description of the appropriateness of each of these four estimates of reliability for different situations, their calculation, interpretation, and relative sizes of correlation coefficients yielded, are available in most measurement and research texts.

## Validity

Validity is the single most critical issue in measurement. When we want to know what is being measured by an instrument and how well it fulfills its function, we are concerned with its validity. *Validity* can be defined as the extent to which the values provided by an instrument actually measure the attributes they are intended to measure. An achievement test, for example, is considered valid to the extent that it produces scores that help us determine how well a student has mastered a subject matter area.

Validity is not a major problem when assessing certain physical properties, such as the length and weight of an object. There is no doubt that a ruler measures length and a merchant's scale measures weight. However, if a researcher wants to study the relationship between personality traits and clothing conformity of adolescents, it is necessary to locate or construct instruments that will accurately measure these two variables as defined in the study. Unlike the direct measures used to assess physical characteristics, instruments designed to measure personality and clothing conformity will be only *indirect* samples of the traits or behaviors. Since so many of the data collection devices used in human ecology investigations are indirect measures, the validity of instruments is of great concern.

Before the general types of validity that have been identified and used in human ecology can be discussed, a few basic points about the validity concept need to be mentioned. First, validity is not a general quality. There may be different validities for a measure depending on its use. An instrument can be valid for one purpose but not another. Second, validity is not an all-or-none phenomenon. It exists in degrees. An instrument may possess high, moderate, or low validity. Third, there is a close relationship between validity and reliability. It is possible to have an assessment tool that is very reliable but does not measure the characteristic for which it was designed. In other words, it can be a consistent index but not measure what it purports to measure. An inconsistent instrument cannot be valid. Even though it does not guarantee satisfactory validity, reliability is a necessary condition for validity. It sets the upper limits on the validity of an instrument.

### Types of Validity

Content Validity. *Content validity,* also termed logical or sampling validity, indicates how well an instrument covers the subject matter, skills, traits, or behaviors under consideration. It is used to determine how an individual would perform at the present time in a given universe of situations of which the instrument constitutes a sample. The questions or situations included must represent the content areas or behavioral patterns to be assessed, and they must be appropriate for the individuals under study and for the circumstances in which they are being used. This type of validity is determined by a nonstatistical, logical process that examines the representativeness, or sampling adequacy, of a measure's content. It involves analyzing the substance, matter, and topics covered to determine if it adequately measures what it is supposed to measure.

A professor of human development who prepares an objective-type test for a unit dealing with theories of development and wishes to determine the instrument's content validity should examine each item on the test for its relevancy to measuring a student's understanding of the theories. If the test is to be high in content validity, it should have a random sample of all items that could possibly be included in a test to measure this area. Unfortunately, a random sample of items from a universe of test content is not possible. Thus, the content validity of test items is necessarily based upon judgments. The professor, either individually or with the assistance of other subject matter specialists, evaluates the representativeness of the items written for the test. To facilitate this task, a *table of specifications* is often prepared to specify the relative emphasis that is to be given to each area and/or expected type of behavioral change (Table 6.1). This requires a

**Table 6.1. Table of Specifications Indicating the Relative Emphasis to be Given to Measurement of a Content Area for a Test of Human Development Theories**

| Subject Matter Content | Types of Behavior | | | |
|---|---|---|---|---|
| | Recall of information | Understanding concepts/ relationships | Application of concepts | Total |
| Psychoanalytic | 6 | 4 | 4 | 14 |
| Neopsychoanalytic | 8 | 6 | 5 | 19 |
| Developmental | 5 | 3 | 2 | 10 |
| Humanistic | 5 | 2 | 2 | 9 |
| Behavioristic | 7 | 5 | 6 | 18 |
| Total | 31 | 20 | 19 | 70 |

careful definition of the content area or trait to be measured, a breakdown of the total area into different categories that make up the content domain, and an examination of the number of items in the various categories to ensure that there are enough questions in each category to discriminate between those subjects who have the knowledge or possess the trait and those who do not (Helmstadter 1964). The correspondence between the content of the instrument and these specificatons is an indication of the measure's content validity.[3]

For many data collection devices, content validity is the only feasible evaluation that can be made initially with regard to an instrument's validity. As might be expected, evaluation of the content validity of achievement tests presents fewer problems than judging content validity of nonintellectual measures.

Closely related to content validity is *face validity.* Face validity is the degree to which an instrument looks valid to the research subject or someone untrained in measurement.[4] It refers to what an instrument seems to meaure on the basis of superficial appearance. Although it is an inadequate index of validity when used alone, and it should never be substituted for more objective kinds of validity evidence, face validity does have a place in measurement and data collection. Indeed, in the initial stages of item development for a research instrument, face validity is about all that a researcher has to go on. But after items have been written, the importance of face validity diminishes except possibly in gaining rapport and in maintaining good public relations with research subjects. If the items seem irrelevant or inappropriate for the stated purpose, the research participants may become uncooperative and unmotivated because they may feel that they are being unfairly assessed. Face validity is also a desirable feature of a measuring instrument because it can affect empirical validity.

Criterion-related Validity. *Criterion-related validity,* sometimes called empirical validity, is concerned with the relationship between test scores, ratings, or observations and one or more external criteria that provide a direct measure of the attribute or behavior being investigated. The association between the results generated by the instrument and the criterion activity is usually expressed by the Pearson product-moment correlation coefficient (or some other form of correlation if both variables are not continuous and interval level) and is commonly referred to as a *validity coefficient.* The magnitude of most validity coefficients tends to be in the low to intermediate range.

One type of criterion-related validity is *predictive validity.* Predictive validity is employed to predict future behavior from the results of a present measurement. When hiring job applicants, this form of validity is useful for predicting their success in a particular position on the basis of a test battery. It also is used in selecting students for admission to college and professional schools (e.g., scholastic aptitude tests).

The method involves administering the test, waiting for the events the test is attempting to predict to occur, and then correlating the test scores with some measure of performance appropriate to the event. Academic achievement, performance in specialized training, and on-the-job performance are among the criteria for validating scores on an instrument. To illustrate, if the *Smith School Readiness Test* is designed to predict performance in the first grade, we would administer the instrument to a large randomly selected group of children at the end of kindergarten and then obtain teacher grades or standardized academic achievement test scores for the youngsters at the end of first grade. The correlation between scores on the readiness instrument and the subsequently obtained criterion measures (i.e., grades or achievement test scores) would represent the predictive validity coefficient for the *Smith School Readiness Test.* The accuracy of the prediction increases as the size of the correlation coefficient increases, so the closer the validity coefficient is to 1.00, the more adequate the *Smith Test* is for predictive purposes. In reality, most validity coefficients normally range from .30 to .70, with those .50 or higher commonly considered acceptable for some purposes (validity coefficients are always lower than reliability coefficients).

It is the magnitude (size) rather than the direction (sign) of the validity coefficient that represents its predictive value. If children making high scores on the *Smith School Readiness Test* (predictor) tended to make high scores on the first grade achievement test (criterion) approximately a year later, and if youngsters scoring low on the predictor measure tended to score low on the criterion measure, the validity coefficient is positive (+). If the association between the two sets of scores is strong, the validity coefficient might be something like .75; if moderate, .45; if weak, .20. If the sign of the validity coefficient is negative (−), this would signify an inverse relationship between the scores on the readiness test and the first grade achievement tests (i.e., children scoring low on one test tended to score high on the other).

The greatest problem in predictive validation is that of obtaining satisfactory external criterion measures. In some cases it may be difficult to identify and obtain criteria, and in other cases their validity may be doubtful. For example, aptitude tests predict future achievement, and grades in a student's college major may predict job success. Yet, what criterion can one use to examine the predictive validity of an artistic or musical aptitude test? What criterion can be used to validate a measure of teacher effectiveness? These can present major measurement problems.

A second type of criterion-related validity is *concurrent validity.* A basic distinction between predictive and concurrent validity is the time period between administration of the instrument and when the criterion measures are obtained. With predictive validity, there is an intervening period between the two, whereas with concurrent validity, the criterion measure can be obtained at or about the same time as the measure being validated. Frequently it is impractical to wait the long period of time necessary for predictive validity, and concurrent validity is used as a substitute. Of course, sometimes the concern is not with predicting future performance but with assessing current status—for which concurrent validity is appropriate.

If we have developed a new paper-and-pencil intelligence test that is relatively brief and inexpensive to administer, we might want to validate it against an older, more established individual test, such as the *Wechsler Intelligence Scale for Children* or the *Stanford-Binet Intelligence Scale,* if the new device is based upon the same theory of intelligence as one of the older instruments. We could administer the new measure and the well-respected *Stanford-Binet* at approximately the same time to a group of subjects. Then we would correlate scores on the new test with those on the criterion (the *Stanford-Binet*), probably using the Pearson product-moment correlation. The resulting correlation coefficient would be an index of concurrent validity of the new intelligence test, or the *current* relationship between the test scores and the criterion.

Criterion measures are not restricted to other test scores. Concurrent measures such as grades or ratings by teachers, job supervisors, and clinicians are just a few of the other possible criterion measures that can be employed in determining concurrent validity. The same principles involved in interpreting a predictive validity coefficient apply to the concurrent validity coefficient. However, the latter establishes a maximum limit for the former, since it is unlikely that scores that do not correlate well with the criterion in the present will correlate with the same criterion at some future time. Consequently, concurrent validity coefficients tend to be higher.

Construct Validity. *Construct validity* is concerned with the degree to which an instrument measures a theoretical construct. Constructs include hypothesized traits or abilities that have evolved from theory, such as intelligence, motivation, anxiety, achievement motivation, mechanical ability, and so on. Since all data collection devices are to some extent impure, and most do not measure exactly what their name implies, it is necessary to determine what an instrument does and does not measure (Cronbach 1984).

Hopkins and Stanley (1981, 106) outline the steps involved in developing a measure of a psychological construct and establishing evidence of its validity:

1. Develop a set of tasks or items based on theory and a rational analysis of the construct.
2. Deduce testable predictions regarding the relationship between the construct and other empirical measures; for example, if the test measures anxiety, we should expect to find some relationship between test scores and clinical ratings of anxiety level, and so on.
3. Conduct studies of these predicted relationships.
4. Eliminate items or tasks that operate contrary to theory (or revise the theory) and proceed again with steps 2 and 3.[5]

These authors describe the measurement of intelligence as a classic example of construct validation. Early attempts to measure the construct used reaction time, auditory memory, and other psychomotor and psychophysical measures. Since performance on these measures was found to be uncorrelated with direct indicators of intelligence, such as grades in school, the early measures were discarded, and over time more cognitively oriented tasks were constructed that were associated with intelligence and with other variables that were logically and theoretically related to intelligence. Gradually the scores correlated as expected with academic achievement, promotion and retention, clinical types of mental subnormality, and so on. Construct validation is a very slow and complex process that requires the accumulation of evidence from many sources.

The technical manuals of many measures, particularly personality inventories, report construct validity. Of the numerous ways to collect evidence for construct validity, one of the simplest methods is to correlate scores derived from the new instrument with scores of other established instruments that reflect the same theory and are considered valid measures of the construct. Another approach is to identify groups that are known to be different on the construct under study and to test the group to see if they do in fact differ significantly on the new measuring device in expected ways. For example, if a clinician rates children as well adjusted and poorly adjusted according to some behavioral theory and personality inventory scores obtained by these youngsters place them into the same categories, the personality instrument is said to have construct validity. When construct validity has been demonstrated, the theory underlying the measure receives support because construct validation involves the appraisal of not only the instrument itself but also the theory behind it.

## USABILITY

Apart from reliability and validity, the two major concerns in evaluating an instrument for research purposes, it is also necessary for the researcher to consider the usability of the data collection device. *Usability* refers to practical considerations such as appropriateness; availability of technical data; ease of administration, scoring, and interpretation; format; availability of equivalent forms; and cost.

## Appropriateness

The researcher must first decide if a questionnaire, interview schedule, or observation guide is suitable for the project. It must consistently and adequately assess the attribute, and it also must be appropriate for the age and type of research subject. Will the data collection procedure place special demands on the subject, such as the ability to read, understand English, follow directions? It would be unfortunate if an elaborately planned project yielded results that reflected level of literacy and not the variable under investigation. Will the instrument selected or developed probe areas that may be considered sensitive to parents, school boards, and the subjects themselves? The instrument, as well as the entire data collection procedure, must meet ethical standards (see Chap. 17). The importance of appropriateness as a criterion in instrument selection cannot be overstated.

## Availability of Technical Data

What do you know about the measuring devices you plan to use? Is technical information available on the instrument? Are reliability, validity, standardization, and other statistical data provided in the test manual and/or have previous studies reported relevant technical data? How has the instrument performed in past research with subjects like yours? A researcher must know as much as possible about the measure he or she is going to use in an investigation. If the instrument is one that you have constructed, how did it fare in your pretesting and in the pilot study? The *Standards for Educational and Psychological Testing,* prepared in 1985 by a joint committee of the American Educational Research Association, the American Psychological Association, and the National Council on Measurement in Education, presents guidelines for the development of reliable and valid instruments and their use; it is a valuable resource for researchers.

## Ease of Administration, Scoring, and Interpretation

The simplicity of administering the test and scoring and interpreting subject responses is a significant usability feature of a data collection device. Regarding *ease of administration:* To minimize subjective judgments by the person collecting the data, are the directions to the researcher clear and complete? If there are subtests, how many are there and is timing critical? Is special training necessary to administer the measure? Some standardized paper-and-pencil intelligence tests, for instance, can be given by classroom teachers to large groups of students, whereas an individual intelligence test requires an examiner with graduate training. When interview, observational, or projective personality techniques are used, some training is always necessary to ensure uniformity of procedure. Departure from predetermined (standard) methods of administering an instrument and collecting data from subjects will affect the reliability and validity of the results.

Closely associated with the ease of administration is the time required for administering the measure. If data are being collected in a school setting, can the instrument be administered during an established class period to avoid administrative inconvenience? If the subjects are young children, will attention span be a problem if the testing session is relatively long? Although a longer measure usually yields more reliable results, with some groups the increased length could cause inattentiveness, boredom, or fatigue. Another time-related consideration in the selection of a data collection technique is imposition on the subject's time. Undoubtedly, length of an interview or observation session can influence participation rate as can the number of items on a mailed self-administered questionnaire in a survey. It is necessary for the researcher to strike a balance between the collection of sufficient data to meet the research objectives and asking too much of research subjects.

The directions for scoring and the *ease of scoring* are other factors that should be taken into account by the researcher. Other things being equal, the researcher should choose an instrument that requires a minimum of time and skill to score, without sacrificing accuracy. Generally, the easier an instrument is to score, the more accurate the scoring. Mechanized scoring, available for an increasing number of measures, has eliminated most scoring problems, has increased accuracy, and has ensured scoring objectivity. A goal for all researchers is to achieve the maximum objectivity possible in scoring. Complete objectivity is attained when two people scoring the same instrument arrive at an identical score. Although this is seldom a problem for objective measures with detailed scoring instructions and scoring keys, instruments that require the personal judgment of the scorer or coder present special difficulties.

*Ease of interpretation* is another important consideration. Most instrument manuals and collateral materials provide information that aids in the interpretation of scores. The clarity with which normative tables are presented and the simplicity with which raw (originally obtained) scores can be transformed into derived scores that indicate a person's relative position in a defined reference group (e.g., standard scores, percentiles, grade equivalents) should be of concern to the researcher (see Chap. 14). The time and training needed to interpret responses also are important factors in instrument selection.

### Format

Format is another point that should receive attention in evaluating the employability of a paper-and-pencil research instrument. The organization of content, typography, clarity of illustrations, and overall visual appeal are important. Bad formatting, particularly poor spacing and placement of items, can create problems in correctly marking answers, and it can lead to fatigue and monotony in the completion of the instrument.

### Equivalent Forms

The availability of equivalent forms of an instrument is extremely important if the experimental design requires a pretest and a posttest. Testing in close succession requires parallel forms. Many commercially published measures, such as achievement tests, provide equivalent forms.

### Cost

Cost sometimes places restrictions on the choice of a data collection technique for a study. Because of budgetary limitations, it may be necessary to use questionnaires instead of face-to-face interviews or observations, group intelligence tests rather than individual tests, and so on. Cost includes not only the financial outlay for the instruments themselves (and possible postage, envelopes, etc.) but also for the personnel to collect the data, score the materials, and interpret the results. The cost of certain instruments is substantially reduced if separate answer sheets and reusable booklets are available.

Although a researcher strives to minimize costs, a measure's reliability and validity and the availability of other pertinent technical information are far more important than cost. It is false economy to select a measure of questionable technical quality just because it is affordable. Adjustments in sample size or reductions in other areas can affect the savings necessary to purchase good instruments with known reliability and validity.

## SOURCES OF INFORMATION ABOUT RESEARCH INSTRUMENTS

In addition to measurement textbooks, there are many sources of information about research instruments that a researcher will find helpful. These include the *Mental Measurements Yearbooks,* numerous other handbooks and related sources in the measurement and evaluation area, professional journals, and test publishers' catalogs.

### *Mental Measurements Yearbooks*

The standard reference for persons seeking information about measuring instruments is Buros's *Mental Measurements Yearbooks* (Buros 1939–1978; Mitchell 1985) and the companion volume, *Tests in Print* (Buros, 1961, 1974; Mitchell 1983).[6] The *Yearbooks* have been published periodically since 1938 and *Tests in Print* since 1961. Separate monographs dealing with specific areas of testing are also available (e.g., *Personality Tests and Reviews, I–II; Reading Tests and Reviews, I–II; Intelligence Tests and Reviews*).

*Mental Measurements Yearbooks* list published instruments along with factual information about each measure (e.g., author, publisher, publication date, price, administration time, appropriate uses, and forms available) and a cumulative bibliography. The outstanding feature of the *Yearbooks* is its inclusion of critical reviews by authorities in the measurement field. Other sections of the *Yearbooks* include reviews of books and monographs dealing with tests and measurements and several indexes (periodical directory and index, publisher's directory and index, index of book titles, index of names, classified index of tests, and score index). *Tests in Print* serves as a master index to the critical reviews, excerpts, and references in the *Mental Measurements Yearbooks* as well as to other monographs about tests in specific subject areas that are published by the Buros Institute of Mental Measurements.

To gain access to updates on instruments covered in the current *Mental Measurements Yearbook* as well as information on new instruments that have recently been developed and that will be published in the next *Yearbook,* the researcher can conduct a computer search using the Mental Measurements Yearbook Database.[7]

### Other Measurement Compendia and Related Sources

In addition to the *Mental Measurements Yearbooks*, there are other sources that list, abstract, or describe published and unpublished measures appropriate for studies in human ecology. These materials, some of which are listed below, should help researchers locate questionnaires, interview schedules, projective techniques, observational systems, and other measures that may be well suited for their research problem and sample. Many of the following are compendia of measuring instruments, and others are devoted in part to the description of available measures.

*Adult Assessment: A Source Book of Tests and Measures of Human Behavior* (Andrulis 1977)

*Biomedical Instrumentation and Measurements* (Cromwell, Weibell, and Pfeiffer 1980)

*British Mirrors: A Collection of Classroom Observation Instruments* (Galton 1978)

*CSE-ECRC Preschool/Kindergarten Test Evaluations* (Hoepfner, Stern, and Nummedal 1971)

*CSE Elementary School Test Evaluations* (Hoepfner et al. 1970)

*CSERBS Test Evaluations: Tests of Higher-order Cognitive, Affective, and Interpersonal Skills* (Hoepfner et al. 1972)

*CSE Secondary School Test Evaluations: Grades 7 and 8,* Vol. 1 (Hoepfner et al. 1974c)

*CSE Secondary School Test Evaluations: Grades 9 and 10,* Vol. 2 (Hoepfner et al. 1974b)

*CSE Secondary School Test Evaluations: Grades 11 and 12,* Vol. 3 (Hoepfner et al. 1974a)

*Current Non-projective Instruments for the Mental Health Field* (Hyman, Woog, and Farrell 1978)

*Directory of Behavior Assessment Techniques* (Hersen and Bellack 1987)

*Directory of Unpublished Experimental Mental Measures,* Vol. 1, 1969–1970 (Goldman and Saunders 1974)

*Directory of Unpublished Experimental Mental Measures,* Vol. 2, 1971–1972 (Goldman and Busch 1978)

*Directory of Unpublished Experimental Mental Measures,* Vol. 3, 1973–1974 (Goldman and Busch 1982)

*Directory of Unpublished Experimental Mental Measures,* Vol. 4, 1975–1976 (Goldman and Osborne 1985)

*Encyclopedia of Clinical Assessment* (2 vols.) (Woody 1980)

*Evaluating Classroom Instruction: A Sourcebook of Instruments* (Borich and Madden 1977)

*The Experience of Work: A Compedium and Review of 249 Measures and Their Use* (Cook et al. 1981)

*Family Assessment Inventories for Research and Practice* (McCubbin and Thompson 1987)

*Family Inventories* (Olson et al. 1985)

*Family Measurement Techniques* (Straus and Brown 1978)

*Guide to Medical Laboratory Instruments* (Ferris 1980)

*Handbook of Family Assessment* (Grotevant and Carlson; in press)

*Handbook of Family Measurement Techniques* (Touliatos, Perlmutter, and Straus; in press)

*Handbook of Measurement and Evaluation in Early Childhood Education* (Goodwin and Driscoll 1980)

*Handbook of Measurement and Evaluation in Rehabilitation* (Bolton 1986)

*Handbook of Psychiatric Rating Scales* (Research and Education Association 1981)

*Handbook of Research Design and Social Measurement* (Miller 1983)

*Handbook of Scales and Indices of Health Behavior* (Reeder, Ramacher, and Gorelink 1976)

*Handbook of Scales for Research in Crime and Delinquency* (Brodsky and Smitherman 1983)

*Improving Educational Assessment and an Inventory of Measures of Affective Behavior* (Beatty 1969)

*Major Psychological Assessment Instruments* (Newmark 1985)

*Measures for Clinical Practice* (Corcoran and Fischer 1987)

*Measures for Psychological Assessment: A Guide to 3,000 Original Sources and Their Applications* (Chun, Cobb, and French 1975)

*Measures of Maturation: An Anthology of Early Childhood Observation Instruments* (3 vols.) (Boyer, Simon, and Karafin 1973)

*Measures of Occupational Attitudes and Occupational Characteristics* (Robinson, Athanasiou, and Head 1973)

*Measures of Political Attitudes* (Robinson, Rusk, and Head 1973)

*Measures of Self Concept, K–12* (Instructional Objectives Exchange 1972)

*Measures of Social Psychological Attitudes* (Robinson and Shaver 1973)

*Measuring Human Behavior: Tools for the Assessment of Social Functioning* (Lake, Miles, and Earle 1973)

*Methods of Measuring Clothing Variables* (Creekmore 1971)

*Mirrors for Behavior: An Anthology of Classroom Observation Instruments,* Vols. 1–14, with supplements (Simon and Boyer 1967–1970)

*News on Tests* (Educational Testing Service)

*Objective Personality and Motivation Tests* (Cattell and Warburton 1967)

*Preschool Test Descriptions: Test Matrix and Correlated Test Descriptions* (Johnson 1979)

*Register of Questionnaires and Attitude Scales* (National Foundation for Educational Research in England and Wales 1976)

*Research Instruments in Social Gerontology* (Mangen and Peterson 1982)

*Scales for the Measurement of Attitudes* (Shaw and Wright 1967)

*Sex-role Attitude Items and Scales from U.S. Sample Surveys* (Mason 1975)

*Sexuality-related Measures: A Compendium* (Davis, Yarber, and Davis 1988)

*Socioemotional Measures for Preschool and Kindergarten Children* (Walker 1973)

*Sociological Measurement: An Inventory of Scales and Indices* (Bonjean, Hill, and McLemore 1967)

*A Sourcebook of Mental Health Measures* (Comrey, Backer, and Glaser 1973)

*Test Collection Bibliographies* (Educational Testing Service)

*Test Critiques,* Vols. 1–7 (Keyser and Sweetland 1985–1988)

*Tests: A Comprehensive Reference for Assessments in Psychology, Education, and Business* (Sweetland and Keyser 1986)

*Tests and Measurements in Child Development: A Handbook* (Johnson and Bommarito 1971)
*Tests and Measurements in Child Development: Handbook II,* Vols. 1–2 (Johnson 1976)
*Tests in Education* (Levy and Goldstein 1984)
*Tests in Microfiche* (Educational Testing Service)
*Women and Women's Issues: A Handbook of Tests and Measures* (Beere 1979)

In addition to these compilations, numerous other books provide helpful information about measuring instruments and the latest data collection techniques in human ecology research.[8]

Another useful source of information about tests and measurements are professional journals that are concerned with assessment. *Educational and Psychological Measurement, Journal of Educational Measurement, Applied Psychological Measurement, Behavioral Assessment, Journal of Personality Assessment, Journal of Psychoeducational Assessment, Journal of Applied Measurement, Applied Measurement in Education, Journal of Clinical Psychology, Measurement and Evaluation in Counseling and Development,* and *Review of Education Research* are only some of the numerous periodicals that publish papers about measuring instruments. Pertinent articles in these and other journals can be identified through the use of bibliographic sources (e.g., *Psychological Abstracts, Education Index*) under such headings as assessment, evaluation, achievement tests, personality measurement, and educational measurement. Although they are not professional journals, informative serials dealing with measurement in the human development and family studies area are *Advances in Psychological Assessment, Advances in Personality Assessment, Advances in Behavioral Assessment of Children and Families,* and *Advances in Family Intervention, Assessment and Theory.*

Up-to-date information on research instruments can also be obtained from test publishers. Most major test publishers will send their latest catalog free of charge. The catalogs usually include descriptions of instruments—their uses, cost, administration time, and scoring services (if available). The researcher may purchase specimen sets of measures that include a copy of the instrument, its manual, and possible supplementary technical information. Depending on the nature of the measure, the purchaser may be required to present credentials documenting that he or she has the necessary training and experience to use the measuring device before the publisher will fill the order.[9] Researchers may also gain access to measures in test libraries of university counseling centers and by contacting other active investigators who maintain test files.

## EVALUATING A RESEARCH INSTRUMENT

The process of selecting observational systems, questionnaires, interview schedules, and projective techniques can be facilitated if the researcher uses a basic outline to organize evaluative information about the various data collection devices being examined. This kind of analysis of the instrument under consideration ensures that no important information is overlooked and allows comparison of the adequacy of one measure with another.[10]

INSTRUMENT EVALUATION OUTLINE

I. General information
   A. Title of the measure
   B. Author(s)
   C. Publisher (and address)
   D. Date(s) of publication
   E. Materials available (forms, levels, etc.)
   F. Administration time
   G. Cost (booklets, answer sheets, scoring services, etc.)
II. Description and purpose of instrument
   A. General type of measure (intelligence, personality, achievement; individual or group)
   B. Population for which designed (ages, grades, special groups, etc.)
   C. Subtests and scores possible
III. Technical features
   A. Item development
      1. Rationale for items
      2. Process of item selection
   B. Norms
      1. Type reported (standard scores, percentiles) and how reported (by age, sex, social class, geographic region, etc.)
      2. Standardization groups (nature, size, manner obtained, etc.)
      3. Adequacy and appropriateness for the research project
   C. Reliability evidence
      1. Type(s) reported (test-retest, equivalent form, interrater, etc.)
      2. Reliability coefficients and size and nature of sample used as basis for calculation
   D. Validity evidence
      1. Type(s) reported (content, criterion-related, construct, etc.)
      2. Validity coefficients and size and nature of sample and external criteria (if applicable) used as a basis for calculation

E. Special comments by the author(s) regarding technical aspects of the measure (cautions, etc.)

IV. Practical features
   A. Ease of administration (procedures, timing, clarity of directions, training necessary, etc.)
   B. Ease of scoring (procedures, clarity of directions, training necessary, etc.)
   C. Ease of interpretation (procedures, clarity of directions, training necessary, etc.)
   D. Adequacy of test manual and collateral materials
   E. Format and other qualitative features of the test materials

V. Evaluations of reviewers and past users of the instrument (from *Mental Measurements Yearbooks*, *Test Critiques,* and other sources, including journal articles reporting research using the measure)

VI. Summary of advantages and disadvantages of the instrument for the research project

## CONSTRUCTING NEW INSTRUMENTS

In spite of the fact that a researcher has hundreds of instruments to select from, there may be no suitable one for assessing exactly what the investigator wants to measure in his or her study. If an appropriate measuring device is unavailable and no existing measures can be adapted satisfactorily for use in a project, it is necessary to construct a new one. Instrument development is a major undertaking. Because it is a highly complex process, only some of the major steps in the construction of a measuring instrument are given here. For this discussion, it is assumed that a paper-and-pencil instrument of some kind is being constructed.

First, the population for which the measure is intended must be identified. Then, the property to be measured is defined and broken down. (A table of specifications, described in the discussion of content validity, is helpful for this purpose.) The next step is to develop items. After the items have been written and arranged in a format that resembles the anticipated final form of the instrument, they are administered to a group of subjects representative of the population for which the instrument is being constructed. Item analyses are subsequently carried out, leading to the elimination of certain questions, the preparation of new items, and the revision of others. The resulting set of items is organized into a new experimental form of the instrument and is pretested with another (larger) analysis group called the standardization or norm group. The questions are again subjected to item analysis, and procedures are followed to obtain the most valid combination of questions. A table of norms, reflecting the scores made by the standardization group, is established. These norms are later used to interpret the scores made by future research subjects.

## Pretesting and Pilot Studies

Some pretesting of instruments is always desirable, but it is absolutely necessary if new measures have been constructed for the study or if existing ones have been adapted. Pretesting helps uncover deficiencies in our measuring devices and allows us to have confidence in the instruments we finally select or develop.

A number of questions are likely to concern the researcher. Does the test elicit valid responses? Will teachers understand the behavioral terms used on a children's rating scale? Will subjects of a particular age, educatonal background, or social class be able to complete a questionnaire on their own, or should the instrument be adapted for administration as a structured interview? If electronic equipment is to be used, does the piece of apparatus accurately present or register stimuli or record subjects' responses with a high degree of accuracy? Is output or measurement of the mechanical device affected by extraneous conditions such as temperature or humidity? If so, what standardized conditions should be adopted to minimize these influences? Although students, friends, and colleagues are frequently solicited to help debug measures, it is preferable to administer the instruments to individuals who are part of the intended population but who will not be included in the final sample.

Ideally, this initial testing of measuring instruments should be expanded into a pilot study covering the whole research process. In the "dress rehearsal" for the main investigation, a small but similar sample is obtained; the actual measures are employed; the data are collected, coded, scored, and analyzed; tentative interpretations are made; preliminary tables and figures are prepared; and a written report is outlined.

In addition to its value in the refinement of measurement devices, pilot work is beneficial because it provides an opportunity for the preliminary examination of hypotheses, which may lead to their modification or elimination and to the development of new hypotheses that may be indicated. It also permits the researcher to check the adequacy of the sample design, data collection techniques, data processing procedures, and methods of analysis, some or all of which may require alteration before the main study is initiated.[11]

Full treatment of the measurement topics discussed in this chapter can be found in most comprehensive tests and measurement books.[12]

## NOTES

1. This example is from Mehrens and Lehmann (1984).

2. Although quite popular, this measure of reliability can sometimes yield estimates that are misleading. For a more complete discussion of observer reliability, including alternatives to interobserver agreement percentage, consult Foster and Cone (1986), Hartmann (1977, 1982), Kazdin (1982), Scott and Hatfield (1985), Suen and Lee (1985), Suen, Ary, and Ary (1986), and Towstopiat (1984).

3. For more information on the use of a table of specifications in instrument development, see Bloom, Hastings, and Madaus (1971), Gronlund (1985), and Helmstadter (1964).

4. See Nevo (1985) for a reexamination of the concept of face validity.

5. See also Campbell and Fiske (1959).

6. There is a newer reference tool published by the Test Corporation of America that is similar to the *Mental Measurements Yearbooks*. *Tests: A Comprehensive Reference for Assessments in Psychology, Education, and Business* (Sweetland and Keyser 1986) provides information on over 3000 instruments, and its companion series, *Test Critiques,* Vols. 1–7 (Keyser and Sweetland 1985–1988), presents evaluations of some of these instruments.

7. There are additional computer search options for test information using other databases, such as the Educational Testing Service Test Collection Database, PSYCINFO, and ERIC.

8. For example, in the nutrition area, see Christakis (1973) and Simko, Cowell, and Gilbride (1984); in education, see Taylor (1984) and selected chapters in Gage (1963), Spodek (1982), Travers (1973), and Wittrock (1984); in child/human development, see Harrington (1986), Hunt and Lindley (1988), Kane and Kane (1981), Knoff (1986), Palmer (1983), Swiercinsky (1985), Touliatos and Compton (1983), Weaver (1984), and Wylie (1974); in family studies, see Cromwell, Olson, and Fournier (1976), Filsinger (1983), Filsinger and Lewis (1981), Gilbert and Christensen (1985), Grotevant and Carlson (1987), Hoffman and Lippit (1960), Holman (1983), Jacob and Tennenbaum (1988), L'Abate and Wagner (1985), O'Leary (1987), and Weiss and Margolin (1986); and in clothing and textiles, see the various publications of the American Society for Testing Materials, such as *ASTM Standards on Color and Appearance Measurement* (ASTM 1984), *ASTM Standards on Chromatography* (ASTM 1981), and *Annual Book of ASTM Standards* (ASTM 1985) as well as the *Federal Test Method Standard No. 191* (US Government Printing Office 1985) and *Technical Manual* (American Association of Textile Chemists and Colorists 1985).

9. For ethical reasons, most test publishers try to restrict sales of measuring instruments to persons who can use and interpret them properly. Major distributing firms print information in their catalogs regarding who may purchase certain instruments because some can be given and interpreted by persons without special training, whereas others require substantial understanding of measurement and an advanced degree in an appropriate profession or membership in a relevant professional association. Here are the qualifications for test purchase outlined in The Psychological Corporation's *Product Directory* (1986, 270–71):

## Qualifications for Test Purchase

Seller's tests are instruments which must be used with professional care. The sale of tests is therefore restricted in accord with the principles stated in *Ethical Standards for Psychologists,* published by the American Psychological Association (APA). To order, write American Psychological Association, 1200 Seventeenth Street, N.W., Washington, D.C. 20036. Some of these basic principles are stated below. Eligibility to purchase tests is determined on the basis of training and experience, and Seller will have the right to rely on the representations of the Purchaser. The Seller reserves the right to require additional evidence of the Purchaser's qualification, and the Seller has the sole right to determine whether a Purchaser is qualified, and under what classification. Members in good standing of the APA and certain other established professional users are exempt from formal registration.

Seller will have the right to withhold or withdraw approval for test purchase where there is evidence of violation of the principles and practices of testing and counseling commonly accepted by professional psychologists and educators. No tests are sold for self-guidance, nor to any individual or organization engaged in testing and counseling by mail. Test users agree to guard against improper use of tests. To protect their value, tests and scoring keys must be kept in locked files or storage cabinets accessible only to authorized personnel.

The rules governing sale of tests to various classes of purchasers are as follow:

**1. Schools, Colleges and Governmental Agencies**

*Accredited schools, colleges, and governmental agencies* may order materials on *official purchase orders* or official stationery, signed by an appropriate administrator.

*Kindergartens, nursery schools, and day-care centers* that are not part of a large accredited school *may* be able to purchase "b" level materials listed under *Resources for Early Childhood* provided that documentation of at least *one* of the following is submitted for registration:

- Registration with the appropriate state educational agency.
- Licensing by the appropriate local government department to operate as an early childhood center.
- Director or Teacher-in-Charge licensed or certified as a teacher of early childhood.

*School teachers and counselors* may purchase tests by official purchase order or with the written authorization of the superintendent, principal, or guidance director. Authorization, on school letterhead, is required for each order.

*Graduate students of accredited universities* may purchase tests for study, research, or practice *only* if the order is countersigned by the professor who assumes responsibility for the proper use of the materials. Authorization, on academic letterhead, is required for each order. Such authorization should include the professor's title and the course or program for which the material will be used.

*Individual staff members* may purchase tests for personal (nonschool) use only if the individual establishes his or her personal qualifications.

. . . . . . . . . . . . . . . . . . . . . . . . . . . . . . . . . . . . . . . .

**2. Business and Industrial Firms**

Business and industrial firms using tests for the selection, training, and promotion of their own employees are asked to note the section of each test titled Requirements for Purchase.

*Level a:* Company purchase orders for tests marked "a"—those commonly used for employment purposes—will be filled promptly. Registration is required for the purchase of b and c level tests.

*Level b:* Available to firms having a staff member who has completed an advanced level course in testing in an accredited university, or its equivalent in training under the direction of a qualified superior or consultant.

*Level c:* Available to firms only for use under the supervision of qualified psychologists, i.e., members of the American Psychological Association or persons with at least a Master's degree in psychology and appropriate training in the field of personnel testing. The qualified person may be either a staff member or a consultant.

**3. Consultants to Business and Industry, Employment Agencies, Vocational Counselors and Psychologists in Private Practice**

. . . . . . . . . . . . . . . . . . . . . . . . . . . . . . . . . . . . . . . . .

**4. Libraries**

. . . . . . . . . . . . . . . . . . . . . . . . . . . . . . . . . . . . . . . . .

**5. Bookstores**

. . . . . . . . . . . . . . . . . . . . . . . . . . . . . . . . . . . . . . . . .

10. Some categories of our outline were suggested by test evaluation forms previously developed by Anastasi (1988), Cronbach (1984), and Goodwin and Driscoll (1980).

11. For an especially good treatment of pretesting and pilot studies, consult Babbie (1973). Also see Ackoff (1953).

12. See Anastasi (1988), Cronbach (1984), Gronlund (1985), Helmstadter (1964), Hopkins and Stanley (1981), Kleinmuntz (1986), Mehrens and Lehmann (1984), and Thorndike and Hagen (1977).

CHAPTER 7

# Major Data Collection Procedures

There are many different ways to obtain information for human ecology research. To acquaint the reader with a wide range of techniques that can be used to collect data, this chapter covers broad categories of data gathering methods: observation, questionnaires, interviews, projective measures, physiological and physical measures. Since a number of sources of research instruments were identified at the end of Chapter 6, only a few examples of specific measurement devices used within these data collection modes are included in this chapter. Synopses of published studies at the end of Chapters 8–12 illustrate the use of some of the techniques discussed here (see summary Table 12.1 at the end of Chap. 12).

Each of the techniques of data collection described is appropriate for certain research problems, study designs, and samples. Since all of them have shortcomings, it is necessary for the researcher to determine which methods will produce the most reliable and valid data. Optimally, more than one method should be employed in a study. In addition, whenever possible, different sources of data and multiple data collectors should be used. Combining methods, sources, and data collectors to investigate the same phenomenon in one study is referred to as *triangulation* (see Chap. 9).

## Observation

Observation is a basic means of learning about the world around us. People are constantly observing activities and the behavior of others. However, accounts of witnesses to crimes and other events reveal that two observers may interpret an incident quite differently and often inaccurately. Such everyday observations are far from scientific. Observation becomes scientific to the extent that it serves a formulated purpose, is planned methodically, is recorded systematically, is related to certain questions or propositions, and is subjected to checks and controls with respect to reliability and validity (Kidder and Judd 1986, 285).

## DATA FROM OBSERVATION

Many different types of data can be obtained through observation. When studying people, we can observe their physical appearance, language behavior (content and structure), paralinguistic behavior (noncontent vocal cues that accompany speech), and kinesic behavior (gestures, posture, facial expressions, interpersonal spacing, touching). In addition to studying ongoing behavior, we can observe the environments in which people live and work—the context of their development and behavior. And we can observe physical traces that people leave behind them, which may reflect something about their behavior, attitudes, and values.

As a data collection technique, observation helps bridge the gap between what people say or believe they would do in a specific situation and what they actually do. Observation may be undertaken in a controlled or uncontrolled setting, it may be visible or concealed, and it may be unstructured or structured.

## SETTINGS FOR OBSERVATION

A researcher may observe behavior in a carefully arranged, controlled laboratory setting where selected variables are isolated and manipulated for study. In such cases, all research subjects are placed in the same, structured situation. For instance, a procedure might be designed to arouse a certain type of feeling to provoke exhibitions of critical behavior. One example is the provocation of aggression by creating conditions designed to annoy the individual.

An advantage of contriving situations in the laboratory is the time saved by not having to wait for the desired conditions to occur in a natural setting. Another advantage is the control the researcher can exercise under these circumstances. A major drawback of the laboratory situation is that it may be quite different from what is encountered in real life. In addition, the narrow sample of behavior that is observed out of context may not represent important behavior patterns in a particular individual's life-style. Observations of an individual based on longer acquaintance may have greater predictive value than those obtained in brief, artificial situations.

Many problems in human behavior are found in the area of personality and social relationships where structured laboratory experiments cannot fully duplicate normal-life situations. These aspects of behavior are more profitably studied under naturally occurring conditions. Observations in field settings, such as the home, classroom, playground, shopping center, or place of employment, are referred to as *naturalistic observations*. Naturalistic observation, a basic technique of field studies, involves taking a representative sample of behavior as it occurs naturally in everyday life. From such samples the researcher estimates typical behavior. Some researchers believe that the best way to understand personality and behavior is to watch people react to the conditions that are most significant for them. If adequate controls have been used, observations carried out in natural settings would be expected to have greater generalizability than those conducted under contrived laboratory conditions.

## ROLE OF THE OBSERVER

In observational studies, the observer can assume one or two roles while recording data: nonparticipant or participant observer. A *nonparticipant observer* takes a position in relation to the research subjects where his or her presence does not disturb the usual functioning and behavior of the group. This approach is typically characterized by concealment behind a one-way mirror or screen to make the observer as inconspicious as possible. Proponents of nonparticipant observation argue that concealment of the observer prevents the observer from becoming a stimulus and affecting the behavior of research subjects. By eliminating observer interference, the subject's behavior is supposedly more natural.

Observation is referred to as *unobtrusive* if the observation process does not affect the behavior of those being studied. Any contaminating influence that an observer has on a subject's behavior is referred to as *reactivity* because the person being observed is "reacting" to the presence of the observer. Generally, any changes produced in what is being studied because of the mere act of measurement is called reactivity. Some authors have indicated that the concern over reactivity is overstated. They have suggested that persons being studied eventually become habituated to the presence of an observer, and there is no need to conceal his or her presence or identity.

An observer who assumes the role of *participant observer* takes part in the activities of the group. The additional responsibilities as observer may or may not be known to the group. The participant observer may live in the same community with the subjects or work in a business or organization to get a "feel" for the meaning of the activities going on. Being part of the group allows the observer to probe more deeply than an outside observer into social and behavioral processes and gain greater understanding for analysis of the problems being studied. The dual role played by the participant observer is very difficult and requires that considerable attention be paid to objectivity as data are collected and recorded.

## UNSTRUCTURED VERSUS STRUCTURED OBSERVATION

### Unstructured Observation

Observational methods of data collection may be unstructured or structured in nature. In unstructured observation, the observer is nonselective in that there are no predetermined ideas regarding what behaviors or events to record. That is, the observer does not impose structure on the observations but rather attempts to obtain a complete record of everything observed during a certain time period. The observer may study one research subject or many subjects simultaneously. The observation period may be only a few minutes or possibly hours. There is no common condition for collecting and recording data.

One popular way to record unstructured observations is with the *anecdotal record.* Anecdotal recordings are brief, objective accounts of a single incident that the observer considers to be significant. Anecdotes are usually written after the fact, and they include a description of the setting, participants, behavior, direct quotations, nonverbal behaviors, and how the episode was concluded.

Another unstructured method of describing behavior and events is the *specimen record.* Specimen recordings are detailed, sequential, narrative accounts of behavior in context (see Ex. 7.1). Since the observer faithfully records everything that takes place during the observation period and also notes his or her inferences, the records are quite lengthy. Using the specimen record, Barker and Wright (1951) required over 400 pages to describe one boy's life during a single day.

A recording technique that combines features of both the anecdotal and specimen record is called the *running record.*

Although unstructured observation provides rich and in-depth descriptions of people's behavior, the data yielded are usually difficult to quantify for research purposes. However, these less structured methods are especially valuable in educational and clinical settings. A primary use of unstructured observation in research is the identification of relevant variables

The room was comfortably warm, the light adequate. It was a cool, bright day. This period immediately follows recess. The children came in from recess, talking and laughing, as they came into the room.

*Writing Spelling Lesson at Blackboard (1)*

*EFU 1 Teacher: Planning Next Activity with Class*

*TIA1* — *Social Contact 1*

2:41 Mrs. Drouet called them to order very briefly and said, "We've talked it over and decided it might be better to do our practice spelling at the board."

She asked if they would like to do that.

*Adult Provides Opportunity for Child*

The class in general indicated that they would.

*Child Accepts Adult's Control*

*TIA1* — *Social Contact 2*

She said pleasantly, "All right, then, you may go to the board."

The class went to the board, with the exception of Raymond Pechter, who sat in his seat.

Raymond Birch took a place at the east blackboard between Douglas Kerr and Susy Norman.

Ben Hutchings was at the south end, then Douglas Kerr, Raymond Birch, and then Susy Norman.

Raymond immediately started to number from one to fourteen on the board in two columns.

He wrote very small letters, much smaller than most of the other children and he left only small spaces between his numbers.

*Getting New Chalk from Teacher (2)*

*EFU 2 Teacher: Giving Chalk to Pupils*

*TIA3* — *Social Contact 3*

Mrs. Drouet said pleasantly from the front of the room, "I think I have some new chalk."

2:42 She said with tolerance, "I suppose everybody will want long chalk if I start to give it to any of you." Many of the children immediately came to get chalk.

Raymond Birch came up eagerly to get his chalk.

The teacher said mildly reproving, "Please, let me take it and give it to you."

I judged that some of them were starting to reach

**Example 7.1.** An excerpt from a specimen record. (Reprinted from R. G. Barker, *The Stream of Behavior,* New York: Irvington, 1963, p. 291. Used by permission.)

to study in greater detail and the generation of hypotheses, both of which are particularly important during the initial stages of a project.

## Structured Observation

In some observational studies, the observer knows in advance what phenomena are to be studied and/or what hypotheses are to be tested. This permits the researcher to structure the observation beforehand by carefully defining all variables and developing a systematic plan to collect and record data obtained in any setting. Structured observation can be employed in either the controlled laboratory or natural field setting. Structured observations are less susceptible to methodological problems than unstructured approaches. Moreover, investigations using structured observation lend themselves more to the checks and controls necessary to establish the reliability and validity of observational data.

### Content of Observations

In a complex situation such as social interaction, no one can expect to observe everything that occurs. The most relevant aspects should be chosen and defined in advance. In planning a structured observational study, an operational definition of the behavior unit being observed or measured must be provided. If observations are to be made of independent behavior in kindergarten children, for example, what actions are to be labeled independent behavior (e.g., the child playing by himself, initiating projects with other children)? The behavior must be described clearly so that an observer can discriminate between it and other similar responses.

### Sampling and Recording Behavior

To be of value in formal research projects, observation should be systematic. Careful planning and control needs to be exercised over such factors as the number of observations, the length of the observation periods, and the interval between them. In structured observation, only designated behaviors are usually sampled.

There are two principal strategies to behavioral sampling: event and time sampling. With *event sampling,* the observer decides on events of a given class to be investigated, carefully defines the behavior involved, identifies the setting in which the event might occur, waits for the event, and then records the episode. Examples of events include children's temper tantrums, aggression, conversations with other people, and customer complaints. Event sampling, which requires counting the number of times the event occurs (it can also include narration), is an effective way to record relatively infrequent as well as frequently occurring events. It generates data that can be statistically analyzed.

With *time sampling,* the observer imposes a systematic time constraint on the observations by specifying when the defined behaviors will be observed and recorded during an observation session (e.g., every 20 seconds, every 5 minutes, or every 10 minutes). To obtain a representative picture of the variable being measured, it is preferable to use many short, well-distributed samples rather than a few longer observation periods. It is also better to collect time samples at randomly selected periods of the day because of the possibility of temporal delimitations of the behavior being studied. Notations are made regarding the presence (1) or absence (0) of the behavior or event at the prescribed intervals. Like event sampling, time sampling yields data that are amenable to quantitative analysis. Additionally, this recording technique provides representative samples of behavior in an economical manner. Major disadvantages are that time sampling lacks continuity and divorces behavior from its context.

## Observational Aids

Observations should be recorded objectively, indicating what actually happened rather than what the observer thought the behavior represented. Immediate recording in precise, concrete, and quantitative terms helps to increase accuracy. The recording of a person's behavior may be faciliated with the use of rating scales, checklists, observational systems, and mechanical aids.

Rating Scales. *Rating scales* provide convenient, systematic procedures for obtaining and recording judgments during the observation process or after the observation is completed. A rating scale is an observational tool that indicates the degree to which a person, process, or thing possesses a characteristic. A numerical value is usually given to descriptive categories, and the observer is provided a sequence of numbers. Example 7.2 is a bipolar numerical rating scale that can be used in education-related research.

A widely used type of rating device is the Likert scale. This numerical rating scale includes statements followed by a five-response continuum, such as *strongly agree, mildly agree, uncertain, mildly disagree,* and *strongly disagree.* Variations include fewer or more response categories. For example, a four-response format might include *very true, tended to be true, tended to be untrue,* and *very untrue.* The observer designates the category that represents his or her response to the descriptive statement. (Several Likert-type rating scales are illustrated in this chapter.)

Some rating instruments do not use numbers at all. Graphic rating scales, for example, divide the trait continuum into spaces which represent the possible number of judgments that can be made. Cues, which consist either of single words or of more complete descriptions, are written along or below the line at each end and often at intermediate points of the scale to

## CLASSROOM OBSERVATION RECORD

### TEACHER CHARACTERISTICS STUDY

Teacher________ No. ____ Sex ____ Class or Subject____ Date____

City ________ School________ Time ____ Observer____

| | | | | | | | | | | Remarks: |
|---|---|---|---|---|---|---|---|---|---|---|
| **Pupil Behavior** | | | | | | | | | | |
| 1. | Apathetic | 1 | 2 | 3 | 4 | 5 | 6 | 7 | N | Alert |
| 2. | Obstructive | 1 | 2 | 3 | 4 | 5 | 6 | 7 | N | Responsible |
| 3. | Uncertain | 1 | 2 | 3 | 4 | 5 | 6 | 7 | N | Confident |
| 4. | Dependent | 1 | 2 | 3 | 4 | 5 | 6 | 7 | N | Initiating |
| **Teacher Behavior** | | | | | | | | | | |
| 5. | Partial | 1 | 2 | 3 | 4 | 5 | 6 | 7 | N | Fair |
| 6. | Autocratic | 1 | 2 | 3 | 4 | 5 | 6 | 7 | N | Democratic |
| 7. | Aloof | 1 | 2 | 3 | 4 | 5 | 6 | 7 | N | Responsive |
| 8. | Restricted | 1 | 2 | 3 | 4 | 5 | 6 | 7 | N | Understanding |
| 9. | Harsh | 1 | 2 | 3 | 4 | 5 | 6 | 7 | N | Kindly |
| 10. | Dull | 1 | 2 | 3 | 4 | 5 | 6 | 7 | N | Stimulating |
| 11. | Stereotyped | 1 | 2 | 3 | 4 | 5 | 6 | 7 | N | Original |
| 12. | Apathetic | 1 | 2 | 3 | 4 | 5 | 6 | 7 | N | Alert |
| 13. | Unimpressive | 1 | 2 | 3 | 4 | 5 | 6 | 7 | N | Attractive |
| 14. | Evading | 1 | 2 | 3 | 4 | 5 | 6 | 7 | N | Responsible |
| 15. | Erratic | 1 | 2 | 3 | 4 | 5 | 6 | 7 | N | Steady |
| 16. | Excitable | 1 | 2 | 3 | 4 | 5 | 6 | 7 | N | Poised |
| 17. | Uncertain | 1 | 2 | 3 | 4 | 5 | 6 | 7 | N | Confident |
| 18. | Disorganized | 1 | 2 | 3 | 4 | 5 | 6 | 7 | N | Systematic |
| 19. | Inflexible | 1 | 2 | 3 | 4 | 5 | 6 | 7 | N | Adaptable |
| 20. | Pessimistic | 1 | 2 | 3 | 4 | 5 | 6 | 7 | N | Optimistic |
| 21. | Immature | 1 | 2 | 3 | 4 | 5 | 6 | 7 | N | Integrated |
| 22. | Narrow | 1 | 2 | 3 | 4 | 5 | 6 | 7 | N | Broad |

**Example 7.2.** A bipolar rating scale. (Reprinted from D. G. Ryans, *Characteristics of Teachers,* American Council on Education, 1960, p. 86, fig. 4. Used by permission.)

help the rater determine precisely where to designate his or her judgment. The mark does not necessarily have to be placed directly above a given cue. Forced choice, another type of nonnumerical rating format, usually requires the observer to choose between two descriptive terms or phrases.

Checklists. *Checklists* also help to objectify observations by providing a uniform way to record data. Whereas a rating scale allows the observer to represent the degree to which a quality is present or the frequency with which a behavior is manifested, a checklist is limited to all-or-none judgments. It is useful when the observer wishes to record whether or not a trait, object, condition, or event is present or whether or not a certain behavior has occurred.

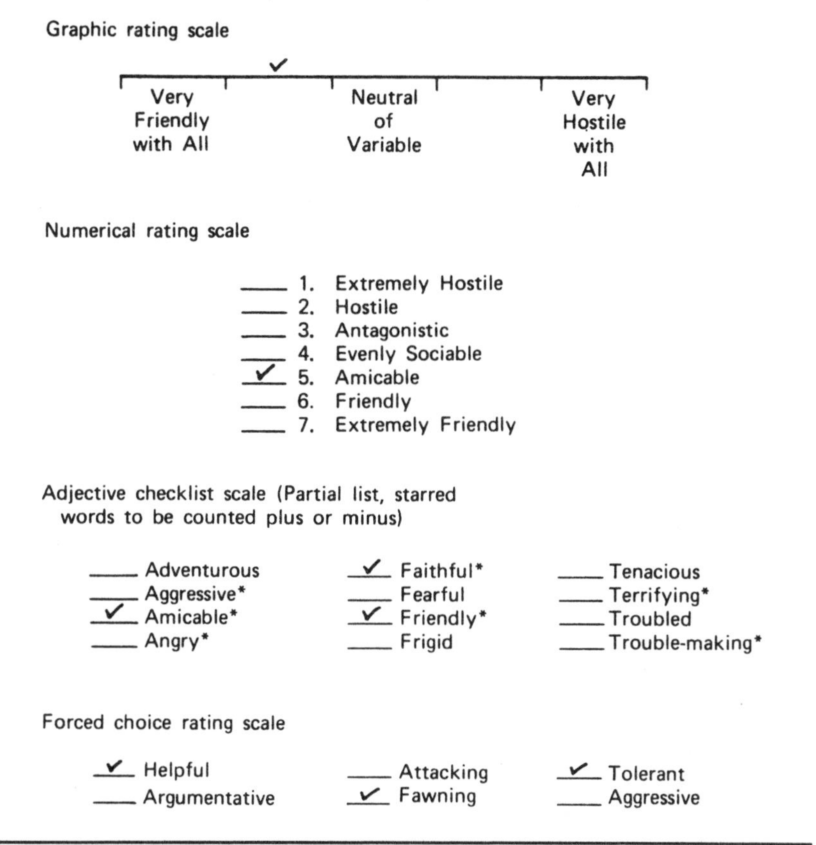


**Example 7.3.** Examples of different kinds of scales for measuring friendliness–hostility. (From N. D. Sundberg, *Assessment of Persons,* Englewood Cliffs, N.J.: Prentice-Hall, 1977, p. 78; an adaptation of J. S. Wiggins, *Personality and Prediction,* 1973, Random House, Inc., p. 311.)

The researcher has many different options when choosing a rating scale or checklist format to record observations. Rating scale and checklist items measuring the same personality dimension are shown in Example 7.3.

Observational Systems. *Observational systems* enable the observer to summarize data by using predetermined categories or lists of behaviors. Two basic recording formats are used: category and sign systems. A *category system* is an observation schedule with a set of carefully defined, mutually exclusive categories of behavior that are directly related to the research objectives. To make the recording manageable, there are usually 10 or less categories. Each unit of behavior observed is put into one and only one category of the system. To ensure exhaustiveness, the recording scheme typically includes a category called *other* or *miscellaneous* for undifferentiated behaviors. The observer indicates the presence or absence of the target behaviors at appropriate intervals in a time-sampling arrangement or uses an event sampling procedure.

Perhaps the best-known and most widely applicable category system is the *Interaction Process Analysis* (IPA). This system, which was developed by Bales (1951), can be used with both natural and laboratory groups. In IPA the observer codes every response made by an individual in a small face-to-face group into 12 categories: shows solidarity, shows tension release, agrees, gives suggestion, gives opinion, gives orientation, asks for orientation, asks for opinion, asks for suggestion, disagrees, shows tension, and shows antagonism. There are six dimensions of interaction, and the sets can be classified as either positive or negative. The dimensions include communication, evaluation, control, decision, tension reduction, and reintegration. Interrelationships among the categories are shown in Figure 7.1.

Another interesting category system, the *Fargo Activity Timesampling Survey* (FATS) was developed for a longitudinal study of obesity in preschool children (Klesges et al. 1984). FATS is an instrument that uses a 10-second interval time sampling procedure to assess a child's discriminable physical activity and the interactions that may influence a youngster's activity level. With a portable event recorder, the observer codes the child's activity level on an 8-point scale (1 = sleeping, 8 = running) and the intensity with which the child engaged in that behavior on a 3-point scale (1 = minimal, 3 = extreme). In addition, if someone encourages or discourages activity in the child during the 10-second interval, the observer codes the agent (mother, father, etc.), the form of interaction (physical or verbal encouragement/discouragement), the child's behavior that was targeted (crawl, walk, etc.), and the child's response to the interactions (crawl, walk, etc.). Operational definitions for the behavioral codes from the training manual (Klesges 1985) are presented in Example 7.4.

A second type of observational system, the *sign system,* is used less often. It lists a relatively large number of behaviors or events that may occur in a specified observation period. Examples of signs are: teacher acknowledges student's response, student uses dictionary, student asks question. These explicitly defined, discrete behaviors, or signs, are listed before the study is initiated and their frequency of occurrence is tallied by the observer. Behaviors that take place but which are not listed are ignored. Sign systems are well suited for the study of behaviors that are infrequent.

Mechanical Aids. *Mechanical aids* are often used by observers to improve the efficiency of recording. Audio recorders have been used in various ways

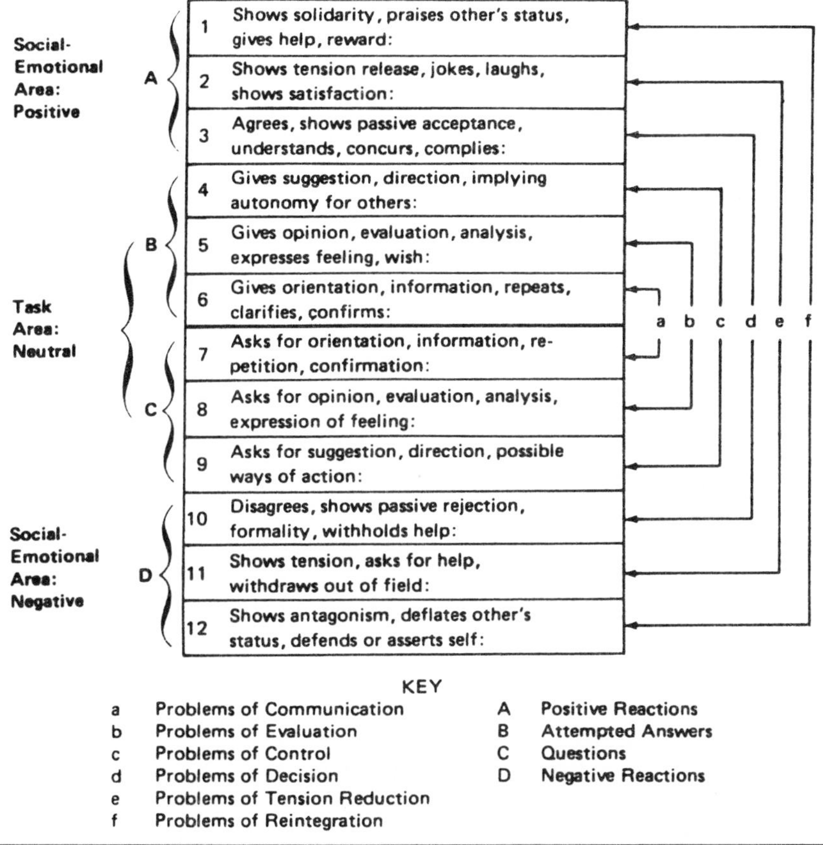


**Figure 7.1.** System of categories used in Bales's *Interaction Process Analysis.* (Reprinted from R. F. Bales, *Interaction Process Analysis,* © 1951 The University of Chicago Press, p. 9, chart 1. Used by permission.)

in observational research, including the recording of an observer's spoken commentary as the behavior or event occurs, the recording of verbal interaction, and cuing time-sampled observations. Radio telemetry has also been employed to carry subjects' verbal behavior by miniature radio transmitter to a sound recorder. Motion picture and videotape techniques are especially appropriate where the social interaction is complex and proceeds so quickly that it is impossible to record everything by any other method. To name only a few of their virtues, both sound and motion picture or videotape recordings are relatively permanent, allow time or event sampling, can be analyzed at the observer's leisure, and permit reliability

Table 2

Operational Definitions for the Fargo Activity Timesampling Survey (FATS)

Parent Interactions

A. *Physical encouragement:* Pats, hugs, kisses, pushes or moves, directs physically, holds and points.
B. *Physical discouragement:* Hits, restrains from action, removes child or object, redirects or moves in another direction, pushes, spanks.
C. *Verbal encouragement:* Suggests, commands, directs, reinforces.
D. *Verbal discouragement:* Forbids, scolds, refuses, punishes, yells.

Child-Initiated Interactions

A. *Requests activity:* Child verbally or physically encourages physical activity. Suggests, commands, directs parents towards physical activity.
B. *Refuses activity:* Child verbally or physically rejects a parental encouragement to be active; child verbally or physically rejects an activity he/she is engaged in and the parent(s) is/are maintaining.

Child Behavior

A. **Sleeping**—(1) *Minimal:* Child is asleep with no or minimal motor activity. (2) *Moderate:* Child is asleep with activity such as rolling, moving arms, or both. (3) *Extreme:* Sleep is accompanied by considerable rocking, moving of arms and legs; e.g., involuntary movements associated with seizures.
B. **Lying down**—(1) *Minimal:* Lying down is associated with no or little movement of the head, trunk, or extremities; e.g., child is lying down on a couch watching others. (2) *Moderate:* Child is moving arms, legs, and/or trunk while lying down; e.g., playing with a toy truck. (3) *Extreme:* Lying down is associated with excessive movement of arms, legs, and/or trunk; e.g., flailing arms or legs wildly; beating the floor; e.g., vigorous play or temper tantrum.
C. **Sitting upright**— (1) *Minimal:* Sitting upright is associated with no or little movement of the head, trunk, or extremities; e.g., sitting up and staring quietly at the television. (2) *Moderate:* Child is moving arms, legs, and/or trunk while sitting up; e.g., playing with blocks, playing "catch." (3) *Extreme:* Sitting upright is associated with excessive movement of arms, legs, and trunk; e.g., excessive arm, leg, or trunk movement; bouncing up and down wildly in anticipation of some positively valent activity.
D. **Crawling**—(1) *Minimal:* Crawling is associated with very slow movement; e.g., a very slow crawl, crawling and stopping repeatedly. (2) *Moderate:* Crawling is associated with considerable motor movement; e.g., consistently crawling with stopping towards a desired goal. (3) *Extreme:* Marked motor movement is associated with the crawling; crawling with high intensity; e.g., fast movement towards a highly desirable or away from a highly undesirable object.
E. **Climbing**—(1) *Minimal:* Climbing on or up something such as furniture very slowly with little physical movement; e.g., crawling slowly up a chair. (2) *Moderate:* Climbing is associated with considerable leg and arm movement; e.g., climbing deliberately for a desired object. (3) *Extreme:* Climbing associated with marked leg, arm and trunk movement; e.g., unusually fast movement towards a desired object.
F. **Standing Still**—(1) *Minimal:* Standing is associated with minimal arm or upper body movement; e.g., standing "at attention." (2) *Moderate:* Standing is associated with movement in arms and/or upper body; e.g., washing dishes, playing "catch." (3) *Extreme:* Standing is associated with marked movements in upper body and/or torso; e.g., waving wildly to get someone's attention; exercises involving upper torson only.
G. **Walking**—(1) *Minimal:* Walking at a very slow pace; e.g., walking slowly and quietly in an attempt to surprise someone. (2) *Moderate:* Walking at a normal rate; e.g., the gait one would observe when asked to retrieve a neutral object. (3) *Extreme:* A very fast-paced walk, usually with fast arm and torso movement but short of trotting or jogging; e.g., the gait observed when a child is told to "walk, don't run" to a positively valent object or area such as a playground.
H. **Running**—(1) *Minimal:* Running at a very slow pace; e.g., trotting, slow skipping, jogging at a minimal level. (2) *Moderate:* Running at a pace equal to medium paced jog or fast skipping. (3) *Extreme:* Excessive motor movement associated with running; e.g., sprinting, running "as fast as you can."

**Example 7.4.** Operational definitions for the Fargo Activity Timesampling Survey (FATS). (Reprinted from R. C. Klesges, "The Fargo-Moorhead Nutrition Project: Training Manual and Procedures," unpublished manuscript, Memphis State University, 1985. Research funded by the National Heart, Lung, and Blood Institute and the Center for Applied Psychological Research, Memphis State University. Used by permission.)

checks. Behavior counters and timing instruments are also valuable observational aids.

Event recorders also have an important place in observational studies. An event recorder is an electromechanical device that registers the occurrence of a particular incident or event. A very popular portable event-recording system that has been used successfully in observation research is Datamyte 900 (Fig. 7.2). Measuring 10″ × 10″ × 2″ and weighing only 4 pounds, it has 14 keys, which allows flexibility in the development of coding schemes for event and time sampling.[1]

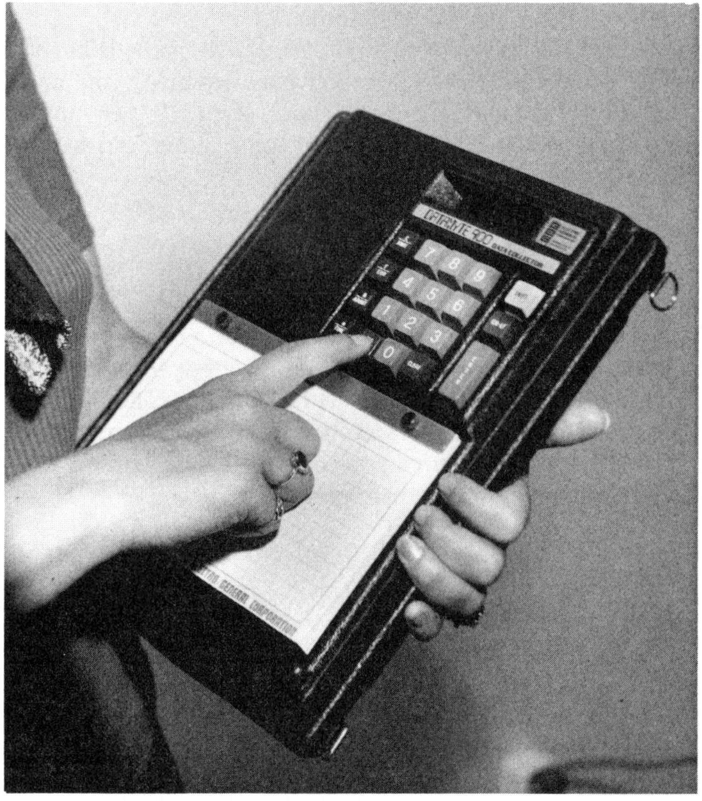


**Figure 7.2.** A hand-held event recorder (Datamyte 900). (Courtesy of Data-Myte Corporation.)

## ADVANTAGES AND LIMITATIONS

The observational method makes it possible to record behavior as it occurs, either in a laboratory or natural setting. It avoids the dependence upon someone else's memory and interpretation of an event. Another merit of observation is that it is independent of the subject's ability or willingness to report. This helps explain its widespread use in the study of young children, mentally ill persons, and others who may be in an inadequate direct source of information. When observations are carried out in everyday settings, they are particularly relevant because they allow the researcher to extrapolate easily from the data. Such naturalistic observations are as close as you can get to real-life situations.

Some limitations associated with observational methods in general include human perceptual errors, observer bias, reactivity, the absence of norms with which to compare data, and susceptibility to unreliability. Another potential problem is cost. Observation studies can be time consuming and expensive.[2]

## OTHER USES OF OBSERVATION

Observation is normally employed as a data collection medium for studying behavior in process, but it can also be put to other uses in research. Two other possibilities of this method of data collection are observation of the environment and observation of physical traces and archival records. The latter may be viewed as a form of "indirect observation" that is relatively uncontaminated by reactivity.

### Observation of the Environment

A person's behavior always occurs someplace, within the limits of a particular environment. That environment is as amenable to assessment as personality and behavior. Observation of the environment provides valuable information regarding the external forces that shape behavior. In studying environments, there are two ways to record the observer's responses (Craik 1970): free and standardized description. In *free description,* the observer describes what is seen in his or her own words. Examples of this narrative approach are ecological descriptions of the home, neighborhood, school, or work unit (Brandt 1972) and behavior setting surveys (Barker 1968; Barker and Wright 1955). In *standardized description* the observer records his or her observations by using more structured means, such as environmental rating scales, checklists, and observational systems (Ex. 7.5).[3]

PHYSICAL ENVIRONMENT INFORMATION – Mark all that apply.

**Playground Facilities/Use/Activities**

- ◯ Playground equipment in new condition.
- ◯ Playground equipment in old condition.
- ◯ Playground equipment seems to be used a lot.
- Playground activity directed by adults:
  - ◯ Always
  - ◯ Sometimes
  - ◯ Never

**Condition of Building**

| Yes | No | |
|---|---|---|
| ◯ | ◯ | Is the school building in good condition? |

**Noise Level**

| Yes | No | |
|---|---|---|
| ◯ | ◯ | Adults seem to have difficulty making themselves heard (have to repeat questions, ask the children to be quiet, etc.) |
| ◯ | ◯ | Children are noticeably disturbed in their work by the noise level. |

**Lighting**

| Yes | No | |
|---|---|---|
| ◯ | ◯ | Physical lighting seems adequate. |
| ◯ | ◯ | Some areas of the room are noticeably lighter/darker than the rest. |

**Heating and Ventilating**

| Yes | No | |
|---|---|---|
| ◯ | ◯ | Some areas of the classroom are noticeably warmer/cooler than the rest. (Direct sunlight, proximity to heating system, etc.) |
| ◯ | ◯ | Classroom is comfortably heated. |

**Displays in Classroom**

| Yes | No | |
|---|---|---|
| ◯ | ◯ | Children's own art on display. |
| ◯ | ◯ | Photographs of the children on display. |
| ◯ | ◯ | Pictures of various ethnic groups on display. |
| ◯ | ◯ | Community events posted. |
| ◯ | ◯ | Other (Specify) → |

NOTE: Do not write outside this box

**Description of Classroom Space**

| Yes | No | |
|---|---|---|
| ◯ | ◯ | Single contained classroom within a building. |
| ◯ | ◯ | Open classrooms. |
| ◯ | ◯ | Portable classrooms. |

**Space per Child**

| Yes | No | |
|---|---|---|
| ◯ | ◯ | Does there seem to be adequate space per child? |

**For each of the items below, mark all that apply:**

① Present
② Used today

**GAMES, TOYS, PLAY EQUIPMENT**

- ①② small toys (trucks, cars, dolls and accessories)
- ①② puzzles, games
- ①② wheel toys
- ①② small play equipment (jumpropes, balls)
- ①② large play equipment (swings, jungle gym)
- ①② children's storybooks
- ①② animals, other nature objects
- ①② sandbox, water table
- ①② carpentry materials, large blocks
- ①② cooking and sewing supplies

**INSTRUCTIONAL MATERIALS**

- ①② Montessori, other educational toys
- ①② children's texts, workbooks
- ①② math/science equipment, concrete objects
- ①② instructional charts

**AUDIO, VISUAL EQUIPMENT**

- ①② television
- ①② record or tape player
- ①② audio-visual equipment

**GENERAL EQUIPMENT, MATERIALS**

- ①② children's own products on display
- ①② displays reflecting children's ethnicity
- ①② other displays especially for children
- ①② magazines
- ①② achievement charts
- ①② child-size sink
- ①② child-size table and chairs
- ①② child-size shelves
- ①② arts and crafts materials
- ①② blackboard, feltboard
- ①② child's own storage space
- ①② photographs of the children on display

**OTHER**

- ①② please specify ......

**Seating Patterns:**

- ◯ Movable tables and chairs for seating purposes.
- ◯ Stationary desks in rows.
- ◯ Assigned seating for at least part of the day.
- ◯ Children select their own seating locations.
- ◯ Teacher assigns children to groups.
- ◯ Children select their own work groups.

**Example 7.5.** A physical environment information checklist. (From *Learning to Look* by Jane Stallings, © 1977 by Wadsworth Publishing Company, Inc. Used by permission of the publisher.)

## Observation of Physical Traces and Archival Records

### Physical Traces

A researcher may study the physical traces of people who have engaged in some type of behavior without having known that evidence they left behind would be used in the future for research purposes. Since they are generally unaffected by reactivity, physical traces are considered unobtrusive measures. There are two classes of physical evidence that are the products of human behavior and characteristics: accretion and erosion traces.

*Accretion traces* refer to the accumulation of material. The best single source on physical traces, *Nonreactive Measures in the Social Sciences* by Webb et al. (1981), provides several examples of these remnants of past behavior and the variables they presumably measure: graffiti on public restroom walls (sexual preoccupation of males and females), position of car radio dials (popularity of radio stations), automobile odometer readings (conservation of energy), dust or smudges on books (reading tastes, book use), and floor areas at archaeological sites (population size). Other examples given by Patterson and Sechrest (1983) are number of pieces of incoming mail received by psychiatric patients (contact with community) and cigarette butts left during a therapy session (client anxiety).

Brandt (1972) points out that another type of physical trace, physical products and material objects of many kinds used by people, may allow the researcher to make inferences about their probable behavior and personality. Archaeologists, anthropologists, and historians have examined artifacts and durable objects to gain clues about people living in earlier times who have left such traces. In a more contemporary sense, a person's material possessions or ways in which one decorates a dormitory room, home, or office may tell something about that individual and his or her life-style.

*Erosion traces* refer to the selective wear on physical objects. To illustrate, toys in a nursery school that show the greatest amount of wear (erosion) are probably those that most of the children prefer. Other examples of this type of use trace, given by Webb et al. (1981), are worn floor tiles around certain museum exhibits (interest in the exhibit), wear on steps (amount of traffic), condition of automobile exteriors (people's driving habits and skills), and food left on cafeteria trays (food intake and waste).

In studying physical traces, a researcher can intervene experimentally to avoid the inconvenience of waiting for deposits or erosions to occur naturally over a long period of time. Intervention by the experimenter can also improve the character of the physical evidence and facilitate the systematic collection of data. It is imperative, however, that these modifications not destroy the nonreactivity of trace techniques by making subjects aware that their behavior is being investigated. Webb et al. (1981) provide several illustrations of planned physical trace measures. Fingerprints on newspaper advertisements, obtained by using special paper that receives prints easily (readershp level); broken glue seals between pages of a publication (pages read); and number and location of noseprints deposited on glass fronts of museum exhibits that are wiped clean at the end of each day (popularity of exhibits and age of viewers) are examples of controlled accretion measures. Controlled erosion measures include the wear on children's shoes, measured at two points in time (activity level), and the wear on public statues whose surfaces have been specially coated (superstitious behavior).

The major advantage of using physical evidence in research is freedom from reactive measurement effects. However, since these indirect indicators are open to misinterpretation, they should be used with caution. Data on remnants, fragments, and products of past behavior should be employed in combination with other data and preferably not as a sole measure of behavior.

### Archival Records

Archival data are data that have been collected in the past and are available for analysis. They are a valuable source of information for researchers who wish to indirectly observe past events through existing materials. One category of archival data is statistical records, including statistical information routinely kept by a society and its institutions, such as political, health, employment, housing, legal, educational, and financial records. A second category of archival data is written records. These include both public and private documents, such as newspapers, magazines, speeches, films, business reports, autobiographies, diaries, and letters. A third category is survey archives of data. Data from surveys conducted by independent social scientists as well as by government, marketing, and opinion poll researchers are often stored in data archives and made available to investigators who wish to do their own analyses. For example, information obtained by the U.S. Bureau of the Census represents a wealth of existing data in a variety of areas for researchers and is available for further analysis.

Archival data are usually considered nonreactive because they are collected by an agency or organization as a part of routine data collection or they are prepared by individuals without awareness that the materials will subsequently serve a research purpose. Yet, some archival data can be somewhat more reactive than others. For instance, information gathered in a survey study by a researcher or data obtained for the U.S. Census are collected in an obtrusive manner because individuals know they are being studied. Generally, however, most types of archival data are viewed as relatively nonreactive.

Other advantages of archival data are their extensiveness, convenience, economy, and in the case of many statistical records, the uniform manner in which the data are collected and maintained. As with physical traces, archival data should be used in conjunction with data obtained through more traditional means and should not be employed as the only source of data unless it is unavoidable (e.g., historical research) (see Chap. 11).

# Questionnaires

In human ecology research, there are times when an investigator is concerned with measuring variables that cannot be observed directly. This can include information about people's current behavior that is not subject to the scrutiny of others, their past behavior, or their attitudes, opinions, and intentions. Most frequently, researchers employ questionnaires or interview techniques to collect such data. *Questionnaires* are instruments that list items or questions to which individuals respond directly. They may include items that are open ended, closed ended, or a combination of the two. For our purposes, questionnaires will be classified on their predominant question and answer format and will be referred to as either open ended or closed ended.

## OPEN-ENDED QUESTIONNAIRES

Questionnaires whose items are posed in an open-ended style permit an individual to respond in his or her own words, thus providing insight into feelings, background, hidden motivations, interests, and so on. These questions can stimulate a person to think about and express what he or she considers to be most important. Examples of open questions are: What is your hobby? What are you planning on naming your child? What do you like about the design of your home? How does your child react when you leave him/her with a baby sitter? In your opinion, what is the most important problem facing our government today? How is your family getting along financially this year compared to last year?

The open-ended question is advisable when the range of answers available to the respondent may not be fully anticipated by the researcher. In this case, restricting the possible answers to the question by using a closed-ended format may result in the subjects' perceiving their options as being more limited than they desire. Although this approach yields comprehensive answers, reliance on the free response requires more effort on the part of the subject (which might reduce participation rates), creates problems for the researcher in coding and tabulation, and achieves lower reliability.

## CLOSED-ENDED QUESTIONNAIRES

Unlike questionnaires featuring an open-ended format with no restrictions on possible answers, questionnaires with closed-ended items have a limited number of appropriate responses that are listed or understood. That is, the universe of possible answers is finite, and the restrictions on that universe are mutually understood and agreed on by the researcher and the subject. There are two types of closed-ended questionnaires: those with nonequivalent-item closed questions (NICQ) and those with summable-item closed questions (SICQ).

### NICQ Questionnaires

An NICQ questionnaire includes independent items or combinations of items that require manipulation of data beyond strict summation. Usually, but not always, the questions seek a piece of information, such as

Do you prefer Product X to Product Y? yes_____ no_____ uncertain_____

What is your sex? male_____ female_____

Did you vote for John Smith? yes_____ no_____

What is your educational attainment? less than high school_____ high school graduate_____ some college_____ college graduate_____

What factor is most important in purchasing a suit? price_____ color_____ current fashion_____ general appearance on me_____

NICQs may also be items that have no preformulated listing of response alternatives. However, the range of acceptable responses is understood equally by the researcher and the respondent. Here are some examples: What brand of cereal do you buy? If the election were held today, which candidate would you vote for? How old are you? What is your occupation? What is your sex? In each of these questions, the possible range of answers is known. For instance, there are a finite number of cereal brands on the market, and candidates for election have been nominated and are on the ballot.

## SICQ Questionnaires

SICQ questionnaires have items of an identical metric that are readily combined through summation to yield a composite score. The responses are structured so that the subject selects an alternative from a list of suggested answers; checks either *yes* or *no,* or *true* or *false;* marks a point on a scale (e.g., from 1 to 5); or ranks statements in terms of importance. Provision may also be made for a person to indicate uncertainty or no opinion. Examples of SICQs are

Do you think our new product is (1) excellent_____ (2) very good_____ (3) good_____ (4) fair_____ (5) poor_____?

How often do you eat green vegetables? more than once a week_____ once a week_____ less than once a week_____ never_____

My friends understand me. true_____ false_____

I am satisfied with my marriage. yes_____ no_____

Rank the following candidates for office in descending order of your preference (1 = highest rank, 4 = lowest rank): _____Jones _____Smith _____Johnson _____Brown

Ease of response, coding, and analysis as well as the relatively limited time required to complete the items are major advantages of closed questions. A disadvantage is that, when unequivocal replies are demanded, a respondent's thinking may be conditioned by the suggestions or may be limited by an incomplete list.

Since both open and closed questions have advantages, many investigators choose to combine the two types of items in a questionnaire. Several questionnaires are illustrated in this chapter (see Exs. 7.6, 7.7, and 7.8).

### Objective Measures

SICQ questionnaires that yield a quantitative score that can be arrived at identically by two or more independent scorers are commonly referred to as objective measures. These instruments include questionnaires that have been constructed with a certain study in mind and those that have been commercially published and are available for widespread use.

Objective measures systematically present the subject with a set of stimuli that requires a limited and structured response. The person is then assigned a numeral or numerals to indicate his or her possession of the attributes that the instrument is supposed to measure. The data are transmitted directly from the subject, eliminating the need for an intervening interpretation between the individual's behavior and the material presented to the data collector (Sundberg 1977). Consequently, there is no subjectivity or personal error on the part of the person collecting the information at the time the data are obtained or scored.

There are two broad classes of objective instruments: measures of maximum performance and measures of typical performance (Cronbach 1984).[4] *Measures of maximum performance* assess what the subject can actually do or how well he or she can perform. Constructed with predetermined correct and incorrect responses, this category includes intelligence, aptitude, and achievement tests. *Measures of typical performance* assess what the subject believes, prefers, or is likely to do in a particular situation. The answers on these measures are "correct" to the extent that they accurately describe what is typical for a person. Instruments included in this category are those that measure personality and interpersonal relations.

Developers of both types of measures provide tables of *norms,* or scores earned by groups of representative subjects. Such instruments with norms are sometimes called standardized measures. (The word standardized also is used to refer to clearly defined data collection, testing, and scoring procedures.) A *standardized measure* is one that is prepared by a uniform procedure; it is composed of a fixed set of questions to be administered by all investigators with the same set of directions and timing constraints; and it has a carefully delineated and consistent scoring procedure. A standardized instrument is typically administered by its developer to a reference group (or groups) in order to establish norms.

Norms are an important part of measurement. Norms are based on actual performance of people, not on predetermined standards of performance. They are a measure of what is (i.e., the status quo) rather than what ought to be. A norm is an average score for a specified group of people—the reference, standardization, or norm group. Norms are usually presented in the form of tables that show a relationship between the *raw scores* (originally obtained scores, e.g., the number of correct responses) and some type of *derived scores* (scores that have been converted from raw scores to units of other scales). Norms reported as derived scores (e.g., *T* scores, grade equivalents, age equivalents, stanines) indicate a subject's standing relative to the normative sample and permit evaluation of his or her performance in reference to other subjects of a given sex, age, grade, or other category. In addition to their usefulness in making these interindividual comparisons, derived scores also provide comparable measures that allow intraindividual (within-individual) comparisons (see Chap. 14).

Measures of Maximum Performance. Measures designed to assess mental capacity have traditionally been referred to as *intelligence tests,* although this term is becoming less widely used. These instruments usually provide an IQ score (or scores if the measure includes subtests).

## DIETARY QUESTIONNAIRE FOR CHILDREN

Name ______________________________

Date ______________________________

1. Does the child eat at regular times each day? ______________
2. How many days a week does he eat—
   - a morning meal? ______________
   - a lunch or midday meal? ______________
   - an evening meal? ______________
   - during the night?† ______________
3. How many days a week does he have snacks—
   - in midmorning? ______________
   - in midafternoon? ______________
   - in the evening? ______________
   - during the night?* ______________
4. Which meals does he usually eat with your family?

   None ______ Breakfast ______ Noon meal ______ Evening meal ______
5. How many times per week does he eat at school, child care center, or day camp?

   Breakfast ______ Lunch ______ Between meals ______
6. Would you describe his appetite as Good? ______ Fair? ______ Poor? ______
7. At what time of day is he most hungry?

   Morning ______ Noon ______ Evening ______
8. What foods does he dislike? ______________

   ______________________________
9. Is he on a special diet now? Yes ______ No ______

   If yes, why is he on a diet? (Check)

   ______ for weight reduction (own prescription)

   ______ for weight reduction (doctor's prescription)

   ______ for gaining weight

   ______ for allergy, specify ______________

   ______ for other reason, specify ______________

   If no, has he been on a special diet within the past year? Yes ______ No ______

   If yes, for what reason ______________
10. Does he eat anything which is not usually considered food? Yes ______ No ______

    If yes, what? ______________ How often? ______________
11. Can he feed himself? Yes ______ No ______

    If yes, with his fingers? ______ with a spoon? ______
12. Can he use a cup or glass by himself? Yes ______ No ______
13. Does he drink from a bottle with a nipple? Yes ______ No ______

    If yes, how often? ______________ At what time of day or night? ______________

* Include formula feeding for young children.

**Example 7.6.** Dietary questionnaire for children. (From *Screening Children for Nutritional Status,* Washington, D.C.: GPO, 1971.)

## DIETARY QUESTIONNAIRE FOR CHILDREN—cont'd

14. How many times per week does he eat the following foods (at any meal or between meals)? Circle the appropriate number:

| | |
|---|---|
| Bacon | 0 1 2 3 4 5 6 7 >7, specify ______ |
| Tongue | 0 1 2 3 4 5 6 7 >7, specify ______ |
| Sausage | 0 1 2 3 4 5 6 7 >7, specify ______ |
| Luncheon meat | 0 1 2 3 4 5 6 7 >7, specify ______ |
| Hot dogs | 0 1 2 3 4 5 6 7 >7, specify ______ |
| Liver—chicken | 0 1 2 3 4 5 6 7 >7, specify ______ |
| Liver—other | 0 1 2 3 4 5 6 7 >7, specify ______ |
| Poultry | 0 1 2 3 4 5 6 7 >7, specify ______ |
| Salt pork | 0 1 2 3 4 5 6 7 >7, specify ______ |
| Pork or ham | 0 1 2 3 4 5 6 7 >7, specify ______ |
| Bones (neck or other) | 0 1 2 3 4 5 6 7 >7, specify ______ |
| Meat in mixtures (stew, tamales, casseroles, etc.) | 0 1 2 3 4 5 6 7 >7, specify ______ |
| Beef or veal | 0 1 2 3 4 5 6 7 >7, specify ______ |
| Other meat | 0 1 2 3 4 5 6 7 >7, specify ______ |
| Fish | 0 1 2 3 4 5 6 7 >7, specify ______ |

15. How many times per week does he eat the following foods (at any meal or between meals)? Circle the appropriate number:

| | |
|---|---|
| Fruit juice | 0 1 2 3 4 5 6 7 >7, specify ______ |
| Fruit | 0 1 2 3 4 5 6 7 >7, specify ______ |
| Cereal—dry | 0 1 2 3 4 5 6 7 >7, specify ______ |
| Cereal—cooked or instant | 0 1 2 3 4 5 6 7 >7, specify ______ |
| Cereal—infant | 0 1 2 3 4 5 6 7 >7, specify ______ |
| Eggs | 0 1 2 3 4 5 6 7 >7, specify ______ |
| Pancakes or waffles | 0 1 2 3 4 5 6 7 >7, specify ______ |
| Cheese | 0 1 2 3 4 5 6 7 >7, specify ______ |
| Potato | 0 1 2 3 4 5 6 7 >7, specify ______ |
| Other cooked vegetables | 0 1 2 3 4 5 6 7 >7, specify ______ |
| Raw vegetables | 0 1 2 3 4 5 6 7 >7, specify ______ |
| Dried beans or peas | 0 1 2 3 4 5 6 7 >7, specify ______ |
| Macaroni, spaghetti, rice, or noodles | 0 1 2 3 4 5 6 7 >7, specify ______ |
| Ice cream, milk pudding, custard or cream soup | 0 1 2 3 4 5 6 7 >7, specify ______ |
| Peanut butter or nuts | 0 1 2 3 4 5 6 7 >7, specify ______ |
| Sweet rolls or doughnuts | 0 1 2 3 4 5 6 7 >7, specify ______ |
| Crackers or pretzels | 0 1 2 3 4 5 6 7 >7, specify ______ |
| Cookies | 0 1 2 3 4 5 6 7 >7, specify ______ |
| Pie, cake or brownies | 0 1 2 3 4 5 6 7 >7, specify ______ |
| Potato chips or corn chips | 0 1 2 3 4 5 6 7 >7, specify ______ |
| Candy | 0 1 2 3 4 5 6 7 >7, specify ______ |
| Soft drinks, popsicles or Koolaid | 0 1 2 3 4 5 6 7 >7, specify ______ |
| Instant Breakfast | 0 1 2 3 4 5 6 7 >7, specify ______ |

16. How many servings per day does he eat of the following foods? Circle the appropriate number:

| | |
|---|---|
| Bread (including sandwich), toast, rolls, muffins (1 slice or 1 piece is 1 serving) | 0 1 2 3 4 5 6 7 >7, specify ______ |
| Milk (including on cereal or other foods) (8 ounces is 1 serving) | 0 1 2 3 4 5 6 7 >7, specify ______ |
| Sugar, jam, jelly, syrup (1 tsp. is 1 serving) | 0 1 2 3 4 5 6 7 >7, specify ______ |

17. What specific kinds of the following foods does he eat most often?

Fruit juices ______________________________

Fruit ______________________________

Vegetables ______________________________

Cheese ______________________________

Cooked or instant cereal ______________________________

Dry cereal ______________________________

Milk ______________________________

Read each statement. Try to put your family or yourself into the situation. Circle the number to the right which best describes how much the statement is like or unlike what your family or you would do in that situation.

**NOT LIKE** means this is **never or not at all like** what your family does.

**SLIGHTLY LIKE** means this is **seldom or slightly like** what your family does.

**SOMEWHAT LIKE** means this is **sometimes or somewhat like** what your family does.

**A LOT LIKE** means this is **usually or a lot like** what your family does.

**EXACTLY LIKE** means this is **always or exactly like** what your family does.

| | Not Like | Slightly Like | Somewhat Like | A Lot Like | Exactly Like |
|---|---|---|---|---|---|
| ·Wants beyond what we seem to be able to afford are often obtained through a special effort to think up new ways to get them . . . . . . . . . . . . . | 1 | 2 | 3 | 4 | 5 |
| ·Once a good money plan (budget) is established, an effort is made to carry it out without being tempted by additional wants . . . . . . . . . . . . . . . . . . . | 1 | 2 | 3 | 4 | 5 |
| ·We often must settle for less than we expect because of emergencies or unexpected events . . . . . | 1 | 2 | 3 | 4 | 5 |
| ·Most really important wants can be worked into plans . . . . . . . . . . . . . . . . . . . . . . . . . . | 1 | 2 | 3 | 4 | 5 |
| ·"Borrowing" from a fund set aside for food, taxes, etc. to buy things not in the budget is avoided . . . | 1 | 2 | 3 | 4 | 5 |
| ·Housing maintenance (repair) is delayed as long as possible because of time or money costs. . . . . . | 1 | 2 | 3 | 4 | 5 |
| ·The children are learning to be creative in reaching goals that at first seem impossible. . . . . | 1 | 2 | 3 | 4 | 5 |

**Example 7.7.** Questionnaire on planning behavior in families. (Adapted from Doris M. Beard, "Morphostatic and Morphogenic Planning Behavior in Families: Development of a Measurement Instrument," Ph.D. diss., Ohio State University, 1975. Used by permission.)

| | Not Like | Slightly Like | Somewhat Like | A Lot Like | Exactly Like |
|---|---|---|---|---|---|
| ·Plans are made for buying something only after it is obvious that time and money are available. . . . . | 1 | 2 | 3 | 4 | 5 |
| ·Money is the primary consideration in the selection of housing for the family . . . . . . . . . . . . . . . | 1 | 2 | 3 | 4 | 5 |
| ·Plans for use of money are frequently changed to take care of new goals. . . . . . . . . . . . . . . . . | 1 | 2 | 3 | 4 | 5 |
| ·Wants beyond what we can afford are either changed to something that costs less or delayed until we can afford them . . . . . . . . . . . . . . . . . . . . . . | 1 | 2 | 3 | 4 | 5 |
| ·We frequently "borrow" money from a fund set aside for food, taxes, etc., to buy things not in the budget. . . . . . . . . . . . . . . . . . . . . . . . . | 1 | 2 | 3 | 4 | 5 |
| ·With the increase in cost of living, we use means other than money to get some of the things we used to buy. . . . . . . . . . . . . . . . . . . . . . . . . | 1 | 2 | 3 | 4 | 5 |
| ·When wants cost more than money is available, wants are reduced to make things balance. . . . . . . . . . | 1 | 2 | 3 | 4 | 5 |
| ·The family wants things we cannot afford. . . . . . | 1 | 2 | 3 | 4 | 5 |

There are several theories of intelligence. That helps explain why there is considerable controversy over the nature of the factors that should be included in the concept and why many instruments labeled as intelligence tests assess various mental functions. Each test reflects the slightly different orientation of the author. For example, some authors view intelligence primarily as an ability to think in abstract terms, while others emphasize the capacity to acquire knowledge, to adapt to new situations, or to solve problems, among other things (Snyderman and Rothman 1987). In addition, tests based on a unifactor theory are constructed to measure primarily a general factor of intelligence, while those based on multiple-factor theories are designed to measure different types of ability, such as verbal, numerical, and spatial intelligence.

Read the following statements and rate <u>each</u> according to the scale given below. Place the number corresponding to your choice in front of each statement. The statements generally refer to a school situation.

Scale: 5. **Almost Always - very few exceptions**

4. **Usually - majority of the time**

3. **Sometimes**

2. **Seldom - not very often**

1. **Almost never - very few exceptions**

_____ •I carefully coordinate the accessories that I wear with each outfit.

_____ •I pay a lot of attention to pleasing color combinations.

_____ •I try on some of the newest clothes each season to see how I look in the styles.

_____ •It's fun to try on different garments and accessories to see how they look together.

_____ •I wear clothes that everyone is wearing even though they may not look good on me.

_____ •When I buy a new article of clothing I try to buy something similar to what my friends are wearing.

_____ •I feel embarrassed when I see someone in clothes that are too tight.

_____ •I feel embarrassed when I see someone in too low cut a dress.

_____ •I am curious about why people wear the clothes they do.

_____ •I wonder why some clothes make me feel better than others.

_____ •Certain clothes make me feel more sure of myself.

_____ •I have more self confidence when I wear my best school clothes.

_____ •I try to buy clothes which are very unusual.

---

**Example 7.8.** Selected items from Creekmore's *Importance of Clothing Questionnaire*. (Reprinted from A. M. Creekmore, *Methods of Measuring Clothing Variables*, Michigan State University Agricultural Experiment Station Project No. 783, 1971. Used by permission of the publisher.)

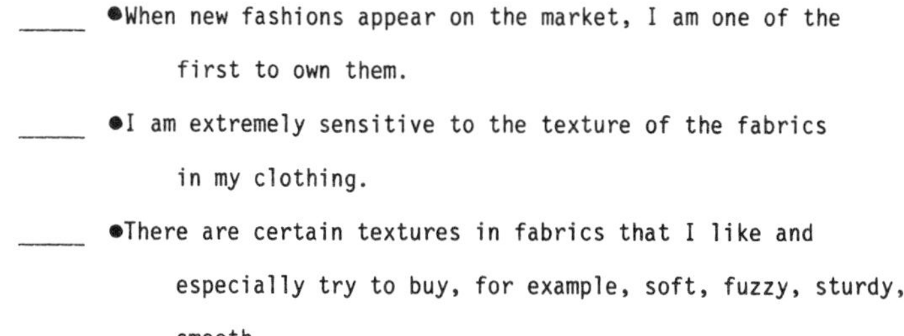

_____ •When new fashions appear on the market, I am one of the first to own them.

_____ •I am extremely sensitive to the texture of the fabrics in my clothing.

_____ •There are certain textures in fabrics that I like and especially try to buy, for example, soft, fuzzy, sturdy, smooth.

Among the most widely used individually administered intelligence tests are the *Wechsler Intelligence Scale for Children, Wechsler Adult Intelligence Scale, Wechsler Preschool and Primary Scale of Intelligence,* and the *Stanford-Binet Intelligence Scale.*[5] Commonly used group intelligence tests include the *Lorge-Thorndike Intelligence Tests, California Test of Mental Maturity, Henmon-Nelson Tests of Mental Ability,* and *Otis-Lennon Mental Ability Test.*

Some people employ the terms *intelligence* and *aptitude* interchangeably. Others make subtle distinctions between them by using intelligence to refer to a general measure and aptitude to mean the measurement of specific factors. Still others use the term *general ability test* because of the overlap among intelligence, aptitude, and achievement test scores. Another distinction is historically based. It is now recognized that intelligence is affected by environmental as well as by hereditary factors and is subject to some change. However, when intelligence tests were first developed, psychologists considered intelligence to be an exclusively innate characteristic. To avoid such an implication, many test developers prefer to call their instruments aptitude tests.

Although there are conflicting opinions, *aptitude tests* are generally considered as measures of one's potential to benefit from training or instruction. Since they predict later performance, the crucial feature of all of them is their predictive validity. Scholastic aptitude tests, for instance, are cognitive measures used to predict success in certain subject matter areas, such as algebra, foreign languages, music, or art, as well as to predict performance in college. Examples of the latter are the *Scholastic Aptitude Test* (SAT) and the *American College Testing Program* (ACT). Other aptitude tests predict vocational success and examine aptitudinal factors that have been found to be important in job performance (e.g., clerical skills, artistic judgment, manual dexterity, mechanical knowledge). Aptitude tests provide single scores or, like the extensively used *Differential Aptitude Tests,* multiple scores.

Unlike aptitude tests that focus on potential and measure the ability to learn new tasks, *achievement tests* assess present levels of knowledge, skills, or performance. Since achievement tests reflect what a person can do right now as a result of exposure to instruction and other past experiences, they are more sensitive to environmental factors than are intelligence or aptitude instruments. Content validity of achievement measures is of utmost importance because they appraise mastery of subject matter. A few standardized achievement tests are the *Comprehensive Tests of Basic Skills, Stanford Achievement Test, Iowa Tests of Educational Development,* and *Wide Range Achievement Test.*

Measures of Typical Performance. The assessment of personality is perhaps the most challenging problem in psychological measurement because human personality is so very complex. There are numerous approaches to personality assessment, most of which are structured paper-and-pencil personality inventories. With these measuring tools, the subject is presented a series of questions dealing with typical feelings and behavior patterns, and the responses are usually scored according to the number of questions he or she answered in a direction purported to display the trait or traits being measured. Some objective inventories measure only one personality dimension, while other devices measure numerous traits. Among the more well-known objective personality instruments are the *California Psychological Inventory, California Test of Personality, Adjective Check List,* and *Minnesota Multiphasic Personality Inventory,* each of which provides scores on multiple dimensions. The *California Psychological Inventory* (Ex. 7.9) is composed of 480 true–false items that are scored for 18 different scales, such as dominance, responsibility, tolerance, and intellec-

| Alternatives | | Item |
|---|---|---|
| True | False | I enjoy social gatherings just to be with people. |
| True | False | I gossip a little at times. |
| True | False | I like poetry. |
| True | False | People often expect too much of me. |
| True | False | My home life was always happy. |
| True | False | Only a fool would vote to increase his own taxes. |
| True | False | I love to go to dances. |
| True | False | Sometimes I feel that I am about to go to pieces. |

**Example 7.9.** Items from *The California Psychological Inventory.* (Reproduced by special permission of the publisher, Consulting Psychologists Press, Inc., Palo Alto, Calif. 94306, from *The California Psychological Inventory* by Harrison Gough, Ph.D. © 1957. Further reproduction is prohibited without the publisher's consent.)

tual efficiency. (Subjective personality measuring techniques will be discussed in the projective measures section of this chapter.)

Instruments measuring attitudes, values, and interests are other types of personality assessment devices frequently used in research. *Attitude scales* measure learned predispositions to respond in a consistent positive or negative manner toward objects, people, ideas, or situations. They place the individual on a continuum from favorable to unfavorable feelings toward any given attitude object. The literature is replete with instruments that have been developed to assess attitudes toward child rearing, family relations, education, ethnic groups, and political and religious issues, to name just a few. In many cases, the assessment device presents a set of statements about the attitude object and asks for an indication of the subject's agreement or disagreement, often by using a Likert rating format, such as *strongly approve, approve, undecided, disapprove,* and *strongly disapprove,* or some other set of related responses that corresponds to numerical values, such as 0 to 4 or 1 to 5.[6] (Rating scales and checklists were mentioned earlier in the description of ways to summarize observations and in the discussion of SICQ questionnaires. They also will be discussed in the section on interviews.)

Another popular way to assess attitudes is with the *semantic differential* (Osgood, Suci, and Tannenbaum 1957). This simple technique presents a single word or concept related to the problem under investigation (e.g., mother, school, love, my job) and asks the subject to indicate his or feelings or perceptions about it. The concept is rated on a seven-point scale between bipolar adjectives, such as interesting–dull, good–bad, strong–weak, fair–unfair, and pleasant–unpleasant. The versatile semantic differential method lends itself to the measurement of numerous research variables. (See Ex. 7.10 of a semantic differential to measure private club image.)

*Value scales* measure a person's beliefs about ideal modes of conduct and ideal terminal goals (Rokeach 1968). Some socially shared standards regarding how an individual should behave include being honest, responsible, independent, loving, and forgiving. Examples of ideal terminal goals are freedom, self-respect, equality, social recognition, and happiness. A commercially available value instrument is the *Study of Values,* which measures the relative prominence of six classes of personal values: theoretical, economic, aesthetic, social, political, and religious (Ex. 7.11). Values, like attitudes, are learned. Both influence human behavior. A person who might have thousands of different attitudes probably has only dozens of values.

*Interest scales* measure the subject's preference for one activity over another. Typically, these self-report devices have the subject decide which of several activities listed in an item he or she prefers most and least. When the preferences are combined, the subject's responses provide a profile of

| | | Extremely | Quite | Slightly | Neither One Nor The Other | Slightly | Quite | Extremely | |
|---|---|---|---|---|---|---|---|---|---|
| PHYSICAL CHARACTERISTICS | dirty | ______: | ______: | ______: | ______: | ______: | ______: | ______: | clean |
| | unattractive decor | ______: | ______: | ______: | ______: | ______: | ______: | ______: | attractive decor |
| | formal atmosphere | ______: | ______: | ______: | ______: | ______: | ______: | ______: | informal atmosphere |
| | noisy | ______: | ______: | ______: | ______: | ______: | ______: | ______: | quiet |
| | loud live music | ______: | ______: | ______: | ______: | ______: | ______: | ______: | no music |
| | crowded | ______: | ______: | ______: | ______: | ______: | ______: | ______: | uncrowded |
| | small | ______: | ______: | ______: | ______: | ______: | ______: | ______: | large |
| CONVENIENCE OF PARKING LOCATION | distant | ______: | ______: | ______: | ______: | ______: | ______: | ______: | near by |
| | long driving time | ______: | ______: | ______: | ______: | ______: | ______: | ______: | short driving time |
| | difficult drive | ______: | ______: | ______: | ______: | ______: | ______: | ______: | easy drive |
| | difficult to find | ______: | ______: | ______: | ______: | ______: | ______: | ______: | easy to find |
| | inadequate parking | ______: | ______: | ______: | ______: | ______: | ______: | ______: | adequate parking |
| MENU OFFERINGS | limited selection | ______: | ______: | ______: | ______: | ______: | ______: | ______: | wide selection |
| | inconsistency in quality and taste | ______: | ______: | ______: | ______: | ______: | ______: | ______: | consistently good quality and taste |
| | offers no wine or mixed drinks | ______: | ______: | ______: | ______: | ______: | ______: | ______: | wide selection of wines and mixed drinks |

**Example 7.10.** Semantic differential to measure private club image. (Reprinted from J. E. Swan and C. M. Futrell, "Increasing the Efficiency of Retailer Image Study," *J. Acad. Mark. Sci.* 8(1980): 51–57, p. 53, exhibit 1. Used with permission of the publisher and the authors.)

| | | Extremely | Quite | Slightly | Neither One Nor The Other | Slightly | Quite | Extremely | |
|---|---|---|---|---|---|---|---|---|---|
| PRICES CHARGED | prices high compared to other restaurants | ______ : | ______ : | ______ : | ______ : | ______ : | ______ : | ______ : | prices low compared to other restaurants |
| | low values for money spent | ______ : | ______ : | ______ : | ______ : | ______ : | ______ : | ______ : | high values for money spent |
| | pricing inconsistent with perceived quality | ______ : | ______ : | ______ : | ______ : | ______ : | ______ : | ______ | pricing consistent with perceived quality |
| | high profit being made | ______ : | ______ : | ______ : | ______ : | ______ : | ______ : | ______ : | low profit being made |
| PERSONNEL | discourteous personnel | ______ : | ______ : | ______ : | ______ : | ______ : | ______ : | ______ : | courteous personnel |
| | unhelpful personnel | ______ : | ______ : | ______ : | ______ : | ______ : | ______ : | ______ : | friendly personnel |
| | inadequate number of personnel | ______ : | ______ : | ______ : | ______ : | ______ : | ______ : | ______ : | adequate number of personnel |
| | slow service | ______ : | ______ : | ______ : | ______ : | ______ : | ______ : | ______ : | fast service |
| | provide minimum service | ______ : | ______ : | ______ : | ______ : | ______ : | ______ : | ______ : | provide maximum service |
| YOUR FRIENDS | unknown to your frients | ______ : | ______ : | ______ : | ______ : | ______ : | ______ : | ______ : | well known to your friends |
| | disliked by your friends | ______ : | ______ : | ______ : | ______ : | ______ : | ______ : | ______ : | well liked by your friends |
| | poorly recommended by your friends | ______ : | ______ : | ______ : | ______ : | ______ : | ______ | ______ : | well recommended by your friends |
| | few friends eat there | ______ : | ______ : | ______ : | ______ : | ______ : | ______ : | ______ : | numerous friends eat there |

**Part I**

8. When witnessing a gorgeous ceremony (ecclesiastical or academic, induction into office, etc.) are you more impressed: (a) by the color and pageantry of the occasion itself, (b) by the influence and strength of the group?

**Part II**

10. Which of the following would you prefer to do during part of your next summer vacation (if your ability and other conditions would permit)
    a. write and publish an original biological essay or article
    b. stay in some secluded part of the country where you can appreciate fine scenery
    c. enter a local tennis or other athletic tournament
    d. get experience in some new line of business

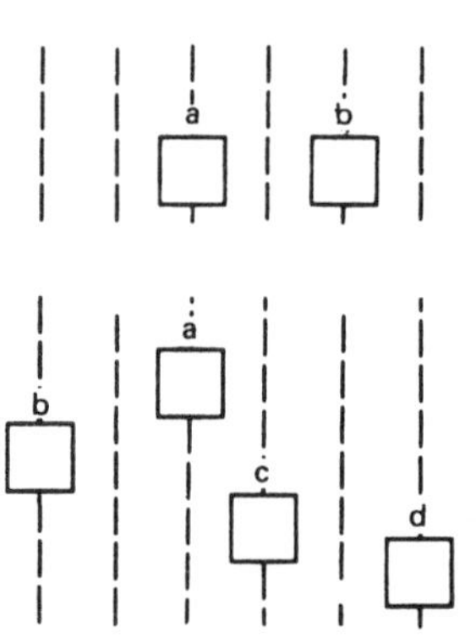


**Example 7.11.** Items from the *Study of Values.* (These materials are reproduced from the *Study of Values* by G. W. Allport, P. E. Vernon, and G. Lindzey, 3d ed., copyright © 1960. Reprinted with permission of the publisher, The Riverside Publishing Company, 8420 W. Bryn Mawr Ave., Chicago, Ill. 60631. All rights reserved.)

strong and weak interests. Instruments such as the *Kuder Preference Record* (*Vocational*), *Kuder Preference Record* (*Occupational*), and *Strong Vocational Interest Blank* have been constructed by determining the patterns of interest of people who are successfully engaged in various occupational areas. The scales are interpreted by comparing the subject's response patterns with those of the normative groups and are a useful means of identifying vocational goals.

Questionnaires may also be used to study social relations. Measures commonly referred to as *sociometric techniques* examine the organization and interaction of social groups. Originally developed by Moreno (1953), this approach usually employs a written questionnaire (or a personal interview) to ask subjects privately to name other persons in the group (e.g., classroom, apartment building, club, industrial setting) whom they like or dislike, desire as companions in a social situation, or prefer as co-workers on a committee or project. Questions, phrased in terms of a specific criterion, might include: Beside whom would you like to sit? Whom would you like to invite to the party? With whom would you like to study? With whom would you prefer to plan this program? Most commonly, each respondent is requested to select two or three other group members as first, second, and third choices.

There are several ways of representing and analyzing sociometric data.[7] One common approach is a graphical procedure called a *sociogram* (Ex. 7.12), which summarizes properties of the group structure and defines so-

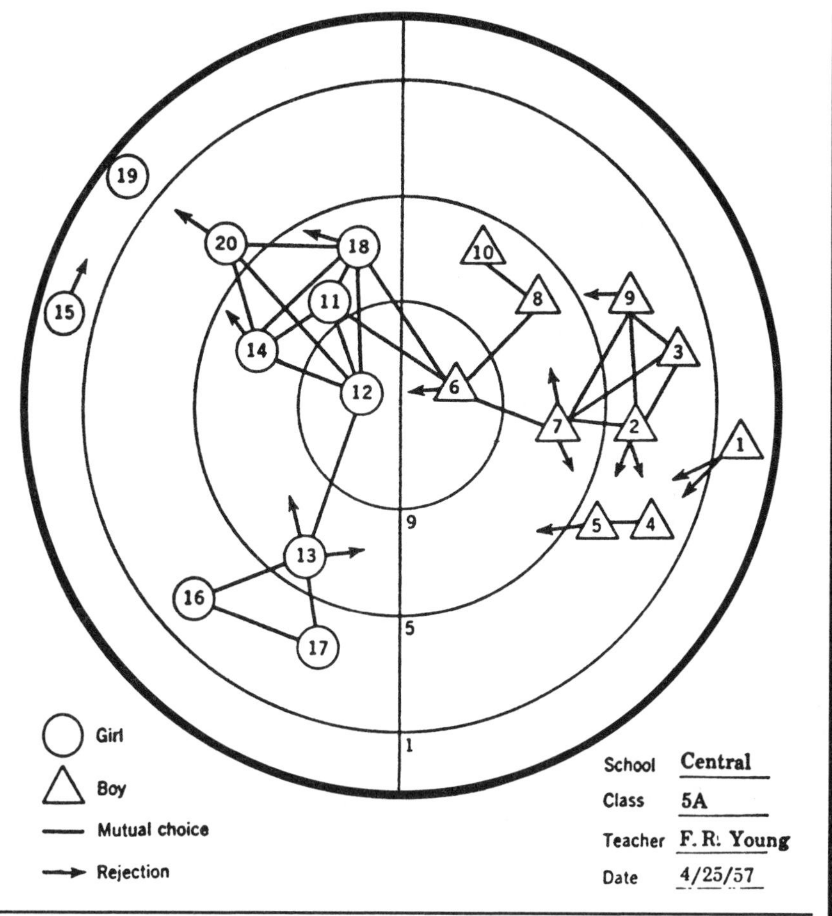


**Example 7.12.** A sociogram. (Reprinted from N. E. Gronlund, *Sociometry in the Classroom,* Harper, 1959, p. 73, fig. 3. Used by permission.)

cial relations by representing individuals with geometric figures and indicating their choices and rejections with lines and arrows to identify "stars" (frequently chosen members), "isolates" (individuals who receive no choices), "rejectees" (individuals who receive negative choices), "cliques" (three or more individuals who choose one another), and so on. When the group being studied is large and there are several choices involved, the diagram often becomes too complex to understand because of the excessive number of lines. In that case, use of a *matrix* is a feasible alternative. There have been several developments in the quantitative analysis of sociometric information, including some rather sophisticated techniques, which make this data collection procedure attractive for the investigation of friendship patterns, social adjustment, prejudice, leadership, and so forth.

An attractive feature of objective measures is that they are a relatively economical means of data collection. Moreover, they yield data that are amenable to quantitative analysis. Of course, their primary virtue is their objectivity. All researchers must attempt to generate data that are as free as possible from subjective bias. Since the judgment or opinion of the data collector or scorer does not influence the results when objective tests and scales are used, reliability problems associated with scoring are eliminated. Objective measurement contributes to replicability. If units of measurement are employed that are understood and can be applied by others, the findings of different investigations using the same objective instruments can be compared. Although objectivity is a distinct advantage of these assessment devices, other considerations in instrument construction may be as important as the achievement of objectivity in scoring.

There are some potential problems associated with the use of objective instruments, particularly measures of typical performance. Two of these are response sets and response styles. *Response sets* are dependent on content and occur when the subject wishes to present a certain picture of himself or herself (e.g., answering items in a socially desirable manner). *Response styles* are generally content independent and refer to a subject's tendency to respond to items in a particular way (e.g., acquiescence, or saying *yes* or *true* to most items.) Both response sets and response styles can have an adverse effect on validity and the interpretation of findings.

## CONSTRUCTING QUESTIONNAIRES

Although instrument development was briefly mentioned in the last chapter, we elaborate here because so many researchers develop their own questionnaires, particularly those measuring typical performance. Great care must be taken in preparing items for questionnaires. Questions must be pretested and revised to eliminate misunderstanding and ambiguities caused by improper wording. To ensure that they will elicit the desired information, a number of points should be kept in mind when constructing these instruments.

Each question should relate to the research problem under investigation. With the possible exception of certain factual information about the subject (i.e., biodata), only those questions should be included that have as their purpose the eliciting of some information to fit the study objectives. The type of question used should be appropriate to the research being conducted. The form of question chosen is determined by the subject matter, the method of administration planned, the sample of people to be studied, and the kind of analysis to be made. The language adopted should be similar to that used and understood by the subjects. Questions must be worded so that they are concrete, specific, relatively brief, and in keeping with the respondent's current level of information and education.

The question content should not be biased (often referred to as loaded) in a particular direction. There should be no suggestion to the subject of the most appropriate answer. An attempt should be made to word questions so that the respondent's tendency to give socially desirable answers is reduced. Since people tend to give answers they know to be socially acceptable, questions dealing with such concepts as motherhood, love, and peace need to be handled carefully, for these terms are desirable ones that everyone is supposed to favor. Similarly, most people are aware that any form of prejudice is disapproved socially. Consequently, no matter what the research subject's true attitude, he or she may give an invalid response when asked for reactions to minority group issues. "Double-barreled" questions (i.e., items covering two or more issues) should also be avoided.

Items should be placed in a logical sequence with provision for smooth transition from one part of the instrument to the next. Finally, the directions on the questionnaire should be clear and complete, and the format should be attractive and well aligned to facilitate reading, increase accuracy, and minimize fatigue.

It is important to try out the questions and procedures on a small scale to determine whether or not they will satisfy the research goals. The *pretesting* of questionnaires is essential because these instruments may have been developed just for the study and may have not had the benefit of extended use and evaluation in previous research. Pretesting should be done with a sample of individuals from a population similar to that to be drawn for the main investigation. Space should be provided on the questionnaire for subjects to indicate the need for additional response alternatives not included in the questionnaire, to comment on ambiguous questions, and so on.

A large sample is not necessary for pretesting. For a well-defined professional group, such as home economics teachers, about 40 or 50 cases may be sufficient. For a more heterogeneous group, such as homemakers, a larger pretest group would be advisable. The results of the trial run should be evaluated with a view toward revising and improving the instrument and the procedures for gathering and analyzing data. Responses to each question should be checked separately, noting items that are frequently left blank or are answered in an unexpected manner. Such items may have been misinterpreted. A brief analysis of the data should be made to determine whether the plan for classifying and quantifying the data to test the hypotheses or answer the research questions will be satisfactory.

A number of sources deal with questionnaires in greater detail.[8]

## ADVANTAGES AND LIMITATIONS

Questionnaires are an economical means of accessing representative samples for research. The instrument is either handed to the subjects or mailed to them. In either case, a minimum of explanation is given. The respondent can take as much time as needed to think about the answers without feeling under pressure to respond. It is an impersonal instrument with standardized instructions and wording. Unusual or personal kinds of activities may be discussed more freely than in an interview. Moreover, there may be less desire on the part of the respondent to try to impress the investigator. Another appeal of the questionnaire is that it requires relatively little skill on the part of the data collector to administer.

Among the limitations of questionnaires are the diversity of meaning that may be attributed to a question by various respondents, the literacy skills that may be required of a person in order to understand the questions and procedures, and the uncertainty of whether an adequate number of responses will be received to represent the population, a problem particularly with mail questionnaires.

# Interviews

The *interview* is a method of person-to-person verbal communication in which one person, the interviewer, asks another person, the respondent, questions designed to elicit information or opinions. It is a conversation with a purpose.

## UNSTRUCTURED VERSUS STRUCTURED INTERVIEWS

Interviews vary with respect to the degree of structure imposed. This leads us to speak of interviews as being unstructured or structured.

### Unstructured Interviews

The unstructured interview is flexible in that the interviewer usually has only an outline of suggested topics, or possibly a general framework of questions, which are geared by the interviewer to the language of the research subject and introduced in any order that suits the situation. Constraints on both the interviewer and interviewee are kept to a minimum. The respondent is encouraged to be open and to express feelings freely. The nonstructured interview does not lend itself well to the testing or verifying of hypotheses, although it is a good tool for exploratory research and a rich source of hypotheses that can later be subjected to more systematic investigation. This style of interviewing also lends itself well to the in-depth study of perceptions, attitudes, and other internal processes. Consequently, it requires considerable training and psychological insight on the part of the interviewer.

The unstructured approach to interviewing usually produces only qualitative data, which are difficult or impossible to analyze statistically. Moreover, the nonuniform procedures used preclude the comparison of results from one interview to another. Each research subject faces a different situation when the unstructured interview is used.

## Structured Interviews

In the structured interview, specific questions are given to each research subject. With this standardized approach, procedures have been formulated prior to the interview and are carefully followed. Even within the structured interview, there may be degrees of structuredness. In some cases, a few questions are open-ended and the researcher is given latitude in ordering and rephrasing them as well as in probing for more information. In most other cases, the person conducting a structured interview uses a rigid interview schedule and handles the interview essentially as a written questionnaire that is presented orally. In this highly structured approach, directions are given in a uniform manner, prespecified questions are presented in a fixed order, interviewee responses are restricted to certain categories (closed ended), transitional phrases are provided word-for-word, and only brief, standard probes are allowed. There is no departure from the schedule by the data collector or the respondent.

In addition to demanding less from the interviewer than in unstructured situations, highly structured interviews have the major advantage of generating data that are amenable to quantification and to reliability checks. Structured interviews are preferable when a large number of interviewers will be collecting data.

The differences between unstructured and structured interviews are shown in Example 7.13, where Gorden (1980) classifies interviews as nonscheduled, moderately scheduled, and highly scheduled. The first corresponds to what we have referred to as unstructured, and the second and third merely represent two subtypes of the structured interview, depending on the degree of structure imposed.

*THE NONSCHEDULED INTERVIEW*

*Instructions to the interviewer:* Discover the kinds of conflicts that the child has had with the parents. Conflicts should include disagreements, tensions due to past, present, or potential disagreements, outright arguments and physical conflicts. Be alert for as many categories and examples of conflicts and tensions as possible.

*THE MODERATELY SCHEDULED INTERVIEW*

*Instructions to the interviewer:* Your task is to discover as many specific kinds of conflicts and tensions between child and parent as possible. The more *concrete* and detailed the account of each type of conflict the better. Although there are 12 areas of possible conflict which we want to explore (listed in question 3 below), you should not mention any area until after you have asked the first two questions in the order indicated. The first question takes an indirect approach, giving you time to built up rapport with the respondent and to demonstrate a nonjudgmental attitude toward teenagers who have conflicts with their parents.

1. What sorts of problems do teenagers you know have in getting along with their parents?
   (Possible probes: Do they always agree with their parents? Do any of your friends have "problem parents"? What other kinds of disagreements do they have?)
2. What sorts of disagreements do you have with your parents?
   (Possible probes: Do they cause you any problems? In what ways do they try to restrict you? Do you always agree with them on everything? Do they like the same things you do? Do they try to get you to do some things you don't like? Do they ever bore you? Make you mad? Do they understand you? etc.)
3. Have you ever had any disagreements with either of your parents over:
   *a.* Using the family car
   *b.* Friends of the same sex
   *c.* Dating
   *d.* School (homework, grades, activities)
   *e.* Religion (church, beliefs, etc.)
   *f.* Political views
   *g.* Working for pay outside the home
   *h.* Allowances
   *i.* Smoking
   *j.* Drinking
   *k.* Eating habits
   *l.* Household chores

**Example 7.13.** Examples of interviews with different degrees of structure. (From R. L. Gorden, *Interviewing,* 3d ed., Dorsey, © 1980, pp. 48–50. Used by permission.)

*Interviewer's explanation to the teenage respondent:* We are interested in the kinds of problems teenagers have with their parents. We need to know how many teenagers have which kinds of conflicts with their parents and whether they are just mild disagreements or serious fights. We have a checklist here of some of the kinds of things that happen. Would you think about your own situation and put a check to show which conflicts you, personally, have had and about how often they have happened. Be sure to put a check in every row. If you have never had such a conflict then put the check in the first column where it says "never."

(*Hand him the first card dealing with conflicts over the use of the automobile, saying,* "If you don't understand any of those things listed or have some other things you would like to mention about how you disagree with your parents over the automobile let me know and we'll talk about it.") (*When the respondent finishes checking all rows, hand him card number 2, saying,* "Here is a list of types of conflicts teenagers have with their parents over their friends of the same sex. Do the same with this as you did with the last list.")

| AUTOMOBILE | *Never* | *Only Once* | *More than Once* | *Many Times* |
|---|---|---|---|---|
| 1. Wanting to learn to drive | | | | |
| 2. Getting a driver's license | | | | |
| 3. Wanting to use the family car | | | | |
| 4. What you use the car for | | | | |
| 5. The way you drive it | | | | |
| 6. Using it too much | | | | |
| 7. Keeping the car clean | | | | |
| 8. Putting gas or oil in the car | | | | |
| 9. Repairing the car | | | | |
| 10. Driving someone else's car | | | | |
| 11. Wanting to own a car | | | | |
| 12. The way you drive your own car | | | | |
| 13. What you use your car for | | | | |
| 14. Other | | | | |

### Types of Questions

Our discussion of the types of questions used in questionnaires also applies to questions intended for interviews. Interview questions, like items in questionnaires, generally fall into the same two categories, closed or open, with the former being more restrictive in nature and the latter allowing the research subject freedom to provide the amount and kind of information he or she wishes.

There are other types of questions: *Lead-in questions* are not directly related to the objectives of the study, but they introduce a relevant subject area by preparing the respondent to give more accurate and valid information. *Filter questions* attempt to determine whether a line of questioning would be appropriate in light of the individual's experiences. *Contingency questions* apply only to those respondents who answered a preceding filter question in a particular manner. *Transition questions* provide a bridge from one topic to another so the research subject will not carry over an inappropriate context from a previous question or will not be confused about the purpose of the interview.

Interview questions tend to be interconnected. The interconnections form a sequence within subtopics or for the entire interview. One type of sequence used in an interview is the funnel sequence. The most general question is asked first (requiring a free response), and then the more restricted questions follow. This approach helps the respondent recall details, so the interviewer is less likely to have to interrupt with specific questions. It is also a good way to begin an interview or initiate a new subtopic. The funnel sequence helps counteract the potential biasing of later responses by introducing more specific questions only as the interview progresses. An inverted funnel sequence of questions is also possible; in it the interviewer begins with items requiring specific responses and then moves to items dealing with broader issues.

## CONSTRUCTING INTERVIEW SCHEDULES

Most of the same considerations in constructing questionnaires (e.g., unambiguous instructions, clear and relevant items, logical order, format, pretesting) also pertain to the preparation of interview schedules. Although most researchers tend to reserve the term *questionnaire* for self-administered questionnaires and the term *interview schedule* for the form used to guide interviewers in questioning and recording a subject's responses, the two terms are often used interchangeably. Indeed, many researchers take an existing questionnaire that is designed for self-completion and present the items orally as an interview-administered questionnaire. Or interviewers ask the respondents to complete the paper-and-pencil questionnaire in their presence. To avoid confusion in the discussion here, interview schedule will mean any predetermined list of instructions and questions used by an interviewer to standardize the interview procedure (Ex. 7.14).

**A: GENERAL ATTITUDES**

A1. (Once again) We are interested in how people are getting along financially these days. Would you say that you and your family are better off or worse off financially than you were a year ago?

| 1. BETTER NOW | 3. SAME | 5. WORSE NOW | 8. UNCERTAIN |
|---|---|---|---|

A2 Why do you say so? ______

A3. Are you people making as much money now as you were a year ago, or more, or less?

| 1. MORE NOW | 3. ABOUT THE SAME | 5. LESS NOW |
|---|---|---|

A4. During the last few months, have you heard of any favorable or unfavorable changes in business conditions? ______

(IF YES) A5. What did you hear? ______

IF NOT CLEAR WHETHER SOME CHANGE R MENTIONS IS FAVORABLE OR UNFAVORABLE, PROBE: "Would (MENTION CHANGE) be favorable or unfavorable?" AND NOTE "favorable" OR "unfavorable".

**B: HOUSING**

B1 Now I'd like to talk with you about things here at home. I am particularly interested in any changes which may have occurred in your housing since last year at this time. When did you move into this (house/apartment)?

______ (YEAR)

B2 How long have you lived here in (COUNTY NAME, e.g., BRONX) county?

______ (YEARS)

B3. Do you (FAMILY UNIT) own this (home/apartment), pay rent, or what?

- ☐ OWNS OR IS BUYING THIS (HOME/APARTMENT) – (GO TO Q. B7)
- ☐ PAYS RENT ON THIS (HOME/APARTMENT) – (GO TO Q. B5)
- ☐ NEITHER OWNS NOR RENTS THIS (HOME/APARTMENT)

**Example 7.14.** Portion of an interview schedule used in a survey of consumers. (Reprinted from G. Katona et al., *Survey of Consumer Finances,* Ann Arbor, Mich.: Institute for Social Research, 1969. Used by permission of the Survey Research Center, University of Michigan.)

Continued

(IF NEITHER OWNS NOR RENTS)

B4. How is that? ______________________________

______________________________

(TURN TO Q. B8)

(IF RENTS)

B5. About how much rent do you pay a month? $________

B6. Do you rent it furnished or unfurnished?

[1.] FURNISHED     [5.] UNFURNISHED

(TURN TO Q. B8)

(IF OWNS OR IS BUYING)

B7. Could you tell me what the present value of this house (farm) is? I mean, about what would it bring if you sold it today?

$________________

(ASK EVERYONE)

B8. Generally speaking, do you think now is a good time or a bad time to buy a house?

[1.] GOOD     [3.] PRO-CON     [5.] BAD     [8.] DON'T KNOW

B9 Why do you say so? ______________________________

______________________________

HS [ ]     HV [ ][ ][ ][ ][ ][ ] (DOLLARS)     R [ ][ ][ ] (DOLLARS)

## ADDITIONS AND REPAIRS

(ASK EVERYONE)

B10. Did you have any expenses for work done on this (house and lot/apartment) in 1968 – things like upkeep, additions, improvements, or painting and decorating? (FARMERS – EXCLUDE FARM BUILDINGS; LANDLORDS – EXCLUDE INCOME PROPERTY)

[ ] YES     [ ] NO – (TURN TO Q. C1)

## INTERVIEW PROCEDURES

Valid data can be collected in an interview if the questions have been well designed and assembled so as to meet the objectives of the research. Interviewing is an art that consists largely of creating a situation in which the respondents will be cooperative and honest. The first requirement for successful interviewing, therefore, is to create a situation in which the research subjects will answer in a reliable and valid manner. When this objective has been met, the interviewer's task is to ask the questions properly to obtain adequate responses and to record those responses accurately and in detail.

### Establishing Rapport

In the initial contact, the subject must be motivated to allow the interview to be conducted. Ordinarily, this sequence of procedures is followed by the interviewer: (a) explanation of the purpose of the research, (b) identification of the group conducting the research, (c) description of the method of selecting the subjects for the sample, (d) specification of the amount of time required of the interviewee, and (e) indication of the confidential nature of the interview. Building rapport in the initial phases of the interview is important in obtaining full cooperation and usable responses.

### Questioning the Respondent

Employing an interview schedule may be compared to an experimenter's use of a laboratory procedure or measuring instrument in a standardized manner. In highly structured interview situations, it is important to ask the questions of each person in exactly the same way. The only instance in which the procedure should vary is when a respondent is unable to understand a question as worded, and it must be repeated (or if necessary, interpreted). Even then, in a structured interview, there are prescribed methods of dealing with these problems, and the interviewer is obligated to handle them in the predetermined manner. If the researcher wants to be able to quantify the data collected and compare the responses of subjects, it is imperative that he or she present the stimulus questions in a standardized fashion. The questions must be identical, and the way they are posed must be identical. There should be no deviation from the interview schedule.

In unstructured or possibly moderately structured interviews where only subjective analyses are planned, the researcher may be permitted to use more flexibility and may tailor questions to the respondents. Sometimes it may be necessary for the interviewer to probe for additional information or to clarify, or make more specific, information that the respondent has already given. This must be accomplished without biasing the data.

When there is a discrepancy between the information given by the respondent and that needed for the study, a skilled interviewer draws upon a variety of probing techniques. Warwick and Lininger (1975) and Gorden (1980) describe a number of such probes. One, the *silent probe,* is the most permissive, and it often is a very productive way of allowing the respondent to proceed in any direction that he or she finds interesting or meaningful. An experienced interviewer waits patiently and confidently for more information, perhaps nodding the head or using an appropriate facial expression during the silent pause. The *encouragement probe* indicates that the interviewer accepts what the respondent has said so far but would like to hear more. Overt encouragement includes remarks such as "yes," "hmmm," and "I see" as well as nonverbal expressions. The *elaboration probe* seeks to obtain more complete or accurate responses from the subject. These probes include ". . . and then?" "What happened next?" "Anything else?" "Tell me more about that." The *clarification probe* specifies the kind of additional information needed. In response to answers that are inconsistent, ambiguous, or contradictory, the interviewer might say, "I am not very clear on what you mean by that—could you be more specific?" The *reflective probe* repeats the interviewee's implicit or explicit statement in an attempt to elicit additional information in a nondirective manner. The interviewer may use reflection in different ways: to repeat words from a previous response, to reflect the meaning or feeling behind the words without actually repeating the words, and to combine several elements from previous responses.

## Recording and Coding the Responses

It is important for the interviewer to record the subject's responses as completely and as accurately as possible. Errors in recording might result from noting something that the interviewee did not say or from failing to record something that was said. Responses should be recorded during the interview. (Recording responses with a pencil is better than using a pen because a pencil allows easy erasures.) Although it takes a fairly skilled interviewer to be able to write intelligent notes while the subject is talking, complete replies may be recorded in several ways, such as by using abbreviations, taking shorthand, or writing key words at the time and completing the details immediately after the interview. Asking for examples or using minor questions are strategies that give the interviewer time for recording the full responses to major questions without long pauses. Using a tape recorder permits a complete and unbiased transcription of the responses later, although it may be impractical under certain circumstances. Of course, permission of the research subject should be obtained if the session is to be recorded.

To ensure a complete record of the interview, all probes used in the course of the interaction should be included because they have a direct effect on the flow of information. At the conclusion of the interview, the interviewer should thank the respondent and ask if there are any further questions about the study.

Although information obtained in highly structured interviews is relatively easy to code once responses have been recorded, data generated by less structured interviews may require considerable effort to tabulate according to a content code. One question from a parent's child-rearing attitudes interview, along with its corresponding interview code, is presented in Example 7.15.

1. All parents have some difficulties in raising children. In general, what has been the hardest thing about child-rearing for you?

| Code | Question 1. Difficulties in raising children | |
|---|---|---|
| 00 | No information, or not covered by code | |
| 01 | Discipline—minding, obeying, making child do something, etc. | |
| 02 | Sibling rivalry, problems between children | |
| 03 | Normal adjustment or developmental problems | Interpersonal—getting along with others |
| 04 | | Responsibility |
| 05 | | Passivity—shy, won't fight back |
| 06 | | Aggressiveness—rowdy, noisy |
| 07 | | Dawdling |
| 08 | | Other |
| 09 | Specific symptoms | Thumbsucking |
| 10 | | Wetting or soiling |
| 11 | | Eating problems |
| 12 | | Nailbiting |
| 13 | | Withdrawal, extreme shyness |
| 14 | | Extreme destructiveness or aggression |
| 15 | | Phobias or fears |
| 16 | | Other |
| 17 | Physical health or illness, safety | |
| 18 | Financial | |
| 19 | Problem within parents | Inadequacy |
| 20 | | Indecision |
| 21 | | Inconsistency between parents |
| 23 | | Lack of patience |
| 23 | | Other |
| 24 | States that he has no problem | |

**Example 7.15.** An interview question and its corresponding codes. (From Carl F. Hereford, *Changing Parental Attitudes through Discussion*. Copyright © 1963 by the Hogg Foundation for Mental Health. By permission of the Univ. of Texas Press.)

## ADVANTAGES AND LIMITATIONS

Among the advantages of an interview is the possibility of obtaining information that very likely could not or would not be obtained by any other method. Someone might be willing to talk about certain family problems, for example, on which he or she would not wish to comment in writing. A person may be willing to spend more time giving information when he or she has direct personal contact than when asked to take time to complete a questionnaire. In some instances, the personal contact encourages cooperation from persons who might neglect to respond to a questionnaire.

Since an interview provides more flexibility in obtaining information than the self-administered questionnaire, it may yield more accurate information and a greater depth of response than could be obtained through a questionnaire. This is particularly true in regard to children and respondents who are poorly educated or are from a low socioeconomic area. These people might have difficulty reading or understanding the questions, or they may not be able to express themselves clearly. An interview can be adapted to the level of understanding of the interviewer.

The interviewer can clarify by repeating or rephrasing questions, by following up leads in responses, or by probing more deeply to obtain a clear picture of the interviewee's ideas. In so doing, however, the interviewer must be careful not to influence the respondent's answer. Through incidental comments and nonverbal behaviors by the interviewee, the researcher is able to collect valuable information that would be impossible to obtain through written replies.

An interview permits greater control regarding the sequence of questions than does a questionnaire. Since questions are hidden from the research subject during an interview, later questions cannot affect earlier replies. Moreover, the respondent cannot consult with someone else about how to answer a question.

As with all data collection techniques, the interview has some possible limitations. The interview procedure can be very costly, especially if a random sample is selected. Employing skilled interviewers and training them are expensive, and the process of interviewing is quite time consuming. In addition to the time actually spent in personal contact with the interviewees when personal interviews are used, time must be allowed for transportation and for either arranging appointments in advance or returning to homes where the person to be visited was not available when first contacted. Evening or weekend hours often must be used in reaching persons who are employed full time.

The respondent may be a limiting factor because he or she is unable to understand the questions or to express ideas clearly, lacks information or is unwilling to reveal what information he or she does have, has an unreliable memory of events, suppresses facts or memories, rationalizes or deliberately distorts responses in order to make a good impression, or has a poor quality of judgments concerning relationships between causes and effects.

Similarly, the interviewer may be a source of bias, directly or indirectly. Errors introduced by the data gatherer may be of several types: omitting a question, rewording a question in a structured interview, giving insufficient time for a respondent to express his or her ideas, failing to probe when necessary or to probe adequately, not listening carefully, giving his or her own interpretation of what the respondent says, and using inadequate or inappropriate motivation. The personal characteristics of the person doing the interviewing, including age, sex, race, social class, and physical appearance, may also influence the responses of the research subjects.

Although this section has concentrated primarily on personal interviews, much of the discussion also applies to interviewing over the telephone (see also Chap. 10). A number of sources can provide readers with more information about interviewing.[9]

## Projective Measures

Projective measures probe into the unconscious depths of the mind and give a more complete picture of personality than is usually possible with most instruments. They do this by using relatively unstructured stimuli for which there are no obvious or socially acceptable responses.

A *projective technique* is one that provides a relatively ambiguous stimulus that the individual is assumed to structure in terms of his or her personality and functioning. When an individual is presented with more objective items, there is little opportunity to project feelings, attitudes, and beliefs. Conversely, a stimulus of low structure has no meaning in itself, and so the individual is forced to "project" something of himself or herself into the response, presumably revealing information about values, needs, attitudes, feelings, and characteristic ways of behaving. The individual has a wide variety of choices when projective measures are used. Through this indirect means of probing personality, the subject gives a personal interpretation or reaction from within, thereby expressing the way he or she perceives the self and the world. The principle of projection may be utilized by getting the subject to respond to words, inkblots, or pictures; to complete partial sentences; to draw pictures; to play with dolls; and so forth.

Projective measures were originally developed for use in clinical psychology, but today applications are being made in many areas within human ecology. Some of the most common projective devices, divided into three broad categories of verbal, visual, and other techniques, are described here.

## VERBAL TECHNIQUES

*Word association,* one of the oldest procedures used in personality study, may well be considered the forerunner of projective techniques. With this verbal projective method, clues to personality of the subject are obtained by analyzing stimulus words on which the subject shows some emotional disturbance or blocking and by examining usualness or unusualness of the subject's responses as compared to the norm for his or her culture or group. In word association, the subject is presented with a word and is asked to respond immediately with the first word that comes to mind. The words expressed presumably indicate feelings and attitudes toward other persons, brands of products, clothing referents, and so on.

*Sentence completion* is another frequently used verbal technique. The projective aspect of this method is that the subject is supplied with an incomplete stimulus (i.e., beginning of a sentence) that he or she is required to complete with a word or phrase. Responses can be analyzed for content, moods, motives, feelings, expectations, attitudes, and so on. The following examples illustrate the usual form that sentence completion instruments take:

If I could have anything . . .
I most dislike . . .
I am happiest when . . .
My mother always . . .
At school . . .
The best thing I like about Product X is . . .

Among the best known sentence completion measures is the 40-item *Rotter Incomplete Sentence Blank.* Another type of completion technique is *story completion,* in which the subject is provided with part of a story and is requested to give the conclusion in his or her own words.

The *third-person technique* is a verbal projective method that asks a subject why another person does a certain thing, thinks a certain way, and so forth. The assumption is that the subject transfers his or her own attitudes to neighbors, friends, co-workers, and others. A variation of this approach was used in the classic marketing study designed to elicit images of products (Haire 1950), in which respondents were asked to write brief descriptions of the personality and character of women who had made out shopping lists for grocery store purchases.

## VISUAL TECHNIQUES

A widely used visual projective technique is the *Rorschach Inkblot Test*. With this instrument, the individual is asked by highly trained persons to respond to inkblots of varying shapes and colors. The subject is shown each card in a series, one at a time, and is asked to tell what he or she sees in it or what it may be. After the individual has responded to each of the cards, a period of inquiry follows in which the psychologist administering the test probes for information to clarify what the subject saw and what aspect of the blot determined the perception. Scoring systems provide for the analysis of both structure and content of responses. The researcher is concerned with the way the subject uses movement, color, shading, and form in determining responses. The need to take interrelationships of various factors into account makes the Rorschach interpretation very complex.

The *Thematic Apperception Test* (TAT), or parts or variants of it, has also been used to a great extent in research studies. The TAT is comprised of a set of vague pictures of relatively low structure to which the subject responds by telling a story about what is happening in each picture, what led up to the scene, and what the outcome will be (Ex. 7.16). The underlying rationale of the TAT is that, in so doing, the individual expresses internal needs and perceived environmental influences.

Although the instrument in its original form is used more in clinical work than in research, the idea behind it has had widespread research use. TAT-like pictures have been used extensively to study needs for achievement, affiliation, and power. A downward extension of the TAT for children (which uses animal figures) is called the *Children's Apperception Test*. A *Clothing TAT* (Rosencranz 1972), developed to examine clothing awareness, consists of a series of seven pictures to which subjects create stories. The drawings depict various incongruities: between clothing of the people in the pictures and other attributes (e.g., age, sex, body build), between clothing of the characters portrayed, and between clothing and the background in the picture.

*Cartoon tests,* sometimes called balloon tests, depict cartoon characters in a variety of situations pertinent to the research problem. Dialog in one or more of the "balloons" is already filled in, and the subject is asked to suggest the missing reply of one of the other characters (Ex. 7.17).

**Example 7.16.** Card 12F of the *Thematic Apperception Test.* (Reprinted by permission of the publishers from *Thematic Apperception Test,* by Henry A. Murray, Cambridge, Mass.: Harvard Univ. Press, copyright © 1943 by The President and Fellows of Harvard College, © 1971 by Henry A. Murray.)

**Example 7.17.** Balloon test. (From S. H. Britt, ed., *Consumer Behavior and the Behavioral Sciences,* copyright © 1966, John Wiley and Sons, p. 49, fig. 2. Reprinted by permission of John Wiley and Sons, Inc.)

## OTHER TECHNIQUES

A third group of projective devices is made up largely of techniques that allow the subject free expression in the form of drawings or play. One drawing technique is the *Draw-a-Person Test.* In this method, the subject is asked to draw a person and then to draw a person of the opposite sex, during which time the examiner takes notes concerning the sequence of body parts drawn and comments on unusual reactions by the subject. Following the drawing session, the subject tells a story about the persons drawn, which is intended to indicate something about the subject's personality and attitudes. Another drawing procedure is the *House-Tree-Person Test.*

*Doll play* is an expressive technique that is well suited for research with young children because it is easy and natural for youngsters to project themselves into the dolls. Doll play has been used successfully with children in nursery school, kindergarten, and early primary grades. The child reveals attitudes toward family members, as well as fears, aggressions, and conflicts. The examiner observes what the child chooses to play with, what the youngster says and does, and any emotional expressions.

## ADVANTAGES AND LIMITATIONS

A primary advantage of projective techniques is that they are largely independent of the subject's self-insight and willingness to reveal inner feelings. The individual is typically unaware of what is being measured. Projective techniques are also not affected by a person's tendency to answer questions in one direction. These measures are especially appropriate with children.

Since projective devices lack objectivity, it is difficult to establish reliability and validity. With objective measures, it is easy for observers to agree on the scoring of responses. When projective instruments are used, it is much more difficult for different judges to come to the same conclusions about an individual's responses. Nevertheless, if they are to be used in research, projective methods must satisfy the same scientific standards as all methods of observation and measurement. They must be subjected to the same type of reliability testing and empirical validation as any other research procedure, even though this may be difficult. Scoring and interpretation of projective techniques can be compared by correlating the judgments made by independent research workers. To the extent that the ratings are in close agreement, objectivity has been achieved. It is generally advisable not to use a projective technique if a more objective instrument is available that adequately measures the same variable. Most projective techniques require a great deal of interpretation and highly specialized training.

The reader is referred to other useful discussions of projective techniques as well as to many good standard texts on measurement in general.[10]

# Physiological and Physical Measures

With the exception of direct observation, all of the techniques of data collection described so far may be considered essentially "indirect" assessments. If we are interested in a subject's inner feelings or internal state, observation may not be direct enough. For example, although we can systematically observe another person's physical appearance, motor response patterns, language, and paralinguistic behavior and can attempt to infer that person's covert feelings (e.g., happiness, anxiety, hostility) or internal state (e.g., nutritional status, stress, physical health), it is often preferable to obtain more direct measurements of these phenomena, if possible. When the hypotheses of a study are physiological or physical in nature, or when a physiological or physical indicator can be measured more directly and precisely, it may be better to use these direct measurements rather than depend on self-reports or observation of external cues.

To illustrate, in clothing and textiles or interior design research, a pupilometer can record changes in pupil size when the subject is presented with a particular color or fabric. Increases in the diameter of the pupils of a person's eyes may serve as an indicator of the positive impact of a stimulus. In nutrition, biochemical analyses performed on blood and urine provide a measure of the concentration of nutrients in the body. In human development, the galvanometer that measures galvanic skin response (GSR) can provide a direct index of emotional arousal or tension. In consumer behavior, an eye camera or an oculometer can track a consumer's eye movements as he or she reads a newspaper advertisement, watches a television commercial, or looks at the packaging of merchandise. With the aid of mechanical devices, other direct assessments of people are possible, including heart or pulse rate, blood pressure, muscle tension, body temperature, and brain wave activity.[11]

Direct physical measurements of nonhuman objects have been methodological mainstays in laboratory research to automatically record observations. A researcher in the clothing and textiles area, for instance, might use an Instron machine to measure the strength of a textile fabric in terms of grams required to break the yarn, or employ a colorimeter to measure small differences in color between samples that are nearly alike.

In summary, the investigator in human ecology has at his or her disposal a variety of data collection techniques to study a wide range of research problems. The type of instrumentation selected, whether it is observation, questionnaires, interviews, projective techniques, or physical or physiological measures, should be appropriate for the problem at hand and the subjects who will comprise the sample. Moreover, the measure must be technically sound. As Bausell (1986, 168) aptly puts it: "The actual form that an instrument takes is not as important as the consistency with which it assigns numbers to individuals or the usefulness of those numbers for the empirical purposes for which they are employed." Finally, the researcher should use multiple methods of data collection in a study whenever possible to strengthen the validity of findings.

## NOTES

1. For a brief overview of equipment and devices to instrument observational study, see Chapter 6 in Touliatos and Compton (1983).

2. Good treatment of direct observation are Bakeman and Gottman (1986), Brandt (1972), Cone and Foster (1982), Evertson and Green (1984), Foster and Cone (1986), Genishi (1982), Gordon and Jester (1973), Hartmann and Wood (1982), Herbert and Attridge (1975), Jackson, Della-Piana, and Sloane (1975), Kent and Foster (1977), McCall (1984), Martin and Bateson (1986), Martinko and Gardner (1985), Medley and Mitzel (1963), Sackett (1978), Touliatos and Compton (1983), Weick (1968, 1985), and Wright (1960).

3. See Chapter 3 in Touliatos and Compton (1983) for an overview of observational strategies appropriate for environmental assessment. Some other relevant sources are Barker (1968), Barker and Schoggen (1973), Bechtel, Marans, and Michelson (1987), Brandt (1972), Craik (1970, 1973), Gump (1975), Proshansky, Ittelson, and Rivlin (1970), and Zeisel (1984).

4. Although many authors simply use the term *tests* to refer to objective measures of maximum performance and reserve the term *questionnaire* for self-report measures of typical performance, we are including objective measures of both maximum and typical performance under the heading questionnaire, specifically in our discussion of summable-item closed question instruments. Objective measures of maximum and typical performance generally meet our criteria for SICQ questionnaires.

5. Complete bibliographic information on well-known instruments cited in this chapter can be obtained from *Tests in Print III* (Mitchell 1983).

6. The Likert-type scale is only one example of a rating scale used in attitude research. For a discussion of attitudes and their measurement, see Dawes and Smith (1985), Edwards (1957b), Henerson, Morris, and Fitz-Gibbon (1978), Mueller (1986), Oppenheim (1966), Schuman and Presser (1981), Shaw and Wright (1967), and Summers (1970).

7. See Lin (1976), Lindzey and Byrne (1968), Gronlund (1959), and Hops and Lewin (1984) for more information concerning sociometric techniques.

8. Details regarding questionnaire construction and use can be found in Belson (1981), Berdie and Anderson (1974), Bradburn and Sudman (1979), Converse and Presser (1986), DeMaio (1983), Dillman (1978, 1983), Frey (1983), Miller (1983), Oppenheim (1966), Payne (1951), Schuman and Presser (1981), Sheatsley (1983), and Sudman and Bradburn (1982). See also Angleitner and Wiggins (1986), Gynther and Green (1982), and Jensen and Haynes (1986) for a discussion of special methodological problems in the construction and evaluation of personality questionnaires.

9. Materials on interviewing by Brenner, Brown, and Canter (1985), Cannell and Kahn (1968), Gorden (1980), Guenzel, Berkmans, and Cannell (1983), Richardson, Snell, and Klein (1965), Somers et al. (1982), Stewart and Cash (1974), Turkat (1986), and Yarrow (1960) are all worth consulting.

10. An especially good treatment of projective techniques is Semeomoff's (1976) *Projective Techniques.* Other related references include Klopfer and Taulbee (1976), Murstein (1965), Rabin (1968, 1981, 1986), and Rabin and Haworth (1960). For a listing of some of the many good texts covering most measurement topics, see Note 12 at the end of Chapter 6.

11. For example, in a recent study Furedy (1987) used heart rate and the T-wave amplitude component of the electrocardiogram to measure mental effort. Epstein (1976), Kallman and Fluerstein (1986), and Katkin and Hastrup (1982) discuss some physiological and physical measures for possible use in research with human subjects.

PART 3

# Research Strategies

CHAPTER 8

# Experiments

Part 3: Research Strategies (Chaps. 8–12) describes several conditions and situations in which subjects are examined. Most of the ways used to categorize research strategies are quite artificial because there are no clear boundaries between strategies. The overlap among research purposes, research settings, and methods of data collection usually makes classification a risky business. Nevertheless, some type of framework is essential to organize and present information in an introductory-level treatment of research. Here, research strategies have been broadly classified as *experimental* or *nonexperimental.*

Experimental approaches are presented in this chapter. Nonexperimental strategies include field studies (Chap. 9), surveys (Chap. 10), and using existing data (Chap. 11). A special category of research, called evaluation studies (Chap. 12), may involve either experimental or nonexperimental approaches. As you will see, there is no completely satisfactory way to classify the many types of strategies, particularly those under the nonexperimental rubric. Synopses of published research that illustrate these research strategies are provided at the end of each chapter (see Summary Table 12.1).

As indicated earlier, research can be undertaken for exploratory, descriptive, and explanatory purposes. This chapter focuses on research whose objective is explanation. When a researcher wishes to move beyond exploration and description and discover causal relationships between variables, the most rigorous research strategy is the *experimental method.* In an experiment, the researcher can examine if use of a certain vitamin supplement results in weight gain or if an instructional strategy in an extension program increases knowledge in a particular area more than another teaching technique.

The most distinctive feature of experimentation is that the researcher intentionally varies one or more variables while holding others constant and then observes the effects of this manipulation. This is quite unlike other forms of investigation where there is no direct control over the variables being studied. For example, in field studies that include no form of researcher intervention, the focus is on *existing* relationships. Similarly, in survey studies, variables such as social class, marital status, intelligence, and attitudes are beyond the researcher's control, cannot be changed for study purposes, and must be investigated retrospectively for their possible effects. Also, in historical research, the events cannot be manipulated by the researcher because they have already taken place, often in the distant past. Only with experiments can the researcher create a controlled situation and deliberately impose conditions to examine cause-and-effect relationships between variables. Extremely well suited for hypothesis testing, experiments help provide straightforward answers to specific questions.

Although there is a tendency to equate experimentation with the laboratory, experiments are not restricted to laboratory settings. They can also be conducted in field settings, where the same principles and procedures apply. A researcher can manipulate variables in both laboratory and nonlaboratory settings. Laboratory experiments are illustrated in **Research Synopses 8.1–8.3,** and field experiments are described in **Research Synopses 8.4, 12.2,** and **12.3.**

## CHARACTERISTICS OF EXPERIMENTS

There are certain major features in most experiments: independent and dependent variables, experimental and control groups, and pretesting and posttesting. The selection and the assignment of research subjects also are important parts of experimental studies.

### Independent and Dependent Variables

In simple terms, the experimental method investigates the causal relationship between variables. To determine if variable X has an effect on variable Y, the researcher purposively manipulates X while controlling other variables that may influence the relationship, and then examines the effect that X has on Y. The variable that is manipulated (by presenting, removing, or varying levels of it) is the *independent variable,* or experimental variable. The presumed effect of the manipulation of the independent variable is called the *dependent variable.* The dependent variable can be a behavior observed directly by the experimenter or a score on a questionnaire. As with all research, independent and dependent variables must be operationally defined.

## Experimental and Control Groups

Experimental designs usually but not necessarily include more than one group. Use of a comparison group helps yield interpretable results by ruling out alternative explanations. The group that is exposed to the independent variable (treatment) is referred to as the *experimental group,* and the group to which the independent variable has not been presented is the *control group.* In principle, the two groups are identical in every respect except that the experimental group receives a certain treatment and the control group does not.

## Pretesting and Posttesting

Another component of many experiments is pretesting and posttesting. At the beginning of the experiment, subjects are observed, interviewed, or given questionnaires to measure the dependent variable.[1] Participants in both the experimental and control groups are treated identically in the pretesting. Following the manipulation of the independent variable with the experimental group, the instrument used earlier as the pretest of the dependent variable (or an equivalent form of it) is again administered to *both* the experimental and control groups. A difference score is calculated between the pretest and posttest measures for each subject in each group, and a mean difference score for the group as a whole is then computed. (The mean change score for the control group serves as a baseline for the amount of change during the course of the experiment that has nothing to do with the treatment.) Under ideal circumstances, the difference score may be considered the change in the value of the dependent variable that is attributable to the independent variable. (Other factors that might contribute to the difference score are discussed under Threats to Experimental Validity.)

## Subject Selection and Assignment

The selection of subjects for experimental research could follow probability sampling procedures described in Chapter 3. Obtaining two random samples from a single population will result in two groups of subjects, one for the experimental group and one for the control group, that differ only by chance. Each group is regarded as being equally representative of the population.

Such a representative sampling plan is rarely adopted in experimental studies for at least three reasons. First, it is quite time consuming to draw random samples. Second, unless the probability samples are relatively large, which is usually not the case in experiments, the samples may differ appreciably just by chance. Third, unlike descriptive research that seeks to describe a population by examining a sample of it, experimental studies are more interested in identifying whether or not an independent variable has made a difference between groups.

Instead of random selection, most experimenters resort to the use of convenience samples, usually voluntary subjects who are then randomly assigned to different groups. Through random assignment to conditions of an experiment, the researcher hopes to eliminate any bias caused by the use of an unrepresentative group (e.g., college student volunteers, or animals that have been purchased from a supplier). However, the problem of generalizability of the results to more heterogeneous populations may still exist.

### Randomization

*Randomization* (a synonym for random assignment) is by far the easiest assignment procedure and the best way to equate groups. Having recruited subjects by whatever means, the researcher numbers all subjects consecutively and uses any method that ensures that a subject has an equal probability of being assigned to any group (condition) in the experiment. Randomization can be accomplished by using a random numbers table (see Chap. 3) or some equivalent procedure, such as flipping a coin or tossing a die.

Random assignment helps neutralize the effects of factors that have not been directly controlled because the researcher is unaware of them or uncertain about which ones should be controlled. Although it is a fact of life that complete control is impossible, by relying on randomness the researcher minimizes bias in the results caused by factors that cannot be held constant. Assuming that the sample is reasonably large, the investigator can feel confident that extraneous factors have been distributed by chance and are similar for all groups. Consequently, any differences found between groups presumably can be attributed to the experimental variable. Most statistical analyses assume randomization.

### Matching

If randomization is not feasible for some reason, the researcher may use *matching* to make groups as comparable as possible. When matching procedures are employed, it is important to know which variables have a sizeable relationship with the dependent variable under study. Sex, age, race, social class, intelligence, and pretest scores on the dependent variable are only some of the variables that can be used in the matching process.

There are different ways to approach matching. For example, the researcher who has identified sex and intelligence as the specific variables on which control is desired selects pairs of subjects who are most equivalent from the pool of available participants: a 20-year-old female with an IQ score between 100 and 120 is paired with another 20-year-old female with an IQ score in the same range. After all subjects in the pool have been paired in this manner, the researcher randomly assigns one member of each set to the experimental group and one to the control group. Unless a limited number of attributes must be controlled, a sizeable pool of available individuals is necessary. Matching extreme cases presents special difficulties.

If there is a problem locating a sufficient number of matched pairs, researchers sometimes turn to a similar but less extensive procedure that guarantees only that proportions or percentages of subjects with the relevant attributes are the same for the different groups at the beginning of the study. Groups, not pairs of individuals, are matched so that each group has the same percentages of blacks and whites, males and females, young and old, or mean scores on the pretest measure of the dependent variable.

Matching can never control all of the relevant factors that randomization can, no matter how many variables are taken into account.[2]

## Blinding

When subjects are being assigned to experimental and control groups, it is preferable that they know only as much about the experimental conditions as is ethically necessary. This principle, referred to as *blinding,* minimizes the impact of expectations held by research subjects that may, in turn, influence results. Certain *demand characteristics* (Orne 1962) of the experiment may guide the subjects' behavior and produce the hypothesized effect. This phenomenon refers to the subjects' perceptions of cues and other information available in the research situation that cause them to speculate about the objectives of the study and the responses expected of them. To ensure that the beliefs and expectations of all subjects are distributed equally among the different groups used in the experiment, the subjects are kept "blind" to the status of the independent variable.

An example of blinding is seen in medical research when the experimental group is given a new drug and the control group is given a placebo, but the subjects do not know which they have received. The placebo is a pill or injection that looks exactly like the real thing but contains an inert substance rather than the medication. A placebo can also be a "theoretically inert" procedure, or treatment (O'Leary and Borkovec 1978). For example, three groups of parents are told that a parent education program they are about to take will help them become more effective disciplinarians with their children. One group (treatment group) receives a structured training program designed with this purpose in mind. The second (placebo group) engages in parenting discussions that past research has shown to have no influence on the use of disciplinary techniques. The third (control group) is put on a waiting list for participation at some future date. When subjects are unaware of their condition (experimental or control), but the experimenter is aware, it is called a *single-blind* experiment.

In addition to potential problems caused by subjects' expectations, another possible source of distortion of results is experimenter expectations.[3] If the experimenter knows who is an experimental or control subject, he or she might unintentionally and subtly treat subjects differently, in addition to the specific ways required to implement the treatment. Experimenter expectations might also influence observations or scoring of the dependent variable if the assessment involves subjective judgments. Applying the same principle of blinding to the experimenter as to the subject in a design is known as a *double-blind*. Neither the subjects nor the experimenter is aware of the treatment that has been administered, thereby minimizing both demand characteristic threats and experimenter effects.

## EXPERIMENTAL DESIGN AND THREATS TO EXPERIMENTAL VALIDITY

In the most general sense, *experimental design* describes the structure of an experiment. It indicates the independent and dependent variables that are to be used and how they are to be operationalized; how the treatment variable is to be systematically manipulated, the interventions timed, and the extraneous variables controlled; the number of groups to be employed and how subjects are to be selected and assigned to groups; how and when the dependent variables are to be measured; and what statistical analyses are to be applied for comparisons. In designing an experiment, the researcher attempts to exert control over all of these elements and to standardize procedures.[4] Only with control can the researcher make decisions about causation.

Different experimental designs vary in their ability to eliminate or control potential sources of invalidity.[5] Some designs are considered "tight," while others are considered "loose." The tighter the design, the more confidence a researcher can have in any causal inferences made from the data. *Pre-experimental designs* are the weakest of the designs. Rigorously controlled *true experimental designs* deal with most of the plausible sources of invalidity. *Quasi-experimental designs,* an approach common in field experimentation, are superior to pre-experimental designs but less rigorous than true experimental designs.

## Threats to Experimental Validity

The validity of findings produced by research in general was discussed in Chapter 3. Here, the focus is on validity issues associated with experiments. *Internal validity* in experimental investigations deals with the question of whether the independent variable was indeed the cause of any differences in the dependent variable found in the groups being studied. It helps rule out competing interpretations. *External validity* refers to the representativeness of a study, or the generalizability of the results to other people, places, and times.

### Internal Validity

Campbell and Stanley (1963) and Cook and Campbell (1979) have identified a number of extraneous (confounding) variables that must be controlled if the effects of the independent variable are to be evaluated unambiguously. The factors described below operate alone or in conjunction with other factors to jeopardize internal validity.

1. *History.* Various unanticipated historical events that occur in the environment while the study is in progress might produce changes in the dependent variables other than those caused by the independent variable. Examples of external intervening events include epidemics, political elections, power failures, noises, and unexpected changes in experimenters.

2. *Maturation.* Maturation refers to the developmental changes that take place within the research subjects—a function of the passage of time. In the course of a study involving a lengthy data collection time span, the participants get older and wiser as a part of normal development and everyday experiences. In short-term experiments, subjects can become tired or bored.

3. *Testing.* In research designs calling for a pretest and posttest to be administered to the same group, taking the initial test might inflate scores on the test given at the conclusion of the study because of a practice effect.

4. *Instrumentation.* Instrumentation denotes changes in the measuring instrument during an experiment. The interviewer may become more experienced or more fatigued, or the observer may become more skillful in identifying categories of behavior or more careless as boredom sets in. Mechanical instruments may undergo changes in calibration as a result of use from pretest to posttest or from experimental to control group.

5. *Statistical regression.* The regression effect is invited by subjects who have either very low or very high scores on the pretest of the dependent variable. Individual scores contain both elements of truth and chance. Because of normal chance variations in individual scores, it is likely that subjects with very high initial scores will score lower on subsequent test-

ings, and those with initially low scores will subsequently improve. This is referred to as regression toward the mean. Thus, if subjects are selected on the basis of having low scores on the pretest, it is likely that their scores on the average will be higher on the second testing, irrespective of the independent variable.

6. *Differential selection of subjects.* When there are initial differences between groups because subjects were not randomly assigned, these differences are likely to continue to operate from pretest and posttest. This is a problem that is associated with the use of intact groups.

7. *Experimental mortality.* If subjects drop out selectively from the experimental or control group before the study is concluded, the differential loss from one of the groups might bias the sample on which complete data are available.

8. *Interactions with selection.* Many of the foregoing factors can interact with characteristics of the groups selected for study. Because of certain selection factors, the effects associated with history, maturation, testing, and so on might not be consistent across all groups in the investigation.

### External Validity

When a researcher is concerned about whether extraneous variables have interacted in some way with the treatment variable to make the study participants unlike members of the population from which they were selected, he or she is thinking about the external validity of the results.

Campbell and Stanley (1963) have identified four factors that limit the generalizability of findings beyond the specific conditions of a particular experiment:

1. *Interaction effects of selection biases and the experimental variable.* Certain characteristics of a sample, such as social class, intelligence, or motivation, might make a group more or less responsive than average to the experimental treatment.

2. *Reactive or interactive effects of pretesting.* The pretest might influence subjects' sensitivity or responsiveness to the experimental stimulus (e.g., by calling attention to issues or problems that might ordinarily go unnoticed).

3. *Reactive effects of experimental procedures.* In addition to other aspects of the research situation (including experimenter expectations), subjects' knowledge that they are being studied might alter normal behavior, possibly affecting the particular behavior under investigation.[6]

4. *Multiple treatment interference.* When the same subjects are repeatedly exposed to a number of experimental treatments,[7] there is the likelihood that the effects of one or more of the pretesting treatments might

carry over and have a delayed effect. This type of interaction is also possible when combinations of an independent variable are used in a study.

Despite these limitations, it is not impossible to produce research results that are both internally and externally valid. A conscientious researcher can design an experiment that eliminates or controls most categories of confounding or, at the very least, can take measures to evaluate potential threats to a study's validity. It is imperative that the investigator be cognizant of these threats and interpret the results accordingly, pointing out the possible rival explanations that might account for the findings.

Internal and external validity have been thoroughly discussed elsewhere (Campbell and Stanley 1963; Cook and Campbell 1979). Complete coverage of the topic is not provided here, but a few examples of ways to enhance experimental validity or to determine if certain factors are present that may have jeopardized validity should be helpful. Problems arising from selection, regression, and selection interactions can generally be avoided by random assignment, which reduces the likelihood that groups are different on relevant dimensions before the experiment. Though not as desirable, matching can help equalize groups. Examining pretest scores is another way to ascertain lack of reasonable equivalence. Regarding the threat of regression toward the mean, the researcher may be able to reduce this unwanted effect by using highly reliable measuring devices.

History, maturation, instrumentation, and testing threats can be isolated by including a control group as part of the design. In this way, both experimental and comparison groups are affected about the same by historical events, maturation, changes in the measuring instrument, and pretesting, with only the experimental subjects being exposed to the treatment. Limiting the duration of an experiment and avoiding rapidly maturing samples (e.g., subjects who might experience growth spurts) are other strategies that help deal specifically with the potential problems of history and maturation, respectively.

Omitting the pretest, disguising it, or using an unobtrusive measure also helps minimize pretest reactivity. Standardization of measurement and data collection procedures can minimize validity threats associated with instrumentation. The training of interviewers, observers, and other persons in the research setting is also beneficial. In studies using direct observation, multiple observers can be employed, and interobserver reliability can be calculated.

Unfortunately, experimental mortality cannot be controlled by randomization or by including a control group. However, keeping the duration of the experiment as short as possible can help counteract some subject loss. Maintaining careful records and documenting who has dropped out for various reasons (e.g., death, illness, change in residence, refusal to cooperate, mechanical equipment failure) are imperative and facilitate the interpretation of findings. To illustrate the importance of mortality, if more low-scoring than high-scoring subjects in the experimental group drop out after taking the pretest, the result will be inflated mean scores on the posttest and reduced mean difference scores because of regression toward the mean. It is important to know if dropouts differ substantially on certain characteristics from those who remain.

The interactive effects of selection biases and the treatment variable can be dealt with through the use of a representative sample of subjects who are randomly selected from a population of interest (i.e., the population to which results are to be generalized) and randomly assigned. Repeated studies of samples from different populations help increase the researcher's confidence that the observed effect of the intervention is not due to its combination with selected characteristics of the subjects.

Replication is the best test of external validity.[8] Some possible remedies for the internal validity threat caused by pretesting also pertain to the confounding effects of pretesting with the experimental variable. The Solomon four-group design, to be discussed later, assesses both pretesting effects and the interaction of testing with the treatment variable.

Reactive effects of experimental procedures, which can hamper generalization, can be evaluated with a post-experimental interview or questionnaire. Through debriefing, the researcher can inquire about demand characteristics that may have been operating within the research setting. Use of placebo control and blinding procedures, deception (if justified) with subsequent debriefing, unobtrusive measures, and naturalistic settings can help combat demand characteristic threats that weaken the validity of research findings. Other reactive effects that result from experimenter expectancy can be countered with blinding techniques, standardization of experimental behaviors extending to the possible use of audiotaped or written instructions, and the use of a "naive" experimenter who is unaware of the hypothesis being tested by the research. Debriefing to determine the subjects' awareness of the hypothesis is helpful not only in identifying demand characteristics but also in assessing experimenter effects.

A summary of the sources of invalidity in different experimental designs is presented in Table 8.1.

## Pre-experimental Designs

Pre-experimental designs are especially vulnerable to experimental validity threats. They are inadequate for most purposes and do not qualify as legitimate experimental designs. Nevertheless, three pre-experimental designs are sometimes employed by persons who are not fully versed in re-

**Table 8.1. Threats to the Validity of Different Experimental Designs**

| | Pre-experimental Designs | | | True Experimental Designs | | | Quasi-experimental Designs | |
|---|---|---|---|---|---|---|---|---|
| Source of Invalidity | One-group posttest | One-group pretest-posttest | Static-group comparison | Pretest-posttest control | Posttest-only control | Solomon four-group | Nonequivalent control group | Time-series |
| *Internal Validity* | | | | | | | | |
| History | – | – | + | + | + | + | + | – |
| Maturation | – | – | ? | + | + | + | + | + |
| Testing | | – | + | + | + | + | + | + |
| Instrumentation | | – | + | + | + | + | + | ? |
| Statistical regression | | ? | + | + | + | + | ? | + |
| Differential selection of subjects | – | + | – | + | + | + | + | + |
| Experimental mortality | – | + | – | + | + | + | + | + |
| Interactions with selection, etc. | | – | – | + | + | + | – | + |
| *External Validity* | | | | | | | | |
| Interaction effects of selection bias and the experimental variable | – | – | – | ? | ? | ? | ? | ? |
| Reactive or interactive effects of pretesting | | – | | – | + | + | – | – |
| Reactive effects of experimental procedures | | ? | | ? | ? | ? | ? | ? |
| Multiple treatment interference | | | | | | | | |

Source: From Donald T. Campbell and Julian C. Stanley, *Experimental and Quasi-experimental Designs for Research*. Copyright © 1963 by Houghton Mifflin Company. Adapted by permission.

search methods or are used when the situation precludes more sophisticated experimentation. The one-group posttest design, the one-group pretest-posttest design, and the static-group comparison are described here to illustrate some of the kinds of rival hypotheses, or alternative explanations, that can be generated by loosely designed studies.

### One-Group Posttest Design

In the one-group posttest design, the researcher administers a treatment to a single group, obtains a posttest score on the dependent variable, and makes an intuitive judgment regarding what would have happened if no treatment had been used. A person conducting a series of parent meetings might show films on child growth and development to the parents and then give the participants a test designed to measure knowledge of children. The parent educator who felt that the mean score on the test was better than it would have been if the films had not been shown at the meetings might conclude that the films were effective in increasing knowledge of child development. Unfortunately, there is no way of knowing if the parents would have scored higher or lower on the test if the films had not been used because there was no baseline to judge against.

### One-Group Pretest-Posttest Design

A slight improvement over the one-group posttest design is the one-group pretest-posttest design, in which a measure of the dependent variable is administered before and after the treatment. A child development knowledge pretest is administered to the parents before showing the films, and a posttest is given after the last film in the series has been viewed. If there is an increase in scores, the parent leader might conclude that the films were responsible for the improvement; but it is impossible to know if the better scores were produced by the experimental treatment or by other factors. Did some of the parents attend public lectures by parenting experts in the community during the time span covered by the study? Did some read child development books or discuss parenting with friends and neighbors? Did some subjects become more knowledgeable about children as a result of dealing with their youngsters on a day-to-day basis during the course of the experiment? Could the content of the pretest have stimulated some parents to learn more about children regardless of the films? Did taking the pretest help some parents score better on the second test?

### Static-Group Comparison

Static-group comparison, also referred to as intact-group comparison, includes a control group, but it does not have pretests (Table 8.2). Using the parent education example again, the parent leader might decide to show child development films to a parent group that is meeting this semester.

**Table 8.2. Comparison of Some Pre-experimental, True Experimental, and Quasi-experimental Research Designs**

| Design | | Pretest | Experimental Condition | Posttest |
|---|---|---|---|---|
| *Pre-experimental* | | | | |
| One-group posttest | Group 1 | | X | X |
| One-group pretest-posttest | Group 1 | X | X | X |
| Static-group comparison | Group 1 | | X | X |
| | Group 2 | | | X |
| *True Experimental* | | | | |
| Pretest-posttest control group | Group 1[a] | X | X | X |
| | Group 2[a] | X | | X |
| Posttest-only control group | Group 1[a] | | X | X |
| | Group 2[a] | | | X |
| Solomon four-group | Group 1[a] | X | X | X |
| | Group 2[a] | X | | X |
| | Group 3[a] | | X | X |
| | Group 4[a] | | | X |
| *Quasi-experimental* | | | | |
| Nonequivalent control group | Group 1 | X | X | X |
| | Group 2 | X | | X |
| Time-series | Group 1 | XXX | X | XXX |

Source: From Donald T. Campbell and Julian C. Stanley, *Experimental and Quasi-experimental Designs for Research.* Copyright © 1963 by Houghton Mifflin Company. Adapted by permission.

[a]Subjects are randomly assigned to these groups.

After the film series has been completed, the parent educator gives a child development knowledge test to that group (the experimental group) and to parents who have signed up for next semester's group (control group). Even if the experimental group received higher scores, nothing definitive can be concluded because, among other things, there was no way of knowing if the two groups were equivalent in their knowledge of child development prior to the study.

## True Experimental Designs

True experimental designs provide the best assurance that most sources of experimental invalidity have been controlled. Three of these true designs will be described.

### Pretest-Posttest Control Group Design

The pretest-posttest control group design includes at least two randomized samples: an experimental group and a control group. Actually, there can be several experimental groups exposed to different treatments, but there is always a control group. We can use the parent education research idea to illustrate the use of the pretest-posttest control group design. Subjects in each group are given a test just prior to the experiment to measure knowledge of child development, but only the experimental group is exposed to the treatment (the films). Afterward, both groups are administered a child development posttest, and the mean difference between the pretest and posttest for each group is compared to determine the effects of the treatment. Appropriate tests of significance are then calculated to see if the obtained difference between the experimental and control groups is sufficiently great to reflect a statistically significant difference rather than a chance occurrence.

This strong design controls for most of the sources of invalidity (history, maturation, statistical regression, differential selection of subjects, etc.) except possibly the interactive effects of pretesting. It is conceivable that the practice of pretesting aroused the interests of the experimental subjects and made them more sensitive to the content of the child development films. Similarly, as a result of the pretesting, control subjects may have been motivated to seek information that was relevant to the study. If the findings for the sample cannot be generalized to the population, the study's external validity is called into question.

### Posttest-Only Control Group Design

In its simplest form, the posttest-only control group design involves a randomly assigned experimental group and a control group. After the experimental group has received the treatment, both groups are measured on the dependent variable, then the scores are compared.

The only difference between this design and the preceding one is the omission of the pretest prior to the onset of the experimental treatment (Table 8.2). The posttest-only control group design may be expanded to include more groups, such as a control group and two or more experimental groups that receive different treatments.

Although pretests are necessary in studies examining *degree* of change, researchers tend to use them in other cases as well, largely out of tradition. There are times when pretests are unnecessary, unavailable, or inconvenient. As long as subjects are allocated to the various groups on a random basis, pretests are usually unnecessary. The omission of pretests eliminates the potential interactive effects of pretesting with the experimental treatment that plague some other designs.

### Solomon Four-Group Design

The Solomon four-group design combines features of the pretest-posttest control group and the posttest-only control group designs. Thus, there are two control groups and two experimental groups (both receiving the same treatment). All groups are administered the posttest, but only one pretested and one unpretested group are exposed to the treatment (Table 8.2). Although this design takes more time and effort, it allows the researcher to determine the main effects of the treatment variable (by comparing posttests for groups 3 and 4) and the interaction effects of pretesting, if any (by comparing groups 2 and 4). In addition to checking on the possible effects and interactions of pretesting, another advantage of this design is replication, since two simultaneous experiments are conducted within one study.

## Quasi-experimental Designs

When the realities of a particular situation preclude true experimentation with its elaborate controls, the researcher may try to incorporate whatever controls are reasonable under the circumstances into what is called a quasi-experimental design. This is often the case with experiments conducted in nonlaboratory environments because control is far more difficult to achieve in field settings than in laboratory settings. Since quasi-experiments only control some of the sources of internal invalidity that true experiments do (Table 8.1), they are considered inferior to true experiments. They cannot rule out rival hypotheses to the extent that true experiments can, and they should be used only if true experimental designs are impractical.

The fundamental difference between quasi-experiments and true experiments is the absence of randomized assignment of subjects to conditions. Both types of designs involve manipulation of the independent variable, and both may include comparison groups.

In research conducted in education settings, for instance, randomization is not always feasible. However, intact groups such as whole classroom groups are usually available for study. Although it is possible to adjust statistically for some of the differences in the composition of these preformed groups that may affect the dependent variables,[9] it is unrealistic to assume that all subject differences can be taken into account. The danger exists that any observed differences in the dependent variable are due to differences in the initial makeup of the groups and not due to the treatment. This lack of equivalence limits the study's inferential powers and requires special caution in the interpretation of findings.

Campbell and Stanley (1963) have suggested several quasi-experimental designs that incorporate a variety of safeguards to eliminate some of the threats to experimental validity. Two of these designs are the nonequivalent control group design and the time-series design.

### Nonequivalent Control Group Design

The nonequivalent control group design, a frequently used quasi-experimental design, is identical to pretest-posttest control group design except intact groups rather than randomly assigned ones are used (Table 8.2). Obviously better than the one-group pretest-posttest pre-experimental design, it is not as desirable as its true experimental control group design counterpart. The use of pretests is very important because it helps initially compare the degree of equivalence of the groups on the dependent variable, thereby providing some control for selection bias. In addition, the researcher normally compares the groups on other factors (e.g., age, sex, race) to determine what influence, if any, they had on the posttest performance.

### Time-Series Design

When a control group cannot be included in a study, another type of quasi-experimental approach, a time-series design, is sometimes considered. This design represents an improvement over the one-group posttest or one-group pretest-posttest pre-experimental design. In addition to a pretest, a series of posttests is used at various stages of the experimental treatment instead of single tests before and after the intervention (Table 8.2). The time-series design can be modified to include two or more introductions of the independent variable or to include two or more intact groups, with one serving as a control group.

## Factorial Designs

Experiments can be designed to deal systematically with more than one independent variable. Indeed, in human ecology, it is acknowledged that human development and behavior are influenced by many different factors. Therefore, by modifying one of the true experimental designs already presented, experiments that more closely approximate the complexity of real-life situations can be set up by using factorial designs that allow the simultaneous comparison of the effects of multiple variables.

In the factorial design, there are at least two independent variables, with a minimum of two levels of each variable (called a $2 \times 2$ factorial). At least one of the independent variables is a treatment variable, while others may represent additional variables (e.g., sex, intelligence) that are included for control purposes (and whose effects can also be studied). Continuing with our parent education example, say there are two parent groups: one group only views child development films, the other group only engages in group discussion on child development topics. If the additional variables of older and younger couples are added, this becomes a $2 \times 2$ design. There can be any number of variables and levels of each, but interpretation of results becomes more difficult as their numbers increase.

The factorial design is attractive for many reasons. Among them, it provides an efficient and economical means of studying multiple variables and of testing several hypotheses within the framework of a single experiment, and it enables the researcher to examine not only the effect of each independent variable separately (main effect) but also its *interaction* (joint effect) with other independent variables. To illustrate the interaction concept, a parent educator may find that the use of films alone has little effect on parents' knowledge of child development, and group discussion alone is equally ineffective. However, a two-variable design would help determine if the combination of a particular technique and younger versus older parents produces an increase in knowledge. It may be that discussions work well with younger parents but not at all with older parents, whereas films are effective with older parents and ineffective with the younger sample. The net result, if data from younger and older parents were combined, would be no difference in the dependent variable. A $2 \times 2$ factorial design, on the other hand, would result in discovering the true nature of the differences.

There is another advantage of factorial designs. By introducing additional relevant variables at different levels, this design broadens the range of generalizability and increases the external validity of an experiment.

## Single-Case Experimental Designs

Although most researchers are concerned about differences between groups of people, some investigators are interested only in comparing a single subject's behavior at different points in time. Single-case research is very common in psychology, education, and social work, and its use has increased in the last few years. The single-case experiment is especially appropriate for research examining behavioral change, such as investigation of the effects of treatment programs like counseling and behavior modification on individual clients (see **Research Synopsis 8.4**). Data are obtained through systematic observation, in either field or laboratory settings, and are analyzed typically through visual inspection of graphed data, although statistical analyses are also used. The case for and against statistical methods in single-subject research remains a source of controversy largely because of the clinical context of most of these studies. The distinction between the clinical and statistical significance of findings continues to divide single-case experimenters.

The initial phase of a single-case experiment involves observing the subject to obtain a baseline assessment, or usual frequency of a target behavior (dependent variable). To be amenable to systematic observation, the behavior under study must be overt and objectively defined by the researcher. The targeted behavior can be measured merely by counting the frequency of its occurrence (i.e., event sampling) or by using some form of time sampling. The baseline stage is called the A phase.

After a reasonably stable estimate of the behavior has been obtained, the researcher applies the treatment in the next stage, or B phase, and continues to measure the dependent variable. The subject's behavior following the intervention is then compared to that observed in the baseline period to determine if the treatment increased or decreased the behavior. In some cases, the goal is to increase a positive response, and in other cases, the objective is to decrease an undesirable behavior. Because the AB design is susceptible to contamination by numerous rival hypotheses (e.g., history, maturation, testing, regression), stronger single-case designs are often adopted to permit a more unambiguous interpretation of causality.

One such option is the ABA design, in which a third time period is added following the experimental treatment. During this second A phase, the independent variable is removed, but the dependent variable is still measured. Since the intervention is withdrawn after the behavioral change has been observed (and the change is likely to be reversed), the ABA strategy is also referred to as a *reversal* design. Efficiency of the intervention is suggested if the level of the targeted behavior during the second A phase is similar to that observed during the initial A phase.

If the independent variable is introduced yet again in a variation of this design called the ABAB design, there is more than one opportunity for the researcher to demonstrate the effects of the experimental treatment. The experimenter can observe if the behavior changes after the treatment variable is introduced (first B phase), if it reverses when the treatment is withdrawn (second A phase), and if the behavior improves when the treatment is reinstated (second B phase). The ABAB design helps rule out the possibility that some concurrent event other than the experimental manipulation has caused the change in behavior. It also avoids ethical problems associated with the elimination of a beneficial intervention and return to a baseline condition.

Other design possibilities for single-case research include multiple-baseline designs, which are essentially several AB designs.[10]

## FIELD EXPERIMENTS

As the name implies, the field experiment is an experiment that is conducted in real-life, not contrived, settings. It is included here rather than in Chapter 9 because the primary criterion for categorizing research strategies in this book is whether or not an investigation is experimental or nonexperimental. The field experiment is clearly an *experiment*. While the setting of a study is a consideration in classifying strategies, it is secondary to the experimental-nonexperimental distinction.

The field experiment combines some of the features of nonexperimental field studies (Chap. 9) and experimentation, but it also possesses some characteristics that depart from both. Like the nonexperimental field study, the field experiment uses natural groupings of subjects in their natural environments—homes, neighborhoods, schools, hospitals, retail stores. But while preserving this advantage of naturalness, the field experimenter purposively manipulates one or more independent variables to examine their causal relations with a dependent variable in much the same way as the laboratory experimenter does. The researcher in a nonexperimental field study is preoccupied only with examining and describing existing relationships among variables in an ongoing social situation without attempting to influence the individuals under investigation or disrupting naturally occuring events. Conversely, the field experimenter carefully structures the study in advance, intrudes into the natural environment, and alters conditions to examine their differential effects. Finally, whereas qualitative (nonnumerical) techniques are quite popular in some nonexperimental field research, such as ethnographic studies, greater attention is given to the quantification of variables in the field experiment, as it is in laboratory experimentation, for the purposes of hypothesis testing.

The field experiment approximates the laboratory experiment in other ways. In principle, the research design of the two is essentially the same. The structure of field and laboratory experiments is similar, as are most of the procedures for data collection, recording, and analysis; but of course, the setting is different.

The lifelike nature of the experimental field situation, considered an asset by many, also presents its share of headaches for the researcher because controlling variables is far more difficult in the field than in the confines of a laboratory. Since there are so many uncontrolled factors involved, the potential is great for contamination of independent variables by extraneous environmental variables. Consequently, careful standardization of conditions and procedures and the use of control groups are especially important.

Manipulation of independent variables and randomization can pose special problems in the field. Pure manipulations of the independent variable are often difficult to achieve, as are pure measures of the dependent variable.[11] There may be obstacles surrounding the use of an experimental treatment, such as when parents of schoolchildren object to a controversial intervention or to the assignment of their youngsters to a control group that does not receive a new, beneficial program. Lack of control over the field situation may extend to the random assignment of subjects to conditions because schools may be reluctant to disrupt intact classroom groups or because organizations may find it difficult to justify breaking up certain work groups to satisfy the researcher's needs. It is unusual, but not impossible, for a field experiment to achieve full experimental control. Field studies are more likely to be quasi-experimental studies.

If some of the potential problems mentioned above can be dealt with satisfactorily, the field experiment becomes a research technique with considerable scientific and practical value. Although it cannot match the precision of a lab experiment, its properties make it a highly regarded method because it features the study of behavior in its natural context while maintaining some of the refinement of laboratory control and manipulation.

### The Natural Experiment

A few words should be said about a special type of field experiment called a natural experiment. A *natural experiment* is the investigation of a naturally occurring event, not affected by the researcher, that is dramatic enough to have a significant impact on people. Nature, government, or society "designs" the natural experiment, with acts of God, changes in government policy, or the joint action of people serving the purpose of the treatment variable. The researcher opportunistically capitalizes on these events that have been activated by natural causes and merely studies their impact. Hurricanes, earthquakes, wartime bombings, political elections, assassinations, and passage of legislation are a few examples of such natural occurrences. The Three Mile Island nuclear accident and the introduction of television into a Canadian community that had never received TV signals before because it was in a geographical blind spot are but two events that presented researchers with opportunities to conduct natural experiments.[12]

Since the natural experiment involves a kind of manipulation of an independent variable, it yields information about causal relationships. It eliminates the problem of artificiality by providing an intervention that has extremely powerful consequences, something that practically or ethically could not be introduced by the researcher in the laboratory or in the planned field experiment. To offset these advantages, the critical events are usually so rare and unexpected that it is seldom possible to plan sufficiently and establish proper controls. Normally, the researcher is forced to study the variables retrospectively in a relatively weak variant of an experimental design.

## ADVANTAGES AND LIMITATIONS

Because it affords greater precision and control, including the manipulation of variables, the experiment puts the researcher in the best position to draw cause-and-effect conclusions, something that is impossible, or certainly difficult, with other research strategies. For this reason, experimentation is considered the hallmark of research methodology.

In spite of its virtues, the experiment has a few drawbacks. Some of these difficulties are solved in part by doing the experiment in laboratory settings, and others by carrying it out in a more natural situation.

Since experiments in each of the two settings have both advantages and disadvantages, they are discussed separately here. Bear in mind, however, that an experiment is an experiment, no matter where it is conducted. The experiment is a research strategy that can be utilized in both laboratory or natural settings.

## The Laboratory Experiment

The major asset of a laboratory experiment is its rigorous control. Control extends to the selection and assignment of subjects, uniformity of procedures, manipulation of selected variables, and control of environmental circumstances and other extraneous variables. In the lab, the researcher can isolate certain factors that occur in the world outside, adjust or vary them to suit his or her study needs, and examine the relationships between variables in great detail under highly controlled conditions. Laboratory experimentation is the preferred choice of many researchers because of its convenience and economy. Most lab experiments are limited in scope, concentrating on only a few variables and involving relatively small samples. Therefore, they are usually easy to carry out and typically cost less than many alternative methods. Another virtue of the laboratory experiment is that it can be replicated fairly easily.

Despite its numerous strengths, the lab experiment has some liabilities. A persistent criticism is the unnaturalness of laboratory situations. The real-life quality of natural conditions is sacrificed in favor of the high degree of control achieved in a synthetic environment. This artificiality may influence the behavior of subjects as well as affect the generalizability of results. Also, the lab situation usually is not amenable to the study of large groups.

Complete control of extraneous factors is impossible, so hazards to internal and external validity may cloud the interpretation of findings in all but the best-designed studies. Variables in the lab usually have a weaker effect than those experienced in everyday settings. Laboratory experiments typically deal with lower or, at best, moderate levels of variables, often making it difficult to find an effect that definitely exists. Some research problems cannot be investigated as controlled experiments because they involve noxious stimuli, trauma, or other conditions that cannot be imposed on research subjects for practical or ethical reasons.

## The Field Experiment

The field experiment has several attractive features. Above all, its life-like settings may increase the generality of findings (external validity), overcoming one of the major shortcomings of laboratory experimentation. It is as close to real life as one can get. Conducting the study in the day-to-day setting helps minimize subject awareness of the experimental treatment and the measured dependent variables. Moreover, it is appropriate for studying problems that cannot be artificially created or that would be changed dynamically if investigated in a laboratory context. Also, the field experiment is useful both for testing theory and for addressing practical problems.

The major disadvantage of this technique is that it usually lacks the precision and control (internal validity) that characterize good laboratory research. Another deterrent is that the field experiment may require more time and effort, in terms of planning, execution, and public relations, than a laboratory experiment. Field experiments also can be more expensive than laboratory experiments. Another drawback is the difficulty of adapting apparatus, materials, and measures of the dependent variable to the field setting so that they blend into the natural environment. This sometimes leads to compromises, for the sake of unobtrusiveness, that adversely affect the overall quality of the experiment.

**SYNOPSIS 8.1**

## Consumer Response to In-store Price Information Environments

Research strategy: Experiment (laboratory)
Data collection technique: Questionnaire

### STATEMENT OF PROBLEM

The primary purpose of this study was to evaluate the impact of different in-store information environments on consumers' processing of price information.

Eight hypotheses were tested in this experiment. For simplification, only one of the hypotheses is illustrated here.

#### HYPOTHESIS

Item marking will decrease errors in recall of the exact prices of products.

### THEORETICAL FOUNDATION

A conceptual model developed by Jacoby and Olson (1977), depicting the steps in the processing of price information, was one of the models used in this study. This model divides consumer reactions to prices into three stages: cognition (encoding of objective price and storage of psychological price), affect (attitude toward price), and behavior (responses to price, such as purchase).

Hypothesis 1 in our illustration involves the cognitive stage. Subjects' familiarity with information influences subsequent processing. Information that is familiar tends to be processed more readily than unfamiliar information because it is compatible with existing cognitive structures (Craik and Lockhart 1972). Because item marking is familiar to consumers and absence of item marking is not, it was hypothesized that item marking will decrease errors in recall of the exact prices of products. (At the time this research was conducted, no major grocery chain had removed item marks from products.)

## METHOD

### SAMPLE

Subjects were female primary household shoppers at least 18 years old in Columbus, Ohio. They were selected on an every-*n*th-name basis from a computerized mailing list compiled by a market research firm. Women selected were telephoned and screened to determine whether they qualified. After agreeing to participate in the experiment, subjects were randomly assigned to eight experimental cells.

### MATERIALS AND PROCEDURES

#### *Laboratory Environment*

A 24-foot grocery aisle was simulated and equipped with 90 different brands and sizes of products in 12 categories.

#### *Questionnaire*

Subjects were asked to recall both the exact and the relative price of products.

#### *Procedures*

During half of the experiment, products were displayed with their item prices. During the other half of the experiment, items were price stamped with a standard ink price marker.

Subjects entered the laboratory individually and were greeted by an experimenter, who disguised the nature of the study, claiming its purpose was to compare shopping habits of women in different cities in the United States. The subject was given a shopping list itemizing 12 product categories. She was instructed to stay within a budget of $10 and to select one brand and size from each category. A stopwatch recorded the total shopping time of each subject.

When the subject left the experimental "shopping" room, another experimenter took her shopping cart and money and directed her into one of three booths to complete the questionnaire. She was asked to rank by price the 12 products she selected in the experimental task and then to recall the exact prices of the products.

After completing the questionnaire, the subject was debriefed by the experimenter, who revealed the true purpose of the research, explained the reason for the disguise, and apologized for the deception.

#### DATA ANALYSIS

The independent variable was level of item marking, which was operationalized as the presence or absence of raw prices on individual items. The dependent variable was a measure of cognitive effects—subjects' recall of relative (ranked) and exact prices of products.

Recalled prices were compared to actual prices and the percentage of recall error was calculated for each product by the following formula:

$$\% \text{ error} = \frac{\text{recalled price} - \text{correct price}}{\text{correct price}}$$

The summary measure was the average percentage of error for the 12 products selected by each subject.

Errors in the ranking of prices (price comparison) were tabulated by counting the absolute differences in rank units between the correct rank and the subject's recalled rank. The summary measure was the total number of rank errors over all sets.

Analysis of variance was the statistic used to examine the effects of item marking on exact-price recall error. Before applying this statistic, a preliminary analysis was conducted of possible intervening variables of encoding time, degree of sensory encoding, and brand loyalty and demographic variables including age. Pearson product-moment correlations showed degree of sensory encoding and age to be significantly correlated with exact-price recall error. Therefore, these variables were controlled in the analysis of variance.

### RESULTS

The item-marking effect had an analysis of variance $F$ value of 5.17, which was significant at $p < .0244$. Thus, the hypothesis was supported. The overall adjusted group mean for item marking was 17.53% error in exact-price recall, contrasted with 21.27% error without item marking.

### CONCLUSIONS AND/OR IMPLICATIONS

To reduce operating costs, managers of grocery stores with electronic scanners may desire to remove price marks from products. The findings from the hypothesis tested suggest that the price removal practice may have an immediate negative consequence. Consumers will notice the absence of item marks and will feel less certain about their knowledge of prices. If price knowledge is important to them, as this study suggests, consumers may be dissatisfied with the retail store and may even change store loyalties.

The author suggested that the methodology employed in this study could also be used to evaluate the effects of other information environments, including nutritional information and safety guidelines.

(Source: V. A. Zeithaml. 1982. *J. Consum. Res.* 8:357–69)

**SYNOPSIS 8.2**

# Influence of Zinc and Iron on Dietary Fluoride Utilization in the Rat

Research strategy: Experiment (laboratory/animal)
Data collection technique: Physical/physiological measurement

## STATEMENT OF PROBLEM

The primary purpose of this study was to provide concepts about the effects of dietary trace element supplementation practices on dietary fluoride bioavailability, especially with respect to fluoride originating from foods prepared in fluorinated water.

More specifically, two experiments were conducted to determine the effect of iron and zinc supplementation on dietary fluoride bioavailability. Experiment 1 was designed to investigate the effect of dietary zinc on fluoride absorption and retention and skeletal concentration of fluoride. Experiment 2 was designed to examine the effect of dietary ferrous iron on fluoride absorption and retention and skeletal concentration of fluoride.

## THEORETICAL FOUNDATION

Fluoride absorption from drinking water is essentially complete, in contrast to a 50%–80% rate from foods. Numerous factors may influence fluoride absorption, including physical interaction between fluoride and food components, physiological state, and interactions between fluoride and other mineral elements. Calcium, magnesium, and aluminum, for example, appear to form insoluble complexes with fluoride (Rao 1984). Iron and zinc can also form insoluble complexes with fluoride, yet many foods are fortified with iron and zinc to improve their nutritional value.

## METHOD

### SAMPLE

The sample in both experiments consisted of six male rats assigned to each of six treatments. The rats were outbred Sprague-Dawley albino rats, with an initial age of 25 days and a weight of 70 grams.

### MATERIALS AND PROCEDURES

*Experiment 1 Diets*

A basal diet without zinc was prepared. From this mix, six individual diets were prepared by adding zinc as $ZnSO_4 \cdot 7H_2O$ and fluoride as NaF, with glucose as a carrier, to provide (a) 6 ppm Zn, (b) 30 ppm Zn, and (c) 150 ppm Zn. Each of these diets had either 2 or 10 ppm F.

*Experiment 2 Diets*

The basal diet for this experiment was identical to that of Experiment 1 except that zinc was added to the mineral mixture (.3846 g $ZnCO_3$) to provide a normal dietary zinc concentration of 12 ppm. Iron was omitted in this experiment, with a small adjustment in sodium chloride addition.

*Procedures*

Six of the rats were assigned to each of the six treatments (diets) in both experiments. Each rat was individually housed in a suspended, stainless-steel cage in a temperature- and light-controlled animal room. They had free access to the powdered diet, provided in glass food jars.

Food intake was measured every 2 days. Intake was also determined daily during metabolic collection periods. Midway through each experiment and again during the sixth week, a 5-day collection of urine and feces was made by using individual stainless-steel metabolic cages. At the end of the sixth week, the rats were killed by decapitation after blood was drawn from the abdominal aorta under light sodium pentobarbital anesthesia. Tibias or femurs of each rat were removed and stored in plastic vials at −20°C.

### DATA ANALYSIS

The fluoride content of urine and ashed bone was determined with a fluoride iron-selective electrode.

In Experiment 1, zinc status was assessed by tibia zinc concentration. Iron status (in Experiment 2) was assessed by liver iron concentration. Atomic absorption spectrophotometry was used for both zinc and iron analyses.

The statistical design was a 2 × 2 factorial with six replicates per treatment. Treatment effects were fluoride, zinc or iron, and interaction of the factors if a significant $F$ value was found for treatment effects.

## RESULTS

There were no significant differences between groups for either food intake or weight gain.

*Experiment 1*

Both the zinc and fluoride content of tibias increased significantly with increasing dietary concentration of zinc and fluoride, respectively. However, the 25-fold range of dietary zinc concentration did not affect either fluoride absorption, fluoride retention, or tibia fluoride concentration. Higher dietary fluoride did result in significantly greater fluoride absorption and retention than lower dietary fluoride.

*Experiment 2*

The results of this experiment—to determine the influence of ferrous iron supplementation on fluoride availability—showed hemoglobin to be significantly higher in the high-fluoride groups of mice compared to the low-fluoride groups. Fluoride did not influence liver iron concentration in this study. Also, both tibia and femur fluoride concentrations increased significantly with higher dietary fluoride concentration. Fluoride absorption and retention were significantly greater in high-fluoride compared to low-fluoride groups. This result was the same as that in Experiment 1.

## CONCLUSIONS AND/OR IMPLICATIONS

The Committee on Dietary Allowances, Food and Nutrition Board (1980) reaffirmed the need for fluoride for optimal human health in their recommendation of a safe and adequate range of intake. Fluoride bioavailability from foods is significantly less than from drinking water. Therefore, researchers in the present study sought to determine fluoride availability under different dietary supplementation practices, especially for persons whose total fluoride intake is from fluorinated water and from foods prepared in fluorinated water. They recommended, from this study with mice, that either iron or zinc be added to foods to improve nutritional value without compromising the availability of food fluoride.

(Source: F. L. Cerklewski and J. W. Ridlington. 1985. © *J. Nutr.* 115:1162–67, American Institute of Nutrition)

SYNOPSIS 8.3

# Social Support and Exploration

Research strategy: Experiment (laboratory)
Data collection technique: Observation (structured)

## STATEMENT OF PROBLEM

The major purpose of this study was to compare the exploratory behavior of children (identified as high-, medium-, and low-exploratory) in independent and adult support sessions.

### HYPOTHESIS

Adult support sessions will increase the frequencies of children's exploratory behaviors.

## THEORETICAL FRAMEWORK

Research shows growing evidence of a substantial relationship between some kinds of social influence and exploratory behavior. These relationships are viewed with respect to Vygotsky's (1978) concept of the "zone of proximal development." In contrast to regarding cognitive capabilities as fixed capacities, he thought of a child's potential in a range between independent task performance and performance in collaboration with a supportive adult or peer. The researcher proposes that if Vygotsky's ideas apply to exploration and curiosity, then assessment of children's exploration in any single context may not reflect potential for exploration accurately.

A survey of the research literature shows that one difference between studies that did and did not show social influences on exploration is the presence of a parent. However, consistent with Vygotsky's theory, the mere presence of a parent may be less important than sensitive, collaborative support provided by the parent.

## METHOD

### SAMPLE

The sample consisted of 97 children attending a middle-class daycare center or kindergarten and first grade classes in a public school in a small heterogeneous city in a southeastern state. The children were all those in the classrooms whose parents returned permission forms (approximately 80%) except for four who refused to participate or were dropped for technical reasons.

## MATERIALS AND PROCEDURES

### *Initial Assessment*

Three novel objects were used to assess children's initial levels of exploration: (a) a drawer box with 18 plastic drawers, each containing a novelty toy; (b) a wooden puzzle box covered with 20 different manipulanda (e.g., a light switch, a slinky spring); (c) a curiosity board covered with 15 manipulanda (e.g., a latch, a plastic box containing a small bell). The toys were presented to the child, who was invited to play with them and ask questions about them.

Children were assigned to high-, medium-, and low-exploratory levels based upon median scores obtained from 263 children in a previous study using the same objects (Henderson 1983). In the present study, children scoring above the median on 10 or more of the variables were classified high-exploratory ($N = 26$); children scoring above the median on 3 or fewer of the variables were considered low-exploratory ($N = 35$); and those scoring above the median on 4 to 9 variables were medium-exploratory ($N = 36$). These assessments were taken approximately 2 weeks before the independent and supportive sessions.

### *Independent and Supportive Sessions*

After the pretest battery was administered, children were randomly assigned to active interest or focusing conditions. Independent sessions followed the same procedures as the initial assessment. In these sessions, experimenters responded to questions by reflecting them, answering briefly if they were repeated, smiling, or nodding in response to comments, but remained as passive as possible. In the supportive sessions, the instructions were the same as for the independent sessions, but then for the *active interest* approach the experimenter moved closer to the table, leaned over with elbows on the table, intently watched the child, and tried to look interested. The *focusing* sessions were designed to model and encourage exploration activity. The experimenter expressed interest in several ways, including pointing out a novel feature of the object every 30 seconds, saying, "Hey, look at that," or making a positive comment about the child's activity. Each of the sessions was videotaped unobtrusively, with recordings being made of the predetermined manipulations of the toys by the subject as well as his or her questions, comments, etc. Time spent playing with the toys was also noted. To ensure standardization of experimental procedures, manipulation checks were carried out by examining videotapes of individual sessions. Interobserver agreement was at least 85% for all variables studied.

## DATA ANALYSIS

The independent variables were independent exploration session, active interest support session, and focusing support session. The dependent variables were children's exploratory behaviors.

Data were analyzed with a 2 (age) × 3 (assessment level) × 2 (active interest versus focusing condition) × 2 (independent versus supportive session) mixed MANOVA, with the last factor repeated.

## RESULTS

The results supported the major hypothesis of a positive effect of the two supportive conditions on exploration behavior. The multivariate main effect of independence versus supportive sessions was significant ($p < .01$), as were the univariate effects for questions, comments, different manipulations, and time exploring. An overall multivariate effect of supportive condition ($p < .05$) reflected univariate differences in favor of the focusing condition (over the active interest condition) for manipulations and time. Many other results of the analyses are also reported in this article.

## CONCLUSIONS AND/OR RECOMMENDATIONS

The primary results of this investigation, the facilitative effect of the supportive conditions on the exploration of young children, were consistent with Vygotsky's concept of the zone of proximal development. The susceptibility of children's exploration to social influences other than those of parents was also an important conclusion of this study. Previous findings on the effects of modeling on exploratory behavior were supported in the greater effect of the focusing condition on manipulations and time spent exploring in this study.

(Source: B. B. Henderson. 1984. *Child Dev.* 55:1246–51)

**SYNOPSIS 8.4**

# A Method for Integrating an Autistic Child into a Normal Public School Classroom

Research strategy: Single-case experiment (field)
Data collection technique: Structured observation (time sampling)

## STATEMENT OF PROBLEM

The purpose of this study was to investigate the feasibility of using behavioral techniques to integrate an autistic child into a normal public school class. (Autism is a syndrome including speech/language disturbances, attentional deficits, and withdrawal and impaired social relationships.)

## THEORETICAL FOUNDATION

A major weakness in the remediation of autism has been the lack of effective classroom educational programs and the almost total exclusion of autistic children from public school programs. However, the recent development of an educational technology for autistic children has resulted in new curricula and classrooms for these children.

At the time this study was conducted, the research in this field concentrated on (a) the one-to-one teaching situation and (b) the formation of special education classes solely for groups of autistic children.

## METHOD

### SAMPLE

The subject for this study was a 5-year-old girl with a primary diagnosis of autism from an agency not associated with the study. The child rarely interacted with anyone and engaged in bizarre autistic mannerisms, including frequent repetitive finger manipulations in front of her eyes and rhythmic manipulation of objects she carried. She also frequently masturbated in class. School officials decided to exclude her from the school system, but she was permitted to remain for the course of this study.

### MATERIALS AND PROCEDURES

The study was conducted in the kindergarten and first grade classrooms of an elementary school in Santa Barbara, California. In addition to the child and a therapist, both classrooms had a teacher, a teacher's aide, and 20 to 30 normal children. An observer was also present to record the data.

Three target behaviors were selected. They were characteristic deficits of autistic children, and they had to be modified before school officials would permit the child to remain in school. The three target behaviors were defined as follows:

(1) *Social behavior:* any response involving direct interaction with another person. Each response was recorded by a check on the data sheet, and the frequency of occurrence during a session constituted the measure of social behavior.

(2) *Self-stimulation:* any stereotyped movement (e.g., rocking, repetitive finger movements, rhythmic manipulation of objects) and gazing at objects such as pencils or lights. This behavior was measured with a stopwatch. Seconds of self-stimulation, cumulated for each observation session, were divided by the total session time to obtain the percentage of time spent on self-stimulatory behavior.

(3) *Verbal response to command:* any appropriate verbal response to a verbal stimulus presented by the teacher or therapist, either directed to the child individually or toward the entire class, requiring a group response.

The three target behaviors were recorded simultaneously in three 4-minute time samples per session, each separated by 9 minutes of no recording, giving a total measurement time of 12 minutes per session. Two sessions were conducted each week.

*Experiment 1*

(Although a second experiment was conducted when the child moved to the first grade and a new teacher, only Experiment 1 will be summarized in this synopsis.)

*Baseline.* Baseline measurements of the child's behavior were taken in the kindergarten classroom (with 20 to 30 other children present) before any intervention. The therapist was introduced as another teacher who would be visiting often in the future.

*Treatment by therapist.* A token economy was employed to dispense rewards easily and unobtrusively in the classroom. Three 1-hour pretraining sessions were used to establish tokens as reinforcers. A white poker chip, to be exchanged for a food reward, served as the token.

In week 4, treatment of social behavior in the classroom was begun. Each occurrence of social behavior by the child was followed by a token and appropriate verbal feedback by the therapist. During weeks 7 to 9, the baseline was reinstated to assess the effects of therapist treatment on social behavior. Treatment was resumed in week 10.

Treatment of self-stimulation was begun in week 10 also. Each occurrence of self-stimulation behavior was followed by removal of a token and the abrupt verbal statement, "No." Absence of self-stimulatory behavior for progressively longer intervals resulted in presentation of a token and a verbal statement, "Good sitting."

Verbal response to command treatment commenced on week 13. The child was awarded a token every time she answered a question requiring a verbal response.

*Training of teacher by therapist.* In weeks 14 and 15, the teacher was trained in general instruction, practice, and feedback techniques regarded to be effective in training teachers in generalized behavior-modification skills with autistic children.

Concurrent with the teacher training, the therapist began to reduce the token reinforcement. The therapist maintained behaviors by social reinforcement and intermittent tokens. During week 15, under the therapist's direction, the teacher began to provide social reinforcement and tokens for appropriate behavior.

*Treatment by teacher without therapist's assistance.* The teacher totally took over treatment beginning with week 16.

## RESULTS

The data showed changes in the child's classroom behavior on all measures. With respect to social behavior, during the baseline 3 weeks, the child exhibited fewer than four social behaviors per session. These behaviors increased immediately when token reinforcement was introduced in week 4. By week 6, a mean of 11.5 social behaviors was recorded. Social behavior in the trained teacher condition remained as high or higher than during treatment by the therapist.

Similar improvements occurred for the other two behaviors measured. Self-stimulating behavior (ranging from 27% to 54% at baseline) decreased to a low of 3% during week 14.

### CONCLUSIONS AND/OR IMPLICATIONS

The child's final performance for each of the three behaviors treated improved sufficiently to ensure her continuation in the public schools. The researchers stated that their results imply that training classroom teachers contributed to the maintenance of treatment behaviors. This conclusion is supported by the fact that two of the three behaviors deteriorated when the child entered first grade with a new teacher (Experiment 2).

Since research on variables contributing to treatment durability is in its infancy, the researchers suggested that continued research in this area should be very important.

(Source: D. C. Russo and R. L. Koegel. 1977. *J. Appl. Behav. Anal.* 10:579–90)

## NOTES

1. This is called *pretesting,* the same term used in Chapters 3 and 6 to indicate evaluation of a measuring instrument before it is employed in gathering data for a study. In the context of experimentation, however, pretesting refers to the actual collection of data by using some instrument to assess the dependent variable before the treatment variable is introduced, and it has nothing to do with judging the adequacy of a measure.

2. Researchers sometimes combine matching with randomization in a procedure called *blocking.* Subjects are intially matched on a key variable (or variables), and members from each block (e.g., males, females) are subsequently assigned to experimental and control groups.

3. Experimenter bias is not confined to research with human subjects. For examples of this phenomenon with laboratory animals, see Cordaro and Ison (1963) and Rosenthal and Lawson (1964). Rosenthal's (1976) *Experimenter Effects in Behavioral Research* is the best general treatment of the topic.

4. When designing a study, the researcher can employ some strategies that will enhance control: randomization, building conditions or factors into the design as independent variables, and holding conditions or factors constant. Another option is *statistical control.* Statistical control involves computational procedures applied to the data when they are being analyzed. Even then, preparation for its use must be done at the time the investigation is planned (Wiersma 1986).

5. Campbell and Stanley's (1963) terminology regarding the classification of experimental designs has been adopted here. The description of these designs and the discussion of factors jeopardizing their validity are drawn heavily from their classic treatise, *Experimental and Quasi-experimental Designs for Research.*

6. The problem of *reactivity* in research was introduced earlier. In an interesting series of studies during the late 1920s at the Western Electric Company's Hawthorne Works in Chicago, researchers found that mere participation in the experiment, rather than the experimental variable, seemed to increase worker productivity. A change in subjects' behavior, presumably attributed to the special attention they receive as participants in a study, is called the *Hawthorne effect.* See Adair (1984) for an interesting paper that reexamines this methodological artifact.

7. When the same subjects are exposed to all treatments, it is known as a *within-subject* design. When research participants are part of either an experimental or control group and experience only one treatment, it is a *between-subjects* design. In the former, comparisons are made within the subject for evidence of change, and in the latter, between subjects from different groups. Many studies contain mixed designs. See Greenwald (1976) for a discussion of these designs.

8. Replication should be done with different groups (preferably heterogeneous ones), at different times, and across different settings.

9. Among these strategies are analysis of covariance (ANCOVA) and use of a factorial design (discussed later in the chapter). In the course of an ANCOVA, the contribution of the one or more covariates (factors) to posttest performance is ascertained. This is done as a check upon the homogeneity of the within-group regression of the covariate(s) upon the criterion. Thus, even though there are distinctions between ANCOVA and a factorial design, both are capable of determining the contribution of initial differences to the posttest performance.

10. For more information on single-case experimentation, consult Barlow and Hersen (1984), Hersen (1982), and Kazdin (1982). Also see Valsiner (1986) for a discussion of individual-based inference methodology.

11. *Simulation* provides an effective way of approximating a set of conditions and artificially manipulating variables, especially those in the natural setting that cannot be controlled for practical or ethical reasons. Formally defined, simulation is "the construction and manipulation of an *operating* model, that model being a physical or symbolic representation of all or some aspects of a social or psychological process" (Dawson 1962, 3). With the help of the computer, simulation can examine the effects of a multiplicity of variable manipulations; reproduce and investigate situations that are rare, costly, or dangerous; and compress or expand time for study purposes. This vicarious approach to experimentation can quickly and efficiently generate large amounts of artificial data. See Abelson (1968), Dutton and Starbuck (1971), Federico and Figliozzi (1981), Graybeal and Pooch (1980), and Guetzkow, Kotler, and Schultz (1972) for an introduction to the topic.

12. The classic study based upon natural experimentation is reported in Festinger, Riecken, and Schachter's (1956) *When Prophecy Fails.* Other reports of natural experiments are in Ball-Rokeach, Grube, and Rokeach (1981), Colombotos (1969), Kasl, Chisholm, and Eskenazi (1981a, 1981b), and Williams (1986).

## CHAPTER 9

# Field Studies

Field studies refer generally to investigations that are carried out in field settings. Field research is the preferred strategy when it is difficult or undesirable to study phenomena out of their natural context. Kerlinger (1986, 372) defines *field studies* as "nonexperimental scientific inquiries aimed at discovering the relations and interactions among sociological, psychological, and educational variables in real social structures."

In this chapter, the term field studies will mean *nonexperimental* investigations, large or small, that study existing relationships and situations of people in their everyday lives and that do not attempt to manipulate or influence the subjects being studied. Today, field research ranges from investigations yielding highly standardized quantitative data in support of hypotheses to interpretative descriptions of social groups in the anthropological tradition.

## TYPES OF FIELD STUDIES

Although there are different ways to classify field studies, one way is to divide them into investigations that require *minimum involvement* of the researcher with subjects and those that require *maximum involvement* with subjects. The first type includes highly focused studies that involve transitory participation in the setting. They necessitate one or only a few visits to the field site and require minimal interaction with subjects other than that which is essential for data collection. The type and amount of data generated does not depend to any great extent on the quality of the interpersonal relationship established by the researcher with the subjects. In fact, if hidden cameras and recorders are used, or if observation is conducted through one-way mirrors, direct interaction may be avoided altogether.

If interviews or questionnaires are employed, the researcher tries to assume a relatively neutral role after having established rapport with the subject. Emphasis is on objectivity and the collection of complete and accurate data, which are usually quantitative in nature. Social exchange unrelated to the objectives of the study is minimized. Most research conducted in field settings falls into this category.

The second type of field study includes what is commonly referred to as ethnographic research. In ethnographic studies, the goal is a complete description and explanation of the culture, community, social institution, or social situation under investigation. They require the researcher to take part in the ongoing activities of the group and to establish very close relationships with the participants and capture their perspective. The researcher lives or works in the setting and becomes an "insider" to acquire a detailed understanding of the people and their activities and beliefs. In ethnographic research, maximum involvement with subjects over an extended period of time is requisite to gaining access to data and to interpreting data. Data are predominantly qualitative.

Since the first type of field research and its typical data collection techniques are discussed in detail elsewhere in the book (see Chaps. 7, 10, 12), this chapter includes only a brief description of these studies. The primary focus of this chapter is on the second type, represented by ethnographic research, with its cultural perspective and distinct methodology. Ethnographic research is experiencing a surge of interest among investigators in different disciplines, as is evidenced by the number of related research articles and books that are appearing in the literature as well as the existence of professional journals that are devoted to ethnography (e.g., *Journal of Contemporary Ethnography, Qualitative Sociology, Anthropology and Education Quarterly*).

## Studies Requiring Minimum Involvement with Subjects

The objective of short-term field studies that require limited interaction between researcher and participants usually is to answer specific research questions or to test preformulated hypotheses. These investigations call for contact with subjects only for the purpose of gathering data (there may be no direct interaction at all, as in unobtrusive observations), necessitate limited time in the field (perhaps only one or two trips to the field for data collection purposes), and lend themselves primarily to the use of quantitative techniques that generate precise numerical data for statistical analysis. Of course, qualitative methods of collecting data may also be used.

This type of field study is further characterized by a rigid research design, greater control by the investigator over the type and range of subject responses, and a probabilistic sampling procedure (unless the field situation precludes it). Usually based upon existing theory, these studies examine variables in a field setting or some aspect of the field situation that is structured enough to answer research questions and test hypotheses.

The researcher who decides to use structured observation in a field setting to test a hypothesis has a detailed plan, knows exactly what to look for before entering the field, and objectively and systematically records the presence or absence of certain events or preselected behaviors without attempting to disrupt variables as they naturally occur (see **Research Synopsis 9.3**). For example, an investigator interested in studying an aspect of children's social behavior in a nursery school situation might use an observational system with precoded categories and record behaviors on a time-sampling or event-sampling basis from an observation booth adjacent to the classroom or from within the classroom itself. A written recording format or a portable electronic digital recording device (see Fig. 7.2) might be used.

Field studies in this category are not limited to structured observation. Some research problems can be investigated in the field by using questionnaires, interviews, projective measures, and so forth (see Chap. 7). The use of multiple methods, including combinations of quantitative and qualitative techniques, should not be overlooked. Studies employing primarily quantitative methods may benefit from the integration of qualitative methods, particularly in the later phases of an investigation. For instance, ambiguous but provocative responses to structured questionnaire items may be followed up to clarify findings through informal interviews. Or a formal interview procedure may identify representative or deviant cases that should be studied more intensively with unstructured observations.

## Studies Requiring Maximum Involvement with Subjects

Ethnographic research requires maximum involvement of the researcher with the subjects. The prototype of ethnographic studies is the classic approach used by anthropologists who investigated preliterate and nonindustrialized cultures in depth by going to some geographic location; living among the people and learning the local language; studying the customs, rituals, and artifacts; and observing intimately the patterns of social interaction in the group. Their efforts culminated in an *ethnography,* or detailed analytic description of life and social structure in another society.[1] Gradually, the anthropological field study model has been adapted by researchers in other disciplines for studying aspects of their own society: its rural communities, urban ghettos, schools, hospitals, prisons, and informal groups.[2] These more recent studies of social institutions and social situations in subsets of larger, contemporary cultural systems have given modern ethnographic research an expanded meaning. There are a number of important considerations in planning and conducting such studies.

### Preliminary Planning and Problem Formulation

In planning ethnographic research, the phenomena to be studied are identified in a very general problem statement (Fig. 9.1). The problem statement may dictate a comprehensive ethnographic inquiry that documents a total way of life, or it may call for a more selective approach that concentrates on one or more aspects of life in the community (Spradley 1980). This vaguely formulated research problem implies foreshadowed

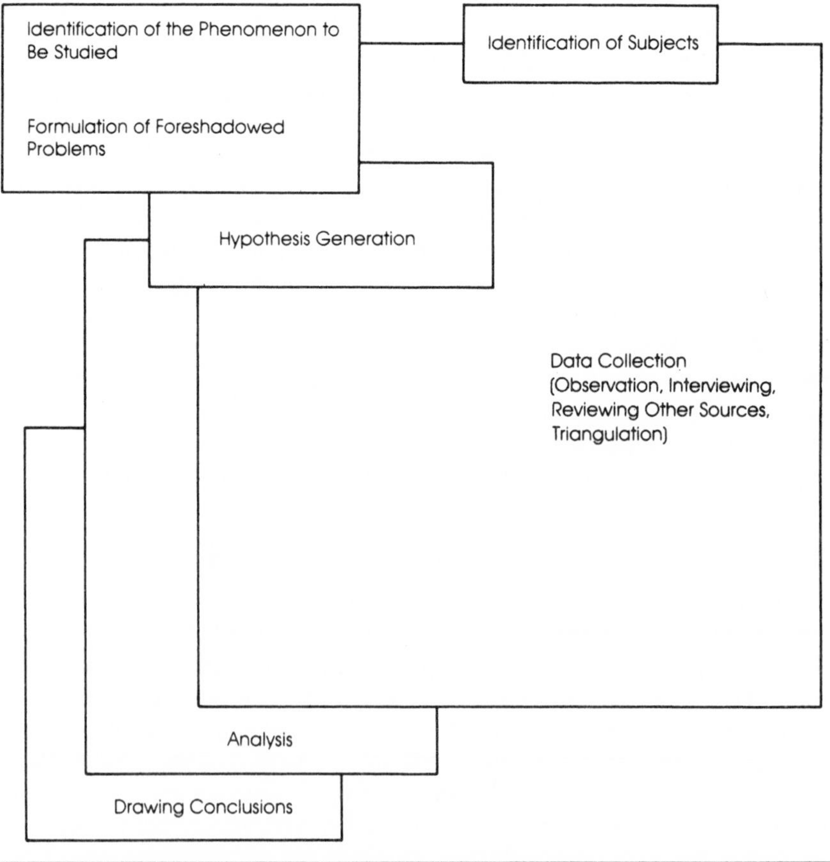


**Figure 9.1.** Activities of the ethnographic research process. (From William Wiersma, *Research Methods in Education: An Introduction,* 4th ed. Copyright © 1986 by Allyn and Bacon, Inc. Reprinted by permission.)

problems that provide a focus of interest for the study. Foreshadowed problems give some direction to the researcher, suggesting what to look for in the field, but they are not restrictive. Development of more specific research ideas may be postponed until additional information is obtained through "scouting expeditions" (Katz 1966), or periods of informal exploratory investigation in which the field researcher visits the proposed site or lives in the setting for a brief time. "Casing" the setting, so to speak, (also called mapping by Schatzman and Strauss 1973) helps the researcher determine the site's suitability and feasibility for the project, identify important variables in the situation, get acquainted with participants, decide on data collection techniques, and possibly obtain some baseline data.

With no formal hypotheses or preset plan of research operations to follow religiously, the ethnographic researcher is free to improvise and make changes as uncertainties of the field setting are encountered. As data collection proceeds, it is common for the researcher operating within this relatively unstructured design to reformulate the problem, generate hypotheses, and revise strategies for gathering information.

### Entering the Field

To conduct an ethnographic study, the investigator needs access to a site, to research subjects, and to documents and records available in the setting. Once a satisfactory research site has been identified, it is necessary to gain entrée to the field setting. Field settings vary in terms of their accessibility for doing ethnographic research (Spradley 1980). Some public places (e.g., street corners, beaches, buses) offer free entry, whereas others are limited-entry (e.g., schools, retirement homes) or restricted-entry (e.g., closed board meetings, hospital operating rooms) settings that require some type of permission before research can be conducted in them.

With few exceptions, before entering the field the researcher prepares a brief written proposal that includes his or her identification, organizational affiliation, and past training and experiences; explains the general nature of the study, procedures, and what will be demanded of the participants; and enumerates ethical safeguards that will be undertaken.[3] Supporting letters of endorsement may accompany the document. When informal groups are to be studied, solicitation of approval will be less official, but sponsorship of informal leaders is essential.

The researcher should expect some degree of negotiation with persons who are empowered to grant or deny access to the setting and be prepared to point out mutual benefits of the study, possibly alter original plans to suit the needs of the host, and even incorporate suggestions by authorities. Inevitably, there are compromises. After this initial clearance, renegotiations may take place. With the passage of time, the hosts might trust the researcher more and provide increased freedom of access. In this sense, field entry may be viewed as a continuous process and not a once-and-for-all decision at the beginning of a study.

### Human Relations and Establishing Rapport

Human relations is an essential part of all research, but nowhere is it more important than in field settings. The project will run more smoothly if amicable interpersonal relations have been established with top officials, other important personnel, or group leaders. Ethnographic studies involve prolonged researcher participation in the group, so field relations can make or break the project. Since the success of these studies depends so much on the willingness of subjects to cooperate, data collection may take a back seat to gaining acceptance and building trust at the beginning of fieldwork. Depending on the extent of disclosure to research subjects, the investigator's entry credentials facilitate the establishment of field relations by assuring participants and, especially, key people in the setting that the researcher is not a school administrator, undercover police office, reporter, or official of some kind who has been sent to spy on them. This goes a long way toward putting the subjects at ease and reducing their inhibitions.

Eliminating these initial concerns helps but does not guarantee smooth entry and the creation of rapport. Building trust is a difficult task that requires a concerted effort on the part of the researcher. It may take time. Social sensitivity, tactfulness, and integrity are requisite to the establishment of goodwill. Demonstrating an interest in the group by learning as much as possible about the inhabitants of the setting (e.g., their language, dress, attitudes, and habits) helps the researcher fit into the group and establish trusting relations. Gaining trust does not assure the researcher full access to all desired information, but it is a necessary condition for the collection of reliable and valid data.

### Assuming Roles in Relation to Field Subjects

There are numerous role choices confronting the researcher. Gold (1958) has described "master roles" that the field researcher can adopt. These are related to whether or not the investigator acknowledges his or her research responsibilities or conceals this fact. Following Gold's terminology, the *complete participant* is a researcher in disguise who becomes a member of a group under false pretenses and actively participates in the situation being studied. This role is selected by a researcher who feels that certain desired information might be withheld from an outsider and/or that the presence of an observer might unduly influence the subjects' behavior. Although the interests of science may be well served, the complete participant role involves deception and raises ethical problems.[4] Consequently, most field researchers assume alternative roles.

In the *participant as observer* role, the researcher shares in the life of the group being studied but makes it known that research is also being done. Activities as a researcher are subordinated to activities as a participant. This is the role taken by most ethnographers.[5]

Since the ethnographic researcher engages in sustained interaction with the group over a period of time, it is also necessary to make other role choices. Through the scouting expedition and other preliminary work, it is usually possible to assess the relationships among the subjects and the existing role structure of the group. This provides clues about where the researcher is most likely to fit within that structure. Naturally, occupancy of certain roles in an ongoing social system may be influenced by personal attributes such as age, sex, race, or certification. As McCall and Simmons (1969, 29) point out, the role adopted by or assigned to the field researcher will have implications for data collection: "Every role is an avenue to certain types of information but is also an automatic barrier to certain other types. The role assumed by the observer largely determines where he can go, what he can do, whom he can interact with, what he can inquire about, what he can see, and what he can be told."

The researcher should assume a role that will provide access to information that is most important for the objectives of the study. This may require some renegotiation of roles as the study develops.[6]

### Collecting, Recording, and Analyzing Data

Earlier a distinction was made between two classes of data collection strategies employed in field studies: qualitative and quantitative techniques. Since qualitative techniques are well suited for ethnographic studies, this section focuses on ways the researcher can collect, record, and analyze these data, with only brief mention of quantitative and mixed methods.

Qualitative Methods of Data Collection. Patton (1980) has referred to qualitative research methods as holistic-inductive approaches used in the context of naturalistic inquiry. Qualitative strategies are *holistic* in that they seek to understand phenomena and situations as a totality and they typically employ multiple data gathering techniques that contribute to a complete picture of a particular situation. Qualitative methods are primarily *inductive* because, unlike in the hypothetico-deductive approach, usually no prior assumptions are made about the relationships among narrowly defined variables and no specific hypotheses are formulated before the study. Instead, the researcher is likely to begin with observations and build toward general patterns, with categories or important dimensions emerging from the data.

Qualitative methods lend themselves well to *naturalistic inquiry,* or the study of phenomena in their naturally occurring state, because data collection is informal. Nonquantitative assessment techniques are especially appropriate not only when there are no predetermined hypotheses but also when hypotheses that have been formulated cannot be operationalized in quantitative terms or when field subjects are likely to alter their normal behavior in response to being studied with standardized measurement techniques (Dooley 1984).

The central technique of qualitative data collection in ethnographic studies is *participant observation,* which immerses the researcher in the everyday lives and activities of the people being studied and at the same time allows him or her to gather relevant information.[7] Participant observation includes wide-focused, informal descriptive observations that may become more selective with the passage of time. While participating in the group and observing, the researcher also conducts unstructured or semistructured interviews and collects and analyzes documents that provide additional information about the cultural scene, group, or social situation. (See **Research Synopses 9.1, 9.2,** and **9.4.**) As data are accumulated by various means, the ethnographer may adapt techniques to the situation and choose to redirect future observations, pursue new lines of investigation through interviews, or locate and examine pertinent documents and records such as journalistic accounts, archives, budgetary records, and official statistics available in the setting. Since the researcher is so "close" to the data being collected, concurrent analysis and interpretation of information are possible.

The flexibility, spontaneity, and open-endedness of participant observation make it ideal for studying many problems in the field. It can provide insights to the researcher that are impossible with other approaches.

Because a diversity of research topics and groups are studied via participant observation, there are no specific guidelines for field investigators to follow. However, Goetz and LeCompte (1984, 112–13) have identified some commonalities among the activities of participant observers across research problems and field sites and have synthesized them into the general framework below. These authors acknowledge that no participant observer will address all of these questions and list them only as possible areas of inquiry.

1. *Who* is in the group or scene? How many people are there, and what are their kinds, identities, and relevant characteristics?
2. *What* is happening here? What are the people in the group or scene doing and saying to one another?
   a. What behaviors are repetitive, and which are irregular? In what events, activities, or routines are people engaged? What resources are used in these activities, and how are they allocated? How are activities organized, labeled, explained, and justified? What differing social contexts can be identified?
   b. How do the people in the group behave toward one another?

What is the nature of this participation and interaction? How are the people connected or related to one another? What statuses and roles are evident in this interaction? Who makes what decisions for whom? How do the people organize themselves for interactions?

c. What is the content of their conversations? What subjects are common, and which are rare? What stories, anecdotes, and homilies do they exchange? What languages do they use for communication, verbal and nonverbal? What beliefs do the content of their conversations demonstrate? What formats do the conversations follow? What processes do they reflect? Who talks and who listens?

3. *Where* is the group or scene located? What physical settings and environments form their contexts? What natural resources are evident, and what technologies are created or used? How does the group allocate and use space and physical objects? What is consumed, and what is produced? What sights, sounds, smells, tastes, and feeling sensations are found in the contexts that the group use?
4. *When* does the group meet and interact? How often are these meetings, and how lengthy are they? How does the group conceptualize, use, and distribute time? How do participants view their past and future?
5. *How* are the identified elements connected or interrelated—either from the participants' point of view or from the researcher's perspective? How is stability maintained? How does change originate, and how is it managed? How are the identified elements organized? What rules, norms, or mores govern this social organization? How is this group related to other groups, organizations, or institutions?
6. *Why* does the group operate as it does? What meanings do participants attribute to what they do? What is the group's history? What symbols, traditions, values, and world views can be found in the group?

Being in the setting for a while should alert the investigator to the locations and times that certain events of interest are likely to occur. Although probability sampling strategies are seldom employed, the researcher attempts to examine behavior across time periods, settings, events, and individuals (Goetz and LeCompte 1984). The ethnographic researcher should also be prepared for unanticipated events that are worthy of careful observation.

Normally, unstructured observations cannot be recorded on the spot in their entirety because comprehensive note taking may disturb the naturalness of the situation. Consequently, note taking is ordinarily done in two stages. In the first stage, the researcher inconspicuously jots down brief notes to stimulate his or her memory when he or she writes up a fuller account later. These jottings include key words, phrases, or quotes, and may incorporate a variety of shortcuts to recording (e.g., shorthand, abbreviations, symbols, diagrams). To deal with the problem of memory distortions, it is helpful if the researcher can retire from the situation for a few moments shortly after an episode or on a regular basis to make field notes either by hand or with the aid of a tape recorder.[8] In the second stage, the temporary notes are converted into permanent field notes as soon as the researcher can arrange to be alone. Transcriptions should occur daily, preferably according to a fixed schedule. Routines are important in the field.

Unstructured observations in the field are supplemented by informal interviews. The field researcher may conduct interviews with selected persons who are willing and able to provide fairly objective information about events the investigator cannot directly observe (e.g., what took place on a particular occasion pertinent to the research) or with members of the group whose personal thoughts, feelings, motives, or interpretations are sought. (The use of key informants as sources of information has been a methodological mainstay in ethnographic investigations.) Although a formal interview schedule is not used, the researcher has a few general points in mind to cover, even though the sequence of questions and their actual wording will depend on the situation. Handwritten notes are made during or soon after the interview unless a tape recorder is utilized. Note taking procedures discussed for unstructured observations also apply to these largely conversational interviews conducted in the field. According to Junker (1960), about one-third of the field researcher's time is spent in recording data, approximately as much as or possibly more time than is spent actually observing and interviewing subjects.

The ethnographic researcher may decide to collect biographical information for analysis from an important individual in the group. This account of a person's life, obtained through in-depth interviewing, is called a *life history.* It helps the investigator understand the development and behavior of an individual in his or her cultural milieu, gain insight into social phenomena from the perspective of the person involved, and relate the abstractions of cultural descriptions to the lives of real people. Researchers employing life history methods supplement the interviews with documents and records, such as diaries, letters, and court records, as well as with information from persons other than the focal subject.[9]

Sampling. Some type of purposive sampling is usually employed in ethnographic research, with individuals (and situations) selected that in the researcher's judgment will yield maximum information and representative findings. McCall and Simmons (1969) have indicated that three types of sampling procedures are typical in field settings, including quota sampling (studying individuals from all categories), snowball sampling (subjects are identified by preceding subjects who have already been studied), and deviant cases (examining cases that do not fit usual patterns), although other authors (e.g., Goetz and LeCompte 1984) suggest additional possibilities. Wiersma (1986) points out that, while random selection of sites may not be applicable (many ethnographic studies are conducted on a single site), random sampling at the site is not completely out of the question. Subjects might be randomly selected for observation or interviewing, and there might be random selection of groups, activities, or blocks of time for study.

Organizing and Analyzing Qualitative Data. The permanent field notes compiled by the researcher, which provide detailed descriptions of people, conversations, and events, form the data for analysis. They contain (a) information about the setting, including date, time, and place; (b) accounts of social interaction, together with their direct quotations, nonverbal behaviors, and duration; (c) the researcher's judgments about what the subjects were thinking or feeling at the time; (d) the investigator's subjective impressions about what he or she saw or heard; (e) notations of possible biases associated with the data due to researcher reactivity or changing roles and relationships in the field; (f) previously omitted information that has now been recalled; (g) reminders to seek additional information in light of data collected that day; and (h) analytic ideas and inferences. Information mentioned in (c) through (h) should be distinguished from the more objective descriptive data in (a) and (b) by setting off the former in parentheses or brackets. Whether the full field notes are handwritten or typed, generous margins are used to allow for making later additions, labeling analytical comments, and giving cross-references. Duplicating copies of the permanent field notes is recommended because it not only guards against loss of data but also permits the researcher to retain one intact copy of raw data in chronological order and to have others for underlining, coding, and clipping and pasting for filing and analysis.

There is no clear line of demarcation between gathering, recording, and analyzing qualitative data. These three processes are intertwined in qualitative research. The inferences and analytic comments made by the researcher in conjunction with field notes on any given day represent beginning analyses. But after being in the field for a certain period of time, the researcher will want to shift the emphasis from data collection to analysis. After the main analysis has begun, however, some limited collection of information may continue, particularly if there are gaps in the data.

Since the collection of qualitative data quickly results in an incredible amount of material, the mass of raw data must be systematically organized and classified so that it can ultimately fit within a set of integrated conceptual categories relevant to the research. One possible way to begin organizing notes has been suggested by Schatzman and Strauss (1973). They recommend that the field investigator label the notes as observational (ON), theoretical (TN), or methodological (MN). *Observational notes* are objective statements telling who said or did what in a situation. When the researcher interprets, infers, or hypothesizes in the notes, they are designated as *theoretical notes. Methodological notes* are those that relate specifically to research operations just completed or ones planned for the future.

Another useful aid in note taking is the preparation of what Schatzman and Strauss call *analytic memos.* If the researcher believes that it may be beneficial to elaborate on a particular TN but does not want to clutter the running record with these lengthy statements, he or she may expand on the TN or integrate several TNs in a fairly abstract statement that helps achieve partial closure on some idea. Analytic memos should be written on a different color paper to distinguish them from regular notes, and they should be filed separately.

Lofland and Lofland (1984) suggest the use of three types of files: mundane files, analytic files, and fieldwork files. *Mundane files,* organized like any business files using concrete categories, help the researcher systematically store information on people, organizations, documents, and forth. *Analytic files* are described by Lofland and Lofland as an "emergent coding scheme" that enables the researcher to extract from and order the mass of raw data included in the field notes. Creation of this separate set of files is a continuous process that requires creativity on the part of the researcher. Analytic files represent the heart of qualitative analysis of field notes. Finally, *fieldwork files* include material written by the investigator on the methodological aspects of the research itself, such as the circumstances under which particular data were collected.

There are many procedures for organizing and filing data that are quite satisfactory. A common pattern followed by ethnographic investigators is to carefully read and reread all notes and then index the material according to topics, variables, or categories in much the same way that one compiles a subject index for a book or designates labels for a filing system in an office. These categories or labels, written in the margins of the chronological field notes, are essentially file headings and serve as the basis for separate files. It is preferable to adopt a flexible classification scheme that can be expanded when new categories must be added or when other categories have to be modified to include subdivisions. Information that bears on the same topic is classified the same and is filed together. A given piece of information in the field notes may be coded in more than one way and will likely be filed under multiple categories. The availability of duplicate copies of the notes allows the researcher to cut up the materials for filing in different locations.

Filing puts the data in order and ensures efficient retrieval of information, both of which are necessary elements in the analytic process. The researcher should expect to do considerable grouping and regrouping of information into different files as analyses proceed and any new data are added. With the creation of more and more files, entries placed under previous headings may have to be moved around. (If lengthy interviews have been undertaken in the study, separate files may be maintained for them, in which case reference is made to the interviews in the permanent field notes.)

Qualitative data are analyzed primarily in nonstatistical ways.[10] The objective in qualitative analysis, according to Dooley (1984, 278–79),

> is to organize the hundreds of pages of raw observational notes into a meaningful mode. The essence of this task is the interconnection of discrete observations within a small number of conceptual categories. It is analogous to a jigsaw puzzle. The researcher fits and refits the pieces according to a variety of preliminary models until there are no or few pieces left over and the fit seems subjectively and logically satisfying.

A few major categories will emerge from the data after the material has been organized into files, read repeatedly, and thought about at length. There is usually a dominant theme that ties most of the categories together and provides an overall analytic structure. Schatzman and Strauss (1973) call this overriding pattern or model a *key linkage.* Once identified, this general scheme helps the investigator determine the significance of the various bits of information on hand and focus increasingly on some data while relegating others to secondary importance. This leads to the writing of an accurate and complete description and analysis of the data called an *analytic description.*[11]

Quantitative and Mixed Methods of Data Collection. Ethnographic researchers use qualitative techniques such as participant observation, key-informant interviewing, and collection of life histories because these methods produce data that reflect the perspectives of the people being studied. Moreover, qualitative approaches may be more appropriate for the investigation of certain phenomena. For example, largely unverbalized opinions of a group may need to be investigated with informal observations, although group opinions normally are assessed with quantitative techniques such as structured questionnaires or structured interviews. Depending on the variables being studied, a qualitative or a quantitative technique may be more suitable for the procurement of information.

Quantitative techniques may also be used to complement qualitative techniques in ethnographic studies (see **Research Synopses 9.1, 9.2,** and **9.4**). To illustrate, certain impressions that emerge from participant observation may suggest the use of quantitative methods (e.g., structured interviews, questionnaires) to provide more exact information, supplement information already gathered, and verify data collected from key informants and through other informal means. Another example is when a researcher engages in unstructured observation until the parameters of a situation are clear and then adopts a more structured approach that incorporates precoded categories involving selected variables. Or perhaps, following conversational interviews with people, the researcher constructs an interview schedule with only relevant questions that yield specific responses which can be easily coded, quantified, and analyzed.

The customary use of multiple methods and data sources, or *triangulation,* in ethnographic studies is a practice that should be encouraged in all research. The combination of methodologies helps the researcher understand the subjects and their environment in an integrative manner and also permits cross-validation of results.[12] The ethnographic researcher has been accurately portrayed in the literature as a methodological pragmatist.

In summary, ethnographic research begins with a minimum of a priori assumptions and theory and follows a flexible research plan. It usually represents an inductive approach in which hypotheses are generated after data collection is under way. It is based on a naturalistic and holistic perspective that studies people in their natural setting over a relatively prolonged period of time and views individuals and their context as a total situation. Ethnographic research seeks to understand people from their own frame of reference, and because of its phenomenological orientation, uses largely unstructured, or qualitative, methods of data collection that assist in tapping the subjective aspects of behavior. Analysis of data is primarily descriptive rather than statistical. However, it must be emphasized that qualitative research and ethnographic research are not necessarily synonymous. That is, not all qualitative studies are ethnographic in nature, nor are ethnographic studies restricted to qualitative techniques. In fact, ethnographic research may use quantitative methods when they are appropriate. Qualitative techniques of gathering data are but one element of ethnographic research, so a researcher can be using so-called ethnographic techniques but not be conducting an ethnographic study. Ethnography is a methodological approach that includes specific techniques of data collection and analysis and whose objective is an in-depth description and interpretation of a culture or a subset of a larger cultural system.

## The Case Study

A type of field study called the *case study* is an in-depth analysis of an individual, a family, a culture, an organization, a program, or an event. Although the single-case methodology has had a long history and has played a significant role in research,[13] the concept of case study has not always been clear in the literature, primarily because it has been put to many uses and its meaning has changed over the years (Platt 1983). As Guba and Lincoln (1981, 371) have noted:

> Many different forms of writing have been labeled "case studies," as the following list suggests: individuals (developmental histories, etiologies of psychopathologies); agencies or organizations (social work agencies, banks, university departments); societies (nude beaches, community influentials); cultures (Trobriand Islanders, Potlatch Indians); movements (Yippies, Zen Buddhists); events (freshman orientations, presidential inaugurations); incidents (strikes, nuclear accidents); methodologies (an instance of use of critical path analysis, an applicaton of geocode analysis); programs (Comprehensive Employment Training Act—CETA, Head Start); projects (development of a new curriculum, a national study of schools, colleges, and departments of education). The range of information that has been included within a case study has varied from a few test scores for an individual to volumes of demographic, social, industrial, and cultural information for an entire society.

To further complicate matters, there is no universally accepted taxonomy for classifying the various types of case studies. Case studies may be undertaken with different purposes in mind, may be pursued at different analytic levels, may require different procedures of the case investigator, and may result in different products (Lincoln and Guba 1985).

Life history interviewing, participant observation, and other ethnographic techniques frequently result in case reports. However, in spite of the close association between case studies, qualitative data, and participant observation, it is important to emphasize that no particular type of research evidence or data collection technique necessarily leads to the production of case studies (Yin 1981).

Yin (1984) argues convincingly for consideration of the case study as a formal research strategy in its own right.[14] He contends that the case study is an approach that is especially well suited for problems seeking to answer *how* and *why* questions about complex, real-life events over which the researcher has little or no control. Conversely, it is not appropriate for questions regarding incidence. Yin (1984, 23) describes the case study more specifically as "an empirical inquiry that investigates a contemporary phenomenon within its real-life context; when the boundaries between phenomenon and context are not clearly evident; and in which multiple sources of evidence are used."

A versatile technique, the case study lends itself to exploratory as well as descriptive and explanatory purposes. Like alternative research strategies, case study research requires the same attention to issues of quality control, such as reliability and validity.

## Basic Designs

In conducting a case study research project, the investigator may consider using either a single-case design or a multiple-case design (Yin 1984). Within each type, there are two additional possibilities based upon the unit of analysis adopted: holistic (single unit) or embedded (multiple units). There are, then, four types of designs: single-case holistic, single-case embedded, multiple-case holistic, and multiple-case embedded.

Single-case designs are usually selected when the case represents a *critical case* (that tests a theory), an *extreme* or *unique case* (that merits careful documentation and analysis), or a *revelatory case* (that provides an opportunity to examine a phenomenon that was previously inaccessible to study). A holistic design that uses a single unit of analysis is chosen if the researcher is interested in understanding the global nature of a phenomenon, whereas an embedded design is chosen if the investigator wishes to examine specific subunits of a phenomenon.

When the case study strategy calls for investigation of more than a single case, it can be considered similar to the use of multiple experiments conducted for purposes of replication. The multiple-case study is inappropriate for certain purposes (e.g., examination of the critical case or the revelatory case). It also requires considerable time, effort, and expense. But when it is justified, a holistic or embedded design can be employed in each individual case involved, as with single-case studies.

## Conducting Case Study Research

Like all investigations, the case study research project begins with definition of a problem. This is followed by specification of the setting for the study (or settings if multiple cases are to be employed). (Procedures associated with selecting and gaining access to a case study site, as well as with establishing and maintaining good public relations in the field, were considered earlier in this chapter.) The general study design is specified in advance, although as with many field studies, the researcher must be flexible and prepared to adapt to changing conditions in the field if necessary. Terms are defined; field procedures are enumerated, including information to be collected and possible sources of evidence; instruments are selected and/or constructed; a timetable is established; methods of data analysis are indicated; and a basic outline for the case study report is formulated, including dummy tables that array categories of data being sought. A detailed plan of this nature enhances reliability, ensures complete data, and also helps the researcher anticipate problems that may be encountered in the course of the investigation. An explicit statement of methods and procedures is particularly important in multiple-case designs, where standardization of procedures across cases is essential. A pilot case study should be carried out to refine methods before data collection for the main study commences.

Evidence for case studies usually necessitates both quantitative and qualitative data, but it may include data that are either exclusively quantitative or exclusively qualitative. Structured and unstructured observations and interviews, participant observation, questionnaires, documents and records, and physical artifacts are all sources of data relevant to case studies. A frequently overlooked possibility in case study research is the incorporation of more traditional research strategies within the case study design. For instance, survey techniques (or even experiments) may be used as a subportion of the case study research project (Yin 1984). The importance of multiple modes of data collection cannot be overemphasized. Additionally, a detailed data base (e.g., case study notes, documents, narratives, tabular materials, microcomputer diskettes, audiotapes) should be created and organized to serve as a physically separate evidentiary base for the case study report.

The area of data analysis for case studies is not especially well developed at this time; it is the most challenging aspect of case study research. However, a few analytic strategies have been outlined by Yin (1984). Before initiating analysis, the researcher typically engages in preliminary manipulations such as placing the data in some temporal scheme; transforming qualitative data into numerical form, if possible, and coding the data; putting data into arrays, matrices, flow charts, and so forth; and calculating frequencies, means, variances, and so on. Usually guided by a general analytic framework (e.g., following theoretical propositions that originally stimulated the study or by using basically a descriptive approach), the investigator pursues more specific analytic techniques, such as pattern-matching, explanation-building, and time-series analysis.[15] Preparation of the case study report is usually the final step in case study research.[16] **Research Synopsis 9.4** provides an example of the case study used as a research strategy.

Case study research is attractive because it allows a comprehensive examination of one or a very few cases. In unique or revelatory cases, the case study is the only feasible way to investigate a phenomenon. The intensive study of a single case is often referred to as *ideographic* research to distinguish it from the investigation of large groups (*nomothetic* research) (Allport 1942). The ideographic approach provides a detailed and integrated picture of a person, a group, or an event—something that is impossible in nomothetic studies with their broader scope and limited number of variables. In large-group research models that focus on average scores and typical performance, information on the individuals who compose those groups is usually masked. While an average score may accurately reflect a group trend, it may not represent an actual score made by any single person in the group. Ideally, the ideographic and nomothetic approaches should be used to complement each other, such as using concrete cases to illustrate statistical findings. Finally, with careful planning, the case study can satisfy descriptive and explanatory research objectives; it is not limited to exploratory investigations designed only to generate ideas and hypotheses.

The literature is replete with objections to the case study. Case study research can be very expensive and time consuming. It normally generates voluminous data that must be organized and analyzed, and strategies for data analysis are not well formulated. A frequent objection is its susceptibility to data collection bias. (In defense of the case study, this same charge can be leveled at other types of field studies that employ observation, self-reports, and archival records as well as at documentary/historical and experimental studies.) The case study has also been criticized for its inability to rule out the influence of extraneous factors, which precludes the conclusive interpretation of data.

The case study has been viewed with skepticism because of its limited power of generalizability, but Yin (1984) believes that this particular argument is not completely founded because unfair comparisons are commonly made between survey research and case study research. In the former, findings from a sample are generalized to a population, but in the latter, results are generalized to theory. Like experiments, he says, case study research relies on analytical and not statistical generalization.

## ADVANTAGES AND LIMITATIONS

Because of the variety of research strategies used in the field, it is difficult to pinpoint advantages and disadvantages common to all nonexperimental field studies. For example, the merits and shortcomings of field investigations may vary according to the data collection procedures used. Most would agree that the pros and cons of certain qualitative methods are not necessarily shared by more structured quantitative techniques. To illustrate, participant observation makes it possible for the researcher to obtain in-depth material, facilitates redirection of inquiry on the basis of incoming data, and lends itself well to the generation of hypotheses. Conversely, participant observation can be criticized for being personally and professionally demanding and time consuming, for producing data that usually require laborious nonmathematical analysis, and for leading to interpretations that may be highly impressionistic. Field studies using quantitative techniques have a predetermined research design that prohibits flexibility of procedures and does not allow the researcher to get as "close" to the data, but they have the advantage of yielding data that are amenable to conventional statistical treatment and hypothesis testing.

Generally, however, field studies are attractive because they are highly realistic, heuristic, and usually less reactive than some other forms of research. They are also relevant to everyday social problems and issues. Additionally, the range of variation and strength of variables are greater in the field than in more artificial settings.

Negatively, nonexperimental field investigations are limited to the examination of relationships already in existence. Furthermore, the field situation is extremely complex, containing numerous variables that cannot be adequately controlled by direct means. Precise measurement of variables is not always possible in the field setting and sampling is more complicated. Other potential problems are feasibility, time and energy required on the part of the researcher, and special ethical problems raised in the field.[17]

RESEARCH SYNOPSIS 9.1

## Place and Personal Identity in Old Age: Observations from Appalachia

Research strategy: Field study (ethnographic)
Data collection techniques: Participant observation, interview (unstructured), diary, photography, cognitive mapping, questionnaire

### STATEMENT OF PROBLEM

The purpose of this study was to explore the phenomenon of attachments to place in old age.

#### HYPOTHESIS

The increasing mobility of current elderly generations is resulting in changing manifestations of attachment to place.

### THEORETICAL FOUNDATION

This study is based upon theoretical and empirical literature regarding sense of place and individuals' attachments to particular locales. Attachment to place is widely acknowledged to be important to the elderly, especially to those over 75 years of age (Gelwicks 1970; Montgomery 1977; Neugarten 1974; O'Bryant 1982).

## METHOD

### SAMPLE

The sample was selected during the first of 3 years of intensive resident participant observation of a panel of elderly residents of Colton, a declining rural Appalachian community, and its surrounding "hollows." Preliminary in-depth interviews were first conducted with 32 elderly persons. A sample panel was selected from this group to provide broad representation of Colton's elderly population. The final panel consisted of 11 women and 4 men ranging from 62 to 91 years of age. Seven participants were young-old (under 75 years of age) and 8 were old-old (over 75 years).

### MATERIALS AND PROCEDURES

The research process in this study involved becoming part of the everyday lives of the subjects (i.e., participating in routine activities and the full array of interactions that constitute the development of any interpersonal relationship).

Once a high level of rapport was established with the subjects, observations and informal tape-recorded interviews, as well as more formal data collection techniques, were used. Over 800 hours of unstructured tape-recorded interviews were supplemented by a variety of measures, including space/time/activity diaries collected over a 2-year period, cognitive mapping tasks, photography (including aerial photography of the area surrounding each participant's home), a significant places inventory, and a treasured personal possessions inventory. In addition, social support network measures were designed to elicit information on the social meaning of place.

### DATA ANALYSIS

Data analysis was primarily inductive. Tape-recorded interviews were transcribed and organized into categories. Data from the more formal measures were also interpreted in relation to the emergent categories.

## RESULTS

Although great variation was found among individual subjects, a pervasive theme of a sense of "insideness" emerged. Insideness appeared to involve a physical, a social, and a psychological or autobiographical affinity with the Colton environment (Rowles 1980).

*Physical insideness* included an inherent body-awareness of every detail of the physical configuration of the Colton environment. Each of these elderly participants had developed an intimate familiarity with environmental barriers, slippery places, etc., providing compensation for an unsteady gait.

A sense of *social insideness* supplemented the physical intimacy. The elderly were integrated within the social fabric of the community.

They became part of a multigenerational social order. At the same time, they were part of an age peer-group "society of the old." This subculture focused on the Senior Center and was sustained through an intensive telephone network and a distinctive set of values and norms of behavior. It was a helping group that invested itself in the welfare of its members.

*Autobiographical insideness* included not only present place but also remembered or "incident" places. It is rarely overtly communicated but is generally taken for granted. Physical proximity, while helpful, is not essential. Subjects had the ability to project themselves into environments displaced in space and/or time. Place, objects, and persons become fused, each becoming an expression of the other.

The analysis of data showed that while the old-old group, with a lengthy residence in the community, had a strong reluctance to relocate, many of the young-old panel members displayed far less vehemence in their reluctance to move, and their attachment to Colton space seemed less intense. This lends support to the hypothesis that increasing mobility of current elderly generations is resulting in changing manifestations of attachment to place. The young-old (under 75 years of age) appeared to be developing identifications with displaced settings that require vicarious involvement.

## CONCLUSIONS AND/OR IMPLICATIONS

It was concluded that relocation for an elderly person constitutes a critical threat to the sense of "insideness" that may pervade his or her relationship with a familiar environment. The investigator stressed that a fundamental reorientation of perspective is needed regarding the nature of old people's transactions with place. Emphasis upon the role of the elderly as passive respondents to their environment should be replaced with a greater emphasis upon their active role in creating places and imbuing them with meaning. The researcher in this study also suggested that practitioners and others concerned with the aging may derive solace from the possibility that components of autobiographical insideness may be transferable. When relocation is absolutely necessary due to declining health or other circumstances, some of the artifacts they surround themselves with may be transferred with them to preserve their identity.

(Source: G. D. Rowles. 1983. *J. Environ. Psychol.* 3:299–313)

RESEARCH SYNOPSIS 9.2

# Home Economists as Cross-cultural Researchers: A Field Study of Ghanaian Clothing Selection

Research strategy: Field study (ethnographic)
Data collection techniques: Participant observation, interview (unstructured), questionnaire, archival records

## STATEMENT OF PROBLEM

The purpose of this study was to combine participant observation procedures from cultural anthropology and social science research methods common to home economics to assess the cross-cultural applicability of the American clothing selection generalization: selection of American dress is based on certain aesthetic, psychological, sociological, economic, and physiological attributes of the clothing.

### HYPOTHESES

1. Ghanaian women will vary significantly in wax cloth selected when analyzed by (a) ethnic group, (b) age, or (c) occupation.

2. Ghanaian women will vary significantly in the relative importance they give to aesthetic, psychological, and sociological clothing attributes when analyzed by (a) ethnic group, (b) age, or (c) occupation.

## THEORETICAL FOUNDATION

The researcher states that the selection of a framework for observing clothing consumers' behavior evolved from the suggestion of anthropologists Bohannan and Glazer (1973, xii), who stated, "We are interested both in the common humanity and in the vastly different kinds of lives that human beings can lead—in the *common problems as well as the different solutions.*" Although cultures have arrived at a variety of visual solutions in their dress, all have followed some cultural criteria in selecting clothing for the body.

## METHOD

### SAMPLE

A sample of 99 women was selected from the Accra Capitol District of Ghana. Initially, these women were selected to represent equal numbers of three occupational groups: working women in traditional occupations, educated professional women in modern occupations, and Ghanaian university students (women aspiring to the modern occupations). The subjects were obtained through three sources. University of Ghana students were randomly chosen from a list of women students provided by the university. Professional women's names were taken from names of women returning to the university to update or further their education and from names of women employed in various professional capacities at the National Women's Training Center near Legon. Names of women in the worker category were obtained through the assistant director of the National Women's Training Center.

### MATERIALS AND PROCEDURES

*Participant Observation*

During the first 2 months of the study, the researcher spent time as a participant observer, with two general questions to guide her inquiry: (1) "Are there certain psychological, sociological, aesthetic, economic, and physiological clothing attributes which are important in selection of Ghanaian wax print textiles?" (2) "Do groups of women in Ghanian society vary in any systematic way in the wax print choices they make and in the relative importance they give to the various clothing attributes in their selection?"

Numerous activities were undertaken in order to provide a holistic picture of the clothing system from design and production, through marketing and selling, to final consumption. Among these activities were observation of wax cloth production; discussion of the Textile Designs Decree of 1973 and the design registration process with the Director of Design Registration and Protection, Ghana Textile Printing Company; review of the United African Company Trade Report Files from 1971 to 1976; observation of cloth distribution to textile traders; and observation of wax cloth apparel used in many occupational, family, and social situations.

In-depth interviews were conducted with 8 wax cloth designers, 10 wax cloth marketing managers, and 7 leading market-women sellers concerning production, distribution, selling, and use of wax cloth. A diary was kept for daily evaluation of personal feelings about interactions and observations to provide insight into the effects of the researcher on the quality of the observations.

Based upon the participant observation experience, three of the five original clothing attributes were selected for further examination: psychological, sociological, and aesthetic. The two hypotheses, stated earlier under Statement of Problem, were formulated for testing.

*Instrumentation*

A questionnaire, refined after pretesting with 18 home science students, was administered to the 99 women subjects. The first section of the instrument dealt with the prestige value and ownership of wax cloth. The second section requested the subject to choose, from among four wax cloth stimuli samples, the one she would most likely wear. The third section required a ranking of reasons for the choice among the stimuli cloths.

#### DATA ANALYSIS

Chi-square analyses were used for significant differences in cloth choices. Spearman rank-order correlations were computed for ranking of reasons for choices. A statistical significance level of $p < .05$ was chosen for this investigation.

## RESULTS

Wax cloth held high prestige value for the women in this study. Chi-square analyses showed no significant difference by age. Wax cloth ownership differed significantly by age ($p < .0001$). One-third of the older women owned more than 30 cloths. By contrast, 70% of the women under age 30 owned less than 20 prints.

In Hypothesis 1, (a) and (b) were supported. Ethnic and age groups differed significantly in the choices they made among stimuli cloths. Younger subjects preferred bright cloth, while older subjects preferred dark or more subdued colors. There were no significant differences among the choices by occupational groupings. Therefore, in Hypothesis 1, (c) was not supported.

Hypothesis 2 was not supported. The ethnic, age, and occupation groups had high correlations in the ranking of their reasons for their choices. These reasons, in order of importance, were aesthetic, psychological, and sociological, but not economic or physiological clothing attributes.

## CONCLUSIONS AND/OR IMPLICATIONS

The feasibility of combining qualitative methods of data collection common to anthropological research with more structured quantitative techniques common to social science research in home economics was demonstrated in a cross-cultural investigation. Several suggestions were made for other researchers planning to conduct fieldwork in other cultures, including a need for awareness of sex-role distinctions in the field community. Also, researchers were cautioned not to formulate definite hypotheses prematurely in field studies of this nature because of the possibility of narrowing the focus of study and precluding a valid assessment of the research problem.

(Source: M. A. Littrell. 1980. *Home Econ. Res. J.* 8:307–16)

**RESEARCH SYNOPSIS 9.3**

# Playground Designs and Preschool Children's Behavior

Research strategy: Field study
Data collection techniques: Observation (structured/time sampling), rating scale

## STATEMENT OF PROBLEM

The primary purpose of this study was to measure the broad range of children's behaviors in different playground environments. Several null hypotheses were tested within the following general null hypothesis:

### HYPOTHESIS

There are no significant differences in the amounts of social, language, or motor behaviors exhibited by children on the higher contemporary design playgrounds, as a group, compared to the amounts of these behaviors of the children on the lower contemporary design playgrounds, as a group.

## THEORETICAL FOUNDATION

In their review of architecturally and educationally related literature on playgrounds, the authors cite numerous conceptual or theoretical rationales for design guidelines for playgrounds. Callecod (1974) evaluated playgrounds in terms of challenge, novelty, and complexity. According to Berlyne (1960) and Ellis (1973), these characteristics should increase arousal and promote play behaviors.

The primary response to recent calls for playground design revisions has been a preference for what Frost (1978) refers to as the "contemporary" playground. In summarizing recent studies of outdoor playgrounds, the authors conclude that (a) children use contemporary playgrounds more than traditional playgrounds, (b) contemporary playgrounds support educationally valuable forms of play, (c) some specific characteristics (e.g., "encapsulation" or arousal level) may promote play behaviors.

## METHOD

### SAMPLE

Six outdoor preschool or day-care playgrounds were rated according to the extent to which they reflect contemporary design suggestions.

Three of the playgrounds received higher ratings and three lower ratings. These six playgrounds served as data collection sites. Schools were similar in fees charged and focus of their curricula.

Subjects were 72 children, 12 from each site. "Older" subjects had an average age of 53.8 months. The average age of the "younger" subjects was 41.8 months. All subjects were similar in family and economic background.

### MATERIALS AND PROCEDURES

*Rating Scale*

A 19-item rating scale was developed for use in determining the extent to which a playground reflected contemporary designs suggested in the contemporary architectural and educational literature. Items on the scale were divided into four areas: social/affective, cognitive, motor, and practical.

Items in the social/affective section were designed to measure playgrounds with characteristics such as providing opportunities for a wide variety of socal interactions, providing privacy when children wish to participate in individual activities or be alone, or promoting feelings of success by providing "clear accomplishment points" (Cohen 1978).

Cognitive items were designed to measure opportunities for children to explore, manipulate, construct, or experiment physically with materials and equipment. This exploration/experimentation behavior is often termed "mess about" in early childhood education literature.

The motor section included items measuring opportunities for body handling, object handling, and movement awareness.

Practical considerations included playground accessibility, protection from outside interference or natural elements, extent to which activities were appropriately joined or separated, and storage and maintenance.

*Observational Technique*

A time-sampling method was used to record children's behavior every 5 seconds for a 2-minute period in one social, one language, and two motor areas.

*Procedures*

Two persons observed each subject simultaneously. Using predetermined categories, such as positive social interaction, negative social interaction, language behavior, vigorous motor behavior, and locomotor behavior (which the researchers define and present in a table in this article), one observer recorded the social and language behaviors and the other recorded the two motor measures. Mean interobserver reliability ranged from .83 to .90. The vast majority of the data was collected in a 5-week period. Each subject was observed on an average of 27.7 minutes.

### DATA ANALYSIS

The independent variable was the extent to which a playground reflected contemporary design suggestions. The dependent variable was children's behaviors.

Data obtained from observations at the higher-rated sites (with more contemporary designs) were compared with data obtained at the lower-rated sites (less contemporary designs). A 2 × 2 × 2 analysis of variance (by design, gender, and age) was used to test the null hypothesis that there were no significant differences in the amounts of social, language, and motor behaviors exhibited by children on the higher contemporary design playgrounds compared to the amounts of these behaviors of the children on the lower contemporary design playgrounds.

## RESULTS

The null hypothesis was accepted. There were no significant differences between the measured behaviors of children on the higher contemporary design playgrounds compared to the lower contemporary design playgrounds. There were also no significant differences related to age. However, there were gender differences. Males exhibited more locomotor behaviors and females more balance behaviors. Males also exhibited more negative social behaviors.

Differences among sites were found when individual sites were compared to one another. Results of a series of 6 × 2 × 2 ANOVAs (individual site, age, gender) revealed significantly greater amounts of positive social, language, vigorous motor, and other desirable motor behaviors at the Site 4 playground. Equipment selection also varied (as measured by amount of time a child interacted with playground materials).

## CONCLUSIONS AND/OR IMPLICATIONS

The authors concluded that there are differences in children's behaviors on different playgrounds, but not strictly according to their reflection of contemporary design suggestions. Aspects of design that appeared to be most important included zonation, encapsulation (enclosed areas), and provision of appropriate materials (vehicles and a flat riding surface in this study).

Recommendations included a change in the forms of adult intervention on playgrounds. Teachers seldom interacted with children on the playgrounds, and at several sites they used the outdoor play period as their "recess from the childen" time. It was suggested that both in-service and pre-service teachers be provided information regarding the potential of outdoor educational environments. The challenge to designers suggested by these researchers is "the provision of environments that offer real rather than cosmetic design differences."

(Source: J. G. Brown and C. Burger. 1984. *Environ. Behav.* 16:599–626)

RESEARCH SYNOPSIS 9.4

# Implementing Organizational Innovations

Research strategy: Field study (case study)
Data collection techniques: Participant observation, observation (structured), interview (unstructured, structured), archival records, questionnaire

## STATEMENT OF PROBLEM

The purpose of this single-case study was to investigate conditions that inhibit and facilitate implementation of organizational change. To accomplish this objective, the study examined the process of implementing a promising educational innovation called the *catalytic role model* that was introduced into an elementary school. (This is a child-centered approach to instruction that requires teachers to radically redefine their roles and change their primary function so that they can serve more as catalysts, or guides.)

## THEORETICAL FOUNDATION

A major explanation for the success or failure of organizational change is that people are initially resistant to change, presumably because they are generally satisfied with the current state of affairs (Argyle 1967). Another aspect of the resistance-to-change rationale is that the success or failure of planned change depends on the ability of leaders or change agents to overcome this resistance. However, the researchers in the present study argue that this explanation may be unsatisfactory because it "ignores important considerations about obstacles to which members who are not resistant to change may be exposed when they make efforts to implement innovations, about the possible importance management, as part of the role set of subordinates, may play in creating or overcoming these obstacles, and about the possibility that members who are not initially resistant to an organizational change may later develop a negative orientation to it." They suggest that in-depth studies of organizations, such as schools, are necessary to examine the importance of this complex set of interrelated factors.

## METHOD

### SAMPLE

The case was a single elementary school that had 11 teachers and 175 students and was located in a low socioeconomic area of a large American city. It was selected for investigation because it was small enough for an intensive study, had a history of innovation, and at the time of the research had an "intense change-oriented atmosphere."

#### MATERIALS AND PROCEDURES

The study was divided into three phases. *Phase 1* (prior to introduction of the innovation and up to the time that implementation was begun) was devoted to defining the role of the field-worker; becoming familiar with the organization, staff, and students; and developing rapport with the people at the school. Additionally, some data collection was conducted. Unstructured interviews were carried out with subject matter specialists, teachers, and administrators to investigate their role perceptions and to obtain information regarding the school's normative climate and social structure. Informal observations were arranged in classrooms 3 days a week (at random times to avoid bias). Also during the initial phase, the research team examined documents and records available at the school (e.g., administrative reports, reports of instructional objectives prepared by teachers, teaching materials, teaching schedules, parent newsletters).

In *Phase 2,* the field investigator shifted the focus of his informal observations and interviews to examine "the attempt to implement the innovation." A few weeks later, structured interviews (using a formal schedule with fixed-choice and open-ended questions) were also incorporated to determine full-time teachers' perceptions about the innovation, barriers, and facilitators to their efforts to implement it, and changes in their feelings and perceptions over time. A modified version of the interview schedule was used with other personnel.

In *Phase 3,* structured classroom observations were undertaken. The teaching staff was also asked to fill out a questionnaire designed to obtain demographic information and data on career aspirations and job satisfaction and to complete the *Edwards Personal Preference Schedule,* a paper-and-pencil personality instrument.

#### DATA ANALYSIS

Data were reported primarily as frequency distributions, percentages, and means.

## RESULTS

Results indicated that there was minimal implementation of the catalytic role model. Among the reasons found were teachers' lack of clarity about the innovation, teachers' lack of skills and knowledge to perform the new role, unavailability of necessary materials and equipment, incompatibility of certain organizational arrangements, and low motivation. The first four factors were present at the beginning of the project and persisted, whereas the fifth one developed between the time that the innovation was announced and final evaluation of its implementation.

## CONCLUSIONS AND/OR IMPLICATIONS

The findings of this important study in innovation theory revealed the inadequacy of the resistance-to-change explanation because of its failure to consider the numerous barriers that can be encountered in the implementation process. It also demonstrated that resistance is not just an important precondition to be considered, but it can develop *after* an innovation has been introduced, even among those who initially held positive feelings about the change.

(Source: *Implementing Organizational Innovations: A Sociological Analysis of Planned Educational Change* by Neal Gross, Joseph B. Giacquinta, and Marilyn Bernstein. Copyright © 1971 by Basic Books, Inc., Publishers. Excerpted by permission of the publisher.)

# NOTES

1. *Ethnography* refers to an investigative mode and to the end product of this research effort.

2. As Goetz and LeCompte (1984) point out, by the 1950s there were fewer and fewer isolated aboriginal groups for anthropologists to study, so they adapted their investigations to industrial societies, a trend already initiated by sociologists in the 1920s and 1930s because of their interest in examining life in North American communities. Thus, the populations of interest and the problems addressed by the two disciplines began to converge, although a few differences in approach and method still remain. For a brief overview of the history of field studies, see Adler and Adler (1987b), Burgess (1982, 1–11; 1984, 11–30), Ellen (1984, 35–61), Goetz and LeCompte (1984), LaRossa and Wolf (1985), and Wax (1971). Examples of traditional ethnographic studies of other cultures include Malinkowski (1922) and Mead (1928). Adaptations of this approach to investigate aspects of American society include Becker et al. (1961), Dalton (1959), Gans (1962), Humphreys (1970), Liebow (1967), and Whyte (1955). See Fetterman (1984), Goetz and LeCompte (1984), Wiersma (1986), and Wilson (1977) for a discussion of educational ethnography.

Some anthropologists have expressed concern over non-anthropologists who claim to be conducting ethnographies. The controversy centers on the use of the term ethnography to describe research that employs only certain elements of traditional ethnography without sufficient attention to the cultural perspective. Goetz and LeCompte (1984, 18) suggest that many of these investigations that are not restricted to the conceptual and theoretical frameworks of cultural anthropology or that use them in combination with other methods and theoretical frameworks be called *quasi ethnographies*. There seems to be no consensus among (non-anthropologist) researchers, however, regarding the exact criteria necessary to label a study an ethnography.

Other distinctions can also be made about ethnographies, which further complicates the definitional problem. For example, some ethnographic studies involve investigation of a culture in all its manifestations (macro-ethnography), while others involve investigation of a social institution or even a social situation (micro-ethnography).

In this chapter, ethnographic research refers to both comprehensive studies of the whole range of experience of a complex society or a community and to studies of familiar social situations. Most ethnographic studies today tend to be limited in scope (i.e., at the micro end of the continuum), investigating a small segment of a culture. To be considered an ethnographic study, micro-ethnographies must be based on extended periods of participant observation and sensitivity to contextual and cultural factors. See Agar (1980), Bernard (1988), Dobbert (1982), Ellen (1984), Goetz and LeCompte (1984), Pelto and Pelto (1978), and Spradley (1979, 1980) for more details about ethnography.

3. A good sample of an entrée letter is included in Schatzman and Strauss (1973, 25–26).

4. See Chapter 17, which deals with ethical problems facing researchers in general and with special dilemmas raised in field studies. (See Note 3, Chap. 17, for specific references.)

5. According to Gold (1958), two other roles are possible, but both are more appropriate for field investigations discussed in the previous section, studies requiring little or no interaction with subjects. The first of these roles is the *observer as participant* role, which is chosen when the researcher's contact with people in the setting will be brief and relatively formal. Often, a researcher enters the field to administer a questionnaire, to conduct a structured interview, or to engage in naturalistic observation on a single occasion. The researcher's scientific intents are clearly established, and the project may even be publicly sponsored. The field investigator interacts with the subjects only to gather data and makes no attempt to establish enduring relationships.

The second role is that of the *complete observer.* Some studies conducted in field settings do not require the researcher to become a participant at all. When the complete observer role is chosen, the researcher does not interact with subjects nor become personally involved with them in any way. Rather, the field investigator studies naturally occurring events unobtrusively in shopping malls, at city zoos, on school playgrounds, or behind the one-way mirror in nursery school settings. Occupying this detached role enables the researcher to observe and record information in an objective and systematic fashion without distraction. Moreover, it minimizes observer intrusiveness. It can be argued, however, that the researcher does not develop full understanding of the people and the processes being studied unless he or she is more intimately involved in the social situation.

6. Janes (1961) contends that the participant observer's role goes through five separate phases, each closely related to the amount and kinds of information people are willing to share with the field researcher. The role "life cycle" includes newcomer, provisional acceptance, categorical acceptance, personal acceptance, and imminent immigrant. For more information on fieldwork roles, see Adler and Adler (1987a), Snow, Benford, and Anderson (1986), and Warren (1988).

7. Defined as such, participant observation closely parallels the role Gold (1958) refers to as participant as observer. For good discusions of participant observation, see Bogdan (1972), Bruyn (1966), Denzin (1978, 182–213), McCall and Simmons (1969), and Spradley (1980).

8. To ensure an accurate and complete record, field researchers are turning increasingly to the use of radio telemetry, still photography, cinematography, videotape recorders, and portable event recorders, as well as conventional sound recorders (see Collier 1970; Michaelis 1955; Touliatos and Compton 1983, 140–56; Werner and Schoepfle 1986). Computers are also being used increasingly to store and manipulate field notes and verbal protocols (see Clark 1987; Hymes 1965; Read 1980; Richards and Richards 1987).

9. The preparation of life histories has been discussed by Denzin (1978, 214–55), Dollard (1935), Faraday and Plummer (1979), Langness (1965), Langness and Frank (1981), Tagg (1985), Taylor and Bogdan (1984), and White (1952). Classic illustrations of this method include Shaw (1930) and Thomas Znaniecki (1927). More modern examples are Bogdan (1974), Bogdan and Taylor (1982), Chambliss (1972), Klockars (1974), and Turkel (1982). The

life history method can be used to study an ongoing life through interviews, as discussed here, or to investigate events in a completed life. The latter approach uses documents and records extensively and is common in documentary/historical research (Chap. 11).

10. Different approaches to qualitative data analysis have been described by Barton and Lazarsfeld (1969), Becker and Geer (1982), Blaxter (1979), Glaser and Strauss (1967), Goetz and LeCompte (1984), Lincoln and Guba (1985), Lofland and Lofland (1984), Miles and Huberman (1984), Patton (1980), Richards and Richards (1987), Schatzman and Strauss (1973), Taylor and Bogdan (1984), and Werner and Schoepfle (1986).

11. Surprisingly, little attention has been given to specific guidelines for writing ethnographies (see Brodkey 1987; Dobbert 1982, 309–18; Marcus and Cushman 1982; Spradley 1980, 161–71; Werner and Schoepfle 1986). However, numerous examples of ethnographic writing are available in the literature (e.g., Spradley and McCurdy 1977).

12. As mentioned in Chapter 7, the use of multitechniques in investigations of the same phenomenon is generally referred to as triangulation. There are different types. *Method triangulation* refers to the collection of data by different means, such as the use of a questionnaire that includes several scales measuring the same thing (within-method) or the use of dissimilar methods, e.g., interviews and observations, to measure the same unit (between-method or across-method). *Data triangulation* refers to the collection of data from different sources and at different times and places. *Investigator triangulation* refers to the use of multiple observers. Rarely achieved in research, *theoretical triangulation* involves the use of more than one theoretical perspective in a study. A "triangulated" study might combine interviewing, observations, standardized tests, and documentary analyses. The goal of triangulation is to strengthen the validity of findings through the congruence and/or complementarity of results from each method (Greene and McClintock 1985). As Webb et al. (1981, 315) have indicated, "When a hypothesis can survive the confrontation of a series of complementary methods of testing, it contains a degree of validity unattainable by one tested within the more constricted framework of a single method."

The best discussions of triangulation are provided by Denzin (1978, 291–307), Jick (1979), and Webb et al. (1981). Other related references include Fetterman (1984), Fielding and Fielding (1986), and Sieber (1973).

13. See Bolgar (1965) and Dukes (1965) for a historical overview of single-case methods.

14. Yin's excellent volume, *Case Study Research,* breaks new methodological ground in that it provides a detailed discussion of the case study from this perspective. The present discussion draws heavily on Yin (1984).

15. For a more extended discussion of case study analytic technique, see Yin (1984), as well as Bromley (1986), Lincoln and Guba (1985), and Miles and Huberman (1984).

16. Both Lincoln and Guba (1985) and Yin (1984) provide good treatments of case reporting.

17. For a more detailed treatment of these issues and other important topics in field studies, see Arnold (1982), Babbie (1986), Bernard (1988), Bogdan and Biklen (1982), Bouchard (1976), Burgess (1982), Ellen (1984), Emerson (1987), Goodenough (1980), Goetz and LeCompte (1984), Johnson (1975), Kirk and Miller (1986), Lincoln and Guba (1985), Lofland and Lofland (1984), Murphy (1980), Schatzman and Strauss (1973), Scott (1965), Taylor and Bogdan (1984), and Werner and Schoepfle (1986).

# CHAPTER 10

# Surveys

Surveys are an extensively used nonexperimental type of research in human ecology. This research strategy has many unique features, including the use of both sampling and questioning, as well as special problems, such as nonresponse, which justify its treatment in a separate chapter. Surveys deal with phenomena as they exist; they do not attempt to alter anything experimentally nor do they involve random assignment of subjects or conditions as in experimental research. As Simon (1978, 190) puts it, "The survey takes the world as it comes." Data for surveys are usually collected by asking people questions in the form of questionnaires or interviews. Survey research is quite versatile and fulfills many purposes.

## OBJECTIVES OF SURVEYS

### Exploration

When an investigator is interested in a problem but does not have enough information about the variables of interest to design a full-fledged study, an exploratory survey may be undertaken. Selltiz, Wrightsman, and Cook (1976) refer to this type of formulative study as an "experience survey." In addition to its value in problem formulation for more precise investigation or for development of hypotheses, the exploratory survey serves other functions, including

> increasing investigators' familiarity with the phenomenon they wish to investigate in a subsequent, more highly structured study, or with the setting in which they plan to carry out such a study; clarifying concepts; establishing priorities for further research; gathering information

> about practical possibilities for carrying out research in real-life settings; providing a census of problems regarded as urgent by people working in a given field of social relations. (Selltiz, Wrightsman, and Cook 1976, 91)

The exploratory probing carried out in the experience survey does not involve probability sampling but does require careful selection of respondents to ensure collection of relevant data. Although exploratory surveys yield descriptive statistics, their primary function is not that of obtaining precise descriptions of selected populations.

## Description

The aim of some surveys is simply to provide accurate information about people—individuals, organizations, cities, nations, or any social group. They seek to arrive at comprehensive quantitative descriptions of the characteristics of some defined population or a sample of that population. In inquiring about the status quo, they ask about what exists without regard for why it exists. Surveys of this nature are the source of information on the incidence of divorce, crime, drug abuse, heart disease, unemployment, and so on. Surveys can describe things or events (e.g., number of hotel rooms in a city, acreage of grain planted, number of microcomputers in a school distirct) as well as people.

One descriptive survey familiar to people in the United States is the decennial census. This enormous project produces a population count that is the basis for assignment of seats to the U.S. House of Representatives and for funding to cities, and it yields demographic data on citizens (e.g., age, sex, race, employment status, income, housing, household composition) for the benefit of government agencies. Surveys that collect evidence concerning the state of affairs are important; they can have significant policy implications for schools, communities, and governmental organizations. They often provide justification for current practices, serve as the basis for formulating new plans to improve conditions and procedures, or help assess the adequacy of status relative to available norms or established standards (Van Dalen 1979).

Most descriptive surveys move beyond the mere collection of data on simple demographic facts. They examine the relationships between variables such as sex and income, occupation and political affiliation, or race and educational attainment. Or they look at the relationships between more complex variables (such as beliefs, attitudes, opinions, preferences, and motivations) and other behaviors. Descriptive surveys may also investigate combinations of those variables that have some theoretical basis. For example, a researcher may use a survey to assess the relationship between educational level and attitudes toward child rearing, race and voting behavior, family living arrangement and school achievement, and sex and self-esteem.[1]

In descriptive surveys designed to study relations, the determination of patterns of relationships is done without an explanatory purpose (i.e., reference to possible causation). However, they usually pose specific questions and may be accompanied by tests of hypotheses.

## Explanation

Descriptive and explanatory surveys share some common features: both require the careful operationalization of variables under study, they may deal with similar data, and they may use some of the same statistical methods. By suggesting fruitful hypotheses, descriptive surveys often provide the foundation for explanatory studies. The major difference between the two surveys is that the primary goal of explanatory surveys is the explanation of relationships and not just the assessment of the incidence, distribution, or interrelationships among variables, although the two functions may be combined in the same study. Whereas descriptive surveys attempt to describe phenomena and possibly show how they go together, explanatory surveys not only try to establish what variables are related but are also concerned with what variables lead to or "cause" other variables. In other words, explanatory surveys attempt to answer why.

The objective of nonexperimental studies such as explanatory surveys is similar to that of experiments—to test hypotheses concerning the possible causal relationship between an independent variable and dependent variable. But in explanatory surveys, unlike experiments, the direct control of variables is impossible. Variables cannot be actively manipulated (either because they are not manipulable or because they occurred before the study began), subjects cannot be randomly allocated to groups, and treatments cannot be assigned to groups at random. The subjects are *already* delinquent, brain damaged, anxious, creative, intelligent, achievement-oriented, users of Brand X toothpaste, or whatever, and the investigator can only examine variables that may be considered antecedents (i.e., possible contributing factors) of these currently existing phenomena (i.e., assumed effects of contributing factors).

If a researcher wants to use a survey approach to study the factors that possibly lead to juvenile delinquency, he or she might examine the relationship of poverty, broken homes, and dimensions of parent-child interaction to delinquent behavior. Unfortunately, an observed relationship may be due to causes other than those the researcher has chosen to emphasize, and alternative hypotheses cannot be ruled out because of the lack of control of a multitude of factors in these nonexperimental studies. Therefore, the researcher may obtain evidence of concomitant variation or relationships and be able to speak comfortably of the "association" (correlation) between variables, but he or she is not in a strong position to discuss unequivocal answers to questions of cause and effect. For this reason, it is better to avoid the term *cause* and, if necessary, use words like *influences* or *leads to* when interpreting findings of an explanatory survey.

Correlation alone cannot completely prove causation.[2] When two variables are correlated, the researcher does not have conclusive evidence that the independent variable caused the dependent variable. He or she must consider the possibility that both are the result of a third variable, that the dependent variable has influenced the independent variable, or that possible independent variables (other than the one being studied) have led to the dependent variable. Causal inferences are hazardous unless the researcher can demonstrate that the variables under investigation covary as stated in the hypothesis, that the cause precedes the effect, and that other possible explanations have been eliminated by holding constant other variables that may have influenced the relationship. Some relatively new powerful statistical techniques that help the researcher make causal inferences from nonexperimental data are available, although results based on these complex analytic methods must generally be interpreted with caution.[3]

Despite the disadvantages of explanatory surveys, relative to experiments, these surveys will continue to be used because so many important research problems cannot be studied experimentally. Indeed, there have been a number of very important survey studies. One such landmark study was the report of Coleman et al. (1966), *Equality of Educational Opportunity*, published as a result of the Civil Rights Act of 1964. Another impressive nationwide survey is the National Assessment of Educational Progress (NAEP), an ongoing investigation of changes over time in the school achievement of U.S. children. Kerlinger (1986) comments that nonexperimental studies like these probably outnumber and outrank experimental studies in importance in the behavioral sciences and education.

## Other Objectives

Aside from the major objectives of exploration, description, and explanation, surveys can be utilized for other related purposes. In evaluation research, surveys are used to assess the impact of new programs, procedures, or policies. Surveys, particularly those using interview and questionnaire methods, are widely employed to obtain pretest and posttest measures of the dependent variable. Compilers of opinion polls use surveys to collect data for prediction studies to forecast elections. Surveys are utilized extensively as a basis, in part, in the construction of measuring instruments. In addition, survey research is employed to develop *social indicators*. These regular reports on the well-being of the general population, its physical and psychological health, leisure-time activities, satisfaction with government services, and so forth, are social and political counterparts to familiar economic indicators (e.g., wholesale price index, unemployment).

## CHARACTERISTICS OF SURVEYS

### Groups Investigated

One way to describe surveys is by the group measured. Survey research that investigates an entire population is called a *population survey* or *census.* Every 10 years, the federal government attempts to survey 100% of the population in the United States (but it always fails to achieve complete participation). For logistical and financial reasons, the population survey is seldom used in research with extremely large groups, but this type of survey is possible with smaller populations. Although there may be an inherent appeal to studying "everyone out there," the utilization of a carefully drawn random sample of a large population can possibly yield more accurate data than a total census.[4]

A *sample survey* deals only with a subset or part of a population. As described in Chapter 3, there are different ways to select samples. Use of an unbiased sample allows the researcher to generalize the results to the population from which the sample was obtained; it is a far more practical approach than a population survey.

Unless otherwise indicated, survey will mean sample survey in this chapter.

### Types of Design

Another way to characterize surveys is by design type. There are two basic designs in survey research: cross-sectional and longitudinal. Both cross-sectional and longitudinal designs attempt to draw temporal conclusions.

In *cross-sectional surveys,* information is collected at a single point in time with the purpose of describing the characteristics of a general sample of a population, identifying differences among particular subgroups, or assessing interrelationships among variables within the sample *as of the time of the study.* Cross-sectional designs take a snapshot of a moment in time where people at various levels that are attainable only through the passage of time can be compared. Examples of cross-sectional surveys are an investigation of attitudes toward marriage and family held by freshmen, sophomore, junior, and senior students in college, and a study of how attitudes toward retirement develop by comparing persons 20–70 years old.

The typical public opinion poll is also a cross-sectional study. Asking people who they plan to vote for in a political election gives an indication of voter sentiment at that particular time. The data can be analyzed by subgroups according to age, sex, social class, race, educational attainment, religious affiliation, and so forth.

Whereas cross-sectional surveys require the collection of data only once, *longitudinal surveys* assess subjects on two or more occasions with the same or similar instruments. They examine stability, development, or change in the subjects across a span of time.

Three primary longitudinal approaches are panel studies, trend studies, and cohort studies. When data are collected at different points in time from the same subjects, who are called the panel, the design is referred to as a *panel survey.* In a *trend survey,* a new sample is drawn at each measurement period to keep up with any changes that may have occurred in the general population. A variation of the trend design is the *cohort survey,* in which specific subpopulations, or cohorts, are examined as they change over time. A cohort is a group of people that have a certain characteristic in common, such as being born in 1950, graduating from college in 1965, or marrying between 1970 and 1975. The same population is involved throughout the research in cohort studies, but a fresh sample is selected every time data are gathered. Although there are many advantages to longitudinal research, a problem that plagues many of these studies is subject attrition.

## Methods of Data Collection

A third way to view surveys is by method of data collection. The primary procedures used to obtain information in survey research are personal interviews, telephone interviews, and questionnaires. Reports such as these are the best avenues for studying opinions, values, past behaviors, and other characteristics that are not directly observable.

### Personal Interviews

Personal interviews were described in Chapter 7, but some of their advantages and disadvantages are summarized here to facilitate comparison with other major survey data collection techniques discussed in this chapter. The *personal interview* is a face-to-face encounter in which an interviewer asks questions verbally and records the subject's answers. It is a flexible procedure that lends itself to the use of visual aids or props (e.g., food models used in 24-hour recall nutrition studies), permits the collection of supplementary information (e.g., respondent's nonverbal behavior, description of the home), allows the interviewer to probe for more information and the respondent to seek clarification of questions, gives the interviewer control over the interview situation, can be conducted with illiterate subjects, and is appropriate for relatively lengthy interaction.

Disadvantages of the face-to-face interview are its high cost in money and time, its susceptibility to interviewer bias and cheating, the need for supervision of interviewers in the field, and the lack of anonymity. Nonresponse also poses problems. If subjects are to be contacted at their homes, the increasing number of households with dual earners away during the day and the fear of crime may affect responses.[5]

**Research Synopsis 10.1** illustrates the use of personal interviews in research.

### Telephone Interviews

Telephone interviews have become a viable alternative to personal interviews now that about 95% of all U.S. households have telephones.[6] Past problems with social class bias in telephone surveys have been substantially reduced. Moreover, with random digit dialing, use of the directory is bypassed, and both listed and unlisted numbers are equally accessible.

Telephone interviews are the quickest way of collecting survey data, and they are far less expensive than personal interviews.[7] They facilitate the use of geographically dispersed and representative samples; surmount certain problems associated with in-the-home surveys by providing access to undesirable neighborhoods and locked apartment buildings as well as by overcoming the reluctance of people to let strangers come into their homes; involve callbacks that do not require travel and excessive time commitment; permit effective monitoring of interviewers, who usually work at a single location, even in national surveys; and may possibly produce more candid answers to sensitive questions by some people because of the impersonality of the procedure.

Recent advances in computer technology have made the telephone an even more attractive option for conducting structured interviews. Computer-Assisted Telephone Interviewing (CATI) enables an interviewer seated at a computer terminal to read the questions shown on the video screen and to enter the responses given by the subject directly into the computer as the interview progresses.[8] The computer is programmed to customize and personalize each interview. Data coding, editing, and tabulation are entirely automated, and certain monitoring features incorporated into CATI facilitate the maintenance of information on completed interviews, retries, and refusals and permit the generation of status reports on the study. It is also possible to monitor interviewer performance by using multiple interviewers located at other terminals. More recently, the human interviewer has been eliminated altogether in telephone surveys, and the subject is interviewed "by computer." The answers to questions are recorded by voice or by having the subject punch certain numbers on the telephone. Some day, the videophone may find its way into survey research, making telephone techniques more like the face-to-face exchange in personal interviews.

Despite its virtues, telephone interviewing has some weaknesses. Although nonresponse is quite low, it is easier for a respondent to terminate an interview (hang up) before it is completed. Broken off interviews are far less common with in-person interviews. Other disadvantages are that the length of the interview is normally restricted to only 10 or 15 minutes, there is a loss of nonverbal information, there is a limit to response alternatives, the phone may be considered inappropriate by some respondents for personal questions unless prior contact has been made, and certain measuring devices that require the physical presence of the instrument, such as pictorial projective techniques or the semantic differential (Chap. 7), cannot be incorporated into the interview.

There may also be some minor differences in response style (e.g., declining to answer, agreeing with everything) between telephone and personal interviews, but research has generally shown that the two methods produce data of comparable quality (Jordan, Marcus, and Reeder 1980; Rogers 1976). Fowler (1984, 78) has pointed out that because of the overall advantages of telephone interviewing, "It is now fair to say that instead of having to justify the telephone as the method of choice, researchers are almost in a position of having to justify why they cannot use the telephone."

**Research Synopsis 10.2** describes a study using telephone interviewing.

### Questionnaires

Chapter 7 described questionnaires in general, so this chapter concentrates primarily on the construction and use of these instruments for distribution through the mail. A questionnaire is a formal list of items that the subject reads and then responds to in writing. It can be administered individually to people who go to a site like a university or research center to participate in a survey, or it can be given to groups of people simultaneously, such as family members in a home, employees in an organization, or students in a single class, a school, or an entire school district. The questionnaire can be delivered to the subject's home or office, left after a few instructions are provided by the researcher, and picked up on a prescribed date, as illustrated in **Research Synopsis 10.3.** It is sometimes used to supplement a personal interview: the questionnaire may be completed by the respondent as part of (during) the interviewing process (see **Research Synopses 10.4** and **12.1**), or it may be left at the end of the face-to-face meeting to be filled out by the subject and returned or picked up later. In many cases, the questionnaire can be sent to the subjects through the mail.

Because of their frequent use in survey research, the remainder of the following section is devoted to mail questionnaires, although many of the comments will pertain to all questionnaire surveys.

Mail Questionnaires. Mail distribution and return of questionnaires has long been a popular data collection technique in research. (**Research Synopsis 10.5** presents a study using mailed questionnaires.) Despite many advantages, a major problem with this method is obtaining a sufficient percentage of responses.

A number of factors influence the return rate (Harvey 1987), not the least of which is the letter of transmittal, or cover letter, accompanying the research materials (Ex. 10.1). The letter of transmittal that is sent originally with the questionnaire should state clearly the purposes of the study so the subject will be motivated to respond. What groups or individuals are being asked to cooperate and the value of the information they can supply should also be stressed. An offer to share the results of the completed study is often effective. If the study can be associated with a professional organization or institution respected by the respondents, the importance of the study may be strengthened. It often is helpful to point out the anonymity of the respondents and the confidentiality with which the data will be handled. The effectiveness of the cover letter is increased if it is brief, typed on the sponsoring organization's letterhead stationery, individually addressed, and signed individually by the researcher.

A number of other factors influence the percentage of mailed questionnaires returned. Greater return is likely when the questionnaire is short, the questions are easy to answer, and it is sent to respondents who are literate and not so mobile that they are unlikely to receive it. Naturally, a stamped envelope should be provided.

In many studies, an attempt is made to follow up the persons from whom no reply has been received. Various procedures are used. A common one is to send a card or letter within a prescribed period after mailing the questionnaire, usually by the return deadline or shortly thereafter. The follow-up card or letter should state in a direct, straightforward manner the significance of the study, the need for obtaining a reply from each person who received the research materials, and the willingness of the researcher to send a duplicate questionnaire in case the other copy is no longer available. Just in case a person has sent a reply while the follow-up letters are being mailed, the letter might say, "If you have not already returned your completed questionnaire . . ."

Even in studies where the replies are anonymous, an identifying number is necessary on each questionnaire or return envelope if a follow-up notice is to be sent to the nonrespondents. As each reply is received, the respondent's name is checked off.

Washington
State University

Department of Sociology / Department of Rural Sociology, Pullman, Washington 99164-4006 / 509-335-8623

Carole Abbott
SW 235 Spruce Street
Pullman, WA 99163

October 9, 1979

Is the place where you live desirable or undesirable? And, what makes it that way? These questions are being asked of people throughout Washington and Oregon this fall.

The high cost of building homes and providing desired community services makes it extremely important to understand the priorities of people in our states. This information is useful to many people, from elected officials to homebuilders, who often must decide which concerns get met and which do not.

Your household is one of a small number, randomly selected in a regionwide sample. In order for the results to truly represent the views of people throughout Washington and Oregon, it is important that each questionnaire be returned, and that about the same number of men and women participate in the study. Thus, we would like for the questionnaire for your household to be completed by the adult female who has (or shares) responsibility for making decisions about the home and community in which you live. If there is no one living in your household who satisfies this description, then the questionnaire should be completed by an adult male who has those responsibilities.

Your answers are confidential. Each questionnaire has an identification number for mailing purposes only, so that we can check each household off the mailing list when their questionnaire is returned. Your name will never be placed on the questionnaire and federal law prevents publication of results or any other use that would allow individuals to ever be identified. This study is completely voluntary. But, we do hope you will complete and return the questionnaire, especially since this is the first study of its kind ever conducted. However, if you choose not to respond, please let us know by returning the questionnaire just as it is.

Results of this research will be made available to elected officials and others concerned with meeting community and housing needs. If you would like a summary of the results, please put "results requested" and your name and address on the back of the return envelope (not on the questionnaire).

I would be happy to answer any questions you might have. Please write or call. My telephone number is (509) 335-8623. Thank you.

Cordially,

Don A. Dillman
Study Director

**Example 10.1.** Sample TDM cover letter. (Cover letter from a Total Design Method [TDM] survey conducted by the Department of Rural Sociology, Washington State University, Pullman, Wash., and Survey Research Center, Oregon State University, Corvallis, Ore., under a grant from the Western Rural Development Center at Oregon State University. Reproduced here by permission of the principal investigators, Don A. Dillman and Robert G. Mason.)

In general, the higher the return rate, the more likely the responses will represent the total group to whom the questionnaires were given. Respondents and nonrespondents might be compared on certain objective characteristics for which information is available. If the two groups are not significantly different on these variables, the sample may be considered representative of the larger population.

Total Design Method. Dillman (1978) has developed a standard set of procedures for questionnaire design and implementation called the *Total Design Method* (TDM). Adherence to details of TDM has consistently resulted in successful questionnaire survey research. Dillman's (1978; 1983, 362) suggested guidelines for questionnaire preparation associated with TDM include

1. Design the questionnaire as a 6½″ × 8¼″ booklet, using white paper to avoid resemblance to advertising brochures. Use of a 16 lb. rather than a 20 lb. paper reduces costs if the materials are to be mailed.
2. Type the questionnaire on 8½″ × 11″ paper and photoreduce it to fit the smaller, less imposing booklet format.
3. On the cover of the booklet, include a title of the project that is stated in a way to promote interest (Ex. 10.2). A descriptive subtitle may further communicate the nature of the research. A neutral but attractive illustration and special instructions to the subject are appropriate for the first page, as is the indication of the sponsoring institution or organization.
4. Do not include questions on the front cover or the back cover. The last page is reserved for a statement of appreciation to the subject, messages regarding sharing the results of the study, and an invitation for additional comments.
5. Arrange questionnaire items so that the initial question is interesting, easy to answer, and applies to all subjects. The most interesting questions and those directly related to the research topic appear first, whereas potentially objectionable items come later. Demographic items are placed at the end of the questionnaire.
6. On each page of the questionnaire booklet, use capital and lowercase letters for questions and uppercase letters only for answers, ask only one question at a time, arrange items vertically, use appropriate transitions, avoid overlap of individual items from one page to the next, and use arrows, indentions, spacing, and other visual cues effectively to provide direction (Ex. 10.3).

In addition, Dillman (1978; 1983, 366–67) has outlined specific TDM implementation procedures, which if followed along with prescribed TDM questionnaire construction guidelines, are capable of producing response

111198

**DO THEY MEET YOUR NEEDS?**

*A regional survey of WASHINGTON and OREGON households*

**Information concerning who should complete this questionnaire is in the letter you received. Your help with this study is greatly appreciated!**

**THE SURVEY RESEARCH CENTER**
**OREGON STATE UNIVERSITY**
**CORVALLIS, OREGON 97331**

**THE DEPARTMENT OF RURAL SOCIOLOGY**
**AND HOME ECONOMICS RESEARCH CENTER**
**WASHINGTON STATE UNIVERSITY**
**PULLMAN, WASHINGTON 99164**

**Example 10.2.** Front cover of a TDM questionnaire booklet. (Cover from a Total Design Method [TDM] mail questionnaire used in survey conducted by the Department of Rural Sociology, Washington State University, Pullman, Wash., and Survey Research Center, Oregon State University, Corvallis, Ore., under a grant from the Western Rural Development Center at Oregon State University. Reproduced here by permission of the principal investigators, Don A. Dillman and Robert G. Mason.)

rates of 60% or higher in mail surveys. The implementation procedures are as follows:

1. Type a one-page cover letter on the sponsoring institution's letterhead (Monarch-sized stationery—10½″ × 7¼″) explaining the significance of the research, the importance of the subject's participation (and its voluntary nature), measures taken to ensure confidentiality, who should and should not fill out the materials, and the reason for the identification number on the front page of the questionnaire booklet (i.e., follow-up) (see Ex. 10.1).

2. Individual names and addresses as well as salutations are typed in the type that matches the multilithed body of the letter. If word processing equipment is available, each letter is individually typed. The exact mailing date is included. The researcher signs each letter individually with a blue ballpoint pen, using enough pressure to cause slight indentations.

3. The research packet, including the cover letter, questionnaire, and business reply or stamped return envelope (6⅜″ × 3½″), is sent first class in a Monarch-sized envelope (7⅜″ × 3¾″) on which the subject's name and address have been individually typed. Address labels are not to be used.

4. One week following the first mailing, the researcher sends a postcard follow-up reminder to all subjects. Exactly 3 weeks after the original mailing, a second cover letter and questionnaire is mailed to subjects who have not yet responded. Seven weeks after the initial mailing, nonrespondents are sent a letter, along with the original cover letter and a replacement questionnaire, by certified mail.

Dillman (1983, 375–76) points out that a questionnaire developed according to TDM guidelines "that is designed to stand entirely on its own in a mail survey, with no direct personal contact, should certainly do no less well when delivered in person to potential respondents." Indeed, with the exception of his recommendations pertaining to the mechanics of mailing and follow-up, all of Dillman's suggestions are applicable even if the questionnaire is directly administered to individuals or to groups of subjects.

Questionnaires are more economical in cost and time than personal interviews; allow respondents to think over items carefully; induce subjects to provide honest answers to embarrassing questions because anonymity can be maintained; eliminate bias due to variations in interviewer characteristics and skills that plague many interview studies; and if designed properly, facilitate the scoring, coding, tabulation, and analysis of subject responses. Problems that beset the use of questionnaires include a literacy requirement, the elimination of subjects with visual handicaps, the lack of opportunity for probing answers or obtaining clarification of ambiguous questions, the generation of answers to open-ended questions that are

# YOUR NEIGHBORHOOD



Q-12 Which one of the following best describes the immediate area, or neighborhood, where your home is located? (Circle number of your answer)

1 COUNTRYSIDE OR ON A FARM
2 A RESIDENTIAL NEIGHBORHOOD WHERE MOST HOMES ARE SIMILAR
3 A RESIDENTIAL NEIGHBORHOOD WITH MIXED TYPES OF HOUSING
4 A NEIGHBORHOOD THAT HAS A FEW STORES OR BUSINESSES
5 A NEIGHBORHOOD THAT IS MOSTLY STORES AND BUSINESSES

Q-13 Here are some words and phrases which might describe your immediate area, or neighborhood. For example, if you think your neighborhood is noisy, please circle the number 1. If you think it is quiet, please circle the number 7. If you feel it is somewhere in between, please circle the numbers 2, 3, 4, 5, or 6 remembering that 1 and 7 represent the extremes of noisy and quiet.

| | | | | | | | | | |
|---|---|---|---|---|---|---|---|---|---|
| A | Noisy. . . . . . . . . | 1 | 2 | 3 | 4 | 5 | 6 | 7. . | Quiet |
| B | Friendly neighbors . . | 1 | 2 | 3 | 4 | 5 | 6 | 7. . | Unfriendly neighbors |
| C | Buildings are poorly kept up. . . . . . . . | 1 | 2 | 3 | 4 | 5 | 6 | 7. . | Buildings are well kept up |
| D | Safe . . . . . . . . . . | 1 | 2 | 3 | 4 | 5 | 6 | 7. . | Unsafe |
| E | A lot of road traffic. | 1 | 2 | 3 | 4 | 5 | 6 | 7. . | No road traffic |
| F | Crowded. . . . . . . . | 1 | 2 | 3 | 4 | 5 | 6 | 7. . | Uncrowded |
| G | Outdoor areas are. . . well kept up . . . . . | 1 | 2 | 3 | 4 | 5 | 6 | 7. . | Outdoor areas are poorly kept up |
| H | A lot of privacy . . . | 1 | 2 | 3 | 4 | 5 | 6 | 7. . | No privacy |
| I | Attractive . . . . . . | 1 | 2 | 3 | 4 | 5 | 6 | 7. . | Unattractive |

Q-14 Now, thinking about the best possible neighborhood in which you could hope to live, where does your present neighborhood stand overall on a scale of one to seven, where a 1 represents the "worst" neighborhood you could possibly live in and 7 represents the "best" possible neighborhood?

1 2 3 4 5 6 7

"worst" "best"

Q-15 If one or two things in your neighborhood could be improved, what things would you like to see happen?

---

**Example 10.3.** Examples of page construction of a TDM questionnaire. (Pages 3 and 4 from a Total Design Method [TDM] mail questionnaire used in survey conducted by the Department of Rural Sociology, Washington State University, Pullman, Wash., and Survey Research Center, Oregon State University, Corvallis, Ore., under a grant from the Western Rural Development Center at Oregon State University. Reproduced here by permission of the principal investigators, Don A. Dillman and Robert G. Mason.)

# HOUSING NEEDS



Q-16 Next we would like to ask some more detailed questions about your home and the extent to which it meets your needs. First, how many rooms do you have in your home or living quarters? (Do not count bathrooms, porches, balconies, foyers, halls, half-rooms, or any part of your house that is rented out to members of another household.)

_____NUMBER OF ROOMS

Q-17 During the winter months how many of these rooms are heated as follows. (Put appropriate number in blanks; total should equal number of rooms mentioned in previous question.)

_____HEATED TO 65° OR HIGHER 24 HOURS A DAY

_____HEATED TO 65° OR HIGHER ONLY PART OF EACH DAY

_____NOT HEATED AT ALL

Q-18 How many bedrooms do you have? (Count rooms used mainly for sleeping even if used for other purposes.)

_____NUMBER OF BEDROOMS

Q-19 How many bathrooms do you have?

_____NUMBER OF BATHROOMS

Q-20 To the best of your knowledge, about when was your home built? We mean first constructed and not when remodeled, added to, or converted. (Circle number of your answer)

1 1975 OR AFTER
2 1970 TO 1974
3 1960 TO 1969
4 1950 TO 1959
5 1940 TO 1949
6 BEFORE 1940

Q-21 Which of these broad categories best describes the number of square feet in your home? Do not include a garage, unfinished basement or spare room rented to members of another household. Just your best estimate is fine.

1 LESS THAN 500 SQUARE FEET
2 501 TO 1000 SQUARE FEET
3 1001 TO 1500 SQUARE FEET
4 1501 TO 2000 SQUARE FEET
5 2001 TO 2500 SQUARE FEET
6 MORE THAN 2500 SQUARE FEET

Q-22 Which of the following best describes how you would feel about moving out of your present home during the next year?

1 NO DESIRE TO MOVE
2 ONLY A SLIGHT DESIRE TO MOVE
3 A DEFINITE DESIRE TO MOVE
4 A VERY STRONG DESIRE TO MOVE

(NOTE: If you OWN the home in which you live please answer the questions on the next page; if you RENT, please skip to page 6.)

shorter and less specific than in interviews, and the likelihood that subjects will change responses after seeing later items.

Mail questionnaires share the advantages and disadvantages of questionnaires in general but have some merits and shortcomings of their own. Questionnaires sent and returned through the mail have geographic flexibility and are good for reaching people who are hard to contact, require no field staff, allow the subject to respond in private at his or her leisure, and eliminate any possible questionnaire proctor bias. In addition to low response rate, a drawback of the mail questionnaire is a dependence on sampling frames such as available mailing lists, which are not always accurate and up-to-date.

The relative merits of personal interviews, telephone interviews, and mail questionnaires are summarized in Table 10.1.

**Table 10.1. Summary of Typical Advantages and Disadvantages of Various Survey Methods**

| | Personal | Mail | Telephone |
|---|---|---|---|
| Standardization of questioning | Low (flexible) | High | Moderate to low |
| Speed of data collection | Moderate | Slow | Fast |
| Cost | High | Low to moderate | Moderate |
| Geographic dispersion | Limited to moderate | Wide | Wide |
| Influence of interviewers | High | None | Moderate |
| Supervision of interviewers | Moderate | None | High |
| Amount of data collected (questionnaire length) | High | Moderate | Low |
| Anonymity of respondent | Low | High | Moderate |
| Ease of callback or follow-up | Difficult | Easy | Easy |
| Response rates | High | Moderate | High |

Source: From *Exploring Marketing Research* by William G. Zikmund. Copyright © 1982 CBS College Publishing, p. 197, table 7.1. Reprinted by permission of CBS College Publishing.

Note: The emphasis is on typical. For example, an elaborate mail survey may be far more expensive than a short personal interview, but this generally is not the case.

## Other Methods

In addition to personal interviews, telephone interviews, and questionnaires, there are other modes of data collection possible in survey research. One promising approach that is closely related to these three methods is computer-interactive techniques. CATI has been mentioned as one type of computer-assisted survey technique in which the interviewer records the subjects' telephone responses directly into a computer by pressing keys on a video terminal. But the *research subject* can also answer questions by interacting directly with the computer in a formal research setting or shopping mall. With automated research questionnaires, the computer is programmed to give instructions and ask questions from a questionnaire constructed by the researcher; it displays the items on the video screen and the subject responds by using the keyboard. The electronic format of the "computerized" questionnaire has several attractive features, including automatically skipping questions if the subject answers a previous one in a particular manner, and randomizing the question order, if desired. After the subject has answered all items, the responses are scored and the results are saved for later analysis.[9]

Surveys can also be conducted via a two-way cable television system, such as the Warner Amex Cable Communication System's QUBE, in which the viewer at home reads questions displayed on the screen and records answers using the cable TV control box.

## ERRORS IN SURVEY RESEARCH

A host of possible survey errors that may influence the final results of a study have been identified in the literature.[10] These errors arise both from sampling and from the data collection process. There are two types of errors associated with sampling: random and systematic. *Random sampling error* is caused by chance variation in different samples drawn from the same population. These errors can be minimized by drawing a sufficiently large sample. *Systematic sampling error* may occur because of inadequate sampling procedures. For example, unrepresentative sampling practices, such as stopping and asking questions of only well-dressed people in a shopping center, or in a household survey, interviewing only those people who are at home when contacted, may bias the sample in a direction away from the population value.

There also are two types of errors associated with the data collection process. *Random data collection error* that may arise from the respondent includes his or her inability to comprehend certain questionnaire items or a failure of memory in answering some questions. The data collector also may produce such errors, which include the interviewer's mistakes in recording answers and inaccuracies in tabulating data. Random data collection errors are sources of unreliability of measurement. *Systematic data collection error* arising from the respondent includes the falsification of answers (so as to look good or avoid embarrassment); the tendency to answer *yes* to all statements, regardless of their content; the disposition to use extremes when responding; or the inclination to provide unusual responses.[11] Other systematic data collection errors are attributable to interviewer effects, missing responses to questionnaire items, and refusals to participate in the study. These errors tend to produce misleading or biased results and may thereby raise concerns about the validity of the data.

Nonresponse is a potentially serious problem and a major issue in surveys. The investigator may draw a large random sample but obtain a low rate of response, which can cause bias in the results. If nonrespondents differ systematically from respondents, the sample will not be representative of the total population.

Schuman and Kalton (1985) describe two types of nonresponse. The first, *total nonresponse,* is due to the researcher's failure to obtain data from everyone selected for inclusion in the sample (i.e., no information is collected from some subjects). Main reasons for total nonresponse are refusals, not-at-homes, ill health or senility, language problems, lost questionnaires, and inadequate or out-of-date addresses on the sampling frames.

The second type, *item nonresponse,* is caused when the research subject does not answer all of the questions asked. The respondent participates in the study and provides some but not all of the information requested. Item nonresponse may be caused by a subject's lack of information to answer a question or by the unwillingness to take the effort to recall the information or to consult necessary records. Or the subject may consider the question to be too embarrassing or to be irrelevant to the survey's objectives. Item nonresponse may also be due to the interviewer's failure to ask a question or to record a response (a problem that is common when complex interview schedules are used) or to the researcher's rejection of a recorded response during data editing because the answer is inconsistent with other answers. Generally then, the level of item nonresponse is related to the nature of the question or to the questionnaire design. Some adjustments are possible that attempt to correct for nonresponse bias.[12]

The survey researcher (and all investigators, for that matter) is obligated to include in his or her research report information regarding the number of subjects who were invited to take part in the study but who could not be contacted, declined, dropped out, or provided incomplete data.[13] If at all possible, the researcher should examine and report any known differences between these subjects and the remaining participants.

## CHOOSING APPROPRIATE SURVEY METHODS

Given the multitude of methodological options in survey research, the investigator is faced with a number of decisions that have implications for the accuracy, credibility, and relevance of data that will be collected. Each research problem will call for different groups to be studied, different design types, and different methods of data collection, so there are no hard and fast rules to fall back on, only general guidelines.

Unless the population to be studied is relatively small, a sample will probably be drawn by using an appropriate technique. If the researcher is interested in a one-time description and/or wants to investigate differences between subpopulations, the cross-sectional approach is usually chosen. If assessing change over time is an objective of the research, one of the longitudinal designs is appropriate. The way in which data are gathered (personal interview, mail questionnaire, etc.) is influenced by the type of information desired, the nature of the population being studied, time factors, and the availability of resources. When equally accurate data are as likely to be produced by one method of data collection as another, the researcher's decision is guided by more practical considerations, such as cost and efficiency. Combining data collection modes (i.e., triangulation) is another alternative that should not be overlooked.

When evaluating the suitability of methods for a study, the researcher needs to take an overall view of the survey process and critically consider all the salient aspects of the project. Fowler (1984, 145) calls this the "total survey design perspective." He explains:

> Total survey design means that when one is designing a survey or evaluating the quality of survey data, one looks at the complete data collection process, not simply at one or two aspects of the survey. The quality of the sample (the frame, the size, the design, the response rate), the quality of the questions as measures, the quality of data collection (especially the use of effective training and supervising procedures), and the mode of data collection constitute a tightly interrelated set of issues and design decisions.

Fowler points out that the cost of eliminating survey error may be high, and certain trade-offs are necessary between feasibility and methodological rigor. It remains for the researcher to decide what design, methods, and level of rigor are acceptable for a particular study purpose.

## CONDUCTING A SURVEY

The several steps in conducting a survey are similar to those taken in other types of research. After identifying a problem, the researcher determines whether a survey is the best way to obtain the desired information. If so, the next decision is whether to study the entire population or a sample of it. Usually, the choice is to sample, thus requiring identification and definition of the target population and selection or construction of a sampling frame. The researcher then develops assessment tools or chooses existing instruments, defines a sampling plan, and designs field procedures. This is followed by a pilot study to pretest measuring instruments and to evaluate planned field procedures. (The importance of pretesting and pilot studies has been repeatedly emphasized, but nowhere is the need more important than in surveys.) Only after instruments are refined, problematic procedures are detected and corrected, and interviewers and other research personnel are trained for their respective roles does the investigator initiate the main survey. The task of data collection for the larger study follows, with provisions for the careful supervision of personnel, including assessment of consistency between interviewers if an interview method is used. Finally, the data are coded, tabulated, and analyzed, and a report that communicates the results and interprets the findings is prepared.

## ADVANTAGES AND LIMITATIONS

Surveys have several advantages. They are a cost efficient way to collect extensive, quantifiable data in a highly standardized manner from a large number of subjects. Because of the structuredness of the data collection process, surveys tend to yield reliable data. They provide one of the few means to collect certain kinds of data, such as attitudes, feelings, beliefs, and past behaviors, all of which are accessible only to the respondent and cannot be observed by the researcher. When carefully executed, surveys are well suited for studies whose aim is to make inferences from a sample to a population.

A few limitations are common to most surveys. Regardless of how carefully the data are collected, the quality of the information and the validity of the findings depend largely on the accuracy and truthfulness of self-reports and/or subjectively reported data. Surveys are vulnerable to various errors associated with sampling and data collection processes. Additionally, survey research places excessive demands on the investigator, including knowledge of sampling techniques, understanding of questionnaire and interview development, expertise in training personnel and in monitoring their performance, and sophistication in statistical analyses. The difficulty in clarifying causation is yet another drawback in survey research.

Because of their popularity as a research strategy, surveys have been given considerable attention in the literature. More complete coverage of survey research is available.[14]

**RESEARCH SYNOPSIS 10.1**

### Social Research Methods Applied to Nutritional Assessment

Research strategy: Survey
Data collection techniques: Interview (structured), physiological/physical measurement

In this article the researchers demonstrate that nutritionists in field situations use easily collected social survey data to explore and evaluate factors that influence nutritional status. Each step in the suggested research design is explained in relation to nutritional evaluation and illustrated by actual procedures used in collecting data in Tanzania.

## STATEMENT OF PROBLEM

The purpose of this study was to explore the interrelationships of the prevalence of protein-calorie malnutrition (PCM) to educational levels of parents, weaning beliefs and practices, location of infant delivery, and size of landholdings.

### HYPOTHESES

1. The low educational attainment of a mother is positively related to home delivery of the infant.
2. The low educational attainment of a mother is positively related to early infant weaning.
3. The mother's belief about the proper age of weaning is positively related to the age of the infant when weaned.
4. The low educational attainment of a father is positively related to the small size of family landholdings.
5. The home delivery of infants is positively related to an increased prevalence of PCM.
6. The early weaning of infants is positively related to an increased prevalence of PCM.
7. The small size of family landholdings is positively related to an increased prevalence of PCM.

## THEORETICAL FOUNDATION

The concept PCM is a complex of syndromes, the etiology of which has been discussed thoroughly by Williams (1965) and Robson et al. (1972). Kwashiorkor is one of these syndromes. First described in 1931, its meaning was derived from a West African Ga language that defined it as a "disease occurring in a young child displaced from his mother by a subsequent pregnancy." Physicians have disagreed on the criteria necessary to establish a diagnosis.

The meaning of PCM to the population is equally important to the nutritional concept. Some children may not be brought to a clinic because the symptoms of kwashiorkor may be considered by the parents to be caused by unknown, supernatural forces affecting the child's life.

## METHOD

### SAMPLE

The sample was drawn from three areas in Tanzania with relatively high-density populations with limited-sized farm holdings. The sampling procedure was based upon accessibility through rural health centers and dispensaries. A representative sample was taken within a 6-mile radius of the particular health center or dispensary where the study was conducted. All leaders living within this 6-mile radius were contacted and asked to identify mothers with infants 5 years of age or younger within their jurisdiction. Each leader was given written instructions for each mother who qualified. This procedure was repeated until a quota of at least 100 mothers was reached for each clinic.

#### MATERIALS AND PROCEDURES

A structured interview and clinical examination were the techniques of data collection.

Clinical examinations were conducted by medical students under the supervision of a pediatrician. Anthropometric measurements were taken by those weighing the children.

After the clinical portion of the study was completed, student nurses and paramedical trainees conducted structured interviews with the mothers. Both groups of interviewers were instructed in interviewing techniques prior to the study. Information relative to all other variables was elicited in the interview.

#### DATA ANALYSIS

In analyzing clinical data, four categories of PCM were established: underweight, kwashiorkor, marasmic-kwashiorkor, and marasmus. Children between 60% and 80% optimum weight levels were categorized as underweight.

Clinical and social data were analyzed for statistical differences by using the chi-square test, with Yates correction factor included in the calculations.

## RESULTS

Out of the seven hypotheses tested, three were found to be significant ($p < .05$). Significant relationships were found between PCM and home delivery. Home delivery (compared to hospital delivery) was positively related to an increase of PCM. The early weaning of infants and small landholdings were also positively related to an increase in PCM.

## CONCLUSIONS AND/OR IMPLICATIONS

The relationship between social phenomena and the nutritional assessment of populations is of particular importance to the nutritionist. This case study, as the authors called it, provided an example of a social research technique that can be used in nutrition surveys. The researchers emphasized that many nutritionists who initiate programs recognize the existence of cultural factors but often use this knowledge on an intuitive or subjective level. They also suggested that baseline data not only can justify proposed programs but also can provide an opportunity to evaluate the success of the programs after their initiation.

(Source: M. Ernster, M. McAleenan, and F. Larkin. 1976. *Ecol. Food Nutr.* 5:143–51)

**RESEARCH SYNOPSIS 10.2**

## Life Status Changes and Changes in Consumer Preferences and Satisfaction

Research strategy: Survey
Data collection technique: Interview (structured/telephone)

### STATEMENT OF PROBLEM

The purpose of this study was to develop and test a theoretical model linking measures of objectively defined changes in consumer life status to changes in brand preferences and overall satisfaction with product and service purchases.

#### HYPOTHESES

1. There is a positive correlation between the number of status changes and the number of changes in brand preferences.
2. There is a positive correlation between the amount of life-style change and the number of changes in brand preferences.
3. The more negative the consequences of the life status change, the higher the level of stress.
4. The more the change in brand preferences, the more the satisfaction with product and service purchases.

### THEORETICAL FOUNDATION

The concept of readiness-to-change is found in various social sciences (e.g., the "teachable moment" in education). However, the concept of consumer readiness-to-change has not been explored previously in a marketing context. The basic behavioral assumption underlying this study is that consumers tend to persist in the thought patterns and behaviors to which they are accustomed. Therefore, bringing about a change in an existing life-style pattern is a formidable challenge.

### METHOD

#### SAMPLE

The subjects were selected through a random sample of telephone numbers from the Los Angeles directory, with the last digit of each selected number replaced by the last digit of the number directly below it. Interviews were conducted at randomized times with the adult who first came to the telephone. The sample consisted of 286 individuals—55% female, 31% never married, and 46% currently married. The sample was considered to represent the census characteristics of the Los Angeles adult population. Twenty percent described their jobs as professional or managerial, 16% as white collar, and 16% as blue collar. The typical respondent was 37.6 years old with 14.5 years of education and had lived in the Los Angeles area for 18 years.

### MATERIALS AND PROCEDURES

An interview schedule was devised and pretested with convenience samples of undergraduate and adult education students in a midwestern community. Telephone interviews were conducted in the fall of 1983.

The question used to test the key dependent variable of changes in brand preferences was, Have you changed your favorite brand in the following 13 product or service categories in the last 6 months, as compared to the 6 months before that? The number of times the respondents reported they had changed a brand preference was used to determine extent of brand preference change.

Status changes were determined with 23 items selected from the *Psychiatric Epidemiology Research Interview* (PERI) scale of 102 life events developed by Dohrenwend et al. (1973). The 23 items consisted of measures in six domains related to school, job, marital status, household composition, residence, and financial status. Respondents were asked whether the impact of each status change was positive or negative and whether it was a major or minor event.

Presence of stress was measured by asking the respondents to answer questions regarding whether they experienced several states (e.g., getting angry, worrying about things) more often, less often, or about the same as they experienced them 6 months before.

To measure life-style, a series of questions was also asked regarding whether respondents had become more or less involved in several activities or had decided to change their appearance through their clothing or hair style in the last 6 months. The number of changes were added to yield an overall index of the total quantity of life-style changes.

For a dissatisfaction measure, respondents were asked whether, compared to 6 months ago, they were satisfied with their purchases more often, less often, or about the same.

### DATA ANALYSIS

The independent variable was status change. The dependent variables were brand preference change, change in satisfaction with product and service purchases, and symptoms of stress. Correlation was the statistic used for testing the hypotheses.

## RESULTS

In the analysis of those cases in which a status change took place, significant correlations were found between unweighted number of status change events and life-style change ($p < .001$), giving support for Hypothesis 1.

A Pearson product-moment correlation coefficient of .38 ($p < .001$) between the amount of life-style change and the number of changes in brand preferences supported Hypothesis 2.

The simple correlation between respondents' evaluation of the life status change and level of stress was negative, with the coefficient being one of the highest in the entire study ($r = -.57, p < .001$). This result supported Hypothesis 3, that the more negative the evaluation of the life status change, the more the respondents reported symptoms of stress. Hypothesis 4 was also supported by the analysis of the data, with a positive correlation between changes in brand preference and purchase satisfaction.

## CONCLUSIONS AND/OR IMPLICATIONS

The researcher concluded that careful specification and testing of the theory in this study suggest that life status change may well represent an important new variable for use in future consumer model-building and research. He pointed out that measures of status change can be found in many existing secondary data sources, including the U.S. Census, or they can be incorporated relatively easily into future consumer studies.

The life changes measure clearly differentiated households according to likelihood of changing. Therefore, such measures should be considered seriously as predictor variables for use in developing market segments.

(Source: A. R. Andreasen. 1984. *J. Consum. Res.* 11:784–94)

**RESEARCH SYNOPSIS 10.3**

# Comparative Evaluation of Manager Performance in Selected Types of Food Services

Research strategy: Survey
Data collection technique: Questionnaire (personally delivered/picked up)

## STATEMENT OF PROBLEM

Among the principal objectives of this study were (a) to design, pretest, and use an instrument for assessing managerial capabilities based on fundamental principles of management and (b) to assess the applicability of the instrument in a comparative evaluation of the manager's performance in various types of food services.

### NULL HYPOTHESIS

There are no significant differences in the mean scores for (a) planning, (b) organizing, (c) directing, (d) communicating, (e) controlling, and (f) decision making among foodservice managers in fast food, restaurant, hospital, nursing home, and school/college types of food services.

## THEORETICAL FOUNDATION

The authors state that, theoretically, a foodservice manager performs functions similar to a manager in any other industry. They also stress the importance of understanding the theory behind these functions in practice, for managers need to adapt to situations as they occur. Their key to success is the degree of skill with which they coordinate the long-term (theoretical) style of management with the flex style, adapting to the realities (Miller 1979).

## METHOD

### SAMPLE

Thirty-eight foodservice managers in five major types of food services participated in the study. Ages ranged from 21 to 63 years.

### MATERIALS AND PROCEDURES

*Instrumentation*

The 30-question multiple-choice questionnaire used in the study consisted of five questions dealing with each of the management functions of planning, organizing, directing, communicating, controlling, and decision making. Subjects were indirectly asked to apply fundamental principles of management through their choices of answers to questions such as the following:

> If there is a complaint from a customer about food service, how would you normally come to know about it?
>
> a. through a waiter/waitress or food server or employees
> b. through complaint/suggestion box
> c. through letters to editor in the newspaper
> d. through your supervisor/boss
> e. through personal contact with the customer

*Procedures*

The questions were carefully pretested before final selection for use in the questionnaire. Items were randomly distributed within the seven-page questionnaire. Demographic data and comments were sought at the end of the instrument.

The questionnaires were personally delivered and collected from 38 randomly selected foodservice managers in the five major types of food service given in the hypotheses. Based on the completeness of information, 30 questionnaires were analyzed, 5 from each type of food service.

#### DATA ANALYSIS

Independent variables were the five major types of food services (fast food, restaurant, hospital, nursing home, and school/college). Dependent variables were managers' mean scores on each of six management functions (planning, organizing, directing, communicating, controlling, and decision making).

Mean scores were calculated for each of the six management functions for each manager. Total mean scores for each function were compared among the managers within the five types of food services by using various sets of analyses of variance.

## RESULTS

Results of the analyses of variance (ANOVA) showed no significant differences within total scores obtained by managers of the five types of food services.

A second set of ANOVAs combined the mean scores of food-service managers in restaurant and fast food service, hospital and nursing homes, and schools/colleges. The managers within these specific groupings had similar responsibilities and clientele. Findings showed significant differences within these groups ($p < .05$). Mean scores obtained by school/college foodservice managers were significantly higher ($p < .05$) than those obtained by fast food service and restaurant managers, indicating better performance by school/college managers.

Inasmuch as the school/college managers also had significantly higher experience and age than the other groups, correlation coefficients were calculated to test for the possible influence of age on the management scores. No significant differences were found.

## CONCLUSIONS AND/OR IMPLICATIONS

It was concluded that the method employed in this study can be used for comparative evaluation and representation of manager performance, as an evaluation tool by supervisors, or by managers for self-appraisal.

(Source: M. A. Khan and H. Al-Obaidy. 1982. *J. Foodservice Sys.* 21:163–70)

RESEARCH SYNOPSIS 10.4

# Energy Conservation: Family Values, Household Practices, and Contextual Variables

Research strategy: Survey
Data collection technique: Questionnaire (interview- and self-administered)

## STATEMENT OF PROBLEM

The purpose of this research was "to determine if there was a difference among the value patterns of husband-wife couples in the adoption rate of household energy conservation practices." A secondary purpose was "to determine if the rate of adoption of conservation practices varied with the level of education, occupational prestige, employment of the wife, and other contextual variables." Although several hypotheses were tested in this study, only one primary hypothesis is illustrated here.

### NULL HYPOTHESIS

There is no significant difference in adoption of energy conservation practice by family values of self-esteem, familism, social responsiveness, and eco-consciousness.

## THEORETICAL FOUNDATION

The theoretical foundation for this study was an ecological systems approach. Cottrell (1955) recognized that the preservation of values is related to the availability of energy. (In Chapter 2, we referred to energy as a broad unifying concept in studying one's relation to the environment.) The ecological systems approach to studying family managerial behavior was proposed by Steidl (1969) and Hook and Paolucci (1970). From this perspective, a change in one part of the system will produce a change in all other parts. The model for this study perceives values as a managerial component, with values clarification and mediation of intrafamilial value conflicts considered to be managerial behavior.

## METHOD

### SAMPLE

The data for the study were collected as part of a larger project, Functioning of the Family Ecosystem in a World of Changing Energy Availability. A multistage probability sample was used, with data collected in a three-county area in Michigan containing diverse government, commercial, and agricultural sectors. A subsample of 157 families with a husband and wife respondent was chosen from this larger project. The selected subsample was found to be representative of the population (Hogan 1976).

## MATERIALS AND PROCEDURES

### *Instrumentation*

A scale of 14 practices was used to measure the adoption rate of energy conservation practices within the household over the past year. The practices included adjusting the thermostat at night, during the day, etc.; turning off lights; and adjusting shades or drapes.

Family values studied were self-esteem, familism, social responsiveness, and eco-consciousness. Within an ecosystem family management framework, these values are considered explicit. The eco-consciousness value represented the interrelationship of human beings and the physical environment. Instruments used to measure these values were the Rosenberg (1965) *Self-esteem Test;* an adaptation of the *Family Concept Inventory* (van der Veen and Novak 1974); a five-item anomie scale by Srole (1956), and items from the Rotter (1966) internal-external control test for the social responsiveness measure. An eight-item measure for eco-consciousness was adapted from two Likert-type scales used as indices of a conceptualization of ecological linkages to the energy situation. Eco-consciousness was defined as the perception of the interrelationship of people and nature.

### *Procedures*

The families in the larger Michigan Agricultural Experiment Station study completed both interview-administered and self-administered questionnaires and received a stipend of $10.

## DATA ANALYSIS

Family scores were computed for energy practices by calculating percentage of conservation practices adopted by the household based on the responses of husband and wife. Family scores for values were based upon the degree of commitment and congruency between the husband and wife on each of the four values. A typology composed of nine types of value configurations was formed, based on the distribution of husband-wife scores above, around, or below the mean. The highest commitment was husband and wife above the mean, while the lowest commitment was for husband and wife below the mean.

Both parametric and nonparametric statistics were used in hypotheses testing. For the null hypothesis considered here (there is no significant difference in adoption of energy conservation practice by family values of self-esteem, familism, social responsiveness, and eco-consciousness), one-way analyses of variance were used to test for differences.

## RESULTS

The eco-consciousness value was found "to be a meaningful predictor of energy conservation behavior." The other three values showed no significant relationships to energy conservation behavior. In the case of eco-consciousness, the null hypothesis of no significant differences was rejected. In families where both husband and wife were highly committed to eco-consciousness, they were high adopters of energy conservation practices, whereas low husband-wife commitment resulted in a low rate of adoption. The $F$ statistic was significant at $p < .05$.

Other portions of the study, not described here, showed that the wife's education, husband's education, and his occupation were related to eco-consciousness.

## CONCLUSIONS AND/OR IMPLICATIONS

The authors concluded that there was support for the family management framework (i.e., an interdependence of value and practice) and that knowledge about interrelationships between people and their physical environment is essential in reaching values and increasing the commitment to eco-consciousness in families.

(Source: M. J. Hogan and B. Paolucci. 1979. *Home Econ. Res. J.* 7:211–18)

RESEARCH SYNOPSIS 10.5

# Characteristics of Adopters and Non-Adopters of Home Computers

Research strategy: Survey
Data collection technique: Questionnaire (mail)

## STATEMENT OF PROBLEM

The purpose of this study was to investigate the nature of persons adopting the home computer (a technological innovation).

### HYPOTHESES

1. Adopters of home computers will be middle-aged, own their residences, and have higher incomes and more education than non-adopters.
2. Adopters of home computers will exhibit a psychographic pro-

file similar to that found for individuals with the low origence/high intellectence traits.

3. Adopters of home computers will have had more experience than non-adopters with other technical consumer products.

## THEORETICAL FOUNDATION

This study is built on Hirschman's (1980a, 1980b, 1981) concept of consumer creativity. Her underlying theme is that high levels of consumer creativity lead to increased adoptive and use innovativeness. She specifies two sources for the generation of innovation—symbolism and technology. A symbolic innovation communicates a different social meaning than it did previously. A technological innovation possesses some tangible features never found before in that product class. Symbolic innovations may be a function of a consumer's desire for a "new look," while technological innovations provide increased functional performance.

Hirschman's conceptualization does not explain possible differences in the type of creativity needed to adopt a technological innovation as opposed to a symbolic one. Welsh's (1975) concept of creativity may provide an explanation. He proposed that creativity is a function of two personality dimensions—*origence,* which emphasizes originality, and *intellectence,* which emphasizes the intellectual.

## METHOD

### SAMPLE

Two mailing lists were obtained, a list of computer clubs from the Apple Corporation and a list of 5000 *Psychology Today* subscribers from a list broker. A list of computer club members was obtained directly from the clubs. Questionnaires to people from both lists were mailed to all geographical areas of the United States, in about the same proportion as the proportion of the region's proportion to the population of the United States as a whole. Within a week of this mailing, a follow-up postcard was sent.

A higher response rate was expected from the computer club members due to their special interest in the topic. Therefore, more questionnaires were sent to *Psychology Today* subscribers. Of the 760 questionnaires mailed to computer club members, 321 were completed and returned (42% response rate). Magazine subscribers returned 318 of 1250 questionnaires (25.4% response rate). Usable questionnaires numbered 639 (32% total response rate). Nonresponse error was investigated through a second mailing to a 10% sample of those who did not answer the first questionnaire. This mailing, consisting of demographic questions, yielded 42 returns (30% of those sampled). These nonrespondents did not differ statistically (through chi-square analysis) demographically from those of either the adopter or non-adopter respondents.

### MATERIALS AND PROCEDURES

A four-page questionnaire consisted of four sections: psychographic, computer-related experience, home computer usage (if applicable), and demographic. In the psychographic section, respondents rated themselves on 60 life-style items on a Likert agree–disagree scale. The majority of these items were taken from a Wells and Tigert (1971) study. A few items were added dealing with time spent in conducting everyday activities and with attitudes toward computers.

A factor analysis was conducted of all 60 psychographic items after the questonnaires were returned, and all items with loadings over .45 were grouped as a factor. A total of 15 factors resulted from this analysis. The second section of the questionnaire covered 19 computer-related experiences.

### DATA ANALYSIS

To determine differences between the two groups (adopters versus non-adopters of home computers), a stepwise discriminant analysis was run (in which the variable that maximizes the Mahalonobis distance between the two groups is used).

## RESULTS

*Hypothesis 1*

The total sample was divided into an analysis subgroup of 439 respondents and a holdout subgroup of 200 respondents. The discriminant function discriminated significantly between the two groups: $\chi^2 = 58.81$, 4 *df*, $p < .001$. The standardized discriminant function was $D = .65$ home ownership + .53 income + .39 education + .39 age. Hypothesis 1 was supported. Adopters of home computers were more likely to be homeowners, with more education and higher incomes, than non-adopters. They were also likely to be middle-aged.

*Hypothesis 2*

Hypothesis 2 was also supported. A profile for computer users was found to be similar to that established by Welsh (1975) for low origence/high intellectence individuals. The standardized discriminant function was $D = .45$ computer attitudes − .40 culinary enthusiast + .36 self-designated opinion leader + .31 information seeker − .29 aesthetic enthusiast + .27 satisfaction with finances + .18 homebody + .15 time spent in everyday activities + .12 credit user. The discriminant function using the psychographic variables was statistically significant ($p < .001$).

From these results, it appears that computer owners were not interested in the arts or cooking or in a great deal of social interaction, as indicated by the homebody result. Adopters also spent more time in everyday activities.

*Hypothesis 3*

This hypothesis, that owners of home computers will have had more experience with the general product class of computer-related products and services than nonowners, was also supported by the data.

### CONCLUSIONS AND/OR IMPLICATIONS

In general, these researchers concluded that their findings support the relationship between consumer creativity and adoptive innovativeness proposed by Hirschman (1980b). They also provided evidence that Welsh's (1975) operationalization of creativity may be helpful in predicting the adoption of different types of innovations. Suggestions for future research included a need for investigations of the role played by the two creativity dimensions (origence and intellectence) in the adoption of different types of innovations.

(Source: M. D. Dickerson and J. W. Gentry. 1983. *J. Consum. Res.* 10:225–35)

## NOTES

1. Kerlinger (1986) calls attributes that are related to membership in social groups, such as sex, income, race, social class, and religious affiliation, *sociological* variables. He refers to opinions, attitudes, and behaviors as *psychological* variables.

2. Establishing causation is difficult under any circumstances, although the greatest risk in inferring causal relationships is found in nonexperimental studies, the least risk in true experimental studies, and intermediate risk in quasi-experimental studies. See Cook and Campbell (1979, 1–36), Krathwohl (1985, 211–28), and Simon and Burstein (1985, 421–41) for good discussions of the extremely complex and controversial concept of cause in both experimental and nonexperimental research.

3. See Blalock (1964), Goodman (1985), Heise (1975), and Kenny (1979) for a discussion of some of these more sophisticated ways of dealing with data generated by nonexperimental research (e.g., linear structural models, path analysis).

4. Babbie (1973) explains why sampling may result in better data. If everyone in the population must be contacted, a sizeable staff of interviewers is usually needed, and the researcher cannot be as selective in the employment of field-workers as he or she would like to be. The extensiveness of the population survey precludes persistent follow-up efforts, which may result in lower response rates. The collection of data for a large project may create measurement problems because of the length of time needed to execute the project. Information obtained from subjects earlier in the survey may be different from that gathered in the latter stages because of changes in the population in terms of the variables being studied due to the passage of time. Finally, the logistics associated with a very large survey (e.g., training and supervising workers, record keeping) may adversely affect the quality of data collected.

5. *Response rate* is defined as the number of subjects who responded divided by the number of subjects sampled. The denominator includes all of the people in the population who were selected for inclusion in the study, whether or not they participated. The numerator includes those who actually provided data.

6. Blankenship (1977), Dillman (1978), Frey (1983), Groves and Kahn (1979), and Lavrakas (1987) provide a helpful overview of telephone interviewing.

7. Availability of the economical WATS telephone service, which provides unlimited long distance calls for a fixed charge, has been a major factor in making telephone interviewing a more viable mode of data collection in surveys.

8. For a discussion of CATI, see Freeman and Shanks (1983), Shangrow (1986), and Shure and Meeker (1978).

9. See Angle (1981), Holden (1985), Johnson (1984), Perlman (1985), and Yarnold et al. (1985).

10. Consult Deming (1944) for what is considered the classic paper on errors in survey research. See also Andersen et al. (1979). Most books dealing with survey research discuss survey error (see Note 14).

11. See Berg (1967), Bradburn (1983), Dijkstra and van der Zouwen (1982), Edwards (1957a), Rorer (1965), and Sudman and Bradburn (1974) for more information dealing with response behavior on questionnaires and in interviews.

12. See Kalton (1983a) and Smith (1983) for a discussion of weighting adjustments possible for total nonresponse and Kalton and Kaspryzk (1982) for a discussion of imputation procedures to treat item nonresponse.

13. See Note 5. Schuman and Kalton (1985) warn that there is variation in the ways nonresponse rate is reported, leading to noncompatibility among surveys.

14. For useful books on survey research, the reader is referred to Babbie (1973), Backstrom and Hursh-César (1981), Dillman (1978), Erdos (1970), Fink and Kosecoff (1985), Fowler (1984), Hyman (1955), Marsh (1982), Miller (1983), Moser and Kalton (1972), Rosenberg (1968), Rossi, Wright, and Anderson (1983), Sonquist and Dunkelberg (1977), Warwick and Lininger (1975), and Weisberg and Bowen (1977). The recent review chapter by Schuman and Kalton (1985) is also worth consulting.

CHAPTER 11

# Using Existing Data

Chapter 7 described the use of physical traces and archival records as unobtrusive data for study, suggesting that existing data are viable sources of information for research. This chapter concentrates on historical methods and secondary analysis of survey data as research strategies to examine data that are already available.

## HISTORICAL RESEARCH

Historical research is concerned with re-creating the past. It inquires about past events, trends, attitudes, and experiences with the objectives of accurately describing and interpreting them as well as of providing a clearer perspective of the present and a basis for predicting the future. According to Reitzel and Lindemann (1982, 169), the aims of historians are similar to those of other researchers: "to produce systematic, reliable statements that either increase the available pool of knowledge about a given topic or bring existing knowledge into a more precise focus by means of new interpretive patterns." Having been developed by ancient Greek historians and philosophers, historical research may be considered the oldest form of true research. In modern times, historical methodology has been greatly refined.

Historical research involves many activities that are common to other scientific investigations and some activities that are unique to this process of inquiry. Like most other research strategies, it operates within an explicit or implicit theoretical framework,[1] and it requires the systematic collection and evaluation of data to test hypotheses or answer research questions. Unlike most other investigations, it depends on data that have been preserved in the past. Historical researchers cannot generate new data, if necessary, nor can they control or manipulate variables the way experimental researchers can. However, as Reitzel and Lindemann (1982, 168) point out, historical researchers have the advantage of being able to "study anything about the past that can be analyzed." Finally, although some historical research has used quantitative methods, historical studies rely primarily on the logical analysis of evidence obtained from documents.[2]

In human ecology, the possibilities for historical investigation seem limitless—the study of clothing, housing and furnishings, food, marriage, child rearing, education, and so on. This makes historical research an attractive option.

Sometimes students also select historical research as an "easy way out"; it may be regarded as an escape from experimental studies, which some students resist. What these students do not realize is that good research demands objective methods and the setting up of specific testable hypotheses or the formulation of research questions. These expectations may in fact be much more difficult to meet in historical investigations because of the nature of the data and the logical analyses involved.

Of course, not all historical studies satisfy these criteria. An examination of the literature reveals that a great many investigations do not meet the requirements of legitimate historical research. Often the historical investigator recites facts but does not synthesize or integrate them into meaningful generalizations; the mere recitation of facts or rehash of what is already known is not historical research. Carefully conducted, historical studies can lead to clarification, correction, or expansion of existing knowledge as well as to the discovery of new knowledge.

## Steps in Historical Research

There are five basic steps in historical research: problem identification, data collection, data evaluation, data synthesis and interpretation, and writing the report.

As with most research, some of the steps in the process may overlap.

### Problem Identification

Identifying a research problem may be challenging, not because of a shortage of historically significant topics, but because of the availability of so much data or of very complex data that require further delimitation of the problem or because of limited data that dictate broadening the scope of the problem. The scope can be varied by increasing or decreasing the geographical area studied, the time span involved, the number of persons investigated, or the categories of human activity examined (Travers 1978).

Since insufficient data will result in inadequate testing of hypotheses and extremely tentative conclusions concerning their confirmation or disconfirmation, Gay (1987) suggests that it is better to investigate a carefully defined problem in depth with one or more specific, well-formulated hypotheses than to study either a broadly-stated problem with vague hypotheses or a problem with virtually untestable hypotheses because of a dearth of available data.

Hypotheses (or questions) are important because they direct the investigator to only relevant sources of information and prevent the waste of time and energy on meaningless data collection. So that the hypotheses will not become too restrictive, some investigators prefer to adopt tentative or working hypotheses that provide necessary structure during the early stages of the study but that can be modified or abandoned later if needed.

### Data Collection

Primary and Secondary Sources. In historical research, source materials may be of two types: primary or secondary. *Primary source materials* include testimony provided by someone who has witnessed a past event firsthand. They can also be written or mechanically reproduced records of past events (e.g., minutes of meetings, sound recordings, photographs, and films) or physical objects used in the past that can be examined directly by the researcher. *Secondary source materials* include accounts or records that are one or more steps removed from the original source; that is, they were prepared by someone who was not actually present to observe what is being described. A newspaper article that reports an interview of someone who has witnessed or participated in an event or material that quotes or paraphrases an author from the writings of that author are secondary sources.

One of the basic rules of historical research is to *use primary sources* if they can be located. Since secondary source materials are subject to a variety of distortions and errors, a researcher should never depend on them if a primary source is available. Like rumors, data that pass through several hands before they reach the investigator may bear little resemblance to the original versions.

Documents and Relics (or Remains). The data for historical research are usually classified as either documents or relics and remains. *Documents* typically are written records, but they may also include pictorial, oral, and mechanical records. Among the many documentary sources of evidence are official records (e.g., laws, vital statistics, minutes of meetings, budgets, annual reports), personal records (e.g., diaries, memoirs, personal letters), orally transmitted records (e.g., folklore, legends, ballads, reminiscences by eyewitnesses or participants in an event), pictorial and mechanical records (e.g., photographs, paintings, sound recordings, videotapes, films) and published records (e.g., newspapers, journal articles, advertisements, books) (Van Dalen 1979, 353–54).[3]

*Relics and remains* are artifacts of historical significance that have been handed down from the past without conscious intention of conveying meaning to future generations.[4] Referred to as "adjuncts to everyday life" by Reitzel and Lindemann (1982, 172), these physical objects include buildings, furniture, clothing, food, pottery, weapons, toys, machinery, and skeletal remains. Often, relics or remains that are available to the researcher reveal more about the past than written records. For example, a school teacher in the early 1800s may have written in his diary about the humane methods of discipline used in his school, whereas the remains of devices for physical punishment in the form of a bundle of switches, iron ruler, and whipping post may reveal the real truth about disciplinary practices.[5] Ideally, the historical researcher combines physical and documentary evidence to study a problem.

In actual practice, documentary analysis is the primary, if not the sole, method employed in most historical investigations.[6] Thus, the "review of literature" (interpreted somewhat more broadly than the usual prelude to other types of research) is considered the data collection technique. With few exceptions (e.g., interviews with participants or observers of an event), there are no measuring instruments. Following a preliminary literature review to initially define the problem, the researcher begins the complex task of identifying, acquiring, and examining various types of written communications to test hypotheses or to answer questions. This major undertaking requires travel to historical archives, libraries with special collections, courthouses, and so on.[7] It also necessitates the careful evaluation of source materials that have been uncovered in the search.

## Data Evaluation

The person who conducts documentary or historical research has seldom witnessed the original events about which he or she is writing, and these events cannot be reproduced. Therefore, it is important to determine the reliability and validity of evidence obtained. The evidence may be incomplete, deliberately biased, or otherwise defective. Since an individual may produce or record only what is considered to be of interest or value, or what one chooses to make known to others, great expenditures of time and effort are often required by the historical investigator to locate complete and accurate information. Whether primary or secondary sources are used, documents and relics should be examined for their authenticity (known as external criticism) and their meaning and accuracy (known as internal criticism). These two processes may be carried on simultaneously.

*External criticism* is concerned with the genuineness of the data. Documents and relics are to the scholar what courtroom witnesses are to a lawyer. Just as the attorney must lay a foundation for the admissability of a document as evidence in court, the researcher must determine if the source materials can be accepted as authentic.

The most important questions raised in the context of external appraisal are When, where, and by whom was the document or relic produced? Since forgeries are common, and there is always the chance of honest errors being made, the form and appearance of historical evidence must be studied. In handwritten documents, authenticated examples of the supposed author's handwriting can serve as a check. Chemical analyses of paper, paint, and glass can be made, artifacts can be carbon dated, and so on.

Apart from determining whether evidence, such as a document, is genuine, the researcher is concerned with the validity of its contents. Through *internal criticism,* the investigator examines the meaning, accuracy, and trustworthiness of the information contained within the document. What was the writer's intent (i.e., the real meaning, as distinguished from literal meaning)? How should obsolete terms and symbolic expressions be interpreted? In addition to determining meaning, the investigator must consider any limitations, motives, and biases that might have led the author to distort or omit information. Was the writer a trained or untrained observer? Do the reports of other independent observers agree with those of this author? Inaccurate reporting might be caused by the use of unreliable sources, including inaccurate documents and undependable informants, or by writing about an event after a lapse of time. Moreover, personal characteristics such as poor health, emotional stress, negligence, incompetence, vanity, or political and other biases are factors that might result in inaccuracies.

Woody (1947, 190) has suggested a number of guidelines for the historical researcher when judging evidence:

> (1) Do not read into earlier documents the conceptions of later times; (2) do not judge an author ignorant of certain events, necessarily, because he fails to mention them (the argument *ex silentio*), or that they did not occur, for the same reason; (3) underestimating a source is no less an error than overestimating it in the same degree, and there is no more virtue in placing an event too late than in dating it too early by the same number of years or centuries; (4) a single true source may establish the existence of an idea, but other direct, competent, independent witnesses are required to prove the reality of events or objective facts; (5) identical errors prove the dependence of sources on each other, or a common source; (6) if witnesses contradict each other on a certain point, one or the other may be true, but both may be in error; (7) direct, competent, independent witnesses who report the same central fact and also many peripheral matters in a casual way may be accepted

for the points of their agreement; (8) official testimony, oral or written, must be compared with unofficial testimony whenever possible, for neither one nor the other is alone sufficient; (9) a document may provide competent and dependable evidence on certain points, yet carry no weight in respect to others it mentions.

## Data Synthesis and Interpretation

After reviewing the materials and establishing their credibility and usefulness, the investigator synthesizes the multitude of facts that he or she has accumulated. *Synthesis* is the process of combining, comparing, and arranging evidence, and making inferences to provide connections between bits and classes of evidence (Shafer 1969, 163).

Although some synthetic activity has gone on in earlier stages of the project, at this time the researcher attempts to make sense out of all of the data. Synthesis requires complete familiarity with the information on hand. Consequently, the investigator reads and rereads data, compares evidence, and makes many tentative combinations and generalizations. As Shafer (1969, 156) points out, the researcher should be especially sensitive to contradictory evidence and be prepared to revise or abandon working hypotheses. Considering all evidence, the investigator "selects for inclusion in his [or her] account those facts that are important and are representative of the total body of evidence—that is, they set forth the pros and cons in true proportion."

The investigator interprets his or her findings in light of original hypotheses and revised or new ones that might have evolved during synthesis as well as within the broader context of existing theory and past research. Because of the relative lack of conclusive evidence in historical research, it is important that the investigator point out deficiencies in the data and acknowledge the possibility of alternative explanations of findings. Although historical researchers are given considerable latitude in their subjective interpretation of results, they should strive for objectivity and qualify their generalizations appropriately.

## Writing the Report

The final step of the research process is preparing a written report, which usually takes the form of a long narrative. Ideas may be organized chronologically, topically, or geographically. Within the latter two arrangements, the treatment is chronological.[8] Decisions also have to be made regarding the amount of space to devote to evidence because the length of an account may indicate emphasis. Reporting historical research is not an easy task because of the burden of incomplete evidence, the need to maintain accuracy, and the desire for an eloquent exposition that will be a contribution to the literature.

Historical investigation is very complex, leading one author to state:

"A historical research study is definitely not for rookies!" (Gay 1987, 185). Gottschalk (1956, 45) explains some of the reasons why historical research is so challenging:

> . . . only a part of what was observed in the past was remembered by those who observed it; only a part of what was remembered was recorded; only a part of what was recorded has survived; only a part of what has survived has come to the historians' attention; only a part of what has come to their attention is credible; only a part of what is credible has been grasped; and only a part of what has been grasped can be expounded or narrated by the historian.

(See **Research Synopsis 11.1** for an example of historical research.)

## Content Analysis

Content analysis is a major methodological tool used in both historical and contemporary documentary research. *Content analysis* is defined by Holsti (1968, 601) as "any technique for making inferences by systematically and objectively identifying specified characteristics of messages." A method of data collection and a method of data analysis, content analysis is similar to structured observation that uses a category system (see Chap. 7), where the researcher directly observes live interaction and records the behaviors in terms of predetermined categories, or views a videotape of the interaction and codes responses after the fact.[9] The content analyst applies his or her categories to information in existing documents such as books, poems, songs, newspapers, magazines, letters, diaries, speeches, films, paintings, and recordings of radio and television programs. Content analysis is also frequently used to analyze transcripts of unstructured interviews, protocols of responses to projective personality measures, and sound and/or videotape recordings of counseling sessions. Content analysis can be either quantitative or qualitative in nature.

With content analysis, a researcher can code communication in terms of its manifest content (what was actually said) or its latent content (its underlying meaning). Coding of the manifest characteristics of messages, such as word frequencies, can be done relatively easily and reliably by humans or by computers. Coding of latent characteristics of texts, such as thematic analysis, is more complicated. A researcher can code one or the other or a combination of the two in a single study.

Krippendorff (1980, 29–31) has identified four features of content analysis that make it a useful research tool. (1) It is an unobtrusive technique. (2) It accepts unstructured material. (3) It is context sensitive and therefore can process symbolic forms. (4) It can cope with large volumes of data.

Applying content analysis to any communication that someone has produced involves a few basic procedures. Although there are many different ways for the researcher to proceed, here is one example. The investigator starts with a research problem and decides on the type of documents to be studied, after which relevant sources are identified. Next the investigator constructs descriptive categories directly related to the research problem and develops precise operational definitions for each category. If the body of material is relatively large, a sample is selected by using one of the techniques described in Chapter 3. For example, a random sample of all programs (noncommercials) aired between 7:00 P.M. and 10:00 P.M. on the three major television networks in one week might be selected by an investigator to code for incidence of violent acts. Or a stratified random sample of editorials published in newspapers throughout the country by state, city size, and average circulation might be drawn for study of favorable or unfavorable assertions about public education. The size of the recording unit to be coded is then designated—single words, themes, sentences, paragraphs, characters, or the whole unit—and the coding system is applied to the unit of context chosen. Finally, the data are analyzed.

Holsti (1968) describes four major systems of enumeration that are commonly used in content analysis. These can be adapted depending on the type of communication being investigated. First, the researcher can look for the appearance or nonappearance of an attribute within sentences, paragraphs, or whole units, depending on the recording unit adopted. Second, the investigator can examine the time or space devoted to a topic, as reflected in the amount of time or coverage allotted in a news broadcast or the headline size and column inches given to newspaper stories dealing with a particular issue. Third, the researcher can measure the characteristics of content by noting the frequency of occurrence of certain key words or ideas in letters, speeches, folktales, books, and so on. Fourth, the content analyst can investigate the intensity of expression to draw inferences about attitudes and values. This approach requires careful study of the intricacies of the language contained in the communication, such as verbal intensity, adverbial modifiers, and tense.

There are several good sources on content analysis,[10] some of which describe the use of electronic computers. Content analysis is illustrated in **Research Synopsis 11.1**.

## SECONDARY ANALYSIS OF SURVEY DATA

Survey data that have been collected by one researcher for a particular purpose may be of value to another researcher who wishes to subject the data to another, or secondary, analysis[11] Perusal of recent issues of professional journals attests to the growing use in research of information previously gathered elsewhere.

Hakim (1982, 1) elaborates on the meaning and scope of secondary analysis:

> Secondary analysis is any further analysis of an existing dataset which presents interpretations, conclusions, or knowledge additional to, or different from, those presented in the first report on the inquiry as a whole or its main results. Secondary analysis will thus include studies presenting more condensed reports (such as social area analysis based on selected social indicators); more detailed reports (offering additional detail on the same topic); reports which focus on a particular sub-topic (such as unemployment) or social group (such as ethnic minority); reports angled towards a particular policy issue or question; analyses based on a conceptual framework or theory not applied to the original analysis; and reanalyses which take advantage of more sophisticated analytic techniques to test hypotheses and answer questions in a more comprehensive and succinct manner than in the original report.

Although secondary analysis has been around for many years, its full utilization with data previously collected through surveys has been facilitated by increased access to computers, by the creation of data archives, and by the development of highly sophisticated techniques for quantitative analysis of survey data.

Archives collect, store, and disseminate machine-readable survey datasets in the same way that a lending library circulates books, with the exception that, once purchased, the researcher retains the copy of the data. Examples of data archives are the Roper Center (University of Connecticut), Laboratory for Political Research (University of Iowa), and U.S. Bureau of Labor Statistics (Washington, D.C.).[12] The Roper Center, for instance, archives datasets for the National Opinion Research Center, Gallup, Yankelovich, and CBS-*New York Times* collections, among others. Archives may specialize in holdings of survey datasets dealing with particular problems, issues, and populations.[13] Some are state, regional, national, or international in scope.

The researcher does not have to depend on major archives to do secondary research. A great deal of already collected data may be conveniently available nearby. Survey information gathered by local or state agencies, school districts, and even research colleagues who are willing to share data are additional valuable sources of survey data for secondary analysis.

A frequently overlooked source of existing data for secondary analyses in human ecology research is the U.S. Census. It is, as Miller (1983, 157) calls it, "a gold mine of data." Census Bureau data include comprehensive enumerations of population and housing characteristics (collected every 10 years) as well as more specialized information on business, manufacturing, transportation, agriculture, and other areas (collected every 5 years). For a fee, interested researchers can obtain magnetic tapes containing data for their own analyses and software for tabulating data. Purchasers of tapes are furnished necessary technical documentation describing the data, indicating the layout of the record format, and explaining the coding system used.

There are two basic types of data tapes available. One includes records based on information obtained directly from the individual respondent, and the other contains only statistical summaries. Miller (1983, 156–57) describes these two data files in greater detail:

> *Basic record tapes.* The tapes containing basic individual records are in nearly all cases confidential; therefore the Bureau cannot sell them but can prepare special tabulations from them. However, certain sets of nonconfidential individual records and punch cards . . . can be purchased from the Bureau. The Bureau has samples of individual records from the 1960 and 1970 Censuses of Population and Housing by removing all information that might make possible identification of any person, household, or housing unit. The Bureau also makes available the nonconfidential returns of some of the public agencies that report on their activities for the Bureau's surveys; for example, information from each building permit-issuing jurisdiction is available on computer tapes.
>
> *Summary tapes.* Many summary tapes are available; these contain small-area totals that were subsequently added together by the computer to obtain the results required for the published tables. Summary tapes are generally useful for further machine processing to obtain totals for areas not shown separately in the published reports or for preparing derived measures (averages, ratios, etc.) for specific geographic areas. The data on these tapes can also be obtained as printouts of the tape content. Such displays are accompanied by technical memoranda explaining the content and organization of the display and supplying identification for the totals.
>
> In addition to the data described above, some files contain the same statistics found in published reports; these files are made available for users who wish to summarize further or to rearrange the published data.

Information about accessing census data is available elsewhere.[14]

**Research Synopses 11.2** and **11.3** illustrate the use of secondary analysis of survey data.

## ADVANTAGES AND LIMITATIONS

There are advantages and disadvantages associated with the utilization of existing data in available documents and surveys (Platt 1981a, 1981b; Riley 1963).

## Existing Documents and Records

A major advantage of available documents is efficiency because the information has already been collected for the researcher. Another is that there is generally an abundance of existing data because our society and others faithfully record their events in different ways. In fact, some information is routinely collected by agencies or organizations in a fairly standardized manner, greatly facilitating subsequent analyses. The abundance of existing data is fortunate because many problems, such as the investigation of historical trends or the study of groups no longer in existence, can only be examined using information that is already available in one form or another. Events in the past cannot be observed directly, and obtaining accurate information about them may not be possible through interviews or questionnaires with people who are still alive.

Much of the existing data is conveniently stored in libraries, where they can be accessed at little or no cost (except possibly for travel expenses). Furthermore, these data can be analyzed and reanalyzed at the researcher's convenience and do not normally require sophistication in quantitative analyses or computer skills. Another positive feature of available documents is that they are generally considered unobtrusive sources, originally prepared without regard for research, and therefore relatively free from the reactivity of measurement.

On the negative side, the investigator using existing documents may encounter difficulties in locating the desired data. Additionally, the researcher has no control over the quality, amount, and storage format of the data. There is always a possibility that the materials chosen for study are biased because of factors such as selective recording and other sources of distortion, although this is seldom a problem with evidence, such as legal records. If there is a shortage of data in an area of interest, the historical researcher cannot generate fresh information. Limited data may require the investigator to employ less acceptable sampling techniques or possibly force him or her to use whatever data are available. A lack of data may also preclude the testing of certain hypotheses or lead to overinterpretation of the data on hand. Finally, information derived from these materials does not lend itself readily to quantitative analysis, except for the application of some content analytic techniques.

## Existing Survey Data

The secondary analysis of existing survey data is attractive for many reasons. By using previously collected survey data, the secondary analyst can realize an enormous savings in money, time, and personnel; can reap the benefits of a large and representative sample; can have access to higher quality data, in some cases, than would be possible otherwise; and can devote more effort to theoretical issues, statistical analyses, and interpretation because it is unnecessary to expend energy in the solicitation of funding and in physically carrying out the survey. Secondary analysis can also enable the investigator to more clearly define the purposes and select appropriate methods for subsequent primary research. A final benefit is that it can help relieve some of the burden placed on respondents as a result of recent overutilization of survey methods. (Our society is rapidly becoming oversaturated with surveys.) In view of shrinking research budgets, there is every reason to believe that the use of secondary analysis of survey data will continue to enjoy popularity among researchers and may increase in the future.

Drawbacks in the use of existing survey data for analysis are that the "old" survey's information may be outdated, its design may be flawed or its instruments of poor technical quality, its data may be inadequately documented, and it may not have addressed all of the questions in which the secondary analyst is interested.

RESEARCH SYNOPSIS 11.1

## Analysis of Historical and Contemporary Dress: An African Example

Research strategy: Using existing data (documentary/historical)
Data collection technique: Archival records/content analysis

### STATEMENT OF PROBLEM

The purpose of this study was to develop a structural method for analyzing dress and to provide specific descriptive data using the method.

### THEORETICAL FOUNDATION

The conceptual framework for this investigation was adapted from components used in linguistic analysis. Sound is fundamental to language. It is divided into discrete units called phonemes. A string of one or more phonemes composes a morpheme, the building block of syntax. The morpheme is the smallest sound/meaning in the structure of language. In the present study, single clothing items are considered the "morphemes" of clothing analysis. In contrast to the minimal sound/meaning of language, clothing items have minimal visual/meaning.

In linguistics, a group of morphemes with information relative to their combination into more complex structures is called a lexicon. In this investigation, all of the clothing items or forms visibly apparent in the data are listed in a lexicon of dress.

From the linguistic literature, Barthes (1967a and 1967b), Bogatyrev (1937/1971), and Faris (1972) view dress and adornment as elements subjected to social prescriptions within a systematic whole. Dress is rule-governed within a sociocultural and temporal context; certain combinations of dress types are found worn under particular conditions. It is presumed that dress differentiates persons according to their social structural characteristics, such as age, sex, religion, marital status, education, and occupation. Meanings are derived by recording and analyzing facts such as the frequency with which particular garments are worn, by whom, and for what occasions.

## METHOD

### SAMPLE

Thirty individuals were studied, comprising five generations of a Yoruba family in Lagos, Nigeria, from 1900 to 1974.

### MATERIALS AND PROCEDURES

The primary data were 607 photographs from the family collections that clearly showed full images of individuals. One family member provided the majority of photographs as well as personal information about the occasions and the individuals pictured. Elderly relatives confirmed and supplemented this information. The photographs were divided into three groups corresponding to political periods within each time span (1900–1939, 1940–1959, 1960–1974).

### ANALYSIS OF DATA

The content analysis of the photographs included the following steps: (a) listing all items worn; (b) calculating frequency with which each item was worn; (c) identifying associations made with items worn most frequently; (d) determining modes related to associations found in step (c) within each time period; (e) identifying items appearing as alternates or additions to model items; and (f) developing rules of dress relating social roles and statuses to use of particular forms of dress.

## RESULTS

Neither a separate results section nor a detailed reporting of findings was given in this article. The purpose of this study was to develop a structural method for content analysis of dress and illustrate the use of the methods with one culture.

The following illustrate "statements about jewelry worn by females in the third period of time" (1960–1974): (a) Wearing two or three pieces of neck jewelry with either indigenous or Western dress indicates a special occasion. (b) Bracelets are optional if indigenous dress is worn by persons who are at home or who are under age 10. (c) If either indigenous or Western dress is worn, then bracelets are also worn by persons over age 16 appearing in public. (d) Bracelets are not worn with Western or indigenous dress at a funeral.

### CONCLUSIONS AND/OR IMPLICATIONS

Although this research focused on the dress of one West African culture, the researchers concluded that the method can be applied to analyze dress in any culture. A series of analyses could provide a base for cross-cultural comparisons. In additon to photographs, other sources of data were suggested, including newspaper and magazine advertisements, mail-order catalogs, and records of department store retail sales.

(Source: B. Wass and J. Eicher. 1980. *Home Econ. Res. J.* 8:319–26)

**RESEARCH SYNOPSIS 11.2**

## Intertype Competition: Restaurants versus Grocery Stores

Research strategy: Using existing data
Data collection technique: Secondary analysis of survey data

### STATEMENT OF PROBLEM

The purpose of this study was to investigate the determinants of competition between grocery stores and restaurants.

Hypotheses were determined to investigate the impact of a set of socioeconomic, environmental, and marketing-mix factors upon the structure of competition in food retailing. Only two of these hypotheses and their analyses will be illustrated in this synopsis.

#### HYPOTHESES

1. As the assortment of restaurant styles broadens relative to the product assortment in the grocery stores, restaurants' share of the market should expand.
2. As the quality of restaurant service improves, they should attract a greater market share. Conversely, as grocery service improves, restaurants should do worse.

## THEORETICAL FOUNDATION

The theoretical foundation for this study draws upon the premise that the structure of competition interacts with marketing strategies employed by firms in determining the profit performance as well as the contribution of those firms to societal welfare (Thorelli 1977). Bucklin (1972, 66) defined market structure as "the manner by which the sale of some commodity is organized by the firms engaged in trading it."

The strategy, structure, performance paradigm has been used by economists for many years (Bain 1968). Scale economics, merger activity, the concentration ratio, and product differentiation are considered to be the key structural features of an industry (Scherer 1980).

The concept of strategic groups of firms is in keeping with the increased concern regarding the appropriateness of "industry boundaries" as defined by the Census Bureau. For example, Newman (1978) indicates that firms competing in the same market need not choose identical corporate strategies. Members of a group compete directly with one another but only indirectly with firms belonging to other strategic groups. Hirschman's (1978) descriptive theory stresses that the relative strength of various department store types depends upon the socioeconomic configuration of the geographical area in which the stores operate. The investigator emphasizes that restaurants and grocery stores represent separate strategic groups competing for consumers' food dollars.

## METHOD

### SAMPLE

Standard metropolitan statistical areas (SMSAs), the geographical units used for this study, were defined as "integrated economic and marketing entities that have little interaction with contiguous areas not part of the SMSA." The data consisted of 228 grocery store and 136 restaurant SMSAs.

### MATERIALS AND PROCEDURES

Data for this study were from those gathered for the *Census of Retail Trade* (U.S. Department of Commerce 1977), the *Marketing Economics Guide* 1977–78, the "Survey of Buying Power 1978," and Marion et al. (1979). Automotive registration figures were by courtesy of the U.S. Department of Transportation and several state Departments of Motor Vehicles.

### DATA ANALYSIS

The independent variables were an assortment of restaurant styles and quality of service. The dependent variable was the distribution of consumer food expenditures between grocery stores and restaurants (restaurants' share of the market). Each of the variables in this study was derived from a factor analysis of the raw data. Details of this analysis, shown in an appendix to the journal article, are summarized in this synopsis.

The general dependent variable consisted of annual dollar sales per restaurant, annual dollar sales per grocery store, number of restaurants per 1000 households, number of grocery stores with payroll per 1000 households, and restaurant sales divided by the total of restaurant sales plus all grocery sales. Assortment of restaurant styles (independent variable) referred to the variety of food preparation styles.

Ordinary least-squares regression was the statistical method used for data analysis.

## RESULTS

The regression analysis showed that as service quality rises, sales in both restaurants and grocery stores rise as predicted (see Hypothesis 2). Also, higher restaurant wages were positively correlated with number of restaurants per household. The author suggested that it must be the case that wages are bid up where there are many restaurants. Higher wages then attract better employees, with an improvement in the quality of restaurant service.

The assortment independent variable behaved as predicted for restaurants (Hypothesis 1), but not for grocery stores. In other words, broadening of the assortment of restaurant styles increased restaurants' share of the market. However, in the sales per grocery store equation, a negative influence resulted. The researcher explained that it may be that as restaurants' share of food sales has grown from 1972 to 1977, grocery stores have responded by offering a wider assortment of merchandise, which inevitably raises grocery prices and may drive customers away. Also, the increase in assortment may not have been sufficiently broad to counter the trend toward eating out.

## CONCLUSIONS AND/OR IMPLICATIONS

From the analyses of all the data in this study, it was generally concluded that the structure of the grocery trade, the restaurant business, and the interaction between the two are determined by a set of socioeconomic, environmental, and marketing-mix factors. The investigator pointed out that the long-term success of restaurant retailing appears to require "investment" in personnel as well as in capital.

Inasmuch as restaurants' share of total sales ranges cross-sectionally from less than 7% to nearly 32%, it is suggested that an understanding of the determinants of interindustry competition may be of value to government officials charged with antitrust enforcement as well as to food retail executives who make strategic marketing decisions for their firms.

(Source: C. A. Ingene. 1983. *J. Retailing* 59(3):49–72)

RESEARCH SYNOPSIS 11.3

# Female-headed Families: An Ecological Model of Residential Concentration in a Small City

Research strategy: Using existing data
Data collection technique: Secondary analysis of survey data

## STATEMENT OF PROBLEM

The purpose of this study was to propose and evaluate an ecological model to compare the effects of the social composition of subareas (distribution of female-headed families) to the effects of spatial and site features.

## THEORETICAL FOUNDATION

The theoretical perspective for this study is that macrolevel processes influence the nature of the housing stock across residential subareas. Processes operating within the housing market allocate different residential consumers to subareas with different housing characteristics. The most powerful or preferred consumers will obtain the most desirable housing (e.g., housing with more internal and external space, in locations with few nonresidential uses and less congested environments). In accord with the ideas of Form (1954), nonresidential consumers are more powerful than residential consumers. The researchers in the present study also contend that female-headed households is one category of small consumers who will not obtain desirable locations because most desirable areas are allocated to more favorable consumers, such as husband-wife families.

The ecological model constructed for this study parallels that of Guest (1972) for examining the effects of site and spatial features on the location decisions of different types of families in the city.

## METHOD

### SAMPLE

A stratified random sample of 230 of the 1575 blocks in the city of Peoria, Illinois, was drawn. Two-thirds of all the housing units in this city were single-family units.

### MATERIALS AND PROCEDURES

Data were taken from the 1970 Census Third Count Summary Tape. The following calculations were made: (a) percentage of female-headed families, (b) percentage of husband-wife families, (c) economic status, (d) percentage of blacks, (e) dwelling density, (f) percentage of five-room units, (g) population potential, (h) nonresidential use, and (i) distance.

#### DATA ANALYSIS

The independent variables were economic status, percentage of blacks, dwelling density, percentage of five-room units, population potential, nonresidential use, and distance. The dependent variables were percentage of female-headed families and percentage of husband-wife families.

Path analysis was used to examine the distribution of female-headed families and to show how different residential features impinge upon the concentration of family types.

## RESULTS

Intercorrelations were computed among the variables. The correlations with the percentage of female-headed families were all in the expected direction. All correlations were statistically significant except for percentage of five-room units and dwelling density. These variables were not significant predictors of the percentage of female-headed families. Correlations with site and spatial variables showed that female-headed families live in less-desirable blocks. Blocks with higher concentrations of female-headed families had low income status, a low percentage of husband-wife families, and a high percentage of black residents. The most important predictors were percentage of blacks and economic status.

Path analysis results revealed more about the locational processes of female-headed families than ordinary multiple regression. The site variables, by themselves, had negative direct effects on the percentage of female-headed families. The spatial variables had no significant effects. However, through the social variables, the site and spatial variables produced associations of female-headed families with locations with undesirable physical features. Another finding suggested that the locational processes of husband-wife families may set the conditions for the residential distribution of female-headed families.

## CONCLUSIONS AND/OR IMPLICATIONS

The results of the path analysis in this study were consistent with the proposed ecological model, which estimated that the social composition of blocks would be important predictors of female-headed families. The lower the economic status of the block, the higher the percentage of female-headed families. Whether this effect was due to discrimination or to the lower economic power of these families was not determined, but the researchers suggested that the effect is important enough to warrant further investigation.

A comparison of this study with the work of Guest (1972), on which the study was based, shows many parallels as well as differences. The most general result is the similarity of the patterns of concentration of female-headed families in a small city to those in a large city. Therefore, it appears that the ecological theories developed by Burgess (1967) and others for large cities may have wider applicability than previously thought, that is, to a wider range of cities and with a finer level of analysis than in past research.

(Source: D. W. Roncek and H. M. Choldin. 1980. *J. Marr. Fam.*42:157–69)

## NOTES

1. For a discussion of theory in historical research, see Gottschalk (1963) and Kocka (1984).

2. For general discussions of data analysis and other aspects in historical research, consult Barzun and Graff (1985), Beringer (1978), Garraghan (1946), Gottschalk (1956), McBreen (1984), Pitt (1972), Platt (1981a, 1981b), Reitzel and Lindemann (1982), and Shafer (1969). Readers interested in quantitative and computer-aided techniques are referred to Aydelotte, Bogue, and Fogel (1972), Beringer (1978, 193–317), Dollar and Jensen (1971), Floud (1973), Rowney and Graham (1969), and Shorter (1971). Also, see Note 10 in this chapter.

3. For a more detailed classification and discussion of the wide range of documents available for research purposes, see Allport (1942), Gottschalk, Kluckhohn, and Angell (1951), Sechrest (1979), and Webb et al. (1981). (Unlike some authors who make fine distinctions between different types of documents, we are using the term in a general sense.) Hakim (1983) and Potvin and Champagne (1986) have dealt specifically with the use of administrative records in research. Jacob (1984) has done a good job of describing strategies for detecting and adjusting analyses for errors in available published data. He also provides useful references on sources and critiques of important datasets. Reynolds (1979, 214–18) discusses some of the ethical considerations in using archival data.

4. Van Dalen (1979, 55) reminds us that an item of evidence may be a relic (remain) or a document, depending on the intention of the producer and the purpose for which it is used. He gives the following example: "A blank form for recording academic studies and achievements . . . is a remain. But, if someone writes the courses, the grades, credits earned, and the name of the student on it, the form conveys information intentionally; thus, it is a document."

5. This example was taken from Good (1963, 191).

6. Documentary analysis is not restricted to historical research. Contemporary documents may also be investigated. See Platt (1981a, 1981b) for a discussion of problems in documentary research.

7. In addition to using the card catalog, indexes, abstracts, journals, theses, dissertations, and other reference tools mentioned in our discussion of the literature review in Chapter 5, the person doing historical research might find it helpful to consult such sources as *Directory of Archives and Manuscript Repositories, Guide to National Archives of the United States, Historical Statistics of the United States: Colonial Times to 1970,* and *Guide to Historical Literature.*

8. Chronological ordering is helpful, particularly if the researcher wishes to identify the circumstances that have possibly led to an event in the past. The issue of causality—as much a problem, if not more of a problem, in historical research as it is in other types of research—has led Barzun and Graff (1985) to state emphatically that history cannot isolate the cause of any event but can reveal only the conditions accompanying its emergence.

9. Content analysis is often considered a form of indirect "observation" and is frequently discussed along with observational study or unobtrusive measures.

10. A thorough discussion of content analysis is given in Berelson (1954), Budd, Thorp, and Donohew (1967), Holsti (1968, 1969), Krippendorff (1980), Mostyn (1985), Ogilvie, Stone, and Kelly (1982), Pool (1959), Rosengren (1981), and Woodrum (1984).

11. The classic book on the topic of secondary analysis of survey data is by Hyman (1972). More recent works are Fraser and Tobin (1985), Hakim (1982), and Kiecolt and Nathan (1985).

12. A more complete listing of data archives is available in Miller (1983, 148–52). Also see Taeuber and Rockwell (1982) for a description of most of the important publicly available datasets.

13. Even though they contain ethnographic materials rather than survey research data such as those found in the archives already identified, the *Human Relations Area Files* (HRAF) are mentioned here because they include valuable cross-cultural data for secondary analysis. This special type of archive contains ethnographies of over 300 cultures around the world, organized into sections such as food and clothing, housing and technology, and individual and family activities. Many researchers have examined different aspects of culture and behavior by analyzing HRAF data and publishing studies based upon these existing materials that are available in paper files, microfiche, punch cards, or magnetic tape. Barry (1980) and Naroll, Michik, and Naroll (1980) have discussed the content, structure, uses, advantages, and limitations of the files. Lagacé (1974) has published a manual for users (available from HRAF, Inc., Box 2054 Y.S., New Haven, CT 06520).

14. There are a number of useful guides to aid the researcher in accessing available census data. Among them are the *1980 Census Users' Guide, Bureau of the Census Catalog, Data User News,* and *1980 Census Indexes.* Specialized guides are included in *Census '80: Continuing the Factfinder Tradition,* published by the U.S. Government Printing Office. For a brief but informative overview of census information and its potential uses by researchers, see Miller (1983, 154–71) and Stewart (1984, 25–57).

CHAPTER 12

# Evaluation Studies

There are two closely related types of investigations that examine the consequences of planned change: social impact assessment (SIA) and evaluation research. Both concerned about the effects of an intervention, these approaches to evaluation fall into the general category of applied research, are conducted in field settings, and make use of multiple methods. The major difference between the two is that *social impact assessment* is mainly prospective and attempts to foresee and minimize unwanted impacts of a proposed intervention, whereas *evaluation research* is primarily retrospective in that it usually takes place after a policy or program has been set in motion (Freudenburg 1986). Also, SIA is typically more multidisciplinary than evaluation research.

## SOCIAL IMPACT ASSESSMENT

Social impact assessment is an outgrowth of environmental impact assessment (which deals with the physical and biological properties of the natural environment). SIA mainly predicts the social consequences of an intervention *before* it is introduced. Therefore, it is anticipatory research that "seeks to place the expectation and attainment of desired outcomes on a more rational and reliable basis" (Wolf 1983, 15). The most important questions for SIA concern who will benefit and who will lose if the proposed action is implemented.

Since people are impacted by policies in different ways—economically, environmentally, commercially, biologically, socially, and psychologically (Finsterbusch 1977)—social impact assessment is necessarily multidisciplinary; it calls for a variety of research methods to determine whether project- or policy-induced changes are likely to be beneficial or detrimental and who will be affected in what ways. It is not uncommon for the probable impacts identified to be both positive and negative, such as when a new freeway or nuclear plant is constructed.

Social impact assessment has traditionally used some sort of cost-benefit analysis, which is appropriate when the economic consequences of a policy are being questioned. This leads to social impact statements indicating whether or not the anticipated monetary costs are justified by expected benefits. However, for a comprehensive analysis of probable impacts, it is necessary to move beyond the straightforward economic cost-benefit format and attempt to balance *social* costs and benefits as well. To achieve this goal, various techniques have been employed, including the use of social indicators, content analysis of archival data, scenario writing, and simulation and gaming.[1]

There are other approaches, but the following description of the elements of a social impact study that uses social indicators is drawn from Finsterbusch (1977), who outlines specific steps required for social impact assessment. First, it is necessary to select policy alternatives for assessment. To narrow the range of alternatives to a manageable number for intensive analysis, the researcher might conduct what Finsterbusch calls a "first-round SIA" based only on judgments by experts obtained through interviews. Another way to decide on alternatives for detailed assessment is to meet with representatives from different interest groups to discuss candidate alternatives. Often only the most likely options are earmarked for further study, but in other cases, widely disparate alternatives are chosen for examination.

Second, the alternatives selected are described in detail.

Third, the research strategy is developed.

Fourth, the probable impacts of each alternative are identified by various means. Finsterbusch suggests the use of a "relevance tree" that systematically classifies impacts based upon social indicators. With this procedure, a potential policy or program can be examined in terms of its economic, political, social, cultural, and environmental impacts on households, communities, organizations and groups, and societal institutions and systems. (The portion of Finsterbusch's relevance tree pertaining to social impacts on households and communities is reproduced in Fig. 12.1.) Utilizing analysts from different disciplines helps reduce the subjectivity of judgments in identifying impacts by using the relevance tree. Impact identification can be accomplished through interviewing experts as well as persons and organizations who will likely be influenced by the policy decision. The most significant impacts are then subjected to more careful examination.

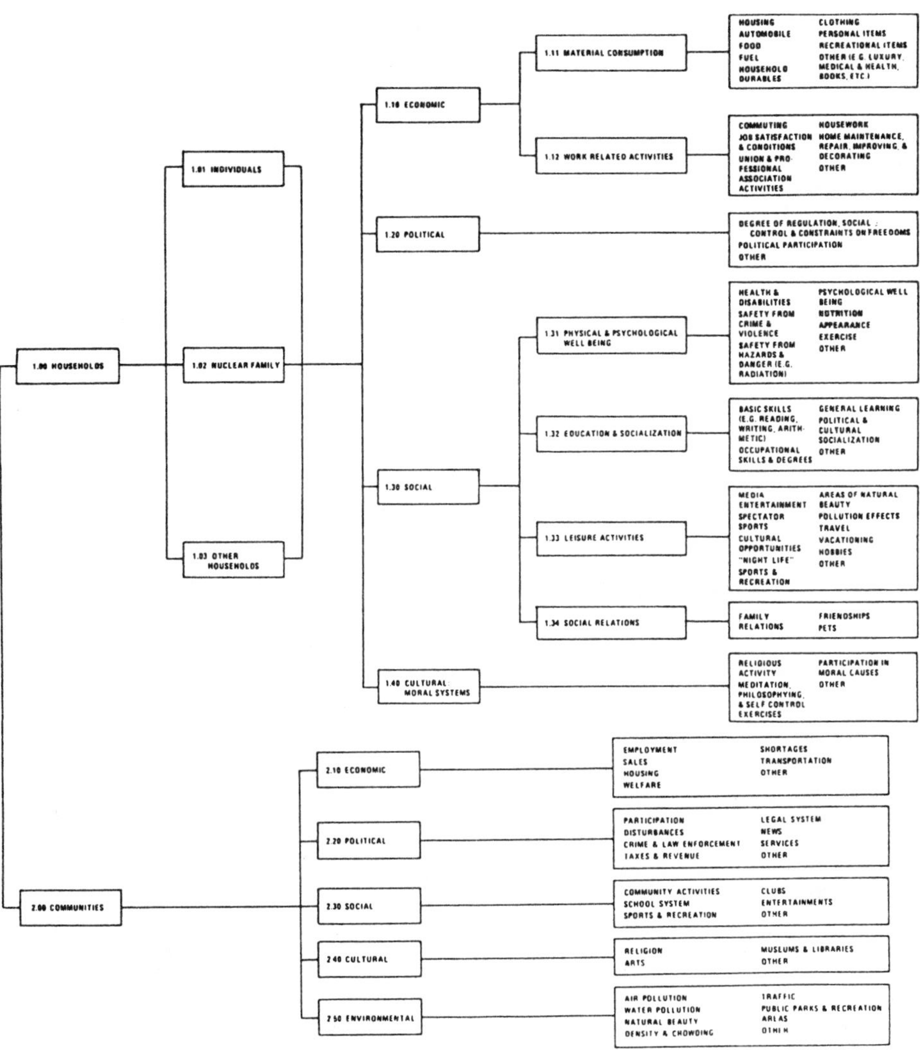


**Figure 12.1.** Portions of an impact relevance tree for social impact analysis. (Reprinted from K. Finsterbusch and C. P. Wolf, eds., *Methodology of Social Impact Assessment,* Stroudsburg, Pa.: Dowden, Hutchinson, and Ross, 1977, p. 6, fig. 1. With permission of Van Nostrand Reinhold.)

Fifth, the magnitude of the anticipated impacts is estimated by using multiple techniques, such as surveys, participant observation, and the analysis of documents and other existing information. Data are analyzed, and conclusions and recommendations are formulated that are based on overall consideration of positive and negative impacts. This is followed by selecting the most appropriate policy alternative, designing the program, and eventually implementing the program. The actual impacts of the program can then be studied by using procedures discussed later under evaluation research.

**Research Synopsis 12.1** is an example of social impact analysis.

## Family Impact Analysis

Also included under the rubric social impact assessment, but with some distinguishing features of its own, is family impact analysis. *Family impact analysis* is concerned specifically with family-related variables. Congressional hearings in the 1970s increased awareness that some bills being introduced in the legislature might be harmful to families (e.g., result in family dissolution), even though the original intent of these government actions was to be helpful and supportive. The potentially counterproductive nature of some of these past economic and social policies was exemplified by the AFDC (Aid to Families with Dependent Children) stipulation that the father be absent from the home before financial assistance is given to the family, the availability of financial aid for institutional but not in-home care of elderly family members, and the disallowance of the child care income tax credit if the care is provided by a relative (Spakes 1983).

Because of the complexity of impact statements involving social and psychological factors and the time necessary for their preparation, as well as the large number of bills introduced at the state and national level each year that affect families in one way or another, it has not been possible to attach family impact statements to very many pieces of legislation under consideration. Consequently, some family analysts have shifted their emphasis and are using this analytic framework primarily as an assessment tool instead of as a predictive tool (Spakes 1983). That is, many persons interested in assessing family policy now utilize family impact analysis as a basis for investigating existing social programs and policies in such areas as adoption, foster care, day care, health, housing, and income maintenance rather than as an anticipatory technique.

Spakes (1983a, 4–7) outlines the steps in family impact analysis: (1) selecting a policy for analysis, (2) clarifying the policy, (3) analyzing how the policy is being implemented, (4) discerning the relationship of the policy to other factors in the social environment, (5) identifying the areas of family functioning most likely to be affected by the policy (membership, economics, socialization/nurturance), (6) measuring the impact, and (7) writing the impact statement. Family impact analysis can be an effective means of determining positive, negative, intended, and unintended effects of programs and policies on families.

Kamerman (1976) identifies several models for family impact analysis, including simulation models using computer analysis, descriptive analytic models employing a combination of quantitative and qualitative methods, descriptive nonquantitative models based upon expert judgment and evaluation, and structured analytic models utilizing checklists.

Stuart (1984, 390–91) describes use of the checklist model for preparing family impact statements in South Australia. Drawing on the procedures developed by the Family Impact Seminar now located at the National Center for Family Studies at Catholic University, the checklist deals with the impact of proposals on important aspects of family functioning and on families at different stages of the life cycle and with different situations and circumstances (e.g., dual earner, non-English speaking).

> The checklist to be completed by each agency consists of a matrix that relates family functions to life cycle and structural considerations. On the vertical axis are listed five areas of family functioning: economic well-being, general well-being, family autonomy, family relationships, and family structure. On the horizontal axis are listed various categories of family composition such as preschool children, school-age children, the aged, and the handicapped and also special family characteristics including such categories as one parent, more than four children, low income, and non-English speaking. The family impact rater is required to fill the appropriate cells in the matrix, indicating a "plus" if the proposal has a generally positive effect and a "minus" if generally negative. The guidelines also state that separate rating sheets may be required for different sections of the community. For example, in a proposal for a rapid transit corridor there might be one sheet for the outer suburbs that would benefit by its use and one for the inner suburbs where houses might be demolished and where there would be more noise in the immediate area of the corridor. For areas in the matrix that have received a negative rating there is to be a statement as to what alternative strategies for achieving the objectives were considered, why they were rejected and, also what remedial measures it would be desirable to undertake.
>
> In addition, the form calls for a statement of what information sources and objective data have been taken into consideration in rating the effects and whether there should be any provision to identify unanticipated effects on families such as the provision for a pilot test, trial implementation, or review procedures. Finally, there is to be a summary statement that brings together the information from the multiple rating sheets. Also, where the assessment conclusions are likely to impact on a specific family style or section of the population, there is to

> be an indication of the appropriate numbers of families affected and the possible extent of the impact on them. The guidelines state that this is particularly important as an aid to decision-making where the proposal is of benefit to some families and had adverse consequences for others.

Although family impact analysis is still in its infancy, there is a growing literature in this area.[2]

## EVALUATION RESEARCH

During the past 25 years or so in the United States, there has been an expansion of public service and social action programs, many of which have required substantial financial support. The national programs created through legislation and the grants by the federal government and private foundations for innovative programs have normally mandated some form of evaluation to judge whether or not the program has produced the desired impact on public health, education, poverty, crime, family planning, housing, and so on. As resources have decreased in recent years, taxpayers have joined the clamor for greater accountability: they are insisting on regular reviews to assess program efficacy. There also has been a growing demand for greater attention to sound evaluation practices. A systematic approach to evaluating programs is necessary to determine which programs should be expanded, modified, or dismantled.

*Evaluation research,* which measures the extent to which programs have followed policy and how well existing programs have achieved goals, can involve all of the methods of data collection described in this book, including quantitative and qualitative techniques, and can make use of nonexperimental as well as experimental, quasi-experimental, and pre-experimental designs.

**Research Synopses 12.2** and **12.3** illustrate evaluation research.

### Evaluation Research and Program Development

Evaluation overlaps with program planning and is embedded in the total process of developing, operating, and analyzing programs. For a program to be evaluable, certain preconditions must be met, as Adams and Schvaneveldt (1985, 320–21) explain:

> First, there needs to be a clearly articulated program structure and operation. Hence there must be a coherent and accurate definition of the program service. Common sense tells us we cannot evaluate what we cannot define. Second, evaluators must be informed as to the spe-

cific goals and proposed effects of the intervention program. Planners, managers and administrators must provide clearly stated short- and long-range goals and objectives void of political rhetoric and ambiguity. And third, the program rationale must provide a clear statement linking program structure and operation to proposed goals and effects. Such justification is a necessary ingredient to determine if the stated program is actually associated with program outcomes. Without a rationale for the proposed connection between program function and program effects (outcome), it is impossible to make any meaningful cause-and-effect evaluation.

Most social action programs include the following steps: (1) determining the need for the program, (2) formulating goals and objectives that are based on identified needs, (3) designing the program to reflect specific goals and objectives, (4) monitoring of program, (5) appraising program outcomes, and (6) analyzing benefits and costs. Although evaluation research may focus on only one or two activities, such as (4) or (5), a comprehensive evaluation involves all of the steps above. Thus, each of these basic evaluation-related activities may be viewed as one stage in the overall evaluation process or as a subtype of evaluation research.

## Types of Evaluation Research

### Needs Assessment

An important first step in program development and an essential type of evaluation research is identification of social problems or unmet needs for which a new or additional program is required. *Needs assessment* refers to the diagnostic procedure that identifies the nature and scope of a problem and the size and location of a target population that requires special services. The population in need may be individuals, families, subcultural groups, organizations, communities, regions, and so on.

The researcher may use existing information, such as descriptive statistics in police, school, mental health, welfare, and unemployment records as well as decennial census data, to obtain indirect indicators or correlates of need. In addition, the investigator may conduct sample surveys to assess incidence and prevalence of a problem or condition. (Incidence refers to the number of new cases, or instances, of a condition [e.g., drug abuse]; and prevalence refers to the total number of existing cases during a specified period of time, irrespective of whether it was "new" in the sense of a first-time occurrence.) Other special surveys might be done to measure the potential beneficiaries of the program, their perceptions of needs, attitudes toward the delivery of available services, and current patterns of utilization of community programs. Surveys might also examine the extent to which professional groups and local agencies are already attempting to deal with the problem or related issues and the success of their efforts. A supplementary means to ascertain need is through community forums in which a cross-section of the potential target population is given an opportunity to express its views directly.

From the information obtained in needs assessment, a program can be developed with clear goals in mind. Specification of goals and operationalization of objectives form the basis for later evaluation.

### Program Monitoring

Once a program has been purposefully designed by using data obtained through needs assessment, it is necessary to investigate progress of the program at periodic intervals. *Program monitoring* (also called formative or process evaluation) examines the dynamics of program operations to evaluate whether or not they are being implemented as prescribed and are delivering the designated services to the target population. In addition to ensuring project conformity, it provides information necessary for fiscal and legal accountability. This continuous, developmental assessment helps improve the ongoing program by uncovering possible shortcomings and resolving problems as well as by identifying positive features that should be retained.

Program monitoring may entail both structured quantitative techniques and more open-ended qualitative methods. Questionnaires may be used to compile routine statistics, such as the number of clients (e.g., patients, students) being served, their characteristics, method of referral, time spent in the program, and benefits from intervention. Increasingly, the recording and storage of these kinds of data are being computerized. Observations and interviews with clients, staff, and program leaders may also be utilized to determine how well a program is functioning in terms of both process and coverage.

### Outcome Assessment

*Outcome assessment* (also called summative evaluation) is carried out at the conclusion of a program to measure the program's results. It seeks to obtain empirical evidence on the extent to which the program accomplished its objectives. When examining the efficacy of a program, it is not uncommon to obtain evidence of both favorable and unfavorable effects as well as unanticipated consequences of the intervention. Regarding the latter, the evaluator might discover that a program to prevent juvenile delinquency was accompanied by higher academic achievement, an increased parental involvement in the schools, and a decreased rate of desertion and divorce. A well-designed and clearly articulated social program is likely to show some effect, even if it is unhypothesized. Care must be taken in interpreting unanticipated results. If enough variables are examined, something will be significant.

Whereas needs assessment and program monitoring employ primarily descriptive methods, program outcome assessment typically involves techniques to gauge the extent to which outcomes have resulted from the intervention. From a scientific vantage point, the ideal model for the evaluation of program outcome is the true experimental design (Chap. 8), which minimizes possible confounding factors and allows the researcher to make causal inferences. Unfortunately, political, ethical, administrative, and budgetary constraints frequently preclude the use of true experimentation and require the researcher to adopt one of the weaker quasi-experimental designs or perhaps a nonexperimental design.

It is quite common for an investigator to examine the outcome of programs without using randomization and experimental manipulation. In these cases, the evaluator undertakes a cross-sectional survey (Chap. 10) with the intention of making post hoc comparisons between program participants and nonparticipants. Comparability between the two groups may be established through matching subjects from the groups on some set of criteria (constructed controls) or through statistical techniques such as ANCOVA and partial correlation (statistical controls).[3]

Pre-experimental designs (e.g., one-group posttest, one-group pretest-posttest) are sometimes also employed in assessing program outcomes, but they lack the precision necessary for ruling out competing explanations of findings. Consequently, conclusions about program outcomes based on these studies are limited.

### Efficiency Analysis

Determining the extent to which a program has produced effects does not necessarily complete the evaluation process. It is usually desirable to go one step further and appraise the efficiency with which a program has fulfilled its objectives. *Efficiency analysis,* including cost-benefit and cost-effectiveness assessments, helps the researcher find out if the results achieved are proportional to the effort expended. *Cost-benefit analysis* assesses the relationship between costs and benefits, or between input (expenditures for personnel, facilities, equipment, materials, etc.) and output (monetary value of program outcomes/impact). The estimate is expressed in monetary terms as the ratio between output and input.

It is often difficult, if not impossible, to place a dollars and cents value on benefits of certain social programs (e.g., reduction in domestic violence, improved mental health). Consequently, *cost-effectiveness analysis* is frequently used instead of cost-benefit analysis as a technique of efficiency assessment. In cost-effectiveness analysis, programs with similar objectives can be compared in terms of output units, such as increases in achievement test scores or reduction in divorce, relative to resources invested in the intervention. But unlike cost-benefit analysis, there is no attempt to monetize program outcomes. It is necessary to attach a monetary value only on the cost of the program.[4]

## Advantages and Limitations

Evaluation research is extremely important because of its contribution to rational decision making in social programming and its potential influence on intervention that may improve the quality of life. While it shares most of the same principles and methods with other types of research, evaluation research has some distinctive features that arise primarily from the conditions under which it is conducted and from its immediate, utilitarian goals.

The realities of the natural setting make evaluation research a very challenging undertaking for many reasons. The questions posed and the variables selected are determined by policy makers, not by the researcher doing the evaluation (evaluator). Program objectives and outcomes are not always clearly operationalized, which makes it difficult to appraise them. Other constraints in the field may preclude sound research practices such as randomization and the use of control groups. Providing the intervention to one segment of the population and withholding it from another is usually not well received by persons staffing the program or by the target group. (Fortunately, there are some ways around this particular problem, such as only delaying the treatment or providing an alternative intervention). Additional record keeping requirements imposed on the organization, unrestricted access to files, regular monitoring of data collection, and other research-related activities often run counter to the priorities of more practice-oriented administrators and people on the staff. These inconveniences caused by the evaluator may lead to subtle resistance or outright noncooperation by those whose program is being evaluated. Interpersonal relationships may be strained further by the continued presence of the evaluator, who will be preparing a report that may eventually terminate the program.

The potential for role conflict on the part of the evaluator is substantial. The evaluator who is an employee of the program (not an outside investigator) is not only answerable to the funding organization's administrator but is also a colleague of the action program staff, some of whom may be reluctant partners in the evaluation process. The interdependent relationships of the evaluator with the administrator and the program staff is crucial to the evaluation task. In the program setting, it is impossible for the evaluator to function autonomously as an objective investigator conducting basic research. The evaluator has at least an indirect investment in the welfare of program beneficiaries, has a commitment to his or her own profession, and has an interest in increasing knowledge about assessing the outcomes of social programs and improving evaluation for the public well-being.

Money and time may produce additional tensions because there is usually too little of each. Typically, the organization expects low-cost evaluations in record time. Seldom is it possible to examine long-term effects, as desirable as this practice may be. In fact, an evaluator is sometimes brought in only after a program is in progress or, worse yet, at the end of a project, thereby necessitating major compromises in evaluation design and methods. Other problems that might emerge in evaluation research are in the areas of utilizing findings and disseminating results.

In spite of some of these obstacles, evaluation research will enjoy increased emphasis in the future and will continue to attract its share of able researchers. According to Lincoln (1985, 251), the practice of evaluation is coming of age, as evidenced by three hallmarks: its coalescence into national organizations; its consideration of subspecializations; and its creation and adoption of standards for professional practice.[5] Growth of the profession toward maturity is also reflected by the appearance of books and handbooks, annual reviews, and journals dealing with evaluation.[6]

## META-ANALYSIS AND PROGRAM EVALUATION

Before concluding the discussion of evaluation studies, a few comments need to be made regarding the increasing role being played by meta-analysis in program evaluation. Described as an approach to literature reviewing in Chapter 5, *meta-analysis* is used to statistically evaluate a set of related empirical studies.[7] In addition to being an attractive alternative to traditional, narrative reviews of the literature, meta-analysis can make a direct contribution to program evaluation by enabling the researcher to quantitatively aggregate the results of previously reported evaluation studies to examine the effects of many different action programs. By integrating the findings of existing studies, an evaluation researcher can obtain some notion of the benefits of social interventions, such as counseling and psychotherapy, educational and marriage enrichment programs, and can learn about the characteristics of intervention techniques that have been associated with varying degrees of success. (See **Research Synopsis 12.4.**)

Evaluation research studies that are alike in certain aspects (e.g., conceptual hypotheses, operational definitions of variables) can be represented in a common metric, such as a percentage, correlation, or probability level. This common value can usually be standardized in order to combine findings across studies.

Although there are many meta-analytic procedures, most can be subsumed under two headings: combination of significance levels and combination of effect sizes.[8] A popular way to synthesize evaluation research is to calculate *effect size*. Although there is no consensus on which effect-size estimate is superior and on how effect size should be interpreted, the most widely used method of comparing two groups is the standardized difference between the treatment- and control-group means. The specific formula adopted depends on the questions being posed by the meta-analyst.

Meta-analysis can also be conducted with nonexperimental studies.

RESEARCH SYNOPSIS 12.1

## Toward an Assessment of the Potential Social Impacts of a Nuclear Power Plant on a Community

Research strategy: Social impact assessment (survey)
Data collection technique: Interview (personal/moderately to highly structured)

### STATEMENT OF PROBLEM

This survey was conducted as a first step of a longitudinal project designed to assess the social impacts of a nuclear power plant. The specific purpose of the survey portion of the project described here was to obtain information about residents' satisfaction with their community, their perception about the quality of their lives, their support for or opposition to the nuclear plant, and their expectations about its effects on the community.

### THEORETICAL FOUNDATION

No theoretical foundation was presented in this article. However, a major goal of the longitudinal project was to supply data for the development of theories and models that might serve as a basis for predicting social impacts of other nuclear generating facilities and, possibly, other large-scale environmental modification projects.

## METHOD

### SAMPLE

A simple random sampling technique was used to select a sample of 350 adult (age 18 and over) citizens of Hartsville, Tennessee, and the surrounding Trousdale County. The median age was 46; average number of school grades completed was 11; 49% were male; 9% were black; 79% were married; and 74% were employed, primarily as salesmen, managers, clerks, farmers, and craftsmen.

### MATERIALS AND PROCEDURES

Personal interviews were conducted in the subjects' homes by trained local female residents. Each respondent was paid $5 for the interview.

The survey included nine general topics: demographic information, satisfaction with neighborhood and community, satisfaction with services available in the community, personal life satisfaction, attitudes toward the nuclear plant and toward Tennessee Valley Authority, perceived likelihood and desirability of events that might accompany construction and operation of the plant, factual knowledge about nuclear power, sources of information about the nuclear plant, and use of specific geographic regions of the community for shopping, socializing, working, recreation, and other activities.

The interview schedule included open-ended questions (e.g., how respondents felt about the community as a place to live and reasons for their view, what they would worry about if the power plant was built) as well as more structured items presented as rating scales, including those using bipolar adjective pairs and Likert formats.

### DATA ANALYSIS

Percentages were computed of respondents' answers to the questions in the survey.

A factor analysis was conducted to examine the interrelations among the subjects' perceptions of anticipated effects of a nuclear plant. A principal components analysis was used, with varimax rotation. All factors with eigenvalues greater than 1.0 were extracted.

Correlation coefficients were calculated between responses to the five-point scale on the "permit construction" question and 18 other variables in the survey, including demographic factors, measures of the perceived quality of life, and perceived likelihood of potential effects of the facility.

## RESULTS

Most subjects were very satisfied with the quality of life in the community and neighborhood. Neighborhoods were rated as extremely "friendly" and "pleasant," with over three-fourths of the respondents marking the extreme point on the scale. Factor analysis of responses on the five-point scale to a list of 24 potential effects of the plant on the community yielded five factors: hazards, economic growth, lower cost of living, social disruptions, and community visibility.

Significant correlations were found between opposition to construction of the plant and four of the demographic variables: being female, being Caucasian, having more years of education, and having lived longer at the current address. None of the four indicators of the perceived quality of life was correlated with opposition to construction. However, opposition to the plant was associated significantly with high estimates of the likelihood of hazards and social disruption and relatively low estimates of the likelihood of economic growth, lower costs, and community visibility.

### CONCLUSIONS AND/OR IMPLICATIONS

The results of this survey indicated that residents of this community were relatively satisfied with life in their community. But they anticipated some undesirable effects with construction of a nuclear plant, such as pollution, radiation hazards, traffic congestion, and crowding in schools. They also expected desirable effects in the form of more jobs, increased business, and better pay, which may outweigh the undesirable effects.

In the next survey of these same people, the researchers hope to discover whether the current levels of opposition to and support for the plant are maintained. The results of both surveys should permit them to monitor changes in social impacts and to analyze the ability of community residents to anticipate outcomes and evaluate their desirability.

(Source: J. W. Lounsbury, E. Sundstrom, C. R. Schuller, T. J. Mattingly, and R. DeVault. 1977. In *Methodology of Social Impact Assessment,* ed. K. Finsterbusch and C. P. Wolf, 265–77. Stroudsburg, Pa.: Dowden, Hutchinson, and Ross. With permission of Van Nostrand Reinhold.)

**RESEARCH SYNOPSIS 12.2**

## An Overview of the National Nutrition Education and Training Program Evaluation

Research strategy: Evaluation research (field experiment)
Data collection technique: Questionnaire

### STATEMENT OF PROBLEM

The purpose of this research was a comprehensive evaluation of the Nutrition Education and Training (NET) program of two states.

### HYPOTHESIS

Program implementation impacts on children's nutrition-related attitudes, beliefs, values, knowledge, and dietary habits/behavior.

## THEORETICAL FOUNDATION

An organizing framework was developed to delineate the components of nutrition education programs and their interactions. The researchers point out that individual nutrition education programs can be designed according to cognitive theory, which holds that children must first learn new information, which then affects their beliefs and feelings about specific nutrition-related behaviors, and finally affects the nutritional behaviors.

Nutritional programs also can be designed around a social environmental perspective. In contrast to changing children's food consumption behavior from classroom learning, this perspective proposes that these behaviors can be changed with new food choices in the cafeteria or increased interest from parents.

## METHOD

### SAMPLE

The states of Nebraska and Georgia were chosen for these field experiments. Although NET programs operate in nearly all states, the researchers chose to evaluate "exemplary" state programs, where they hoped to find positive results because at the time of the studies many state programs were not fully implemented. Also, they wished to determine NET accomplishments under the best circumstances and to provide NET practitioners with information on the effects of two very different programs that had already undergone a good deal of development.

In Nebraska, data were collected, through a randomized evaluation design, from over 2300 children in 96 classrooms distributed across grades 1–6 in 20 schools. Thirteen schools served as treatment schools and seven as control schools. Nebraska's program followed a centralized model, with uniform materials and training at local sites.

In Georgia, the research design consisted of nonrandom selection of treatment schools that were already participating in NET and control schools that were not in the program. Approximately 1400 children in grades 1–8, distributed across seven school districts, constituted the sample. Georgia used a decentralized model, which provided guidance, resources, and a framework for nutrition education, but local project directors decided which activities to implement.

### MATERIALS AND PROCEDURES

The evaluation team in Nebraska administered a battery of instruments on three occasions. All children took a pretest, then a posttest 10 weeks later. A subsample of NET and non-NET children also completed a subset of the instruments 10 months later as a follow-up measure of retention and/or delayed change. The battery of instruments measured nutrition knowledge, attitudes, and behaviors.

The same procedures were used in the Georgia evaluation. However, since these schools used different curricula and materials, measuring instruments were designed to detect general impact on nutrition knowledge, attitudes, and reported habits rather than changes specific to a particular curriculum.

### DATA ANALYSIS

The researchers do not describe the method of data analysis, but references to status reports and final reports of the evaluation projects are given at the end of the article.

## RESULTS

In the Nebraska study, "strong positive impacts" were found on NET children's nutrition-related knowledge across several different curriculum-specific and standardized measures of knowledge and across grades 1–6. The effects on nutrition knowledge were larger and more consistent in grades 4–6 than in grades 1–3. The researchers point out that the curriculum in grades 4–6 was primarily knowledge-oriented, in contrast to an experience-oriented curriculum in grades 1–3. In grades 4–6, NET children were more willing than non-NET children to taste unfamiliar foods. No strong, program-related effects were found on measures of food attitudes, reported food habits, or overall plate waste.

In the Georgia evaluation study, results showed the program had strong positive effects on nutritional knowledge, especially in grades 1–4. No strong program-related impacts were found on food attitudes or self-reported food habits.

## CONCLUSIONS AND/OR IMPLICATIONS

The authors stressed that, while the findings from evaluations of the NET programs in Nebraska and Georgia are important, it is difficult to generalize from them. Therefore, they also drew upon evaluations of nutrition education programs in California, Pennsylvania, West Virginia, and from a five-state study. In summary, positive effects of a nutritional education program on nutritional knowledge appear almost universal, but effects on attitudes, food preference, plate waste, and other behavioral matters are inconsistent across studies and are confined to specific grade and food-item combinations.

Recommendations included more emphasis in the future on the training of school foodservice personnel and the development of integrated programs, as well as on program monitoring and evaluation materials. Provision of technical assistance in program evaluation was also suggested.

(Source: R. G. St.Pierre and V. Rezmovic. 1982. *J. Nutr. Ed.* 14(2): 61–65, © Society for Nutritional Education)

**RESEARCH SYNOPSIS 12.3**

## An Evaluation of a Parent Education Program for Fathers of School-aged Children

Research strategy: Evaluation research (field experiment)
Data collection techniques: Questionnaire, interview (structured), projective measure

### STATEMENT OF PROBLEM

The purpose of this study was to develop and evaluate a parent education program for fathers of school-aged children.

#### NULL HYPOTHESIS

There are no significant differences between the experimental group of fathers, who were given a parent education program, and a control group of fathers on (a) fathers' communication skills, (b) children's perceptions of their relationships with their fathers, and (c) family systemic effects (assessed in terms of fathers' and mothers' family concepts).

### THEORETICAL FOUNDATION

The reciprocal relationships between husbands' and wives' paid and family work has been described in a model developed by Pleck (1977). With wives increasing their paid work, a reduction in their family work is needed to avoid role overload, with a corresponding increase in family work by husbands to pick up the slack. However, research results indicate that husbands' participation in family work continues to be low compared to that of their wives.

Although it is believed that men's participation in the parenting aspect of family work may be facilitated by educational intervention, parent education for fathers is a badly neglected area. A review of the literature on parent education reveals numerous approaches that can be classified according to their pedagogical method and theoretical orientation.

Theoretically, programs have been developed from client-centered (Dreikurs and Soltz 1964; Gordon 1976), behavioral (Patterson 1971), and other orientations.

## METHOD

### SAMPLE

Eleven married Caucasian fathers with at least one child between the ages of 6 and 12 years volunteered to participate in the study. They were recruited from announcements distributed by churches, schools, health and social service agencies, and businesses serving a Boston neighborhood. Using the same procedures, a nonequivalent control group, with reasonably comparable demographic characteristics, was recruited from two suburban communities.

### MATERIALS AND PROCEDURES

The parent education program consisted of eight 3-hour sessions held weekly and emphasized the development of communication skills. An advanced doctoral candidate, with skills training and experience in group work, led the group. The program included both didactic and experimental components. The format for the skill training sessions was based upon the work of Ivey (1971).

This study was a quasi-experimental nonequivalent control group design. Both the experimental and control groups of fathers, their wives, and one of their children were pretested and posttested on the dependent measures before and after the parent education program. These measures were fathers' communication skills, children's perceptions of their relationships with their fathers, and family systemic effects (assessed in terms of fathers' and mothers' family concepts).

The *Sensitivity to Children Scale* (STC) (Stollak 1968) and the *Porter Acceptance Scale* (PAS) (Porter 1954) were used to assess fathers' communication skills. The STC scale consists of 16 problem situations. The PAS is a 40-item multiple-choice questionnaire subdivided into four subscales that are combined to give an overall acceptance score.

A 31-item schedule (Doyle 1981) was used in the children's interviews to determine their relationships with their fathers. A second measure of this variable was a projective device, the *Kinetic-Family-Drawing* (KFD), in which the child was asked to draw his/her family doing something (Burns and Kaufman 1972).

Family systemic effects were assessed with the *Family Concept Test* (FCT) developed by van der Veen (1965).

### DATA ANALYSIS

The independent variable was the parent education program. The dependent variables were the fathers' communication skills, children's perceptions of their relationships with their fathers, and family systemic effects.

Analysis of covariance was the statistic used to analyze data from the STC, the PAS, and the FCT, with the pretest scores as the covariants. The choice of this method was based upon its ability to test significance after adjusting for initial differences between the experimental and control groups. The Fisher's exact test was used to analyze the data from the structured child interview and the KFD.

## RESULTS

The findings revealed an improvement in fathers' communication skills after the parent education program. Fathers in the experimental group (who received the parent education program) improved significantly more ($p < .05$) than control group fathers on the STC score and significantly reduced their undesirable responses. No significant differences were found between the groups on the total STC score nor on the subscales.

There were also significant differences between the experimental and control groups on children's perceptions of their relationships with their fathers. Significantly more children whose fathers participated in the parent education program—compared to control group children—were judged to have perceived positive changes in their relationship with their fathers.

The family satisfaction of fathers in the education group decreased significantly ($p < .01$) compared to control subjects.

## CONCLUSIONS AND/OR IMPLICATIONS

The researchers concluded that this evaluation of the skills training program for fathers shows that the program has promise, especially in the ability of the program to encourage fathers to apply their skills to their relationships with their children. They also cautioned that the findings must be regarded as somewhat tentative, particularly since the participants were volunteers and the *N* was small. They suggest that subsequent evaluations should include follow-up assessment and an attempt to refine the measures for the assessment of children's perceptions.

(Source: R. F. Levant and G. F. Doyle. 1983. *Fam. Relat.* 32:29–37. Copyrighted 1983 by the National Council on Family Relations, 1910 West County Road B, Suite 147, St. Paul, Minn. 55113. Used with permission.)

RESEARCH SYNOPSIS 12.4

# Bringing the Review of Literature into the Age of Quantification: Meta-analysis as a Strategy for Integrating Research Findings in Family Studies

Research strategy: Meta-analysis

## STATEMENT OF PROBLEM

The purpose of this study was to present a meta-analysis of research on the effectiveness of the Minnesota Couple Communication Program (CCP).

Several specific questions were raised: Does CCP have a positive effect? Are couples who participated in CCP superior to those who had no treatment? Are couples who participated in CCP superior to those who had no treatment after controlling for group differences at pretest? Are couples who participated in CCP superior to couples who participated in some alternative treatment program?

## THEORETICAL FOUNDATION

Meta-analysis, a quantitative method for integrating research literature across studies, was developed by Glass (1977) and his associates (Glass, McGaw, and Smith 1981). It involves identifying a common metric in order to combine results across studies. Most meta-analysts calculate *effect size,* the difference between two means divided by a standard deviation (Cohen 1977). The specific formula for calculating effect size varies with the question being addressed. The use of effect size is not limited to studies where mean differences have been calculated between experimental and control groups. Correlational data can be transformed into a difference between means or vice versa. It is important to select a group of studies with common independent and dependent variables and/or hypotheses.

## METHOD

### SAMPLE

The sample consisted of the 20 CCP studies (out of 26 completed) that were available in some published form through August 1981. These 20 studies represent 34 different CCP groups and include 294 couples who participated in CCP, 202 untreated couples, and 63 couples who participated in an alternative treatment.

### MATERIALS AND PROCEDURES

The CCP is a structured, 12-hour program that was developed to teach communication skills to couples (Miller, Nunnally, and Wackman 1976).

The findings of the 20 CCP studies were grouped according to questions and type of measure. All attitudinal measures were self-report and all behavior measures were based on coded observations of couple interaction. Measures were scored in a consistent direction, so that a positive effect size always indicated a favorable change (e.g., increased marital satisfaction).

### DATA ANALYSIS

Delta was the form used to calculate effect size: $M_t - M_c/SD_c$. An effect size of .35 or below was considered small, .36 to .65 was moderate, and .66 or above was large. (See Cohen 1977, 20–27, for a discussion of delta). Inasmuch as sampling distributions have not been determined, no significance tests are available for delta.

Before a study was omitted due to lack of statistical information, papers on statistical technology were consulted that described strategies for retrieving the necessary information to calculate effect size. Statistics such as *t*, *F*, and chi-square can be converted to correlations and then to effect sizes. Tables in Cohen (1977) can be used for these conversions. However, it is difficult to recover enough information to calculate effect size from studies using nonparametric statistics, since they do not include basic concepts of means and standard deviations.

Following is an example of the specific formula used for one of the questions asked in this meta-analysis study, Does CCP have a positive effect?

$$ES = \frac{M \text{ Exp Post} - M \text{ Exp Pre}}{SD \text{ Exp Post}}$$

(The mean of the CCP group at pretest is subtracted from the mean for the CCP group at posttest and divided by the standard deviation of the CCP group at the posttest.)

## RESULTS

In answer to the question, Do couples change? a comparison was made between the pretest and posttest and between the pretest and follow-up test. In almost all measures used, positive change occurred in couples experiencing CCP.

Another result included a large difference between CCP and no-treatment groups in the use of positive communication behaviors ($ES = 1.16$).

## CONCLUSIONS AND/OR IMPLICATIONS

The author concluded that the application of meta-analysis techniques to the review of literature is an innovation made necessary by the pressure of an ever-increasing number and complexity of primary research studies. The development of family studies, like the rest of the social sciences, has moved from the qualitative to the quantitative. It is time to recognize the importance and power of applying quantitative methodology to the literature review process. Also, meta-analysis can produce a more precise phrasing of hypotheses in research. Theoretical propositions can be expressed not only in terms of expected direction but also in terms of expected size of effect.

(Source: K. S. Wampler. 1982. *J. Marr. Fam.* 44:1009–23)

# NOTES

1. Finsterbusch and Wolf (1977), Finsterbusch, Llewellyn, and Wolf (1983), and Soderstrom (1981) illustrate techniques that have been used in social impact assessment. For a recent review of the literature on SIA, see Freudenburg (1986). Also see Leistritz and Ekstrom (1986) for an international bibliography of social impact assessment and mitigation.

2. For more information regarding family impact analysis, see Kamerman (1976) and Spakes (1983a, 1983b). Special issues of *Journal of Marriage and the Family* (Nye and McDonald 1979) and *Journal of Family Issues* (Cherlin 1984) deal specifically with family policy.

3. For a concise discussion of comparative designs for assessment of program outcome, see the excellent book by Rossi and Freeman (1985). Bentler and Woodward (1979) also provide a lucid presentation of nonexperimental evaluation research.

4. This is a simplified treatment of a complex topic. The reader is referred to Levin (1983), Thompson (1980), and Yates (1985) for more information about efficiency analysis.

5. See ERS Standards Committee (1982), Joint Committee on Standards for Educational Evaluation (1982), and Lincoln (1985).

6. Several good sources that provide an overview of evaluation research are available, including Bernstein and Sheldon (1983), Cook and Shadish (1986), Cook, Leviton, and Shadish (1985), Cronbach (1982), Cronbach et al. (1980), Franklin and Thrasher (1976), Guba and Lincoln (1981), Patton (1986), Rossi and Freeman (1985), Rutman (1984), Struening and Brewer (1983), Suchman (1969), and Weiss (1972). Other materials address subtypes of evaluation research, such as needs assessment, in greater detail: Burdge (1983), McKillip (1987), Neuber et al. (1980), Warheit, Bell, and Schwab (1977). Still others deal primarily with data collection (Burstein, Freeman, and Rossi 1985) or with qualitative methods in particular, (Fetterman 1984; Fetterman and Pitman 1986; Patton 1980). A few references are also available that provide more of a "how-to-do-it" approach: Fink and Kosecoff (1980a, 1980b) and Herman (1988). Palumbo (1987) addresses the politics of program evaluation.

An increasing number of journals are now devoted exclusively to the area, including

*Evaluation, Evaluation Practice, Evaluation Review, Evaluation and the Health Professions, Evaluation in Education, Evaluation and Program Planning, Educational Evaluation and Policy Analysis,* and *New Directions for Program Evaluation.* Sage Publications, Inc. publishes a review series, *Evaluation Studies Review Annual,* that provides a sample of vital concerns, important research topics, and contemporary issues in the field.

7. See Glass, McGaw, and Smith (1981), Hunter, Schmidt, and Jackson (1982), Rosenthal (1984), Strube and Hartmann (1983), and Wolf (1986) for a more complete discussion of meta-analysis.

8. Another approach has limited current use. It is the voting or box-score method, in which studies are sorted into three sets based on their findings: significantly positive, significantly negative, and nonsignificant. If a plurality of studies falls into one of these three categories, the modal category is assumed to give the best representation of the outcomes of research in the area. As Hedges and Olkin (1980) show, this simple form of meta-analysis has several drawbacks.

**Table 12.1. Summary of Research Synopses Illustrating Different Research Methods, Chapters 8–12**

| Synopsis | Research Strategy | Data Collection Technique(s) | Other Features | Titles and Author(s) | Source |
|---|---|---|---|---|---|
| **8.1** | Experiment (laboratory) | Questionnaire | Systematic sampling, use of deception and debriefing, ANOVA | Consumer Response to In-store Price Information Environments (Zeithaml) | *Journal of Consumer Research* |
| **8.2** | Experiment (laboratory) | Physiological/physical measurement | Animal subjects, factorial design, ANOVA | Influence of Zinc and Iron on Dietary Fluoride Utilization in the Rat (Cerklewski and Ridlington) | *Journal of Nutrition* |
| **8.3** | Experiment (laboratory) | Observation (structured) | Interobserver reliability calculated, MANOVA | Social Support and Exploration (Henderson) | *Child Development* |
| **8.4** | Experiment/single-case (field) (Experiment [field], *see also* **12.2, 12.3**) | Observation (structured/time sampling) | Multiple-baseline design, interobserver reliability calculated | A Method for Integrating an Autistic Child into a Normal Public School Classroom (Russo and Koegel) | *Journal of Applied Behavior Analysis* |
| **9.1** | Field study/ethnographic | Participant observation, interview (unstructured), diary, photography, cognitive mapping, questionnaire | Use of sound recorder; primarily inductive data analysis | Place and Personal Identity in Old Age: Observations from Appalachia (Rowles) | *Journal of Environmental Psychology* |
| **9.2** | Field study/ethnographic | Participant observation, interview (unstructured), questionnaire, archival records | Chi-square, Spearman rank-order correlation | Home Economists as Cross-cultural Researchers: A Field Study of Ghanaian Clothing Selection (Littrell) | *Home Economics Research Journal* |
| **9.3** | Field study | Observation (structured/ time sampling), rating scale | Interobserver reliability calculated, ANOVA | Playground Designs and Preschool Children's Behavior (Brown and Burger) | *Environment and Behavior* |

Table 12.1. *continued*

| Synopsis | Research Strategy | Data Collection Technique(s) | Other Features | Titles and Author(s) | Source |
|---|---|---|---|---|---|
| **9.4** | Field study/case study | Participant observation, observation (structured) interview (unstructured, structured), archival records, questionnaire | Use of a "critical case" to test a theory | *Implementing Organizational Innovation* (Gross, Giacquinta, and Bernstein) | Same |
| **10.1** | Survey | Interview (structured), physiological/physical measurement | Chi-square test | Social Research Methods Applied to Nutritional Assessment (Ernster, McAleenan, and Larkin) | *Ecology of Food and Nutrition* |
| **10.2** | Survey | Interview (structured/telephone) | Random sampling of numbers from telephone directory; bivariate and multiple equation analyses | Life Status Changes and Changes in Consumer Preferences and Satisfaction (Andreasen) | *Journal of Consumer Research* |
| **10.3** | Survey | Questionnaire (personally delivered/picked up) | Correlation, ANOVA | Comparative Evaluation of Manager Performance in Selected Types of Food Services (Khan and Al-Obaidy) | *Journal of Foodservice Systems* |
| **10.4** | Survey | Questionnaire (interview-and self-administered) | Multistage probability sampling, ANOVA (and post-hoc tests), ANCOVA, MCA, multiple regression, reliability coefficients reported for the different instruments used with the study sample | Energy Conservation: Family Values, Household Practices and Contextual Variables (Hogan and Paolucci) | *Home Economics Research Journal* |

Table 12.1. *continued*

| Synopsis | Research Strategy | Data Collection Technique(s) | Other Features | Titles and Author(s) | Source |
|---|---|---|---|---|---|
| **10.5** | Survey (*see also* **12.1**) | Questionnaire (mail) | Chi-square, factor analysis, discriminant analysis | Characteristics of Adopters and Non-Adopters of Home Computers (Dickerson and Gentry) | *Journal of Consumer Research* |
| **11.1** | Using existing data (documentary/historical) | Archival records/content analysis | Use of photographs | Analysis of Historic and Contemporary Dress: An African Example (Wass and Eicher) | *Home Economics Research Journal* |
| **11.2** | Using existing data | Secondary analysis of survey data | Factor analysis, regression | Intertype Competition: Restaurant Versus Grocery Stores (Ingene) | *Journal of Retailing* |
| **11.3** | Using existing data | Secondary analysis of survey data | U.S. Census data, stratified random sampling, path analysis | Female-headed Families: An Ecological Model of Residential Concentration in a Small City (Roncek and Choldin) | *Journal of Marriage and the Family* |
| **12.1** | Social impact assessment (survey) | Interview (personal/moderately to highly structured) | Simple random sampling, percentages, factor analysis, Pearson product-moment correlation | Toward an Assessment of the Potential Social Impacts of a Nuclear Power Plant on a Community (Lounsbury et al.) | *Methodology of Social Impact Assessment* |
| **12.2** | Evaluation research (field experiment) | Questionnaire | Randomized evaluation design in one study, nonrandom selection of treatment schools that were already participating in the program for the second study | An Overview of the National Nutrition Education and Training Program Evaluation (St. Pierre and Rezmovic) | *Journal of Nutrition Education* |

**Table 12.1.** ***continued***

| Synopsis | Research Strategy | Data Collection Technique(s) | Other Features | Titles and Author(s) | Source |
|---|---|---|---|---|---|
| **12.3** | Evaluation research (field experiment) | Questionnaire, interview (structured), projective measure (drawing) | Quasi-experimental (nonequivalent control group design), ANCOVA, Fisher's Exact Test | An Evaluation of a Parent Education Program for Fathers of School-aged Children (Levant and Doyle) | *Family Relations* |
| **12.4** | Meta-analysis | | Effect sizes calculated | Bringing the Review of Literature into the Age of Quantification: Meta-analysis as a Strategy for Integrating Research Findings in Family Studies (Wampler) | *Journal of Marriage and the Family* |

PART 4

# Data Preparation and Analysis

CHAPTER 13

# Preparing Data for Analysis

Assuming that the researcher has selected one or more of the methods of data collection described in Chapter 7, has collected data, and has scored questionnaires, interview schedules, observations, and other information in his or her possession, the researcher now must assemble and organize the raw data and put them into forms that permit quantitative analyses. Between data collection and analysis some intermediate steps must be performed: establishing categories and coding data, preliminary editing, entering data into the computer, computer editing, and using a computer program.

## ESTABLISHING CATEGORIES AND CODING DATA

The task of classifying data is essentially "one of reducing a wide variety of idiosyncratic items of information to a more limited set of attributes composing a variable" (Babbie 1986, 331). The reduction of data to simplify the handling of a large number of research subject responses and the transformation of any nonnumerical data into categories with numerical codes are necessary before any statistical analyses can be attempted. As might be expected, the classification and coding of objective information presents fewer problems for the researcher than dealing with more conceptual information.

### Basic Coding Strategies

There are two basic coding strategies. In the first, the *coding scheme* (the system of numerical codes that represents and classifies items or variables) is derived from the research problem or the theory underlying the investigation and is developed in advance of data collection. Following a *deductive method,* the researcher begins with conceptual definitions, operationalizes the terms, and constructs appropriate indexes, such as questions with specific response alternatives. The alternatives (answers) are either precoded with numbers printed beside them or are listed so that a numerical code can later be assigned to each. Research participants are able to classify themselves on a questionnaire or checklist with these preconstructed categories in much the same way as they would answer a multiple-choice test. Or the investigator can observe the subject's behavior and simultaneously code the observational data into categories. If a structured interview is used for data collection, the researcher can use the preexisting codes to report categories of responses to oral questions as they are asked in the interview situation.

In the second approach to coding, categorization follows data collection. There is no preconceived coding scheme. Only after a sufficiently large number of responses have been obtained for an item are codes assigned to the responses. For example, in a questionnaire study, a researcher might examine the answers of 50 to 100 subjects or more to an open-ended question, list the responses that occurred at least 15% of the time, and use these as the response alternatives and the basis for a coding scheme for that particular item. An *inductive method* of coding, this approach is often employed in interview and questionnaire studies with open-ended questions. It is also used in observational studies that produce comprehensive narrative records (as opposed to those utilizing precoded observer systems) and in some research utilizing data from existing documents.

Sometimes the two coding strategies are combined, such as when extensive responses are obtained, concepts are induced from the data, and a second set of data is collected that is better formulated, more specific, and directly related to the concepts under investigation (Weick 1968).

In all cases, the coding scheme should relate closely to the research problem, contain code categories that are exhaustive and mutually exclusive, and possess sufficient detail. *Exhaustiveness* refers to a classification system in which every response can be categorized. This may require the use of a special category called "other" or "miscellaneous." *Mutual exclusiveness* means that every piece of information is classified into one and only one category. The criterion of *sufficient detail* underscores the importance of having enough categories to ensure that important distinctions of a detailed nature can be made. As a general rule, it is better to have too many categories than too few; the number of categories can always be reduced later. If the researcher begins with a few broad categories, finer distinctions are lost entirely. It is important to bear in mind that the final number of categories used in the analyses may be limited by the sample size and planned statistical techniques.

## Illustration of Coding Schemes

Because of the importance of describing the sample in one's study and the potential usefulness of biographical information as variables in research, most investigators routinely collect *biodata* on their subjects through the use of a questionnaire or demographic checklist of some kind. Here are examples of just a few questions that might be asked on a biographical questionnaire. The respondent would be requested to fill in the necessary information or circle the number of the alternative that best answers the question.

1. What is your college major?
   1 = vocational home economics education
   2 = family and child development
   3 = fashion, clothing, and textiles
   4 = nutrition and foods
   5 = family resource management
   6 = interior design
   7 = other (explain)__________
2. What is your age in years?________
3. What is your sex?
   1 = male
   2 = female
4. What is your racial or ethnic group?
   1 = white (except Hispanic)
   2 = black
   3 = Hispanic
   4 = Native American
   5 = other (explain)__________
5. Who did you live with while you were growing up?
   1 = both biological parents
   2 = biological mother only
   3 = biological father only
   4 = biological mother and stepfather
   5 = biological father and stepmother
   6 = adoptive parents
   7 = relatives
   8 = other (explain)__________
6. How many brothers and sisters do you have?__________
7. What is your birth order position?
   1 = oldest
   2 = middle
   3 = youngest
   4 = only child
8. How much education did your father complete?
   1 = less than high school
   2 = high school
   3 = some college
   4 = associate degree
   5 = bachelor's degree
   6 = graduate degree
   7 = other (explain)__________
9. What was your father's occupation?
   ____________________
10. What were the reasons for selecting your major area of study?
   ____________________

Question 2, specifying age in years, will yield a number (e.g., 18, 20, 40). Similarly, Question 6 will lead to such responses as 0, 2, 4, or 7, indicating how many siblings the subject has. The numbers called for in these two items are actual numbers that stand for their respective quantities (they are ready to be analyzed). Conversely, the numbers the subject circles in answer to precoded Questions 1, 3, 4, 5, 7, and 8 represent an arbitrary numerical code decided on by the researcher. The code digit 1 in these six questions has the various meanings of vocational home economics education, male, white, both biological parents, oldest, and less than high school. There was no special reason for choosing 1 to represent these meanings; the investigator could have selected any number.

On Question 9, the subject is asked to write in the father's occupation. Since there are an extremely large number of possible answers to this open-ended question (there are several thousand occupations), the researcher can simplify the handling of these narrative data by adopting a preestablished coding scheme such as Hollingshead's (1975) *Four Factor Index of Social Status* or Duncan's *Socioeconomic Index* (Duncan 1961; Featherman and Stevens 1982).

For postcoding, another option is to devise a new coding scheme, especially for the project, to code the recorded responses. For example, the investigator might classify the diverse responses to Question 9 according to these categories: 1 = professional and technical, 2 = managerial and proprietary, 3 = clerical and sales, 4 = skilled, 5 = semiskilled, 6 = unskilled, 7 = unemployed, and 8 = other (explain)__________. By using the numeric codes 1 through 8, the researcher reduces the answers to a more practical number and translates them into a form that facilitates analysis.

Another possibility for classifying responses to Question 9 might be to distinguish among occupations that represent different sectors of the economy (e.g., manufacturing, commerce, education, health). (Frequently, occupational information is combined with responses from other personal background items dealing with educational attainment and income to calculate an index of socioeconomic status.) The nature of the research problem and the analyses planned for the study will help determine what coding scheme works best.

Since the coders must exercise judgment in the classification of open-ended responses according to the coding scheme, it is imperative that those doing the coding be carefully trained. Additionally, the investigator should perform reliability checks at regular intervals to ensure intercoder reliability if more than one coder is used.

Sometimes, as with Question 10, a single item allows multiple responses. Since narrative answers are invited to the question, What were the reasons for selecting your major area of study? the researcher might want to look over the completed questionnaires to see what answers were actually written in a certain percentage of the time. Recall that in such cases the investigator notes the most frequent responses (e.g., those given 15% of the time), assigns a numerical code to each, and uses these as a basis for coding the item (usually done during the editing phase). Since the number of categories for this open-ended question will have to be limited for practical purposes and all responses will probably not fit the codes, it is necessary to include a code labeled "other" to accommodate infrequent answers.

Of course, the researcher who is familiar with the literature on vocational choice can avoid some of the difficulties associated with an open-ended item like Question 10. The investigator might be able to identify 10 reasons that have been typically cited for selection of academic major in past research (e.g., challenging, potential salary, service to society). These could be provided on the questionnaire as alternative answers to the question with accompanying codes. The subject might be asked to select only three. Or the researcher could list all 10 with blanks (rather than numerical codes) beside each, with instructions to check as many as apply. In effect, Question 10 would then become 10 different little questions with a 1 subsequently coded for each question checked (to indicate *yes*) or a 2 if it is not checked (to indicate *no*). Again, one of the alternatives (i.e., little questions that could be checked) should be "other" or "miscellaneous" to ensure exhaustiveness of categories.

As mentioned, it is preferable to code data with as much detail as possible so that later, the combination of categories used to code an item remains an option. Looking at Question 9, the occupational categories could subsequently be combined into 1 = professional and 2 = nonprofessional. Likewise, the eight living arrangement categories in Question 5 could be coded simply as 1 = both biological parents and 2 = not both biological parents. The educational attainment categories of Question 8 could be collapsed into dichotomous categories with the codes 1 = no college degree and 2 = college degree. Some of the categories on Questions 4, 5, and 8 may even be dropped altogether if there are no subjects in them or if there are insufficient cases for analysis.

The various considerations in coding scheme construction discussed above apply equally to demographic-type items and to more conceptual items in human ecology research. The former were used as examples for the sake of simplicity and because biodata are applicable to research in all of the specialty areas of human ecology.

## Codebook Construction

After the coding scheme has been developed for the data, the next step is to assemble a codebook. A *codebook* identifies all units of information or variables in the study; tells the code number assigned to describe the answer, rating, score, or observation if an actual data value is not utilized; and specifies where this information is located in the data record (Ex. 13.1). The term *column* is normally used when referring to the position of data elements. A collection of related data elements constitutes a *field;* that is, a field is the group of columns used to code a variable. A collection of fields for a research subject constitutes a *record,* and a set of records for an entire sample of subjects is called a *file.*

Once the codebook has been assembled and the data have been coded,

LINE 1

| Column | Description |
|---|---|
| 1-3 | Subject identification number |
| 4 | College major |
| | 1= Vocational home economics education |
| | 2= Family and child development |
| | 3= Fashion, clothing, and textiles |
| | 4= Nutrition and foods |
| | 5= Family resource management |
| | 6= Interior design |
| | 7= Other |
| 5-6 | Age in years |
| 7 | Sex |
| | 1= male |
| | 2= female |
| 8 | Racial/ethnic group |
| | 1= white (except Hispanic) |
| | 2= black |
| | 3= Hispanic |
| | 4= Native American |
| | 5= Other |
| 9 | Living arrangement |
| | 1= both biological parents |
| | 2= biological mother |
| | 3= biological father |
| | 4= biological mother and stepfather |
| | 5= biological father and stepmother |

**Example 13.1.** Partial example of a codebook.

| Column | Description |
|---|---|
| | 6= adoptive parents |
| | 7= relatives |
| | 8= other |
| 10-11 | Number of siblings |
| 12 | Birth order position |
| | 1= oldest |
| | 2= middle |
| | 3= youngest |
| | 4= only child |
| 13 | Father's education |
| | 1= less than high school |
| | 2= high school |
| | 3= some college |
| | 4= associate's degree |
| | 5= bacholor's degree |
| | 6= graduate degree |
| | 7= other |
| 14 | Father's occupation |
| | 1= professional and technical |
| | 1= managers and proprietors |
| | 3= clerical and sales |
| | 4= skilled workers |
| | 5= semiskilled workers |
| | 6= unskilled workers |
| | 7= unemployed |
| | 8= other |

| Column | Description |
|---|---|
| . . . | . . . |
| 18-20 | Overall grade point average |
| 21-23 | Grade point average in major field |
| 24-25 | Coopersmith Self-Concept score |
| 26-27 | CPI -- Do |
| 28-29 | CPI -- Cs |
| 30-31 | CPI -- Sy |
| . . . | . . . |
| 60-61 | CPI -- Fe |
| 62 | FES-1 |
| 63 | FES-2 |
| 64 | FES-3 |
| . . . | . . . |
| 80 | FES-19 |

**LINE 2**

| Column | Description |
|---|---|
| 1 | FES-20 |
| . . . | . . . |
| 71 | FES-90 |
| 72-80 | Blanks |

many researchers prepare a *coding sheet* (Ex. 13.2) to increase speed and accuracy of data entry, although doing so may introduce transcription errors. Except for limitations imposed by some computer programs, a line of the coding sheet could include 100, 150, or 200 columns;[1] however, for ease of data handling, many standard coding sheets are 80 columns long. (It also may be a carryover from the now obsolete 80-column punch cards.)

For the following discussion, it is assumed that the data file is contained on disk or tape. Punch cards have been used in the past for both

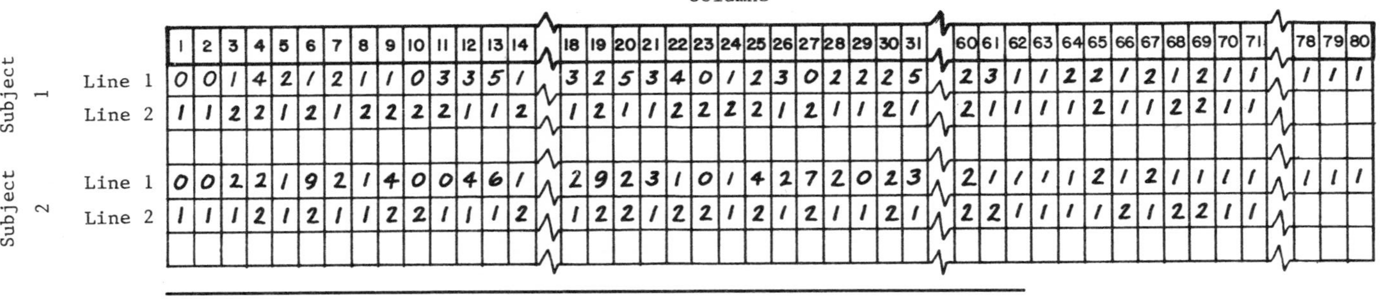

Columns

| | | 1 | 2 | 3 | 4 | 5 | 6 | 7 | 8 | 9 | 10 | 11 | 12 | 13 | 14 | 18 | 19 | 20 | 21 | 22 | 23 | 24 | 25 | 26 | 27 | 28 | 29 | 30 | 31 |
|---|---|---|---|---|---|---|---|---|---|---|---|---|---|---|---|---|---|---|---|---|---|---|---|---|---|---|---|---|---|
| Subject 1 | Line 1 | 0 | 0 | 1 | 4 | 2 | 1 | 2 | 1 | 1 | 0 | 3 | 3 | 5 | 1 | 3 | 2 | 5 | 3 | 4 | 0 | 1 | 2 | 3 | 0 | 2 | 2 | 2 | 5 |
| | Line 2 | 1 | 1 | 2 | 2 | 1 | 2 | 1 | 2 | 2 | 2 | 2 | 1 | 1 | 2 | 1 | 2 | 1 | 1 | 2 | 2 | 2 | 2 | 1 | 2 | 1 | 1 | 2 | 1 |
| | | | | | | | | | | | | | | | | | | | | | | | | | | | | | |
| Subject 2 | Line 1 | 0 | 0 | 2 | 2 | 1 | 9 | 2 | 1 | 4 | 0 | 0 | 4 | 6 | 1 | 2 | 9 | 2 | 3 | 1 | 0 | 1 | 4 | 2 | 7 | 2 | 0 | 2 | 3 |
| | Line 2 | 1 | 1 | 1 | 2 | 1 | 2 | 1 | 1 | 2 | 2 | 1 | 1 | 1 | 2 | 1 | 2 | 2 | 1 | 2 | 2 | 1 | 2 | 1 | 2 | 1 | 1 | 2 | 1 |
| | | | | | | | | | | | | | | | | | | | | | | | | | | | | | |

| | | 60 | 61 | 62 | 63 | 64 | 65 | 66 | 67 | 68 | 69 | 70 | 71 | 78 | 79 | 80 |
|---|---|---|---|---|---|---|---|---|---|---|---|---|---|---|---|---|
| Subject 1 | Line 1 | 2 | 3 | 1 | 1 | 2 | 2 | 1 | 2 | 1 | 2 | 1 | 1 | 1 | 1 | 1 |
| | Line 2 | 2 | 1 | 1 | 1 | 1 | 2 | 1 | 1 | 2 | 2 | 1 | 1 | | | |
| | | | | | | | | | | | | | | | | |
| Subject 2 | Line 1 | 2 | 1 | 1 | 1 | 1 | 2 | 1 | 2 | 1 | 1 | 1 | 1 | 1 | 1 | 1 |
| | Line 2 | 2 | 2 | 1 | 1 | 1 | 1 | 2 | 1 | 2 | 2 | 1 | 1 | | | |
| | | | | | | | | | | | | | | | | |

**Example 13.2.** Partial example of a coding sheet.

data entry and storage but are rarely encountered in modern computer systems.

Example 13.1 is a portion of a codebook that was prepared for an investigation of family background, personality, and achievement of human ecology majors. The first several columns correspond to information provided by research subjects on a personal background questionnaire. (Some of these items were used in the preceding section.) Columns 1–3 are designated for the subject's research identification number.[2] A three-digit field is employed because there are more than 100 but fewer than 1000 subjects. The numerical code that represents the participant's academic major is entered in column 4. The actual number reflecting age in years is put in columns 5–6. Sex, racial or ethnic group, and living arrangement are given appropriate code digits in columns 7, 8, and 9, respectively. Number of siblings is identified in columns 10–11. A two-digit field is necessary because it is possible to have 10 or more siblings, but in most cases it will be a single-digit entry that must be prefixed by a zero or a blank space to make it fit the two-digit field. For example, one sibling may be entered as 01 or as a blank followed by a 1. The codes for birth order position, father's occupation (as well as for items dealing with mother's occupation and subject's current marital status that are not shown here) each employ only a single-digit code.

Cumulative grade point average and average in the major area of study are put in columns 18–20 and 21–23, respectively. Since the decimal point is in a constant position for these variables, it can be eliminated without affecting the data. (With many computer programs, the position of the decimal point is specified when communicating the data layout to the computer.) A three-digit field is maintained for grade point averages, so a 3.25 average is entered as 325, a .95 average as 095, and so on. Columns 24–25 are designated for total scores on the *Coopersmith Self-esteem Inventory,* a paper-and-pencil questionnaire used in the study. Columns 26–61 are to be used for scores on the 18 *California Psychological Inventory* (CPI) scales, each of which is reported as a two-digit entry.[3]

The Coopersmith and CPI scores are to be entered after the two instruments have been hand-scored. For the *Family Environment Scale* (FES), however, the researcher has chosen to record subject responses for each of the 90 FES items and to let the computer score this particular measure. Noting responses to all items on the family instrument will allow certain computations (e.g., factor analysis). Since the questionnaire items are answered by the subjects as *true* or *false,* the code digit 1 is entered for items marked *true* and 2 for those marked *false,* beginning with FES item 1 in column 62. The data for a single subject (or case) will not go on one line, so an additional line must be used. On the second line, FES item 20 is entered in column 1, FES item 21 in column 2, and so on through column 71 until responses to all FES questions have been included. Columns 72–80 are left blank for all subjects (because there are no more data).

## PRELIMINARY EDITING

Not only must the data be in suitable form but they must also be as free from error as possible if further processing is to proceed without delay. Some editing, or inspection and correction, of data is always necessary.

Preliminary manual editing is a first step. The researcher must check the raw data to see whether or not the subjects complied with directions included within the measuring instrument or if the interviewers or observers followed all of the guidelines for the collection and recording of information. For instance, if a self-administered questionnaire or a checklist was filled out by the respondents, the investigator should scan the completed instrument to see if more than one answer was given to single-response items; if implausible values were written in as answers; if items, sections, or whole pages were left blank; if unclear responses need clarification; or if there was an obvious response bias, such as answering all of the items or most of them *yes, no,* or *undecided.* It may be necessary to drop some subjects from the sample.

A few comments should be made about *blanks* because of the potential problems they can pose when a computer program is used for analysis. It is not uncommon for a respondent to fail to answer an item for some reason or for the investigator to be unable to note a valid score for every research subject on each questionnaire or subtest. At the preliminary editing stage, it is best to assign a predetermined numerical code value for items or scores left blank; otherwise it will not be possible to determine if a blank was intentional, if it was a result of a coding error, or if it was caused by a key operator's inadvertent failure to enter a number in the column. Since blanks are often treated by the computer as zeros and the zero is a valid digit and an appropriate response for certain items, the analysis may be distorted. It is important that the investigator determine how blanks are interpreted by the computer program that will be used. Contingent upon the program, the researcher may choose to use blanks for spacing purposes and ease of visualization in inspecting data.

It is better to detect and eliminate errors at this early data editing phase of the study than to postpone corrections until later, although some subsequent "data cleaning" is usually necessary. Typically, the manual editing of raw data just described is reinforced later by a computer edit. The researcher should summarize detailed editing specifications in writing so that they can be uniformly followed. This also ensures that editing instructions are available for later reference. It is good practice for the investigator to fully document *all* steps in the research process.

## ENTERING DATA INTO THE COMPUTER

Before the data are accessible to the computer for analysis, they must be in machine-readable form. According to Karweit and Meyers (1983), there are two basic types of data entry techniques: transcriptive and source. With *transcriptive data entry* techniques, the data are prepared on documents at the source and subsequently transcribed to a form suitable for computer processing or for direct entry into the computer. With *source data entry* techniques, data are recorded directly in machine-readable form, doing away with the need for transcription of data.

### Transcriptive Data Entry

In transcriptive data entry, data may first be transferred to columns of a code sheet by following guidelines indicated in the codebook. Using the preassigned codes and defined card fields described earlier for the human ecology student research (Ex. 13.1), the partial code sheet in Example 13.2 illustrates data for two subjects.

If precoded and designed with extreme care, some questionnaires and interview schedules may be self-coding, thus eliminating the need for initially hand copying data onto separate coding sheets and making it possible for the data to be keyed directly from the instrument itself. Although the use of precoded instruments may increase data entry time, it helps minimize transcription errors incurred by incorrect copying in the preparation of coding forms. The layout of such questionnaires should be simple and clear to allow an orderly and uninterrupted visual flow from one item response to the next. The placement of blanks for responses along a column on the left-hand or right-hand side of the page, for example, makes the direct-keying method easier by alleviating the problem of looking for the next question in a sequence. The number of each item should be identical to the column location where the information is to be keyed. Before the completed questionnaires are keyed for direct entry, careful editing of all documents is required and open-ended questions, if used, should be coded.

#### Keying Operations

The most common means of transcriptive data entry involves using a terminal to key data onto magnetic tape or disk.[4] This approach has displaced traditional punch card equipment. It bypasses the process of initially recording data on cards and then converting cards to tape. If data are recorded onto tape or disk, they can be used immediately by a computer system (mainframe or microcomputer).

## Source Data Entry

Source data entry techniques avoid transcriptive procedures altogether. The data are recorded directly in a form suitable for computer processing, thus obviating the need for personnel and time to transcribe the data and avoiding errors due to mistranscription.

Of the source data entry techniques, the *optical marker reader* (OMR), which can read and translate a mark-sense card, has generated the greatest interest and use among researchers. Marks, representing responses to individual items, are made with special soft-lead pencils in designated spaces on the preprinted document. The sheet or "card" is subsequently read into the computer, the marks are sensed photoelectrically, and they are recorded on another medium or directly transmitted to the computer. The size and layout of mark-sense sheets vary according to the needs of the research project. The responses (marks) can be made on a separate answer sheet, or they can be made beside the item on the document itself. Although lightly marked answers, stray marks, and erasures can create problems for the machine, errors can be reduced by furnishing adequate instructions and by visually inspecting the documents. With certain programs, some editing can be done as the sheets are read, and those sheets with unreadable answers are rejected, examined later, and possibly corrected or omitted.

A second type of optical reading procedure, the *optical character reader* (OCR), reads handwritten, printed, or typed data. Although it is a promising technique, it has not been widely adopted in research.

A means of recording data directly in a machine-readable form that is being used with increasing frequency among investigators conducting observational studies is the *portable event recorder* (see Chap. 7). These battery-powered instruments, which consist of a keyboard and memory device, allow researchers to key predetermined codes into memory while they are observing the behavior or event. The recorded data are later transferred to tape or "dumped" onto disk storage on the computer.

*Automated interviewing* also uses source data entry. Using a terminal, the interviewer keys responses as the subject answers telephone interview questions. A variation of this approach is the *computerized questionnaire,* where questionnaire instructions, questions, and alternative item responses with numerical codes are presented to research subjects sitting at computer terminals. The subjects read the questions projected on the video screen and enter responses themselves by keying in their answers on the terminal typewriter.

Regardless of the data entry method used, it is essential that the researcher get into the habit of making duplicate copies of everything (codebooks, coding sheets, magnetic tapes, drafts of manuscripts submitted for typing, etc.) and maintaining them at separate locations to guard against loss by fire, theft, and so forth. Raw data should also be retained.

## COMPUTER EDITING

As indicated earlier, the researcher ordinarily engages in two types of editing before analyzing data. The first, or preliminary editing, is largely a clerical process done by hand. The second uses the computer to locate input errors; it is sometimes referred to as *data cleaning*. Errors introduced after preliminary editing (i.e., associated with data processing) are more expensive to correct. These coding and keying errors must be identified and rectified. Unfortunately, the verification process does not uncover and correct all of these errors.

There is one error detection procedure that is facilitated by the computer but is not considered computer editing in the strict sense. It is called *visual verification*. The researcher has the computer print out all of the data and then visually inspects columns for glaring errors. The columns should line up neatly, and the investigator should be able to detect undefined or unusual codes in certain columns, locate columns in which data appear that should be blank (i.e., those in which data have not been assigned), or identify instances in which data have been shifted to the right or left. Of course, if the sample is large and/or there are many variables per subject, visual inspection of the computer file can be quite tedious.

A common type of error detection procedure done by computer is to generate frequency distributions of all variables. This is done in order to identify unusual or incorrect coding that needs to be followed up. For instance, if it is known that a particular school district whose student population is being studied has approximately the same number of black and white students enrolled, and the frequency distribution for race reveals a marked imbalance in number of subjects in the two groups, the researcher can examine the data for possible coding errors or check with interviewers, questionnaire proctors, testers, and so on for any irregularities in data collection that may help explain the discrepancy.

Another procedure is for the researcher to specify the possible values associated with each column and to ask the computer to indicate which columns contain an illegal code. If the column designated for sex of a particular respondent has a 3 entered in it and that variable should have coded either 1 (male) or 2 (female), the computer can scan the data and print out the subject identification number. Then, the researcher is able to consult the raw data for that subject to determine what the value should have been. If the 3 was a transcription error, it is corrected. If the numerical code (3) actually was the response on the biodata sheet, the investigator might contact the subject, if possible, to clarify the response; discard the response and handle it as missing data; or delete the subject from the sample.

Another frequently used computer edit is to examine whether the logical constraints of the data have been violated. A subject who has responded that he or she is an only child on a birth order item should report 00 on the sibling number item. If that subject indicates, say, two brothers and sisters, it is clear that an error has been made on one of the two items, and the discrepancy must be resolved. Or if a subject codes an item *yes* that asks if he or she was born in the United States and then fills in the name of a foreign country in the succeeding item requesting the country of birth if not born in the United States, it is a signal that something is wrong. In both instances, the researcher goes back to the original questionnaire filled out by the subject to investigate further.

Hoinville and Jowell (1977) have indicated that most computer editing checks can be subsumed under five principal categories: structure checks (all information is available for each subject), valid coding range checks (only codes within the valid range have been entered), omission checks (responses to all questions are provided by the subject), filter checks (certain questions have been answered only by certain subjects and not others), and logic checks (presence of one response has set limits on another response).

## USING A COMPUTER PROGRAM

After corrections have been made in the computer file and another printout reveals that they have all been incorporated, the data may be considered "clean." The researcher is then free to proceed to the next step: statistical analysis. Ordinarily, considerable thought has already been given to the matter of analysis, so most of the appropriate statistical techniques have been identified for the data on hand, and the appropriate computer package has been selected. All that usually remains for the researcher at this phase of a study is to tell the computer exactly what to do once it has all of the numbers necessary for calculation.

The detailed set of instructions given to the computer that causes it to perform certain operations is called a *program* (sometimes also referred to as *software* to distinguish it from physical equipment, or *hardware)*. A wide range of programs is already available for different kind of analyses. These "canned" programs compute everything from means, standard deviations, correlations, and $t$ tests to more advanced procedures such as multivariate statistics. Since appropriate programs exist for most research problems in human ecology, rarely must an investigator write an original program for a study. However, even with a canned procedure, it is necessary for the researcher to communicate with the software and to provide data formats, code specifications, procedures to be performed, and so forth. For instance, in the earlier grade point average example, the researcher specifies the location of the decimal point.

Computer centers generally have statistical processing packages, such as the Statistical Package for the Social Sciences/SPSS^x (SPSS Inc. Staff 1983), Biomedical Computer Programs/BMDP (Dixon and Brown 1983), and Statistical Analysis System/SAS (SAS Institute 1985). Each of these packages has a detailed user's manual that describes its data management capabilities, statistical procedures, program limitations, storage requirements, and guidelines for invoking various operations. It is imperative that the researcher using one of these packages obtain the appropriate user's manual and become familiar with its content.

After a program that is suited to the project is chosen, the researcher creates a *command file* according to directions in the user's manual to control the processing of data. Commands indicate such information as the number of cases; number of variables; where the data are to be found on the record layout; how to handle missing values; nature of the statistical analysis and between what variables; and at what point to begin the operation, read input data, and terminate the run. Errors in the commands or in their sequencing may cause the program not to run as planned. When that occurs, the program is corrected, and it is run as many times as needed until it is completed successfully.

## SUGGESTIONS FOR EFFECTIVE COMPUTER UTILIZATION

The first consideration for the researcher is whether or not computer support is required for the study. For practical purposes, use of the computer becomes a necessity if there are a large number of variables and subjects or the analysis is complex. To derive maximum advantage from the computer center, the investigator should make this decision before finalizing the research design.

Assuming that a computer will be used, the researcher should establish contact with a computer center resource person, perhaps in the user's service division; obtain written procedures for using the facility; and find out information such as the nature of support that is possible; the training classes that are offered; what kinds of statistical packages are available; what costs and billing procedures are; and how computer time is scheduled.

Before discussing specifics of the study with the computer center resource person, the investigator should formulate the research problem and put it in writing, avoiding conceptual terms and using operational definitions and examples of concepts that can be understood by someone unfamiliar with the subject matter area. A flow chart might help illustrate the specific steps of the study.

Although there is usually ample assistance from computer center personnel and faculty advisers, it is necessary for the researcher to take the responsibility for becoming familiar with fundamental concepts and terminology of computers and data processing through formal course work, computer short courses, and self-directed reading. Only then will the investigator derive maximum benefit from computer technology in his or her research.

## FUNCTIONAL COMPONENTS OF A COMPUTER SYSTEM

Since the physical and electronic principles of computer operation are extremely complicated and beyond the scope of this book, this is only a brief and simplified description of the computer as part of the broad overview of the computer system. In general terms, the digital computer is a data processing machine that can perform various mathematical and logical operations with incredible speed in accordance with preprogrammed instruction and without human intervention during the processing. A computer system performs input, processing, and output functions; it is made up of input devices, a central processing unit (arithmetic-logic unit, control unit, primary storage unit), secondary storage devices, and output devices (Fig. 13.1).

After the data intended for analysis and the computer program have been entered into the computer (by using the input devices discussed in this chapter), both the data and the instructions are forwarded to a storage unit where they are held for later use. Since internal memory (the *primary storage unit*) has limited capacity, most of the data and programs are stored in external units (*secondary storge devices* such as magnetic disks, magnetic tapes, or punched cards). However, information in external storage must first be transferred to the primary storage unit before it can be used in processing.

The instructions of the computer program are called forth one at a time by the *central processing unit* (CPU), which interprets them and sends data to the *arithmetic-logic unit* with directions to perform certain functions. The CPU, which coordinates the timing and operation of the entire system, is considered the "brain" of the computer. It transfers information back and forth between one part of the computer to another, as required.

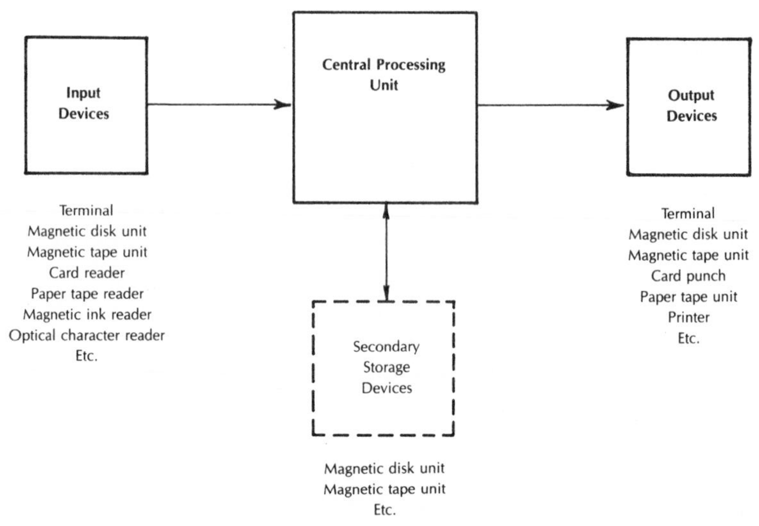


**Figure 13.1.** Components of a computer system.

The arithmetic-logic unit does the adding, subtracting, multiplying, and dividing, as well as other logical operations.

When the processing is complete, the computer program tells the CPU to output the results using an *output device.* (Output is the end product of computer processing.) While most output of concern to the researcher will be printed on paper, output can also be stored on magnetic disks or tapes, punched on cards, or displayed on monitors.

## Microcomputers

Microcomputers (often called personal computers) are increasingly available to the researcher. Over the past few years, computational power has dramatically increased while the cost of such power available in small units has been reduced substantially. At the time of writing, a microcomputer complete with 256–640K (1 K = 1024 bytes of memory), a floppy disk drive and hard disk (for increased data storage capability), monitor, and dot matrix printer can be purchased for approximately $1000–$2000.

As indicated earlier, such microcomputers can be used as terminals to communicate with the more powerful university mainframe. Additionally, many statistical packages that will run on microcomputers are available. By using these packages, the researcher can complete the statistical analyses for a project entirely on the microcomputer. Of course, the investigator should first consider the nature of the project, the volume of data, and the type of analyses to be performed before deciding whether to use the university mainframe or a microcomputer.

## STRENGTHS AND LIMITATIONS OF COMPUTERS

The computer is a marvelous research device. It can perform conventional statistical calculations at incomprehensible speeds, with basic operations measured in microseconds (millionths of a second) and nanoseconds (billionths of a second). It minimizes much of the time-consuming and tedious work associated with data analysis while ensuring almost complete accuracy of calculations. It has made complicated analyses practical and even commonplace. Not very long ago, advanced statistics such as multiple regression and factor analysis were considered prohibitive by many investigators. Needless to say, the computer has had an enormously positive impact on the quantitative aspect of research.

But we should not view the computer only in terms of its data organization, statistical, and hypothesis testing capabilities. By handling so many variables simultaneously, the computer helps the researcher identify complicated patterns and relationships that might otherwise go undetected. These, in turn, lead to new hypotheses. The computer has also played an important role in information retrieval for literature searches, data collection, word processing, and content analysis. The versatility of the computer has not only facilitated research, it also has encouraged better research.

However, the computer is just a research tool. It cannot think or reason for itself. In spite of its many virtues, the computer cannot formulate research problems, select variables to investigate, choose appropriate measuring devices, gather data, specify an appropriate analysis, and interpret the results. These are the researcher's responsibility. Above all, it cannot compensate for inadequate data, poor research design, selection of an inappropriate program, or an investigator's lack of knowledge of the statistical and analytical principles underlying a particular program. It is sad but sometimes true that the easily obtained output of the computer can motivate overdependence and uncritical use of the machine. Actually, with the advent of computers, researcher expertise may be more important than ever before.

If the investigator selects an inappropriate analysis or makes a mistake in instructions, the computer will not know. An obedient servant of the researcher, it will faithfully execute the analyses even though the results may be meaningless. This has led to the use of an acronym in computer circles: GIGO, or Garbage In, Garbage Out. In the hands of a competent investigator who understands the capabilities and limitations of the machine, the computer has limitless potential.[5]

## NOTES

1. The researcher should be aware of any limitations on record length and of any column placement requirements of the program being used.

2. The code for each variable in the study represents a field. Thus, columns 1–3 (research identification number) are field 1, column 4 (subject's major) is field 2, and so on.

3. If a minus score were possible with these instruments, it would be necessary to allocate a column for the negative sign. However, with most computer programs, the plus sign for positive scores would not have to be used.

4. Increasingly, researchers are entering data into the computer by using terminals. Terminals exist in several forms. All have a keyboard, used for input, that is similar to the one on a typewriter but that also may have special function keys. In addition, terminals have an output device. CRT terminals provide a video display monitor, which allows the investigator to view the data as they are being input, thereby facilitating data editing. A terminal may have, either in place of or in addition to the monitor, a printer to provide hard copy of the data. Data entered on the terminal are transmitted to the main computer over lines (either phone lines or lines dedicated specifically to the terminal). The data files created are stored on magnetic tape or disk for future access.

Microcomputers may also be used as terminals. Assuming the data are processed on the university's mainframe, the data may be entered by using a microcomputer that is connected to the mainframe, typically by a modem and telephone lines.

5. For a more detailed treatment of computers and data processing, see Blissmer (1985), Brownell (1985), Heise (1981), Kindred (1982), Madron, Tate, and Brookshire (1987), Parker (1984), Popkin and Pike (1981), Schnake (1985), Schrodt (1984), Vazsonyi (1980), and Walsh (1981). Preparing data for analysis is well explained in Babbie (1986) and Sonquist and Dunkelberg (1977).

CHAPTER 14

# Analyzing Data

Before collecting data and preparing them for analysis, the researcher should consider the statistical methods that will enable him or her to analyze the data and eventually interpret the results. Ideally, analysis should be planned, in consultation with a faculty adviser, statistician, and computer resource person, at the time the research is designed. The design of the study and the hypotheses formulated will guide the investigator with respect to the proper breakdown and analysis of data.

Since the objective of this book is not to teach statistical computation but to provide an orientation to some basic statistical concepts that are needed in conducting and interpreting research, the following material is not intended to be a thorough discussion of statistics. Other available sources provide a more comprehensive treatment of statistical methodology.[1] Persons planning to do research will need to complete formal courses in statistics.

*Statistics* has multiple meanings. To the layperson, the term usually means statements of numerical facts, such as the percentage of student athletes who graduate from college, the number of live births in a state, the average income of a typical family of four, or the median age at first marriage for females. To the researcher, statistics refers primarily to a method of dealing with data. It is a tool that helps the investigator handle quantitative facts or observations, including techniques for organizing, summarizing, and analyzing information, as well as for making generalizations and inferences from data (McCall 1975).

There are two major functions served by statistics: description and inference. *Descriptive statistics* facilitate comprehension and presentation of the jumbled mass of information collected by presenting the data in an efficient and meaningful summary form. They organize, reduce, and summarize single variables or the relationships among variables for subjects on whom data have been collected. Descriptive statistics are of special value during the initial stages of analysis. Some studies are designed to achieve only this descriptive function. *Inferential statistics* are concerned (a) with estimating values of parameters in a population on the basis of data obtained on samples taken from the population and (b) with testing hypotheses concerning relationships among variables in the population.

## DESCRIPTIVE STATISTICS

### Categorizing the Data

The categorization of data is the preliminary step in any analysis. (This topic was touched on in the discussion of coding data.) Categorization is a useful technique for partitioning the data and reducing the items of information under investigation to a more manageable form and number.

Kerlinger (1986, 127–30) recommends that a method of classification follow certain fundamental rules. First, the analytic paradigm selected should be consistent with the research questions to be answered or hypotheses to be tested. Second, the categories should be exhaustive, with all subjects fitting into existing categories. Third, the categories should be mutually exclusive and independent. Fourth, each category (variable) should be derived from its own classificatory principle; that is, variables such as sex and social class are treated separately for classification purposes and can each be placed on only one dimension. Fifth, categorization on one level of discourse (i.e., ideas that have a logical connection to each other) are categorized together. However, ideas outside that categorization must remain separate from the overall grouping unless some logical means of connection can be established.

Categories should be small enough to ensure homogeneity of all cases falling within a single category. However, sample size must be large enough to permit the differentiation of cases into various categories. If a good job of coding data has already been done, the task of categorizing the data at this stage of the research process is minimized.

### Frequency Distribution

If you collected intelligence test scores on 100 students and simply wrote them down on a sheet of paper as you received them, say, from a counselor's office (probably in alphabetical order by student last name), the data would be unorganized. It would be difficult to have a clear picture of the group of scores. To organize this mass of data into a more readable and understandable form, the scores may be presented as a frequency distribution. Such a distribution, as the name implies, is the number of cases falling into different categories. A frequency distribution of scores (or intervals of score values) is made by placing the values in numerical order from largest to smallest and indicating the frequency with which each value occurs. Sometimes, rather than noting a long list of scores with only one or two subjects obtaining one particular score, the scores may be more clearly presented by grouping them into a smaller number of categories in intervals of 5 or 10 points or some other arbitrary cutting point, depending on the number and range of scores (Table 14.1).

**Table 14.1. Grouped Frequency Distribution of Achievement Scores Attained by 40 Female College Students**

| Score | Frequency |
|---|---|
| 80–89 | 8 |
| 70–79 | 12 |
| 60–69 | 10 |
| 50–59 | 6 |
| 40–49 | 4 |

In addition to raw frequency distributions and grouped frequency distributions, the investigator can describe the variable distribution in terms of percentages, such as the percentage of subjects who are male and female or who are in various academic majors. The researcher is not limited to the tabular presentation of data to reflect the distribution of a variable. Graphing techniques can also be used as supplementary visual aids (but never substitutes) for this purpose (see Chap. 16).

## Measures of Central Tendency

Large numbers of measures are difficult for the eye and mind to group and understand. Consequently, an entire distribution of measures is often summarized by characteristic values called *measures of central tendency,* which represent central points in the frequency distribution around which scores tend to cluster. The most commonly used measures of central tendency are the mean, median, and mode.

### Mean

The *mean,* frequently called the arithmetic mean, is the most stable and reliable index of central tendency. It is the arithmetic average computed by adding all of the scores in a distribution and then dividing by the number of cases. This summary statistic is appropriate for interval- or ratio-level data. Calculation of the mean is one of the initial steps in analysis that later permits more advanced statistical treatment of data.

### Median

The *median* is a point (not necessarily a score) in a distribution, above and below which half of the scores lie. When an odd number of untied scores is involved, this point is identical with the value of the middle score when they are ranked (e.g., 5, 7, **8**, 9, 15). When no singular data point represents the middle score, formulas available in most statistics books are used. For example, some distributions contain an even number of untied scores (e.g., 10, 14, 17, 24) or an odd number of scores where no one person has the middle score (e.g., 1, 2, 3, 3, 4, 5, 6). Since the median is less sensitive to extreme values than the mean, it is more appropriate when there are a few extremely high or low scores in a distribution. The median, which requires data that are at least ordinal level (see Chap. 3) can be used in certain statistical tests where the mean is inappropriate.

### Mode

The *mode* is the score, value, or interval in a distribution that occurs most often. Used less by researchers than either the mean or median to characterize centrality, the mode is a very rough estimate that can be determined for all levels of measurement. For nominal data (Chap. 3), it is the only measure of central tendency that can be calculated. Examples of the mode include the most frequent score made on a test, the brand of detergent bought by most homemakers, and the most common age of children in a class. If more than two scores share the same highest frequency, the distribution is said to be *multimodal.* The special case of two scores with the same (highest) frequency is called a *bimodal* distribution.

For good perception of the data in any research project, it is advisable for the researcher to calculate all three measures of central tendency when appropriate. If the distribution of scores is fairly symmetrically distributed around a central point, the mean, median, and mode will be similar (they will be identical in a perfectly symmetrical distribution). In such circumstances, the mean should be the choice because of its many desirable properties and the advanced statistical computations it allows.

## Measures of Variability

Although measures of central tendency give important information by summarizing the level of a group of scores, to describe the distribution fully we must also know how the scores are spread about the central value. Measures providing this essential information about the dispersion (scattering) of scores are called *measures of variability.* Whereas indicators of central tendency are points in a distribution, measures of variability designate distance or number of units on the scale of scores. The concept of variability is very important in statistical methods.

### Range

The simplest measure of dispersion is the *range.* A crude descriptive index, the range is the distance or difference between the highest and lowest score in a series. (If the highest score is 50 and the lowest is 20, the range is 50 − 20, or 30.) Since the range is determined by only two scores and ignores all the others, it can convey misleading information concerning total variability if one or both of the extreme scores differ markedly from other scores. The range is more meaningful when combined with other measures.

A more stable measure of variability is the *interquartile range.* This is obtained by splitting the distribution into four equal parts, or quartiles. Quartiles are values below which 25%, 50%, and 75% of the scores lie. The score at the lower (25%) quartile ($Q_1$) is then subtracted from the score at the upper (75%) quartile ($Q_3$). Independent of the effects of extreme cases, it reflects the range of the middle 50% of the scores in a symmetrical distribution. The interquartile range is most likely to be used in situations where the median and percentiles are applicable.

### Variance and Standard Deviation

Just as the interquartile range is linked with the median, the variance and standard deviation are measures of the spread of a set of scores around the mean. Both of these measures of dispersion are based on the differences (deviation) between each individual score in a series and the mean for that distribution. Simply stated, the *variance* is the sum of the squared deviations of each score from the mean of the distribution divided by the number of scores; and the *standard deviation* (*SD*) is the positive square root of the variance. Thus, if the variance is 16, the standard deviation would be 4. Both concepts are very useful in describing a distribution and are requisite to further statistical procedures.

If the range of one series of scores exceeds another, the spread or differences between the scores and the mean will tend to be larger, and the standard deviation will have a higher value. A relatively high standard deviation indicates that the scores are more widely scattered about the mean (they are more heterogeneous), while a lower standard deviation means that the scores are less spread out (they are more homogeneous).

The standard deviation should always be reported as a companion measure with the mean (and along with sample size) because the mean by itself gives incomplete information. If variability is considerable, the measure of central tendency loses some of its meaning. Together, measures of centrality and variability provide a clearer picture of the major features of a distribution and allow adequate interpretation of the data.

## The Normal Distribution

When many variables in human ecology are measured and plotted, their frequency distributions often approximate what is called a *normal distribution,* or normal frequency curve. These approximations are seen in the height and weight of people; intelligence, aptitude, and achievement scores; and calories consumed, for example. There are thousands of situations in which "nature behaves generally according to the rule of the normal frequency curve" (Leedy 1985, 177).

Although there are many different normal distributions, only the population mean and standard deviation are needed to describe any particular one. If a large sample has been selected on a probability basis, the data will typically distribute in a form resembling a bell-shaped, symmetrical configuration (Fig. 14.1) whose mean, median, and mode are identical and divide the distribution into equal parts. Score values are represented on the baseline (horizontal axis), and frequencies (or number of cases) are indicated by the area under the curve (vertical axis). This graphic version of the distribution illustrates that the majority of scores cluster around the mean, where the curve reaches its maximum height, while the rest taper off gradually toward both extremes. Theoretically, the tails extend to infinity in both directions and never touch the baseline. The mathematically defined theoretical normal distribution plays a prominent role in statistics and research.

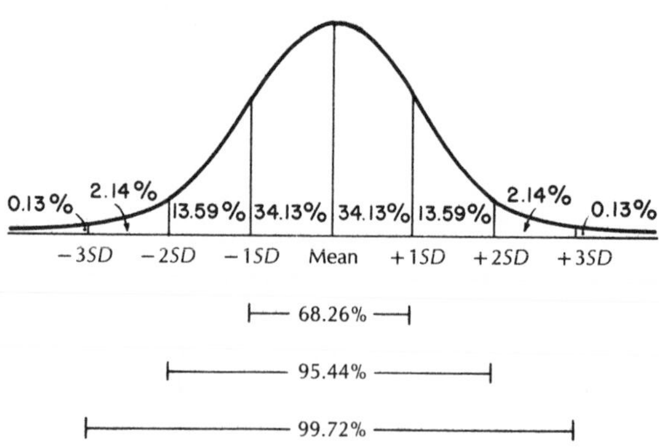


**Figure 14.1.** Percentage areas between standard deviations under the normal curve.

The standard deviation is an important characteristic of the normal curve and can be best understood in relation to the ways in which data tend to distribute themselves theoretically in the distribution. Taking into account the distance between every individual score and the mean, the standard deviation divides the normal curve into a number of equal units. All of the scores in a normal distribution are included in the total area under the curve, which can be divided into parts representing percentages of the whole. These parts, measured along the baseline from the mean, are standard deviation units. Each unit of standard deviation corresponds to a fixed proportion of the area under the curve, or frequency of cases, that lie between the mean and given *SD* unit. In a normal distribution (Fig. 14.1), at least 34.13% of the scores are included between the mean and +1 *SD* (to the right).[2] Since the distribution is symmetrical, between the mean and −1 *SD* (to the left), 34.13% of the cases are also found. Between the mean and +2 *SD*, 47.72% of the cases are located; and similarly, between the mean and −2 *SD*, 47.72%. Between the mean and +3 *SD* are found 49.86% of all cases, and between the mean and −3 *SD*, 49.86%. Thus, 68.26% (34.13% + 34.13%) of all scores fall within ±1 *SD* of the mean, 95.44% (47.72% + 47.72%) within ±2 *SD* of the mean, and 99.72% (49.86% + 49.86%) within ±3 *SD* of the mean. Six *SD* units, then, account for almost all of the cases; only 0.26% fall beyond ±3 *SD* from the mean (a total of 26 cases [13 + 13] in 10,000).

Although the relationship of the standard deviation unit to the distribution of scores does not technically apply to groups of scores that are not normally distributed, many frequency distributions in human ecology are at least roughly normal and are assumed to be normal for statistical purposes. In these instances, the concept of standard deviation continues to have essentially the same meaning, and it is possible to make descriptive statements about the frequency of any range of values in a population. To illustrate, in a distribution of aptitude test scores with a mean of 70 and a *SD* of 8, 68.26% of all cases would have a score between 54 and 86 (±2 *SD*); and 99.72% would have a score between 46 and 94 (±3 *SD*). (These hypothetical test scores are shown under the normal curve in Fig. 14.2.) Using the percentages associated with the various *SD* units, any individual's position relative to the entire distribution can be determined by examining how far, in *SD* units, that person's score deviates from the mean score for the total group. All that is needed is for the researcher to compute the mean and standard deviation for the distribution.

In a normal distribution, an equal number of cases fall on both sides of the mean. Since it is symmetrical, its skewness is said to be zero. (As already indicated, the mean, median, and mode in such a distribution are identical.) But some distributions take on nonsymmetrical shapes. If there is a preponderance of high scores and only a few low scores, the distribu-

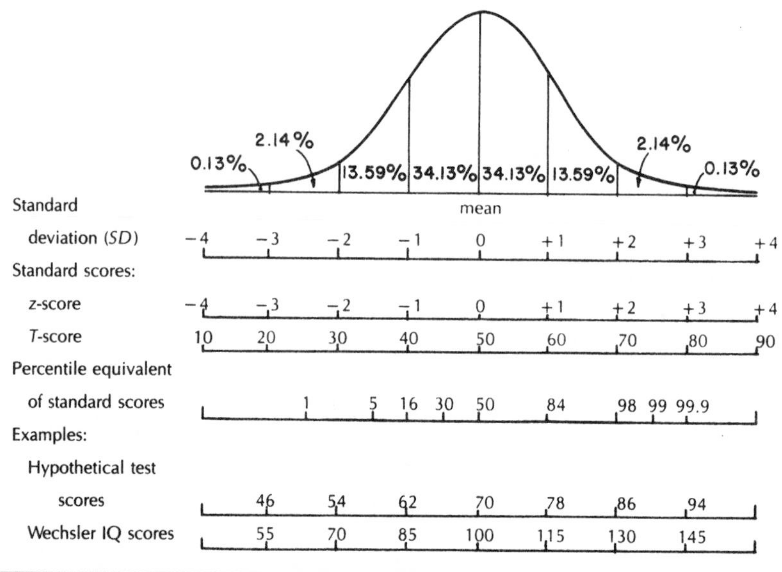


**Figure 14.2.** The normal curve and examples of distributed scores.

tion is referred to as *negatively skewed* ("tail" points to the left), with the median being larger than the mean. Conversely, if there are disproportionately more low scores, the distribution is referred to as *positively skewed* ("tail" points to the right), and the median is less than the mean.

The form of a distribution has implications for the use of particular measures of central tendency and for the selection of statistical tests. Many statistical methods make assumptions about the nature of the distribution of scores.

## Measures of Relative Position

### Standard Scores

Using the normal curve, it is possible to determine how many standard deviation units a given raw score is above or below the mean. When raw scores taken from a normally distributed population are converted into units of standard deviation, they become *standard scores.*

There are several advantages to transforming raw scores into standard scores. It permits the comparison of a score with the entire distribution, thereby giving the score relative meaning. In other words, it tells what the score means—whether it is high or low in relation to other scores—something we cannot discern from a raw score. In addition, any score given in standard deviation units has comparable meaning from one set of scores to another. If someone scored 1 *SD* above the mean on a performance measure and 2 *SD* above the mean on a separate measure of verbal ability, we can say that the individual is better in the verbal area.

A distribution of standard scores follows its origin, or raw, score distribution, but standard score distributions always have a mean of zero and an *SD* of 1. This theoretical distribution is referred to as the *standard normal distribution,* or standard normal curve. All normally distributed populations can be transformed into a standard normal curve, whose characteristics are the same as those of any normal distribution (i.e., 68.26%, 95.44%, and 99.72% of the scores are within ±1 *SD*, ±2 *SD*, and ±3 *SD* of the mean, respectively). When the raw scores of a normal distribution are expressed as standard scores, they will conform to the standard normal distribution. Each raw score corresponds to a location on the baseline of the standard normal curve.

*z* Score. A basic standard score is the *z* score.[3] Since the standard normal distribution has a mean of zero and an *SD* of 1, a score falling at 1 *SD* above the mean is called a *z* score of +1 (Fig. 14.2). A person who scored directly at the mean does not vary from the mean in terms of standard deviation and would therefore have a corresponding *z* score of zero. If the original score placed the individual at 2 *SD* below the mean, the *z* score would be −2. Any observations that can be made about *z* scores will be the equivalent of similar statements involving the corresponding raw scores in the original population, as long as that population is normally distributed.

*T* Score. Among other types of standard scores that are based upon the relationship of the standard deviation unit to the score values in a normal distribution is the *T* score. The *T* score is a *z* score that has been converted to a distribution whose mean is 50 and *SD* is 10. It overcomes some of the problems caused by possible fractional and negative values. Someone whose raw score has been converted to a *T* score of 45 would be −.5 *SD* units away from the mean. A *T* score of 70 would place the individual +2 *SD* above the mean.

### Percentile Rank

Since standard scores are frequently difficult for some people to interpret, another way (popularized by commercial test publishers) to describe a score in relation to other scores is with the *percentile rank*. Percentile rank refers to the percent of all scores falling at or below a given raw score. A subject who has obtained a score that places him or her at the 84th percentile has scored equal to or better than 84% of all cases and is 1 *SD* above the mean (i.e., only 16% scored higher). A score at the 50th percentile (the median) is at the middle of the distribution.

One disadvantage with the percentile rank scale is the differences between scores are uneven, with the units being greater at the upper and lower ends of the distribution than in the middle. Unlike *z* scores, which represent an interval-level scale, percentiles are ordinal measurements. Therefore, a difference in one percentile point at the middle of the distribution does not mean the same thing as the identical difference at either extreme of the distribution. In terms of raw scores, the difference between the 98th and 99th percentile is larger than the difference between the 50th and the 51st percentile.

### Wechsler Deviation IQ Score

The normal curve is commonly used in reporting and interpreting IQ test results. The *Wechsler deviation IQ* has a mean of 100 and an *SD* of 15. Thus, at +1 *SD* from the mean, the IQ score is 115; at −1 *SD*, the IQ score is 85, and so on.

Standard scores like the *z* score and *T* score and other measures based on the normal curve provide units of measurement that have comparable meaning from one instrument to another (Fig. 14.2). For example, an individual who scored 86 on the hypothetical test, was 2 *SD* above the mean, had a *z* score of +2, had a *T* score of 70, and was at the 98th percentile. Provided that we know the mean and standard deviation, we could transform and include in Figure 14.2 any normally distributed score and be able to determine the score that corresponds to various standard deviation units.

## Measures of Relationships

The discussion of descriptive statistics so far has focused on the examination of one variable at a time (univariate analysis). Human ecology researchers, however, are usually interested not only in investigating scores on a single variable in one distribution but also in studying the relations among scores of two or more variables from different distributions. The degree of association between variables is referred to as *correlation.*

### Correlation and Correlation Coefficients

The direction and the magnitude of a relationship are usually expressed in terms of a numerical index called a *correlation coefficient.* Regarding direction: if both sets of data tend to vary together (covary) in the same way, the pattern is called a positive relationship. An increase in one variable is accompanied by an increase in the other, and a decrease in one is associated with a decrease in the other. That is, those scoring high on one distribution tend to score high on the other; those scoring in the middle range on one tend to score in the middle on the other distribution; and those scoring low on one also tend to score low on the other. Positive correlations would probably be found between height and weight, grade point average and rank in graduating class, IQ scores and academic achievement, and educational attainment and income. The plus sign that indicates the positive nature of the relationship is usually omitted, so a correlation coefficient without a sign is taken to be positive.

A negative (inverse) relationship signifies that as one variable increases, the other decreases; that is, persons scoring high on one distribution tend to score low on the other, and persons scoring low on one tend to score high on the other. Negative correlations would likely be found between days on a diet and body weight, altitude and oxygen availability, amount of alcohol consumed and motor coordination, and time spent studying and number of errors on an exam. Inverse correlations are prefaced with a minus sign.

The values of some variables do not covary at all. For instance, hair length and intelligence are uncorrelated. Such correlations are said to be zero.

The magnitude (strength) of a relationship is indicated by the numerical value of the correlation coefficient, which typically is reported as a two-digit decimal. Correlation coefficients can take values ranging from a perfect negative relationship (−1.00) through zero to a perfect positive relationship (+1.00). If the absolute value of the coefficient is relatively high (regardless of sign), it is a strong association. Thus, correlation coefficients of .70 or −.55 suggest a relationship of greater magnitude than .45. A correlation coefficient of zero indicates that there is absence of a relationship (Table 14.2).

In human ecology research, perfect positive or perfect negative relationships are seldom achieved with a sample of any appreciable size. Zero relationships are also rare. Usually, the correlation coefficient takes on an intermediate value.

**Table 14.2. Different Degrees of Correlation Illustrated with Hypothetical Scores by Six Children on Two Separate Tests**

| $r = -1.00$ | | $r = .00$ | | $r = 1.00$ | |
|---|---|---|---|---|---|
| Test A | Test B | Test A | Test B | Test A | Test B |
| 60 | 10 | 60 | 50 | 60 | 60 |
| 50 | 20 | 50 | 20 | 50 | 50 |
| 40 | 30 | 40 | 10 | 40 | 40 |
| 30 | 40 | 30 | 60 | 30 | 30 |
| 20 | 50 | 20 | 40 | 20 | 20 |
| 10 | 60 | 10 | 30 | 10 | 10 |

Pearson's *r*. The most commonly used correlation coefficient is the *Pearson product-moment correlation coefficient* (*r*). Pearson's *r* is employed to assess the relationship between two variables when both are continuous, have been measured on an interval or ratio scale, and are normally distributed.

It indicates the degree to which two variables can be described by a straight line when plotted graphically as a *scattergram* (or scatter diagram). Scatter diagrams enable the researcher to visually examine the degree of association between two variables and to get an intuitive feel for the data as well as an indication of the direction (sign) of the relationship. Scatter diagrams are double-entry or two-dimensional graphs in which the subject's score on one measure (variable) is plotted on the vertical axis and his or her score on the other variable is plotted on the horizontal axis. A dot placed at the intersection of these two points represents the pair of scores of one subject. Although the scattergram can be prepared by hand for relatively small samples, computer programs are available for this purpose.

The Pearson *r* is an estimate of the degree to which the data points tend to disperse (scatter) in the scatter diagram (Fig. 14.3). As the points tend to deviate from a straight line, the magnitude of the relationship decreases. The closer the points are to a straight line, the larger the absolute value of the correlation. When the correlation is perfect, the data points fall in a straight line.[4]

Sometimes the plotted data reveal an underlying trend that is not characterized by a straight line but rather by a curve. Such nonlinear trends are referred to as *curvilinear relationships*. Although the curve can take different forms, a type of curvilinear trend often reported in the research literature is represented by the bending or flattening of the curve. The flattening means that as the scores on one variable increase, the scores on the second variable also increase up to a certain point; beyond that point, further increases in scores on the first variable are associated with decreases in scores of the other (i.e., inverted U shape). Examples of this type of curvilinear trend include the relationship between amount of stress and productivity or between chronological age and hours of sleep required.

Since the Pearson correlation coefficient is inappropriate for expressing the association between two sets of variables that are not linear, when *r* is used with nonlinear data, it always results in an underestimate of the relationship. Even if the true relationship is strong, the calculated *r* can be extremely low in such cases. Statistical procedures are available for relationships that a scatter diagram reveals are nonlinear as well as for those that do not meet the other minimum assumptions of the Pearson *r*.

Other Correlation Coefficients. Choice of the type of correlation coefficient to examine the association between two variables depends on several

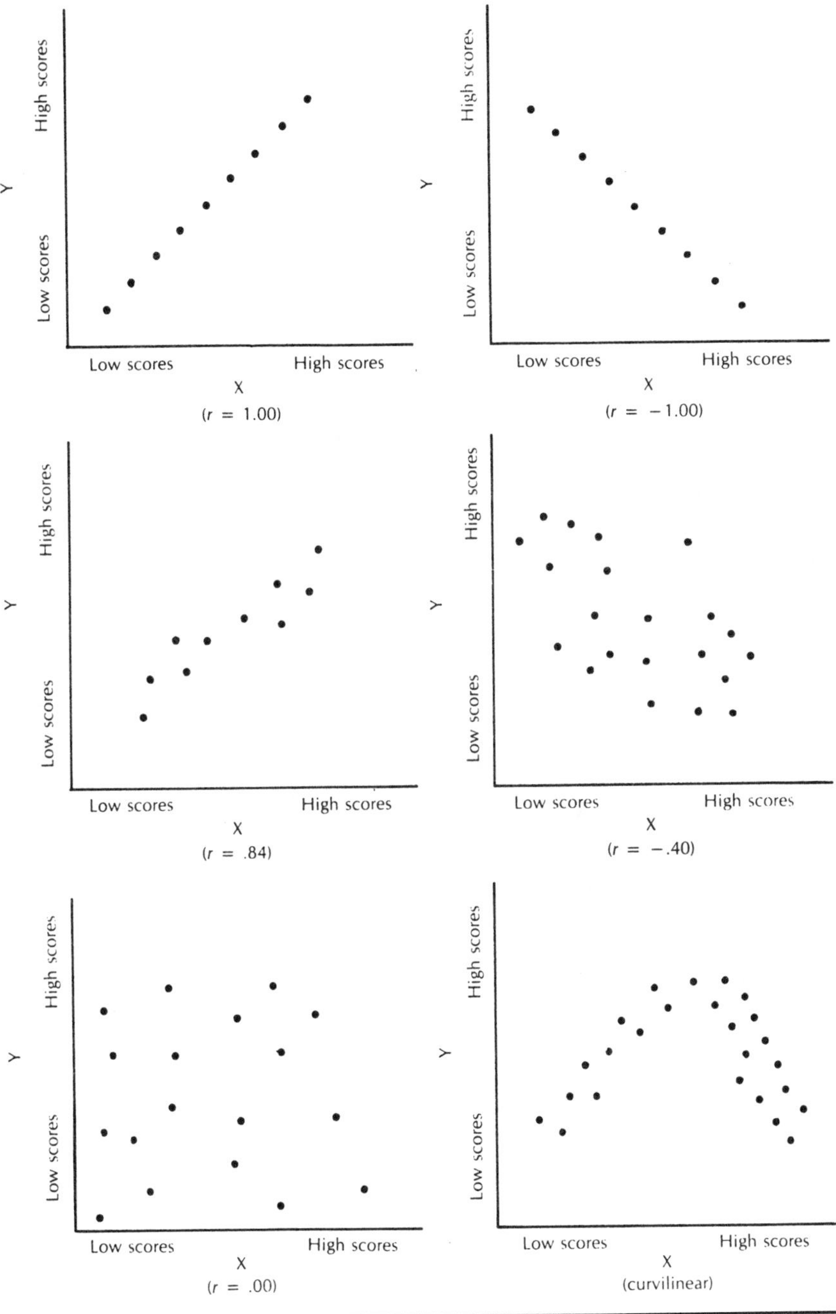


**Figure 14.3.** Scatter diagrams of different degrees of relationship between two variables (hypothetical data).

factors, such as kind of measurement scales used (nominal, ordinal, interval, ratio), nature of the underlying distribution (continuous or discrete), and characteristics of the distribution of scores (linear or nonlinear) (Elifson, Runyon, and Haber 1982, 189). For instance, when data are ordinal, *Spearman's rank-order correlation coefficient,* or rho ($r_s$) can be employed. An alternative for handling data in the form of ranks is *Kendall's tau* ($\tau$), which contains a correction for ties. The *point biserial correlation coefficient* ($r_{pb}$) can be utilized when one variable is a dichotomy and the other is either interval- or ratio-level. When both variables are true dichotomies, the *phi coefficient* ($\phi$) is appropriate.

### Multivariate Techniques Using Correlation

There are times when a *bivariate analysis,* which includes the techniques discussed thus far, is inappropriate or insufficient for a researcher's needs. Rather than examine the relationships between only two variables, the investigator may wish to look at several variables at the same time. Examining three or more variables simultaneously to determine the nature of their relationships is called *multivariate analysis.* Several multivariate techniques are based on correlation.

The *partial correlation,* which is an extension of the Pearson *r,* allows us to investigate the association between two variables by holding constant another variable (or variables) that the researcher suspects is also involved in the relationship. If we are studying the correlation between height and weight of people, for example, we would probably want to hold chronological age constant (i.e., partial out the effects of this extraneous factor) because of its possible influence on the relationship under investigation. We probably will find that the correlation of height and weight, which is around .80, will be reduced to approximately .60 when the factor of age is nullified. When not statistically controlled, the age variable makes the correlation between height and weight spuriously large.

*Multiple correlation,* another application of Pearson's *r,* enables the researcher to look at the relationship between one variable and a combination of other variables taken together to determine what the relative weights of the different variables are in producing the obtained relationship. Success in college, for instance, might be multiply correlated with aptitude test scores, high school grade point average, number of advanced science and math courses taken, and parental attitudes toward education.

*Multiple regression* follows essentially the same logic as multiple correlation. With the multiple regression procedure, the value of a criterion variable, such as college success, is predicted from the combined knowledge of several other variables (aptitude test scores, grades, etc.). In addition, the relative contribution of each independent variable as a predictor can be assessed.

*Canonical correlation analysis,* a generalization of multiple regression, examines a set of independent variables and a set of dependent variables and generates new variables to describe the relationship. One set might include demographic variables (e.g., family size, social class) and the other set include scores on different subscales of a personality adjustment inventory.

*Path analysis,* also derived from multiple regression, is a technique that breaks down a linear relationship and graphically presents the "paths" of possible causal relationships among variables by using a structural model involving all of the variables of interest. A causal hierarchy is developed that indicates that some variables may possibly cause others but cannot be caused by them. In addition to providing quantitative estimates of the network of causal influences, the procedure also helps the researcher clarify a mental picture of the causal system and provides a way of organizing his or her work (Simon and Burstein 1985, 330).

Another technique that employs correlation to study multiple variables is *factor analysis.* This procedure examines an array of correlation coefficients for a set of variables and seeks to identify the underlying structure among the several variables. It reduces variable complexity by rearranging and clustering the variables that are intercorrelated to create a smaller and more manageable set of components. The new components (variables) are called *factors.* A researcher who has collected a wide variety of data on college students and is interested in determining the minimum number of variables that account for college success might use factor analysis to reduce and organize the data.[5]

### Interpreting Correlation

Questions frequently arise regarding the interpretation of correlations. What is a high, medium, or low correlation? Although there are differences of opinion, some researchers consider a correlation coefficient of .70 to .90 as high, .40 to .70 as moderate, .20 to .40 as low, and less than .20 as negligible.[6] The real issue, however, is the magnitude of the relationship in the context of the variables being studied. To evaluate the size of a correlation, it is necessary to be familiar with the research literature in order to know what levels of correlation have been previously reported on similar data. For example, in Chapter 6 the use of the correlation coefficient as an index of reliability and validity of measuring instruments was mentioned. For measuring instruments a validity coefficient in the .40 to .60 range is considered relatively high, whereas a reliability coefficient in this range would be unacceptable—we would hope that reliability would be .90 or higher. Again, the question of a high or low correlation coefficient cannot be divorced from its context.

Correlation can also be interpreted by squaring it and then multiplying by 100 to determine the amount of overlap or common variance between the two measures (*coefficient of determination*, or $r^2$). When squared, a correlation of .50 between two sets of scores yields a value of .25, which is equivalent to 25%. Thus, 25% of the variability in one variable is shared by the other, or 25% of all of the factors associated with a score on one variable is also associated with scores on the other. This also means that 75% of the variance in one variable is *not* estimated by the other (Table 14.3).

**Table 14.3. Interpreting the Importance of Correlation**

| Relationship | ($r$) Correlation Coefficient | ($r^2$) Variance Explained | | Remarks about Variance |
|---|---|---|---|---|
| Negligible | <.20 | Up to .04 | = | Up to 4% of the variation in one measure is explained by its relationship with another measure. |
| Low-to-definite | .20–.40 | Up to .16 | = | Up to 16% of the variation explained. |
| Moderate-to-substantial | .40–.70 | Up to .49 | = | Up to 49% of the variation explained. |
| High | .70–.90 | Up to .81 | = | Up to 81% of the variation explained. |
| Very high | >.90 | Over .81 | = | Over 81% of the variation in one measure is explained by its relationship with another measure. |

Source: From C. H. Backstrom and G. Hursch-César, *Survey Research*, 2d ed. (New York: Wiley, 1981), p. 367; where it had been adapted from J. P. Guilford, *Fundamental Statistics in Psychology and Education* (New York: McGraw-Hill, 1965), p. 145. Reprinted by permission of Macmillan and McGraw-Hill.

Another question asked about correlations is, How strong must a correlation be to allow us to conclude that one variable caused the other? The answer is simple. No matter what magnitude, we are on shaky ground if we infer causality on the basis of correlation alone. Correlations do not necessarily imply causal relationships, they only indicate that a relationship of some magnitude and direction exists between variables. Even when researchers use highly sophisticated quantitative analysis with correlational data in a nonexperimental study, any causal interpretations must be made with appropriate qualifications.[7]

A final note of caution should be added about the importance of the unit of analysis to the interpretation of correlational data. When relationships are found based on group data, it is not always appropriate to similarly interpret those results for individuals with different combinations of personal characteristics and levels of performance. For example, a researcher might find that poverty and delinquency rates are correlated when measured at the state level. While this indicates that a relationship between these variables exists for many members of this group, it may be misleading to infer from these aggregate data the interrelationship between poverty and delinquency for all group members.

A researcher who makes assertions about individual subjects from group data is committing what is called the *ecological fallacy.*[8] The converse of this error is the *individualistic fallacy,* when a researcher erroneously infers aggregate-level relationships from individual-level relationships. Both problems in the interpretation of correlation can be avoided if the investigator collects, analyzes, and interprets data that pertain to the unit of analysis specified in his or her hypotheses.

The correlation coefficient is a versatile statistic. It can be applied in many different ways in research: as a descriptive statistic to describe the relationship between variables; as an index of the reliability and validity of a research instrument; in prediction, since correlation allows us to predict one variable from knowledge of another variable or from a combination of variables; and in inferential statistics.

## INFERENTIAL STATISTICS

Descriptive statistics describe aspects of the particular group under investigation. The objective of many studies, however, is to generalize findings to a larger group from a subset of that group. In most cases, a researcher is unable to compute descriptive measures of a population because data for the entire group are unavailable for study. The use of inferential (sampling) statistics makes it possible to infer something, on the basis of empirical probability, about population characteristics (*parameters*) from corresponding sample characteristics (*statistics*). Naturally, statistical inference would be unnecessary if the researcher could study the whole population and obtain actual population values.

### Uses of Inferential Statistics

There are two primary uses of inferential statistics. One is to estimate a population parameter from evidence collected on a random sample (e.g., central tendency, variability). Two types of estimates are possible: point and interval. A *point estimate* is a single statistic, calculated from one sample, that is considered a good indication of the corresponding parameter. If the sample mean is 44.5, this single sample value is the point estimate of the population mean. The major drawback with this approach is that there is no way to determine the amount of error that the researcher is likely to make in the estimate. A more frequently used procedure for estimating parameters is called *interval estimation.* Rather than specifying a point, the researcher uses sample data to define a confidence interval (band) within whose limits a population value, such as a mean, falls. Then, the investigator can assert with a certain degree of confidence that the actual population mean lies within specific limits.

A second use of inferential statistics is testing hypotheses of no difference or no relationship among variables in the population. (Recall the two types of hypotheses posed by the researcher: the research, or alternate, and the null.) The research hypothesis states the difference or relationship the investigator expects to find with the data. The null hypothesis (the one actually tested) states that there is no difference or relationship between two sets of scores—i.e., the difference (or relationship) between the two values is zero.

If the null hypothesis is rejected, the obtained difference is regarded as not being due only to chance (but likely due to the variables under study). The difference is larger than that expected based upon chance alone and is therefore significant (real). When no support is found for the null hypothesis, the investigator indirectly obtains evidence for its alternate (the research hypothesis) and regards the research hypothesis as probably true.

If the null hypothesis is accepted, the difference is attributable to chance and is not statistically significant. This leads the investigator to infer that the research hypothesis is probably false. (Examples of hypothesis testing are provided in hypothetical studies described in conjunction with parametric and nonparametric techniques later in this chapter and in the research synopses at the ends of Chaps. 8–12.)

## Levels of Significance

Inference is not absolutely certain; it is based upon probability theory. When using inferential procedures or tests of significance, the researcher needs to know the likelihood that sample results also apply to the population concerned. There must be a basis for deciding whether differences are sufficiently large that their occurrence cannot be attributed to chance or so small that their occurrence on the basis of normal fluctuations caused by sampling error is relatively probable. That criterion is the *significance level,* or level of significance (alpha, or alpha level). Prior to testing the hypothesis, the investigator sets the significance level to indicate the maximum risks he or she is willing to take of making an error when concluding that there is a difference attributable to the research situation and not to chance. In practice, researchers sometimes report the highest significance level attained.

Commonly used alpha levels are .05 and .01. If the .05 level of significance is selected, the likelihood of obtaining the observed difference due to chance is less than 5 times in 100; that is, if a study were conducted 100 times, spurious conclusions could be drawn in fewer than 5 of the trials. At the .01 level of significance, the same results would be obtained in at least 99 of 100 replications of the study. The lower the alpha level, the greater degree of confidence the researcher can have in the findings. An investigator reporting the results of a study typically refers to them as being statistically significant at the .05 level (if that was the alpha level chosen in advance). If the results do not achieve the .05 cutoff point, they are not statistically significant, and the researcher reports that no difference or relationship was demonstrated. (Phrases like "almost significant" or "trends toward significance" should be avoided in reporting nonsignificant findings.)

### Type I and Type II Errors

There are two statistical decisions that can be made in hypothesis testing. First, the investigator can reject the null hypothesis when a predetermined alpha level, such as $p < .05$ or $p < .01$, is achieved. This leads to the assertion of the research hypothesis. Second, the researcher can fail to reject the null hypothesis when the data do not come out significantly different (i.e., fail to reach the predetermined alpha level).

In making decisions regarding the null hypothesis, one of two types of error is possible. When the researcher does not reject a true hypothesis or rejects a false hypothesis, there is no error (Table 14.4). But the researcher can make the mistake of rejecting the null hypothesis when it is actually true. Falsely rejecting the hypothesis is called a *Type I,* or alpha ($\alpha$), error. The probability of rejecting a true hypothesis is represented by the level of significance, or alpha level. As the alpha level decreases, the probability of falsely rejecting a true null hypothesis decreases. The researcher who is willing to risk rejection of the null hypothesis when it is true only 5 times out of 100 or less adopts the .05 level. If the commission of a Type I error might have serious practical consequences (e.g., medical studies, pharmaceutical investigations, and other research that will impact large numbers of people), the researcher can adopt a more conservative level of confidence,

**Table 14.4. Errors in Hypothesis Testing**

| | Researcher's Decision | |
|---|---|---|
| Actual Situation | Accept null hypothesis | Reject null hypothesis |
| Null hypothesis is true | correct | Type I error |
| Null hypothesis is false | Type II error | correct |

such as the .01 level, where there is a 1 in 100 chance of making an error. (It should be noted that attaining significance at any given level [e.g., $p < .05$, $p < .01$] is a function of both sample size and the variability of the data. The smaller the standard deviation and the larger the sample size, the greater the chance that a relatively small difference between group means will be found to be statistically significant.)

If the researcher fails to reject the null hypothesis when it is false, a second type of error is possible: the *Type II,* or beta ($\beta$), error. The probability of an erroneous acceptance of a false hypothesis requires calculation and is seldom reported in studies, although Type II errors are more common than Type I errors. As a general rule, the lower the level of significance used to reject the null hypothesis (and the less likelihood of a Type I error), the greater the risk of a Type II error, and vice versa. The two errors are inversely related.[9] So, if the .01 level of significance is applied, there is more protection against a Type I error than with the .05 level, but there is a greater chance of committing a Type II error with the former rather than with the latter.

Ordinarily, researchers prefer the more conservative position of failing to claim a result when it is true rather than claiming a result when it is not true. This explains why relatively low levels of significance, such as .05, .01, and even .001, continue to be used (and why relatively fewer Type I errors are made). Since the researcher can never really know if a particular investigation that yields significant results is accurate, it is worthwhile to replicate studies to increase confidence that a Type I error has not been made.

## Parametric and Nonparametric Tests

There are two groups of tests available to the researcher for testing hypotheses: parametric and nonparametric. The appropriateness of each type within certain conditions is explained here.

### Parametric Tests

Employed more often in research, parametric tests make certain basic assumptions about the nature of the population from which the sample was obtained and about the values of the parameters. Parametric inferential procedures assume that the data are normally distributed, that the dependent variables are continuous and measured on an interval or ratio scale (see Chap. 3), and that if two or more populations are being investigated, the variance or spread within the group is equal (homogeneous). When all assumptions are met, parametric tests are extremely powerful techniques that minimize the risk of a Type II error. Their superiority is related to the fact that they make maximum use of the information available in the data (e.g., mean, variance, standard deviation).

Of the parametric techniques available for use in inferential analysis, three are discussed here: *t* test, analysis of variance, and Pearson *r*.

The *t* Test. The *t* test is a parametric statistical technique that compares two means to determine if the difference between them is real or due to chance. As an illustration of a *t* test for independent samples, consider a hypothetical study of the effects of a diet supplement on weight gain. The null hypothesis is that there is no significant difference in weight between students receiving a diet supplement (Group 1—Experimental group) and students not receiving the supplement (Group 2—Control group). The level of significance (or critical region for rejection) selected is .05 ($p < .05$). This means the probability of incorrectly concluding no effect of diet supplement on weight gain is to be .05 or less.

To test the hypothesis of no significant difference between weights of the two groups, the mean weights of the two groups are computed and a *t* test is performed for difference between means. This determines the likelihood of the two means being drawn from the same population. In this study, the mean weight of Group 1 (receiving diet supplement) is 99.2. The mean weight of Group 2 is 102.3. Through a mathematical process, a *t* value of −1.31 is calculated for the data. A statistical table indicates that the critical region for rejection at the .05 level is 2.05; that is, the hypothesis of no difference between means can be rejected only if the *t* value is less than −2.05 or greater than 2.05. Since the *t* value obtained (−1.31) is not less than −2.05, the researcher fails to reject the hypothesis. The conclusion must be that there is no significant difference in weight between the two groups.

If a *t* value had been obtained within the critical region of rejection, the hypothesis could have been rejected. Then, the researcher could have assumed that the difference in weight between the groups was significant and that the probability of the difference being due to chance was less than .05. If the investigator selected the .01 level of significance, a larger difference between the sample means would have been needed to reject the hypothesis.

Analysis of Variance. The *analysis of variance* (ANOVA) has wider application than the *t* test in that it permits the simultaneous comparison of two *or more* means to determine if there are any statistically significant differences between them.[10] The procedure examines the amount of variability that is attributable to variation between the groups and to variation within the groups. The between-group variation is divided by the within-group variation, and the resulting ratio is called an *F* value. The computed *F* ratio is evaluated by referring to appropriate tables with critical values. If the *F* ratio exceeds the cutoff point for a designated level of significance, the test is statistically significant, and the null hypothesis can be rejected: The means are not all considered equal. If the calculated *F* value is smaller than the critical value required for statistical significance, the null hypothesis is not rejected. It is concluded that the difference in sample means is due to random sampling fluctuation.

Here is a hypothetical study that should help illustrate a simple application of ANOVA. (More complex analysis variance models, such as multivariate analysis of variance, or MANOVA, are also available.) A family researcher is interested in investigating the effectiveness of three different approaches to parent education (group discussion, written materials, lecture method). The null hypothesis is that there is no difference among the population means of parents receiving the three types of training. The level of significance is set at .05. If the *F* ratio is significant at the .05 level, the null hypothesis is rejected, indicating that there are significant differences within the total set of data. This suggests that not all methods of parent education yield the same results (as measured by a parenting skills inventory or some other measure).

However, ANOVA does not tell the researcher how the means differ. It would be helpful to know if every method of parent education differs from every other method or if there are differences between some and not between others. Duncan's multiple range test, Tukey's HSD, and Scheffe's test are commonly used to identify the specific differences, thereby allowing the investigator to conclude that one specific type of parent education is more or less effective than another.

The Pearson *r*. Inferential statistics are employed to examine relationships, as well as differences between means. Earlier, correlation was presented as a descriptive statistic that indicates the strength of a relationship between two or more variables. The Pearson *r*, a parametric technique, can also be used to test hypotheses about the association of variables in the population, based upon sample *r*'s, and therefore can be considered here in the context of inferential techniques. A special table for evaluating the significance of *r* is available in most statistics books. This table provides minimum *r*'s to achieve significance at different probability levels, for different degrees of freedom ($N - 2$, or number of pairs of scores minus two).

A null hypothesis often investigated in correlational studies is that the population coefficient is zero[11] (that is, there is no correlation in the population regardless of the value that the researcher has obtained for the sample). To test this hypothesis, the researcher compares the calculated *r* with the table value. For example, if the *N* is 20 (and degrees of freedom are 18), the table reveals that the *r* must be at least equal to .4438 to be significant at the .05 level. If the obtained *r* is .50, the researcher can reject the null hypothesis of no significant relationship and conclude that the sample was drawn from a population in which the true correlation differs from zero. There is only a very small probability that the observed sample coefficient could have been obtained if there were no relationship between the populations of values.

When data do not meet the minimum parametric assumptions and Pearson's *r* is inappropriate, other measures of relationship are available. One such nonparametric technique is called Spearman's rho.

## Nonparametric Tests

Nonparametric tests, unlike their parametric counterparts, make no assumptions about the population under investigation. Often called distribution-free statistics, they do not assume normality of the population distribution or require equal group variances. In contrast to parametric methods, they are used with variables expressed in nominal or ordinal (rather than interval) form. And they are appropriate for very small samples, although they are often used with relatively large samples when underlying assumptions have not been met. Nonparametric tests, which involve frequencies and medians (but not means), are simpler to calculate, especially when the sample is small to moderate in size. The major drawback is that nonparametric tests are less powerful than their parametric analogs.[12] Nonparametric tests increase the chance of a Type II error because they are less sensitive to small differences and are less able to detect that such differences might be statistically significant. (Sources that describe nonparametric techniques in detail are available.[13])

Chi-square. The *chi-square* ($\chi^2$) test is a widely used nonparametric procedure to determine whether a single sample is different from a hypothetical distribution or whether two or more distributions differ from each other. For example, it can be employed to examine whether there are differences in the numbers or frequencies of people responding in certain ways.

Using a one-sample design, a group of people may be asked if they prefer Brand A or Brand B diet cola, and the frequencies of people preferring Brand A and those preferring Brand B may be compared with a hypothetical distribution. With the chi-square technique, one can determine the probability that the frequencies observed differ from expected theoretical frequencies. In the diet cola survey, from a sample of 50 people, it is expected that 25 people would prefer Brand A and that 25 would prefer Brand B. In the chi-square test, these are called the *expected* frequencies (the number that would be expected to occur by chance). If 20 out of 50 people in the survey actually preferred Brand A and 30 out of 50 people preferred Brand B, these preferences are the *observed* frequencies. The question to be asked is, Do the observed frequencies differ sufficiently from the expected frequencies to justify rejection of the null hypothesis? If the two frequencies do differ, the null hypothesis is rejected, and it is concluded that there is a preference for Brand B over Brand A.

The chi-square can also be used in a two-sample or more-than-two-sample design to determine whether observed distributions differ from one another. In such cases, the difference (or differences) in distribution between the groups is tested. Frequencies are entered in cells in a contingency table (Table 14.5), and the computation of chi-square is based on the row and column frequencies. In Table 14.5, the expected frequencies are found by multiplying the column totals by the row totals and dividing by the grand total. Specifically, the expected frequency for males preferring Brand A would be (52 × 44)/95, or 24.1. Expected frequencies are determined for every cell in the table. The differences between the observed and expected frequencies are summed and are the basis for the chi-square. If the value of chi-square is high enough, the null hypothesis is rejected.

**Table 14.5. 3 × 2 Contingency Table of Diet Cola Brand Preference by Sex**

| Brands | Male | Female | Total |
|---|---|---|---|
| A | 32 | 12 | 44 |
| B | 14 | 22 | 36 |
| C | 6 | 9 | 15 |
| Total | 52 | 43 | 95 |

A statistical table provides the critical values of chi-square needed to reach significance at $p < .05$, $p < .01$, and so forth. The appropriate statistical table reveals that the computed value of $\chi^2$, which is 10.67 in this case, is significant beyond the .01 level. Thus, the null hypothesis is rejected, and we can conclude that males and females differed in their preferences for brands of diet cola more than could be expected by chance.[14]

Additional nonparametric tests are mentioned in the next section.

## Selecting an Appropriate Statistical Test

The statistical test a researcher selects for a study depends on the nature of the hypothesis and the required assumptions previously discussed. For example, if the investigator wants to determine if the difference between groups is significant, and parametric assumptions have been met (interval-level data, normal distribution, homogeneous variance), the *t* test is usually chosen when there are two groups, and analysis of variance is employed when there are more than two groups. If less than interval-scale measurement is achieved and/or the parametric assumptions are not satisfied, a nonparametric analysis is used. The Mann-Whitney *U* test is the nonparametric analog to the parametric *t* test for independent (uncorrelated) samples, and the Kruskal-Wallis ANOVA is the nonparametric counterpart of the one-way ANOVA in parametric measurements. The nonparametric chi-square test has no parametric analog for the investigation of difference.

A researcher who is interested in testing a hypothesis about the relationship between variables would use the Pearson product-moment correlation if conditions have been met to justify the use of parametric analysis. Otherwise, Spearman's rank-order correlation or the contingency coefficient, both nonparametric statistics, may be used to examine relationships.

A summary of hypotheses and the statistical tests that are appropriate for their investigation follows. The listing is abridged and somewhat oversimplified and is only intended to indicate some of the principal considerations necessary before selecting a statistical test.[15]

### STATISTICAL TEST SELECTION

Hypothesis: differences in means

*Parametric analysis:* examines means; parametric assumptions are met

1. *t* test: compares the means of two groups
2. One-way ANOVA: compares the means of three or more groups
3. Etc.

Hypothesis: differences in frequencies

*Nonparametric analysis:* examines frequencies; parametric assumptions are not met

1. Mann-Whitney *U* test: compares two independent groups where data have been measured on an ordinal scale
2. Kruskal-Wallis ANOVA: compares the distributions of three or more independent samples
3. Chi-square test: examines differences between an observed number and the expected number of responses, people, or objects that fall into two or more categories
4. Etc.

Hypothesis: relationships between variables

*Parametric analysis:* examines relationships; parametric assumptions are met

1. Pearson product-moment correlation (*r*): measures the association between two variables
2. Multiple correlation (*R*): examines the relationship between a dependent variable and two or more independent variables

3. Etc.

*Nonparametric analysis:* examines relationships; parametric assumptions are not met

1. Spearman's rho ($r_s$): examines rank-order correlation between two variables
2. Contingency coefficient ($C$): examines the association between two sets of attributes when only nominal information about one or both sets is available
3. Etc.

## NOTES

1. Numerous introductory and intermediate texts dealing with statistical procedures are appropriate for human ecology research: Bruning and Kintz (1977), Cox (1987), Daniel (1987), Dowdy and Wearden (1983), Edwards (1984), Ferguson (1981), Guilford and Fruchter (1977), Hays (1988), and Hinkle, Wiersma, and Jurs (1988), Steel and Torrier (1980), and Zar (1984).

2. An *SD* actually tells the *minimum* number of cases within a specific range. To prevent redundancy the phrase "at least" before 34.13% , etc., has been omitted in the remainder of the discussion.

3. The calculation involves subtracting the mean raw score from the raw score and dividing the difference by the standard deviation of the original distribution. Thus, if the mean raw score is 100 and its standard deviation is 10, a raw score of 125 is equivalent to a $z$ score of 2.5.

4. This line is referred to as a *regression line.* It is a line that is the best possible linear representation of the points in a scatter diagram. It minimizes the squared distances between the several points and the line. (See any statistics text for the steps in computing regression lines.)

5. Good treatment of these and other multivariate techniques are presented in Dillon and Goldstein (1984), Hair et al. (1984), Kachigan (1982), and Pedhazur (1982).

6. Such interpretations should be used only if the correlation coefficient is statisically significant.

7. An increasing number of researchers are using these advanced methods. Even with path analysis, the investigator can only say that, given a particular model, some variables may possibly cause others but cannot be caused by them. Although the investigator can conclude that a particular model of causation is compatible with the data, he or she cannot *prove* that a variable is caused by other variables (Miller and Wilson 1983).

8. Robinson's (1950) classic study using the 1930 U.S. Census data revealed that the correlation between race and literacy was larger at the aggregate level than the correlation between the same variables measured on the individual level. Firebaugh (1978) has reanalyzed these data to determine the source of cross-level bias. For an advanced treatment of ecological inference, see Langbein and Lichtman (1978).

9. Simultaneous reduction of the two types of errors, without affecting one another, is possible by using very large samples and/or by minimizing sampling variability.

10. Unlike the *t* test, ANOVA also has the advantage of allowing the examination of *interactions* (the effect of two independent variables operating together on the dependent variable, apart from the main effect of each independent variable).

11. Some other possible hypotheses involving the correlation coefficient are that the two population correlation coefficients are equal or that the coefficient is a specified value other than zero.

12. Some researchers argue that parametric techniques are robust enough to yield valid results even when all assumptions are not met. Consequently, they continue to apply the more powerful parametric procedures to most research problems unless the populations are markedly nonnormal, the variances excessively heterogeneous, or the sample sizes extremely small. Others advocate the use of nonparametric techniques whenever assumptions are violated. See also Note 3, Chapter 3.

13. For a lucid presentation of nonparametric techniques, consult Siegel and Castellan (1988). Other references are Bradley (1968), Gibbons (1985), and Kraft and Van Eeden (1968).

14. The artificial data for this example were adapted from Siegel (1956, 104–7).

15. Decision matrices or decision trees for use in selecting appropriate statistical tools are presented in many statistics and research texts. For a comprehensive guide to the selection of appropriate statistics or techniques for application in different analyses, see Andrews et al. (1981).

PART 5

# Research Communication

CHAPTER 15

# Writing Research Proposals

Proposal writing is an important part of the research enterprise. A person who plans to conduct research will also need to know how to prepare proposals because a proposal of some kind is often required before initiating a study. Researchers may be unable to undertake an investigation without financial support and must submit a request for funding from a foundation or government agency. Also, students preparing to do a master's thesis or doctoral dissertation are normally expected to present a proposal and receive approval from their research advisory committee before initiating their project.

Even when a formal proposal is not required, it is beneficial to develop such a written plan outlining the intended study. Doing so helps ensure a feasible design that, when implemented, will likely yield interpretable findings of possible scientific value. Considering the related literature and thinking about sampling, instrumentation, possible logistical problems, statistical analyses, and so on permits formulation of a comprehensive statement of the rationale underlying the project and a description of the procedures the researcher plans to follow. If a detailed proposal has been developed, the task of preparing a final research report is partly done. The introduction, literature review, and method will be fairly complete and can be easily adapted into the preliminary sections of a manuscript submitted as a journal article or can be converted into opening chapters of a thesis or dissertation.

Only a brief introduction to two types of proposals is presented here: research grant proposals and thesis or dissertation proposals. There is considerable overlap between them because most proposals contain similar content, and many of the same principles apply to proposals submitted for funding and to those submitted in partial fulfillment of academic degrees.

## RESEARCH GRANT PROPOSALS

Outside funding of research is critical to the advancement of human ecology. Unfortunately, it is far more difficult today than in recent years to obtain sponsored project funds because (1) "real dollars" available from allocating organizations have either declined or stabilized (Coleman 1984; Hall 1977); (2) the relative importance of the federal government as a source of funding has decreased (Hall 1977); (3) the number of organizations and individuals applying for grant money has increased (White 1975); and (4) funding agencies have become more critical in their assessment of proposals and have adopted more stringent criteria and sophisticated review methods, not only because of shrinking resources but also because of negative experiences with some projects that have not produced the results they promised (Lefferts 1982).

As White (1975, vii) indicates, these recent trends have important implications for securing research support: "Grant seekers today must be prepared to meet powerful competition. Not only must they be well trained and competent in their fields of specialization, but they must be skilled in identifying the most likely sources of funding and able to make presentations that stand out among the vast and increasing tide of applications now flooding all grant-making organizations."

### Activities in the Grant Proposal Process

A general outline of the activities involved in proposal development, based upon a model developed by Hall (1977), is presented in Figure 15.1.[1] Some of these activities will be discussed further.

#### Locating Funding Sources

Identification of the most appropriate funding source for a particular project is an important first step in obtaining support for research. There are two major categories of funders: private foundations and government agencies. Read (1986, 3) defines a private foundation as a "nongovernmental, nonprofit organization having a principal fund of its own, managed by its own trustees and directors, and established to maintain or aid charitable, educational, religious, or other activities serving the public good, primarily by making grants to other nonprofit organizations." Each foundation usually has restrictions on the types of programs that can receive support, the geographical area within which support may be granted, the minimum and maximum amount of awards, and the types of organizations that qualify for funding (Lefferts 1982).

Government funders, on the other hand, include federal, state, and local agencies that operate with public tax dollars. Like private founda-

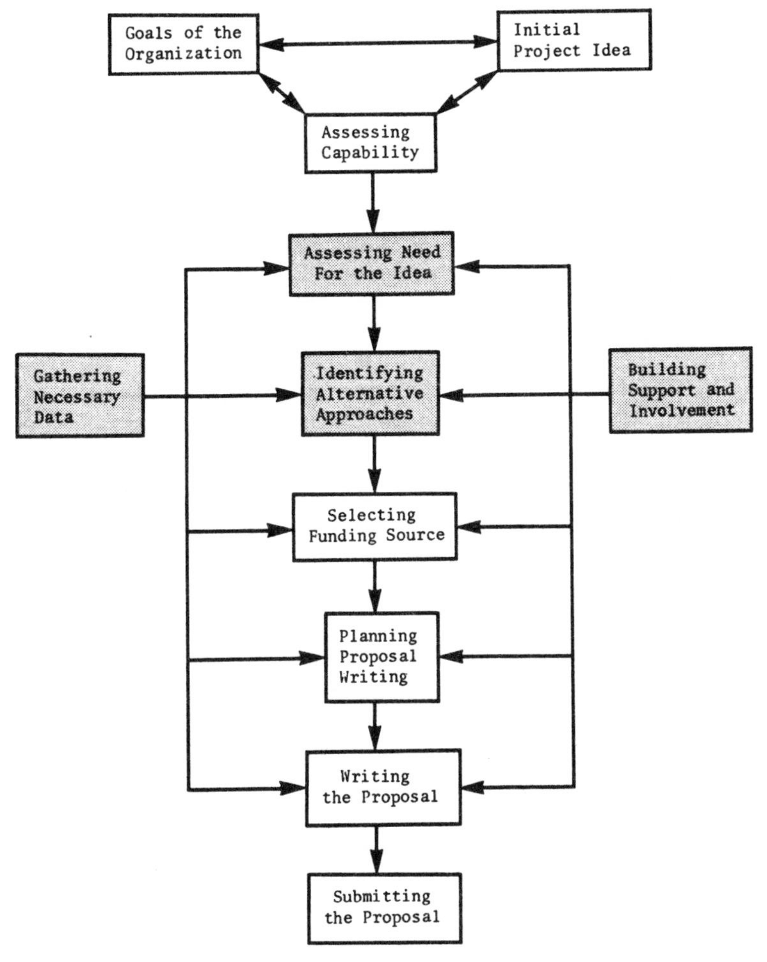


**Figure 15.1.** Model for proposal development. (Reprinted from M. Hall, *Developing Skills in Proposal Writing,* 2d ed., Portland, Ore.: Continuing Education Publications, 1977. Used by permission.)

tions, they disburse grants and other monies to nonprofit organizations and individuals. But unlike foundations that are free to determine the types of projects they will support, government agencies are restricted by legislative appropriations and authorizations. Guidelines for obtaining government monies are highly structured, with detailed proposals and extremely formal review processes.

In addition to foundations and government agencies, other sources of research funding include corporations, individuals, religious bodies, community organizations, professional associations, and local groups. However, the primary sponsor of funded research in this country is the federal government.

Determining funding sources that might be receptive to a proposal is facilitated by reference tools available in many libraries. These materials are usually kept in the reference section, although some large libraries may have a separate funding information center. In addition, offices of research and sponsored projects of major research universities frequently maintain their own libraries of materials for use in identifying grantors. Only a few of the many resources for locating appropriate grantmakers will be mentioned here.

Directories. Some of the better-known comprehensive directories that describe foundations, characterize their program interests, and indicate financial and personnel data are *The Foundation Directory, Foundation Grants Index Annual, National Data Book,* and *Source Book Profiles.* The first three are also available as databases online. Company-sponsored funders are listed in *Taft Corporate Giving Directory* as well as in some of the foundation directories (e.g., *Source Book Profiles*). Researchers interested in seeking support from foundations outside the United States may consult the *International Foundation Directory* and *Directory of European Foundations.* Other directories include foundations that share special program interests. Another resource, *Foundation Grants to Individuals,* is devoted exclusively to foundation grant opportunities for individual applicants, including support for research projects.

The bible of federal government domestic-assistance and grant programs is the *Catalog of Federal Domestic Assistance.* Published by the Office of Management and Budget, it describes more than a thousand programs administered by approximately 50 agencies. A computerized retrieval system based upon the *Catalog,* called FAPRS (Federal Assistance Program Retrieval), is also available to grantseekers. The *Guide to Federal Funding for Social Scientists* is another directory for government funding sources. The *Annual Register of Grant Support,* the *Directory of Research Grants,* and the APA *Guide to Research Support* are three additional reference tools that include information about both government and foundation funding sources.

Periodicals. Periodicals offer up-to-date information on sources of funding for particular research problems. Some contain information about government funding, such as the *Commerce Business Daily* (announcing all government requests for proposals, or RFPs, that exceed $25,000), the *Federal Register* (supplementing and updating the *Catalog of Federal Domestic Assistance* five days per week), and the *Federal Grants and Con-*

*tracts Weekly* (containing the latest RFPs, closing dates for grant programs, etc.). *Foundation News* (bimonthly) and *Foundation Grants Index Bimonthly* cover private funding, and *Funding Review* (quarterly) covers both private and government funding. Other periodicals dealing with grantmakers, grantmaking activities, and current trends include *Grants Magazine* (quarterly), *Grantsmanship Center News* (bimonthly), and *Grassroots Fundraising Journal* (bimonthly).

### Selecting a Potential Funder

Before deciding to submit a research proposal to a funding source, a general rule of thumb is for the proposer to know as much about the potential grantor as possible. Here are some of the questions that need to be answered about each funder being considered:

> What current trends exist, resulting in limitations, restrictions, and/or potential future opportunities for individual applicants? Although no one can provide you with guarantees, how good are your chances? Try to find out about the competition: Who was awarded funding in the latest year of record? Might they be reapplying this year? What percentage of applicants do these grant recipients represent? Who are the important decision makers employed by the funder? What review process do they follow? How long will it take? When will you be notified about their decision regarding your proposal? What style of approach should you adopt? What politics and/or proper etiquette are involved? (Margolin 1983, 82–83)

Above all, the proposal must lie within the scope of the funder's program (Krathwohl 1977).

### Contacting the Funder

Once a potential funding source has been identified, it is good practice to call and make an appointment with an appropriate program officer or other important staff member. As Lefferts (1982, 103) has emphasized, "There is no substitute for personal contact and visibility with funders so that they know whom they are dealing with; thus the proposal becomes more than a written document." Bauer (1984) estimates that chances for a successful application are increased 300% when the researcher contacts the funding source before the proposal is written.

In addition to having an opportunity to "sell" the idea firsthand, preproposal contact allows the proposer to learn more about the funder's mission, special programs, and hidden agenda, if any, as well as necessary guidelines and policies. It helps the researcher tailor the proposal to the funding source. Whether the contact is by telephone or in person, it should be brief and to the point. If at all possible, an appointment should be made and the researcher should visit the funding source in person. Considerable preliminary planning is necessary to maximize the benefits of this information exchange.[2] Not enough can be said about the importance of these and other preapplication activities. To improve chances of proposal acceptance, a great deal of work must be done in advance of writing the proposal.[3]

Before taking the time and effort to prepare a full-blown proposal, many researchers prefer to send some type of summary statement first to find out if the funder is interested. This brief proposal is sometimes referred to as a concept paper, letter of inquiry, or letter proposal. The *letter proposal* format is being used increasingly by government and private funders as part of the application process. Some grantmaking agencies require the concept paper and use it as an initial screening device. They will not forward the lengthy application packet to an applicant unless they like the ideas presented in the preproposal and the proposed research is clearly eligible for support under one of their programs. Many private foundations, particularly smaller ones, may not have the staff or time to review longer proposals and may base their funding decisions exclusively on these one- or two-page letter proposals.[4]

## Preparing the Research Grant Proposal

### General Characteristics of the Grant Proposal

When the researcher thinks an idea may lead to funding and/or feels encouraged by the preproposal contact with the potential funder, he or she prepares a formal proposal. The document is written in clear and concise language and is arranged in a logical sequence, with continuity from one section to the next. Organization of a proposal is enhanced by the use of proper headings and subheadings that allow a reviewer to follow the proposer's train of thought and understand the critically important steps of the project. The text is not cluttered with excessive details; it includes only essential information. Appendixes are used for auxiliary information.[5] Since proposals are often reviewed by a multidisciplinary panel of judges, not all of whom are completely knowledgeable about the topic, technical jargon is kept to a minimum. Finally, the proposal is written in the future tense because the study has not yet been done.

### Organization and Content of the Proposal

Most research grant proposals require essentially the same information, although organization of the document and the number and names of the headings may vary. It is important to follow the format suggested by the funding source.

There are several parts to a grant proposal. The *introduction* is normally used to tell very briefly the general nature and scope of the problem, where the research will be conducted, the method, and the significance of the study. (The more detailed presentation of these items comes in later sections.) In addition, the introduction can be used to establish the credibility of the researcher and the applying organization, if this is possible within a reasonable amount of space. Otherwise, such information may be relegated to an appendix.[6]

The *problem statement* (or statement of need) presents the need for the study and includes some quantitative documentation as well as a survey of related literature. This section of the report gives the researcher an opportunity to demonstrate knowledge of previous work in the field and show how past investigators have not met the need that the proposed study will satisfy.

The *objectives* section indicates what the study will accomplish and includes specific hypotheses or questions to be answered.

The *procedures* section describes how objectives will be met and how hypotheses and questions will be addressed. Information about design issues, such as the proposed sample, instrumentation, and statistical analyses, is presented.[7] A time schedule is usually included to illustrate when certain activities (e.g., data collection, analysis) will begin and end. (See Ex. 15.1 for a simplified timetable.)

The *budget* section indicates how much money will be needed and the manner in which it will be spent to meet the study objectives. Government agencies expect very detailed budgets and provide their own forms for the researcher to complete, whereas private foundations are normally less structured and require relatively less budgetary detail. Separate budget explanation sheets may be used to justify certain expenditures. (See Ex. 15.2 for a simplified hypothetical budget.)

Other sections dealing with personnel and with facilities and equipment may be included if these items were not discussed in other parts of the

| Activity | Month | | | | | | | | | | | |
|---|---|---|---|---|---|---|---|---|---|---|---|---|
| | 1 | 2 | 3 | 4 | 5 | 6 | 7 | 8 | 9 | 10 | 11 | 12 |
| 1. Selection of Sample | x | | | | | | | | | | | |
| 2. Collection of Data | | x | x | x | x | | | | | | | |
| 3. Preparation of Data for Analysis | | | x | x | x | x | | | | | | |
| 4. Analysis of Data | | | | | | | x | x | | | | |
| 5. Preparation of Report | | | | | | | | | x | x | x | x |

**Example 15.1.** Sample timetable for a proposed 1-year study.

| | | Amount |
|---|---|---|
| I. Direct Costs | | |
| A. Personnel salaries | | |
| 1. Project director: Dr. John Doe | | |
| (½ released time for 24 mos. @ $35,000/yr.) | $35,000 | |
| 2. Dr. Jane Wilson | | |
| (¼ released time for 24 mos. @ $30,000/yr.) | 15,000 | |
| 3. Research assistant: Mr. Joe Johnson | | |
| (24 mos. @ $7,000/yr.) | 14,000 | |
| 4. Research assistant: Ms. Mary Jackson | | |
| (12 mos. @ $7,000/yr.) | 7,000 | |
| 5. Secretary, to be appointed | | |
| (half-time for 24 mos. at $15,000/yr.) | 15,000 | $86,000 |
| B. Employee fringe benefits (25% of salary for Drs. Doe and Wilson only); 25% x $50,000 | 12,500 | 12,500 |
| C. Consultants | | |
| 1. Dr. John Jones, Asst. Prof. of Statistics and Research, Local University. 2 days @ $200/day | 400 | |
| 2. Dr. Mary Smith, Prof. of Home Economics, State College, 4 days @ $250/day | 1,000 | 1,400 |
| D. Travel (trips to research site for data collection, etc.; 60 miles @ 22¢ x 75 | 990 | 990 |
| E. Supplies and Materials | 2,500 | 2,500 |
| F. Equipment | 800 | 800 |
| G. Communications | | |
| 1. Postage | 200 | |
| 2. Long distance calls | 250 | 450 |
| H. Services | | |
| 1. Xeroxing | 250 | |
| 2. Data entry | 250 | 500 |
| I. Publication Costs | 600 | 600 |

**Example 15.2.** Sample budget for a proposed 2-year study.

| | | |
|---|---|---|
| J. Other Direct Costs | | |
| 1. Computer time (2 hrs. at $150/hr.) | 300 | 300 |
| K. Subtotal Direct Costs | | 106,040 |
| II. Indirect Costs | | |
| Calculated at 56% of salaries and wages, | | |
| excluding fringe benefits (56% x $86,000) | | 48,160 |
| III. Total Project Cost | | $154,200 |

document. Under *personnel,* the researcher discusses individuals needed for execution of the study, their responsibilities, and their qualifications. In the *facilities and equipment* section, the researcher indicates special facilities and equipment that are necessary.[8]

Throughout the proposal writing process, the researcher must remember that he or she is trying to convince the allocating agency that the proposed study is important and consistent with its grantmaking goals and that the applicant is competent and the right person to carry out the investigation.

Figure 15.2 presents a summary by Hall (1977, 90) of the major components of a proposal and the type of information provided in each.

### Evaluating the Adequacy of a Grant Proposal

After the proposal has been written, it is advisable to review the document carefully before submitting it. Lauffer (1983, 145) recommends this brief checklist for determining the adequacy of a proposal:[9]

- Are the important points easily discovered in skimming the proposal?
- Has the applicant made a convincing case for a specific local need, outlined a realistic plan for meeting that need, and demonstrated that it is the agency best positioned to carry out the plan?
- Are the stated objectives clearly reflected in the sections on procedures, personnel, and budget?
- Does the proposal present an honest, factual picture of the applicant agency and of the resources and personnel available for the project? Are the "plus" factors emphasized, but without exaggeration?
- Is the presentation grammatical, clear, and concise, avoiding jargon, overblown phraseology, and unexplained abbreviations?
- Have all requirements of the funding agency been met?

There are many good sources dealing with proposal writing, and sample grant proposals are available in the literature.[10]

| Topic | Information to Be Provided |
|---|---|
| Title Page | Title of project, name of applicant and organization, name of agency submitted to, inclusive dates of project, total budget request, signatures of authorized personnel approving submission from the local agency. |
| Abstract | Summary of the proposal with at least some reference to the major points in the statement of need, objectives, procedures, evaluation, and dissemination components. Should stress the end-products. Usually 250 to 500 words. |
| Problem Statement (or Statement of Need) | Clear and precise statement of the problem to be addressed and the need for its solution. Should establish *significance, relevance, timeliness, generalizability* and *contribution* of the project. *Innovativeness* of proposed methodology may also be substantiated. Usually includes references to previous research or earlier works. Statistical data describing the need is also cited. In research proposals, this component may have a separate section labeled "related research" which includes more lengthy discussion of previous studies. |
| Objectives | A very specific indication of the proposed outcomes of the project stated as objectives, hypotheses and/or questions. May also state over-all goals of project. Should flow logically from the identified needs/problems. |
| Procedures | How the objectives will be met or the hypotheses/questions tested. In non-research projects this section usually starts with description of the over-all approach and then gets into details about methodology, participants, organization and time-lines. In a research project, one usually describes design, population and sample, data and instrumentation, analysis, and time schedule. The section should end with clear identification of both short-term and long-term end-products expected. |
| Evaluation* | Details the means by which the local agency and the funding source will know the project has accomplished its purposes. State purpose of evaluation, type of information to be collected, details on instruments, data collection, analysis and utilization and tells how results will be reported. Evaluative criteria should be provided for each objective. |
| Dissemination* | How will products and findings be shared with others? Frequently this section also details reports to be given to the funding source. |
| Facilities & Equipment | Facilities and equipment required and how these will be provided. This section may also describe any unique equipment or facilities available to the local agency which will facilitate the project. |
| Personnel | Who are the personnel that will work on the project and what will they do? What are their backgrounds and credentials? If new staff are needed, how many and of what type? How will they be selected? In a research proposal, this section may also include a description of the project's administrative organization. Individuals to serve as consultants should also be identified, their backgrounds described and use justified. |
| Budget | Cost of the project. Usually divided into categories such as personnel, supplies and materials, travel, data processing, facilities or equipment and indirect costs. |

*These categories may or may not be included in research proposals, or if required, can be discussed as elements of the procedures component.

**Figure 15.2.** The major components of a proposal. (Reprinted from Mary Hall, *Developing Skills in Proposal Writing*, 2d ed., Portland, Ore.: Continuing Education Publications, 1977. Used by permission.)

## Reasons Why Grant Proposals Succeed or Fail

Grant proposals are approved or not approved for several reasons. Margolin (1983, 214–15) has identified five general ingredients that seem to be common to most successful proposals. A successful proposal

- Delivers an important idea *and* addresses a significant problem of society at large.
- Indicates that the applicant has chosen an outstanding approach to solve the problem and a reasonable plan for implementation.
- Assures the funder that the applicant is capable of success.
- Shows that the proposal is, indeed, within the scope of the funder's activities and will serve in an immediate way to advance the grantmaking goals of the particular funder to which it is addressed.
- Sets forth anticipated results that seem to justify the costs and the time estimated to accomplish the project.

There are some definite reasons why proposals are not recommended for support.[11] Margolin (1983, 234) gives 10 reasons why most grant proposals are turned down:

- Inadequately presented statement of need—perceived by funder as either not a significant issue or as one of such magnitude that a few grant dollars would barely make a dent in the problem.
- Objectives are ill defined—put forward as vague goals or as personal aims.
- Procedures are confused with objectives.
- Lack of integration within the text among components of the proposal.
- The funder does not accept proposals from unaffiliated individuals.
- The funder knows that the proposed idea has already been tried and failed.
- The funder approves of the concept but believes that the applicant is not the proper individual to conduct the project or that the institution with which the applicant is affiliated is not suitable.
- The individual has adopted a poor approach and appealed on an emotional or a political rather than a factual basis.
- The idea costs too much.
- The funder does not have enough information.

If a grant proposal is unsuccessful, the researcher should contact the funding source to find out why it was turned down. Government agencies are obligated to provide this information, but private foundations are also usually willing to reveal the factors that led to rejection. It is possible for a good proposal not to be funded because of unexpected reductions in the funder's budget, and the applicant needs to know this. Reapplication in the following grantmaking cycle may not be out of the question. Reviewers' written comments or more informal feedback on the grant proposal can help the researcher identify weak (as well as strong) points of the proposal. All is not lost if something is learned from one's mistakes.

A specimen research grant proposal is presented in Example 15.3 at the end of the chapter.

## THESIS AND DISSERTATION PROPOSALS

Satisfying the research requirements for a graduate degree can be a personally fulfilling experience because of the sense of accomplishment associated with independent thinking and with addressing a problem and achieving its solution. It can also be professionally rewarding because of the skills developed in the process and the possible contributions to knowledge that a scholarly job of research can make.

The failure of some students to complete their thesis or dissertation can often be traced directly to the lack of proper planning before the research was initiated. Although certain external and/or personal obstacles may impede the student researcher's progress toward a completed thesis or dissertation, a carefully developed proposal, which provides direction for the study and a basis for the final research report, facilitates completion of the report and increases the probability that the student will gain a research-based graduate degree.[12]

Allen (1973, 34) admonishes students: "Prepare your proposal well, and you will have little chance of becoming lost in your work." Madsen (1983, 36) echoes Allen's sentiments when he emphatically states, "There is no question that care lavished on the formal proposal will be repaid a thousand times."

### Functions of the Proposal

According to Locke and Spirduso (1976, 1–2), a thesis or dissertation proposal serves at least three functions:

1. *Communication*. The proposal serves to communicate the student's research plans to those who give consultation and advice. The proposal is the primary resource upon which the thesis or dissertation committee must base the functions of consultation, advice, and, ultimately, consent. Both the quality of assistance obtained and the economy of consultation depend directly upon the clarity and thoroughness of the proposal.
2. *Plan*. The proposal serves as a plan for action. All empirical research consists of careful, systematic, and preplanned observations of some restricted set of phenomena. The acceptability of results is

judged exclusively in terms of the adequacy of the methods employed in making, recording, and interpreting the planned observations. The plan for observations, with its supporting arguments and explications, is the qualitative basis on which the thesis or dissertation will be judged.

A thesis or dissertation can be no better than the plan of investigation—methodology or procedures—employed. Hence, an adequate proposal sets forth the plan in step-by-step detail. The existence of a detailed plan that incorporates the most careful anticipation of problems to be confronted and contingent courses of action is the most powerful insurance against oversight or ill-considered choices during the execution phase of the investigation. The hallmark of a good proposal is a level of thoroughness and detail sufficient to permit another investigator to replicate the study, that is, to perform the same planned observations with results not substantially different from those the author might obtain.

3. *Contract.* A completed proposal, approved for execution by the sponsoring committee, constitutes a bond of agreement between the student and his advisors. The approved proposal describes a study that, if conducted competently and completely, should provide the basis for a report that would meet all standards for acceptability. Subsequent changes, introduced either by the student or by the committee, should be made only with the full knowledge and concurrence of all parties. Substantial changes should be supported by arguments for absolute necessity or compelling desirability. In all but rare instances, revision of the proposal should be completed prior to the collection of data.

## Overview of the Proposal Process

Although procedures vary widely, the proposal process usually begins when the student has a problem area or tentative topic in mind and meets with a professor to talk about it. That professor typically is someone with whom the student has had an ongoing relationship and would possibly like to have serve as a research adviser for the thesis or dissertation. The meeting may lead to further crystallization of the problem and the professor's encouragement for the student to put the ideas in writing in the form of a five- or six-page outline. This will enable them to have something more concrete to work with and talk about the next time they meet.

After further discussions, the student incorporates the professor's suggestions and any other changes resulting from the student's reading, and polishes the outline. If there has been only tacit agreement that the professor plans to be the research adviser, he or she may agree to serve at this time. The two then consider which faculty may have a contribution to make to the study.[13] After identifying potential research advisory committee members, the student distributes a copy of the revised outline to each one. These professors discuss the proposed project with the student, make recommendations, and indicate a willingness to be on the committee if they are interested and can find time.[14] Finally, the research adviser, who will function as the thesis or dissertation committee chair, obtains feedback from them and, if appropriate, gives the student permission to prepare a formal proposal for presentation and defense before the full commitee.[15] During proposal writing, the student uses committee members for consultation, but the primary resource person continues to be the research adviser, or committee chair.

### Selecting and Formulating a Research Problem

Selecting and formulating a thesis or dissertation problem is a developmental process. Through previous course work, outside readings, and interactions with colleagues and professors, the student identifies areas of interest that may lead to suitable topics for study. Discussions with the person the student would like to direct the study and with other professors who are being considered for the research advisory committee contribute to further development of the problem (see following section).[16] Even after the research adviser has been chosen and the research committee has been appointed, refinement of the problem continues during proposal writing and possibly following defense if the proposal is rejected or approved with conditions that require further revisions.

### Choosing a Research Adviser and Research Committee

Choosing a research adviser and the rest of the research committee and working effectively with them are crucial elements in writing a proposal and eventually preparing an acceptable thesis or dissertation. The student, in conjunction with this advisory team, will develop the research problem, prepare a proposal, conduct the research, and write the final report. The committee will also pass judgments on the student's abilities as a master's or doctoral candidate, a researcher, and a professional (Long, Convey, and Chwalek 1985, 56). Thus, the research committee performs two roles: adviser and judge (Allen 1973, 28).

The Research Adviser. The person who directs a student's thesis or dissertation research is referred to by different names, including research adviser, committee chair, thesis or dissertation director, or major professor. As chair of the research committee, the research adviser provides overall direction for the student, serves as the student's sponsor, coordinates interaction of the group, mediates major disagreements between committee members and the student or among committee members, handles official paper work with the department and graduate school, and so forth.

Procedures for selecting a professor to chair the graduate research committee depend on the department and institution. Often an academic adviser is designated when the student is admitted to the graduate program, and he or she also later serves as the research adviser when the student reaches the thesis or dissertation stage. Some departments assign one person to function as an academic adviser for all students in a particular area of specialization until pre-thesis or pre-dissertation requirements have been met (e.g., completion of preliminary exams), at which time another person is chosen or designated research adviser.

Other departments use what Allen (1973, 41) calls the "natural-selection" method. They encourage graduate students to become acquainted with as many professors as possible (through their courses, teaching or research assistantships, and social contacts) and to seek an informal adviser from among them. When the student is ready to begin thinking seriously about preparing the proposal, he or she asks that person to serve as a research adviser, or the professor offers to direct the student's research. Although the major criterion used by most students when seeking to identify a professor for this role is similarity of research interests, there are other considerations. Do you get along with this person and work effectively together? Do you respect and trust this person? Is this person held in high regard by faculty in the department and on campus? Is this person accessible? Is this person well organized, conscientious, and thorough? Is this person reasonably prompt in responding to requests and returning written material? Is this person tenured or likely to receive tenure? Does this person plan to retire or take a sabbatical (or other leave of absence) during the time you will be conducting the investigation?

The Research Committee. The process for choosing other members of the research committee also varies considerably, and students should find out what the local policy is early in their graduate work. Committee members are selected with the objective of achieving a balance of skills and expertise. For example, if the committee chair is primarily a theoretician, it is advisable to include a first-rate research methodologist on the committee. For all quantitative studies, there must be someone who is knowledgeable about statistics and research design.

Most of the same qualities sought in a research adviser are important for other committee members. A harmonious, competent group, with complementary strengths, that has an active interest in the area under study represents the ideal. Although the chair will play the dominant role on the advisory team, other committee members are important and should be chosen with care. The research committee will be with the student every step of the way, from proposal development through final defense of the thesis or dissertation.

### Writing the Proposal

Since there is no standardized format or universally accepted guidelines for preparation of thesis and dissertation proposals, the student should consult the research adviser or academic department for assistance. Regarding length of the document, some departments expect 10–20 pages or less, whereas others require the equivalent of preliminary chapters of the final report. There are reasons why a relatively detailed proposal is preferred over a superficial one. It helps ensure that the student will fully consider the problem, the literature, the methodology, and so on. A more detailed proposal will also allow thorough evaluation and effective guidance by the research committee.

Substantial writing done at this stage of the thesis or dissertation process is seldom wasted because most of the information included in the proposal will become a part of the final report in some form or another. Alterations that may have to be made are the addition of references, revisions in the method section to incorporate changes from the proposed to actual procedures finally employed, changes in writing tense from future to past or present, expansion of some sections, and so forth.

Information relating to thesis and proposal writing that is discussed elsewhere in this book (e.g., scientific writing, reviewing the literature, selecting measuring instruments) will not be repeated here. However, a sample proposal format with annotation that is presented here summarizes some of the important components of a thesis or dissertation proposal. The type of investigation planned will dictate the organization and content of the document; for instance, a proposal for an experimental study will differ from a proposal for a historical study. (See Ex. 15.4 at the end of the chapter for a specimen proposal.)

1. Title page—The title page includes the proposed title (indicating main variables and subject population), author's name, degree sought, institution, date, and names of research committee members (with the committee chair clearly identified).
2. Table of contents—A table of contents may be included to provide an organizational framework for the proposal.
3. Introduction
   a. Statement of the problem—A succinct statement of the nature of the problem is made early in the introduction. A brief presentation of the background of the problem and potential significance of the study is also given.
   b. Review of related literature—A well-integrated presentation of relevant theory and research indicates the current state of knowledge related to the problem. The section concludes with a brief summary of the literature and its implications, which builds a case for the

study and provides a context for the hypotheses or questions that follow.

c. Hypotheses or research questions—Hypotheses or research questions are precisely stated.

4. Method
   a. Subjects—The population from which participants for the research will be selected is defined (e.g., characteristics, size). (The method for drawing the sample is usually described in the procedures section, but in some cases it may be done here.)
   b. Instruments (and/or materials and apparatus)—Measuring instruments planned for use in the study are described in detail (including evidence of their reliability and validity), along with the purposes for which they will be employed. If a new measure will be developed for the investigation, procedures for its construction and its evaluation are explained, including plans for pretesting. (If field testing of instruments has already been done, results may be included here, in a separate pilot study section, or in the appendix.) This is also the place where any special equipment, devices, or other materials to be used in carrying out the study are specified.
   c. Procedures—This part of the proposal describes in chronological order the steps that will be necessary to conduct the investigation and how they will be done (e.g., sample selection, data collection, treatments, debriefing). It also indicates precautions that will be taken to prevent physical, mental, or social harm to participants (specimen consent forms, etc., are put in the appendix).
   d. Design and analysis—The proposed research design and planned statistical techniques for data analysis are described. (Sample tables and figures, which may be placed in the appendix, explicitly label all variables and help the student and the committee to think through the measurements, relationships, and comparisons the study will produce.)
5. References—References cited in the proposal are listed in alphabetical order by first author.
6. Appendix—The appendix includes copies of measuring instruments; descriptions of apparatus; transcripts of directions to subjects; results of pilot studies that have already been conducted; sample forms for the protection of human subjects; expected, or "dummy," tables and figures; and possibly a trial table of contents for the final report. It also includes a time schedule for executing the research, with actual dates given for completion of major activities in the thesis or dissertation process.

There are several good sources that treat thesis and dissertation proposal development in greater detail.[17]

Form approved
OMB No. 0925-0001

DEPARTMENT OF HEALTH AND HUMAN SERVICES
PUBLIC HEALTH SERVICE

**GRANT APPLICATION**

FOLLOW INSTRUCTIONS CAREFULLY

| LEAVE BLANK | | |
|---|---|---|
| TYPE | ACTIVITY | NUMBER |
| REVIEW GROUP | | FORMERLY |
| COUNCIL/BOARD *(Month, year)* | | DATE RECEIVED |

1. TITLE OF APPLICATION *(Do not exceed 56 typewriter spaces)*
Family Therapy versus Traditional Therapy for Drug Abusers

2. RESPONSE TO SPECIFIC PROGRAM ANNOUNCEMENT ☐ NO ☐ YES *(If "YES," state RFA number and/or announcement title)*
Family Therapy and Prevention Research, NIH Guide for Grants & Contracts; 11(8),8/19/83

3. PRINCIPAL INVESTIGATOR/PROGRAM DIRECTOR

3a. NAME *(Last, first, middle)*
Joanning, Harvey H.

3b. SOCIAL SECURITY NUMBER
481-62-2618

3c. POSITION TITLE
Associate Professor & Director,
Marriage & Family Therapy Program

3d. MAILING ADDRESS *(Street, city, state, zip code)*
Department of Home & Family Life
Texas Tech University
Lubbock, Texas 79409

3e. DEPARTMENT, SERVICE, LABORATORY OR EQUIVALENT
Department of Home & Family Life

3f. MAJOR SUBDIVISION
College of Home Economics

3g. TELEPHONE *(Area code, number and extension)*
(806) 742-3674

4. HUMAN SUBJECTS
☐ NO ☒ YES { ☐ Exemption # ________ OR ☒ Form HHS 596 enclosed

5. RECOMBINANT DNA
☒ NO ☐ YES

6. DATES OF ENTIRE PROPOSED PROJECT PERIOD
From: July 15, 1984 Through: July 14, 1988

7. DIRECT COSTS REQUESTED FOR FIRST 12-MONTH BUDGET PERIOD *(from page 4)*
$

8. DIRECT COSTS REQUESTED FOR ENTIRE PROPOSED PROJECT PERIOD *(from page 5)*
$

9. PERFORMANCE SITES *(Organizations and addresses)*
Texas Tech University
Lubbock, Texas 79409

10. INVENTIONS *(Competing continuation application only)*
☒ NO ☐ YES { ☐ Previously reported OR ☐ Not previously reported

11. APPLICANT ORGANIZATION *(Name, address, and congressional district)*
Texas Tech University
Lubbock, TX 79409
Congressional District 19

12. TYPE OF ORGANIZATION
☒ Public. Specify ☐ Federal ☐ State ☐ Local
☐ Private Nonprofit
☐ For Profit *(General)*
☐ For Profit *(Small Business)*

13. ENTITY IDENTIFICATION NUMBER
756002622

14. ORGANIZATIONAL COMPONENT TO RECEIVE CREDIT FOR BIOMEDICAL RESEARCH SUPPORT GRANT
Code 20 Description

15. OFFICIAL IN BUSINESS OFFICE TO BE NOTIFIED IF AN AWARD IS MADE *(Name, title, address and telephone number.)*
Eugene Payne
Vice President for Finance & Administration
Texas Tech University
Lubbock, TX 79409
(806) 742-2196

16. OFFICIAL SIGNING FOR APPLICANT ORGANIZATION *(Name, title, address and telephone number)*
J. Knox Jones, Jr.
Vice President for Research & Graduate Study
Texas Tech University
Lubbock, TX 79409 (806) 742-2152

17. PRINCIPAL INVESTIGATOR/PROGRAM DIRECTOR ASSURANCE: I agree to accept responsibility for the scientific conduct of the project and to provide the required progress reports if a grant is awarded as a result of this application. Willful provision of false information is a criminal offense *(U.S. Code, Title 18, Section 1001).*

SIGNATURE OF PERSON NAMED IN 3a *(In ink. "Per" signature not acceptable)* | DATE

18. CERTIFICATION AND ACCEPTANCE: I certify that the statements herein are true and complete to the best of my knowledge, and accept the obligation to comply with Public Health Service terms and conditions if a grant is awarded as the result of this application. A willfully false certification is a criminal offense *(U.S. Code, Title 18, Section 1001).*

SIGNATURE OF PERSON NAMED IN 16 *(In ink. "Per" signature not acceptable)* | DATE

PHS 398 (Rev. 5/82)

**Example 15.3.** Specimen research grant proposal from which specific dollar amounts have been deleted. (Adapted from Harvey H. Joanning, "Family Therapy versus Traditional Therapy for Drug Abusers," a grant application submitted to the National Institute on Drug Abuse in 1983. Used by permission.)

PRINCIPAL INVESTIGATOR/PROGRAM DIRECTOR: Joanning, Harvey H.

## ABSTRACT OF RESEARCH PLAN

ːY PROFESSIONAL PERSONNEL ENGAGED ON PROJECT

| NAME | POSITION TITLE | DEPARTMENT AND ORGANIZATION |
|---|---|---|
| Harvey Joanning | Principal Investigator and Associate Professor | Department of Home and Family Life, Texas Tech University (TTU) |
| William Quinn | Co-Principal Investigator and Assistant Professor | Department of Home and Family Life, TTU |
| Rudolfo Arrendondo | Co-Investigator and Associate Professor | Department of Psychiatry TTU School of Medicine |
| Judith Fischer | Co-Investigator and Associate Professor | Department of Home and Family Life, TTU |

BSTRACT OF RESEARCH PLAN: State the application's long-term objectives and specific aims, making reference to the health relatedness of the oject, and describe concisely the methodology for achieving these goals. Avoid summaries of past accomplishments and the use of the first person. ne abstract is meant to serve as a succinct and accurate description of the proposed work when separated from the application. **DO NOT EXCEED HE SPACE PROVIDED.**


The central concerns of this research project are to assess the relative effects of three therapeutic procedures on the drug abusing behavior of adolescents, on the use or nonuse of drugs by their younger siblings, and on the dynamics of their families.

The study will compare a family therapy model based on Strategic and Structural Family Therapy; a traditional (representative) drug abuse treatment model based on Adlerian Individual Psychology, Reality Therapy and social skills training; and an attention control model containing information commonly disseminated in drug education programs.

Another concern of the study is to assess the relative impact of these therapies on Anglo and Hispanic populations. Of particular interest is whether certain therapies affect Anglo or Hispanic populations differently.

The study will employ a pretest-posttest-control group design with repeated extended follow-up. Several areas of response will be assessed to determine the effects of treatment: 1) the degree of use or non use of drugs by adolescent drug abusing and younger sibling members of subject families; 2) the impact of drug use on the interpersonal behavior and school performance of adolescent abusers; 3) the degree of satisfaction with marital or family systems as expressed by members of those systems; 4) the quality of family functioning as rated by outside judges; and 5) the ability of subject families to deal with stress.

Effects of treatment will be analyzed using multivariate analysis of covariance for unrelated dependent measures followed by appropriate univariate procedures. Additional analyses including chi square and analysis of variance will be used to test for pretest differences on demographic and dependent variables, therapist effects, and impact of treatments on younger siblings.


VERTEBRATE ANIMALS INVOLVED ☒ NO ☐ YES If "YES," identify by common names and underline primates.

## TABLE OF CONTENTS

*Number pages consecutively at the bottom throughout the application. Do not use suffixes such as 5a, 5b. Type the name of the Principal Investigator/Program Director at the top of each printed page and each continuation page.*



SECTION 3. Appendix *(Six sets) (No page numbering necessary for Appendix)*

Number of publications: 8    Number of manuscripts: 1

Other items *(list)*:

Support Letters from:

1. Lubbock Independent School District
2. Department of Psychiatry
3. Department of Family Practice

Vitae
Demographic Sheets
Copies of Measures

☒ Application Receipt Record, Form PHS 3830
☒ Form HHS 596 if Item 4, page 1, is checked "YES" and no exemptions are designated.

PRINCIPAL INVESTIGATOR/PROGRAM DIRECTOR: Joanning, Harvey H.

## DETAILED BUDGET FOR FIRST 12 MONTH BUDGET PERIOD DIRECT COSTS ONLY

| FROM | THROUGH |
|---|---|
| | |

DOLLAR AMOUNT REQUESTED *(Omit cents)*

| ERSONNEL *(Applicant organization only)* | | TIME/EFFORT | | | | |
|---|---|---|---|---|---|---|
| NAME | POSITION TITLE | % | Hours per Week | SALARY | FRINGE BENEFITS | TOTALS |
| | Principal Investigator | | | | | |
| | | | | | | |
| | | | | | | |
| | | | | | | |
| | | | | | | |
| | | | | | | |
| | | | | | | |
| | | | | | | |
| | | | | | | |
| | | | | | | |
| | | | | | | |
| | | | | | | |
| | | | | | | |
| | | | | | | |
| SUBTOTALS → | | | | | | |

| | | |
|---|---|---|
| ONSULTANT COSTS | | |
| QUIPMENT *(Itemize)* | | |
| UPPLIES *(Itemize by category)* | | |
| RAVEL | DOMESTIC | |
| | FOREIGN | |
| ATIENT CARE COSTS | INPATIENT | |
| | OUTPATIENT | |
| LTERATIONS AND RENOVATIONS *(Itemize by category)* | | |
| CONSORTIUM/CONTRACTUAL COSTS | | |
| OTHER EXPENSES *(Itemize by category)* | | |
| TOTAL DIRECT COSTS *(Also enter on page 1, item 7)* → | | $ |

PHS 398 (Rev. 5/82) PAGE 4

PRINCIPAL INVESTIGATOR/PROGRAM DIRECTOR: Joanning, Harvey H.

## BUDGET FOR ENTIRE PROPOSED PROJECT PERIOD
## DIRECT COSTS ONLY

| BUDGET CATEGORY TOTALS | | 1st BUDGET PERIOD (from page 4) | ADDITIONAL YEARS SUPPORT REQUESTED | | | |
|---|---|---|---|---|---|---|
| | | | 2nd | 3rd | 4th | 5th |
| RSONNEL (Salary and ıge benefits.) oplicant organization only) | | | | | | |
| ɪNSULTANT COSTS | | | | | | |
| ɪUIPMENT | | | | | | |
| ɪPPLIES | | | | | | |
| TRAVEL | DOMESTIC | | | | | |
| | FOREIGN | | | | | |
| PATIENT CARE COSTS | INPATIENT | | | | | |
| | OUTPATIENT | | | | | |
| -TERATIONS AND ENOVATIONS | | | | | | |
| ɔNSORTIUM/ ɔNTRACTUAL COSTS | | | | | | |
| THER EXPENSES | | | | | | |
| OTAL DIRECT COSTS | | | | | | |

**OTAL FOR ENTIRE PROPOSED PROJECT PERIOD** *(Also enter on page 1, item 8)* → $

JSTIFICATION (Use continuation pages if necessary): Describe the specific functions of the personnel and consultants. If a recurring annual increase personnel costs is anticipated, give the percentage. For *all* years, justify any costs for which the need may not be obvious, such as equipment, foreign avel, alterations and renovations, and consortium/contractual costs. For any additional years of support requested, justify any significant increases in ıy category over the first 12 month budget period. In addition, for COMPETING CONTINUATION applications, justify any significant increases over ıe current level of support.

Principal Investigator: Oversee the project, supervise staff, determine priorities, oversee the budget; prepare papers; advanced doctoral-level research coordinator: conduct data collection, code and analyze data, assist in project administration; graduate therapy coordinator: schedule therapists and clients, monitor therapy sessions to ensure adherence to models; therapists: conduct therapy sessions, maintain contact with subjects to ensure session attendance; clerk/typist: prepare materials, type papers and correspondence, keypunch data, operate computer/word processor. During the first and second year one research coordinator, one therapy coordinator, and twelve therapists will be used to collect data or conduct the treatments; during the third and fourth year, one research coordinator and one research assistant will be used to conduct follow-up testing, code and analyze data, maintain contact with subjects. Throughout the study, the research assistants and therapists will be at the doctoral level reflecting the need for advanced skills to handle treatments and data analysis. Computer and research consultant costs are included throughout the study due to the anticipated large volume and complexity of data analysis. Personnel costs increase each year, reflecting projected 10% raises and the advanced level of graduate students employed. A computer, printer, cable, and modem is included to facilitate and increase the accuracy of data collection and analysis, increase the speed of analysis, store and reproduce instruments . . .

PRINCIPAL INVESTIGATOR/PROGRAM DIRECTOR: Joanning, Harvey H.

## BIOGRAPHICAL SKETCH

Give the following information for key professional personnel listed on page 2, beginning with the Principal Investigator/Program Director. Photocopy this page for each person.

| NAME | TITLE | BIRTHDATE (Mo., Day, Yr.) |
|---|---|---|
| Joanning, Harvey H. | Associate Professor | October 22, 1947 |

EDUCATION *(Begin with baccalaureate or other initial professional education and include postdoctoral training)*

| INSTITUTION AND LOCATION | DEGREE *(circle highest degree)* | YEAR CONFERRED | FIELD OF STUDY |
|---|---|---|---|
| Briar Cliff College, Sioux City, IA | B.A. | 1969 | Psychology |
| University of Iowa, Iowa City, IA | M.A. | 1972 | Counseling Psychol. |
| University of Iowa, Iowa City, IA | Ph.D. | 1973 | Counseling Psychol. |

RESEARCH AND/OR PROFESSIONAL EXPERIENCE: Concluding with present position, list in chronological order previous employment, experience, and honors. Include present membership on any Federal Government Public Advisory Committee. List, in chronological order, the titles and complete references to all publications during the past three years and to representative earlier publications pertinent to this application. **DO NOT EXCEED TWO PAGES.**

Academic and Counseling Positions:

1970-71 Practicum Student, University Counseling Service, University of Iowa
1972-73 Intern, University Counseling Service, University of Iowa
1973-74 Staff Member, University Counseling Service, University of Iowa
1974-76 Psychologist, University Counseling Center, Texas Tech University
1977- Assistant Professor (77-80); Associate Professor (1980-), Department of Home & Family Life and Psychologist, University Counseling Center, Texas Tech University

Administrative Experience:

1977- Director, Marriage Family Development Center (a division of the University Counseling Center), Texas Tech University
1980- Director, Marriage and Family Therapy Doctoral Program, Department of Home and Family Life, Texas Tech University

Publications:

Joanning, H. The academic performance of Vietnam veteran college students. Journal of College Student Personnel, 1975, 16, 10-13.
Joanning, H. Behavioral rehearsal in the group treatment of socially nonassertive individuals. Journal of College Student Personnel, 1976, 17, 313-318.
Nathan, E., Joanning, H., Duckro, P., & Beal, D. Differential effectiveness of written and verbal communications in modifying students' perceptions of the counseling center's role. Journal of Counseling Psychology, 1978, 25, 242-245.
Duckro, P., Joanning, H., Nathan, E., & Beal, A. A religious concerns factor of the counseling appropriateness check list. Journal of College Student Personnel, 1978, 19, 450-452.

. . . . . . . . . . . . . . . . . . . . . . . . . . . . . . . . . . . . . . . . . . .

Brock, G., & Joanning, H. Structured communication training for married couples: A comparison of the relationship enhancement program and the couple communication program. Journal of Marriage and Family Therapy, in press.

Honors:
1983 American Association for Marriage and Family Therapy Outstanding Postgraduate Research Contribution Award. Co-Recipient with Greg W. Brock, Ph.D.

## OTHER SUPPORT

*(Use continuation pages if necessary)*

For each of the professionals named on page 2, list, in three separate groups: (1) active support; (2) applications and proposals pending review or funding; (3) applications and proposals planned or being prepared for submission. Include *all* Federal, non-Federal, and institutional grant and contract support. If none, state "none." For each item give the source of support, identifying number, project title, name of principal investigator/program director, time or percent of effort on the project by professional named, annual direct costs, and entire period of support. (If part of a larger project, provide the titles of both the parent project and the subproject and give the annual direct costs for each.) Describe the contents of each item listed. If any of these overlap, duplicate, or are being replaced or supplemented by the present application, delineate and justify the nature and extent of the scientific and budgetary overlaps or boundaries.

PRINCIPAL INVESTIGATOR/PROGRAM DIRECTOR:
(1) ACTIVE SUPPORT:

Joanning, Harvey

none

Quinn, William

none

Arredondo, Rudolfo

none

Fischer, Judith L.

Tentative title: Adolescent Self Esteem and Social Competence Proposal
This proposal does not overlap, duplicate, or supplement the present application.

PRINCIPAL INVESTIGATOR/PROGRAM DIRECTOR: Joanning, Harvey H.

## RESOURCES AND ENVIRONMENT

ACILITIES: Mark the facilities to be used at the applicant organization and briefly indicate their capacities, pertinent capabilities, relative proximity ıd extent of availability to the project. Use "other" to describe the facilities at any other performance sites listed in Item 9, page 1, and at sites for eld studies. Using continuation pages if necessary, include an explanation of any consortium arrangements with other organizations.

☐ Laboratory: N/A

☐ Clinical: The Marriage and Family Development Center will house the treatment portion of the study. Marriage and Family Development Center consists of 14 interview rooms, 3 group rooms, a large reception area and audio/video systems in each room.

☐ Animal: N/A

☐ Computer: The Texas Tech Computer Center maintains and operates a National Advance System, AS/6 computing system in a batch and teleprocessing (interactive terminal and RJE) environment. The computer uses card, disk, and tape input and has the capability for storing data and programs on disk. . .

☐ Office: The College of Home Economics at Texas Tech University will provide ample office space for conduct of this investigation. The facility is one of the largest of its kind, and research projects have top priority in space allocation.

☐ Other (__________):

MAJOR EQUIPMENT: List the most important equipment items already available for this project, noting the location and pertinent capabilities of each.

Audio-video equipment already in place will be used to record therapy sessions and evaluations. The only other equipment necessary for this project is the standard office equipment necessary for the conduct of a social science investigation. Office space, file cabinets, and chairs, desks, etc. will be furnished for the project by the Department of Home and Family Life and College of Home Economics at Texas Tech University.

ADDITIONAL INFORMATION: Provide any other information describing the environment for the project. Identify support services such as consultants, secretarial, machine shop, and electronics shop, and the extent to which they will be available to the project.

Although the Department of Home and Family Life is equipped with modern word processing equipment to facilitate the development of manuscripts and reports stemming from this research, this equipment is overused and insufficient to meet the varied needs of the department. The Department of Home and Family Life will have in place by April, 1984 a Telex Executive CRT Terminal (TC-178-2) and Telex Hard Copy Printer (TC-286-60CPS) connected to the main frame computer to provide data analysis and additional high speed word processing capability to add convenience to research in the College facility. With the large faculty in the Department it is anticipated that this equipment will be in heavy use. An IBM Display Writer and Printer . . .

## Introduction

Due to the large amount of relevant literature reviewed to provide an adequate threoretical and research base for this study, the Significance section exceeds the three page limit. A five page Significance section is included.

## A. Specific Aims

The specific aims of this study are to assess the impact of a family systems therapy, a traditional therapy, and an attention control condition on: 1) the drug abusing behavior of adolescents, 2) on the use or nonuse of drugs by younger siblings of these adolescents, and 3) on the dynamics of families of these adolescents. The family systems therapy will be based on Strategic and Structural Family Therapies. The traditional therapy will be representative of approaches currently used to treat adolescent drug abusers and will be based on Adlerian Individual Psychology, Reality Therapy, and three models of social skills training. The attention control condition will be educational in nature and consist of information commonly disseminated in drug education programs. A secondary aim of the study is to assess the relative impact of these three therapies on Anglo and Hispanic populations.

The study will employ a pretest-posttest-control group design with 6 month, 12 month, and 24 month follow-up. The relative impact of Family Systems Therapy, Traditional Therapy, and Attention Control Therapy will be assessed. Research into the effectiveness of systems oriented family interventions indicates long term family wide impact of such therapy. The results of this study are expected to indicate that the Family Systems Therapy employed in this study will prove more effective than Traditional Therapy in the treatment of drug abuse. The Traditional Therapy to be used in this study is representative of current intervention procedures for treating adolescent drug abusers, focuses on adolescents outside their family system, emphasizes change in behaviors and cognitions adolescents use in dealing with peers, and does little to change the social network in which the adolescent functions over the long term. Consequently, the Family Systems Therapy with its focus on permanent and pervasive social network changes (i.e., family, relatives, and peers) is expected to impact more significantly on the drug behavior of adolescent abusers and their younger siblings as well as on the overall dynamics of their families. Specifically the Family Systems Therapy is expected to be more effective than Traditional or Attention Control Therapies in: 1) decreasing the use of drugs among adolescent abusers; 2) preventing abuse among younger siblings of abusers; 3) improving school performance (grades, conduct, teacher evaluations); 4) improving subject families' overall satisfaction with family life (intimacy, cohesiveness); 5) and improving subject families' ability to cope with internal and external stress.

The relative impact of the three treatment conditions on Anglo and Hispanic families cannot be predicted due to the lack of prior research in this area. However, the findings of this study will give clearer direction to practitioners interested in how best to serve these two large subpopulations.

In summary, the proposed study will provide a significant research contribution by evaluating the effectiveness of these methods for treating adolescent drug abuse and by comparing the impact of these therapies on two large segments of the United States population

NCIPAL INVESTIGATOR/PROGRAM DIRECTOR OR AWARD CANDIDATE *(Last, first, middle)* | SOCIAL SECURITY NUMBER

Joanning, Harvey H. | 481-62-2618

## B. Significance

The adolescent years bring with them dramatic physical changes, sharp shifts in social adjustment, and a new set of confusing expectations. The resultant creation of emotional anxiety in adolescents accompanied with a push toward independence, leads many youths to experimentation with alcohol and drugs. According to a 1978 national survey of drug use among high school seniors (NIDA/Johnston et al., 1979) by twelfth grade, only about 10 percent of youth have never used any substance. While the number of young adult drug abusers, overall, may decline in the next decade, it remains difficult to estimate the parameters of the drug abuse problem of the adolescent group (NIDA/Richards, 1981). Further, the National Survey on Drug Abuse: 1979 (NIDA/Miller) indicates that the trend patterns observed do not appear to indicate that a point of saturation has been reached. Indeed the Health and Human Services Third Annual Report (1980) states that by the end of the 1970's drug use had evolved from an epidemic to endemic situation. However, drug treatment follow-up studies with adolescents have been scarce and of those done, questions about reliability and validity arise (Held, 1978; Schmelter & Kern, 1978).

In a NIDA published catalog of treatment research (1981), eight out of the total twelve articles listed under "treatment assessment" are based on data obtained from the Drug Abuse Reporting Program (DARP). Yet, less than 20 percent of the DARP sample was under 18, therefore, allowing little use of these studies' results when looking at the adolescent drug abuser. As a result, much literature has been directed toward suggesting NIDA provide additional resources and funding to assist in the design and data analysis of large scale investigations of drug abuse among adolescents (e.g., NIDA/Lettieri & Ludfori, 1982).

Given the above limitations, the DARP follow-up research indicated favorable outcomes for methadone maintenance program (MM), therapeutic communities (TC) and outpatient drug free treatments (DF) as compared to outpatient detoxification clinics and intake only comparison groups (NIDA/Simpson & Sells, 1982; Simpson, 1981).

. . . . . . . . . . . . . . . . . . . . . . . . . . . . . . . . . . . . . . .

Some authors have recognized the need to intervene with the parents of drug abusing adolescents. Caroff, Lieberman, & Gottesfeld (1970) point to the need of encouraging the parents to become involved and provide support to the adolescent. They emphasize the importance of re-educating the parents to untangle confusions about normal adolescence. The therapist functions as a link in the communication between parents and adolescents. The authors stress that separation (i.e., into a residential community) for these young people is premature--they must have the protective environment of the parents. Solow and Cooper (1974) describe how the adolescent comes to the point of crisis in trying to cope and deal with his/her development tasks of resolving inner tensions and separating from parents. After a treatment plan has been developed for the adolescent, the parents are seen with a psychiatric social worker in a consultant role. The parents, in this process, become able to facilitate the resolution of the adolescent conflict, and aid the adolescent in his/her search for an identity.

In a novel therapeutic approach, paradoxical intention was used effectively with a drug abusing adolescent (Morelli, 1978). In this approach (c.f. Haley, Weakland, Watzlawick, Lazarus, & Frankl) the symptom (i.e., drug abuse) is prescribed as the cure. However, the author notes the possible danger of this approach with drug abusers in that those individuals high in external locus of control,

| PRINCIPAL INVESTIGATOR/PROGRAM DIRECTOR OR AWARD CANDIDATE *(Last, first, middle)* | SOCIAL SECURITY NUMBER |
|---|---|
| Joanning, Harvey H. | 481-62-2618 |

. . . . . . . . . . . . . . . . . . . . . . . . . . . . . . . . . . . . . . . . .

Many programs incorporate vocational and social integration elements. Sackstein (1981), in an international perspective on the subject, indicates that the more successful drug rehabilitation programs include vocational evaluation, job counseling guidance, job preparation, vocational training, and selective placement.

Several programs have incorporated multiple treatment modalities within one general program. Gottheil, Rieger, Farwell, and Lieberman (1977) describe a program where both individual and family techniques were utilized with drug abusing adolescents. Group methods provided opportunities for attempting less destructive alternative styles of coping. More expressive forms of treatment--music, art, role

. . . . . . . . . . . . . . . . . . . . . . . . . . . . . . . . . . . . . . . . . .

As indicated previously, the current research regarding adolescent drug abuse has several limitations--tendency for samples to be of the young adult age (18-22); overemphasis on opiate drug abuse (NIDA/Glenn, 1981); and an emphasis toward research with the medical model context and its emphasis on the individual (Clayton, 1979). Further, very few treatment programs/studies have included adequate statistical analysis of their outcome results. Descriptive accounts of limited sample sizes abound in the literature. Because substantial evidence is accumulating about the significant role the family plays in the drug abuse of its members (NIDA/Hendin, Polliger, Ulman, & Carr, 1981), and because there is an increase in the adolescent non-opiate cohort (NIDA/Richards, 1981), there is a strong need for the study of family oriented treatment with non-opiates among adolescents and their families.

In addition to the need to focus on adolescent abusers in general, more information as to the impact of drug abuse on members of Hispanic families is needed.

Recent government reports project that between the present and 1995, a decline in the number of young adult drug abusers can be expected among most subgroups in the U.S. with one notable exception, the non-white young adult population. Much of this can be attributed to the rapidly growing Hispanic population (NIDA Research Monograph 35, 1981). Demographers generally agree that Hispanic Americans will be the largest minority in the U.S. by 1990. Much of the rapidly growing Hispanic population is the result of large scale immigration due to lack of employment opportunities in Latin America (Falicov, 1982). Between 1961 and 1976, Latin Americans were by far the largest immigrant group to the U.S. (NIDA Research Monograph 35 1981).

. . . . . . . . . . . . . . . . . . . . . . . . . . . . . . . . . . . . . . . . . .

While the effectiveness of brief family systems oriented therapy has been demonstrated with families of Black American drug abusers (Stanton & Todd, 1981), no major study has systematically tested brief systems therapy on families of Hispanic drug abusers. The need for such research is obvious.

. . . . . . . . . . . . . . . . . . . . . . . . . . . . . . . . . . . . . . . . . .

To summarize, this study would be of primary significance because of its ability to compare the relative impact of traditional and family systems based drug abuse treatment/preventive programs on adolescents. Of secondary significance would be the study's inclusion of a large percentage of Hispanics in the subject pool, thus allowing cross-cultural comparison of treatment impact.

INCIPAL INVESTIGATOR/PROGRAM DIRECTOR OR AWARD CANDIDATE *(Last, first, middle)* | SOCIAL SECURITY NUMBER

Joanning, Harvey H. | 481-62-2618

## C. Preliminary Studies

### 1. Work Completed

The principal investigator has completed several therapy outcome studies (Brock & Joanning, 1983; Joanning, 1976, 1982; Avery, Thiessen, & Joanning, 1983). The methodology proposed for this study was developed in these earlier studies. The co-investigators have also completed studies relevant to this proposal. Quinn has conducted research in the area of family therapy (Protinsky, Quinn, & Elliot, 1982; Quinn & Keller, 1981, 1983). These studies focus on family system therapies and provide conceptual and therapeutic background for this proposal. Quinn has recently edited a book on inter-generational family relationships and interventions. This theoretical and empirical volume will provide conceptual material for the proposal. Fischer has researched the processes involved in adolescent development. Most relevant to this study is her work with the family systems impact on the existence or nonexistence of a disturbed adolescent in the family (Fischer, 1980).

### 2. Work in Progress

Quinn has a clinical journal article in progress focusing on rites of passage in families of adolescents. Joanning is preparing a behavioral rating scale for publication which assesses the quality of communication in marital and family relationships.

3. Several of the papers cited above are included in the appendix.

PRINCIPAL INVESTIGATOR/PROGRAM DIRECTOR OR AWARD CANDIDATE (Last, first, middle): Joanning, Harvey H.

SOCIAL SECURITY NUMBER: 481-62-2618

## D. Experimental Design and Methods

### 1. Overview of Experimental Design

This study is a comparison of family therapy and traditional drug abuse counseling for the treatment of adolescent drug abusers. The goal of the study is threefold: 1) to decrease or eliminate drug abuse among adolescents between the ages of 13 and 19, 2) to prevent the incidence of drug abuse among younger siblings of these same adolescent drug abusers, and 3) to assess the relative impact of different therapies on Anglo and Hispanic populations. The design of the study provides for a pretest, a treatment period during which three different intervention groups will be conducted, an immediate posttest, as well as extended follow-up testings at periods of six months, one year, and two years following completion of treatment period. During each testing period all subjects will be administered a variety of self-report instruments, will become involved in an analogue social situation designed to allow specific behavioral observations, and will be assessed through the use of third party reports of information relevant to the stated goals of the project. During the treatment period families will be exposed to one of three interventions for a period of ten to twelve weeks. All members of the family residing in the home will be involved in assessment. Single parent families, low income families, and members of cultural or ethnic minorities will be included in the study.

Subject families will be randomly assigned to one of three intervention programs: 1) a systems oriented family therapy based on Structural and Strategic family therapy, 2) traditional drug abuse counseling based on existing drug abuse treatment programs, and 3) a minimal impact family intervention implementing a classroom discussion group format. The minimal impact family intervention will act as an attention control for the study. This control group is designed to allow for the effects of increased attention to the family while minimizing the chance of actual change due to the intervention. The control condition is based on drug information programs found in many schools. Therapists for the study will consist of six male and six female third and fourth year doctoral students with a minimum of four years experience in the field of psychotherapy. Dependent measures for the study will be instruments and assessment devices with established validity and reliability.

### 2. Participants

The sample will consist of 90 families assigned at random to one of three intervention procedures. Each family will consist of at least one drug abusing adolescent between the ages of 13 and 19 years, one sibling younger than the abuser, and one parent. The abuser will have had at least a three month history of inappropriate use of illicit drugs other than alcohol. Marijuana abusers will have used the drug at least three times weekly for three months. Only those alcohol abusers who use alcohol <u>in combination</u> with other illicit drugs will be included in the sample. Families from lower-lower class through upper-middle class will be included in the sample.

. . . . . . . . . . . . . . . . . . . . . . . . . . . . . . . . . . . . . . .

Subject families will be drawn primarily from the caseloads of the Substance Abuse Treatment Center (SATC) at St. Mary's Hospital and the Marriage and Family Development Center (M&FDC) at Texas Tech University.

3. Treatments

Group One: Family Systems Therapy

a. Rationale

Non-behavioral family therapy has emerged as an effective treatment model in recent years. Gurman and Kniskern (1978) reported that this modality demonstrated superiority in two-thirds of the studies in which it was evaluated and had equal results in comparison with the remainder of studies. These findings, as well as even more recent reports (see Gurman & Kniskern, 1981), point to the significance of engaging the family in treatment for a broad scope of "individual" symptoms. This study will demand (using direct as well as gentle approaches) that the (1) adolescent drug abuser, (2) parent(s) or guardian of the IP, and (3) children including at least one younger sibling, will attend some or all of the therapy sessions.

There are several important reasons for using family systems therapy in treating families with a drug abuser. Most central is that abuse in this theoretical model is viewed as part of family process. Abusive

. . . . . . . . . . . . . . . . . . . . . . . . . . . . . . . . . . . . . . .

b. Structural/Strategic Treatment Model of the Present Study

The model of treatment in this study draws from the structural and strategic schools of family therapy. Both of these schools see families as rule-governed systems which operate within a given set of tolerance limits for departure from those rules. However, the schools tend to

. . . . . . . . . . . . . . . . . . . . . . . . . . . . . . . . . . . . . . .

c. Description of the Treatment

. . . . . . . . . . . . . . . . . . . . . . . . . . . . . . . . . . . . . . .

Group Two: Traditional Drug Therapy

a. Rationale

. . . . . . . . . . . . . . . . . . . . . . . . . . . . . . . . . . . . . . .

b. Model of Therapy

. . . . . . . . . . . . . . . . . . . . . . . . . . . . . . . . . . . . . . .

PRINCIPAL INVESTIGATOR/PROGRAM DIRECTOR OR AWARD CANDIDATE *(Last, first, middle)* | SOCIAL SECURITY NUMBER

Joanning, Harvey H. | 481-62-2618

Group Three: Attention Control Treatment

a. Rationale

. . . . . . . . . . . . . . . . . . . . . . . . . . . . . . . . . . . . . .

b. Treatment Outline by Session

. . . . . . . . . . . . . . . . . . . . . . . . . . . . . . . . . . . . . .

4. Measures

a. Self-report

(1). Dyadic Adjustment Scale (DAS) (Spanier, 1976). This 32-item measure has acceptable psychometric properties and is useful in providing a global assessment of marital functioning. The four subscales account for 94% of the covariance among items (Spanier & Thompson,

. . . . . . . . . . . . . . . . . . . . . . . . . . . . . . . . . . . . . .

(2). Family Adaptability and Cohesion Evaluation Scales II (FACES II) (Olson, Portner, & Bell, 1982). This 30-item self-report instrument

. . . . . . . . . . . . . . . . . . . . . . . . . . . . . . . . . . . . . .

(3). Parent-Adolescent Communication (Barnes & Olson, 1982). Communication is most fully recognized by systems theory (conceptual framework of family therapy proposed), and by therapists, researchers and

. . . . . . . . . . . . . . . . . . . . . . . . . . . . . . . . . . . . . .

(4). F-Copes (Family Coping Strategies) (McCubbin, Larsen, & Olson, 1982). This 30-item measure assesses family adaptation to stress. This scale taps effective problem-solving approaches and behaviors.

. . . . . . . . . . . . . . . . . . . . . . . . . . . . . . . . . . . . . .

(5). Social Support Inventory (SSI) (McCubbin, Patterson, Rossman, & Cooke, 1982). This 71-item measure is an assessment of available

. . . . . . . . . . . . . . . . . . . . . . . . . . . . . . . . . . . . . .

b. Observation

. . . . . . . . . . . . . . . . . . . . . . . . . . . . . . . . . . . . . .

The dimesions of interactional categories on the CRS will represent the systemic properties of families and attend to family restructuring using the family systems therapy proposed. This scale complements the

. . . . . . . . . . . . . . . . . . . . . . . . . . . . . . . . . . . . . . .

INCIPAL INVESTIGATOR/PROGRAM DIRECTOR OR AWARD CANDIDATE *(Last, first, middle)* | SOCIAL SECURITY NUMBER

Joanning, Harvey H. | 481-62-2618

c. Unobtrusive IP Measures

(1). Urinalysis tests will be performed in the lab at the TTU Health Sciences Center. Families will be asked randomly to bring in the IP (telephone call) at least once per week for four weeks, less frequently (every other week) during the latter stage of therapy.

. . . . . . . . . . . . . . . . . . . . . . . . . . . . . . . . .

d. Unobtrusive Family Measures

(1). School records of siblings living at home will be kept; these include school attendance, school performance, and comments on any unusual or acting out behavior.

. . . . . . . . . . . . . . . . . . . . . . . . . . . . . . . . .

5. Therapists

The treatment staff will consist of six male and six female, third and fourth year doctoral students in a Ph.D. graduate program accredited by the

. . . . . . . . . . . . . . . . . . . . . . . . . . . . . . . . . . . . . .

6. Procedure

a. Recruitment. MDFC has been the site for four major outcome studies in the last five years. Each of these studies has attracted thirty-five or more

. . . . . . . . . . . . . . . . . . . . . . . . . . . . . . . . . . . .

b. Pretesting and Assignment. Each time 15-24 families become available for treatment, pretesting will be conducted during a two-week period prior to the first week of treatment. Screening of all families to determine the

. . . . . . . . . . . . . . . . . . . . . . . . . . . . . . . . . . . .

c. Treatment Period. Treatment will commence each time 15-24 families are available (5-8 per treatment condition). The Family Systems Therapy will

. . . . . . . . . . . . . . . . . . . . . . . . . . . . . . . . . . . .

d. Study Management. A study of this magnitude and complexity obviously requires careful and coordinated management. The organization chart given below indicates which study personnel are responsible for which

. . . . . . . . . . . . . . . . . . . . . . . . . . . . . . . . . . . .

e. Posttesting and Follow-up Testing. An immediate posttest will be held for each family within a two-week period following termination of therapy.

. . . . . . . . . . . . . . . . . . . . . . . . . . . . . . . . . . . .

## E. Human Subjects

1. Subject Characteristics

Ninety families will be recruited for the study. Ages will range across the life span. Males, females, adults, and children will be studied. Primarily Anglo (white) and Hispanic individuals will be involved. Any family will be included if the family contains a drug abusing adolescent member(13-19) and at least one parent and one younger sibling.

2. Sources of Research Material

Material gathered will include: 1) paper and pencil self-report inventories completed by individual family members; 2) teacher, parent, and adolescent ratings of the adolescent's behavior; 3) school attendance records and grades of all children of the family still in school; 4) juvenile court records of adolescents who have appeared before the court; 5) drug screen urinalysis. All of these data and records will be secured for research purposes only and will not be disclosed other than as anonymous summary statistical information.

3. Recruitment of Subjects/Consent

Subjects will be recruited through announcements distributed in schools and churches, through media announcements, and by self referral or referral by area professionals. Interested families will be given written and verbal explanations of the 1) general nature of the study; 2) subject family participation in the study; 3) general nature and purpose of measure taken; 4) reasons for gathering school and court records; 5) benefits, hazards, and precautions of the study; and 6) limits of liability of the investigators and therapists. A formal consent form detailing the information just listed will be signed by the parent or parents in each family who agree to participate. A copy of the consent form will be made available to the family. All consent forms and explanations will be available in English or Spanish. All explanations will be provided by one of the Principal Investigators, Co-Investigators, or the Research Coordinator. All the procedures just described will be included as part of a screening interview conducted at the Substance Abuse Treatment Center of St. Mary's of the Plains Hospital.

4. Potential Risks and Procedures of Minimizing Risks

   a. Physical. No physical risks are likely. No physically invasive measures or treatments are planned. The possibility of physical abuse exists in the families studied; however, that risk will have existed prior to the beginning of the study. The study should be helpful in reducing the probability of abuse if it does exist, due to the treatments employed.

   b. Psychological. The psychotherapeutic interventions to be used in the study present the risk of psychological stress as family members come to grips with the reality of problems in their lives and the difficulties of overcoming these problems. However, because the interventions are designed to

NCIPAL INVESTIGATOR/PROGRAM DIRECTOR OR AWARD CANDIDATE *(Last, first, middle)* | SOCIAL SECURITY NUMBER

Joanning, Harvey H. | 481-62-2618

7. Data Analysis and Interpretation

Preliminary analysis of pretest data will be accomplished by conducting a one-way ANOVA across each pretest demographic variable and each dependent measure by treatment group (Family Systems Therapy, Traditional Drug Treatment, Attention Control). The demographic variables are SES level, educational

. . . . . . . . . . . . . . . . . . . . . . . . . . . . . . . . . . . . . . . .

8. The Research Staff

The project will be headed by the Principal Investigator. He will be assisted by the Co-Principal Investigator although the Principal Investigator will be ultimately responsible for representing the study to outside

. . . . . . . . . . . . . . . . . . . . . . . . . . . . . . . . . . . . . . . .

9. Time Line for the Research

July 15, 1984 - August 31, 1984

Preparation time including:

1) Manual preparation
2) Hiring of staff
3) Course preparation

. . . . . . . . . . . . . . . . . . . . . . . . . . . . . . . . . . . . . . . .

June 1, 1988 - July 14, 1988

1) Data analysis and study write-up for pretest to 24 month follow-up findings
2) Final grant report to NIDA

10. Equipment

All interview rooms and audio/video equipment are available. Consumable supplies such as test materials, file folders, computer and communication services, as well as staff, will be needed. A micro-computer with appropriate software will be needed for data storage and word processing.

11. Principal Investigator Assurance

The undersigned agrees to accept responsibility for the scientific and technical conduct of the research project and for provision of required progress reports if a grant is awarded as a result of this application.

__________________ Date

__________________ Principal Investigator

be therapeutic, the stresses induced will be lessened as therapy progresses.

c. Legal. Adolescents entering the study, and in some cases the parents, will be at risk if illicit drugs are actively being used. Obviously, the illicit drug users in the family are always at risk of arrest. While in treatment, adolescents might bring illicit drugs to the therapy session or be under the influence of such drugs. University Legal Counsel has advised us that Texas law requires only that we attempt to prevent the use of illicit drugs (the major point of the therapy provided). We will not be required to inform the legal authorities of drug possession or use. Texas law clearly gives professionals the option of deciding whether or not to inform legal authorities of the offense. If a professional decides that not disclosing illicit drug use is in the best interest of the drug user and the treatment program, he or she need not report the offense. Consequently, no legal risk exists for an adolescent or parents who enter the study.

d. Confidentiality. Academic records, teacher evaluations, and court records will be solicited for use as outcome measures. Any time any information about a person is gathered, confidentiality is lessened or jeapordized. Simply asking for information such as grades or observed effects of drug use in the classroom alerts the contact person (e.g., teacher) that the person involved may be using drugs; consequently, confidentiality is violated. Several safeguards will be used to limit threats to confidentiality. Scores on measures and statistics drawn from school or court records will be stored in computer memory by code number rather than by name. Matching lists of code numbers and names will be secured in a locked file in the Principal Investigator's office. The Research Coordinator will use code numbers only on all measures and records collected and will turn over all matching lists on a daily basis. In regard to teachers becoming aware of an adolescent's potential use of drugs, that awareness can be regarded an asset as well as a risk in that knowing a teacher is observing may limit drug use in the classroom or on the school campus. In summary,although threats to confidentiality exist, the precautions described above should minimize those risks.

5. Benefits vs. Risks

The benefits possible for families and adolescent abusers entering this study are great--increased satisfaction with personal and/or family life; reduced risk of drug addiction, health problems or emotional problems. All reasonable and practical precautions will be taken by the investigators and therapists to reduce or eliminate risks. Consequently, the benefits of participating in the study can reasonably be expected to far outweigh the risks.

PRINCIPAL INVESTIGATOR/PROGRAM DIRECTOR OR AWARD CANDIDATE *(Last, first, middle)* Joanning, Harvey H.

SOCIAL SECURITY NUMBER 481-62-2618

I. Literature Cited


Abelsohn, D. Dealing with the abdication dynamic in the post-divorce family: A context for adolescent crisis. Family Process, 1983, 22, 359-383.

Alexander, B.K., & Dibb, G.S. Opiate addicts and their parents. Family Process, 1975, 14, 499-514.

Amini, F., Salasnek, S., & Burke, E.L. Adolescent drug abuse: Etiological and treatment considerations. Adolescence, 1976, 11, 281-299.

Amini, F., Zilberg, N.J., Burke, E.L., & Salasnek, S. A controlled study of inpatient vs.outpatient treatment of delinquent drug abusing adolescents: One year results. Comprehensive Psychiatry, 1982, 23, 436-444.

Ansbacher, H.L., & Ansbacher, R.A. The Individual Psychology of Alfred Adler. New York: Harper, 1956.

Aponte, H.J., & Van Deusen, J.M. Structural family therapy. In A.S. Gurman and D.P. Kniskern (Eds.), Handbook of Family Therapy. New York: Brunner/Mazel, 1981.

Brock, G., & Joanning, H. Structured communication training for married couples: A comparison of the relationship enhancement program and the couple communication program. Journal of Marriage and Family Therapy, in press.

Brock, R.C., & Whitehead, P.C. "414": A therapeutic community for the treatment of adolescent amphetamine abusers. Corrective and Social Psychiatry and Journal of Applied Behavior Therapy, 1973, 19, 10-19.

Bourne, P.G., & Ramsey A.S. The therapeutic community phenomenon. Journal of Psychedelic Drugs, 1975, 7, 203-207.

Campos, R. Family therapy and the Chicano drug abuser. In Drug Abuse from the Family Perspective. DHHS Publication No. (ADM) 80-910, 1980.

Caroff, P., Lieberman F.,& Gottesfeld, M.L. The drug problem: Treating preaddictive adolescents. Social Casework, 1970, 59, 527-532.

Chitwood, D.D., Wells K.S., & Russe, B.R. Medical and treatment definitions of drug use: The case of the adolescent user. Adolescence, 1981, 16, 817-829.

. . . . . . . . . . . . . . . . . . . . . . . . . . . . . . . . . . . . . . . . . . .

Vaillant, G.E. A 12-year follow-up of New York narcotic addicts: III. Some social and psychiatric characteristics. Archives of General Psychiatry, 1966a, 15.

Vaillant, G.E. Parent-child cultural disparity and drug addiction. Journal of Nervous and Mental Disease, 1966b, 142, 534-539.

PERCEIVED-AGE ASCRIPTIONS AS A FACTOR

IN THE SOCIAL-ROLE PERCEPTION

AND SOCIAL-ROLE BEHAVIOR OF

PRESCHOOL CHILDREN IN A

MIXED-AGE SETTING

by

Libby Balter Blume

A proposal for a dissertation to be submitted

in partial fulfillment of the requirements

for the degree of

Doctor of Philosophy

Texas Tech University

1986

Advisory Committee:

Nancy J. Bell (co-chair)
Connie Steele (co-chair)
Janet Schrock
Gwendolyn T. Sorell
Betty S. Wagner

---

**Example 15.4.** Specimen dissertation proposal. (Adapted from Libby B. Blume, "Perceived-age Ascriptions as a Factor in the Social-Role Perception and Social-role Behavior of Preschool Children in a Mixed-age Setting," dissertation proposal, Texas Tech University, 1986. Used by permission.)

## TABLE OF CONTENTS

# I. INTRODUCTION

## Statement of the Problem

Researchers interested in the study of preschoolers' social relationships have been guided by both social-psychological and cognitive-developmental theories in interpreting differences in interactions among cross-age partners (Feldman & Ruble, 1981). Social cognition theorists have proposed that children's emerging social-cognitive concepts mediate their interpersonal interactions (Serafica, 1982). From this perspective, the child's perceptions of other people influence subsequent behavior with them. A representation of others is constructed by the perceiver using a cognitive structure, often termed a "social schema" (Taylor & Crocker, 1981), that consists of information from the social environment regarding prototypical interactions with another person. Theoretically, as children develop social schemas they are able to realize that the relative age of an interactional partner is a strong indicator of future behavior.

The proposed study will utilize constructs borrowed from schema theory (Taylor & Crocker, 1981) to examine: (1) children's use of social category information to infer the age-group membership of others, (2) children's use of social-role ratings of others' past behaviors, and (3) children's tacit knowledge of social relations as evidenced in their behaviors in natural settings. This study is designed to examine the effect of preschool children's ascriptions of age categories on their perceived and enacted social roles in an attempt to explore the link between cognitive and social factors in the interpersonal environment. If preschool children can ascribe age categories to their peers (such as "young" or "old"), they would also be able to use that conceptual framework accurately to guide behavior.

Specifically, this study will investigate the effects of the perceived age of social partners on preschool children's social-role perceptions and behavior in a mixed-age classroom.

## Related Literature

Research on preschool children's social understanding includes studies of age categorization, social-role perception, and social-role behavior (Shantz, 1983).

### Children's Concepts of Age Categories

The investigation of children's concepts of age categories is analogous to research on children's person perception. It has been demonstrated that preschoolers are able to discriminate representative human stimuli by age (Edwards, 1984), although young children are likely to confuse height with age (Edwards, 1984; Kuczaj & Lederberg, 1977).

### Children's Concepts of Social Roles

The study of preschool children's concepts of age-related social roles typically uses hypothetical stories about people, dolls, or photographs representing various age groups. Preschoolers over 3 years old are able to understand behavioral roles (Watson & Fischer, 1980); however, when stories were told to children involving four social-role functions (showing, helping, giving, and playing), children nominated older-child dolls for "showing" and "helping," same-age dolls for "playing," and infant dolls for "playing" and "giving" (Edwards & Lewis, 1979). In a pilot study for the proposed research, children from a mixed-age classroom were assessed using Edwards and Lewis's (1979) categories of social-role behaviors and an array of uniformly-photographed portraits of familiar classmates (Blume, 1986). Social-role preferences by age of classmates were consistent with previous findings.

## Children's Social-Role Behaviors

Social-role interactions between children who differ in age have been the focus of many investigations of preschool-age and school-age children (Dunn, 1983; French, 1984). In both literatures, the enactment of complementary age roles among children who are younger or older has been demonstrated. Most of these studies, particularly those examining social-role behaviors among preschool-age dyads, have used observational techniques as the primary method of data collection.

## Rationale

Experimental research has been conducted regarding the development of children's ability to judge age, as well as to attribute social roles to prototypic dolls, photographs, or descriptions of people. Such data suggest that preschool children are able to discriminate age categories. However, no data exist that systematically describe the effect of perceived age-group membership of familiar playmates on preschool children's social-role perception and behavior. The data from studies of mixed-age peer and sibling interaction suggest that children are perceptive of age differences and enact social-role behaviors in a complementary relationship to the role of a cross-age partner (Dunn, 1983;

Watson & Fischer, 1980). Older children are more likely to take a leadership role by directing activity, whereas younger children are more likely to follow their partners (Hartup, 1983).

Although observed age-related role behaviors have been shown in recent peer and sibling interaction research (Abramovitch, Corter, Pepler, & Stanhope, 1986; Stoneman, Brody, & MacKinnon, 1984), preschool children's social-role attributions have been documented in person-perception investigations only with unfamiliar peers (Edwards & Lewis, 1979). Laboratory studies of the age categorizations of preschool children also have used only unfamiliar stimuli (Edwards, 1984). Researchers have not examined the attribution of social roles by preschool-aged children to familiar classmates for whom, theoretically, age categories can be more accurately discriminated than for unfamiliar children.

The dimension of familiarity has been described as an important factor in the child's social system (Lewis, Feiring, & Kotsonis, 1984; Oden, Hertzberger, Mangione, & Wheeler, 1984). However, in most studies of childhood social cognition, the presence of others as social agents has usually been in the form of hypothetical people engaging in make-believe social acts in an unfamiliar social context and, thus, is likely to hold no subjective meaning for the child (Chandler, 1982). Use of unfamiliar social contexts and stimulus materials has been blamed for the equivocal and contradictory findings of many person-perception studies (Bearsion, 1982).

The proposed study is designed to investigate children's understanding and enactment of mixed-age peer relationships by utilizing a social-psychological analysis of preschoolers' ability to make age-related discriminations of their familiar classmates.

Research Question

This study will examine how children's perceptions of their classmates as older or younger group members of a preschool class affect their observed social-role behaviors and ratings of classmates on three social-role functions: showing, helping, and sharing. Two predictions will be tested:

Hypotheses

(1) Mean ratings of classmates perceived as older on the social roles of Show, Help, and Share will be higher than the mean ratings of classmates perceived as younger.

(2) Subjects will more frequently engage in the Follower-Style social-role behaviors of Learner, Managee, and Receiver with children perceived as older than with children perceived as younger, and will more frequently engage in the Leader-Style social-role behaviors of Teacher, Manager, and Giver with children perceived as younger than with children perceived as older.

## Significance of the Study

The proposed study will indicate whether or not preschool children discriminate age distinctions within a mixed-age preschool classroom and perceive age-related differences in social roles. Such findings would suggest that age-category representations may enable subjects to group familiar children together on the basis of social schemas for "young" or "old" social roles and that preschoolers over 3 years of age are able to cognate such schemas to guide their perceptions and behaviors with familiar partners.

The study will serve to extend previous data on siblings' social-role behaviors and on school-age children's social-role perception of familiar classmates to the domain of peer relations. Thus, it will address the developmental implications of mixed-age preschool programs and family interaction settings in which young children may be provided with unique opportunities for social-cognitive development.

## II. METHOD

### Sample

Subjects for this study will be 30 children between the ages of 36 and 72 months who are attending one of two mixed-age preschool programs in the fall of 1986. The socio-economic status of families in the preschool program is middle class, based on parental occupations. Each of the four classrooms that will be included enrolls 16 children, 50% male and 50% female, with an age range of from 18 months to 6 years. Each classroom is staffed by a baccalaureate-level head teacher and shares the same educational curriculum.

Parents of all subjects will be required to sign an informed consent form as required by the University Human Subjects Committee. Only children whose parents have consented to allow their participation will be included as subjects; however, children under 36 months of age will serve as social targets in the observation of subjects' social-role behaviors and will also be rated by each subject on two person-perception rating tasks. All children will have been in the same classroom for 1 month when the study begins.

## Measures and Procedures

The study will be composed of three data collection phases: (1) assessment of person perception; (2) observation of social-role behavior during interaction in the mixed-age preschool classroom; and (3) measurement of variables to be used as controls in the analyses, including cognitive ability, language skills, social competence level, and height.

### Assessment of Person Perception

During the fifth week of the preschool program, subjects will be asked to categorize themselves and their classmates as "older" versus "younger" and to rate them on three social-role functions: "showing," "helping," and "sharing." Previous age discrimination studies have utilized either a paired comparison procedure that requested subjects to judge pictorial stimuli on the basis of "which is the youngest (or oldest)" or a sorting procedure that required subjects to classify pictorial stimuli by age group: "baby," "child," or "adult" (Edwards, 1984). In this study, the age categorization task will utilize a forced-choice sorting procedure (Perceived-Young/ Perceived-Old) with stimulus photographs of familiar classmates.

The age-categorization task will be used to generate two lists of targets per subject: (1) a group of target children perceived by a subject as young; and (2) a group of target children perceived by the subject as old. Since the number categorized as young or old will be potentially different for each subject, these totals will be used to compute percentage scores on the factors of social-role perception and social-role behavior.

Following the categorization of each stimulus photograph, subjects will rate each classmate (including self) using a pictorial rating scale designed for the study. Each of three picture cards will consist of unisex portrayals of ambiguously-aged preschool children engaging in three complementary social-role behaviors representing older vs. younger social-role prototypes: "Showing another child where to play" vs. "Being shown where to play;" "Teaching another child how to use a new toy" vs. "Wanting to learn how to use a toy;" and "Giving a toy to another child" vs. "Getting a toy from another child." The relative position of the older vs. younger prototypical role behaviors on the right or left side of the picture card will be alternated. Each of the six line drawings will have a large and a small circle drawn below it that will be used in scoring on a 4-point ordinal scale (Harter & Pike, 1984) reflecting degree of prototypically-older social-role behavior (see Appendix A).

Subjects will also complete a retest of a randomly selected subset of four target children (two from each perceived-age group) on both the age categorization and the social-role rating task to assess the stability of subjects' responses.

## Observation of Social-Role Behavior

During the 2 weeks immediately following administration of the person-perception tasks, two trained coders (blind to the hypotheses of the study) will code observations of children's social-role behaviors in the mixed-age preschool classroom. The observational coding system will be adapted from a sibling interaction study conducted by Stoneman, Brody and MacKinnon (1984). The two observers will code the occurrence of six social-role behaviors and the target child or children with whom the focal child is engaged. The categories of Manager/ Managee; Teacher/ Learner; and Giver/ Receiver will represent three pairs of complementary social-role behaviors that correspond to the three social roles (Show/ Help/ Share) assessed by the rating task described above.

Observers will record event-frequencies of social-role behaviors with a target group consisting of the classmates whom the subject previously rated on the person-perception tasks. Based on each subject's prior classification of children on the age-categorization task, the names of specific targets will be recorded onto individualized coding sheets (See Appendix B).

Observers will code social-role behaviors during five 10-minute sessions over a 2-week period. They will use an event-sampling observational method to record one of six mutually-exclusive social-role behaviors with a certain target or targets in which one of the following conditions is met: (1) a verbal or gestural communication occurs; or (2) a change in activity, material, location, or partner occurs. If a minimum of 40 coded behaviors has not occurred with both "perceived-older" and with "perceived-younger" target children, additional 10-minute event-samples will be collected on subsequent days until a cumulative total of 40 interactions with each age group has been recorded.

Observers will be trained through practice coding sessions using videotapes until a minimum of .85 agreement is reached on all codes. For overall reliability estimates, inter-rater reliability will be calculated as percent agreement on each social-role category summed across the 2-week coding period (Hartmann, 1977).

### Measurement of Control Variables

Perceived-age ascriptions, social-role perception, and observed social-role behaviors are the major variables of interest in the study. The variables of height, cognitive processing ability, language ability, and social competence will be considered potential control variables.

Height will be defined as the measurement, in inches, of subjects at the beginning of the study; cognitive processing ability will be assessed by the Mental Processing Composite scale of the Kaufman Assessment Battery for Children (Kaufman & Kaufman, 1983); language ability will be measured by the Language Quotient score on the Preschool Language Scale (Zimmerman, Steiner, & Pond, 1979); and social competence scores will be percentile ranks on the California Preschool Social Competency Scale (Levine, 1969; Elzey & Lewis, 1969).

## Design and Analyses

The study will utilize a mixed-model analysis of variance design. Preliminary correlational analyses will be conducted to assess the relationship of the control variables to the major dependent variables of the study: age-categorization, social-role perception, and social-role behavior.

Two mixed-model analyses of variance (ANOVA) will be conducted. The first hypothesis of the study will be tested by a 2 x 2 x 3 mixed-model ANOVA with gender as the between-groups factor and Perceived-Age and three social-role ratings (Show, Help, Share) as the repeated measures. The second hypothesis will be tested by a 2 x 2 x 6 mixed-model ANOVA with gender as the between-groups factor and the six social-role behaviors (Manager, Managee, Teacher, Learner, Giver, Receiver) as the repeated measures. (See Appendix C for sample tables and figures.)

## REFERENCES


Abramovitch, R., Corter, C., Pepler, D. J., & Stanhope, L. (1986). Sibling and peer interaction: A final follow-up and a comparison. Child Development, 57, 217-229.

Bearison, D. J. (1982). New directions in studies of social interaction and cognitive growth. In F. C. Serafica (Ed.), Social development in context. New York: Guilford.

Blume, L. B. (1986, March). Perceived social functions and peer interactions in a mixed-age play context. Paper presented at the biennial meetings of the Southwestern Society for Research in Human Development. San Antonio, TX.

Brody, G. H., Stoneman, Z., MacKinnon, C. E., & MacKinnon, R. (1985). Role relationships and behavior between preschool-aged and school-aged sibling pairs. Developmental Psychology, 21, 124-129.

Chandler, M. J. (1982). Social cognition and social structure. In F. C. Serafica (Ed.), Social-cognitive development in context. New York: Guilford.

Dunn, J. (1983). Sibling relationships in early childhood. Child Development, 54, 787-811.

Edwards, C. P. (1984). The age group labels and categories of preschool children. Child Development, 55, 440-452.

Edwards, C. P., & Lewis, M. (1979). Young children's concepts of social relations: Social functions and social objects. In M. Lewis & L. A. Rosenblum (Eds.), The child and its family. New York: Plenum.

French, D. C. (1984). Children's knowledge of the social functions of younger, older, and same-age peers. Child Development, 55, 1429-1433.

Harter, S., & Pike, R. (1984). The pictorial scale of perceived competence and social acceptance for young children. Child Development, 55, 1969-1982.

Hartmann, D. P. (1982). Assessing the dependability of observational data. In D. P. Hartmann (Ed.), New directions for methodology of social and behavioral science: No. 14. Using observers to study behavior. San Francisco: Jossey-Bass.

Hartup, W. W. (1983). Peer relations. In E. M. Hetherington (Ed.), Handbook of child psychology: Vol. 4. Socialization, personality, and social development. New York: Wiley.

Kaufman, A. S., & Kaufman, N. L. (1983). K-ABC interpretive manual. Circle Pines, Minn.: American Guidance Service.

Kuczaj, S. A., & Lederberg, A. R. (1977). Height, age, and function: Differing influences on children's comprehension of "younger" and "older." Journal of Child Language, 4, 395-416.

Lewis, M., Feiring, C., & Kotsonis, M. (1984). The social network of the young child: A developmental perspective. In M. Lewis (Ed.), Beyond the dyad. New York: Plenum.

Oden, S., Herzberger, S. D., Mangione, P. L., & Wheeler, V. A. (1984). Children's peer relationships: An examination of social processes. In J. C. Masters & K. Yarkin-Levin (Eds.), Boundary areas in developmental psychology. New York: Academic Press.

Serafica, F. C. (Ed.). (1982). Social-cognitive development in context. New York: Guilford.

Shantz, C. U. (1983). Social cognition. In J. H. Flavell & E. Markman (Eds.), Handbook of child psychology: Vol. 3. Cognitive development. New York: Wiley.

Stoneman, Z., Brody, G. H., & MacKinnon, C. (1984). Naturalistic observations of children's activities and roles while playing with their siblings and friends. Child Development, 55, 617-627.

Taylor, S. E., & Crocker, J. (1981). Schematic bases of social information processing. In E. T. Higgins, C. P. Herman, & M. P. Zanna (Eds.), Social cognition: The Ontario symposium, Vol. 1. Hillsdale, N.J.: Erlbaum.

Watson, M. W., & Fischer, K. W. (1980). Development of social roles in elicited and spontaneous behavior during the preschool years. Developmental Psychology, 16, 483-494.

Zimmerman, I. L., Steiner, V. G., & Pond, R. E. (1979). Preschool language scale manual (rev. ed.). Columbus, Ohio: Merrill.

## APPENDIX A

### Sample Social-Role Rating Item

| MANAGEE | MANAGER |
| --- | --- |
| Is ____________ someone who needs to be shown where to play? | Is ____________ someone who shows others where to play? |

# APPENDIX B

## Sample Observation Coding Sheet

Name of subject ______ S# ______ Age-mo ______ Observer ______ Date ______ Time begin/end ______

PERCEIVED YOUNG

| | MANAGER | MANAGEE | TEACHER | LEARNER | GIVER | RECEIVER | NOTES |
|---|---|---|---|---|---|---|---|
| | | | | | | | |
| | | | | | | | |
| | | | | | | | |
| | | | | | | | |
| | | | | | | | |
| | | | | | | | |
| | | | | | | | |
| | | | | | | | |
| | | | | | | | |
| | | | | | | | |
| | | | | | | | |
| | | | | | | | |
| | | | | | | | |
| | | | | | | | |
| | | | | | | | |

PERCEIVED OLD

| | MANAGER | MANAGEE | TEACHER | LEARNER | GIVER | RECEIVER | NOTES |
|---|---|---|---|---|---|---|---|
| | | | | | | | |
| | | | | | | | |
| | | | | | | | |
| | | | | | | | |
| | | | | | | | |
| | | | | | | | |
| | | | | | | | |
| | | | | | | | |
| | | | | | | | |
| | | | | | | | |
| | | | | | | | |
| | | | | | | | |
| | | | | | | | |
| | | | | | | | |
| | | | | | | | |

COMMENTS ON OVERALL OBSERVATION/DAY:

## APPENDIX C

### Sample Tables and Figures

Pearson Product-Moment Correlations Between Social-Role Ratings of Perceived-Young and Perceived-Old Targets and Subjects' Height, Mental Processing, Language Ability, and Social Competence Scores.

| SUBJECT MEASURES | TARGET SOCIAL-ROLE RATINGS | | | | | |
|---|---|---|---|---|---|---|
| | Perc-Young: Show | Perc-Old: Show | Perc-Young: Help | Perc-Old: Help | Perc-Young: Share | Perc-Old: Share |
| Height | | | | | | |
| Mental Processing | | | | | | |
| Language Ability | | | | | | |
| Social Competence | | | | | | |

*$p < .05$

Analysis of Variance Comparing Social-Role Behaviors with Perceived-Young and Perceived-Old Classmates by Male and Female Subjects.

| SOURCE OF VARIANCE | df | SS | *F* | *p* |
|---|---|---|---|---|
| Social-Role Behavior | 5 | | | |
| Gender by Social-Role Behavior | 5 | | | |
| Social-Role Behavior by Subject (Error) | 130 | | | |
| Perceived-Age Group by Social-Role Behavior | 5 | | | |
| Gender by Perceived-Age Group by Social-Role Behavior | 5 | | | |
| Perceived-Age Group by Social-Role Behavior by Subject (Error) | 130 | | | |
| TOTAL | 335 | | | |

Social-Role Ratings on Show, Help, and Share for Perceived-Young and Perceived-Old Classmates

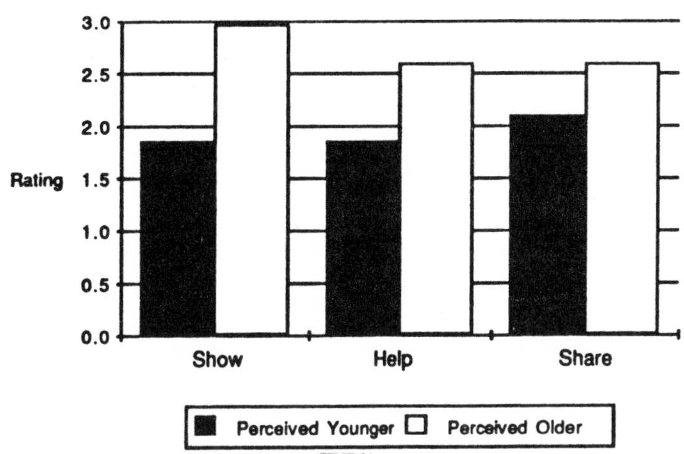


APPENDIX D

Proposed Timeline

| | |
|---|---|
| Proposal Approved by Human Subjects Committee | May, 1986 |
| Assessment Materials Prepared & Pilot Tested | June-July, 1986 |
| Parental Consent Forms Signed | August, 1986 |
| Data Collection | September-October, 1986 |
| Revision of Introductory Chapter | September, 1986 |
| Revision of Methods Chapter | October, 1986 |
| Data Analysis | November-December, 1986 |
| Write Results Chapter | January, 1987 |
| Write Discussion Chapter | February, 1987 |
| Draft to Dissertation Advisor | March 1, 1987 |
| Revised Draft to Committee | April 1, 1987 |
| Final Examination | April 10, 1987 |
| Corrections and Final Typing | April 30, 1987 |
| Dissertation Submitted to Graduate Dean | May 1, 1987 |

# NOTES

1. There is some overlap in activities of the process and omission of steps for certain types of proposals. Much like the research process discussed in Chapter 3, there is an underlying sequence to activities associated with proposal development, but these activities do not always follow an orderly progression from one step to another.

2. Bauer (1984, 1985) has done a thorough job of outlining steps involved in contacting a funding source, including calling the grantor on the phone (making appointments, arranging a phone interview); visiting the funding source (who should go, what to bring); questions to ask at the meeting; and keeping records of telephone and/or person-to-person contacts.

3. See Bauer (1985) for a discussion of the effective use of *advocates* to increase proposal acceptance rate. These are people who can help the researcher by providing expertise in certain areas, writing endorsement letters, talking to funding agencies for the researcher and arranging appointments, and accompanying the researcher to meet potential funders.

Bauer also suggests that the researcher explore the possibility of communicating with previous grantees and past reviewers, as well as obtaining copies of proposals recently funded by the agency, to increase grant success.

4. There are differences of opinion regarding the virtues of a letter proposal. Some authors recommend its use as a first step, and others believe that unless it is required it may be disadvantageous. Arguments favoring the letter proposal are that it allows the researcher to inquire about the possible interest of several different funders with a minimum of time and effort, it increases the possibility of a quick response, and it provides the researcher an opportunity to modify the proposal if the funding agency is interested but desires certain changes. A possible disadvantage is that the brevity of the proposal may obscure the importance of the proposed study. Since this may be the grant applicant's only contact with the agency, the letter must be a good one. Researchers who are well known in the field may be more likely to be invited to submit a full-length proposal (Lefferts 1982, 114; Margolin 1983, 209–11).

Examples of letter proposals are presented in some of the sources listed in Note 10. A particularly good one is illustrated in Bauer (1985, 34–35).

5. An appendix may include such material as tables, graphs, and supporting statistical data; vitae of key personnel; endorsement letters; capability statements (see Note 6); and certifications (e.g., assurance of compliance with federal regulations such as the protection of human subjects, care and use of animals, etc.)

6. A separate *capability statement* is advisable with major proposals and is usually incorporated into an appendix. Lefferts (1982, 30) points out that "organizational credibility can be established by a variety of techniques: history, prior experience and successes, availability of supporting resources, support of cooperating groups, references to the organization's work or to the importance of the addressed problem to already credible groups (for example, commissions)."

7. Evidence is included in the proposal that all study procedures have been examined and approved by an institutional review committee to ensure protection of the rights and welfare of subjects (see Chap. 17).

8. The total proposal package typically includes a cover letter, title page, abstract, project narrative, and appendix.

9. Hall (1977, 327–29) and Krathwohl (1977, 5–12) have provided more comprehensive proposal checklists.

10. Sources on grant proposal writing include Bauer (1984, 1985), Coleman (1984), Conrad (1980), Dermer (1980), Guba (1963), Hall (1977), Krathwohl (1977), Lauffer (1983), Lefferts (1982), Kiritz (1980), Locke, Spirduso, and Silverman (1987), Margolin (1983), McAdam, Maher, and McAteer (1982), and White (1975). Sample grant proposals (some with critiques) are presented in Bauer (1984, 1985), Caplovitz (1982), Coleman, Keller, and Pfeffer (1982), Ezell (1981), Lefferts (1982), Locke, Spirduso, and Silverman (1987), and White (1983). See also "The Grants Clinic" section of *Grants Magazine* for examples of successful proposals.

11. The classic study of weaknesses in grant proposals was conducted by Allen (1960). He examined 605 unsuccessful National Institutes of Health proposals reviewed during the 12-month period that ended June 1959. Allen identified a total of 26 shortcomings related to the problem, the research approach, the researcher, or other miscellaneous matters.

More recent sources that have discussed funding decisions for grants include Norman (1986) and Oetting (1986). See also Chalfant and Nitzman (1965), Cole and Cole (1981), Cole, Cole, and Simon (1981), Laveck et al. (1974), Smith (1963), and Townsend (1974).

12. Sternberg (1981), Long, Convey, and Chwalek (1985, 1–19), and Madsen (1983, 1–8) discuss problems faced by students during the thesis or dissertation process.

13. At some institutions, the entire committee (including the research adviser) is appointed, and the student has no input in their selection. Another practice is for the graduate school to appoint its own representative to each research committee to ensure that minimal standards are maintained. The size of committees also varies. Typically, there are two to four committee members in addition to the chair, one of whom is from outside the department but in a related field.

The research adviser will be familiar with the expertise of faculty members and will also know about any personality conflicts that might exist among faculty being considered for the advisory committee.

14. These professors will expect to see their suggestions incorporated into the formal proposal. The student should get into the habit of taking notes at all conferences with committee members. Immediately after the proposal defense, it is especially important for the student and research adviser to summarize points made by the committee at the hearing. The summary should then be circulated among individual committee members to verify recommendations and achieve a consensus on expected changes.

15. For a good discussion of proposal defense, see Long, Convey, and Chwalek (1985, 103–10). Also see Gardner and Beatty (1980, 83–86), Locke, Spirduso, and Silverman (1987, 53–57), and Sternberg (1981, 81–84).

16. In addition to the four criteria for evaluating a research problem presented in Chapter 4, Allen (1973, 22–23) adds additional questions (see especially nos. 14–24) that the student should ask when selecting a research topic.

17. See Allen (1973, 33–42), Davitz and Davitz (1967), Gardner and Beatty (1980), Locke, Spirduso, and Silverman (1987), Long, Convey, and Chwalek (1985, 67–110), Madsen (1983, 35–62), Sternberg (1981, 72–107), and Veldman (1971). Specimen proposals with commentaries are available in Leedy (1985), Locke, Spirduso, and Silverman (1987), and Madsen (1983).

CHAPTER 16

# Writing Research Reports

The results of a study must be communicated in some way if they are to be of value to others. Documenting what happened in an investigation enhances progress in a field by adding new information to the body of knowledge and allowing the possibility of verification, describing methodological innovations, indicating unsuccessful approaches to a research problem that can be avoided in the future, reducing the likelihood of needless repetitions, and providing a historical function (Matheson, Bruce, and Beauchamp 1974, 215).

The forms that research reports can take range from theses and dissertations to technical reports, conference papers, journal articles, and full-length monographs. This discussion will concentrate primarily on the preparation of manuscripts for submission to professional journals, since many of the guidelines for periodical articles also pertain to final reports that appear in other communication media. There are, of course, slightly different preferred styles among the various journals, as there are among the non-periodical reporting modes.

This chapter does not deal with the fundamentals of good writing (grammar, word usage, punctuation, etc.),[1] the different guidelines published in the various style manuals,[2] the physical preparation of manuscripts,[3] or all of the details associated with scientific writing.[4] Rather, the presentation is kept fairly general in the trust that the reader will consult the appropriate sources recommended in the chapter notes.

# GENERAL PRINCIPLES OF SCIENTIFIC WRITING

## Basic Considerations

Before discussing the organization and content of research reports, a few general comments should be made regarding scientific writing. Research reporting requires accuracy, clarity, and conciseness. The task is best served by simple language (not literary flair). Simple writing is not necessarily dull. Research reporting also necessitates careful documentation. References are used to support statements in the report and to indicate that material has been borrowed or quoted from another source.

Since the report deals with events that have already happened, the past tense is utilized to a great extent unless it is obviously inappropriate. The past tense is ordinarily used to describe the procedure and both the past tense and present perfect tense are employed in the literature review (e.g., "Jones found" or "Research has demonstrated"). The present tense may be used in the discussion and conclusions (e.g., "The data indicate") or in referring to material that is currently being presented in a table or figure (e.g., "Table 1 presents").

The third-person, passive voice (e.g., "ANOVA was employed" or "A telephone survey was conducted by the authors") continues to be used in most scientific writing because it contributes a formal and impersonal tone to the report. But there is a gradual trend away from this norm in some professional journals, with the substitution of the less awkward active voice and use of the first person. Unless skillfully employed, however, there is a danger that constant use of *I* or *we* may distract the reader from the content of the document. The rationale behind the use of the passive voice is that it "plays down the person; it emphasizes the fact" (Leedy 1985, 245).

## Nondiscriminatory Language

When preparing written reports, the researcher should also be sensitive to the use of language that may reinforce questionable attitudes and assumptions about certain groups of people. Two areas of special concern in scientific writing are sexist language and racial/ethnic bias.[5]

### Use of Nonsexist Language

The use of nonsexist language in writing has recently received considerable attention, due largely to the efforts of the American Psychological Association (APA), which has prepared guidelines for nonsexist language in APA journals. Sexism in writing falls into two categories according to the APA (1983, 44): problems of designation and problems of evaluation. These two terms are explained as follows:

> *Problems of designation.* When you refer to a person or persons, choose words that are accurate, clear, and free from bias. Long established cultural practice can exert a powerful, insidious influence over even the most conscientious author. For example, the use of *man* as a generic noun can be ambiguous and may convey an implicit message that women are of secondary importance. You can choose nouns, pronouns, and adjectives to eliminate, or at least to minimize, the possibility of ambiguity in sex identity or sex role.
>
> *Problems of evaluation.* Scientific writing, as an extension of science, should be free of implied or irrelevant evaluation of the sexes. Difficulties may derive from the habitual use of cliches or familiar expressions, such as "man and wife." The use of *man* and *wife* together implies differences in freedom and activities of each and may inappropriately prompt the reader to evaluate the roles. Thus, *husband* and *wife* are parallel, and *man* and *woman* are parallel, but *man* and *wife* are not.

Both types of sexism are subdivided into ambiguity of referent (when it is not clear whether the writer means one or both sexes) and stereotyping (when the writer implies unsupported or biased evaluation of the sexes). With practice, researchers can overcome these problems.[6]

### Avoidance of Racial/Ethnic Bias

Equally important in scientific writing is the avoidance of racial and ethnic bias. The APA (1983, 44–45) classifies racially/ethnically biased language into two categories—designation and evaluation—the same way it categorizes sexist language. The first problem refers to preferences for nouns referring to the racial or ethnic group. Deciding what to call a group can be difficult because of changes over time and disagreement about the preferred name even by members of the group in question (e.g., Mexican American, Chicano, Hispanic). The researcher must ascertain how the sample identifies itself with respect to race and ethnicity.[7]

The second problem frequently arises when the researcher uses one group (usually his or her own) as a universal standard against which other groups are judged, without the benefit of supporting data. When presenting findings, the researcher should refrain from using language that implies evaluation (e.g., culturally disadvantaged) when it is intended to describe one group rather than to compare groups. The APA (1983, 45) recommends the following test of implied evaluation: "Substitute another group (e.g., your own) for the group being discussed. If you are offended by the revised statement, there is probably bias in the original statement."

## ORGANIZATION AND CONTENT OF RESEARCH REPORTS

Although there is some variability in the research literature concerning the number of headings and names given to the different sections of a report, most reports have the following components: title, abstract, introduction, method, results, discussion, and references. If used, tables and figures are included after the references. Two possible variations of this typical structure are placing the abstract at the end of a report and calling it a summary, and combining results and discussion in brief articles.

### Major Components of a Research Report

Following a general format like the one given here ensures that essential elements will be reported in all investigations and that the scientific community will derive maximum information and benefit from each study. Use of a fairly standardized format for articles (and other reports) and conventional headings to organize the material also helps the reader to locate specific information quickly without having to examine the entire paper.

This format is appropriate for both experimental and nonexperimental studies:

1. Title—Brief and informative statement of the content of your research
2. Abstract—Summary of 3–6 below
3. Introduction—The problem you investigated and why you did the study
4. Method—The procedures you used
5. Results—Your findings
6. Discussion—The meaning of your findings
7. References—Materials cited in the report
8. Tables and figures—Tabular or figural summarization of bodies of data

#### Title

The title of a report should clearly indicate what the study is about. It should identify the primary variables investigated and possibly the population studied. Misleading titles are an inconvenience to consumers of the research literature, and they present special problems for information services that use titles as a guide to report content for indexing and abstracting.

The title should be concise (12–15 words maximum) without sacrificing accuracy (e.g., "Effect of Parent Discussion Groups on Parenting Skills" or "Diet of Elementary School Children in Four Texas Communities"). Only key words should be included, and all unnecessary words (e.g., A Study of, An Experiment on, or An Analysis of) should be eliminated. The *Publication Manual* of the APA (1983, 22) emphasizes that "A title should be fully explanatory when standing alone." The investigator usually waits until the end to finalize the title.

### Abstract

An abstract is an easily comprehensible summary in an encapsulated form (usually 100–150 words or less) of the most important elements of the study: problem (purpose of the investigation), method (subjects, instruments, and procedures), results (major findings, including statistical significance levels), and conclusions/implications (what was discussed). It is prepared after other sections of the report have been written.

Placed immediately after the title, an abstract is simply a miniature picture of the study. If a famous oil painting of museum size were photographed and reduced to the size of a small snapshot, the same general features would be recognizable even though specific details would no longer be evident. In the same manner, when the final document is reduced to an abstract, the essential framework is retained. An abstract should not attempt to present details of the data or to introduce findings that have not been discussed elsewhere in the report.

An abstract is extremely important and should be prepared with great care because it is the most widely read part of the report. Researchers usually consult abstracts when reviewing the literature to see if an article is relevant and whether they should read the full report. Abstracts must be accurate and concise, but maximally informative, because they are also used by information retrieval systems.[8]

### Introduction

By virtue of its location at the beginning of the document, the introduction ordinarily is not given a heading. (Other sections do carry headings.) An introduction provides the context for a study by starting with a very broad view of the problem and presenting important background material. Step by step, it moves from this general orientation to progressively narrower issues that provide a rationale for the study, justify selection of the particular combination of variables (variables may be conceptually defined in this section), and lead to the specific problem and statement of precise hypotheses or research questions.[9]

The progression from general to specific is accomplished through discussion of the broadest conceptualization of the problem first, then followed by relevant theory, classic studies, more recent studies, and finally, significant investigations that are considered immediate precursors to the study at hand. Typically, the literature review becomes more and more detailed as these latter studies are cited.

In theses and dissertations, an entire chapter may be devoted to the review of literature; but in professional journals, only the most pertinent sources are included because of limited periodical space and readers' presumed familiarity with related works, especially important theories and landmark studies. For the sake of brevity, the author may refer to review articles that summarize past research, if they are available. It may be possible to cover the literature with only a few studies that have built effectively on past research.

Although styles vary, sources are cited in the text of the report, usually by indicating the author's last name and year of publication. For example, "Jones (1987) has indicated. . ." or "Other researchers have disagreed with this line of reasoning (e.g., Adams 1968; Smith and Jones 1976; Taylor 1985)."

Once an overview of theoretical and conceptual issues has been presented and the major findings of relevant research have been summarized, it should be possible to see how the current study (and each hypothesis) has evolved from previous knowledge and debates in the literature. Toward the end of the introductory section, the researcher indicates how the study is similar to past investigations and, perhaps more significantly, how it departs from previous research (i.e., What is different or original about the current investigation? Why is it important? Why is it being done? Why is it being done this way?). The researcher concludes the introductory section by specifically stating the hypotheses.

### Method

This section tells how the study was conducted. The sample, design, procedures, reliability and validity of measuring instruments, ethical safeguards, and data analysis are described. The Method section should be detailed enough for the reader to assess the appropriateness of the methodology for testing the hypotheses and to judge the reliability and validity of the findings. Carefully written and identifying and operationalizing all variables and procedures, it should serve as a blueprint for someone who wants to repeat the study.

Since this section includes so much information, it is ordinarily divided into subsections. The number of subsections, their headings, and how they are combined is determined by characteristics of the study being reported, the author's preferences, and the journal to which the paper is being submitted. The subsections that appear in most reports are Subjects (or Sample), Materials (or Instruments, Measures, Apparatus, etc.), and Procedures. In addition, when fairly complex or innovative statistical analyses or research designs are employed or whenever the researcher deems it appropriate, a separate Data Analysis or Design subsection may be included in the Method section. (In some cases, the nature of the analyses and design is self-evident, since the findings are presented in the Results section that follows.)

Subjects. The Subjects subsection describes the participants in the study, indicating the total number and how many were in each subgroup (or assigned to each experimental condition), the major demographic characteristics (age, sex, race/ethnicity, educational background, and other relevant information); the population from which they were taken; how they were selected (including inducements for participation); and the number of subjects who did not complete the study (and reasons). In addition to information regarding subject loss, refusal rates and return rates (especially important in surveys) are usually reported here or in the Procedures subsection. If animals are used, the same attention to detail is necessary (age, sex, strain, weight, maintenance conditions, etc.). Unless the reader knows how the sample was drawn and who the subjects were, it is impossible to determine to what extent the results can be generalized.

Materials. The Materials subsection, also frequently headed Instruments, Measures, or Apparatus, specifies all data collection instruments (tests, observational systems, interview schedules, etc.) or equipment (machines, equipment, devices) used in carrying out the investigation. Well-established measures require minimal description because most researchers are already familiar with them. It may be necessary only to cite references for them and to briefly mention their reliability and validity. However, measuring instruments such as questionnaires or observational systems specially developed for the study must be described in detail, including pretesting procedures, item format, evidence of reliability (e.g., Cronbach's alpha, interrater reliability), and scoring information. Sample items are normally presented for previously untried instruments and may also be included for more established ones. (The entire questionnaire or interview schedule is sometimes given in an appendix.)

Similarly, when standard equipment is utilized, it is necessary only to provide the name, model number, and manufacturer of the apparatus. Use of homemade equipment (or complex apparatus) necessitates careful description and may even require inclusion of a drawing to avoid confusion.

Procedures. The Procedures subsection provides a step-by-step description, from beginning to end, of what happened to the subjects and of exactly how the data were collected (familiar standard procedures need not be enumerated in detail). It describes the setting or conditions, how subjects were assigned to groups (if relevant), the instructions to the research participants, the experimental manipulations (if any), and the manner in which the subjects' behavior or responses were recorded and when the measurements were taken. Reliabilities are documented here if they were not included in the Materials subsection or in the Results section.

The Procedures subsection should include how the researcher dealt with ethical problems.[10] If the procedures raised ethical issues, their inclusion in the study should be justified. For example, if the subjects were deliberately misinformed about the objectives or methods of the investigation, the researcher must justify these procedures and explain how subjects were told about this afterward (see Chap. 17). The investigator can assure the reader that informed consent was obtained, anonymity was ensured, and so forth. If animals were used as subjects, it is appropriate to tell how the researcher complied with guidelines for the use of nonhuman animals in research.

### Results

The Results section of the report presents the outcome of the study in a straightforward manner—without interpretation. Optimally, presentation of the findings should be so factual (objective) that another investigator faced with the same problem and data would write very nearly the same report of results. In this section, the statistical procedures used typically are mentioned first, then the data are described and summarized by using descriptive statistics such as ranges, means, and standard deviations. The presentation of results often continues by reporting findings by hypotheses. Structuring the presentation in this manner ensures a logical approach (i.e., consistent with the way in which the problem was developed in the introduction and in the same order in which the hypotheses were originally stated). The researcher indicates that the data supported acceptance or rejection of the various hypotheses and provides information about the inferential statistics for each result (name of the statistical test employed, the calculational value, degrees of freedom, and significance level).

Main results are given and only then are more detailed or peripheral findings indicated. Findings that are inconsistent with the hypotheses are also reported. Results may be summarized in tabular or graphic form and incorporated into this section if data are extensive and/or if they can be presented more clearly and economically through these visual media. Although tables and figures are placed at the end of the report, the author indicates in the running text where the table or figure should go when the article is published.

### Discussion

In the Discussion section, the researcher interprets findings and draws conclusions. In addition, he or she may make recommendations. In brief reports, the results and discussion may be combined into one section. The investigator has considerably more freedom of expression in this part of the report than in the Results section, as long as the presentation is based directly on the data. That is, the researcher can "take off from the data," as Fox (1969, 742) points out, because the discussion is only "data-based," not "data-bound" as are the results.

Normally, the Discussion section begins with a (very) brief restatement of the study's purpose and a summary of support or nonsupport found for the hypotheses. Inferences are then made, results are qualified, findings are examined in terms of previous theory and past investigations, implications are discussed, conclusions are drawn, and suggestions for future research and other recommendations are offered.

*Interpretation* of findings can be difficult. The researcher might be faced with negative results, inconsistent results, apparently meaningless results, or expected results. Whatever the case, he or she is obligated to accept the findings and interpret the data.[11] In interpreting data, the researcher asks two basic questions: What do the results mean? What is the significance of the findings? The general frame of reference for interpreting results is the established rationale for the study (i.e., past theory and research) and the stated hypotheses or research questions.[12] But within this broad framework, the investigator is free to examine certain facts, identify important relationships, qualify findings, and generalize from the results. While the researcher should not overinterpret the data, neither should he or she underinterpret them.

Since there is likely to be at least some ambiguity and even contradictory findings within a study, the researcher must look at these and try to account for them. The investigator needs to be mindful of factors that might have influenced the results, such as sampling techniques, controls, adequacy of the measuring instruments, methods of data collection, and statistical procedures. Although methods and procedures were justified earlier in the research process, at the interpretation stage methodological issues should be reconsidered in light of actual findings. Potential shortcomings in certain aspects of the study design and their implications should be honestly addressed. In interpreting the data, the researcher should consider rival explanations, resulting from internal validity problems, that could have accounted for the results.

An issue in interpretation that is frequently overlooked is that of practical versus statistical significance. A researcher is obliged to address the practical meaning, as well as the statistical significance, of his or her findings. If statistically significant results have been found, the researcher has some confidence (with known probability) that the findings were not accidental. But practical significance of the findings might be another matter altogether. Are the results useful or meaningful? Statistical significance does not necessarily guarantee practical significance, as Ellinstad and Heimstra (1974, 118–19) point out:

> It is quite possible to design and conduct behavioral studies that statistically detect the most trivial differences between groups of individuals. Assume, for example, that we conducted a study comparing the reaction times of males and females and found that the difference in mean reaction time for the two groups is only .02 seconds, but that the result is significant at the $\alpha$ level of .01. It is entirely possible that a difference this small would be deemed significant, particularly if the groups were relatively large. It is extremely difficult, however, to imagine a situation in which a difference of .02 seconds would make any practical difference in the performance of either men or women.

In the Discussion section, the researcher also tries to arrive at *conclusions* that achieve a final synthesis or integration of the myriad details already presented. Conclusions likewise provide some definitive answers regarding the original research problem. They should include generalization that are warranted by the evidence obtained in the study, and they should be kept within the boundaries established by the purposes and limitations of the research. They help incorporate the study into the structure of current knowledge and contribute something to the field.

Finally, the researcher may offer *recommendations* concerning future research and/or the implementation of findings. The investigator often suggests profitable areas for further research that might resolve confusion or contradictions in the results (e.g., refinements, replications, extensions, etc.). Because of the cyclical nature of research, these recommendations will undoubtedly motivate future studies. Some investigations have greater potential for action than others and lend themselves more to concrete recommendations for practice, in which case the researcher includes the suggestions. Experience gained through careful and devoted attention to a specific problem over an extended period of time places the researcher in a position where he or she has much to offer other people who are interested in related problems.

Kidder and Judd (1986, 430–31) have aptly described the research report as a document that is usually written in the "shape" of an hour glass. They indicate that "it begins with broad general statements, progressively narrows down to the specifics of your particular study, and then broadens out again to more general considerations." Within this shape, the research report has continuity. The discussion is based upon the presentation of results that is linked to the hypotheses that are derived from past theory and research outlined in the introduction. Moreover, the discussion at the end of the report uses the literature cited at the beginning of the report. Consequently, in the course of writing and rewriting, the researcher will move back and forth from results to hypotheses, discussion to results, discussion to introduction, and so on.

### References

In the References section, references cited in the paper must be listed alphabetically, according to the (first) author's last name. If the researcher consulted a particular source but did not specifically refer to it in the main body of the report, it is not listed. Journal articles, books, chapters in books, technical reports, conference papers, and other information sources follow slightly different bibliographic forms. Following APA style, samples of entries for a book, a journal article, and a chapter in a book are

Kerlinger, F. N. (1986). *Foundations of behavioral research* (3rd ed.). New York: Holt.

Brown, J. G., & Burger, C. (1984). Playground designs and preschool children's behaviors. *Environment and Behavior, 16,* 559–626.

Rheingold, H. L. (1982). Ethics as an integral part of research in child development. In R. Vasta (Ed.), *Strategy and techniques of child study* (pp. 305–324). New York: Academic Press.

There are numerous other reference styles. Style *B* of *The Chicago Manual of Style* (13th ed.) has been used in this book.

### Tables and Figures

Tables. A table is a systematic array of numbers (or words) that displays values in rows and columns (Mullins 1980, 48). When specific numbers are necessary for clarity and the series of numbers is of manageable size, a table may be an effective medium for the presentation and summarization of data in an organized manner. Mullins (1980, 47) recommends the use of tables instead of narrative when

- They make a point more clearly than you can make it in text alone.
- The information is not duplicated in the text or in other tables, equations, or illustrations.
- In the text you want to discuss the information and perhaps draw conclusions.
- Writing the information in text would take at least three times as much page space (this criterion is especially important in documents being prepared for publication).

The principal goals of table construction are accuracy, neat appearance, and ease of interpretation. These goals are more likely to be achieved when a table is simple, presenting one main idea and only a few facts related to it. A cardinal rule in table preparation is to provide as much information as possible in a compact format but not too much to confuse the reader. If a table is unwieldy, it should be broken up into two or more smaller tables.

A table should be a self-contained display of information and not be dependent on the text for meaning or clarity. It should complement textual material and not duplicate it. Therefore, care should be taken in developing a brief but explanatory title for the table and in labeling the rows and columns. All abbreviations should be explained. A table should clearly indicate the variables for which the data are being presented, the subjects on whom the data were collected (and any subgroups), the sample size (*N*), and the statistics included in the table. Its function is to provide an overview of important details. The textual discussion, on the other hand, should provide generalizations based upon the tabulated material that help the reader understand the information in a table even if the reader does not examine the table itself. Tabular data should always be organized so that they parallel the presentation of material in the text and they do not introduce terminology that has not already been discussed.

Brief tabular material can be placed directly in the context of the report as an informal table introduced by a sentence that is followed by a colon. But in most cases involving more extensive data, a formal table is constructed on a separate manuscript page. A table should appear only after it has been mentioned in the text so that the reader is aware of the nature of the data to be presented. The researcher should break the text and instruct the editor and printer to insert it as near the point of first reference as possible (e.g., Insert Table 1 here). Tables are numbered consecutively throughout the research report (e.g., Table 1, Table 2, etc.).

Table 16.1 is an example of a simple layout of the most important components of a table. The table is numbered, and the title is understandable without referring to the text. Looking at the title, the reader is alerted to the type of data that is to be displayed and the nature of the sample. The rows are labeled BPC Dimensions to signify that data will be given for each of the *Behavior Problem Checklist* dimensions in the five rows below. Column headings indicate that the columns are organized by sex of child and that they present means and standard deviations for the various BPC

**Table 16.1. Example of a Table Layout for Means and Standard Deviations of *Behavior Problem Checklist* (BPC) Scores of Fourth Grade Boys and Girls**

| | Boys[a] | | Girls[b] | |
|---|---|---|---|---|
| BPC Dimensions | Mean | *SD* | Mean | *SD* |
| Conduct problems | 3.22 | 4.78 | .91 | 1.88 |
| Personality problems | 1.39 | 2.49 | 1.30 | 2.08 |
| Inadequacy-immaturity | 1.04 | 1.66 | .77 | 1.42 |
| Socialized delinquency | .25 | .77 | .15 | .48 |
| Psychotic signs | .25 | .58 | .09 | .35 |

[a]*N* = 176
[b]*N* = 169

scores. If there are no data for a particular column, it is customary to leave the space blank or to use dots or dashes. The zero value should never be used to denote an omission. Footnotes are placed immediately under the table to provide additional information and/or to explain exceptions, omissions, and abbreviations or symbols. When tests of significance are being presented, the probability levels ($p < .05$, $p < .01$, etc.) are usually given in a footnote. Although styles vary, footnotes are often preceded by a superscript lowercase letter.

Generous spacing and careful arrangement of data are essential for effective tables. Everything is double spaced. All decimal points are aligned in the columns. Horizontal rules can be used to improve the legibility of a table by breaking up the data into logical groupings. However, rulings should be minimized and white space used as a substitute whenever possible. Vertical rules should be employed sparingly because of the problems they cause for the printer. Vertical rulings are never used at the sides of tables. All rules should be drawn in pencil.

Figures. It is often easier to convey information by figures than by verbal or tabular presentation. Figures include graphs, charts, drawings, diagrams, photographs, and other illustrations. Figures help the reader see at a glance complicated ideas and complex patterns or relationships that might require extensive textual explanation. Although they do not replace written descriptions, figures can facilitate explanation and interpretation of research results. Generally, figures should be used instead of text when they meet the criteria for tables listed in the preceding section.

As with tables, figures are inserted following the point of initial reference in the report (when published) and are numbered consecutively in the text. If symbols are used in the illustration, a legend or key is necessary. The word *Figure* or *Fig.* (along with its number) usually appears below the illustration with a caption. The caption may serve both as a title for the figure and as a brief explanation of the figure's contents. There are several acceptable styles, but the researcher should follow the specific guidelines of the target journal.

Each figure should be placed on a separate sheet of high quality white drawing paper. Black india ink should be used. Letters should not be typed or written freehand unless you are a professional artist. A lettering stencil or pressure-sensitive tape with letters, symbols, and different patterns of lines and dots (available in art supply stores) produces high quality figures. Difficult illustrations should be prepared professionally.

Graphs are the most widely used type of figure in research reports. Graphs can be used to clarify numerical data, to present relationships among variables, to reveal trends or changes over a period of time, or to show how a total is made up of its component parts. To be effective, these visual aids must be accurate, simple, and clear. The APA (1983, 95) *Publication Manual* lists seven characteristics of a good figure. A good figure (1) augments rather than duplicates the text; (2) conveys only essential facts; (3) omits visually distracting detail; (4) is easy to read—its elements (type, lines, labels, etc.) are large enough to be read with ease in the printed form; (5) is easy to understand—its purpose is readily apparent; (6) is consistent with and is prepared in the same style as similar figures in the same article, that is, the lettering is of the same size and typeface, lines are of the same weight, and so forth; and (7) is carefully planned and prepared.

Different types of graphs can illustrate data in human ecology research. Among them are bar, line, pictorial, scatter, and pie graphs (see Fig. 14.3 and Ex. 16.1). A *bar graph* is a commonly used device composed of vertical or horizontal bars (oblong boxes). The bars can extend vertically with the bases at the bottom (sometimes also called a column graph), or the bars can be horizontal with the zero position at the left. The width of the bar is arbitrarily set by the researcher and is the same for all bars. Quick to prepare and easy to understand, the bar graph is useful for illustrating sizes or amounts at different times, comparing aspects of several items at the same time, or showing parts of a whole at one point in time. It is also a popular way of representing frequency distributions. The height or length of the bar indicates the number of cases in a particular category, and that number may be written on each bar.

Because of its suitability for displaying relatively small numbers of entities, the vertical bar graph is the choice of many researchers. When all of the bars are of equal length (representing 100% for each group), they are referred to as compound bars, or 100% bars. The hatched or shaded areas within each bar that show the size of its components should be indicated in the same order on each bar. The reader is then able to make visual comparisons by looking at the areas filled in by similar hatchings on the component portions.

A *line graph* is frequently employed for plotting continuous data to illustrate trend and movement. In single-subject experimental designs, for example, a line graph can summarize the course and results of a behavior modification treatment program. Or it can demonstrate learning curves or changes in test scores over time.

The *pictorial graph* (pictograph) often starts with a bar graph, and an appropriate symbol is selected to fill in the bar and add to its appeal. To be effective, the symbol must be clear, interesting, and closely associated with the idea. Whenever possible, the symbol should be small enough so that one whole symbol stands on the shortest bar. Each symbol represents 10, 100, or some other unit of children, food, or whatever is being shown. Increasing numbers are shown by adding more symbols of equal size rather than by increasing the size of the symbol.

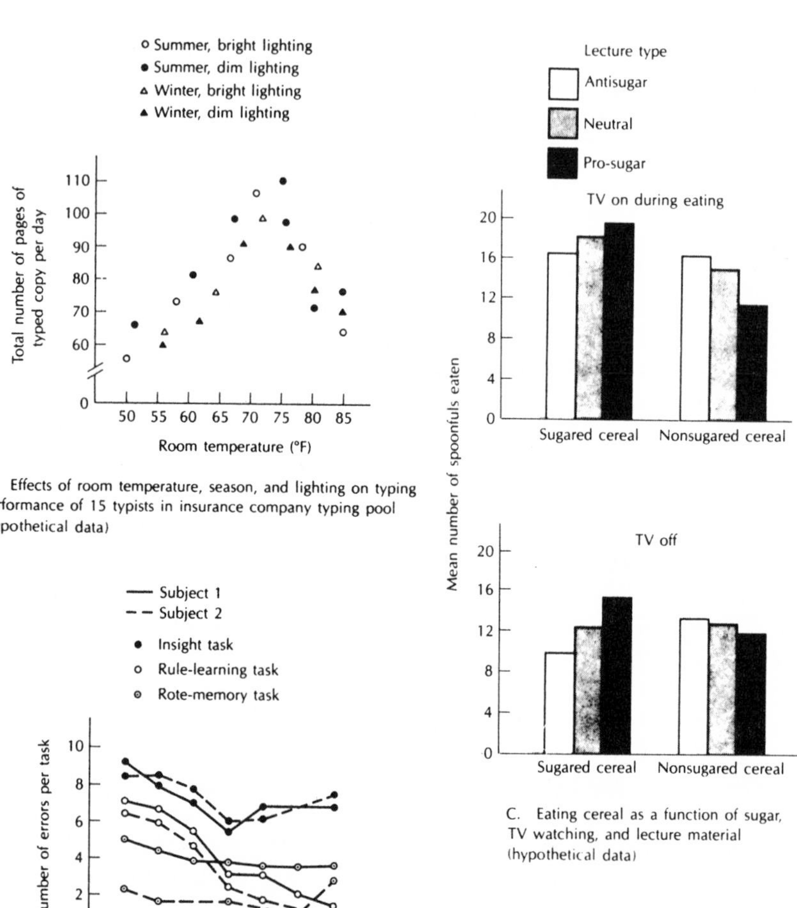


A. Effects of room temperature, season, and lighting on typing performance of 15 typists in insurance company typing pool (hypothetical data)

B. Relationships between age and type of task for two rats (hypothetical data)

C. Eating cereal as a function of sugar, TV watching, and lecture material (hypothetical data)

**Example 16.1.** Scatter (*A*), line (*B*), and bar (*C*) graphs of hypothetical data. (From *Understanding Behavioral Research* by Nancy S. Harrison © 1979 Wadsworth Publishing Company, Inc. Used by permission.)

A *scatter graph* (scatter diagram) consists of data, unconnected by lines, representing the intersection of two variables. It provides a visual depiction of a relationship (see Fig. 14.3 and Ex. 16.1).

A *pie graph* (circle graph) shows how an entire area or volume is divided. A 100% graph, it presents percentages and proportions. It is sometimes used in the form of a three-dimensional silver dollar to show a family (or national) budget or the way in which money has been spent. For materials having not more than five or six parts, a pie graph may make an attractive, simple presentation. The largest segment is usually shaded the lightest and is often placed at the top. Other sections follow in a clockwise direction according to their size, and each is progressively darker. A picture or symbol may be used in each segment along with the printed name of the category and the numerical size. If space within the circle is too small, the labels or pictures may be placed outside. Emphasis may be given to one portion by cutting it and withdrawing it slightly from its normal position in the circle. The area for each segment must be of correct size. The proper number of degrees on the circumference of the circle should be measured with a protractor.

In addition to graphs, figures include charts, line drawings, and photographs. *Charts* are an effective visual medium in which to present the relationships among the components of an object, a group, or a system. A chart is usually made up of boxes connected with lines. A good example is a flow sheet that represents the chronology of a process (see Fig. 16.1) or an organizational chart that shows the relationship of various parts of an organization. These types of diagrams are used to illustate such matters as the relative positions of authority, the flow of work in an organization, or the number of persons being admitted to or dropping out at different stages of a process.

If *line drawings* are utilized, they should be prepared by a professional artist, and they should include the minimum amount of detail to convey the necessary information. Among their many uses, pen-and-ink drawings (and diagrams) are sometimes employed to illustrate an apparatus used in an experiment.

*Photographs* are used least frequently. To be effective, they must be glossy prints of professional quality. An artificial background, a sharp focus, and good lighting are necessary to make the elements of the picture distinct. Most researchers resort to line drawings rather than photographs because of the inevitable loss of detail when a print is reproduced. Not all journals have sufficiently high quality reproduction standards for photographs.

A flow chart is presented in Figure 16.1 to help the researcher decide what kind of figure (or table) is appropriate to display data. A number of

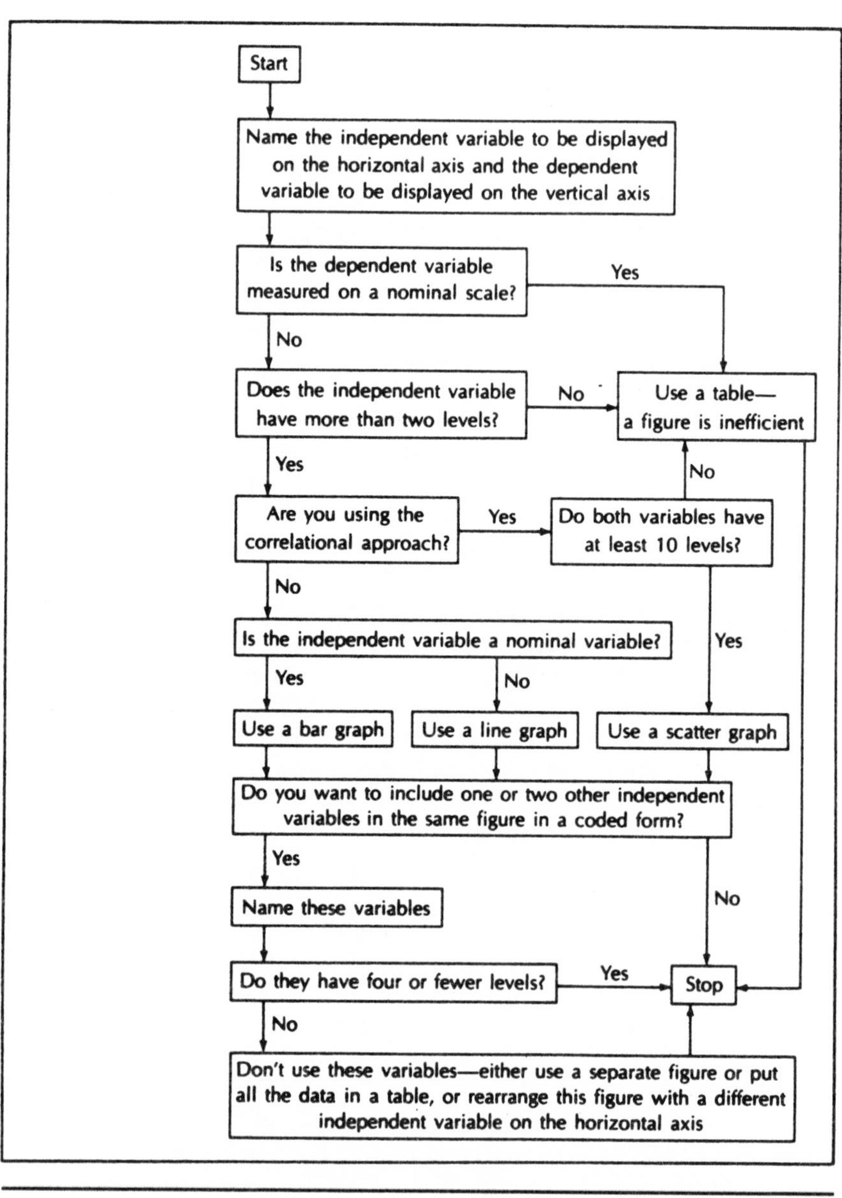


**Figure 16.1.** Flow chart for deciding which kind of figure (if any) is appropriate for illustrating data. (From *Understanding Behavioral Research* by Nancy S. Harrison © 1979 by Wadsworth Publishing Company, Inc. Used by permission.)

good sources are available that deal with the preparation and the use of figures and tables.[13]

## CRITERIA FOR EVALUATING RESEARCH REPORTS

Because of space limitations, a "model" research report from the literature is not reproduced in this chapter. Good examples can be found in reputable journals.[14] However, some general criteria for evaluating the content and organization of most research reports are given here. Other authors have offered similar guidelines.[15]

1. Title—Is it concise (12–15 words) and clear? Is it informative (e.g., includes major independent and dependent variables, population being studied)?
2. Abstract—Is it approximately 100–150 words (depending on the journal)? Does it highlight the important points made in the report (problem, method, major results, major conclusions)?
3. Introduction—Is the problem adequately conveyed? Is the literature cited relevant, up-to-date, complete, and well organized? Is the status of current knowledge clear? Are conceptualization and rationale of the study explicit? Is the significance of the problem established? Does the section conclude with a brief overview of the problem and a formal statement of hypotheses or research questions?
4. Method—Does it indicate the procedures used to investigate the problem, including information about subjects, materials, or apparatus; precisely what was done (in chronological order) to the subjects; and analyses to be conducted? Are relevant variables defined? Are reliability and validity of the instruments reported? Is the research design adequately described? Is observance of ethical standards indicated?
5. Results—Are methods of data analysis indicated (if not included in the Method section)? Are results given for all procedures stated in the Method section? Are results of the analyses presented clearly?
6. Discussion—Is there an initial, brief statement of essential findings to orient the reader? Is the discussion confined to what can be concluded from the data reported in the Results section? Are findings accurately interpreted in the context of preexisting knowledge presented in the introduction? Are limits of generalization from the data indicated? Is there reference to future research that should be done, and are specific reasons given for these additional studies? Are the conclusions clear? If given, do recommendations logically follow the results and conclusions?
7. References—Are only those references cited in the text included in the reference list? Are the references alphabetized by last name of first

author and in ascending order by year of publication if there are two sources by the same author(s)?

8. Tables and figures—Do they summarize and illustrate data in a more efficient and informative manner than can be conveyed in the text? Do they supplement, but not duplicate, information in the body of the report? Are they well constructed and easy to read? Can they be understood without having to read the explanation in the text?
9. Overall presentation—Is the report concise and clearly written? Is the organization of material logical, and does it move smoothly from one section to another? Is the tone of the report objective? Is discriminatory language avoided? Is the report prepared according to the manuscript specifications of the target journal (e.g., APA or ASA style)?

## STUDENT THESES AND DISSERTATIONS

Although the primary concern in this chapter has been the preparation of research articles, many of the suggestions mentioned are also relevant to graduate theses and dissertations. The principles of good scientific writing and the suggestions for organization and presentation of technical material may be applied to all research reports. However, since the graduate schools at most universities give detailed guidelines and prescribe their own format that must be carefully followed, and major professors closely monitor the writing of their thesis and dissertation students, no attempt has been made here to deal specifically with research reports submitted in partial fulfillment of advanced degrees. Copies of master's theses and doctoral dissertations cataloged in the university library or available in the academic department provide examples of student research reports and can serve as a guide for what is acceptable at a particular institution.

A number of published sources present a good overview of the thesis and dissertation process.[16]

## NOTES

1. Among the many good books on effective use of the English language are Bates (1980), Bernstein (1965), McKay and Rosenthal (1980), Ross-Larson (1982), Strunk and White (1979), and Zinsser (1985).

2. The APA (1983) *Publication Manual* is, in our opinion, the best style manual available and the easiest for authors to follow. Other style guides include Campbell, Ballou, and Slade (1986), *CBE Style Manual* (1983), *The Chicago Manual of Style* (1982), Turabian (1987), and *U.S. Government Style Manual* (1973). Different academic specialties have their own style requirements, as do individual journals. Most institutions also prescribe guidelines for theses and dissertations.

3. Most of the references cited in Notes 2 and 4 provide information on the mechanics of physically preparing research reports. Numerous informative references are available on *word processing* and automation in writing. The reader is referred to Brownell (1985, 71–141), Fluegelman and Hewes (1983), McKenzie (1984), Mullins (1980, 23–44), Stultz (1982), and Zinsser (1983). For authors following APA or CBE guidelines for manuscript preparation, word processing software (Manuscript Manager) using these editorial styles is available from Pergamon Press, Inc. See also Blau (1984) and Staff of the University of Chicago Press (1987).

4. For a more detailed treatment of writing scientific material, see Barrass (1978), Becker (1986), Day (1983), Hill and Cochran (1977), Huth (1987), Katz, Kapes, and Zirkel (1980), Magistrale, Bond, and Fulwiler (1987), Maimon et al. (1981), Mullins (1977, 1980), Skillin and Gay (1974), and Sociology Writing Group, UCLA (1986), as well as the APA (1983) *Publication Manual.*

For a discussion of orders of authorship in scientific writing, see APA (1981), Bridgewater, Bornstein, and Walkenbach (1981), Spiegel and Keith-Spiegel (1970), and Winston (1985).

5. Although we plan to focus on sex and racial/ethnic bias, researchers should be equally concerned about language that is free of age, heterosexist, and disability bias. More detailed treatment of racially and ethnically biased language, as well as new guidelines for avoiding ageist, heterosexist, and handicapping language, will be included in the fourth edition of the APA *Publication Manual.*

The International Association of Business Communicators' (1982) publication, *Without Bias,* provides guidelines for nondiscriminatory communication concerning age and disability (as well as sex, race, and ethnicity).

6. Readers are referred to Miller and Swift (1988), Moulton, Robinson, and Elias (1978), and Sorrels (1983), as well as to the APA (1983, 45–49) guidelines, for more information on nonsexist language.

7. See Lampe (1982, 1984), Moore (1976), and Yankauer (1987), as well as APA (1983, 44–45).

8. See APA (1983, 23–24), Cremmins (1982), Day (1983, 22–25), and McGirr (1978) for more details on abstracting.

9. Subsequently, we will refer simply to hypotheses when we mean hypotheses *or* research questions.

10. Since there are undeniable methodological consequences of different ethical procedures in research, the ethical safeguards employed should be indicated in the Method section (see Adair, Dushenko, and Lindsay 1985). As one example, parental informed consent may introduce bias in child subject samples (see Frame and Strauss 1987) and must be mentioned. Additionally, description of these practices in the report reinforces the importance of adherence to ethical regulations in the profession. Currently, some journals are quite lax about requiring disclosure of ethical measures taken, whereas others insist at least that the author indicate in the cover letter accompanying the manuscript (but not in the report) that ethical standards have been met.

11. It is important to note that the disconfirmation of hypotheses may be as important to scientific progress as confirmation.

After the study begins, information gleaned from the data must not affect the stated hypotheses or the analyses being used to evaluate them. Similarly, the investigator must not increase sample size to obtain a desired level of significance.

12. Some issues that are usually addressed when considering findings relative to existing knowledge in the field include: Are the findings consistent with theory? Are the results similar to those of previous studies? If not, what are the differences and how can they be explained? What new questions are raised by the results?

13. Sources on how to design tables and graphs include Babbie (1986, 341–59), Caplovitz (1983, 191–215), Houp and Pearsall (1980), Lefferts (1981), Lockwood (1969), Mullins (1980), Schmid and Schmid (1979), Selby (1979), Spear (1969), and Zeisel (1985), as well as those cited in Notes 2 and 4.

14. Adams and Schvaneveldt (1985), Borchardt and Francis (1984), Craig and Metze (1986), Hardyck and Petrinovich (1975), Harrison (1979), Meyers and Grossen (1978), and Mouly (1978) present sample reports in their textbooks, some with helpful running commentaries. The APA (1983) *Publication Manual* also presents a model report to illustrate application of APA style.

15. The most comprehensive checklist of this nature is provided by Krathwohl (1985). Best (1981), Borg (1987), Isaac and Michael (1981), Joseph and Joseph (1979), Katzer, Cook, and Crouch (1982), Miller (1983, 611–13), Mouly (1978), and Ward, Hall, and Schramm (1975) have also outlined criteria for evaluating research and reports of research. White (1987) has discussed the importance of reference list accuracy. For a brief discussion of suggestions to improve manuscripts submitted to professional journals, see Boor (1986).

16. See Allen (1973), Balian (1983), Long, Convey, and Chwalek (1985), Madsen (1983), Martin (1980), Sternberg (1981), Sugden (1973), Teitelbaum (1982), and Yates (1982).

PART 6

# Ethical and Professional Responsibilities

CHAPTER 17

# Ethical Considerations in Human Ecology Research

This book emphasizes that human ecology is the study of human beings in interaction with their near environment, with the basic mission of improving the quality of human life. With this focus, researchers in human ecology should be aware of the need to protect all research participants.

A great deal of attention has been devoted to the sociopolitical rights of various groups of people who historically have been denied many rights and privileges—blacks, women, consumers, and children. For example, the rights of children have been directly implicated in numerous social issues, such as adoption policies, foster home placement, child labor, child abuse, desegregation, intelligence testing, and compulsory schooling (Feshbach and Feshbach 1978). Coverage of rights in this book will be limited primarily to those involved in procedures used to study people.

More recently, animal rights groups are calling for more stringent control over the use of animals in research. Some have advocated prohibiting their use completely.

Many of the ethical issues regarding research subjects being debated among the public, academic and professional researchers, and the government are complex and many-sided. We must be concerned not only with the rights of research participants but also with the medical and social benefits to be gained through research findings.

## ETHICAL CODES OF PROFESSIONAL ASSOCIATIONS

Thirty-nine associations have been identifed with codes of ethics that can be classified according to whether or not they contain materials explicitly dealing with protection of human subjects in research. Twenty-one give some recognition of problems in this area either through codes of ethics, letters, or documents (Bower and de Gasparis 1978). This chapter includes summaries and selected portions of the codes of ethics of the American Anthropological Association (AAA), American Psychological Association (APA), American Sociological Association (ASA), and the Society for Research in Child Development (SRCD).[1]

## American Anthropological Association

In its *Professional Ethics* the AAA (1983, 1) includes the following statements in its preamble:

> Anthropologists work in many parts of the world in close personal association with the peoples and situations they study. Their professional situation is, therefore, uniquely varied and complex. They are involved with their discipline, their colleagues, their students, their sponsors, their subjects, their own and host governments, the particular individuals and groups with whom they do their field work, other populations and interest groups in the nations within which they work, and the study of processes and issues affecting general human welfare. In a field of such complex involvements, misunderstandings, and conflicts, the necessity to make choices among conflicting values are bound to arise and to generate ethical dilemmas. It is a prime responsibility of anthropologists to anticipate these and to plan to resolve them in such a way as to do damage neither to those whom they study nor, in so far as possible, to their scholarly community. Where these conditions cannot be met, the anthropologist would be well-advised not to pursue the particular piece of research.

The following sections are taken from the "Ethical Principles of Psychologists" (APA 1981, 633 and 637–38).*

> Psychologists respect the dignity and worth of the individual and strive for the preservation and protection of fundamental human rights. They are committed to increasing knowledge of human behavior and of people's understanding of themselves and others and to the utilization of such knowledge for the promotion of human welfare. While pursuing these objectives, they make every effort to protect the welfare of those who seek their services and of the research participants that may be the object of study. They use their skills only for purposes consistent with these values and do not knowingly permit their misuse of others. While demanding for themselves freedom of inquiry and communication, psychologists accept the responsibility this freedom

*From American Psychological Association, "Ethical Principles of Psychologists," *American Psychologist* 36:633–38. Copyright 1981 by the American Psychological Association. Reprinted by permission of the publisher.

requires: competence, objectivity in the application of skills, and concern for the best interests of clients, colleagues, students, research participants, and society. In the pursuit of these ideals, psychologists subscribe to principles in the following areas: 1. Responsibility, 2. Competence, 3. Moral and Legal Standards, 4. Public Statements, 5. Confidentiality, 6. Welfare of the Consumer, 7. Professional Relationships, 8. Assessment Techniques, 9. Research with Human Participants, and 10. Care and Use of Animals.

Acceptance of membership in the American Psychological Association commits the member to adherence to these principles.

Psychologists cooperate with duly constituted committees of the American Psychological Association, in particular, the Committee on Scientific and Professional Ethics and Conduct, by responding to inquiries promptly and completely. Members also respond promptly and completely to inquiries from duly constituted state association ethics committees and professional standards review committees.

*Principle 9: Research with Human Participants*

The decision to undertake research rests upon a considered judgment by the individual psychologist about how best to contribute to psychological science and human welfare. Having made the decision to conduct research, the psychologist considers alternative directions in which research energies and resources might be invested. On the basis of this consideration, the psychologist carries out the investigation with respect and concern for the dignity and welfare of the people who participate and with cognizance of federal and state regulations and professional standards governing the conduct of research with human participants.

a. In planning a study, the investigator has the responsibility to make a careful evaluation of its ethical acceptability. To the extent that the weighing of scientific and human values suggests a compromise of any principle, the investigator incurs a correspondingly serious obligation to seek ethical advice and to observe stringent safeguards to protect the rights of human participants.

b. Considering whether a participant in a planned study will be a "subject at risk" or a "subject at minimal risk," according to recognized standards, is a primary ethical concern to the investigator.

c. The investigator always retains the responsibility for assuring ethical practice in research. The investigator is also responsible for the ethical treatment of research participants by collaborators, assistants, students, and employees, all of whom, however, incur similar obligations.

d. Except in minimal-risk research, the investigator establishes a clear and fair agreement with research participants, prior to their participation, that clarifies the obligations and responsibilities of each. The investigator has the obligation to honor all promises and commitments included in that agreement. The investigator informs the participants of all aspects of the research that might reasonably be expected to influence willingness to participate and explains all other aspects of the research about which the participants inquire. Failure to make full disclosure prior to obtaining informed consent requires additional safeguards to protect the welfare and dignity of the research participants. Research with children or with participants who have impairments that would limit understanding and/or communication requires special safeguarding procedures.

e. Methodological requirements of a study may make the use of concealment or deception necessary. Before conducting such a study, the investigator has a special responsibility to (i) determine whether the use of such techniques is justified by the study's prospective scientific, educational, or applied value; (ii) determine whether alternative procedures are available that do not use concealment or deception; and (iii) ensure that the participants are provided with sufficient explanation as soon as possible.

f. The investigator respects the individual's freedom to decline to participate in or to withdraw from the research at any time. The obligation to protect this freedom requires careful thought and consideration when the investigator is in a position of authority or influence over the participant. Such positions of authority include, but are not limited to, situations in which research participation is required as part of employment or in which the participant is a student, client, or employee of the investigator.

g. The investigator protects the participant from physical and mental discomfort, harm, and danger that may arise from research procedures. If risks of such consequence exist, the investigator informs the participant of that fact. Research procedures likely to cause serious or lasting harm to a participant are not used unless the failure to use these procedures might expose the participant to risk of greater harm, or unless the research has great potential benefit and fully informed and voluntary consent is obtained from each participant. The participant should be informed of procedures for contacting the investigator within a reasonable time period following participation should stress, potential harm, or related questions or concerns arise.

h. After the data are collected, the investigator provides the participant with information about the nature of the study and attempts to remove any misconceptions that may have arisen. Where scientific or humane values justify delaying or withholding this information, the investigator incurs a special responsibility to monitor the research and to ensure that there are no damaging consequences for the participant.

i. Where research procedures result in undesirable consequences for the individual participant, the investigator has the responsibility to detect and remove or correct these consequences, including long-term effects.

j. Information obtained about a research participant during the course of an investigation is confidential unless otherwise agreed upon in advance. When the possibility exists that others may obtain access to such information, this possibility, together with the plans for protecting confidentiality, is explained to the participant as part of the procedure for obtaining informed consent.

*Principle 10: Care and Use of Animals*

An investigator of animal behavior strives to advance understanding of basic behavioral principles and/or to contribute to the improvement of human health and welfare. In seeking these ends, the investigator ensures the welfare of animals and treats them humanely. Laws and regulations notwithstanding, an animal's immediate protection depends upon the scientist's own conscience.

a. The acquisition, care, use and disposal of all animals are in compliance with current federal, state or provincial, and local laws and regulations.

b. A psychologist trained in research methods and experienced in the care of laboratory animals closely supervises all procedures involving animals and is responsible for ensuring appropriate consideration of their comfort, health, and humane treatment.

c. Psychologists ensure that all individuals using animals under their supervision have received explicit instruction in experimental methods and in the care, maintenance, and handling of the species being used. Responsibilities and activities of individuals participating in a research project are consistent with their respective competencies.

d. Psychologists make every effort to minimize discomfort, illness, and pain of animals. A procedure subjecting animals to pain, stress, or privation is used only when an alternative procedure is unavailable and the goal is justified by its prospective scientific, educational, or applied value. Surgical procedures are performed under appropriate anesthesia; techniques to avoid infection and minimize pain are followed during and after surgery.

e. When it is appropriate that an animal's life be terminated, it is done rapidly and painlessly.

## American Sociological Association

In its *Code of Ethics,* the ASA (1984, 1) includes the following statements in its preamble:

> . . . As a discipline committed to the free and open access to knowledge and to self regulation through peer review and appraisal, sociology shares with other disciplines the commitment to the pursuit of accurate and precise knowledge and to public disclosure of findings. However, because sociology necessarily entails study of individuals, groups, organizations and societies, these principles may occasionally conflict with more general ethical concerns for the rights of subjects to privacy and for the treatment of subjects with due regard for their

integrity, dignity and autonomy. This potential conflict provides one of the justifications for a code of ethics.

The styles of sociological work are diverse and changing. So also are the contexts within which sociologists find employment. These diversities of procedures and context have led to ambiguities concerning appropriate professional behavior. These ambiguities provide another justification for this code. . . .

The "Sociological Research and Practice" section (pp. 1–3) covers these topics: (a) objectivity and integrity, (b) sociologists' use of their disciplinary roles, (c) cross-national research, (d) work outside of academic settings, and (e) respect for rights of research populations.

The introduction to the topic of cross-national research (p. 2) states:

Research conducted in foreign countries raises special ethical issues for the investigator and the professional. Disparities in wealth, power, and political systems between the researcher's country and the host country may create problems of equity in research collaboration and conflicts of interest for the visiting scholar. Also, to follow the precepts of the scientific method—such as those requiring full disclosure—may entail adverse consequences or personal risks for individuals and groups in the host country. Finally, irresponsible actions by a single researcher or research team can eliminate or reduce future access to a country by the entire profession and its allied fields.

Another section is "Publications and Review Process."

## Society for Research in Child Development

In its "Ethical Standards for Research with Children," the SRCD (1973) lists 21 principles. Some points made in selected principles are these:

The child must be free to participate or not (a freedom which is to be based on informed consent on the part of the child, its parents or guardians, and those persons whose interaction with the child is a focus of inquiry).

The investigator must honor all commitments and not harm the child either physically or psychologically.

Full disclosure is the ideal. When a particular methodology requires deception, a committee must give prior approval, and corrective action must be taken afterward.

All information must be kept confidential.

Special safeguards must be taken when consulting institutional records.

Because the investigator's words may carry unintended weight with parents and children, caution should be exercised in reporting results.

## LEGISLATION

### The Buckley Amendment

Many of the ethical guidelines developed by the professional associations were translated into law when the Buckley Amendment became effective in November 1974. This amendment, entitled Protection of the Rights and Privacy of Parents and Students, was introduced by Senator James Buckley as an amendment to the 1974 elementary and secondary education bill (General Education Provisions Act).

The Buckley Amendment requires institutions, under the penalty of losing federal funds, to provide parents and students aged 18 or enrolled in college access to all official files, records, and data containing information directly related to the students. This material specifically includes, but is not necessarily limited to, identifying data; academic work completed; level of achievement (grades, standardized achievement scores); attendance data; scores on standardized intelligence, aptitude, and psychological tests; interest inventory results; health data; family background information; teacher or counselor ratings and observations; and verified reports of serious or recurrent behavior patterns.

This amendment also gives parents and eligible students the right for a hearing to challenge any portion of the records that may appear "inaccurate, misleading, or otherwise inappropriate." Confidentiality of the records is assured by prohibiting schools from releasing them to third parties without a parent's or student's written consent.

The U.S. Office of Education and professional organizations have set up guidelines for use in complying with this law. Critics of the Buckley Amendment object to its lack of clarity in areas such as letters of recommendation, "official" files, and research. The curbs on data-gathering activities and the protection of "personally identifiable" data, such as social security numbers, could hamper evaluation and make longitudinal research studies virtually impossible (Trotter 1974). A federal attorney commented that "research will be much more cumbersome administratively and that the opportunity for naturalistic experimentation will be eliminated" (Davis 1975). The amount and kinds of data maintained by schools also may be curtailed.

The Buckley Amendment was presented and passed because thousands of letters were sent to national organizations by parents who expressed concern with their children's records being given to third parties by schools (Davis 1975). In proposing his amendment, Senator Buckley cited examples of abuses in the preparation and handling of student records. These examples point up the serious consequences of a nonscientific approach to observing and recording data on children. On the other hand, many professional researchers are suffering from the results of these abuses. It has been suggested that it may be in order to press for the passage of legislation to protect the rights of ethical researchers (Davis 1975).

### National Research Act of 1974

The National Research Act of 1974 mandated the establishment of the National Commission for the Protection of Human Subjects of Biomedical and Behavioral Research to make recommendations to the Health, Education, and Welfare Department (HEW, which is now HHS, Health and Human Services) concerning guidelines for the protection of human research subjects. It also stipulates that any institution applying for funds from HEW must have established an institutional review board "to review all biomedical and behavioral research involving human subjects conducted at or sponsored by" the institution. Such reviews are to consider (1) whether the research subjects are at risk, (2) whether the risks are outweighed by any benefit to the subject or by the importance of knowledge gained, (3) that the right and welfare of the subjects will be adequately protected, (4) that legally effective informed consent will be obtained, and (5) that the research will be reviewed at timely intervals.

The National Commission for the Protection of Human Subjects of Biomedical and Behavioral Research (1977) submitted a report entitled *Report and Recommendations—Research Involving Children.*

## INFORMED CONSENT

A federal regulation (Federal Register 1981, 8389) defines the elements of informed consent as follows:

> 1. A statement that the study involves research, an explanation of the purposes of the research and the expected duration of the subject's participation, a description of the procedures to be followed, and identification of any procedures which are experimental;
> 2. A description of any reasonably foreseeable risks of discomfort to the subject;
> 3. A description of any benefits to the subject or to others which may reasonably be expected from the research;
> 4. A disclosure of appropriate alternative procedures or courses of treatment, if any, that might be advantageous to the subject;
> 5. A statement describing the extent, if any, to which confidentiality or records identifying the subject will be maintained;
> 6. For research involving more than minimal risk, an explanation as to whether any compensation and an explanation as to whether any medical treatments are available if injury occurs and, if so, what they consist of or where further information may be obtained;

7. An explanation of whom to contact for answers to pertinent questions about the research and research subjects' rights, and whom to contact in the event of a research-related injury to the subject; and

8. A statement that participation is voluntary, refusal to participate will involve no penalty or loss of benefits to which the subject is otherwise entitled, and the subject may discontinue participation at any time without penalty or loss of benefits to which the subject is otherwise entitled.

The 1981 federal regulations provide for the recognition that not all social research can be conducted with informed consent (Sieber 1982a). An institutional review board may approve a consent procedure that omits or alters some of the informed consent elements if the research does not involve more than minimal risk to subjects, if the rights and welfare of subjects will not be adversely affected, and if (whenever appropriate) additional pertinent information is provided the subjects after participation.

In addition, the 1981 federal regulations exempt many categories of social research from institutional review board examination. These exemptions include all research not funded by the U.S. Department of Health and Human Services; research on "normal educational practices" that is conducted in schools; and survey and interview research and research employing cognitive, diagnostic, aptitude, and achievement tests *except* where individual subjects can be identified. Inasmuch as federal regulations are amended periodically, the researcher is responsible for being informed of current regulations prior to conducting research studies.[2] (Informed consent for children as research subjects is discussed in a later section.)

## PRIVACY AND CONFIDENTIALITY

Maintaining privacy and confidentiality is an ethical obligation of researchers and others having access to personal information about human beings. Privacy applies to persons, and confidentiality applies to data. Privacy is maintained when people can control who has access to information about them or who may intrude into their lives. Confidentiality, an extension of the concept of privacy, refers to agreements between individuals that limit others' access to private information. A research subject may agree to disclose private information if the researcher promises not to provide others with access to data that would identify individual subjects (Sieber 1982a).

Various threats to the individual's rights to privacy do occur. In some instances, information is obtained about people without their knowledge. In other instances, information may be obtained with the informed consent of the subject and passed on to third parties by the investigator at a later time. Requests for individual information gathered through research may come from many sources, including the research participant's friends and relatives, employers, teachers, data banks, and law enforcement officers.

### Subpoena of Confidential Records

No promise made by a researcher to maintain confidentiality of data can legally withstand a subpoena from a court of law (unless the researcher is willing to refuse and accept the consequences), although the Privacy Commission has recommended to Congress that government-collected or government-sponsored research data be protected by statute so that data for research could not be used against a research subject. Some states have enacted statutes that protect certain types of research data in limited areas, but none of the statutes applies to all of social research. Both research data and consent forms can be subpoenaed. Therefore, consent forms sometimes protect the researcher at the expense of the research participant. In studies such as those dealing with prostitution, alcohol and drug abuse, gambling, and criminal behavior, a subpoena could be fateful for the research participant (Bond 1978).

### Social Responsibility versus Ethical Procedures

A dilemma with serious implications for the issues of privacy and confidentiality involves discovering, during the progress of research, personal problems of the subject that the investigator believes need the attention of others. In such cases with children, the question is often raised as to whether parents, teachers, or others should be notified (Keith-Spiegle 1976). Guidelines of the SRCD (1973, 5) state: "When, in the course of research, information comes to the investigator's attention that may seriously affect the child's well-being, the investigator has the responsibility to discuss the information with those expert in the field in order that the parents may arrange the necessary assistance for the child."

## EQUIPMENT AND TECHNOLOGY

Advances in scientific technology have made it possible to observe and record data on the characteristics and behavior of individuals to the extent that the public is expressing increasing concern over threats to personal freedom. Concealable tape recorders, small photographic and TV cameras, extension telephones, one-way vision screens, drugs, and computerized information in data banks are examples of widely used techniques.

Data banks are especially threatening to the maintenance of confidentiality. A *data bank* is defined as "any collection of coded information about individuals that is kept in a form so that the information is easily retrievable, often by automatic means" (APA 1973, 93). Because access to data is so much easier when data are computerized than when they are retained in manual records and because the researchers and others collecting data lose control of their data, ethical concerns arise. If information in the data bank identifies individuals, the data could be used to the disadvantage of these individuals; people with access to the data may not be adequately trained to interpret the data; and the data may be used later for purposes for which the subjects did not consent. Before contributing data to data banks, investigators must assure themselves that safeguards exist to protect confidentiality and the anonymity of the subjects.

In addition to research data, many other types of information are stored in data banks, including employee records, medical records, and credit information. Departments or agencies of the federal government as well as many private agencies maintain files on billions of people. In a 1974 report of a four-year study on the extent and nature of personal data collection in federal agencies, a Senate Subcommittee on Constitutional Rights commented that 54 agencies had reported 858 data banks containing more than 1.25 billion records on individuals (Kelley and Weston 1975).

The use of automated data systems is the wave of the future in health care. In about half of the states, psychiatric information in data banks has been directly matched to names or social security numbers. However, a better trend is emerging in some states where community health centers are refraining from placing identifiable personal confidential information in computer data banks. Some are using code numbers assigned at the treatment facility and are decoding the information only at the mental health facility where the person is served (Kelley and Weston 1975).

## PROBLEMS WITH SOME RESEARCH DESIGNS, STRATEGIES, AND SETTINGS

Professional ethics in conducting research have been discussed primarily with respect to general ethical guidelines of informed consent to participate in such research, anonymity of subjects, and confidentiality of data. The actual design of the research studies and the reliability and validity of the instruments used are seldom mentioned in ethical guidelines. The issues of adequate experimental design, analysis procedures, and interpretation of results are often considered to be different from ethical issues. Yet, as Rutstein (1969, 524) explains: "When a study is in itself scientifically invalid, all other ethical considerations become irrelevant. There is no point in obtaining 'informed consent' to perform a useless study. A worthless study cannot possibly benefit anyone, least of all the experimental subject himself. Any risk to the patient, however small, cannot be justified. In essence, the scientific validity of a study on human beings is in itself an ethical principle."

There are some special problems associated with certain research designs, strategies, and settings.

## Field Studies

Studying behavior in natural settings presents ethical problems, particularly when individuals are observed through the use of one-way vision screens or other equipment without their knowledge or consent, or through the participant observation method if the observer has not been identified as someone doing research.[3] In an attempt to overcome subjects' self-conscious control or concealment of real feelings when the presence of an observer is known, some researchers mingle secretly with subjects, become participants with them (as patients, drug addicts, etc.), and establish relationships with them in order to elicit information. There is little need for ethical concern when participant observers clearly identify themselves and their purposes upon joining the group (Brandt 1972). Children are routinely subjected to observation through one-way vision screens, in many instances without their knowledge.

Disguised and undisguised participation studies range along a continuum, so there is no absolute cutoff where they definitely become unethical. There is no general agreement among social scientists about whether disguised participant observation is justified. However, Diener and Crandall (1978, 125–26) suggest several safeguards to minimize detrimental effects if a researcher decides to proceed with a disguised observation study:

> 1. Deceive as little as possible. Do not deceive subjects when it serves little purpose, and remember that it is better to let others draw incorrect conclusions or simply be ignorant of your scientific study than to actively lie.
>
> 2. Enter private spheres with the maximum informed consent consonant with the research goals. When a private sphere has been observed without the participants' knowledge, obtain their informed consent post hoc whenever possible.
>
> 3. Plan procedures that absolutely guarantee subject anonymity, especially in published reports. One safeguard, especially where sensitive information is reported, is to let the subjects read a draft of the report and point out any passages they feel were given in confidence or any statements that might jeopardize their anonymity.
>
> 4. Review the potential influences of the observers on the group and rework the study if any negative consequences are foreseen.

5. Fully inform research assistants about the research before it begins and give them free choice whether to participate.

6. Consider whether the study could cause indignant outrage against social science, thus hampering other research endeavors. If so, consider canceling the study or using a different methodology.

## Experiments

As indicated in Chapter 8, the purpose of experiments is to test hypotheses about the effects of certain treatments or interventions on specific characteristics of individuals or objects. In most experiments, the treatment is given to the experimental group but not to the control group. As mentioned in Chapter 12, ethical questions may exist when an intervention believed to be useful is withheld from subjects who are in need of the benefits of the treatment. For example, a longitudinal study comparing the effects of an inadequate diet on the cognitive development of children who received supplemental diets (experimental group) and children who are "naturally" poorly nourished (control group) would raise ethical questions, especially since the deleterious effects of malnutrition on cognitive development have already been established. One solution in both biomedical and psychological research is to use the best known treatment on the control group for comparison with the effects of the experimental treatment (Rutstein 1969). In studies of shorter duration, another possibility is to provide the treatment to the control group after the investigation is completed, thereby meeting the scientific need of not contaminating the data and at the same time meeting the ethical need of providing a beneficial intervention to all subjects.

Deception is another issue in many experimental investigations.

Discussions of these and other ethical problems in experiments are discussed at length in the literature.[4]

## Surveys

Nonexperimental studies such as surveys face the major ethical problem of privacy and confidentiality. Obtaining a valid sample usually requires access to lists or files that may in itself breach privacy or confidentiality. Then, once the subject is contacted, the researcher must be able to guarantee that these rights will be safeguarded. This is especially important in view of the fact that most survey research requires voluntary cooperation. Before any data can be collected in a survey, such as an interview study, the respondents should be provided certain essential information, including the sponsoring organization and the name of the person collecting the data, the general purpose of the study and how the data will be used, the extent to which responses are confidential, and the voluntary nature of the study and the respondents' freedom to omit questions they prefer not to answer. Since minimal risks are usually incurred in surveys, research consent forms are not always used.

Fowler (1984, 137) has outlined eight standard procedures that minimize breaches of confidentiality:

> 1. All people who have access to the data or a role in the data collection should be committed in writing to confidentiality.
>
> 2. Minimize links between answers and identifiers. Names or addresses are the most common identifiers. Often names are not required in order to execute a proper survey. When they can be avoided, many survey organizations do not use names in any part of the research process. When there are specific identifiers such as names or addresses, they are put on pieces of paper (or coversheets) that can be separated physically from the interview schedule in which the actual survey responses are recorded.
>
> 3. Completed interview schedules should not be accessible to nonproject members.
>
> 4. Identifiers should be removed from completed questionnaires if nonstaff people are going to look at them; it is common to remove them as soon as possible in any case.
>
> 5. Individuals who could identify respondents from their profile of answers, such as supervisors in the case of a survey of employees or teachers in the case of a survey of students, should not be permitted to see the actual questionnaire responses.
>
> 6. The actual data files usually will have some kind of an ID number for each respondent. The link between the ID number and the sample addresses or the identifiers should not be available to general users of the data file.
>
> 7. During analysis, researchers should be careful about presenting data for very small categories of people who might be identifiable.
>
> 8. When a project is completed, or when use of the actual survey questionnaire is over, it is the responsibility of the researcher to see to the eventual destruction of completed survey research instruments, or their continuing secure storage.

Sieber (1982a, 147) has indicated that survey researchers have developed a variety of approaches in order to protect privacy and confidentiality: "For example, some social scientists have employed empirical methods to assess what subjects consider as private and to learn under what conditions students are willing to disclose private information candidly. Some have developed a range of sampling methods that minimize invasion of privacy without jeopardizing the validity of the sample. Others have fought legal shields or other procedures that protect data from subpoena. Still others have devised statistical and procedural devices for collecting and maintaining data that do not include unique identifiers but that retain scientific usefulness nevertheless."[5]

## Behavior Modification Research

Behavior modification (sometimes called behavioral technology, behavior therapy, applied behavior analysis, contingency management, or conditioning therapy) is being used increasingly in schools, clinics, mental hospitals, vocational and industrial settings, and social planning. Behavior modification involves measuring the occurrence of the behavior to be changed and of the desired behavior. It is based on a model of human behavior that assumes that human behavior follows natural laws and that behavior is an adaptation of people to their circumstances. Moreover, it holds that behavior can be changed or modified through the application of learning principles. Behavior modification research generally involves observation in the setting where the problem behavior occurs (Stoltz et al. 1978).

The practice of behavior modification and behavior modification research (typically single-case designs) are fraught with ethical questions, for many view such control over people as a machinelike process suppressing individual freedom. Critics have expressed concern over some of the technical terms used, such as *shaping, reinforcement,* and *control,* and over the use of punishment or unpleasant stimuli or denial of privileges. Proponents argue that all types of psychological interventions attempt to control people's behavior. Less formally, people's behavior is also controlled or influenced by education, advertising, and political campaigns. As Bandura (1975, 185) puts it, "The basic moral question is not whether man's behavior will be controlled, but rather by whom, by what means, and for what ends."

Both the courts and Congress have been actively involved in issues dealing with behavior modification. The Senate Subcommittee on Constitutional Rights of the Committee of the Judiciary published a report of over 600 pages based upon a three-year investigation of behavior modification. This report documents the extent of federal support for behavior modification research, criticizes the government's involvement in such projects, and calls for "continuing legislative oversight . . . to ensure that constitutional rights and privacy are well protected" when behavior modification is used (U.S. Congress 1974). The National Commission for the Protection of Human Subjects (1975) was also charged with investigating the implications for the protection of subjects of "research advances such as behavior modification."

The APA established a Commission on Behavior Modification that identified issues of importance in considering psychological interventions:

identification of the client; definition of the problem and selection of goals; selection of the intervention method; accountability; evaluation of the quality of the psychologist and the intervention; record keeping and confidentiality; protection of client's rights; assessment of the place of research in therapeutic settings.[6]

### Longitudinal Research

The major features distinguishing longitudinal research from most other types of research is the continuation of the relationship between the investigator and subject over an extended period of time, even for many years. Maintaining confidentiality becomes more difficult when subjects must be contacted over a period of years. A coded system (with identities of subjects secured in a locked file with access limited to authorized personnel only) is most commonly used to protect confidentiality. Since losing subjects is a serious problem in a longitudinal study, the researcher too often pressures subjects to remain involved in the study.

### Cross-cultural Research

In addition to problems encountered in various research settings and designs, the researcher conducting investigations in other cultures may face some different ethical dilemmas. For instance, cross-cultural research usually involves situations in which the researcher and the subjects do not share the same culture (i.e., language, customs, laws, value systems). Therefore, in these investigations, the investigator should strive to understand and demonstrate respect for the local culture and the values of the people being studied. Moreover, the researcher should be sensitive to possible political uses of the findings and be prepared to explain any such implications. Bochner (1980) has recommended two general ethical principles of cross-cultural research with human subjects. First, the researcher should not do anything that might harm the subjects or lower their self-esteem. Second, participation in the study should enrich the participants in some way and benefit the culture providing the data materially, practically, or theoretically.[7]

## DECEPTION

*Informed consent* implies that a subject has been told about the procedures to be followed in a study in which he or she has been asked to agree to participate. Yet, *concealment* (withholding information from the subject) and *deception* (misinforming the subject) are frequently practiced by behavioral scientists. Deception is difficult to defend unless it is absolutely essential for the validity of the research findings that the subject be unaware of what is being investigated.

Diener and Crandall (1978, 72) give fictitious behavioral experiments as examples similar to those actually staged by psychologists. The following example was designed to confirm a theory about how adults react to and protect small children. It is a good illustration of the use of deception in research:

> Sunbathers soak up the warm Florida sunshine while children build sand castles and collect shells up and down the beach. The water is warm and calm; swimmers float lazily about as a group of teen-agers splash by. Suddenly the beach erupts into pandemonium, as the cry "Shark!" sounds out. Swimmers rush madly for shore; parents scramble to grab confused children who are playing in the shallow water. Everyone who is safely on the beach stares toward the azure water, trembling, trying to spot the shark or perhaps a victim of his jaws.

### Debriefing

In dealing with college students and adults, investigators typically handle the ethical problems of studies involving deception by a *debriefing* procedure (carefully explaining the reason for the deception after the study is over). (Mills 1976 has provided some general instructions for debriefing.) In research with young children, debriefing is not an adequate solution, for a full explanation of procedures to them is seldom desirable (Smith 1967). However, results of one study on the effects of deception and debriefing on fifth grade children's attitudes concluded that children generally viewed participation favorably and that debriefing, in contrast to encouraging children's skepticism, influenced children to view the value of experimentation more positively (Weissbrod and Mangan 1978). Generally positive evaluations of experiments involving deception and debriefing also were made in a study of college students' reactions (Gerdes 1979).

## USE OF CHILDREN IN RESEARCH

Although some of the principles of SRCD (1973) were mentioned earlier, further discussion about children as research subjects is pertinent. Attitudes toward children's rights fall within two different frameworks, one dealing with their rights to be nurtured and one dealing with their rights to self-determination. The issues involved are complex and the opinions diverse. Children are persons, not objects, but they do not have the experience and judgment of adults. Therefore, the right of self-determination must be related to the developmental level of the child and the type of determination or judgment required of him or her. Children's rights also depend upon cultural values and norms.

In considering children's rights as research subjects, the application of informed consent becomes an important issue involving the question of their capacity for self-determination. HEW (HHS) guidelines specify that no child of "sufficient understanding" should be required to take part in a nonbeneficial research activity without giving consent (or assent) (National Commission for the Protection of Human Subjects 1975). The assessment of sufficient understanding creates a problem. Such a determination must be based upon our current knowledge of the child's cognitive development. The requirement of consent by parents or legal guardians prior to research participation of children is intended to protect the rights of those whose capacity is not sufficiently developed for informed consent. However, parental consent is sufficient only for infants and very small children. For older children, both parental consent and the consent of the child are required.

The establishment of a specific chronological age for sufficient understanding for informed consent is unsatisfactory because children's rates of development differ. However, the Buckley Amendment provides parents of children and students aged 18 or enrolled in college access to students' official records, and the British Medical Research Council specifies age 12 as the age criterion for sufficient understanding. HEW (HHS) has proposed that the "age of discretion" for children be set at 7 years.

Ferguson (1978) sets forth some special considerations that apply to four developmental groups. For research with infants and toddlers, she believes that only parental consent is necessary. If preschool and primary-age children are used, both parental consent and a very general explanation of the activity to the child (e.g., "We want to find out more about how children play or what they think about things") are required. With preadolescents (school-age children), informed consent should be obtained directly from the youngsters, including the signing of appropriate consent forms, after parental consent has been granted. For purposes of research participation, adolescents should be treated as adults, although those who are still minors legally must also have consent of their parents. Since children pose special problems for investigation, in addition to the matter of informed consent, those planning to do research with children are obliged to consult some of the many good references on this topic.[8]

## USE OF ANIMALS IN RESEARCH

An explosive conflict is brewing between animal rights groups, some of which protest any use of animals in research, and the biomedical and social scientific community, who point out that animal research is basic to programs in the fields of medicine and human behavior and development.[9] It is generally agreed that regulations and inspection procedures governing the care and treatment of laboratory animals should be tightened.

### Federal Animal Welfare Act of 1966

Although the Federal Animal Welfare Act of 1966 does not cover actual research, it addresses various aspects of transporting, selling, and housing some animals used in research. Under this act, all animals housed by universities, medical schools, hospitals, and research centers are monitored by the U.S. Department of Agriculture. USDA representatives make unannounced inspections regarding standards for housing, feeding, cleanliness, ventilation, and veterinary medical care.

### American Association for Accreditation of Laboratory Animal Care

The American Association for Accreditation of Laboratory Animal Care has been sponsored by the scientific community since 1965. Its rigorous standards are followed by approximately 450 institutions. Many research centers also have their own internal review committees for inspection of animal facilities and insurance of humane treatment of animals.

### U.S. Public Health Service

A two-year review by NIH (National Institutes of Health) of an animal care policy adopted in 1979 resulted in a new policy, which took effect in November 1985. The 1985 policy requires recipients of Public Health Service research grants to conform to more stringent standards. NIH (which is part of the Public Health Service) is charged with the administration of the policy. The policy is expected to have a broad impact on biomedical researchers, since nearly one-half of NIH-supported research projects involve the use of live animals.

The 1985 policy differs from the 1979 policy in five major areas (McDonald 1985):

> Institutions will be required to designate an official who is responsible for the institution's laboratory-animal program. In addition, a veterinarian qualified in laboratory-animal medicine must participate in the program.

The roles and responsibilities of the university committees responsible for reviewing institutions' animal programs will be upgraded and expanded. Also, the committees must now include a person not affiliated with the institution, a veterinarian with training or experience in the care and use of laboratory animals, a practicing scientist with experience in research involving animals, and a member whose primary concerns are in a nonscientific area.

Institutions will be required to provide the NIH detailed information about their programs for the care and use of research animals. NIH officials said the information will be used to assess an institution's commitment to animal welfare and its ability to comply with the agent's policy.

Each institution's animal-care committee will be required to review and approve sections on the care and use of animals that are contained in grant applications. Agency officials said they will not support research involving animals until such approval is documented.

Institutions that are not accredited by the American Association for Accreditation of Laboratory Animal Care will be required to conduct a self-assessment of their animal-research programs according to criteria listed in the *NIH Guide for the Care and Use of Laboratory Animals*. Deficiencies in an institution's program must be reported to the NIH and must be corrected within a specified amount of time.

## 1986 American Psychological Association Guidelines

The APA (1986) recently adopted comprehensive guidelines for the use of nonhuman animals (vertebrates) in research. The guidelines are based upon APA (1981) Principle 10, "Care and Use of Animals," presented earlier in the chapter. Some of the points addressed in the new guidelines are summarized here:

1. General (e.g., compliance with relevant international, federal, state, local, and institutional laws and regulations; posting of guidelines; reporting of violations)
2. Personnel (e.g., supervision by a researcher experienced in the care and use of lab animals, consultation and inspection by a veterinarian, maintenance of records of procedures with animals)
3. Facilities (e.g., conformity with specifications in the *NIH Guide for the Care and Use of Laboratory Animals,* utilization of local institutional animal care and use committees)
4. Requisition of animals (e.g., breeding of animals for lab use, lawful acquisition of animals, procedures for taking animals from the wild)
5. Care and housing of animals (e.g., healthful conditions; enriching environments, where possible)

6. Justification of the research (e.g., clear scientific purpose, prior approval of a review committee, consideration of alternatives to use of animals)

7. Experimental design (e.g., suitability of the species for the research, use of species that will suffer the least discomfort, utilization of the minimum number of animals necessary)

8. Experimental procedures (e.g., anesthetization of animals during procedures, close supervision of surgical procedures, employment of minimal deprivation procedures)

9. Field research (e.g., minimization of harmful effects on the population, plants, and animals in the area; respect for property and privacy of inhabitants in the area; procurement of necessary permits for research with endangered species)

10. Educational use of animals (e.g., review by animal care and use committee, utilization of audio-visual and other alternatives, instruction in the ethical use of animals in research)

11. Disposition of animals (e.g., use of alternatives to euthanasia; use of humane procedures where euthanasia is indicated; verification of death before disposal according to existing legislative, health, environment, and other concerns)

All investigators using animals in research should become thoroughly familiar with these guidelines.

## RESEARCH ON ENVIRONMENTAL STRESS

The area of human ecology dealing with environmental stressors such as crowding poses special ethical problems for researchers. The majority of the research studies on crowding have been laboratory studies conducted in university settings with "nonvulnerable" subjects. The generalization of findings from this population to "vulnerable" populations in the real world may be invalid, resulting in social injury. Scientific validity requires empirical evidence of any adverse effects of crowding, but the scientist is obligated to avoid causing harm to subjects. Yet, study of vulnerable populations in their natural settings poses threats to privacy and autonomy, since these populations have little control over investigators, who could observe, misinterpret, and publish information about their lives (Loo 1982). Of course, it is these populations that are most likely to live under crowded conditions, so studies of them have much greater social relevance and benefits. The major dilemma for researchers of environmental stress, therefore, involves a conflict between their responsibility to society and their responsibility to the welfare of research participants.

A *vulnerable population* is a population of persons who, relative to the majority of society, have less power, opportunity, or freedom to determine outcomes in their lives or to make decisions that affect their situation because of their age, physical or mental condition, race, economic or political position, or captive status. Loo (1982) suggests numerous procedures for protecting participants' rights in conducting case studies with vulnerable populations in crowding research in both laboratory and cultural settings. In the concluding paragraph, Loo (1982, 125) states, "The solution lies in conducting scientifically valid research, using procedures that are sensitive to the populations studied, conducting research in a setting that is appropriate to the variables studied and to the populations most likely to be affected by the research findings."

## ETHICAL CONSIDERATIONS IN RESEARCH SPONSORSHIP

Funds for use in conducting research in human ecology may be received from numerous organizations in the public and private sectors of society: federal and state governments; institutions (e.g., hospitals, school systems); or from private industries (e.g., drug producers, the food industry, hotel industry, retailers). Ethical concerns arising from this research sponsorship include questions regarding the sponsor's mission and administrative controls, the misuse of research results by the sponsoring organization, the possible restriction on access to research data, and the responsibility for publishing or otherwise using research results. The investigator should ensure that the scientific integrity of the research process is not compromised by such influences. Before undertaking sponsored research, the investigator should be informed of the funding organization's expectations concerning the immediate and open publication of research findings and of any possibility of delayed publication or censorship of results.

## RISKS VERSUS BENEFITS

The literature on ethical guidelines for use in studying humans is replete with concerns for the need to protect subjects participating in investigations from physical and psychological harm. Relatively less consideration is given to the benefits accruing from such participation, although federal regulations do specify that the risk to subjects should be weighed against the benefits from proposed research.

One's attitudes regarding risks versus benefits in considering approaches to scientific study depend not only upon one's views of science, but also upon one's general ethical philosophy. Schlenker and Forsyth

(1977) have examined and contrasted three philosophical positions on the nature of ethics within the context of psychological research: teleology, deontology, and skepticism.

*Teleology* considers the balancing of the potential benefits of research (e.g., advancement of science, beneficial technological applications, advantages to subjects) against the potential costs (e.g., harm to subjects, detrimental technological applications). The APA's *Ethical Principles in the Conduct of Research with Human Participants* maintains a teleological position: "The general ethical question always is whether there is a negative effect upon the dignity and welfare of the participants that the importance of research does not warrant" (APA 1973, 11).

The *deontology* ethical position involves the adherence to rigid, universal rules that hold irrespective of the situation or consequences. Theologian Paul Ramsey (1970) is close to the deontology position in asserting that the ethical justification for research must rest with the rigid application of the patient-benefiting principle. For example, in research with young subjects, proxy consent (by parents) is acceptable only when the child stands to benefit from the experimental procedure.

In contrast, *skepticism* denies the ability to apply universal rules and asserts the individuality of moral codes.

It is impossible to do justice to such an important topic in a brief chapter. Therefore, the reader is encouraged to consult some of the numerous references available on research ethics and to stay abreast of recent developments in this area through professional journals and organizational newsletters.[10] It is a special privilege to conduct research—one that requires a professional attitude and strict adherence to ethical guidelines.

## NOTES

1. Other codes of professional ethics and practices that are relevant to research in human ecology include those by the National Council on Public Polls, the American Association for Public Opinion Research (both of these lists of guidelines have been reproduced in Frey 1983), and the Division of Developmental Psychology of the APA (APA, Division 7, 1968). The reader should write directly to these and other associations for their latest codes of ethics.

2. Most universities, and even some academic departments within institutions, have research committees to review *all* proposed studies involving live subjects, whether the investigation is funded or nonfunded. See Beauchamp et al. (1982, 329–415) and Ceci, Peters, and Platkin (1985) for further discussion of the use of institutional review boards and the regulation of research.

3. For sources that deal with the special problems associated with field studies, see Appell (1978), Emerson (1981), Filstead (1970), Kimmel (1988), LaRossa, Bennett, and Gelles (1981),

Punch (1986), Ruback (1986), Rynkiewich and Spradley (1976), Sieber (1982b), van Maanen (1983), Webb et al. (1981), and Whyte (1984, 193–223). For references on the ethics of evaluation studies, see Conner (1982), Diener and Crandall (1978, 127–47), Fetterman (1984, 211–35), Warren (1980), and Windle and Neigher (1978).

4. See Diener and Crandall (1978, 127–47), Riecken and Boruch (1974, 245–69), Roberts (1983), and Sieber (1982a).

5. See Sieber (1982a) for specific illustrations of these methods; also Kelman (1982, 79–82) and Tremblay and Dillman (1977) for discussions of the ethical dilemmas faced by survey researchers.

6. For a discussion of these and other issues, see Feldman and Peay (1982), Stolz (1975), and Stolz et al. (1978).

7. Ethical considerations in cross-cultural research are addressed in Diener and Crandall (1978, 101–15), Reynolds (1979, 218–24), Tapp (1972), and Tapp et al. (1974).

8. Cooke (1982), Ferguson (1978), Frankel (1978), Rheingold (1982), Rosen, Rekers, and Bentler (1978), and Smith (1967) are only a few of the many good references in this area. Of course, researchers using children as subjects should also become acquainted with the SRCD (1973) and APA, Division 7 (1968) guidelines.

9. Space limitations preclude presentation of both sides of this argument. Researchers who are anticipating the use of animals in their research should become familiar with the literature in this area, however. Coile and Miller (1984), Fox (1986), Garfield (1984), Miller (1985), Rollin (1985), Russell and Burch (1959), and Ryder (1975) are representative of the books and articles written on the topic.

10. Some good general references on ethical guidelines for research are Beauchamp et al. (1982), Boruch and Cecil (1979), Bower and de Gasparis (1978), Diener and Crandall (1978), Reynolds (1979, 1982), Sieber (1982a, 1982b), Sjoberg (1967), and Useem and Marx (1983). An informative paper on ethical regulations and their impact on research practice has been written by Adair, Dushenko, and Lindsay (1985).

For a discussion of researcher's ethical and social responsibility to conduct investigations that are free from sexist and heterosexist bias, see Stark-Adamec and Kimbell (1984) and Morin (1977). Also see the recent guidelines prepared by special task forces of the American Psychological Association on avoiding sexism (APA in press) and heterosexism (APA 1986) in the design and interpretation of research.

Scarr (1988) has discussed the potentially negative consequences of overprotecting under-represented groups in research by avoiding socially sensitive issues (e.g., gender and racial differences). She argues for the forthright study of these issues, even though it might yield politically uncomfortable results.

CHAPTER 18

# Professional Responsibilities for Research

To commemorate the 75th anniversary of the American Home Economics Association (AHEA) in 1984, the Policy Board for the *Home Economics Research Journal* (*HERJ*) decided to devote the March and June issues of *HERJ* to special topics considered important to researchers within the profession. All of the papers submitted for these issues "challenge the profession to give a higher priority to research activity and to the development of scholars in a profession which has its primary focus on improving the quality of life of all people" (Ritchey and Lovingood 1984, 251). "Research is the foundation and lifeblood of any profession" (Hawthorne, Woodburn, and Powell 1984, 491).

The same challenge was expressed in preparation for the 50th AHEA anniversary in 1959: "Challenge: To expand research and focus it on the needs of individuals and families" (AHEA 1959, 12).

Another example of professional responsibility for research is stated in the Summary of Recommendations of the 1978 HERAPP (Home Economics Research Assessment, Planning and Projections) study (Ritchey 1978, 3):

> Research in home economics is important to the growth and development of the profession, but is most important for the solution of critical problems confronting families and individuals in a complex and rapidly changing society. Based upon the data obtained through the HERAPP study, the following recommendations are essential for the continued improvement and development of research in home economics:
>
> The home economics profession must place a higher priority on research and scholarly activities.

The base of funding for all areas of home economics research must be increased.

The base of funding for home economics research must be broadened.

Home economics must become a viable, supported component of the agricultural experiment station–land-grant system.

Research support should be directed toward the most important problem areas.

## DEVELOPING PERSONNEL FOR RESEARCH

Development of research personnel is the key to a research enterprise in any discipline. Research provides the foundation on which teaching in the classroom and in the community should be based. Establishing and publishing research goals are of little value unless the goals are translated into action. This generation must recruit and prepare the researchers of tomorrow (Clark 1972).

### Undergraduate Study

It is in the undergraduate years that students build their foundation of theoretical knowledge in basic and applied disciplines and, it is hoped, in scientific methods of inquiry and approaches to problems. Graduate programs should build on the tools and skills acquired at the undergraduate level toward a higher level of sophistication. Therefore, introduction of research courses at the undergraduate level is recommended.

The importance of theory cannot be overemphasized. Theory, whether explicit or implicit, is involved in every step of the investigative process from initial premise to final interpretation of data. In an article in the *HERJ,* McCullers (1984, 523) points out that "a major concern. . .was the belief that home economists have avoided the use of theory in research, and that we have been paying an intolerable price for doing so in terms of the stature and recognition accorded home economics research within the scientific community." One reason for the relative absence of theory from home economics research has to do with inadequate training in research and particularly in theory (McCullers 1984). Courses in both the basic and applied disciplines should be based upon the theories developed for understanding of those disciplines.

### Graduate Study

Graduate study at the doctoral level is oriented toward research and creative scholarship. The Ph.D. is often referred to as a research degree. However, simply producing a dissertation is not enough. The graduate student should have the opportunity to learn and experience the processes of research and critical inquiry in many more ways. This means having a good foundation in appropriate methods of inquiry, statistics, computer usage, search and retrieval, proposal formulation, and writing (Lund 1984).

Questions have been raised regarding the increasing use of non-thesis options in master's programs. When given a choice between an all-course program and one involving research and a thesis, most students choose the non-thesis option. The reasons for this choice merit careful study (Schlater 1970).

### In-service Training

Completion of a graduate program and receipt of a degree is only the beginning of a research career. In most scientific disciplines, postdoctoral work as an assistant or research associate with an experienced researcher is a customary route toward building research experience and a publication record.

Researchers also must update and upgrade their skills constantly. Appropriate opportunities are available through short courses and seminars, national and regional workshops, college courses that can be audited or taken for credit, sabbatical and other work leaves of absence, and so on.

## MAKING A COMMITMENT TO RESEARCH

The challenge to home economics to give a higher priority to research has been emphasized, but leaders in other disciplines are also expressing the need for reordering priorities. An editorial in a recent news issue of the Committee on Science of the American Association for Clinical Chemistry stated: "Clinical chemists must assume new responsibilities in research if our discipline is not to be relegated to an area of merely technology. . . . We shall not experience the professional status and recognition that we feel is our due until we contribute creatively to our own areas of expertise" (Labbe 1982, 4).

The process of acquiring existing knowledge is different from the process of producing new knowledge and ideas. It is the latter process that we should be fostering in teaching and service programs. In this way, we can integrate our research, teaching, and service programs, and our roles can change from that of purveyors and consumers of information to that of creative producers of new knowledge and ideas to solve personal and societal problems.

### Research Leadership

One of the six factors identified by Montgomery and Ritchey (1975) contributing to the limited number of home economics research publications was the failure of administrators to place adequate emphasis on faculty research. They tended to regard research as something to be done after teaching, extension, and/or administrative activities. Yet, it is the administrators (department heads and deans) who must create the atmosphere for research. A favorable research atmosphere is most often set by administrators who have the philosophy that research is important and who have research skills and experience themselves.

Administrators can provide encouragement and support to researchers through allocation of resources and other rewards that place research in high priority. These resources and rewards take the form of financial support; providing time for research in the faculty members' assignment loads; providing support staff, such as secretaries, technicians, and graduate assistants; and merit evaluations for salaries, tenure, and promotions. Most university systems regard research and publication high on the priority list for promotion recommendations.

## FINANCING RESEARCH

A good deal of research is accomplished by committed researchers in spite of inadequate time, facilities, and financial support. However, graduate research assistantships offered by college departments provide help for the researcher as well as experience and financial remuneration for the graduate student. Information regarding both teaching and research assistantships may be obtained directly from the institution offering the graduate program.

Some of these research assistantships are funded by the universities offering the graduate programs. Others are supported by funds received by faculty researchers from the U.S. government, private foundations, business and industry, and so forth. Fund seeking is often referred to as the "art of grantsmanship." The process is time consuming and very competitive. The probability of success increases with one's knowledge and experience regarding the "working of the system." Research proposals must sell the funding agency on the relevance of the proposed research to the agency's mission, the training and qualifications of the researchers, the adequacy of the research facilities to be used, the justification of the budget, and the creativity and potential of the research to the advancement of science. The graduate years are not too early to learn the art of grantsmanship.

## DISSEMINATING RESEARCH FINDINGS

The researcher's responsibilities do not end with conducting a research project and analyzing data. The results of a study must be communicated to the scientific community. In most instances, the findings should also be communicated in a popular form to the public if they are to make the greatest impact on society and the quality of life and fulfill this mission of the science of human ecology.

# References


Abelson, R. P. 1968. Simulation of social behavior. In *Handbook of social psychology,* vol. 2., 2d ed., ed. G. Lindzey and E. Aronson, 274–356. Reading, Mass.: Addison-Wesley.

Ackoff, R. L. 1953. *The design of social research.* Chicago: Univ. of Chicago Press.

Adair, J. G. 1973. *The human subject.* Boston: Little, Brown.

______. 1984. The Hawthorne effect. *J. Appl. Psychol.* 69:334–45.

Adair, J. G.; Dushenko, T. W.; and Lindsay, R. C. L. 1985. Ethical regulations and their impact on research practice. *Am. Psychol.* 40:59–72.

Adams, G. R., and Schvaneveldt, J. D. 1985. *Understanding research methods.* New York: Longman.

Adler, P. A., and Adler, P. 1987a. *Membership roles in field research.* Newbury Park, Calif.: Sage.

______. 1987b. The past and the future of ethnography. *J. Contemp. Ethnog.* 16:4–24.

Agar, M. H. 1980. *The professional stranger.* New York: Academic Press.

______. 1986. *Speaking of ethnography.* Beverly Hills: Sage.

Albrecht, K., and Zemke, R. 1985. *Service America!* Homewood, Ill.: Dow Jones–Irwin.

Allen, E. M. 1960. Why are research grant applications disapproved? *Science* 132:1532–34.

Allen, G. R. 1973. *The graduate student's guide to theses and dissertations.* San Francisco: Jossey-Bass.

Allport, G. W. 1942. *The use of personal documents in psychological science.* New York: Social Science Research Council.

American Anthropological Association. 1983. *Professional ethics.* Washington, D.C.: AAA.

American Association of Textile Chemists and Colorists. 1985. *Technical Manual.*

American Educational Research Association, American Psychological Association, and National Council on Measurement in Education. 1985. *Standards for educational and psychological testing.* Rev. ed. Washington, D.C.: American Psychological Association.

American Home Economics Association. 1959. *Home economics new directions.* Washington, D.C.: AHEA.

American Psychological Association. 1973. *Ethical principles in the conduct of research with human participants.* Washington, D.C.: APA.

______. 1981. Ethical principles of psychologists. *Am. Psychol.* 36:633–38.

______. 1983. *Publication manual.* 3d ed. Washington, D.C.: APA.

______. 1986. *Guidelines for the ethical conduct in the care and use of animals.* Washington, D.C.: APA.

______, Division 7. 1968. Ethical standards for developmental psychologists. *Newsletter,* 1–3.

______, Task Force on Non-Heterosexist Research. 1986. *Avoiding heterosexist bias: Guidelines for ethical and valid research.* Washington, D.C.: APA.

______, Task Force on Nonsexist Research. In press. Guidelines for avoiding sexism in research. *Am. Psychol.*

American Society for Testing Materials. 1985. *Annual book of ASTM standards.* Parts 32 and 33. Philadelphia: ASTM.

American Sociological Association. 1984. *Code of ethics.* Washington, D.C.: ASA.

Anastasi, A. 1988. *Psychological testing*. 6th ed. New York: Macmillan.

Andersen, R.; Kasper, J.; Frankel, M.; and Associates. 1979. *Total survey error.* San Francisco: Jossey-Bass.

Andreasen, A. R. 1984. Life status changes and changes in consumer preferences and satisfaction. *J. Consum. Res.* 11:784–94.

Andrews, F. M.; Klem, L.; Davidson, T. N.; O'Malley, P. M.; and Rogers, W. L. 1981. *A guide for selecting statistical techniques for analyzing social science data.* Ann Arbor, Mich.: University of Michigan, Institute for Social Research.

Andrulis, R. S. 1977. *Adult assessment.* Springfield, Ill.: Thomas.

Angle, H. V. 1981. The interviewing computer: A technology for gathering comprehensive treatment information. *Behav. Res. Methods Instrum.* 13:607–12.

Angleitner, A., and Wiggins, J. S. 1986. *Personality assessment via questionnaire.* New York: Springer-Verlag.

*The annual guides to graduate study.* 1971. Princeton, N.J.: Peterson's Guides, Inc.

Appell, G. 1978. *Ethical dilemmas in anthropological inquiry.* Waltham, Mass.: Crossroads.

Argyle, M. 1967. The social psychology of social change. In *Social theory and economic change,* ed. T. Burns and S. B. Sells, 87–101. London: Tavistock.

Argyris, C.; Putnam, R.; and Smith, D. M. 1985. *Action science.* San Francisco: Jossey-Bass.

Arnold, D. O. 1982. Qualitative field methods. In *Qualitative methods,* vol. 2 of *A handbook of social science methods,* ed. R. B. Smith and P. K. Manning, 49–78. Cambridge, Mass.: Ballinger.

Atherton, P., and Christian, R. W. 1977. *Librarians and online services.* New York: Knowledge Industry.

Aydelotte, W. O.; Bogue, A. C.; and Fogel, R. W. 1972. *The dimensions of quantitative research in history.* Princeton, N.J.: Princeton Univ. Press.

Babbie, E. R. 1973. *Survey research methods.* Belmont, Calif.: Wadsworth.

———. 1986. *The practice of social research.* 4th ed. Belmont, Calif.: Wadsworth.

Backstrom, C. H., and Hursh-César, G. 1981. *Survey research.* 2d ed. New York: Wiley.

Badia, P., and Runyon, R. P. 1982. *Fundamentals of behavioral research.* Reading, Mass.: Addison-Wesley.

Bain, J. 1968. *Industrial organization.* 2d ed. New York: Wiley.

Bakeman, R., and Gottman, J. M. 1986. *Observing interaction.* New York: Cambridge Univ. Press.

Bales, R. F. 1951. *Interaction process analysis.* Chicago: Univ. of Chicago Press.

Balian, E. S. 1983. *How to design, analyze, and write doctoral research.* Lanham, Md.: University Press of America.

Ball-Rokeach, S. J.; Grube, J. W.; and Rokeach, M. 1981. Roots. *Public Opin. Q.* 45:58–68.

Bandura, A. 1975. The ethics and social purposes of behavior modification. In *Annual review of behavior therapy, theory and practice,* vol. 3, ed. C. M. Franks and G. T. Wilson. New York: Bruner/Mazel.

Bangert-Drowns, R. L., 1986. Review of developments in meta-analytic method. *Psychol. Bull.* 99:388–99.

Barker, R. G. 1960. Ecology and motivation. In *Nebraska symposium on motivation,* ed. M. R. Jones, 1–50. Lincoln: Univ. of Nebraska Press.

———. 1968. *Ecological psychology.* Stanford, Calif.: Stanford Univ. Press.

Barker, R. G., and Schoggen, P. 1973. *Qualities of community life.* San Francisco: Jossey-Bass.

Barker, R. G., and Wright, H. F. 1951. *One boy's day.* New York: Harper.

———. 1955. *Midwest and its children.* New York: Row and Peterson.

Barlow, D. H., and Hersen, M. 1984. *Single case experimental design.* 2d ed. New York: Pergamon.

Barrass, R. 1978. *Scientists must write.* London: Chapman and Hall.

Barry, H. 1980. Description and uses of the Human Relations Area Files. In *Handbook of cross-cultural psychology,* vol. 2, ed. H. C. Triandis and J. W. Berry, 445–78. Boston: Allyn and Bacon.

Barthes, R. 1967a. *Elements of semiology.* London: Jonathan Cape.

______. 1967b. *Systeme de la mode.* Paris: Editions du Seriel.

Barton, A. H., and Lazarsfeld, P. F. 1969. Some functions of qualitative analysis in social research. In *Issues in participant observation,* ed. G. J. McCall and J. L. Simmons, 163–96, 239–44. Reading, Mass.: Addison-Wesley.

Barzun, J., and Graff, H. F. 1985. *The modern researcher.* 4th ed. New York: Harcourt.

Bates, J. D. 1980. *Writing with precision.* 3d ed. Washington, D.C.: Acropolis Books.

Bates, M. J. 1984. Locating elusive science information. *Spec. Libr.* 75:114–20.

Bauer, D. G. 1984. *The "how to" grants manual.* New York: Macmillan.

______. 1985. *The complete grants sourcebook for higher education.* New York: Macmillan.

Bausell, R. B. 1986. *A practical guide to conducting empirical research.* New York: Harper.

Beatty, W. H., ed. 1969. *Improving educational assessment and an inventory of measures of affective behavior.* Washington, D.C.: Association for Supervision and Curriculum Development.

Beauchamp, T. L.; Faden, R. R.; Wallace, R. J., Jr.; and Walters, L. R. 1982. *Ethical issues in social science research.* Baltimore: Johns Hopkins Univ. Press.

Bechtel, R. B.; Marans, R. W.; and Michelson, W. 1987. *Methods in environmental and behavioral research.* New York: Van Nostrand Reinhold.

Becker, H. S. 1986. *Writing for social scientists.* Chicago: Univ. of Chicago Press.

Becker, H. S., and Geer, B. 1982. Participant observation. In *Field research,* ed. R. G. Burgess, 239–50. London: George Allen and Unwin.

Becker, H. S.; Geer, B.; Hughes, E.; and Strauss, A. 1961. *Boys in white.* Chicago: Univ. of Chicago Press.

Beere, C. A. 1979. *Women and women's issues.* San Francisco: Jossey-Bass.

Belson, W. A. 1981. *The design and understanding of survey questions.* Aldershot, Hants, Eng.: Gower.

Bentler, P. M., and Woodward, A. 1979. Nonexperimental evaluation research. In *Improving evaluations,* ed. L. E. Datta and R. Perloff, 71–102. Beverly Hills: Sage.

Berdie, D., and Anderson, J. 1974. *Questionnaire design and use.* Metuchen, N.J.: Scarecrow Press.

Berelson, B. 1954. Content analysis. In *Handbook of social psychology,* vol. 1, ed. G. Lindzey, 488–522. Reading, Mass.: Addison-Wesley.

Berg, I. A. 1967. *Response set in personality assessment.* Chicago: Aldine

Beringer, R. E. 1978. *Historical analysis.* New York: Wiley.

Berlyne, D. E. 1960. *Conflict, arousal, and curiosity.* New York: McGraw-Hill.

______. 1971. *Aesthetics and psychobiology.* New York: Appleton-Century-Crofts.

Bernard, H. R. 1988. *Research methods in cultural anthropology.* Newbury Park, Calif.: Sage.

Bernstein, I. N., and Sheldon, E. B. 1983. Evaluation research. In *An introduction to social research,* vol. 1 of *A handbook of social science methods,* ed. R. B. Smith, 93–132. Cambridge, Mass.: Ballinger.

Bernstein, T. M. 1965. *The careful writer.* New York: Atheneum.

Best, J. W. 1981. *Research in education.* 4th ed. Englewood Cliffs, N.J.: Prentice-Hall.

Biernacki, P., and Waldorf, D. 1981. Snowball sampling. *Sociol. Methods & Res.* 10:114–63.

Bierstedt, R. 1959. Nominal and real definitions in sociological theory. In *Symposium on sociological thoery,* ed. L. Gross, 121–44. New York: Harper.

Blackwell, R. D., and Talarzyk, W. 1983. Life-style retailing. *J. Retailing* 59(4): 7–26.

Blalock, H. M., Jr. 1964. *Causal inferences in nonexperimental research.* Chapel Hill: Univ. of North Carolina Press.

Blankenship, A. B. 1977. *Professional telephone surveys.* New York: McGraw-Hill.

Blau, G. L. 1984. Editing in style. *Behav. Res. Methods, Instrum., Comput.* 16:28–31.

Blaxter, M., ed. 1979. The analysis of qualitative data. Special issue of *Sociol. Rev.* 27:649–827.

Blissmer, R. H. 1985. *The computer annual.* New York: Wiley.

Bloom, B. S.; Hastings, J. T.; and Madaus, G. F. 1971. *Handbook on formative and summative evaluation of student learning.* New York: McGraw-Hill.

Bochner, S. 1980. Unobtrusive methods in cross-cultural experimentation. In *Handbook of Cross-Cultural Psychology,* vol. 2, ed. H. C. Triandis and J. W. Berry, 319–88. Boston: Allyn and Bacon.

Bogatyrev, P. 1937/1971. *The functions of folk costume in Moravian Slovakia.* Trans. Richard G. Crum. Paris: Mouton Press.

Bogdan, R. 1972. *Participant observation in organizational settings.* Syracuse: Syracuse Univ. Press.

______. 1974. *Being different.* New York: Wiley.

Bogdan, R., and Biklen, S. K. 1982. *Qualitative research for education.* Boston: Allyn and Bacon.

Bogdan, R., and Taylor, S. 1982. *Inside out.* Toronto: Univ. of Toronto Press.

Bohannan, P., and Glazer, M., eds. 1973. *High points in anthropology.* New York: Knopf.

Bolgar, H. 1965. The case study method. In *Handbook of clinical psychology,* ed. B. B. Wolman, 363–413, Chicago: Rand McNally.

Bolton, B., ed. 1986. *Handbook of measurement and evaluation in rehabilitation.* 2d ed. Baltimore: Brookes.

Boor, M. 1986. Suggestions to improve manuscripts submitted to professional journals. *Am. Psychol.* 41:721–22.

Bond, K. 1978. Confidentiality and the protection of human subjects in social science research. *Am. Sociol.* 13:1–50.

Bonjean, C. N.; Hill, R. J.; and McLemore, S. D. 1967. *Sociological measurement.* San Francisco: Chandler.

Borchardt, D. H., and Francis, R. D. 1984. *How to find out in psychology.* New York: Pergamon.

Borg, W. R. 1987. *Applying educational research.* 2d ed. White Plains, N.Y.: Longman Inc.

Borgatta, E. F., and Bohrnstedt, G. W. 1980. Level of measurement. *Sociol. Methods & Res.* 9:147–60.

Borich, G. D., and Madden, S. K. 1977. *Evaluating classroom instruction.* Reading, Mass.: Addison-Wesley.

Boring, E. P., ed. 1945. Symposium on operationism. *Psychol. Rev.* 52:241–94.

Boruch, R. F., and Cecil, J. S.. 1979. *Assuring the confidentiality of social science data.* Philadelphia: Univ. of Pennsylvania Press.

Bouchard, T. J., Jr. 1976. Field research methods. In *Handbook of industrial and organizational psychology,* ed. M. D. Dunnette, 363–413. Chicago: Rand McNally.

Bower, R. T., and de Gasparis, P. 1978. *Ethics in social research.* New York: Praeger.

Boyer, E. G.; Simon, A.; and Karafin, G., eds. 1973. *Measures of maturation.* 3 vols. Philadelphia: Research for Better Schools.

Bradley, J. 1968. *Distribution-free statistical tests.* Englewood Cliffs, N.J.: Prentice-Hall.

Bradburn, N. M. 1983. Response effects. In *Handbook of survey research,* ed. P. H. Rossi, J. D. Wright, and A. B. Anderson, 289–328. New York: Academic Press.

Bradburn, N. M., and Sudman, S. 1979. *Improving interview method and questionnaire design.* San Francisco: Jossey-Bass.

Brandt, R. M. 1972. *Studying behavior in natural settings.* New York: Holt.

Brenner, M.; Brown, J.; and Canter, D. 1985. *Research interview.* London: Academic Press.

Bridgewater, C. A.; Bornstein, P. H.; and Walkenbach, J. 1981. Ethical issues and the assignment of publication credit. *Am. Psychol.* 36:524–25.

Bridgman, P. W. 1927. *The logic of modern physics.* New York: Macmillan.

Brodkey, L. 1987. Writing ethnographic narratives. *Writ. Commun.* 4:25–50.

Brodsky, S. L., and Smitherman, H. O., eds. 1983. *Handbook of scales for research in crime and delinquency.* New York: Plenum.

Bromley, D. B. 1986. *The case-study method in psychology and related disciplines.* New York: Wiley.

Bronfenbrenner, U. 1977. Toward an experimental ecology of human development. *Am. Psychol.* 32:513–30.

______. 1979. *The ecology of human development.* Cambridge: Harvard Univ. Press.

Brooks, A., and Touliatos, J. In press. Computerized literature searching for home economics practitioners and researchers. *Journal of Home Economics.*

Brown, J. G., and Burger, C. 1984. Playground designs and preschool children's behavior. *Environ. Behav.* 16:599–626.

Brownell, B. A. 1985. *Using microcomputers.* Beverly Hills: Sage.

Bruning, J. L., and Kintz, B. L. 1977. *Computational handbook of statistics.* 2d ed. Glenview, Ill.: Scott, Foresman.

Bruyn, S. 1966. *The methodology of participant observation.* Englewood Cliffs, N.J.: Prentice-Hall.

Bucklin, L. 1972. *Competition and evolution in the distributive trades.* Englewood Cliffs, N.J.: Prentice-Hall.

Budd, R. W.; Thorpe, R. K.; and Donohew, L. 1967. *Content analysis of communication.* New York: Macmillan.

Bullock, R. J., and Svyantek, D. J. 1985. Analyzing meta-analysis. *J. Appl. Psychol.* 70:108–15.

Burdge, R. J. 1983. Community needs assessment and techniques. In *Social impact assessment methods,* ed. K. Finsterbusch, L. G. Llewellyn, and C. P. Wolf, 191–213. Beverly Hills: Sage.

Burgess, E. W. 1967. The growth of the city. In *The City,* ed. R. E. Park, E. W. Burgess, and R. McKenzie, 47–62. Chicago: Univ. of Chicago Press.

Burgess, R. G. 1982a. Approaches to field research. In *Field research,* ed. R. G. Burgess, 1–11. London: George Allen and Unwin.

______, ed. 1982b. *Field research.* London: George Allen and Unwin.

______. 1984. *In the field.* London: George Allen and Unwin.

Burns, R. C., and Kaufman, S. H. 1972. *Actions, styles, and symbols in Kinetic-Family-Drawings (KFD).* New York: Brunner/Mazel.

Buros, O. K., ed. 1939–1978. *Mental measurements yearbook.* Vols. 1–8. Highland Park, N.J.: Gryphon.

______, ed. 1961. *Tests in print.* Highland Park, N.J.: Gryphon.

______, ed. 1974. *Tests in print II.* Highland Park, N.J.: Gryphon.

Burstein, L.; Freeman, H. E.; and Rossi, P. H., eds. 1985. *Collecting evaluation data.* Beverly Hills: Sage.

Callecod, R. L. 1974. Play preferences of selected grade school children on varying types of playground equipment. Master's thesis. Urbana, Ill.: University of Illinois.

Campbell, D. T., and Fiske, D. W. 1959. Convergent and discriminant validation by the multitrait-multimethod matrix. *Psychol. Bull.* 56:81–105.

Campbell, D. T., and Stanley, J. C. 1963. *Experimental and quasi-experimental designs for research.* Chicago: Rand McNally.

Campbell, W. G.; Ballou, S. V.; and Slade, C. 1986. *Form and style.* 7th ed. Boston: Houghton Mifflin.

Cannell, C. F., and Kahn, R. L. 1968. Interviewing. In *Handbook of social psychology,* vol. 2, 2d ed., ed. G. Lindzey and E. Aronson, 526–95. Reading, Mass.: Addison-Wesley.

Cannon, W. B. 1932. *The wisdom of the body.* New York: Norton.

Canter, D. 1977. *The psychology of place.* New York: St. Martin's Press.

Caplovitz, D. 1983. *The stages of social research.* New York: Wiley.

Cattell, R. B., and Warburton, F. W. 1967. *Objective personality and motivation tests.* Urbana, Ill.: Univ. of Illinois Press.

*CBE style manual.* 1983. 5th ed. Bethesda, Md.: Council of Biology Editors.

Ceci, J. J.; Peters, D.; and Plotkin, J. 1985. Human subjects review, personal values, and the regulation of social science research. *Am. Psychol.* 40:994–1002.

Cerklewski, F. L., and Ridlington, J. W. 1985. Influence of zinc and iron on dietary fluoride utilization in the rat. *J. Nutr.* 115:1162–67.

Chalfant, J. C., and Nitzman, M. 1965. Shortcomings of grant applications to the Handicapped Children Research Program. *Except. Child.* 32:180–85.

Chambliss, W. 1972. *Boxman.* New York: Harper.

Chein, I. 1981. An introduction to sampling. In *Research methods in social relations,* 4th ed., ed. L. H. Kidder, 418–44. New York: Holt.

Chein, I.; Cook, S. W.; and Harding, J. 1948. The field of action research. *Am. Psychol.* 3:43–50.

Chen, C., and Schweizer, S. 1981. *Online bibliographic searching.* New York: Neal-Schuman.

Cherlin, A. 1984. Special issue on family policy. *J. Fam. Issues* 5:155–288.

*The Chicago manual of style.* 1982. 13th ed. Chicago: Univ. of Chicago Press.

Christakis, G., ed. 1973. Nutritional assessment in health programs. *Am. J. Public Health* 63 (suppl.).

Chun, K. T.; Cobb, S.; and French, J. R. P., Jr. 1975. *Measures for psychological assessments.* Ann Arbor: Survey Research Center of the Institute for Social Research, University of Michigan.

Clark, C. M. 1987. Computer storage and manipulation of field notes and verbal protocols. *Anthropol. Educ. Q.* 18:56–58.

Clark, H. E., ed. 1972. Actualizing our research potential in home economics. *Home Econ. Res. J.* 1:49–61.

Cochran, W. 1977. *Sampling techniques.* 3d ed. New York: Wiley.

Cohen, J. 1977. *Statistical power analysis for the behavioral sciences.* Rev. ed. New York: Academic Press.

Cohen, S. 1978. Environmental load and the allocation of attention. In *Advances in environmental psychology,* vol. 1. Hillsdale, N.J.: Erlbaum.

Coile, D. C., and Miller, N. E. 1984. How radical animal activists try to mislead humane people. *Am. Psychol.* 39:700–01.

Cole, J. R., and Cole, S. 1981. *Peer review in the National Science Foundation.* Washington, D.C.: National Academy of Sciences.

Cole, S.; Cole, J. R.; and Simon, G. A. 1981. Chance and consensus in peer review. *Science* 214:881–86.

Coleman, J. E. et al. 1966. *Equality of educational opportunity.* Washington, D.C.: GPO.

Coleman, W. E. 1984. *Grants in the humanities.* 2d ed. New York: Neal-Schuman.

Coleman, W.; Keller, D.; and Pfeffer, A., eds. 1982. *A casebook of grant proposals in the humanities.* New York: Neal-Schuman.

Collier, J. 1970. *Visual anthropology.* New York: Holt.

Colombotos, J. 1969. Physicians and medicare. *Am. Sociol. Rev.* 34: 318–34.

Committee on Dietary Allowances, Food and Nutrition Board. 1980. Fluoride. In *Recom-*

*mended dietary allowances,* 9th ed., 156–59, 178. Washington, D.C.: National Academy of Sciences.

Compton, N. H. 1964. Body-image boundaries in relation to clothing fabric and design preferences of a group of hospitalized psychotic women. *J. Home Econ.* 56:40–45.

Comrey, A. L.; Backer, T. E.; and Glaser, E. M. 1973. *A sourcebook for mental health measures.* Los Angeles: Human Interaction Research Institute.

Comroe, J. H., and Dripps, R. D. 1976. Scientific basis for the support of biomedical sciences. *Science* 192:105–111.

Conant, J. B. 1951. *Science and common sense.* New Haven: Yale Univ. Press.

Cone, J. D., and Foster, S. L. 1982. Direct observation in clinical psychology. In *Handbook of research methods in clinical psychology,* ed. P. C. Kendall and J. N. Butcher, 311–54. New York: Wiley.

Cone, J. D., and Hayes, S. C. 1976. The submerged discipline of environmental psychology. Paper presented at Annual Convention of the Midwest Association for Behavioral Analysis, Chicago.

Conner, R. F. 1982. Random assignment of clients in social experimentation. In *The ethics of social research,* vol. 1, ed. J. E. Sieber, 57–77. New York: Springer-Verlag.

Conrad, D. L. 1980. *The quick proposal workbook.* San Francisco: Public Management Institute.

Converse, J. M., and Presser, S. 1986. *Survey questions.* Beverly Hills: Sage.

Cook, J. D.; Hepworth, S. J.; Wall, T. O.; and Warr, P. B. 1981. *The experience of work.* New York: Academic Press.

Cook, T. D., and Campbell, D. T. 1979. *Quasi-experimentation.* Chicago: Rand McNally.

Cook, T. D.; and Shadish, W. R., Jr. 1986. Program evaluation. In *Annual review of psychology,* vol. 37, ed. M. R. Rosenzweig and L. W. Porter, 193–232. Palo Alto, Calif.: Annual Reviews, Inc.

Cook, T. D.; Leviton, L. C.; and Shadish, W. R. 1985. Program evaluation. In *Handbook of social psychology,* vol. 1, 3d ed., ed G. Lindzey and E. Aronson, 699–777. New York: Random House.

Cooke, R. A. 1982. The ethics and regulation of research involving children. In *Handbook of developmental psychology,* ed. B. B. Wolman. Englewood Cliffs, N.J.: Prentice-Hall.

Cooper, H. M. 1984. *The integrative research review.* Beverly Hills: Sage.

Corcoran, K., and Fischer, J. 1987. *Measures for clinical practice.* New York: Free Press.

Cordaro, L., and Ison, J. R. 1963. Psychology of the scientist: X. *Psychol. Rep.* 13:787–89.

Cottrell, F. 1955. *Energy and society.* Westport, Conn.: Greenwood Press.

Cox, C. P. 1987. *A handbook of introductory statistical methods.* New York: Wiley.

Craig, J. R., and Metz, L. P. 1986. *Methods of psychological research.* 2d ed. Monterey, Calif.: Brooks/Cole.

Craik, F. I., and Lockhart, R. S. 1972. Levels of processing. *J. Verbal Learn. Verbal Behav.* 2:671–84.

Craik, K. H. 1968. The comprehension of the everyday physical environment. *J. Am. Inst. Plann.* 34:29–37.

______. 1970. Environmental psychology. In *New directions in psychology,* vol. 4, ed. K. H. Craik et al., 3–121. New York: Holt.

______. 1973. Environmental psychology. In *Annual review of psychology,* vol. 24, ed. P. H. Mussen and M. R. Robinson, 403–22. Palo Alto, Calif.: Annual Reviews, Inc.

Creekmore, A. M. 1971. *Methods of measuring clothing variables.* Michigan Agricultural Experiment Station Project 783. East Lansing: Michigan State University.

Cremmins, E. T. 1982. *The art of abstracting.* Philadelphia: ISI Press.

Cromwell, L.; Weibell, F. J.; and Pfeiffer, F. A., eds. 1980. *Biomedical instrumentation and measurements.* 2d ed. Englewood Cliffs, N.J.: Prentice-Hall.

Cromwell, R. E.; Olson, D. H.; and Fournier, D. G. 1976. Diagnosis and evaluation in marital and family counseling. In *Treating relationships,* ed. D. H. Olson. Lake Mills, Ia.: Graphic Publishing.

Cronbach, L.J. 1951. Coefficient alpha and the internal structure of tests. *Psychometrika* 16:297–334.

———. 1982. *Designing evaluation of educational and social programs.* San Francisco: Jossey-Bass.

———. 1984. *Essentials of psychological testing.* 4th ed. New York: Harper.

Cronbach, L. J. et al. 1980. *Toward reform of program evaluation.* San Francisco: Jossey-Bass.

Csikszentmihalyi, M., and Rochberg-Halton, E. 1981. *The meaning of things.* New York: Cambridge Univ. Press.

Dalton, M. 1959. *Men who manage.* New York: Wiley.

Daniel, W. W. 1987. *Biostatistics.* 4th ed. New York: Wiley.

Darwin, C. 1859/1964. *The origin of species.* Facsimile ed. Intro. and bibli. by Ernst Mayr. Cambridge: Harvard Univ. Press.

Davis, C. M., Yarber, W. L., and Davis, S. L., eds. 1988. *Sexuality-related measures.* Lake Mills, Iowa: Graphic Publishing.

Davis, C. R. 1975. The Buckley regulations. *Educ. Res.* 4:11–13.

Davis, G., and Parker, C. A. 1979. *Writing the doctoral dissertation.* Woodbury, N.Y.: Barron.

Davitz, J. R., and Davitz, L. J. 1967. *A guide for evaluating research plans in psychology and education.* New York: Teachers College Press.

Dawes, R. M., and Smith, T. L. 1985. Attitude and opinion measurement. In *Handbook of social psychology,* vol. 1, 3d ed., ed. G. Lindzey and E. Aronson, 509–66. New York: Random House.

Dawson, R. E. 1962. Simulation in the social sciences. In *Simulation in social science,* ed. H. Guetzkow. Englewood Cliffs, N.J.: Prentice-Hall.

Day, R. A. 1983. *How to write and publish a scientific paper.* 2d ed. Philadelphia: ISI Press.

DeMaio, T. J., ed. 1983. *Approaches to developing questionnaires.* Statistical Policy Working Paper 10. Washington, D.C.: GPO.

Deming, W. E. 1944. On errors in surveys. *Am. Sociol. Rev.* 9:359–69.

Denzin, N. K. 1978. *The research act.* 2d ed. New York: McGraw-Hill.

Dermer, J. 1980. *How to write successful foundation presentations.* Hartsdale, N.Y.: Public Service Materials Center.

Dickerson, M. D., and Gentry, J. W. 1983. Characteristics of adopters and non-adopters of home computers. *J. Consum. Res.* 10:225–35.

Diener, E., and Crandall, R. 1978. *Ethics in social and behavioral research.* Chicago: Univ. of Chicago Press.

Dijkstra, W., and van der Zouwen, J. 1982. *Response behaviour in the survey-interview.* New York: Academic Press.

Dillman, D. A. 1978. *Mail and telephone surveys.* New York: Wiley.

———. 1983. Mail and other self-administered questionnaires. In *Handbook of survey research,* ed. P. H. Rossi, J. D. Wright, and A. B. Anderson, 359–77. New York: Academic Press.

Dillon, W. R., and Goldstein, M. 1984. *Multivariate analysis.* New York: Radius Press.

Dixon, W. J., and Brown, M. B., eds. 1983. *BMDP-83: Biomedical computer programs, P-series.* Rev. ed. Berkeley: Univ. of California Press.

Dobbert, M. L. 1982. *Ethnographic research.* New York: Praeger.

Dohrenwend, B. S.; Krasnoff, L.; Askenasy, A.; and Dohrenwend, B. P. 1973. Exemplifica-

tion of a method for sealing life events. *J. Health Soc. Behav.* 19:205–29.
Dollar, C. M., and Jensen, R. J. 1971. *Historian's guide to statistics.* New York: Holt.
Dollard, J. 1935. *Criteria for the life history.* New Haven: Yale Univ. Press.
Dooley, D. 1984. *Social research methods.* Englewood Cliffs, N.J.: Prentice-Hall.
Douty, H. 1963. Influence of clothing on perception of persons. *J. Home Econ.* 55(3): 197–202.
Dowdy, S., and Wearden, S. 1983. *Statistics for research.* New York: Wiley.
Downs, R., and Stea, D. 1973. *Image and environment.* Chicago: Aldine.
Doyle, G. F. 1981. *Research protocols for father training project.* Unpublished manual, Kennedy Hospital for Children, Brighton, Mass.
Dreikurs, R., and Soltz, V. 1964. *Children.* New York: Hawthorne.
Drew, C. J., and Hardman, M. L. 1985. *Designing and conducting biomedical research.* New York: Pergamon.
Dukes, W. F. 1965. $N = 1$. *Psychol. Bull.* 64:74–79.
Duncan, O. D. 1961. A socioeconomic index for all occupations. In *Occupations and social status,* ed. A. J. Reiss, Jr. et al. New York: Free Press.
Dutton, J. M., and Starbuck, W. H. 1971. *Computer simulation of human behavior.* New York: Wiley.
Educational Testing Service. *News on tests.* Princeton, N.J.: ETS.
______. *Test collection bibliographies.* Princeton, N.J.: ETS.
______. *Tests in microfiche.* Princeton, N.J.: ETS.
Edwards, A. L. 1957a. *The social desirability variable in personality assessment and research.* New York: Holt.
______. 1957b. *Techniques of attitude scale construction.* New York: Appleton.
______. 1984. *Experimental design in psychological research.* 5th ed. New York: Harper.
Ehrlich, P., and Ehrlich, A. 1970. *Population, resources, environment.* San Francisco: Freeman.
Elifson, K. W.; Runyon, R. P.; and Haber, A. 1982. *Fundamentals of social statistics.* Reading, Mass.: Addison-Wesley.
Ellen, R. F., ed. 1984. *Ethnographic research.* London: Academic Press.
Ellingstad, V., and Heimstra, N. 1974. *Methods in the study of human behavior.* Monterey, Calif.: Brooks/Cole.
Ellis, M. J. 1973. *Why people play.* Englewood Cliffs, N.J.: Prentice-Hall.
Emerson, R. M. 1981. Observational field work. In *Annual review of sociology,* vol. 7, ed. R. H. Turner, 351–78. Palo Alto, Calif.: Annual Review, Inc.
______. 1987. Four ways to improve the craft of fieldwork. *J. Contemp. Ethnog.* 16:69–89.
Ennis, R. H. 1964. Operational definitions. *Am. Educ. Res. J.* 1:183–201.
Epstein, L. H. 1976. Psychophysiological measurement in assessment. In *Behavioral assessment,* ed. M. Hersen and A. S. Bellack, 207–32. New York: Pergamon.
Erdos, P. L. 1970. *Professional mail surveys.* New York: McGraw-Hill.
Ernster, R.; McAleenan, M.; and Larkin, F. 1976. Social research methods applied to nutritional assessment. *Ecol. Food Nutr.* 5:143–51.
ERS Standards Committee. 1982. Research society standards for program evaluation. *New Dir. Program Eval.* 15(Sept.): 7–19.
Evertson, C. M., and Green, J. L. 1984. Observation as inquiry and method. In *Third handbook of research on teaching,* ed. M. C. Wittrock, 119–61. New York: Macmillan.
Ezell, S., ed. 1981. *The proposal writer's swipe file.* Washington, D.C.: Taft Corporation.
Faraday, A., and Plummer, K. 1979. Doing life histories. *Sociol. Rev.* 27:768–73.
Faris, J. C. 1972. *Zuba personal art.* London: Gerald Duckworth.
Featherman, D. L., and Stevens, G. 1982. A revised socioeconomic index of occupational status. In *Social structure and behavior,* ed. R. M. Hauser et al. New York: Academic Press.

*Federal Register.* January 26, 1981. *Rules and regulations* 46: 16, p. 8389.

*Federal test method standard no. 191, 1985.* Washington, D.C.: GPO.

Federico, P. A., and Figliozzi, P. W. 1981. Computer simulation of social systems. *Sociol. Methods Res.* 9:513–33.

Feldman, M. P., and Peay, J. 1982. Ethical and legal issues. In *International handbook of behavior modification and therapy,* ed. A. S. Bellack, M. Hersen, and A. E. Kazdin, 231–61. New York: Plenum.

Ferguson, G. A. 1981. *Statistical analysis in psychology and education.* 5th ed. New York: McGraw-Hill.

Ferguson, L. R. 1978. The competence and freedom of children to make choices regarding participation in research. *J. Soc. Issues* 34:114–21.

Ferris, C. 1980. *Guide to medical laboratory instruments.* Boston: Little, Brown.

Feshbach, N. D., and Feshbach, S. 1978. Toward an historical, social and developmental perspective on children's rights. *J. Soc. Issues* 34:1–7.

Festinger, L.; Riecken, H.; and Schachter, S. 1956. *When prophecy fails.* Minneapolis: Univ. of Minnesota Press.

Fetterman, D. 1984. *Ethnography in educational evaluation.* Beverly Hills: Sage.

Fetterman, D., and Pitman, M. A., eds. 1986. *Educational evaluation.* Beverly Hills: Sage.

Fielding, N. G., and Fielding, J. L. 1986. *Linking data.* Beverly Hills: Sage.

Filsinger, E. E. 1983. *Marriage and family assessment.* Beverly Hills: Sage.

Filsinger, E. E., and Lewis, R. A., eds. 1981. *Assessing marriage.* Beverly Hills: Sage.

Filstead, W. J., ed. 1970. *Qualitative methodology.* Chicago: Markham.

Fink, A., and Kosecoff, J. 1980a. *An evaluation primer workbook.* Beverly Hills: Sage.

———. 1980b. *An evaluation primer workbook.* Beverly Hills: Sage.

———. 1985. *How to conduct surveys.* Beverly Hills: Sage.

Finsterbusch, K. 1977. The potential role of social impact assessments in instituting public policies. In *Methodology of social impact assessment,* ed. K. Finsterbusch and C. P. Wolf, 2–12. Stroudsburg, Pa.: Dowden, Hutchinson, and Ross.

Finsterbusch, K., and Wolf, C. P., eds. 1977. *Methodology of social impact assessment.* Stroudsburg, Pa.: Dowden, Hutchinson, and Ross.

Finsterbusch, K.; Llewellyn, L. G.; and Wolf, C. P., eds. 1983. *Social impact assessment methods.* Beverly Hills: Sage.

Firebaugh, G. 1978. A rule for inferring individual-level relationships from aggregate data. *Am. Sociol. Rev.* 43:557–72.

Floud, R. 1973. *An introduction to quantitative history.* Princeton, N.J.: Princeton Univ. Press.

Fluegelman, A., and Hewes, J. J. 1983. *Writing in the computer age.* New York: Doubleday.

Flugel, J. C. 1950. *Psychology of clothes.* London: Hogarth Press.

Folkman, S., and Lazarus, R. 1980. An analysis of coping in a middle-aged community sample. *J. Health Soc. Behav.* 21:219–39.

Form, W. H. 1954. The place of social structure in the determination of land use. *Soc. Forces* 32:317–23.

Foster, S. L., and Cone, J. D. 1986. Design and use of direct observation procedures. In *Handbook of behavioral assessment,* ed. A. R. Ciminero, K. S. Calhoun, and H. E. Adams, 253–324. New York: Wiley.

Fowler, F. J., Jr. 1984. *Survey research methods.* Beverly Hills: Sage.

Fox, D. J. 1969. *The research process in education.* New York: Holt.

Fox, M. A. 1986. *The case for animal experimentation.* Berkeley: Univ. of California Press.

Frame, C. L., and Strauss, C. C. 1987. Parental informed consent and sample bias in grade-school children. *J. Soc. Clin. Psychol.* 5:227–36.

Frankel, M. S. 1978. Social, legal, and political responses to ethical issues in the use of children as experimental subjects. *J. Soc. Issues* 34:110–13.

Franklin, J. L., and Thrasher, J. H. 1976. *An introduction to program evaluation.* New York: Wiley.

Fraser, B. J., and Tobin, K., eds. 1985. *Secondary analysis and large-scale assessments.* Perth: Western Australia Institute of Technology.

Freeman, H. E., and Shanks, J. M., eds. 1983. The emergence of computer-assisted survey research. Special issue of *Sociol. Methods Res.* 12:115–230.

Freudenburg, W. R. 1986. Social impact assessment. In *Annual review of sociology,* vol. 12, ed. R. H. Turner and J. F. Short, Jr., 451–78. Palo Alto, Calif.: Annual Reviews, Inc.

Frey, J. H. 1983. *Survey research by telephone.* Beverly Hills: Sage.

Frick, E. 1980. *Library research guide to history.* Ann Arbor, Mich.: Pierian Press.

Frost, J. L. 1978. The American playground movement. *Childhood Educ.* 54:176–82.

Furedy, J. J. 1987. Beyond heart rate in the cardiac psychophysiological assessment of mental effort. *Human Factors* 29:183–94.

Gage, N. L., ed. 1963. *Handbook of research on teaching.* Chicago: Rand McNally.

Gaito, J. 1980. Measurement scales and statistics. *Psychol. Bull.* 87:564–67.

Galton, M. 1978. *British mirrors.* Leicester, Engl.: University of Leicester.

Gans, H. 1962. *Urban villagers.* New York: Free Press.

Gardner, D. C., and Beatty, G. J. 1980. *Dissertation proposal guidebook.* Springfield, Ill.: Thomas.

Gardner, P. L. 1975. Scales and statistics. *Rev. Educ. Res.* 48:43–57.

Garfield, E. 1984. Animal experimentation. *Curr. Contents* 16(5): 3–13.

______. 1987a. Reviewing review literature. Part 1. Definitions and uses of reviews. *Curr. Contents* 19(18):3–6.

______. 1987b. Reviewing review literature. Part 2. The place of reviews in scientific literature. *Curr. Contents* 19(19):3–8.

Garraghan, G. J. 1946. *A guide to historical method.* New York: Fordham Univ. Press.

Gay, L. R. 1987. *Educational research.* 3d ed. Columbus, Ohio: Merrill.

Gelwicks, L. E. 1970. Home range and use of space by an aging population. In *Spatial behavior of older people,* ed. L. A. Pastalan and D. H. Carson, 148–61. Ann Arbor: University of Michigan–Wayne State University Institute of Gerontology.

Genishi, C. 1982. Observational research methods for early childhood education. In *Handbook of research in early childhood education,* ed. B. Spodek, 564–91. New York: Free Press.

Gerdes, E. P. 1979. College students' reactions to social psychological experiments involving deception. *J. Soc. Psychol.* New York: Houghton-Mifflin.

Gibbons, J. D. 1985. *Nonparametric statistical inference.* 2d ed. New York: Marcel Dekker.

Gibson, J. 1979. *The ecological approach to visual perception.* New York: Houghton Mifflin.

Gilbert, R., and Christensen, A. 1985. Observational assessment of marital and family interaction. In *The handbook of family psychology and therapy,* vol. 2, 961–88, ed. L. L'Abate. Homewood, Ill.: Dorsey.

Glaser, B., and Strauss, A. 1967. *Discovery of grounded theory.* Chicago: Aldine.

Glass, G. V. 1977. Integrating findings. In *Review of research in education,* vol. 5, ed. L.S. Shulman, 351–79. Itasca, Ill.: F. E. Peacock.

Glass, G. V.; McGaw, B.; and Smith, M. L. 1981. *Meta-analysis in social research.* Beverly Hills: Sage.

Goetz, J. P., and LeCompte, M. D. 1984. *Ethnography and qualitative design in educational research.* New York: Academic Press.

Gold, R. L. 1958. Roles in sociological field observations. *Soc. Forces* 36:217–33.

Goldman, B. A., and Busch, J. C., eds. 1978. *Directory of unpublished experimental mental measures.* Vol. 2. New York: Human Sciences Press.

———. 1982. *Directory of unpublished experimental mental measures.* Vol. 3. New York: Human Sciences Press.

Goldman, B. A., and Osborne, W. L., eds. 1985. *Directory of unpublished experimental mental measures.* Vol. 4. New York: Human Sciences Press.

Goldman, B. A., and Saunders, J. L., eds. 1974. *Directory of unpublished experimental mental measures.* Vol. 1. New York: Behavioral Publications.

Goldstein, M., and Goldstein, I. 1984. *The experience of science.* New York: Plenum.

Good, C. V. 1963. *Introduction to educational research.* 2d ed. New York: Appleton-Century-Crofts.

Goodenough, W. H. 1980. Ethnographic field techniques. In *Handbook of cross-cultural psychology,* vol. 2, ed. H. C. Triandis and J. W. Berry, 29–56. Boston: Allyn and Bacon.

Goodman, L. A. 1985. *Analyzing qualitative-categorical data.* Ed. M. Jay. Lanham, Md.: University Press of America.

Gorden, R. L. 1980. *Interviewing.* 3d ed. Homewood, Ill.: Dorsey.

Gordon, I. J., and Jester, R. E. 1973. Techniques of observing teaching in early childhood and outcomes of particular procedures. In *Second handbook of research on teaching,* ed. R. M. W. Travers. Skokie, Ill.: Rand McNally.

Gordon, T. 1976. *Parent effectiveness training in action.* New York: Bantam.

Gottschalk, L. 1956. *Understanding history.* New York: Alfred Knopf.

———, ed. 1963. *Generalization in the writing of history.* Chicago: Univ. of Chicago Press.

Gottschalk, L.; Kluckhohn, C.; and Angell, R. 1951. *The use of personal documents in history, anthropology, and sociology.* New York: Social Science Research Council.

Graybeal, W. J., and Pooch, U. W. 1980. *Simulation.* Cambridge, Mass.: Winthrop.

Green, B. F., and Hall, J. A. 1984. Quantitative methods for literature reviews. In *Annual review of psychology,* vol. 35, ed. M. K. Rosenzweig and L. W. Porter, 37–54. Palo Alto, Calif.: Annual Reviews, Inc.

Greene, J., and McClintock, C. 1985. Triangulation in evaluation. *Eval. Rev.* 9:523–45.

Greenwald, A. G. 1976. Within-subjects design. *Psychol. Bull.* 83:314–20.

Greenwald, A. G.; Pratkanis, A. R.; Leippe, M. R.; and Baumgardner, M. H. 1986. Under what conditions does theory obstruct research progress? *Psychol. Rev.* 93:216–29.

Gronlund, N. E. 1959. *Sociometry in the classroom.* New York: Harper.

———. 1985. *Measurement and evaluation in teaching.* 5th ed. New York: Macmillan.

Gross, N.; Giacquinta, J. B.; and Bernstein, M. 1971. *Implementing organizational innovations.* New York: Basic Books.

Grotevant, H. D., and Carlson, C. I. 1987. Family interaction coding systems. *Fam. Process* 26:49–74.

———. In press. *Handbook of family assessment.* New York: Guilford Press.

Groves, R. M., and Kahn, R. L. 1979. *Surveys by telephone.* New York: Academic Press.

Guba, E. G. 1963. Guides for the writing of proposals. In *Educational research,* ed. J. A. Culbertson and S. P. Hencley, 289–305. Danville, Ill.: Interstate Printers and Publishers.

Guba, E. G., and Lincoln, Y. S. 1981. *Effective evaluation.* San Francisco: Jossey-Bass.

Guenzel, P. J.; Berkmans, T. R.; and Cannell, C. F. 1983. *General interviewing techniques.* Ann Arbor, Mich.: Institute for Social Research.

Guest, A. M. 1972. Patterns of family location. *Demography* 9:159–71.

Guetzkow, H.; Kotler, P.; and Schultz, R. L. 1972. *Simulation in social and administrative science.* Englewood Cliffs, N.J.: Prentice-Hall.

Guilford, J. P., and Fruchter, B. 1977. *Fundamental statistics in psychology and education.* 6th ed. New York: McGraw-Hill.

Gump, P. V. 1975. Ecological psychology and children. In *Review of child development research,* vol. 5, ed. E. M. Hetherington, 75–126. Chicago: Univ. of Chicago Press.

Gynther, M. D., and Green, S. B. 1982. Methodological problems in research with self-report inventories. In *Handbook of research methods in clinical psychology,* ed. P. C. Kendall and J. N. Butcher. New York: Wiley.

Hair, J. F.; Anderson, R. E.; Tatham, R. L.; and Grablowsky, B. J. 1984. *Multivariate data analysis.* New York: Macmillan.

Haire, M. 1950. Projective techniques in marketing research. *J. Mark.* 14: 649–52.

Hakim, C. 1982. *Secondary analysis in social research.* London: George Allen and Unwin.

______. 1983. Research based on administrative records. *Sociol. Rev.* 31:489–519.

Hall, E. T. 1966. *The hidden dimension.* New York: Doubleday.

Hall, J. L. 1981. *Online bibliographic databases.* London: Aslib.

Hall, M. 1977. *Developing skills in proposal writing.* 2d ed. Portland: Continuing Education Publications.

Hannon, B. 1975. Energy conservation and the consumer. *Science* 189:95–102.

Hansen, M. H.; Hurwitz, W. N.; and Madow, W. G. 1953. *Sample survey methods and theory.* New York: Wiley.

Hardyck, C., and Petrinovich, L. F. 1975. *Understanding research in the social sciences.* Philadelphia: Saunders.

Harrington, R. G., ed. 1986. *Testing adolescents.* Kansas City: Test Corporation of America.

Harrison, N. S. 1978. *Understanding behavioral research.* Belmont, Calif.: Wadsworth.

Hartmann, D. P. 1977. Considerations in the choice of interobserver reliability estimates. *J. Appl. Behav. Anal.* 10:103–16.

______. 1982. Assessing the dependability of observational data. In *Using observers to study behavior,* ed. D. P. Hartmann. San Francisco: Jossey-Bass.

Hartmann, D. P., and Wood, D. D. 1982. Observational methods. In *International handbook of behavior modification and therapy,* ed. A. S. Bellack, M. Hersen, and A. E. Kazdin, 109–38. New York: Plenum.

Harvey, L. 1987. Factors affecting response rates to mailed questionnaires. *J. Mark. Res. Soc.* 29:341–53.

Hawley, A. 1950. *Human ecology.* New York: Ronald Press.

Hawthorne, B. E.; Woodborn, M.; and Powell, J. A. 1984. Research process and achievement. *Home Econ. Res. J.* 12:490–98.

Hays, W. L. 1988. *Statistics.* 4th ed. New York: Holt.

Hedges, L. V., and Olkin, I. 1980. Vote-counting methods in research synthesis. *Psychol. Bull.* 88:359–69.

Heise, D. R. 1975. *Causal analysis.* New York: Wiley.

______, ed. 1981. Special issue on microcomputers and social research. *Sociol. Methods Res.* 9:395–536.

Helmstadter, G. C. 1964. *Principles of psychological measurement.* New York: Appleton.

Hempel, C. G. 1952. *Fundamentals of concept formation in empirical science.* Chicago: Univ. of Chicago Press.

Henderson, B. B. 1983. Patterns and correlates of individual differences in exploration and curiosity. Unpublished manuscript.

______. 1984. Social support and exploration. *Child Dev.* 55:1246–51.

Henerson, M. E.; Morris, L. L.; and Fitz-Gibbon, C. T. 1978. *How to measure attitudes.* Beverly Hills: Sage.

Herbert, J., and Attridge, C. 1975. A guide for developers and users of observation systems and manuals. *Am. Educ. Res. J.* 12:1–20.

Herman, J. L., ed. 1988. *Program evaluation kit.* 2d ed. Newbury Park, Calif.: Sage.

Hersen, M. 1982. Single-case experimental designs. In *International handbook behavior modification and therapy,* ed. A. S. Bellack, M. Hersen, and A. E. Kazdin, 167–203. New York: Plenum.

Hersen, M., and Bellack, A. S. 1987. *Dictionary of behavioral assessment techniques.* New York: Pergamon.

Hill, M., and Cochran, W. 1977. *Into print.* Los Altos, Calif.: William Kaufman.

Hinkle, D. E.; Wiersma, W.; and Jurs, S. G. 1988. *Applied statistics for the behavioral sciences.* 2d ed. New York: Houghton-Mifflin.

Hirschman, E. C. 1978. A descriptive theory of retail market structure. *J. Mark.* 28:34–38.

———. 1980a. Consumer creativity. In *Theoretical developments in marketing,* ed. C. W. Lamb, Jr., and P. M. Dunna, 162–65. Chicago: American Marketing Association.

———. 1980b. Innovations, novelty seeking, and consumer creativity. *J. Consum. Res.* 7:283–95.

———. 1981. Symbolism and technology as sources for the generation of innovations. In *Advances in Consumer Research,* vol. 9, ed. A. Mitchell, 537–41. St. Louis: Association for Consumer Research.

Hoepfner, R.; Conniff, W. A., Jr.; Hufano, L.; Bastone, M.; Ogilvie, V. N.; Hunter, R.; and Johnson, B. L., eds. 1974a. *CSE secondary school test evaluations: Grades 11 and 12.* Vol. 3. Los Angeles: Center for the Study of Evaluation, University of California–Los Angeles.

Hoepfner, R.; Conniff, W. A., Jr.; McGuire, T. C.; Klibanoff, L. S.; Stangel, G. F.; Lee, H. B.; and Rest, S., eds. 1974b. *CSE secondary school test evaluations: Grades 9 and 10.* Vol. 2. Los Angeles: Center for the Study of Evaluation, University of California–Los Angeles.

Hoepfner, R.; Conniff, W. A., Jr.; Petrosko, J. M.; Watkins, J.; Erlich, O.; Todaro, R. S.; and Hoyt, M. F., eds. 1974c. *CSE secondary school test evaluations: Grades 7 and 8.* Vol. 1. Los Angeles: Center for the Study of Evaluation, University of California–Los Angeles.

Hoepfner, R.; Hemenway, J.; DeMuth, J.; Tenopyr, M. L.; Granville, A. C.; Petrosko, J. M. Krakower, J.; Silberstein, R.; and Nadeau, M., eds. 1972. *CSERBS test evaluations.* Los Angeles: Center for the Study of Evaluation and Research for Better Schools.

Hoepfner, R.; Stern, C.; and Nummedal, S. G., eds. 1971. *CSE-ECRC preschool/kindergarten test evaluations.* Los Angeles: Center for the Study of Evaluation and Early Childhood Research Center, University of California–Los Angeles.

Hoepfner, R.; Strickland, G.; Stangel, G.; Jansen, P.; and Patalino, M., eds. 1970. *CSE elementary school test evaluations.* Los Angeles: Center for the Study of Evaluation, University of California–Los Angeles.

Hoffman, L. W., and Lippitt, R. 1960. The measurement of family life variables. In *Handbook of research methods in child development,* ed. P. H. Mussen, 945–1013. New York: Wiley.

Hogan, M. J. 1976. Energy conservation. Ph.D. diss. Michigan State University.

Hogan, M. J., and Paolucci, B. 1979. Energy conservation. *Home Econ. Res. J.* 7:211–18.

Hoinville, G., and Jowell, R. 1977. *Survey research practice.* London: Heinemann Educational Books.

Holahan, C. J. 1978. *Environment and behavior.* New York: Plenum.

———. 1982. *Environmental psychology.* New York: Random House.

Holden, G. W. 1985. Analyzing parental reasoning with microcomputer-presented problems. *Sim. Games* 16:203–10.

Hollingshead, A. B. 1975. Four factor index of social position. Unpublished manuscript. New Haven: Yale University.

Holman, A. M. 1983. *Family assessment.* Beverly Hills: Sage.

Holsti, O. R. 1968. *Content analysis.* In *Handbook of social psychology,* vol. 2, ed. G. Lindzey and E. Aronson, 596–692. Reading, Mass.: Addison-Wesley.

______. 1969. *Content analysis for the social sciences and humanities.* Reading, Mass.: Addison-Wesley.

Hook, N., and Paolucci, B. 1970. Family as ecosystem. *J. Home Econ.* 62:315–18.

Hopkins, K. D., and Stanley, J. C. 1981. *Educational and psychological measurement and evaluation.* 6th ed. Englewood Cliffs, N.J.: Prentice-Hall.

Hops, H., and Lewin, L. 1984. Peer sociometric forms. In *Child behavioral assessment,* ed. T. H. Ollendick and M. Hersen, 124–47, New York: Pergamon.

Houp, K. W., and Pearsall, T. E. 1980. *Reporting technical information.* 4th ed. New York: Macmillan.

Humphreys, L. 1970. *Tearoom trade.* Chicago: Aldine.

Hunt, T., and Lindley, C. J., eds. 1988. *Testing older adults.* Kansas City: Test Corporation of America.

Hunter, J. E.; Schmidt, F. L.; and Jackson, G. B. 1982. *Meta-analysis.* Beverly Hills: Sage.

Huth, E. 1987. *How to write and publish papers in the medical sciences.* 2d ed. Philadelphia: ISI Press.

Hyman, H. 1955. *Survey design and analysis.* Glencoe, Ill.: Free Press.

______. 1972. *Secondary analysis of sample surveys.* New York: Wiley.

Hyman, R. B.; Woog, P.; and Farrell, H. K. 1978. *Current non-projective instruments for the mental health field.* New York: Atcom.

Hymes, D. H., ed. 1965. *The use of computers in anthropology.* London: Mouton.

Ingene, C. A. 1983. Intertype competition. *J. Retailing* 59(3): 49–72.

Instructional Objectives Exchange. 1972. *Measures of self concept, K–12.* Rev. ed. Los Angeles: Instructional Objectives Exchange.

International Association of Business Communicators. 1982. *Without bias.* 2d ed. New York: Wiley.

Isaac, S., and Michael, W. B. 1981. *Handbook in research and evaluation.* 2d ed. San Diego: Edits Publishers.

Ivey, A. E. 1971. *Microcounseling.* Springfield, Ill.: Charles C. Thomas.

Jackson, D. A.; Della-Piana, G. M.; and Sloane, H. N., Jr. 1975. *How to establish a behavior observation system.* Englewood Cliffs, N.J.: Educational Technology Publications.

Jackson, G. B. 1980. Methods for integrative reviews. *Rev. Educ. Res.* 50:438–60.

Jacob, H. 1984. *Using published data.* Beverly Hills: Sage.

Jacob, T., and Tennenbaum, D. 1988. *Family assessment.* New York: Plenum.

Jacoby, J., and Olson, J. 1977. Consumer response to price. In *Moving ahead in attitude research,* ed. Y. Wind and M. Greenberg. Chicago: American Marketing Association.

Jaeger, R. M. 1984. *Sampling in education and the social sciences.* New York: Longman.

Janes, R. W. 1961. A note on phases of the community role of the participant-observer. *Am. Sociol. Rev.* 26:446–50.

Janke, R. V. 1985. Three new online directories. *Database* 8(4): 6–9.

Jensen, B. J., and Haynes, S. N. 1986. Self-report questionnaire and inventories. In *Handbook of behavior assessment,* ed. A. R. Ciminero, K.S. Calhoun, and H. E. Adams, 150–175. New York: Wiley.

Jick, T. D. 1979. Mixing qualitative and quantitative methods. *Adm. Sci. Q.* 24:602–10.

Johnson, C. W. 1984. Microcomputer-administered research. *Educ. Psychol. Meas.* 44:165–67.

Johnson, H. W. 1979. *Preschool test descriptions.* Springfield, Ill.: Thomas.

Johnson, J. M. 1975. *Doing field research.* New York: Free Press.

Johnson, O. G. 1976. *Tests and measurements in child development.* 2 vols. San Francisco: Jossey-Bass.

Joint Committee on Standards for Educational Evaluation. 1982. *Standards for evaluation of educational programs, projects, and materials.* Boston: Allyn and Bacon.

Jordan, L. A.; Marcus, A. C.; and Reeder, L. 1980. Response styles in telephone and household interviewing. *Public Opin. Q.* 44:210–22.

Joseph, M. J., and Joseph, W. D. 1979. *Research fundamentals in home economics.* 2d ed. Minneapolis: Burgess.

Jung, C. G. 1965. The need for roots. *Landscape* 14(2): 1.

Junker, B. H. 1960. *Field work.* Chicago: Univ. of Chicago Press.

Kallman, W. M., and Feuerstein, M. J. 1986. Psychophysiological procedures. In *Handbook of behavioral assessment,* ed. A. R. Ciminero, K. S. Calhoun, and H. E. Adams, 325–50. New York: Wiley.

Kalton, G. 1983a *Compensating for missing data.* Ann Arbor, Mich.: Survey Research Center, University of Michigan.

———. 1983b. *Introduction to survey sampling.* Beverly Hills: Sage.

Kalton, G., and Kasprzyk, D. 1982. Imputing for missing survey responses. In *Proceedings of the section on survey research methods,* 22–31. Washington, D.C.: American Statistical Association.

Kamerman, S. 1976. *Developing a family impact statement.* New York: Foundation for Child Development.

Kane, R., and Kane, R. 1981. *Assessing the elderly.* Lexington, Mass.: D. C. Heath.

Kaplan, A. 1964. *The conduct of inquiry.* San Francisco: Chandler.

Kaplan, S. 1976. Adaptation, structure and knowledge. In *Environmental knowing,* ed. G. T. Moore and R. G. Golledge, 32–45. Stroudsburg, Pa.: Dowden, Hutchinson and Ross.

Karweit, N., and Meyers, E. D., Jr. 1983. Computers in survey research. In *Handbook of survey research,* ed. P. H. Rossi, J. D. Wright, and A. B. Anderson, 379–414. New York: Academic Press.

Kasl, S. V.; Chisholm, R. F.; and Eskenazi, B. 1981a. The impact of the accident at the Three Mile Island on the behavior and well-being of nuclear workers: Part I. *Am. J. Public Health* 71:472–83.

———. 1981b. The impact of the accident at the Three Mile Island on the behaviors and well-being of nuclear workers: Part II. *Am. J. Public Health* 71:484–95.

Katkin, E. S., and Hastrup, J. L. 1982. Psychophysiological methods in clinical research. In *Handbook of research methods in clinical psychology,* ed. P. C. Kendall and J. M. Butcher, 387–425. New York: Wiley.

Katz, D. 1966. Field studies. In *Research methods in the behavioral sciences,* ed. L. Festinger and D. Katz, 56–97. New York: Holt.

Katz, S. B.; Kapes, J. T.; and Zirkel, P. A. 1980. *Resources for writing for publication in education.* New York: Teachers College Press, Columbia University.

Katzer, J.; Cook, K. H.; and Crouch, W. W. 1982. *Evaluating information.* 2d ed. Reading, Mass.: Addison-Wesley.

Kazdin, A. E. 1982. *Single-case research designs.* New York: Oxford.

Keith-Spiegel, P. 1976. Children's rights as participants in research. In *Children's rights and the mental health professions,* ed., G. P. Koocher, 53–81. New York: Wiley.

Kelley, V. R., and Weston, H. B. 1975. Computers, costs, and civil liberties. *Soc. Work* 20:15–19.

Kelman, H. C. 1982. Ethical issues in different social science methods. In *Ethical issues in social science research,* ed. T. L. Beauchamp, R. R. Faden, R. J. Wallace, Jr., and L. Walters, 40–98. Baltimore: Johns Hopkins Univ. Press.

Kendler, H. H. 1981. The reality of operationism. *J. Mind Behav.* 2:331–41.

Kennedy, J. R. 1979. *Library research guide to education.* Ann Arbor, Mich.: Pierian Press.

Kenny, D. A. 1979. *Correlation and causality.* New York: Wiley.

Kent, A., ed. 1977. *Encyclopedia of library and information service.* New York: Marcel Dekker.

Kent, R. N., and Foster, S. L. 1977. Direct observational procedures. In *Handbook of behavioral assessment,* ed. A. R. Ciminero, K. S. Calhoun, and H. E. Adams, 279–328. New York: Wiley.

Kerlinger, F. N. 1979. *Behavioral research.* New York: Holt.

______. 1986. *Foundations of behavioral research.* 3d ed. New York: Holt.

Ketterer, R. F.; Price, R. H.; and Politser, E. 1980. The action research paradigm. In *Evaluation and action in the social environment,* ed. R. H. Price and P. E. Politser. New York: Academic Press.

Keyser, D. J., and Sweetland, R. C., eds. 1985–1988. *Test critiques.* Vols. 1–7. Kansas City: Test Corporation of America.

Khan, M. A., and Al-Obaidy, H. 1982. Comparative evaluation of manager performance in selected types of food services. *J. Foodservice Syst.* 21:163–70.

Kidder, L. H., and Judd, C. M. 1986. *Research methods in social relations.* 5th ed. New York: Holt.

Kiecolt, K. J., and Nathan, L. E. 1985. *Secondary analysis of survey data.* Beverly Hills: Sage.

Kilgour, F. G.; Long, P. L.; Landgraf, A. L.; and Wyckoff, J. A. 1972. The shared cataloging system of the Ohio College Library Center. *J. Libr. Autom.* 5:157–83.

Kimmel, A. J. 1988. *Ethics and values in applied social research.* Newbury Park, Calif.: Sage.

Kindred, A. R. 1982. *Introduction to computers.* 2d ed. Englewood Cliffs, N.J.: Prentice-Hall.

Kiritz, N. 1980. *Program planning and proposal writing.* Los Angeles: Grantsmanship Center.

Kirk, J., and Miller, M. L. 1986. *Reliability and validity in qualitative research.* Beverly Hills: Sage.

Kirk, T. G. 1978. *Library research guide to biology.* Ann Arbor, Mich.: Pierian Press.

Kish, L. 1965. *Survey sampling.* New York: Wiley.

Kleinmuntz, B. 1986. *Personality and psychological assessment.* Malabar, Fla.: Krieger.

Klesges, R. C. 1985. The Fargo-Moorhead nutrition project. Unpublished manuscript, Memphis State University.

Klesges, R. C.; Coates, T. J.; Moldenhauer-Klesges, L. M.; Holzer, B.; Gustavson, J.; and Barnes, J. 1984. The FATS. *Behav. Assess.* 6:333–45.

Klockars, C. B. 1974. *The professional fence.* New York: Free Press.

Klopfer, W. G., and Taulbee, E. S. 1976. Projective tests. In *Annual review of psychology,* vol. 27, ed. M. R. Rosenzweig and L. W. Porter, 543–67. Palo Alto, Calif.: Annual Reviews, Inc.

Knoff, H. M. ed. 1986. *The assessment of child and adolescent personality.* New York: Guilford Press.

Kocka, J. 1984. Theories and quantification in history. *Soc. Sci. Hist.* 8:169–78.

Kraft, C. H., and Van Eeden, C. 1968. *A nonparametric introduction to statistics.* Englewood Cliffs, N.J.: Prentice-Hall.

Krathwohl, D. R. 1977. *How to prepare a research proposal.* 2d ed. Syracuse: Syracuse University Bookstore.

______. 1985. *Social and behavioral science research.* San Francisco: Jossey-Bass.

Krippendorff, K. 1980. *Content analysis.* Beverly Hills: Sage.

Kuder, G., and Richardson, M. 1937. The theory of estimation of test reliability. *Psychometrika* 2:151–60.

Kuhn, T. S. 1970. *The structure of scientific revolutions.* 2d ed. Chicago: Univ. of Chicago Press.

L'Abate, L., and Wagner, V. 1985. Theory-derived, family-oriented test batteries. In *The handbook of family psychology and therapy,* vol. 2, ed. L. L'Abate, 1006–31. Homewood, Ill.: Dorsey.

Labbe, P. 1982. Committee on Science, American Association for Clinical Chemistry.

Lagacé, R. O. 1974. *Nature and use of the HRAF Files.* New Haven: HRAF, Inc.

LaGrange, C. 1981. OCLC's interlibrary loan subsystem. *Ref. Serv. Rev.* 9:61–68.

Lake, D. G.; Miles, M. B.; and Earle, R. B., Jr. 1973. *Measuring human behavior.* New York: Teachers College Press.

Lake Placid Conference on Home Economics. *Proceedings of the fourth annual conference, 1902.* Washington, D.C.: American Home Economics Association.

Lampe, P. E. 1982. Ethnic labels. *Ethn. Racial Stud.* 5:542–48.

———. 1984. Mexican Americans. *Hisp. J. Behav. Sci.* 6:77–85.

Langbein, L. I., and Lichtman, A. J. 1978. *Ecological inference.* Beverly Hills: Sage.

Langness, L. L. 1965. *The life history in anthropological science.* New York: Holt.

Langness, L. L., and Frank G. 1981. *Lives.* Novato, Calif.: Chandler and Sharp.

LaRossa, R., and Wolf, J. H. 1985. On qualitative family research. *J. Marr. Fam.* 47:531–42.

LaRossa, R.; Bennett, L. A.; and Gelles, R. J. 1981. Ethical dilemmas in qualitative family research. *J. Marr. Fam.* 43:303–13.

Lauffer, A. 1983. *Grantsmanship.* 2d ed. Beverly Hills: Sage.

Laveck, C. C. et al. 1974. Recipients of research grants for NICHD. *Pediatrics* 53: 706–11.

Lavrakas, P. J. 1987. *Telephone survey methods.* Newbury Park, Calif.: Sage.

Lazarus, R. S. 1966. *Psychological stress and the coping process.* New York: McGraw-Hill.

Lazarus, R. S., and Cohen, J. B. 1977. Environmental stress. In *Human behavior and environment,* vol. 2, ed. I. Altman and J. Wohlwill, 80–127. New York: Plenum.

Lazerwitz, B. 1968. Sampling theory and procedures. In *Methodology in social research,* ed. H. M. Blalock, Jr., and A. B. Blalock, 278–328. New York: McGraw-Hill.

Leedy, P. D. 1985. *Practical research.* 3d ed. New York: Macmillan.

Lefferts, R. 1981. *Elements of graphics.* New York: Harper.

———. 1982. *Getting a grant in the 1980s.* 2d ed. Englewood Cliffs, N.J.: Prentice-Hall.

Leistritz, F. L., and Ekstrom, B. 1986. *Social impact assessment and management.* New York: Garland.

Levant, R. F., and Doyle, G. F. 1983. An evaluation of a parent education program for fathers of school-aged children. *Fam. Relat.* 32:29–37.

Levin, H. M. 1983. *Cost-effectiveness.* Beverly Hills: Sage.

Levy, P., and Goldstein, H. 1984. *Tests in education.* New York: Academic Press.

Levy-Leboyer, C. 1982. *Psychology and environment.* Beverly Hills: Sage.

Lewin, K. 1936. *Principles of topological psychology.* New York: McGraw-Hill.

———. 1946. Action research and minority problems. *J. Soc. Issues* 2:34–46.

Lewin, M. 1979. *Understanding psychological research.* New York: Wiley.

Liebow, E. 1967. *Tally's corner.* Boston: Little, Brown.

Lin, N. 1976. *Foundations of social research.* New York: McGraw-Hill.

Lincoln, Y. S. 1985. The ERS standards for program evaluation. *Eval. Program Plann.* 8:251–53.

Lincoln, Y. S., and Guba, E. G. 1985. *Naturalistic inquiry.* Beverly Hills: Sage.

Lindzey, G., and Byrne, D. 1968. Measurement of social choice and interpersonal attractiveness. In *Handbook of social psychology,* vol. 2, 2d ed., ed G. Lindzey and E. Aronson, 452–525. Reading, Mass.: Addison-Wesley.

Linton, R. M. 1968. Strategy for improvement of the status of man in his environment. *Proceedings of symposium on human ecology.* Warrenton, Va.: HEW.

Littrell, M. A. 1980. Home economists as cross-cultural researchers. *Home Econ. Res. J.* 8:307–16.

Locke, L. F., and Spirduso, W. W. 1976. *Proposals that work.* New York: Teachers College Press.

Locke, L. F.; Spirduso, W. W.; and Silverman, S. J. 1987. *Proposals that work.* 2d ed. Newbury Park, Calif.: Sage.

Lockwood, A. 1969. *Diagrams.* Vista, N.Y.: Watson-Guptill.

Lofland, J., and Lofland, L. H. 1984. *Analyzing social settings.* 2d ed. Belmont, Calif.: Wadsworth.

Long, T. J.; Convey, J. J.; and Chwalek, A. R. 1985. *Completing dissertations in the behavioral sciences and education.* San Francisco: Jossey-Bass.

Loo, C. M. 1982. Vulnerable populations. In *The ethics of social research,* vol. 1 of *Surveys and experiments,* ed. J. E. Sieber, 105–26. New York: Springer-Verlag.

Lounsbury, J. W.; Sundstrom, E.; Schuller, C. R.; Mattingly, T. J.; and DeVault, R. 1977. Toward an assessment of the potential social impacts of a nuclear power plant on a community. In *Methodology of social impact assessment,* ed. K. Finsterbusch and C. P. Wolf, 265–77. Stroudsburg, Pa.: Dowden, Hutchinson, and Ross.

Lund, L. A. 1984. Promoting excellence through successful journal publishing. *Omicron Nu Newsl.* 23 June 1984. Haslett, Mich.

Lynch, K. 1960. *The image of the city.* Cambridge: MIT Press.

McAdam, R.E.; Maher, M.; and McAteer, J. F. 1982. *Research and project funding for the uninitiated.* Springfield, Ill.: Charles C. Thomas.

McBreen, E. L. 1984. Historical research in home economics. *Home Econ. Res. J.* 12:539–49.

McCall, G. J. 1984. Systematic field observation. In *Annual review of sociology,* vol. 10, ed. R. H. Turner and J. F. Short, Jr., 263–82. Palo Alto, Calif.: Annual Reviews, Inc.

McCall, G. J., and Simmons, J. L., eds. 1969. *Issues in participant observation.* Reading, Mass.: Addison-Wesley.

McCall, R. B. 1975. *Fundamental statistics for psychology.* 2d ed. New York: Harcourt.

McClelland, D. C.; Atkinson, J. W.; Clark, R. A.; and Lowell, E. L. 1953. *The achievement motive.* New York: Appleton.

McCubbin, H. I., and Thompson, A. I. 1987. *Family assessment inventories for research and practice.* Madison, Wisc.: Family Stress, Coping and Health Project, University of Wisconsin.

McCullers, J. C. 1984. The role of theory in research. *Home Econ. Res. J.* 12:523–38.

McDonald, K. 1985. U.S. announces more stringent standards for treatment of laboratory animals. *Chron. Higher Educ.* 15 May 1985, 10.

McGirr, C. J. 1978. Guidelines for abstracting. *Tech. Commun.* 25(2): 2–5.

McKay, S., and Rosenthal, L. 1980. *Writing for a specific purpose.* Englewood Cliffs, N.J.: Prentice-Hall.

McKenzie, A. T., ed. 1984. *A grin on the interface.* New York: MLAA.

McKenzie, R. 1925. The ecological approach to the study of the human community. In *The city,* ed. R. Park and E. Burgess. Chicago: Univ. of Chicago Press.

McKillip, J. 1987. *Need analysis.* Newbury Park, Calif.: Sage.

McLuhan, M. 1964. *Understanding media.* New York: New American Library.

McMillan, P. 1981. *Library research guide to sociology.* Ann Arbor, Mich.: Pierian Press.

Madron, T. W.; Tate, C. N.; and Brookshire, R. G. 1985. *Using microcomputers in research.* Beverly Hills: Sage.

Madsen, D. 1983. *Successful dissertations and theses.* San Francisco: Jossey-Bass.

Magistrale, A.; Bond, L.; and Fulwiler, T. 1987. *Writer's guide.* Lexington, Mass.: D.C. Heath.

Maimon, P.; Belcher, G. L.; Hearn, G. W.; Nodine, B. F.; and O'Connor, F. W. 1981. *Writing in the arts and sciences.* Boston: Little, Brown.

Malinowski, B. 1922. *Argonauts of the Western Pacific.* London: Routledge and Kegan Paul.

Mandler, G., and Kessen, W. 1959. *The language of psychology.* New York: Wiley.

Mangen, D. J., and Peterson, W. A., eds. 1982. *Research instruments in social gerontology.* Vols. 1–3. Minneapolis: Univ. of Minnesota Press.

Manheim, H. L. 1977. *Sociological research.* Homewood, Ill.: Dorsey.

Mann, T. 1987. *A guide to library research methods.* New York: Oxford Univ. Press.

Marcus, G. E., and Cushman, D. 1982. Ethnographics as texts. In *Annual review of anthropology,* ed. B. J. Siegel, A. R. Beals, and S. A. Tyler, 25–69. Palo Alto, Calif.: Annual Reviews, Inc.

Margenau, H. 1950. *The nature of physical reality.* New York: McGraw-Hill.

Margolin, J. B. 1983. *The individual's guide to grants.* New York: Plenum.

Marion, B. et al. 1979. *The food retailing industry.* New York: Praeger.

*Marketing Economics Guide.* 1977–1978. New York: Marketing Economics Institute.

Marsh, C. 1982. *The survey method.* London: George Allen and Unwin.

Martin, P., and Bateson, P. 1986. *Measuring behaviour.* New York: Cambridge Univ. Press.

Martin, R. 1980. *Writing and defending a thesis or dissertation in psychology or education.* Springfield, Ill.: Thomas.

Martinko, M. J., and Gardner, W. L. 1985. Beyond structured observation. *Acad. Manage. Rev.* 10:676–95.

Mason, K. O. 1975. *Sex-role attitude items and scales from U.S. sample surveys.* HEW Publication Number ADM 75-248. Rockville, Md.: National Institute of Mental Health.

Matheson, D. W.; Bruce, R. L.; and Beauchamp, K. L. 1974. *Introduction to experimental psychology.* 2d ed. New York: Holt.

Maxwell, S. E., and Delaney, H. D. 1985. Management and statistics. *Psychol. Bull.* 97:85–93.

Mead, M. 1928. *Coming of age in Samoa.* New York: William Morrow.

Medley, D. M., and Mitzel, H. E. 1963. Measuring classroom behavior by systematic observation. In *Handbook of research on teaching,* ed. N. L. Gage, 247–328. Skokie, Ill.: Rand McNally.

Mehrabian, A. 1976. *Public places and private spaces.* New York: Basic Books.

Mehrabian, A., and Williams, M. 1969. Nonverbal concomitants of perceived and intended persuasiveness. *J. Pers. Soc. Psychol.* 13:37–58.

Mehrens, W. A., and Lehmann, I. J. 1984. *Measurement and evaluation in education and psychology.* 3d ed. New York: Holt.

Melson, G. F. 1980. *Family and environment.* Minneapolis: Burgess.

Merton, R. K. 1951. The social psychology of housing. In *Current trends in social psychology.* Pittsburgh: Univ. of Pittsburgh Press.

———. 1957. *Social theory and social structure.* Glencoe, Ill.: Free Press.

Meyers, L. S., and Grossen, N. E. 1978. *Behavioral research.* 2d ed. San Francisco: Freeman.

Michaelis, A. R. 1955. *Research films in biology, anthropology, psychology, and medicine.* New York: Academic Press.

Miles, M. B., and Huberman, A. M. 1984. *Qualitative data analysis.* Beverly Hills: Sage.

Mill, R. C., and Morrison, A. M. 1985. *The tourism system.* Englewood Cliffs, N.J.: Prentice-Hall.

Miller, C., and Swift, K. 1988. *The handbook of nonsexist writing.* 2d ed. New York: Lippincott and Crowell.

Miller, D. C. 1983. *Handbook of research design and social measurement.* 4th ed. New York: Longman.

Miller, J. 1979. Theory versus realism in management. *Food Serv. Mark.* 41:25.

Miller, N. E. 1985. The value of behavioral research on animals. *Am. Psychol.* 40:423–40.

Miller, P. McC., and Wilson, M. J. 1983. *A dictionary of social science methods.* New York: Wiley.

Miller, S.; Nunnally, E. W.; and Wackman, D. B. 1976. Minnesota couples communication program (MCCP). In *Treating relationships,* ed. D. H. L. Olson. Lake Mills, Ia.: Graphic Publishing.

Mills, J. 1976. A procedure for explaining experiments involving deception. *Pers. Soc. Psychol. Bull.* 2:3–13.

Mitchell, J. 1986. Measurement scales and statistics. *Psychol. Bull.* 100:398–407.

Mitchell, J. V., Jr., ed. 1983. *Tests in print III.* Lincoln: Univ. of Nebraska Press.

______. 1985. *Ninth mental measurements yearbook.* Lincoln: Univ. of Nebraska Press.

Montgomery, J. E. 1977. The housing patterns of older people. In *The later years.* Monterey, Calif.: Brooks/Cole.

Montgomery, J. E., and Ritchey, S. J. 1975. Home economics research. *J. Home Econ.,* 67(1): 35–39.

Moore, R. B. 1976. *Racism in the English language.* New York: Council on Interracial Books for Children/Racism and Sexism Resource Center for Educators.

Moreno, J. L. 1953. *Who shall survive?* 2d ed. New York: Beacon House.

Morin. S. F. 1977. Heterosexual bias in psychological research on lesbianism and male homosexuality. *Am. Psychol.* 32:629–37.

Morrison, B. M., and Gladhart, P. 1976. Energy and families. *J. Home Econ.* 68:15–18.

Moser, C., and Kalton, G. 1972. *Survey methods in social investigation.* 2d ed. New York: Basic Books.

Mostyn, B. 1985. The content analysis of qualitative research data. In *The research interview,* ed. M. Brenner, J. Brown, and D. Canter, 115–45. London: Academic Press.

Moulton, J.; Robinson, G. M.; and Elias, C. 1978. Sex bias in language use. *Am. Psychol.* 33:1032–36.

Mouly, G. J. 1978. *Educational research.* Boston: Allyn and Bacon.

Mueller, D. J. 1986. *Measuring social attitudes.* New York: Teachers College Press.

Mullins, C. J. 1977. *A guide to writing and publishing in the social and behavior sciences.* New York: Wiley.

______. 1980. *The complete writing guide.* Englewood Cliffs, N.J.: Prentice-Hall.

Murphy, J. T. 1980. *Getting the facts.* Santa Monica, Calif.: Goodyear.

Murstein, B. I., ed. 1965. *Handbook of projective techniques.* New York: Basic Books.

Nachmias, D., and Nachmias, C. 1987. *Research methods in the social sciences.* 3d ed. New York: St. Martin's Press.

Nagel, E. 1961. *The structure of science.* New York: Harcourt.

Naroll, R.; Michik, G. L.; and Naroll, F. 1980. Holocultural research methods. In *Handbook of cross-cultural psychology,* vol. 2, ed. H. C. Triandis and J. W. Berry, 479–521. Boston: Allyn and Bacon.

National Commission for the Protection of Human Subjects. 1975. *Children and the mentally disabled as research subjects.* Washington, D.C.: National Commission.

National Commission for the Protection of Human Subjects in Biomedical and Behavioral Research. 1977. *Report and recommendations.* HEW Publications (05)77-0004. Washington, D.C.: GPO.

National Foundation for Educational Research in England and Wales. 1973, 1976. *Register of questionnaires and attitude scales.* Slough, Berkshire, England: NFER.

NCA-5. 1986. Research priorities statement. Committee of Agriculture Experiment Station Home Economics Administration in the North Central Region. Mimeographed.

Neuber, K. A.; Atkins, W. T.; Jacobson, J. A.; and Reuterman, N. A. 1980. *Needs assessment.* Beverly Hills: Sage.

Neugarten, B. L. 1974. Age groups in American society and the rise of the young-old. *Ann. Am. Acad.* 415:187–98.

Nevo, B. 1985. Face validity revisited. *J. Educ. Meas.* 22:287–93.

Newman, H. 1978. Strategic groups and the structure performance relationship. *Rev. Econ. Stat.* 60:417–27.

Newmark, C.S. 1985. *Major psychological assessment instruments.* Boston: Allyn and Bacon.

Noblit, G. W., and Hare, R. D. 1988. *Meta-ethnography.* Newbury Park, Calif.: Sage.

Norman, K. L. 1986. Importance of factors in the review of grant proposals. *J. Appl. Psychol.* 71:156–62.

Nurius, P. S., and Yeaton, W. H. 1987. Research synthesis reviews. *Clin. Psychol. Rev.* 7:695–714.

Nye, F. I., and McDonald, G. W., eds. 1979. Family policy. Special issue of *J. Marr. Fam.* 41:447–684.

O'Bryant, S. L. 1982. The value of home to older persons. *Res. Aging* 4:349–63.

Oetting, E. R. 1986. Ten fatal mistakes in grant writing. *Prof. Psychol.: Res. Pract.* 17:1–4.

Ogilvie, D. M.; Stone, P. J.; and Kelly, E. F. 1982. Computer-aided content analysis. In *Qualitative methods,* vol. 2 of *Handbook of social science methods,* ed. R. B. Smith and P. K. Manning, 219–46. Cambridge, Mass.: Ballinger.

O'Leary, K. D., ed. 1987. *Assessment of marital discord.* Hillsdale, N.J.: Erlbaum.

O'Leary, K. D., and Borkovec, T. D. 1978. Conceptual, methodological, and ethical problems of placebo groups in psychotherapy research. *Am. Psychol.* 33:821–30.

Oliver, L. W., and Spokane, A. R. 1983. Research integration. *J. Couns. Psychol.* 30:252–57.

Olson, D. H.; McCubbin, H. I.; Barnes, H.; Larsen, A.; Muxen, M.; and Wilson, M. 1985. *Family inventories.* Rev. ed. Minneapolis: Family Social Science Department, University of Minnesota.

Oppenheim, N. A. 1966. *Questionnaire design and attitude measurement.* New York: Basic Books.

Orne, M. T. 1962. On the social psychology of the psychological experiment. *Am. Psychol.* 17:776–83.

Osgood, C.; Suci, G.; and Tannenbaum, P. 1957. *The measurement of meaning.* Urbana: Univ. of Illinois Press.

Palmer, J. O. 1983. *The psychological assessment of children.* 2d ed. New York: Wiley.

Palumbo, D. 1987. *The politics of program evaluation.* Newbury Park, Calif.: Sage.

Park, R., and Burgess, E. 1921. *Introduction to the science of sociology.* Chicago: Univ. of Chicago Press.

______, eds. 1925. *The city.* Chicago: Univ. of Chicago Press.

Parker, C. S. 1984. *Understanding computers and data processing today and tomorrow.* New York: Holt.

Parten, M. 1950. *Surveys, polls, and samples.* New York: Harper.

Patterson, D. R., and Sechrest, L. 1983. Nonreactive measures in psychotherapy outcome research. *Clin. Psychol. Rev.* 3:391–416.

Patterson, G. R. 1971. *Families.* Champaign, Ill.: Research Press.

Patton, M. Q. 1980. *Qualitative evaluation methods.* Beverly Hills: Sage.

______. 1986. *Utilization-focused evaluation.* 2d ed. Beverly Hills: Sage.

Payne, S. L. 1951. *The art of asking questions.* Princeton, N.J.: Princeton Univ. Press.

Pedhazur, E. J. 1982. *Multiple regression in behavioral research.* 2d ed. New York: Holt.

Pelto, P.J., and Pelto, G. H. 1978. *Anthropological research.* Cambridge, Engl.: Cambridge Univ. Press.

Perlman, G. 1985. Electronic surveys. *Behav. Res. Methods, Instru., Comput.* 17:203–5.

Perry, L. S., and Dana, R. H. 1985. Macroconceptual analysis of psychological literature. *Prof. Psychol.: Res. Pract.* 16:354–62.

Peters, M., and Robinson, V. 1984. The origins and status of action research. *J. Appl. Behav. Sci.* 20:113–24.

Pfaffenberger, A.; Franklin, R. A.; and Echt, S. 1983. Computer searching in the field of home economics. *J. Vocat. Home Econ. Educ.* 1:49–60.

Pitt, D. C. 1972. *Using historical sources in anthropology and sociology.* New York: Holt.

Platt, J. 1981a. Evidence and proof in documentary research: 1. *Sociol. Rev.* 29:31–52.

______. 1981b. Evidence and proof in documentary research: 2. *Sociol. Rev.* 29:53–66.

______. 1983. The development of the "participant observation" method in sociology. *J. Hist. Behav. Sci.* 19:379–93.

Pleck, J. H. 1977. The work-family role system. *Soc. Probl.* 24:417–27.

Plihal, J., and Brown, M. 1969. *Evaluation materials.* Minneapolis: Burgess.

Pool, I. 1959. *Trends in content analysis.* Urbana: Univ. of Illinois Press.

Popkin, G. S., and Pike, A. H. 1981. *Introduction to data processing.* 2d ed. Boston: Houghton-Mifflin.

Popper, K. R. 1963. *Conjectures and refutations.* New York: Harper.

Porter, B. 1954. Measurement of parental acceptance of children. *J. Home Econ.* 46(3):177–84.

Potvin, L., and Champagne, F. 1986. Utilization of administrative files in health research. *Soc. Indic. Res.* 18:409–23.

Proshansky, H.; Ittelson, W.; and Rivlin, L., eds. 1970. *Environmental psychology.* New York: Holt.

Punch, M. 1986. *The politics and ethics of fieldwork.* Beverly Hills: Sage.

Rabin, A. I., ed. 1968. *Projective techniques in personality assessment.* New York: Springer.

______. 1981. *Assessment with projective techniques.* New York: Springer.

______. 1986. *Projective techniques for adolescents and children.* New York: Springer.

Rabin, A. I., and Haworth, M. R., eds. 1960. *Projective techniques with children.* New York: Grune and Stratton.

Raj, D. 1972. *The design of sample surveys.* New York: McGraw-Hill.

Ramsey, P. 1970. *The patient as person.* New Haven: Yale Univ. Press.

Rand Corporation. 1955. *A million random digits with 100,000 normal deviates.* Glencoe, Ill.: Free Press.

Rao, G. S. 1984. Dietary intake and bioavailability of fluoride. In *Annual review of nutrition,* ed. W. J. Darby, 115–36. Palo Alto, Calif.: Annual Reviews, Inc.

Rapoport, A. 1982. *The meaning of the built environment.* Beverly Hills: Sage.

Rapoport, R. N., ed. 1985. *Children, youth, and families.* New York: Cambridge Univ. Press.

Read, P. E., ed. 1986. *Foundation fundamentals.* 3d ed. New York: Foundation Center.

Read, M. W. 1980. Ethnographic field-notes and interview transcripts. SRU Working Paper 8. Cardiff: Sociology Research Unit.

Reed, J. G., and Baxter, P. M. 1983. *Library use.* Washington, D.C.: American Psychological Association.

Reeder, L. G.; Ramacher, L. G.; and Gorelink, S. 1976. *Handbook of scales and indices of health behaviors.* Pacific Palisades, Calif.: Goodyear.

Reitzel, J. M., and Lindemann, B. 1982. Historical evidence. In *Qualitative methods,* vol. 2 of *Handbook of social science methods,* ed. R. B. Smith and P. K. Manning, 167–96. Cambridge, Mass.: Ballinger.

Research and Education Association. 1981. *Handbook of psychiatric rating scales.* 2d ed. New York: REA.

Reynolds, P. D. 1971. *A primer in theory construction.* Indianapolis: Bobbs-Merrill.

______. 1979. *Ethical dilemmas and social science research.* San Francisco: Jossey-Bass.

______. 1982. *Ethics and social science research.* Englewood Cliffs, N.J.: Prentice-Hall.

Rheingold, H. I. 1982. Ethics as an integral part of research in child development. In *Strategies and techniques of child study,* ed. R. V. Vasta, 305–24. New York: Academic Press.

Richards, L., and Richards, T. 1987. Qualitative data analysis. *Aust. New Zeal. J. Soc.* 23:23–35.

Richardson, S.; Snell, B.; and Klein, D. 1965. *Interviewing*. New York: Basic Books.
Riecken, H. W., and Boruch, R. F., eds. 1974. *Social experimentation*. New York: Academic Press.
Riley, M. W. 1963. *A case approach*. Vol. 1 of *Sociological research*. New York: Harcourt.
Ritchey, S. J. 1978. *HERAPP report*. Blacksburg, Va.: Virginia Polytechnic Institute and State University.
Ritchey, S. J., and Lovingood, R., eds. 1984. Home economics research. Special issue of *Home Econ. Res. J.* 12:251–432.
Roberts, L. 1983. Experimental design. In *An introduction to social research*, vol. 1 of *Handbook of social sciences methods*, ed. R. B. Smith, 325–63. Cambridge, Mass.: Ballinger.
Robinson, J. P., and Shaver, P. R. 1973. *Measures of social psychological attitudes*. Rev. ed. Ann Arbor: Institute for Social Research University of Michigan.
Robinson, J. P.; Athanasiou, R.; and Head, K. B. 1973. *Measures of occupational attitudes and occupational characteristics*. Rev. ed. Ann Arbor: Institute for Social Research, University of Michigan.
Robinson, J. P.; Rusk, J. G.; and Head, K. B. 1973. *Measures of political attitudes*. Rev. ed. Ann Arbor: Institute for Social Research, University of Michigan.
Robinson, W. S. 1950. Ecological correlations and the behavior of individuals. *Am. Sociol. Rev.* 15:351–57.
Robson, J. R.; Larkin, F. A.; Sanchetto, A. M.; and Tadayyon, B. 1972. *Malnutrition*. New York: Gordon and Breach.
Rogers, T. F. 1976. Interviews by telephone and in person. *Public Opin. Q.* 40:51–65.
Rokeach, M. 1968. *Beliefs, attitudes, and values*. San Francisco: Jossey-Bass.
Rollin, B. E. 1985. The moral status of animals in research. *Am. Psychol.* 40:920–26.
Roncek, D. W., and Choldin, H. M. 1980. Female-headed families. *J. Marr. Fam.* 42:157–69.
Rorer, L. 1965. The great response-style myth. *Psychol. Bull.* 63:129–56.
Rosen, A. C.; Rekers, G. A.; and Bentler, P. M. 1978. Ethical issues in the treatment of children. *J. Soc. Issues* 34:122–36.
Rosenberg, M. 1965. *Society and the adolescent self-image*. Princeton, N.J.: Princeton Univ. Press.
______. 1968. *The logic of survey analysis*. New York: Basic Books.
Rosencranz, M. L. 1972. *Clothing concepts*. New York: Macmillan.
Rosengren, K. E. 1981. *Advances in content analysis*. Beverly Hills: Sage.
Rosenthal, R. 1976. *Experimenter effects in behavioral research*. New York: Irvington.
______. 1984. *Meta-analytic procedures for social research*. Beverly Hills: Sage.
Rosenthal, R., and Lawson, R. 1964. A longitudinal study of the effects of experimenter bias on the operant learning of rats. *J. Psychiatr. Res.* 2:61–72.
Rosenthal, R., and Rosnow, R. L. 1969. *Artifact in behavioral research*. New York: Academic Press.
______. 1975. *The volunteer subject*. New York: Wiley.
Rossi, P. H., and Freeman, H. E. 1985. *Evaluation*. 3d ed. Beverly Hills: Sage.
Rossi, P. H.; Wright, J. D.; and Anderson, A. B. 1983. *Handbook of survey research*. New York: Academic Press.
Ross-Larson, B. 1982. *Edit yourself*. New York: Norton.
Rotter, J. B. 1966. Generalized expectancies for internal versus external control of reinforcement. *Psychol. Monogr.* 80:1–28.
Rowles, G. D. 1980. Growing old "inside." In *Transitions of aging*, ed. N. Datan and N. Lohmann, 152–70. New York: Academic Press.
______. 1983. Place and personal identity in old age. *J. Environ. Psychol.* 3:299–313.
Rowney, D. K., and Graham, J. Q. 1969. *Quantitative history*. Homewood, Ill.: Dorsey.
Ruback, R. B. 1986. Ethical and legal aspects of applied social psychological research in field

settings. In *Advances in applied social psychology,* vol. 3, ed. M. J. Saks and L. Saxe. Hillsdale, N.J.: Lawrence Erlbaum.

Rummel, J. F. 1964. *An introduction to research procedures in education.* 2d ed. New York: Harper and Row.

Russell, J. A., and Mehrabian, A. 1976. Environmental variables in consumer research. *J. Consum. Res.* 3:62–63.

Russell, W., and Burch, R. 1959. *The principles of humane experimental technique.* London: Methuen.

Russo, D. C., and Koegel, R. L. 1977. A method for integrating an autistic child into a normal public school classroom. *J. Appl. Behav. Anal.* 10:579–90.

Rutman, L., ed. 1984. *Evaluation research methods.* 2d ed. Beverly Hills: Sage.

Rutstein, D. D. 1969. The ethical design of human experiments. *Daedalus* 98:377–82.

Ryder, R. 1975. *Victims of science.* London: David-Poynter.

Rynkiewich, M. A., and Spradley, J. P. 1976. *Ethics and anthropology.* New York: Wiley.

Sackett, G. 1978. *Observing behavior.* 2 vols. Baltimore: University Park Press.

St. Pierre, R. G., and Rezmovic, V. 1982. An overview of the national nutrition education and training program evaluation. *J. Nutr. Educ.* 14(2): 61–65.

Sanford, N. 1970. Whatever happened to action research? *J. Soc. Issues* 26(4): 3–23.

SAS Institute, Inc. 1983. *SAS user's guide: Basics, version 5.* Rev. ed. Cary, N.C.: SAS Institute.

Sax, G. 1968. *Empirical foundations of educational research.* Englewood Cliffs, N.J.: Prentice-Hall.

Scarr, S. 1988. Race and gender as psychological variables. *Am. Psychol.* 43:56–59.

Schatzman, L., and Strauss, A. L. 1973. *Field research.* Englewood Cliffs, N.J.: Prentice-Hall.

Scherer, F. 1980. *Industrial market structure and economic performance.* Chicago: Rand McNally.

Schlater, J. D. 1970. *National goals and guidelines for research in home economics.* East Lansing: Michigan State University.

Schlenker, B. R., and Forsyth, D. R. 1977. On the ethics of psychological research. *J. Exp. Soc. Psychol.* 13:369–96.

Schmid, C. F., and Schmid, S. E. 1979. *Handbook of graphic presentation.* 2d ed. New York: Wiley.

Schnake, M. A. 1985. *The world of computers and data processing.* St. Paul: West.

Schrodt, P. A. 1987. *Microcomputer methods for social scientists.* Beverly Hills: Sage.

Schuman, H., and Kalton, G. 1985. Survey methods. In *Handbook of social psychology,* vol. 1, 3d ed., ed. G. Lindzey and E. Aronson, 635–97. New York: Random House.

Schuman, H., and Presser, S. 1981. *Questions and answers in attitude surveys.* New York: Academic Press.

Scott, M. M., and Hatfield, J. G. 1985. Problems of analyst and observer agreement in naturalistic narrative data. *J. Educ. Meas.* 22:207–18.

Scott, W. R. 1965. Field methods in the study of organizations. In *Handbook of organizations,* ed. J. G. March, 261–304. Chicago: Rand McNally.

Sechrest, L., ed. 1979. *Unobtrusive measures today.* San Francisco: Jossey-Bass.

Selby, P. H. 1979. *Using graphs and tables.* New York: Wiley.

Selltiz, C.; Wrightsman, L. S.; and Cook, S. W. 1976. *Research methods in social relations.* 3d ed. New York: Holt.

Selye, H. 1956. *The stress of life.* New York: McGraw-Hill.

______. 1976. *Stress in health and disease.* Woburn, Mass.: Butterworth.

Semeomoff, B. 1976. *Projective techniques.* New York: Wiley.

Shafer, R. J. 1969. *A guide to historical method.* Homewood, Ill.: Dorsey.

Shangraw, R. F., Jr. 1986. Telephone surveying with computers. *Eval. Program Plann.* 9:107–11.

Shaw, C. 1930. *The jack roller.* Chicago: Univ. of Chicago Press.

Shaw, M. E., and Wright, J. M. 1967. *Scales for the measurement of attitudes.* New York: McGraw-Hill.

Sheatsley, P. B. 1983. Questionnaire construction and item writing. In *Handbook of survey research,* ed. P. H. Rossi, J. D. Wright, and A. B. Anderson, 195–230. New York: Academic Press.

Sheehy, E. P. 1976. *Guide to reference books.* 9th ed. Chicago: American Library Association.

Shorter, E. 1971. *The historian and the computer.* Englewood Cliffs, N.J.: Prentice-Hall.

Shure, G. H., and Meeker, R. J. 1978. A minicomputer system for multiperson computer-assisted telephone interviewing. *Behav. Res. Methods Instrum.* 10:196–202.

Sidowski, J. B., and Lockard, R. B. 1966. Some preliminary considerations in research. In *Experimental methods and instrumentation in psychology,* ed. J. B. Sidowski, 3–32. New York: McGraw-Hill.

Sieber, J. E., ed. 1982a. *Surveys and experiments.* Vol. 1 of *The ethics of social research.* New York: Springer-Verlag.

———. 1982b. *Fieldwork, regulation, and publication.* Vol. 2 of *The ethics of social research.* New York: Springer-Verlag.

Sieber, S. D. 1973. The integration of fieldwork and survey techniques. *Am. J. Sociol.* 78:1335–59.

Siegel, S. 1956. *Nonparametric statistics.* New York: McGraw-Hill.

Siegel, S., and Castellan, N. J. 1988. *Nonparametric statistics.* 2d ed. New York: McGraw-Hill.

Silverman, I. 1977. *The human subject in the psychological laboratory.* New York: Pergamon.

Simko, M. D.; Cowell, C.; and Gilbride, J. A. 1984. *Nutrition assessment.* Rockville, Md.: Aspen.

Simon, A., and Boyer, E. G., eds. 1967–1970. *Mirrors for behavior.* Philadelphia: Research for Better Schools.

Simon, J. L. 1978. *Basic research methods in social science.* 2d ed. New York: Random House.

Simon, J. L., and Burstein, P. 1985. *Basic research methods in social science.* 3d ed. New York: Random House.

Sims, L.; Paolucci, B.; and Morris, P. 1972. A theoretical model for the study of nutritional status. *Ecol. Food Nutr.* 1:197–205.

Sjoberg, G., ed. 1967. *Ethics, politics, and social research.* Cambridge, Mass.: Schenkman.

Sjoberg, G., and Nett, R. 1968. *A methodology for social research.* New York: Harper and Row.

Skillin, M. E., and Gay, R. M. 1974. *Words into type.* 3d ed. Englewood Cliffs, N.J.: Prentice-Hall.

Slonim, M. J. 1960. *Sampling in a nutshell.* New York: Simon and Shuster.

Smith, G. R. 1963. A critique of the proposals submitted to the Cooperative Research Program. In *Educational research,* ed. J. A. Culbertson and S. P. Hencley, 277–87. Danville, Ill.: Interstate Printers and Publishers.

Smith, H. W. 1975. *Strategies of social research.* Englewood Cliffs, N.J.: Prentice-Hall.

Smith, M. B. 1967. Conflicting values affecting behavioral research with children. *Am. Psychol.* 22:377–82.

Smith, T. W. 1983. The hidden 25 percent. *Public Opin. Q.* 47:383–404.

Snow, D. A.; Benford, R. D.; and Anderson, L. 1986. Fieldwork roles and informational yield. *Urban Life* 14:377–408.

Snyderman, M., and Rothman, S. 1987. Survey of expert opinion on intelligence and aptitude testing. *Am. Psychol.* 42:137–44.

Society for Research in Child Development, 1973. Ethical standards for research with children. *Newsletter,* Winter, 3–5.

Sociology Writing Group, UCLA. 1986. *A guide to writing sociology papers.* Lexington, Mass.: D. C. Heath.

Soderstrom, E. J. 1981. *Social impact assessment.* New York: Praeger.

Somers, R. H.; Manheimer, D. I.; Kleman, M. T.; and Mellinger, G. D. 1982. Structured interviews. In *Qualitative methods,* vol. 2 of *Handbook of social science methods,* ed. R. B. Smith and P. K. Manning, 145–61. Cambridge, Mass.: Ballinger.

Sommer, R. 1969. *Personal space.* Englewood Cliffs, N.J.: Prentice-Hall.

Sonquist, J. A., and Dunkelberg, W. C. 1977. *Survey and opinion research.* Englewood Cliffs, N.J.: Prentice-Hall.

Sorrels, B. D. 1983. *The non-sexist communicator.* Englewood Cliffs, N.J.: Prentice-Hall.

Spakes, P. 1983a. Family impact analysis. *Soc. Casework* 64:3–10.

______. 1983b. *Family policy and family impact analysis.* Cambridge, Mass.: Schenkman.

Spear, M. E. 1969. *Practical charting techniques.* New York: McGraw-Hill.

Spiegel, D., and Keith-Spiegel, P. 1970. Assignment of publication credits. *Am. Psychol.* 25:738–45.

Spodek, B., ed. 1982. *Handbook of research in early childhood education.* New York: Free Press.

Spradley, J. P. 1979. *The ethnographic interview.* New York: Holt.

______. 1980. *Participant observation.* New York: Holt.

Spradley, J. P., and McCurdy, D. W. 1977. *Conformity and conflict.* 3d ed. Boston: Little, Brown.

SPSS Inc. Staff. 1983. *SPSS user's guide.* New York: McGraw-Hill.

Srole, I. 1956. Social integration and certain corollaries. *Am. Sociol. Rev.* 21:709–16.

Staff of the University of Chicago Press. 1987. *Chicago guide to preparing electronic manuscripts.* Chicago: Univ. of Chicago Press.

Stark-Adamec, C., and Kimball, M. 1984. Science free of sexism. *Can. Psychol.* 25(1): 23–34.

Steel, R. G. D., and Torrier, J. H. 1980. *Principles and procedures of statistics.* 2d ed. New York: McGraw-Hill.

Steidl, R. E. 1969. An ecological approach to the study of family managerial behavior. In *Proceedings of conference on the family.* Pennsylvania State University.

Stevens, S. S. 1951. Mathematics, measurements, and psychophysics. In *Handbook of experimental psychology,* ed. S. S. Stevens, 1–49. New York: Wiley.

Stewart, C. J., and Cash, W. B. 1974. *Interviewing.* Dubuque, Ia.: Wm. C. Brown.

Stewart, D. W. 1984. *Secondary research.* Beverly Hills: Sage.

Stokols, D., ed. 1977. *Perspectives on environment and behavior.* New York: Plenum.

______. 1978. Environmental psychology. In *Annual review of psychology,* vol. 29, ed. M. R. Rosenzweig and L. W. Porter, 253–95. Palo Alto, Calif.: Annual Reviews, Inc.

______. 1982. Environmental psychology. In *The G. Stanley Hall lecture series,* vol. 2, ed. A. Kraut, 155–205. Washington, D.C.: American Psychological Association.

Stollack, G. A. 1968. A measure of parent sensitivity to children. Unpublished manuscript. Michigan State University.

Stolz, S. B. 1975. Ethical issues in research on behavior therapy. In *Issues in evaluating behavior modification,* 239–56 ed. W. S. Wood. Champaign, Ill.: Research Press.

Stolz, S. B. et al. 1978. *Ethical issues in behavior modification.* San Francisco: Jossey-Bass.

Straus, M. A., and Brown, B. W. 1978. *Family measurement techniques.* 2d ed. Minneapolis: Univ. of Minnesota Press.

Strube, M. J., and Hartmann, D. P. 1983. Meta-analysis. *J. Consult. Clin. Psychol.* 51:14–27.

Struening, E. L., and Brewer, M. B., eds. 1983. *Handbook of evaluation research.* Beverly Hills: Sage.

Strunk, W., Jr., and White, E. B. 1979. *The elements of style.* 3d ed. New York: Macmillan.
Stuart, A. 1984. Family impact statements in South Australia. *J. Fam. Issues* 5:383–99.
Stultz, R. A. 1981. *The word processing handbook.* Englewood Cliffs, N.J.: Prentice-Hall.
Suchman, E. A. 1969. *Evaluative research.* New York: Russell Sage Foundation.
Sudman, S. 1976. *Applied sampling.* New York: Academic Press.
Sudman, S. and Bradburn, N. M. 1974. *Response effects in surveys.* Chicago: Aldine.
______. 1982. *Asking questions.* San Francisco: Jossey-Bass.
Sudman, S., and Kalton, G. 1986. New developments in the sampling of special populations. In *Annual review of sociology,* vol. 12, ed. R. H. Turner, Palo Alto, Calif.: Annual Reviews, Inc.
Suen, H. K., and Lee, P. S. C. 1985. Effects of the use of percentage agreement on behavioral observation reliabilities. *J. Psychopathol. Behav. Assess.* 7:221–34.
Suen, H. K.; Ary, D.; and Ary, R. M. 1986. A note on the relationship among eight indices of interobserver agreement. *Behav. Assess.* 8:301–3.
Sugden, V. M. 1973. *The graduate thesis.* New York: Pitman.
Summers, G. F., ed. 1970. *Attitude measurement.* Chicago: Rand McNally.
Sundberg, N. D. 1977. *Assessment of persons.* Englewood Cliffs, N.J.: Prentice-Hall.
Survey of Buying Power 1978. *Sales and Marketing Management Magazine.*
Sweetland, R. C., and Keyser, D. J., eds. 1986. *Tests.* 2d ed. Kansas City: Test Corporation of America.
Swiercinsky, D. P., ed. 1985. *Testing adults.* Kansas City: Test Corporation of America.
Taeuber, R. C., and Rockwell, R. C. 1982. National social data series. *Rev. Public Data Use* 10:23–111.
Tagg, S. K. 1985. Life story interviews and their interpretation. In *The research interview,* ed. M. Brenner, J. Brown, and D. Canter, 163–99. London: Academic Press.
Tansley, A. G. 1935. The use and abuse of vegetational concepts and terms. *Ecology* 16:284–307.
Tapp, J. L. 1972. Symposium on ethical considerations in the conduct of cross-cultural research. In *First IACCP international conference abstracts,* ed. J. Dawson, 358–59. Hong Kong: University of Hong Kong.
Tapp, J. L.; Kelman, H. C.; Triandis, H. C.; Wrightsman, L. S.; and Coelho, G. V. 1974. Continuing concerns in cross-cultural ethics. *Int. J. Psychol.* 9:231–49.
Taylor, R. L. 1984. *Assessment of exceptional children.* Englewood Cliffs, N.J.: Prentice-Hall.
Taylor, S. J., and Bogdan, R. 1984. *Introduction to qualitative research methods.* 2d ed. New York: Wiley.
Teitelbaum, H. 1982. *How to write a thesis.* New York: Monarch Press.
Thomas, W. I., and Znaniecki, F. 1927. *The Polish peasant in Europe and America.* Chicago: Univ. of Chicago Press.
Thompson, M. S. 1980. *Benefit-cost analysis for program evaluation.* Beverly Hills: Sage.
Thorelli, H. 1977. *Strategy and structure = performance.* Bloomington: Indiana Univ. Press.
Thorndike, R. L., and Hagen, E. 1977. *Measurement and evaluation in psychology and education.* 4th ed. New York: Wiley.
Tigert, D. I.; Lathrope, R.; and Bleeg, M. 1971. The fast food franchise. *J. Retailing* 47:81–90.
Toffler, A. 1970. *Future shock.* New York: Random House.
Touliatos, J., and Compton, N. H. 1983. *Approaches to child study.* Minneapolis: Burgess.
Touliatos, J.; Perlmutter, B. F.; and Straus, M. A. In press. *Handbook of family measurement techniques.* Newbury Park, Calif.: Sage.
Townsend, T. H. 1974. Criteria grantors use in assessing proposals. *Found. News* 15(2[March/April]): 33–38.
Towstopiat, O. 1984. A review of reliability procedures for measuring observer agreement. *Contemp. Educ. Psychol.* 9:1–20.

Travers, R. M. W., ed. 1973. *Second handbook of research on teaching.* Chicago: Rand McNally.

______. 1978. *An introduction to educational research.* 4th ed. New York: Macmillan.

Tremblay, K. R., and Dillman, D. A. 1977. Research ethics. *Humboldt J. Soc. Relat.* 5:65–84.

Trotter, S. 1974. Buckley sparks controversy, gives students access to school files. *APA Monitor,* 5.

Turabian, K. L. 1987. *A manual for writers of term papers, theses, and dissertations.* 5th ed. Chicago: Univ. of Chicago Press.

Turkat, I. D. 1986. The behavioral interview. In *Handbook of behavioral assessment,* ed. A. R. Ciminero, K. S. Calhoun, and H. E. Adams, 104–49. New York: Wiley.

Turkel, S. 1982. *Working.* New York: Avon.

Turner, J. H. 1986. *The structure of sociological theory.* 4th ed. Homewood, Ill.: Dorsey.

Underwood, B. J. 1957. *Psychological research.* New York: Appleton.

U.S. Congress. Senate Committee on the Judiciary, Subcommittee on Constitutional Rights. 1974. *Individual rights and the federal role in behavior modification.* Washington, D.C.: GPO.

U.S. Department of Agriculture. 1981. *National plan for new initiatives in home economics.* Washington, D.C.: USDA.

U.S. Department of Commerce. 1977. *Census of retail trade.* Washington, D.C.: GPO.

*U.S. government style manual.* 1973. Rev. ed. Washington, D.C.: GPO.

Useem, M., and Marx, G. T. 1983. Ethical dilemmas and political considerations. In *An introduction to social research,* vol. 1 of *A handbook of social science methods,* ed. R. B. Smith, 169–200. Cambridge, Mass.: Ballinger.

Valsiner, J., ed. 1986. *The individual subject and scientific psychology.* New York: Plenum.

Van Dalen, D. B. 1979. *Understanding educational research.* 4th ed. New York: McGraw-Hill.

van der Veen, F. 1965. The parent's concept of the family unit and child adjustment. *J. Couns. Psychol.* 12:196–200.

van der Veen, F., and Novak, A. I. 1974. The family concept and the disturbed child. *Am. J. Orthopsychiatr.* 44:763–72.

Van Maanen, J. 1983. On the ethics of fieldwork. In *An introduction to social research,* vol. 1 of *A handbook of social science methods,* ed. R. B. Smith, 227–51. Cambridge, Mass.: Ballinger.

Vazsonyi, A. 1980. *Introduction to data processing.* 3d ed. Homewood, Ill.: Irwin.

Veldman, D. J. 1971. *Writing a thesis or dissertation proposal in the behavioral sciences.* Fort Worth: American Continental Publishing Co.

Vygotsky, L. S. 1978. *Mind in society.* Cambridge: Harvard Univ. Press.

Walker, D. K. 1973. *Socioemotional measures for preschool and kindergarten children.* San Francisco: Jossey-Bass.

Wallace, W. 1971. *The logic of science in sociology.* Chicago: Aldine Atherton.

Walsh, M. E. 1981. *Understanding computers.* New York: Wiley.

Wampler, K. S. 1982. Bringing the review of literature into the age of quantification. *J. Marr. Fam.* 44:1009–23.

Wapner, S. 1981. Transactions of person-in-environments. *J. Environ. Psychol.* 1:223–39.

Ward, H. W.; Hall, B. W.; and Schramm, L. F. 1975. Evaluation of published educational research. *Am. Educ. Res. J.* 12:109–28.

Warheit, G. J.; Bell, R. A.; and Schwab, J. J. 1977. *Needs assessment approaches.* Rockville, Md.: National Institute of Mental Health.

Warren, C. A. B. 1980. Data presentation and audience. *Urban Life* 9:282–308.

______. 1988. *Gender issues in field research.* Newbury Park, Calif.: Sage.

Warwick, D. P., and Lininger, C. A. 1975. *The sample survey.* New York: McGraw-Hill.

Wass, B., and Eicher, J. 1980. Analysis of historic and contemporary dress. *Home Econ. Res. J.* 8:319–26.

Watkins, S. M. 1984. *Clothing.* Ames: Iowa State Univ. Press.

Wax, R. 1971. *Doing fieldwork.* Chicago: Univ. of Chicago Press.

Weaver, S. L., ed. 1984. *Testing children.* Kansas City: Testing Corporation of America.

Webb, E. J.; Cambell, D. T.; Schwartz, R. D.; Sechrest, L.; and Gove, J. B. 1981. *Nonreactive measures in the social sciences.* 2d ed. Boston: Houghton Mifflin.

Weick, K. E. 1968. Systematic observational methods. In *Handbook of social psychology,* vol. 1, 2d ed., ed. G. Lindzey and E. Aronson, 357–451. Reading, Mass.: Addison-Wesley.

———. 1985. Systematic observational methods. In *Handbook of social psychology,* vol. 1, 3d ed., ed. G. Lindzey and E. Aronson, 567–634. New York: Random House.

Weisberg, H. F., and Bowen, B. D. 1977. *An introduction to survey research.* San Francisco: Freeman.

Weiss, C. H. 1972. *Evaluation research.* Englewood Cliffs, N.J.: Prentice-Hall.

Weiss, R. L., and Margolin, G. 1986. Assessment of marital conflict and accord. In *Handbook of behavioral assessment,* 2d ed., ed. A. R. Ciminero, K. S. Calhoun, and H. E. Adams, 561–600. New York: Wiley.

Weissbrod, C. S., and Mangan, T. 1978. Children's attitudes about experimental participation. *J. Soc. Psychol.* 106:69–72.

Wells, W., and Tigert, D. 1971. Activities, interests, and opinions. *J. Advert. Res.* 11:27–35.

Welsh, G. S. 1975. *Creativity and intelligence.* Chapel Hill, N.C.: Institute for Research in Social Science, University of North Carolina.

Werner, O., and Schoepfle, G. M. 1986. *Systematic fieldwork.* Vols. 1 and 2. Beverly Hills: Sage.

White, A. 1987. Reference list inaccuracies. *J. Couns. Dev.* 66:195–95.

White, R. W. 1952. *Lives in progress.* New York: Dryden.

White, V. 1975. *Grants.* New York: Plenum.

———, ed. 1983. *Grant proposals that succeeded.* New York: Plenum.

Whyte, W. F. 1955. *Street corner society.* 2d ed. Chicago: Univ. of Chicago Press.

———. 1984. *Learning from the field.* Beverly Hills: Sage.

Wiener, N. 1954. *The human use of human beings.* New York: Doubleday Anchor.

Wiersma, W. 1986. *Research methods in education.* 4th ed. Rockleigh, N.J.: Allyn and Bacon.

Williams, C. D. 1965. The etiology of malnutrition. *Proceedings of the First Western Nutrition Congress,* 1:20.

Williams, M. E. 1985. *Computer-readable databases.* Chicago: American Library Association.

Williams, T. M. 1986. *The impact of television.* New York: Academic Press.

Wilson, S. 1977. The use of ethnographic techniques in educational research. *Rev. Educ. Res.* 47:245–65.

Windle, C., and Neigher, W. 1978. Ethical problems in program evaluation. *Eval. Program Plann.* 1:97–108.

Windley, P. G. 1975. Environmental dispositions. In *Theory development in environment and aging,* ed. P. G. Windley, T. O. Byerts, and F. G. Ernst, 127–41. Washington, D.C.: Gerontology Society.

Winston, R. B., Jr. 1985. A suggested procedure for determining order of authorship in research publications. *J. Couns. Dev.* 63:515–18.

Wittrock, M. C., ed. 1984. *Third handbook of research on teaching.* Washington, D.C.: American Educational Research Association.

Wohlwill, J. 1976. Environmental aesthetics. In *Human behavior and environment,* vol. 1, ed. I. Altman and J. Wohlwill, 37–86. New York: Plenum Press.

Wolf, C. P. 1983. Social impact assessment. In *Social impact assessment methods,* ed. K. Finsterbusch, L. G. Llewellyn, and C. P. Wolf, 15–33. Beverly Hills: Sage.

Wolf, F. M. 1986. *Meta-analysis.* Beverly Hills: Sage.

Woodrum, E. 1984. "Mainstreaming" content analysis in social science. *Soc. Sci. Res.* 13:1–19.

Woody, R. H., ed. 1980. *Encyclopedia of clinical assessment.* 2 vols. San Francisco: Jossey-Bass.

Woody, T. 1947. Of history and its methods. *J. Exp. Educ.* 15:175–201.

Wright, H. F. 1960. Observational child study. In *Handbook of research methods in child development,* ed. P. H. Mussen, 71–139. New York: Wiley.

Wylie, R. 1974. *The self concept.* Vol. 1. Rev. ed. Lincoln: Univ. of Nebraska Press.

Yankauer, A. 1987. Hispanic/Latino—What's in a name? *Am. J. Public Health* 77:15–17.

Yaremko, R. M.; Harari, H.; Harrison, R. C.; and Lynn, E. 1986. *Handbook of research and quantitative methods in psychology.* Hillsdale, N.J.: Erlbaum.

Yarnold, P. R.; Dubinsky, B.; Marguus, G.; Khait, I.; and Berman, Z. 1985. Datamatic. *App. Psychol. Meas.* 9:431.

Yarrow, L. J. 1960. Interviewing children. In *Handbook of research methods in child development,* ed. P. H. Mussen, 561–602. New York: Wiley.

Yates, B. T. 1982. *Doing the dissertation.* Springfield, Ill.: Charles C. Thomas.

______. 1985. Cost-effectiveness analysis and cost-benefit analysis. *Behav. Assess.* 7:207–34.

Yates, F. 1981. *Sampling methods for censuses and surveys.* 4th ed. New York: Macmillan.

Yin, R. K. 1981. The case study crisis. *Adm. Sci. Q.* 26:58–65.

______. 1984. *Case study research.* Beverly Hills: Sage.

Zar, J. H. 1984. *Biostatistical analysis.* 2d ed. Englewood Cliffs, N.J.: Prentice-Hall.

Zeisel, H. 1985. *Say it with figures.* 6th ed. New York: Harper and Row.

Ziesel, J. 1984. *Inquiry by design.* New York: Cambridge Univ. Press.

Zeithaml, V. A. 1982. Consumer response to in-store price information environments. *J. Consum. Res.* 8:357–69.

Zinsser, W. 1983. *Writing with a word processor.* New York: Harper.

______. 1985. *On writing well.* 3d ed. New York: Harper.

# Index